CW00552786

GERMAN HANDGUNS

GERMAN HANDGUNS

The Complete Book of the Pistols and Revolvers of Germany, 1869 to the Present

IAN V. HOGG

Greenhill Books, London
Stackpole Books, Pennsylvania

German Handguns
First published 2001 by Greenhill Books, Lionel Leventhal Limited, Park House, 1 Russell Gardens, London NW11 9NN
and
Stackpole Books, 5067 Ritter Road, Mechanicsburg, PA 17055, USA

British Library Cataloguing in Publication Data
Hogg, Ian V. (Ian Vernon), 1926?
German handguns: the complete book of the pistols and revolvers of Germany, 1869 to the present
1. Pistols – Germany – History – 19th century 2. Pistols – Germany – History – 20th century
I. Title
683.4′32′0943

ISBN 1-85367-461-3

Library of Congress Cataloging-in-Publication Data available

Edited, designed and typeset by Roger Chesneau
Printed and bound in Great Britain by Butler and Tanner Limited, Frome, Somerset

CONTENTS

INTRODUCTION

My interest in German pistols and revolvers can be said to have begun in 1940, when there was a distinct possibility that, along with the rest of the population of Great Britain, I might acquire first-hand knowledge of the subject in the near future whether I wanted to or not. In the event, my knowledge remained theoretical for the time being and, indeed, for some years, since the Army, in its inscrutable wisdom, sent me to the Far East. But as my military career took a more technical turn and I was able to gain access to a wider spectrum of weapons, it became possible to build on that early theoretical knowledge by handling and firing the various weapons and ammunition, studying the operation, measuring velocities and pressures and delving into histories, interrogation reports, trials reports and every other reference I could find.

This book is based upon one I wrote thirty years ago, and it covered German pistols from 1870 to 1945. There were two reasons for this time-scale: the first was that the market at the time was for World War II literature, and the second was that the German pistol world was in such a turmoil at that time that sorting out who was doing what, and why, looked like being a great deal of non-cost-effective work. Moreover, in those days the primary interest was military-historical rather than technical-historical.

The subsequent thirty years have seen a varied assortment of new designs appear in Germany, and there has also been a great amount of historical research carried out by firearms enthusiasts, so that far more is now known about the early days of pistol design. As a result of this, we can now throw caution to the winds and include details of pistols from 1869 to 1999—a period which was determined by, at the farther end, the first metallic-cartridge weapons, and at the closer end by the fact that it had to stop somewhere and the end of the millennium seemed a suitable place to draw the line.

Perhaps the first thing that stands out in this book is the predominance of the automatic pistol in Germany. There are comparatively few native designs of revolver. I think that in the nineteenth century, when revolvers were the only handguns, the German market was satisfied by imports from Belgium and Britain—a combination of countries which could cover every facet of the market from the cheapest to the most expensive. The only German maker to get a foothold in this market appears to have been Pickert, with his range of inexpensive household revolvers, and, as far as the military market went, the Reichsrevolver, designed by the Firearms Commission to the Army's specification, was perfectly satisfactory in an era when all the best officers wore swords.

The first working automatic pistol appears to have been developed in Austria, but the first practical automatic to meet with any degree of commercial success was the German Borchardt, after which every German gunmaker worth his salt set about developing an automatic. Some of these achieved little commercial success, but this was a matter of economics rather than defective design. As the reader will see in these pages, German automatic pistols came in all shapes and sizes, but very few were technical failures. However, this is not to say that the successful designs sold by the thousand from day one: far from it. Even the mighty Mauser was the recipient of some grim and damning reports from testing commissions in its early days, but Mauser, and men like him, were alert to every nuance of criticism and took steps to identify a defect and correct it as rapidly as possible. The competition was fierce and the rewards were great: national military acceptance was the early goal, but after Georg Luger cornered that particular market, foreign military acceptance was the next prize. After that the police and commercial market opened for a different class of weapon—and bear in mind, of course, that in those far-off and carefree days the purchase of a pistol was a simple matter of laying down the money and picking the pistol you wanted: there was no need to ask anyone's permission or explain why you wanted, needed or desired a pistol. (But, of course, if you misused the pistol then the State would invite you to stand on a trapdoor with a rope around your neck.)

All of which explains, to some degree, why there was such a proliferation of automatic pistol designs prior to 1914; then another burst of energy in the 1929–39 period; and then another in the 1970s when terrorism became a growth industry and the Federal German Police laid down some fairly positive statements about what they did and did not want in a future police pistol. At the same time, there has been an increase of interest in sporting revolvers, but this has largely been satisfied by designs which owe very little to German originality and almost everything to American influence, and I think that this is simply a question of manufacturing convenience. The Americans have refined the revolver to the ultimate: there have been one or two attempts in the past fifty years to try to invent a new revolver, but none has lasted the course. Smith & Wesson and Colt between them laid down what the revolver ought to be in the late 1890s, and nothing very much in the way of innovation has taken place since then. There is no point in re-inventing the wheel, and taking the American designs as a model is no more than good commercial sense.

With the automatic pistol, however, native design has predominated. It had to: there is not a great deal of non-German automatic pistol design about, and once one has said 'Colt/Browning' one has summed up the competition, since very little else from outside Germany has achieved any prominence. And when I say 'Colt/Browning' I am referring to the dominant system of operation, and not to the manufacturers. Astra, Star, SIG, Tanfoglio, Sphinx—they all base their designs on the Colt/Browning dropping barrel, and, again because it makes economic sense, this has begun to appear in German designs too.

Another thing which stands out from the study of these pages is the transient nature of the gunsmith's trade. Today we are in the age of conglomerates and consortia; but many of the weapons in these pages were made by small concerns in the days when small was beautiful but nobody thought it very noteworthy. And, contrary to accepted legend, it also appears that wars are not the harvest time for gunmakers. Most of these firms seem to have gone to the wall either during a war or in the economic slump which invariably follows one. Of course, most of these small firms relied entirely upon the sporting and general population, and not the military market. Sporting and such activities suffer when the would-be sportsman is off to the wars, leaving the poor gunmaker in a vulnerable position when the slump comes. Furthermore, in the last quarter of the twentieth century repressive legislation and political correctness have taken their toll in the trade.

I am not foolish enough to think that I have tracked and pinned down every German pistol made during the chosen period. There are two or three which have been left out because there is doubt as to whether they actually were made in Germany and, if so, when and by whom. Moreover, with some of the volume producers of cheaper revolvers, such as Pickert, there is a high probability that one or more of their sub-sub-variations has been missed or overlooked. Aficionados of the Broomhandle and the Luger will doubtless debate my classification and selection, but a little friendly argument now and again is good for the liver.

Before leaving the reader to the study of German pistols and revolvers, I would like to acknowledge the assistance given to me by various people, notably John Walter, the West Midlands Constabulary, the Royal Military College of Science, the School of Infantry Museum and, of course, the Ministry of Defence Pattern Room at Nottingham and its Curator, Herbert Woodend and Assistant Curator Richard Jones. Without the facilities offered by these people and establishments to examine, dismantle, photograph, and in some cases fire the various weapons seen in these pages, this would be a very thin book indeed.

Ian V. Hogg
Upton-upon-Severn

GERMAN HANDGUNS A-Z

ADLER

Adler Waffenwerke Max Hermsdorff, Zella St Blasii

The Adler is a confusing weapon. Three separate people designed, made and sold the pistol, and each of them attached his name, in one way or another, so that responsibility (or blame) is difficult to apportion with any accuracy. It appears to have been the original brainchild of a patentee named Haussler; his name always appears on the pistol in that context. However, Max Hennsdorff took out German Patent 176909 of 22 August 1905, which depicts the Haussler design and makes modifications to it, and it is this patent which, strictly speaking, covers the Adler pistol. The third party in the business is the company of Engelbrecht & Wolff, whose name also appears on the pistol; and this is the firm which actually made the weapons.

Below: The Adler pistol, left side, showing the safety catch and gas escape port.

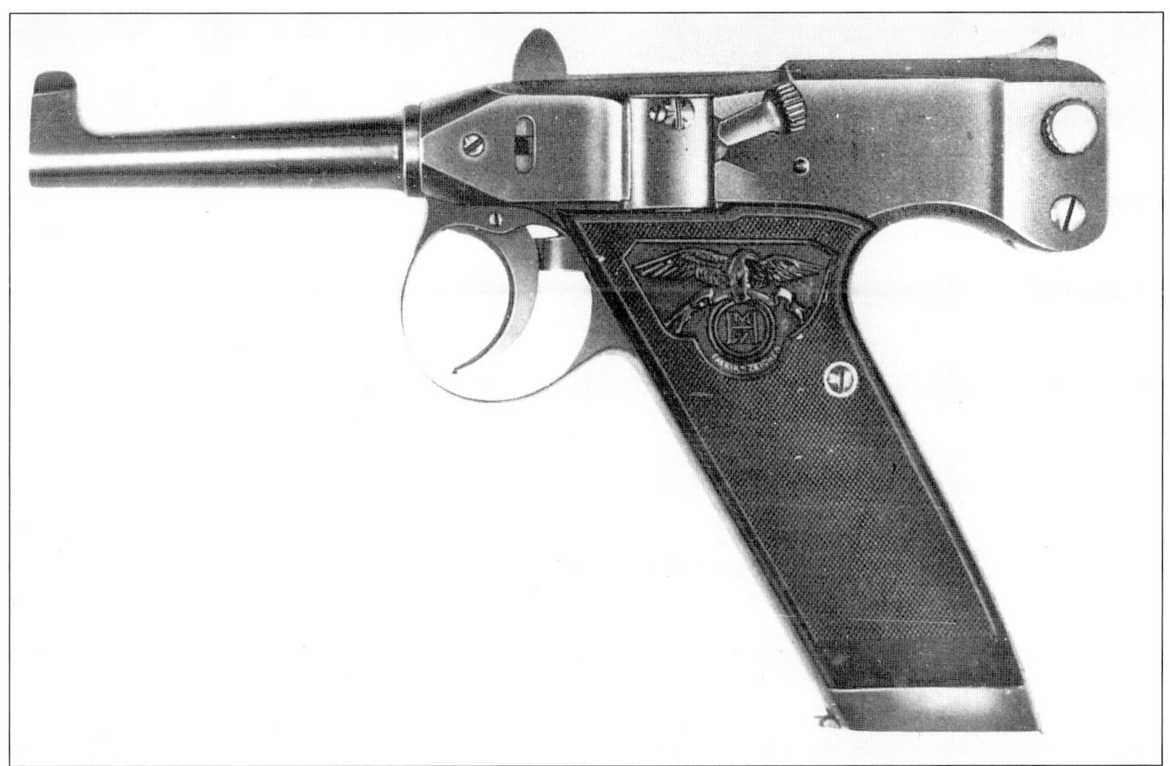

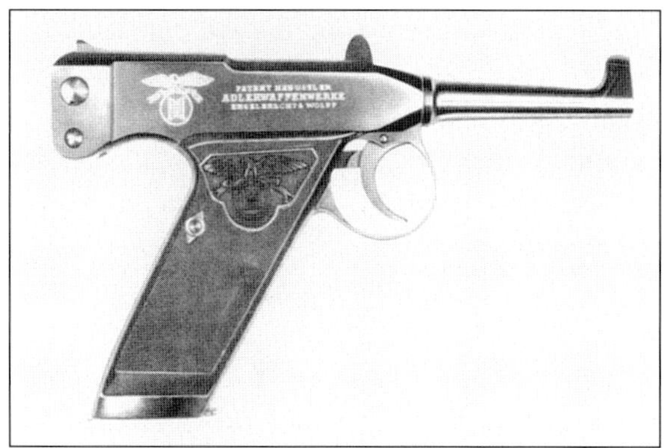

Above: Right side of the Adler pistol.

Finally there is the Adlerwaffenwerke, which appears to have been purely a sales organisation.

In fact, very few pistols were made, since it was not a particularly good design and could not compete in the markets of the day: production began early in 1906 and had finished by 1907, with a total of fewer than 2,000 pistols made. It was a blowback pistol using a reciprocating bolt inside a square-section receiver, with a prominent cocking knob protruding from a slot in the top. The grip was well raked, but there was an excessive overhang at the rear, reminiscent of the Borchardt, which makes the pistol an awkward handful. Another point against it was that it was chambered for a special cartridge, the 7.25mm Adler, a bottle-necked cartridge which was made only by one firm (Rheinische Metallwaren und Maschinenfabrik of Sömmerda) and never adopted by any other gunmaker.

The Adler patent appears to be concerned with a simple blowback mechanism, but the principal novelty, and doubtless that upon which the patent's claims were founded, rests in the construction of the receiver. The rear end is closed by a right-angled unit, pivoted at the bottom of the frame and locked by a transverse pin above, so that the unit forms the rear and top of the receiver, and supports a guide rod for the return spring. The pistol is striker-fired, and a safety catch on the left of the frame locks the trigger linkage. An unusual feature is the vertical slot in the receiver's left sidewall at the chamber mouth: this allows inspection of the bolt face and enables one to see if there is a cartridge in the chamber. Doubtless it would also act as a gas escape in the event of a case failure.

Routine stripping of the Adler is quite easy and also quite unusual. At the rear of the receiver there are two cross bolts; the upper one is a locking bolt, the lower one a pivot. After removing the magazine and ensuring that the pistol is empty, simply grip the pistol so that the top of the receiver is firmly held and then press the upper bolt and drive it out to the right side. This will release the rear end and top of the receiver, and by carefully removing the hand, the top can be raised and folded back and down so as to expose the return spring and its

7.25mm Adler

Method of operation	Blowback, striker-fired
Safety devices	Manual catch on left side of receiver
Magazine type	Single-column detachable box in butt
Position of catch	Bottom rear of butt
Magazine capacity	8 rounds
Front sight	Fixed blade
Rear sight	Fixed V-notch
Overall length	7.55in (192mm)
Barrel length	3.39in (86mm)
Number of grooves	6
Direction of twist	Right-hand
Empty weight	24.2oz (685g)
Markings	Right of receiver: 'PATENT HAUSSLER ADLERWAFFENWERKE ENGELBRECHT & WOLFF' with an eagle surmounting a monogram of 'MHZ' (Max Hermsdorff Zella); this eagle badge is repeated on the grips
Serial number	On top of receiver

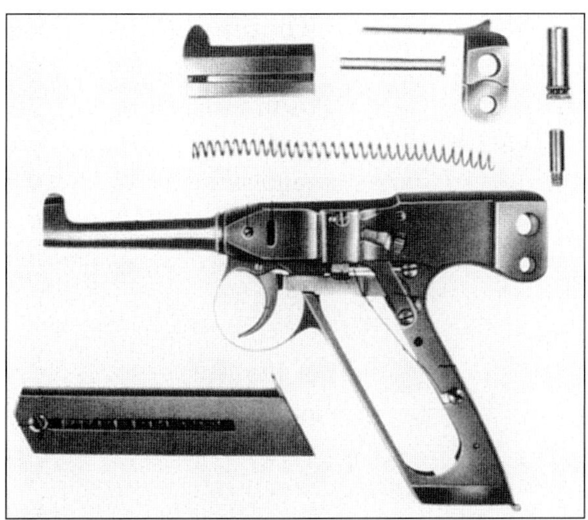

Above: The Adler stripped to its basic components.

guide rod. The rod, spring and bolt can now be withdrawn from the rear of the receiver. The firing pin and spring are removed by unscrewing the bush in the rear of the bolt. Removal of the butt grip plates, by the usual screws, allows access to the fairly simple lockwork and safety catch mechanism. To reassemble the gun, simply insert the bolt, return spring and guide rod into the receiver and fold over the top section, ensuring that the return spring guide rod slips into its locating bush on the rear face of the receiver cover. Insert the cross bolt from the right side.

ALFA

Brand name of A. L. Frank of Hamburg. This company was an importer and distributor of pistols and other sporting firearms, but not a manufacturer. The name Alfa is a popular choice and will be found on weapons ranging from simple and cheap revolvers to complex heavy machine guns, but only revolvers and one repeating pistol bearing this name and with German or Belgian proof marks can be attributed to Frank. The revolvers are the usual cheap Belgian imports—short-barrelled Bulldog models in particular—but the repeating pistol is a four-barrelled model in .230 calibre which has sufficient similarity to the Regnum of August Menz (q.v.) that I feel safe in the belief that it was a cheaper version of the Regnum made to Frank's order.

The Alfa pistol has four barrels, one above the other, in a block which is pivoted to the frame of the pistol and released by a catch on top of the frame so as to tip down and expose the chambers. After loading, the block is tipped back and locked in place, after which a safety catch on the side can be applied. When the weapon is ready to fire the catch is released and successive pulls on the trigger release four firing pins in turn to fire the four barrels. There does not appear to be any method of extraction other than poking the empty cases out with a pencil or some similar instrument. No dimensions are available as no specimen has been located.

The majority of Alfa pistols seen in catalogues appear to be profusely ornamented and fitted with mother-of-pearl grips, suggesting that they were offered as ladies' self-defence weapons.

ANSCHUTZ, J. G.

J. G. Anschutz GmbH, Ulm/Donau

Established in 1865 and today best known as a rifle maker, J. G. Anschutz also made a long-range competition pistol in .22 calibre. This was called the Exemplar and was actually the bolt-action from the Anschutz Model 64 (left-handed) rifle fitted to a 250mm barrel and given a pistol stock. It was available either as a single-shot weapon or as a 5-shot magazine repeater in .22 Long Rifle or four-shot in .22 Winchester Magnum Rimfire.

Right, upper: The Anschutz Exemplar Hornet pistol, showing the left-handed bolt action.
Right, lower: The Anschutz Rekord-Match model of 1933, from a contemporary catalogue. (John Walter)

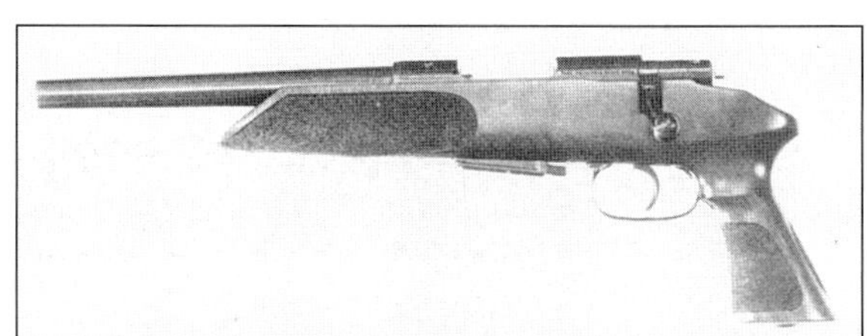

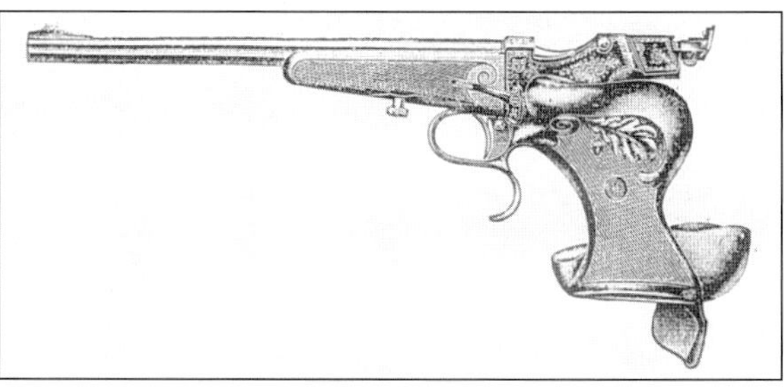

It was followed, in 1989, by the Exemplar Hornet, a similar design based upon the Model 54 left-handed rifle action, chambered for the .22 Hornet cartridge and fitted with telescope mounts but no iron sights. The design is quite simple, a well-shaped pistol grip and short wooden stock supporting the bolt action and about one-third of the barrel. The fit and finish are of high quality. This is a large and heavy pistol, and is primarily designed for long-range silhouette shooting and hunting.

Dismantling comprises little more than removing the bolt by pressing down the retaining catch on the right of the receiver and withdrawing the bolt to the rear. By grasping the body of the bolt and turning the safety catch to the 'S' position, the component parts are freed and can be dismantled. By removing the two screws in front of the magazine and behind the trigger guard the barrel and receiver can be lifted from the stock.

Anschutz Exemplar Hornet

Calibre	.22 Hornet (5.6 × 35R)
Method of operation	Bolt action, striker-fired
Safety devices	Wing type safety catch on cocking piece of bolt
Magazine type	Detachable box ahead of trigger guard
Position of catch	Behind magazine housing
Magazine capacity	5 rounds
Front sight	None
Rear sight	None; telescope mounts provided
Overall length	19.375in (492mm)
Barrel length	10.00in (254mm)
Number of grooves	6
Direction of twist	Right-hand
Empty weight	4lb 7oz (2.013kg)
Markings	Left side of receiver: 'J. G. ANSCHUTZ ULM/DONAU'; top of barrel: 'Cal .22 Hornet FACTORY LOAD ONLY'
Serial number	On left of receiver

ANSCHUTZ, Udo

U. Anschutz, Zella Mehlis

Udo Anschutz manufactured single-shot 'free' target pistols between 1927 and 1939. Although to a standard basic design, they were invariably highly customised to the demands of individuals, and nominally identical models often exhibit startling differences. The Rekord-Match 1933 and Rekord-Match 210 models both used Martini hinged-block actions and were chambered for the .22 Long Rifle cartridge. Target sights of various patterns were fitted and the stocks and grips were to individual requirements.

BEHOLLA

Becker & Hollander, Suhl
Waffenfabrik August Menz, Suhl
Stendawerke Waffenfabrik GmbH, Suhl
H. M. Gering & Cie, Armstadt

This pistol takes its name from the firm of Becker & Hollander of Suhl, the principal man-

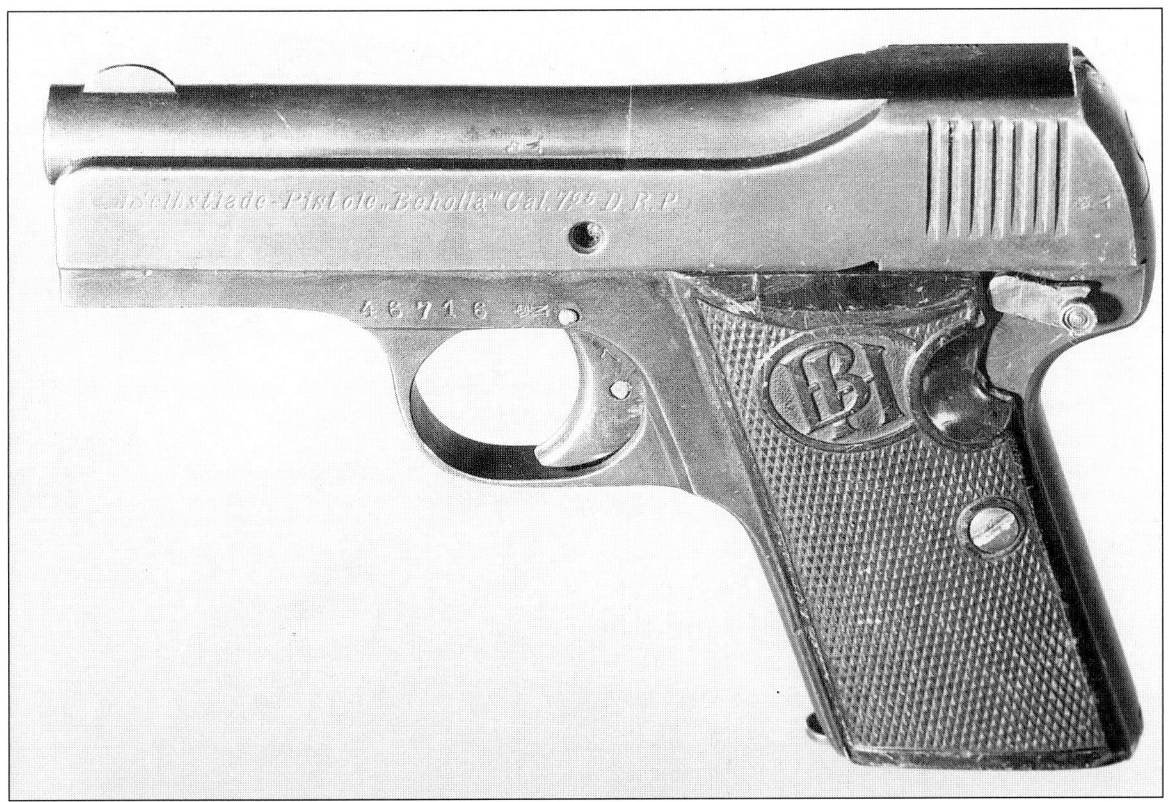

Above: The Beholla pistol. Note the hole in the slide, which gives access to the barrel locking pin.

ufacturers. During World War I it was taken into military use as a substitute standard weapon and was manufactured in a number of establishments, often being given a fresh name in the process—Stenda (the actual designer of the pistol), Leonhardt or Menta. It is a straightforward blowback pistol of the pocket class, marginally capable of combat performance, being robust enough to withstand the rough and tumble of military use and with a bullet that just manages to be disabling. The only remarkable feature of its construction is the method of barrel attachment, and recourse to a bench vice and toolkit is required in order to dismantle the weapon.

The general design is common enough, with a barrel attached firmly to the frame and an open topped slide-cum-breech block with arms extending alongside and in front of the barrel to hold the recoil spring.

To dismantle the gun, first remove the magazine and operate the slide to ensure that it is not loaded. Then procure a hammer and a thin drift or parallel punch. Halfway along the slide, on each side, is a hole through which a pin can be seen. This pin secures the barrel in the frame and, until the barrel is removed, nothing can be done. With the gun suitably supported—preferably in a vice—use the hammer and drift to drive out the pin through the frame holes from right to left. Now push back the slide until the safety catch can be turned up into a notch in the lower edge of the slide, thus locking the slide back against the pressure of the recoil spring. The barrel can now be pushed straight back (this may demand the application of the hammer—protecting the muzzle with some absorb-

Beholla Pistol

Calibre	7.65mm Browning
Method of operation	Blowback, striker-fired
Safety devices	Manual catch on left rear of grip
Magazine type	Single-column detachable box in butt
Position of catch	Bottom rear of butt
Magazine capacity	7 rounds
Front sight	Fixed blade
Rear sight	Fixed V-notch
Overall length	5.50in (140mm)
Barrel length	2.88in (73mm)
Number of grooves	6
Direction of twist	Right-hand
Empty weight	22.5oz (637g)
Markings	Left of slide: 'Selbstlade-Pistole "Beholla" Cal. 7,65 D.R.P.' or '"MENTA" KAL. 7,65' or 'Selbstlade Pistole "Leonhardt" ' or 'WAFFEN-FABRIK STENDAWERKE SUHL I/TH'; right of frame: 'STENDAWERKE G.m.b.H. WAFFENBAU SUHL' or 'BECKER & HOLLANDER WAFFENBAU SUHL' or 'H. M. GERING ARNSTADT' (Menta pistols carry no maker's name); grips: Stenda pistols carry 'STW' moulded into the top of the grips
Serial number	Full number on left of frame; last two or three digits on trigger, on dovetail lug of barrel and on underside of slide near muzzle

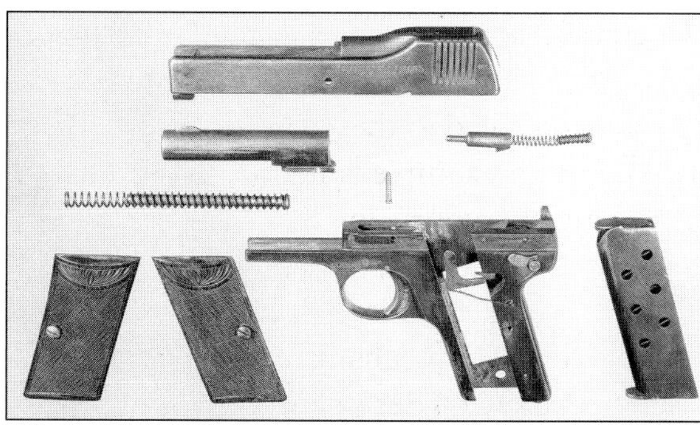

Above: The Menta dismantled. The Beholla, Stenda and Leonhardt are exactly the same.

ent cushion—to overcome years of inaction) so that the dovetail section beneath the breech slides clear of its mounting in the frame. Once free, it can be lifted clear. Then, gripping the slide, depress the safety catch and allow the slide to go forward until it clears the frame. Then remove the recoil spring and its guide rod. No further stripping is recommended.

Reassembly is simply a reversal of the above procedure.

BERGMANN

Th. Bergmann, Werk Gaggenau, Suhl

Theodor Bergmann was among the earliest manufacturers of automatic pistols, though he was principally an entrepreneur and the actual design of weapons was done by employees, notably Louis Schmeisser. Bergmann's first pistol patent was taken out in conjunction with Otto Brauswetter, a watchmaker of Szegedin, Hungary, in June 1892 and related to a long-recoil automatic pistol which was never manufactured. The first pistol to appear under the Bergmann name was a delayed blowback weapon in which the bolt engaged with an in-

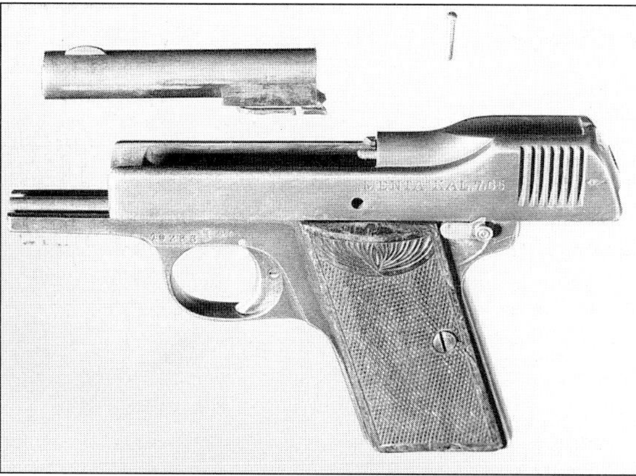

Left: With the slide drawn back, the pin is driven out and the barrel removed from this Menta pistol (which is a Beholla under a different name).

clined face in the receiver, which gave the desired delay in breech opening. Of the few made, one was supplied to the Swiss Army for trial in 1893, but no example is known to exist today.

During the course of the Swiss trial Bergmann made some improvements to his design, and removed the dubious delay system to adopt a pure blowback mechanism. This became the Model of 1894 or Bergmann No 2, and one of its more remarkable features was the absence of an extractor, the empty case (which was sharply tapered and had no rim of any sort) being blown from the chamber by residual pressure as the bolt opened and ejected by striking the top round in the magazine and being bounced out, clear of the feedway. The system worked, on the whole, surprisingly well so far as extraction went, but was less efficient in the matter of ejecting the case clear of the gun. The Bergmann chamber carried a gas escape on the right-hand side to permit the safe escape of gas should a case rupture occur on firing—not unknown in those days—and this port tended to unbalance the gas pressure ejecting the case. Hence the path of the ejected case was far from predictable and the result was that cases often failed to clear the feedway and jammed the returning bolt.

A more significant defect is that, without positive extraction, unloading an unfired cartridge becomes a difficult task. In theory it should fall out if one opens the bolt and points the pistol upwards, but in practice—and particularly if there have been previous rounds fired, leaving the chamber dirty—the cartridge stays in place and has to be ejected by poking something suitable down the muzzle. When the calibre is 5mm, something sufficiently thin and rigid is not always readily available.

Bergmann No 2, 1894

Calibre	5mm Bergmann No 2 1894
Method of operation	Blowback, hammer-fired
Safety devices	Manual catch on left side of receiver
Magazine type	Single-column, clip-loaded, side-opening
Position of catch	On magazine cover
Magazine capacity	5 rounds
Front sight	Fixed blade
Rear sight	Fixed V-notch
Overall length	11.02in (280mm)
Barrel length	5.31in (135mm)
Number of grooves	6
Direction of twist	Right-hand
Empty weight	36.3oz (1,030g)
Markings	Right of magazine cover: 'PISTOLET BERGMANN'; left side of frame: 'PATENT S.G.D.G.'; on right side of frame, behind trigger, is a badge representing a miner (*Bergmann*) carrying a pick-axe and lantern
Serial number	On barrel and on frame below breech

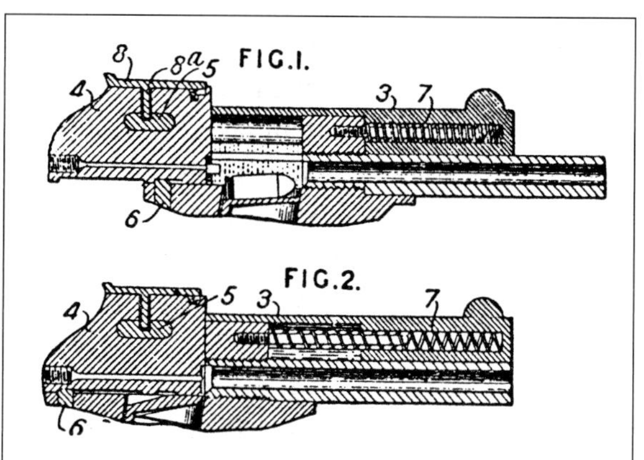

Left: Patent 16329, 22 July 1902, Theodor Bergmann. Although credited to Bergmann, this was much more likely to have come from the drawing board of Louis Schmeisser. It relates to a blowback pistol firing from an open bolt—a somewhat rare concept. Fig. 1 shows the bolt, which has a fixed firing pin, open and retained by the sear. Pulling the trigger released the bolt to go forward, collect a round from the magazine, chamber it and fire it, as in Fig. 2. The bolt was then blown back to be caught by the sear once more. In the form shown here it never got further than the Patent Office, but the germ of the idea remained with Schmeisser and reappeared with his 1916 Bergmann MP18 submachine gun.

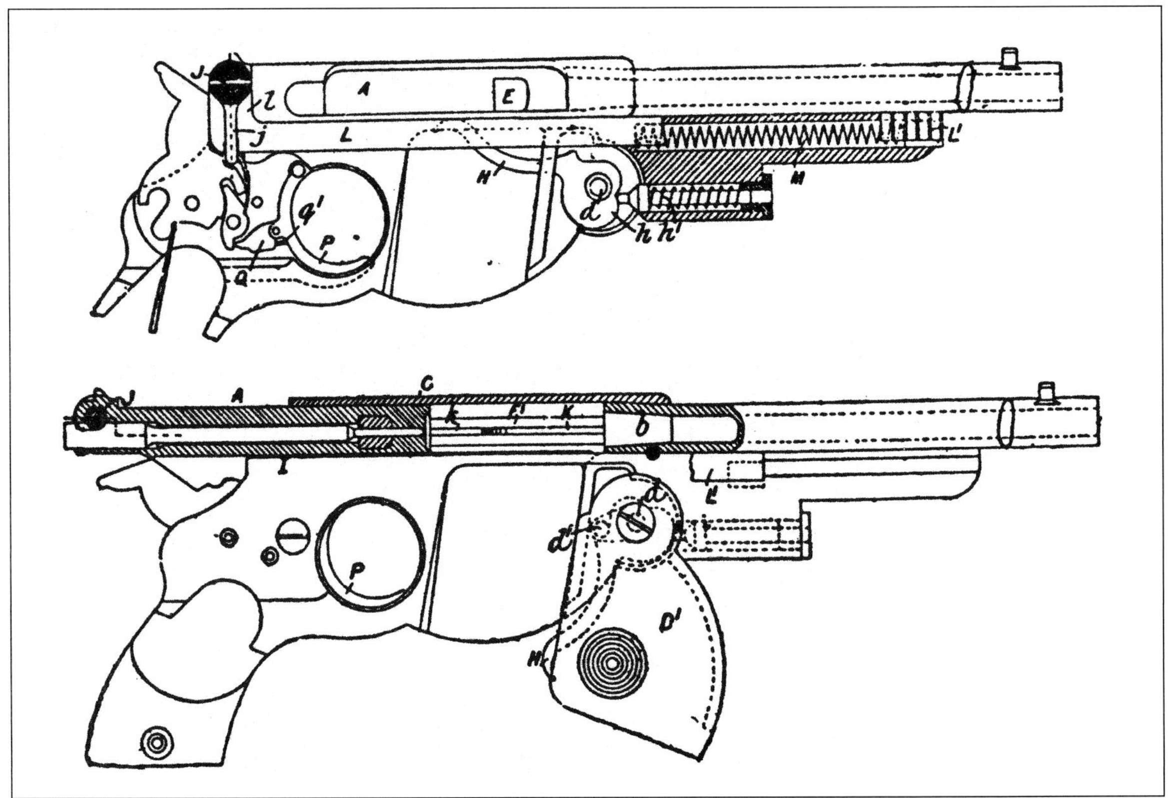

Above: Patent 13070, 5 July 1894, Eisenwerk Gaggenau. Eisenwerk Gaggenau was Theodor Bergmann's trading name, so we may be fairly sure that this came from the end of Louis Schmeisser's pencil. Although not Bergmann's first pistol patent, this is substantially his master patent for the group of blowback pistols he produced in the latter half of the 1890s.

To accompany the 5mm No 2 model, for those who required something rather more powerful, there were the 6.5mm Bergmann No 3 and the 8mm Bergmann No 4 pistols. Mechanically they were the same as the 5mm version, firing non-grooved, non-rimmed cartridges loading from a clip, and they differed solely in dimensions and calibre. The 5mm model was sold as an indoor 'saloon' target pistol and the 6.5mm as more of a general-purpose weapon, and the 8mm was put forward as a potential military arm. However, although all three were accurate and pleasant to shoot (according to contemporary reports), they made no great impression on the market place.

It would not be unreasonable to assume that their poor sales might have been due to the eccentric ejection system. In any event, within a year or so Bergmann abandoned his system, developed conventional rimless cartridges and fitted positive extractors and ejectors to his pistols. The new cartridges were identified as the Model 1896 pattern, and the change took place before any of the three calibres had reached a serial number of 1000.

The model described here is the 6.5mm No 3; as noted, the 5mm No 2 and 8mm No 4 versions are identical in principle, differing only in dimensions and, in some cases, in the method of attachment of the barrel. The bolt is a hollow lightweight steel unit with the firing pin running inside it. In all Bergmann models the firing pin is completely free and without a spring,

Right, upper: The 5mm Model 1896 is typical of all the early Bergmann pistols.
Right, lower: Right side of the 6.5mm Bergmann No 3, showing the magazine opened to receive a clip of cartridges and the bolt drawn back.

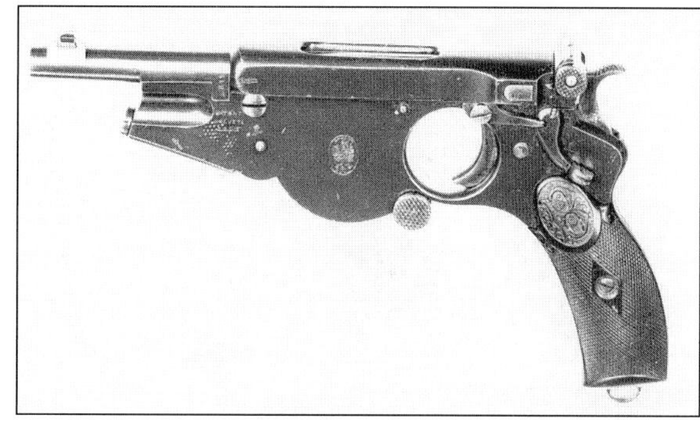

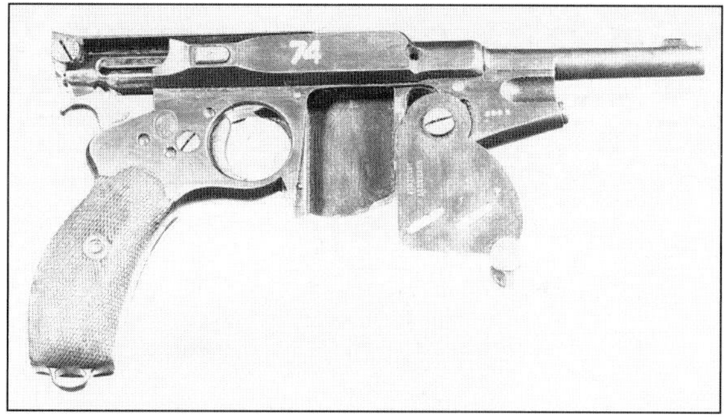

being so light as to be pushed to the rear by the resistance of the chambered cartridge without even indenting the primer cap. An external hammer strikes the pin when released by the trigger. The weak point of the design lies in the magazine, which is really an adaptation of the Mannlicher clip system used with several contemporary military rifles. A spring-loaded arm is used to force cartridges up through a light metal clip to a position where the bolt can strip the cartridge from the magazine; the magazine is loaded by swinging open a side plate (this action also pulling the feed arm down and clear), dropping the loaded clip into the magazine recess and closing the plate to bring the arm to bear on the bottom cartridge. The clip, provided with a finger loop which protrudes through the bottom of the magazine, can now be withdrawn downwards, leaving the cartridges in place, or it can be left in position, in which case it falls clear when the last round is loaded into the chamber. The system is reasonably good when the clip is left in place but, when withdrawn, the excess space in the magazine allows the cartridges to shuffle about and usually jam under the pressure of the spring arm.

Bergmann No 3, 1896

Calibre	6.5mm Bergmann No 3 1894
Method of operation	Blowback, hammer-fired
Safety devices	Manual catch on left side of receiver
Magazine type	Single-column, clip-loaded, side-opening
Position of catch	On magazine cover
Magazine capacity	5 rounds
Front sight	Fixed blade
Rear sight	Fixed V-notch
Overall length	10.03in (255mm)
Barrel length	4.40in (112mm)
Number of grooves	6
Direction of twist	Right-hand
Empty weight	31.0oz (880g)
Markings	Left side of magazine: a badge representing a miner (*Bergmann*) carrying a pick-axe and lantern; left side of frame, close to the chamber: 'PATENT BREVETE S.G.D.G.'; on top of breech slide: 'PISTOLET BERGMANN'
Serial number	On barrel and on frame below breech

To dismantle the Bergmann, after clearing the gun, remove the cross-screw at the rear of the bolt and withdraw it to the right. Tip the gun, cock the hammer and shake out the firing pin. Now press out (in either direction) the cross-bolt retaining the bolt unit and allow the recoil spring to come out; pull back and remove the bolt, and then remove the bolt cover by lifting the rear end while unhooking the front edge. Beneath the breech on the left side is the barrel locking screw; remove this and the barrel is free to be unlocked by rotating it through 180° and sliding it out to the front. At the front of the frame is a hollow screw; removing this allows a rod and spring to slide out, releasing tension on the magazine cover. Take out the cover pivot screw and the cover and magazine follower arm can be lifted off. There is no necessity to proceed further and strip the lockwork for normal cleaning, though the method of stripping is apparent on examination. To reassemble the weapon the reverse order is followed.

If, when the gun is assembled, it is desired to hold the bolt to the rear, this can be done by pulling it fully back and then pressing the trigger, allowing the hammer to rise and lock into a notch on the lower surface of the bolt. To release the bolt, the hammer must be pressed back to the cocked position with the thumb.

The later models of these pistols used a conventional extractor and grooved cartridge case, which considerably improved their reliability; in the 5mm and 8mm calibres—and, occasionally, in the 6.5mm calibre—the barrel was screwed into the frame instead of employing the turn-and-pull system just described.

Below: The 6.5mm Bergmann No 3 seen in dismantled condition.

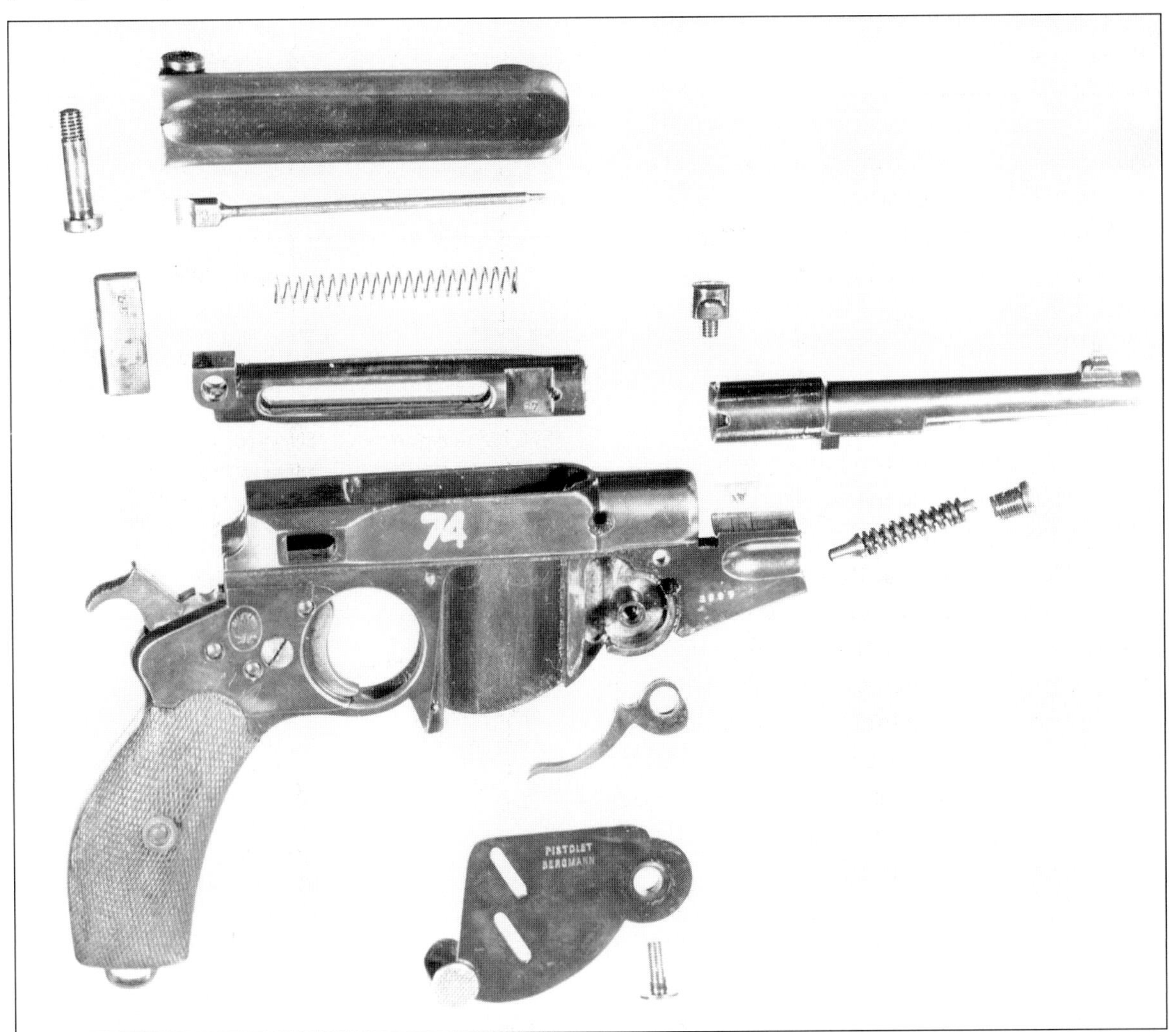

Above: The 10mm model was submitted to the British Army for test in 1902; the design is that of the earlier 7.8mm No 5, with a locked breech and a removable magazine.

Even though the improved design sold in greater quantity that the earlier models, the market was slow; much of this, of course, was due to the pure novelty of the automatic pistol and doubtless the cost compared to the myriad cheap revolvers available at that time. What was needed was a fat military contract, but no military force would even look at a small-calibre blowback pistol.

In 1897 Bergmann patented a locked-breech version of his design in which the barrel and breech were locked together on firing and recoiled as one unit for some 6mm, after which a cam face on the frame moved the bolt sideways to unlock it. The barrel movement was stopped by a frame lug, allowing the bolt to continue to the full extent of its travel. On return, the bolt was forced back into alignment with the barrel by a flat spring and then carried the barrel back into battery. The general design and appearance was similar to that of the blowback pistols, except that the magazine was of the rather more practical removable box, fitted ahead of the trigger guard in a similar manner to the better-known Mauser. Bergmann now put this design into production as his M1897 pistol or No 5. It was in 7.63mm calibre and the cartridge was very similar to the 7.63mm Mauser's, but with a longer neck; to avoid confusion Bergmann called it the 7.8mm No 5. The pistol's butt was shaped like a revolver butt and was prepared for a detachable shoulder stock. A very few were equipped with long barrels and chambered for a special high-velocity cartridge; these were always fitted with the shoulder stock and were termed 'carbines', being another example of the attempt to market a handy weapon for game shooting. It is open to doubt whether these models were ever contemplated as cavalry weapons.

For reasons which no doubt seemed good at the time, Bergmann now chose to step back, and he abandoned his detachable box magazine to return to the side-loading clip system of his earlier design. Allied to the locked breech, this appeared as the Bergmann No 7 pistol in 1899, chambered for a new 8mm cartridge which eventually became the 8mm Simplex and

Bergmann No 4, 1894

Calibre	8mm Bergmann No 4 1894
Method of operation	Blowback, hammer-fired
Safety devices	Manual catch on left side of receiver
Magazine type	Single-column, clip-loaded, side-opening
Position of catch	On magazine cover
Magazine capacity	5 rounds
Front sight	Fixed blade
Rear sight	Fixed V-notch
Overall length	10.03in (255mm)
Barrel length	4.40in (112mm)
Number of grooves	6
Direction of twist	Right-hand
Empty weight	31.4oz (890g)
Markings	Left side of magazine: a badge representing a miner (*Bergmann*) carrying a pick-axe and lantern; left side of frame, close to the chamber: 'PATENT BREVETE S.G.D.G.'; on top of breech slide: 'PISTOLET BERGMANN'
Serial number	On barrel and on frame below breech

Bergmann No 5, 1897

Calibre	7.8mm Bergmann No 5, 1897
Method of operation	Recoil, laterally locked, hammer-fired
Safety devices	Manual catch on left side of receiver
Magazine type	Detachable box, charger-loaded
Position of catch	Beneath frame, ahead of magazine
Magazine capacity	5 rounds
Front sight	Fixed blade
Rear sight	Fixed V-notch
Overall length	10.62in (270mm)
Barrel length	3.94in (100mm)
Number of grooves	6
Direction of twist	Right-hand
Empty weight	40.75oz (1,155g)
Markings	Monogrammed 'B' moulded into the buttplates; no other markings on specimen examined
Serial number	On barrel and on frame below breech

bore no relation to his earlier 8mm No 4 cartridge.

Neither the 5 nor the 6 appealed to the military, and after trying the No 6 in 7.5mm and 7.65mm calibres with no success, Bergmann reverted to his No 5 design but somewhat more robustly built and chambered for a potent 10mm cartridge, offering this to the British Army in 1902. (It is perhaps worth comment that this was the first attempt by anybody to promote a 10mm cartridge; and it was to be more than sixty years before the calibre was accepted.) As ever, the British were adamant that nothing less than .45in could be effective as a military cartridge and turned the 10mm Bergmann down.

BERGMANN-BAYARD

In 1901 Bergmann had patented a machine gun design using a vertically moving locking piece to secure the breech; he now adapted this locking system to his No 5 pistol (which he now called the Mars) and produced a new cartridge, the 9mm No 6, and with this he at last achieved his aim.The design was adopted by the Spanish Army, but, with success in Bergmann's grasp, fate dealt a cruel blow.

Throughout all these years, Bergmann's manufacturing capacity had been small, and more or less confined to making prototypes and experimental weapons; production was always performed by a sub-contractor, the V. C. Schilling company in Suhl. Now, in 1904, as Bergmann was about to make arrangements for the manufacture of pistols for Spain, Schilling was bought out by the Heinrich Krieghoff company and the long-standing agreement with Bergmann was abruptly terminated. Since he could not possibly fulfil the contract from his own small factory in Gaggenau, Bergmann sold his contract to the Belgian firm Anciens Établissements Pieper and quit the pistol business to concentrate on making machine guns.

The Pieper company made some small changes in the pistol, mainly to suit their manufacturing convenience, and also some slight dimensional changes in the cartridge, and both then became known as the 9mm Bergmann-Bayard, 'Bayard' being the Pieper trademark. They completed the Spanish contract and then went on to market the pistol commercially, se-

Below:The 9mm Bergmann-Bayard, with magazine removed.

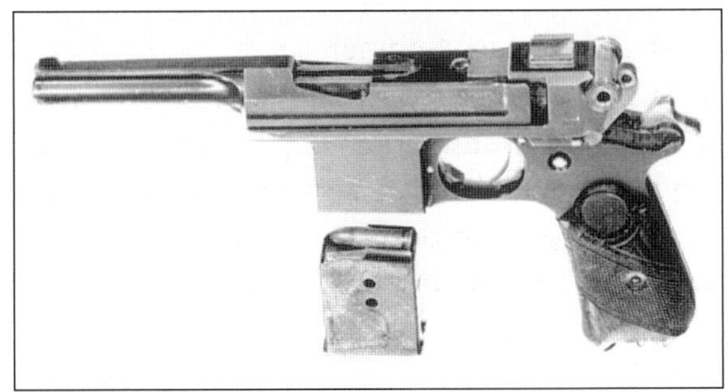

Bergmann-Bayard Model 1908

Calibre	9mm Bergmann-Bayard
Method of operation	Recoil, vertically locked, hammer-fired
Safety devices	Manual catch on left side of receiver
Magazine type	Detachable box, charger-loaded
Position of catch	On magazine cover
Magazine capacity	6 rounds
Front sight	Fixed blade
Rear sight	Fixed V-notch
Overall length	9.84in (250mm)
Barrel length	4.02in (102mm)
Number of grooves	6
Direction of twist	Right-hand
Empty weight	35.8oz (1015g)
Markings	On left side: 'BREVETE S.G.D.G. ANCIENS ETABLISSEMENTS PIEPER HERSTAL LIEGE BERGMANN'S PATENT'
Serial number	On right side of frame, ahead of the hammer

curing a contract from Denmark in 1910 and another from Greece in 1913, though this latter was suddenly stopped when the Germans occupied Belgium in 1914. Pieper never resumed production after 1918, but the Danes had a slightly modified version made in the 1920s, some of which were manufactured in Belgium and others in Denmark. The Spanish Army gave up the pistol in 1920, but retained the cartridge (calling it the 9mm Largo) until the 1980s.

Theodor Bergmann retired in 1910 and died in 1915. The business continued under the guidance of Hugo Schmeisser (the son of Louis, who had left the company in 1912), and in about 1912 Schmeisser began producing an automatic pistol which bore no similarity to the earlier Bergmann designs but leaned more towards the Browning 1906 pattern. The Taschen Pistole (Pocket Pistol) appeared in four models: No 2 and No 3 were in 6.35mm calibre and were both full-slide blowback pistols of quite conventional form. The difference was that the No 3 had a deeper butt frame and a magazine containing nine rounds instead of the six of the No 2.

The No 4 and No 5 models were of the same basic design but the No 4 was in 7.65mm Browning and the No 5 in 9mm Browning Short calibres. But it seems that production of these pistols was slow to start and was then terminated by the outbreak of war providing the Bergmann factory with more important things to do, and thus all these models are relatively scarce.

Hugo Schmeisser left Bergmanns in 1919 and went to Haenel; the Bergmann company appears to have continued in operation and to have prepared to bring the Taschen Pistolen back into production. At the same time, the company acquired some sort of interest in a one-hand pistol developed by a Pole named Witold Chylewski, resident in Hungary. How Bergmanns became involved in this is not recorded, but the result was that a highly modified Taschen Pistole with the essential one-hand cocking system of Chylewski was produced as the Bergmann Einhand in late 1919 or early 1920.

Below: The Bergmann-Bayard dismantled.

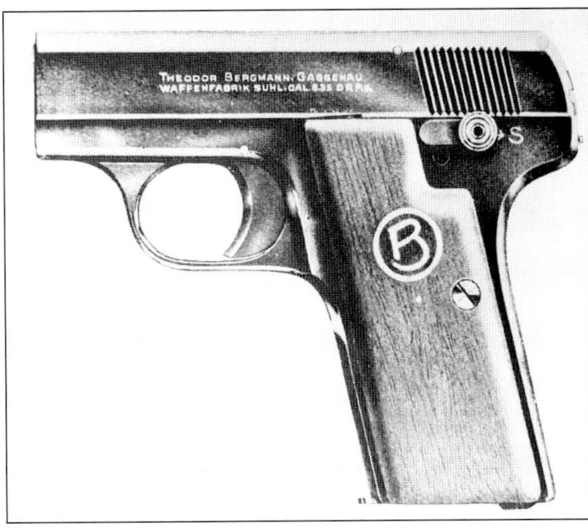

Above: The 6.35mm Taschen Modell Bergmann shows a reversion to a more conventional sort of design.

However, by this time the Bergmann concern appears to have been drifting aimlessly with no guiding hand at the helm. In the aftermath of war, industries were reorganising and combining into more economic units, and as part of this turmoil the Bergmann name and factory were acquired by the Lignose Pulverfabrik, which was busy snapping up various small independent firms and combining them into the A. G. Lignose-Berlin. Their subsequent exploitation of the Bergmann name and the Taschen and Einhand pistols is detailed under the Lignose heading on a later page, and in the entry on Bergmann Erben below.

Bergmann Taschen Modell 3

Calibre	6.35mm Browning
Method of operation	Blowback, single-action, striker-fired
Safety devices	Manual catch on left rear of frame
Magazine type	Single-column detachable box in butt
Position of catch	At heel of butt
Magazine capacity	9 rounds
Front sight	None
Rear sight	Groove in slide top
Overall length	4.72in (120mm)
Barrel length	2.16in (55mm)
Number of grooves	6
Direction of twist	Right-hand
Empty weight	16.75oz (475g)
Markings	Left of slide: 'THEODOR BERGMANN. GAGGENAU WAFFENFABRIK SUHL.'; right of slide: 'MODELL III KALIBER 6,35'
Serial number	On right side of frame

BERGMANN ERBEN

Th. Bergmanns Erben GmbH, Suhl

As if the affairs of Th. Bergmann are not already sufficiently convoluted, we must now examine the activities of a fresh company bearing the Bergmann name, though in truth it had nothing whatever to do with Bergmann. As noted above, in 1920 the Bergmann company was absorbed by the A.G. Lignose-Berlin. The firm appears to have prospered, so much so that in 1937 it extended its reach and acquired the Menz company of Suhl, incorporating the Menz pistol designs into its product line but identifying them as products of 'Theodor Bergmanns Erben'. 'Erben' translates as 'heirs' or 'successors', and this name appears to be little more than an attempt to profit from the goodwill extant in the Bergmann name, since there is no connection between Bergmann and these pistols.

The first models, in 7.65mm calibre, were the Bergmann Erben Spezial, which was simply the contemporary Menz P&B Spezial which had been in production at the time of the takeover. The 7.65mm Bergmann Erben Model 2 resembled the P&B Spezial but with some minor details changed; for example, the magazine release was a push-button in the front left edge of the grip instead of the usual spring catch at the heel of the butt. This pistol was also produced in 9mm Short chambering.

Above: The Bergmann Erben Model 2 was more or less a Menz Model 2 with some cosmetic changes.

Numbers of 6.35mm Liliput pistols were also produced as the Model 1 and can only be distinguished from the Menz product by the monogrammed medallions on the grips, which bear crossed pistols and 'Th B Suhl'. For further details on the pistols, see the Menz entry.

The 6.35mm Bergmann Erben Model 2 was the only original design, and even that had a distinct Menz look about it, since it resembled a shortened and lightened version of the 7.65mm Menz Model 2 with a somewhat more tapered front end to the slide and frame. The slide top was stepped, so that the initial reaction is to think it is an exposed barrel, but it is a full-slide design. There are no special tricks about dismantling: merely pull back the slide as far as it will go, lift, and pass forward over the barrel.

Bergmann Erben Model 2

Calibre	6.35mm Browning
Method of operation	Blowback, single-action, striker-fired
Safety devices	Manual catch on left rear of frame
Magazine type	Single-column detachable box in butt
Position of catch	At heel of butt
Magazine capacity	7 rounds
Front sight	Fixed blade
Rear sight	Groove in slide top
Overall length	4.88in (124mm)
Barrel length	2.60in (66mm)
Number of grooves	6
Direction of twist	Right-hand
Empty weight	14.5oz (410g)
Markings	Left of slide: 'THEODOR BERGMANN ERBEN WAFFEN-FABRIK SUHL'; right of slide: 'MODELL II KALIBER 6,35'
Serial number	On right side of frame

BORCHARDT

Ludwig Loewe, Berlin
Deutsche Waffen- und Munitionsfabrik, Berlin

Hugo Borchardt was born in Magdeburg in 1844 and emigrated to the United States in 1860. Nothing is known of his activities until 1865, when he first appears as Superintendent of Works (or factory manager) of the Pioneer Breech-Loading Arms Company, a fairly responsible position for a young man of 21 and evidence that he must have spent the intervening years learning the machinist's trade. The Pioneer company soon collapsed and Borchardt moved to the Singer Sewing Machine Company and then to Colt's Patent Firearms Company. After a few months with Colt he moved once more, this time to the Winchester Arms Company, where he became involved in the design of revolvers.

Several of Borchardt's prototype revolvers survive, though it is doubtful if he was entirely responsible for the design. Winchester were keen to develop a revolver to use as a bargaining counter with Colt, who had begun marketing a lever-action rifle. The ploy worked: Colt stuck to making pistols and Winchester to making rifles. By that time, however, Borchardt had moved once again, becoming factory Superintendent for the Sharps Rifle Company in 1876,

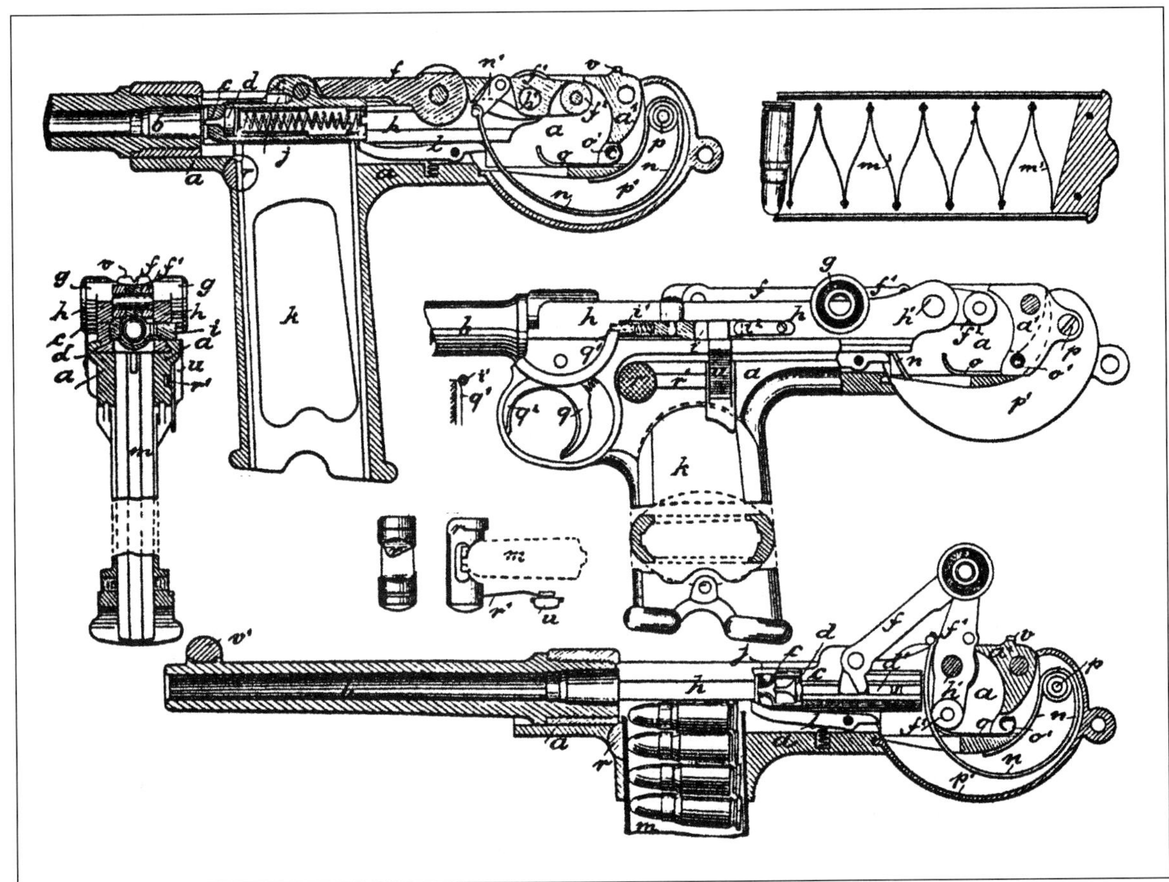

Above: Patent 18,774, 6 October 1893, Hugo Borchardt. This was Borchardt's pistol patent that shows his application of the Maxim toggle lock, his placing of the magazine inside the butt and, most particularly, his clock-spring recoil arrangement.

where he designed a very successful rifle. But the company was under-capitalised and went into liquidation in 1880, leaving Borchardt without a job. He left the United States and went to Hungary to work for the Hungarian arsenal in Budapest, becoming works manager by 1889. It is probable that during this period he saw demonstrations of the Maxim machine gun, then being touted around Europe, and, impressed by the toggle locking system used in the Maxim, began working an a design of automatic pistol.

He returned, briefly, to the USA in 1891, but after that his movements become a mystery. He took out German patents for his pistol in September 1893, and there is evidence that Borchardt pistols were being manufactured by the Ludwig Loewe factory in Berlin in July of that year. But the precise relationship between Borchardt and Loewe is not clear: the best estimate is that he approached Loewe as a private individual, gained Loewe's agreement to finance and produce the pistol as licensee, and was thereafter retained by Loewe as a designer and consultant.

What is in no doubt is that Borchardt's pistol was a viable, commercially successful, locked-breech automatic pistol. As to being the first automatic pistol of all, there is room for suspecting that the Bergmann No 2 of 1894 might take that position; unfortunately there are no surviving production or sales records that would settle the argument.

The operation of the pistol is based upon Maxim's toggle lock, though applied in a different manner. The barrel is attached to a 'barrel extension', a metal framework extending back from the chamber and acting as a guide to the movement of the bolt. A toggle—two steel 'limbs' joined by a hinge—lies behind the bolt, one limb being attached to the bolt and the other to the rear end of the barrel extension. They act like a human leg: when straight, the arrangement resists pressure; once the knee is bent the resistance ceases. In this case, when the cartridge is fired, the rearward movement of the cartridge case due to the gas pressure is resisted by the straight leg of the two toggle limbs, and the impulse is delivered to the rear end of the barrel extension. At the same time, the normal recoil effect causes the entire barrel, barrel extension, bolt and toggle to move backwards. After a short distance, the central hinge of the toggle strikes a ramp on the pistol frame and thus the 'knee' is forced to bend, whereupon the gas pressure inside the chamber drives the case backwards, opening the bolt, folding up the toggle and placing a return spring under tension. The cartridge case is ejected and the return spring now pulls the toggle back down to the straight-line position. In so doing it drives the bolt forward to strip a fresh round from the magazine (in the butt—another first for Borchardt) and ram it into the chamber. The toggle drops flat, the firing pin has been cocked, and the pistol is ready to fire once more.

The Borchardt has an odd appearance as the butt is almost central, there appearing to be as much pistol behind the firer's hand as in front of it. The butt is at right angles to the axis of the bore and, together with the rear overhang, leads to an inconvenient grip. This overhang is largely due to the difficulty which Borchardt found in designing a suitable return spring system, bearing in mind that he was tilling virgin ground and had nobody from whom to copy. His solution was to adopt a coiled leaf spring, rather like a clock mainspring, which is curled up in the prominent housing at the rear of the pistol. This spring is hooked to spurs on the rear limb of the toggle in such a fashion that the rising of the toggle increases the tension on the spring, which later reasserts itself and closes the breech. It can readily be appreciated that the adjustment of this spring is a most critical feature of the assembly of this pistol. Unlike a

Below: The Borchardt of 1894—elegant engineering, ingenious design, but a somewhat impractical combat weapon.

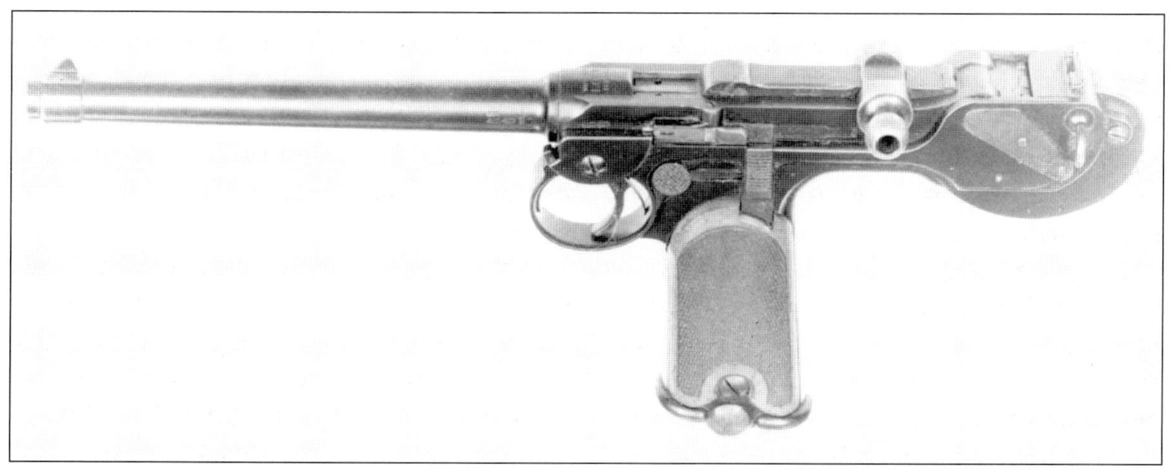

coil spring, it cannot be shortened or replaced by a longer one—it has to be exactly the correct length and tension when made—and, once fitted, it has to be adjusted to operate at the correct tension. This delicacy of action, together with the round-to-round variations in chamber pressure and recoil force which were common with the early smokeless powders, makes the self-loading action of the Borchardt somewhat less than reliable—though, of course, it was a notable advance for its day.

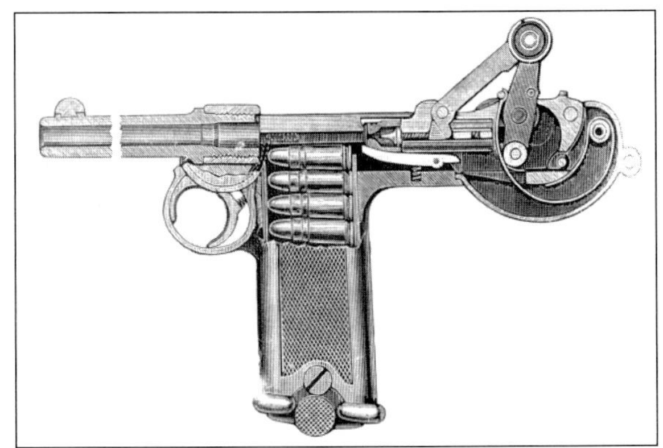

Above: The toggle mechanism of the Borchardt pistol.

The Borchardt cartridge resembles the Mauser 7.63mm round but is very slightly smaller and it is sometimes possible to chamber Mauser rounds in the Borchardt pistol, although the power of the Mauser round is more than the Borchardt was designed to accept; the toggle-joint action is particularly sensitive to the ammunition used, and the combination of Mauser rounds and the Borchardt pistol cannot be recommended. It has been reported that a very few models were actually chambered and provided with stronger recoil springs to suit them to 7.63mm Mauser cartridges (in about 1913), but in spite of diligent research no positive confirmation of this has appeared. There are also reports that models of this pistol have been seen chambered for the 7.65mm Parabellum cartridge, but, again, there is no firm evidence of this and I am not entirely convinced.

An extract from *Arms and Explosives* for April 1920 is of interest here. In a review of Captain H. B. C. Pollard's book *Automatic Pistols*, the reviewer reminisces as follows:

'We don't think he quite does justice to Borchardt's cartridge, for though he credits it with being the father of those which followed it, he would have said more in praise had he heard certain remarks of the inventor, in which Borchardt claimed that he could not move with the design of the pistol until he had materialised a cartridge capable of withstanding the entirely novel conditions imposed by automatic loading. Some further remarks Borchardt made proved the existence of a certain amount of soreness against Mauser who, taking the cartridge worked out by Borchardt, found the construction of an improved pistol to fire it an easy matter, for he had also the faults of the other to guide his design. We do not submit this addendum in the spirit of criticism, since nobody but those who were engaged in the arms trade at the time could appreciate first the incredulity and then the amazement which accompanied the exhibition by Mr. H. F. L. Orcutt at his Cannon Street offices of the hand-made model of the pistol, which was passed round during the time when the tools were being prepared for quantity production.'

Henry Orcutt was the London agent for Ludwig Loewe, and it is unfortunate that the writer omitted to note the date on which this hand-made model was exhibited, but more recent research by John Walter suggests that it may have been in the late spring of 1895.

In the matter of stripping the Borchardt, the best advice I have ever heard came from a highly professional gentleman who, when I was examining his Borchardt during a hurried visit, said 'Are you going to strip it?' 'I don't think I will,' I replied, 'as I haven't much time.' 'Thank God,' he replied, 'I stripped it once and took two days to get it all back together and working properly.' Today the ease of stripping and maintaining a weapon is usually paramount in the designer's mind from the moment he picks up his pencil, and many promising weapons of the past have failed to gain acceptance because of neglect of this feature. However, in Borchardt's day this was a minor consideration compared with getting a working pistol, and this can be seen when attempting to take a pistol of this type to pieces for the first time.

To dismantle the Borchardt then—if you really must—first ensure that the magazine is removed, the gun empty and the striker forward. Then grasp the recoil spring housing securely, remove the screw therein and then allow the housing to come away from the pistol (under control, since the recoil spring is tending to force it off). Pull the housing clear and unhook the recoil spring from its anchorage on the toggle. Do not attempt to remove the recoil spring from the housing. The side covers on the frame may now be lifted clear to expose the toggle anchor pin, which can then be pushed out. (It may be said at this point that familiarity with stripping the Luger is an asset when dealing with the Borchardt.) Next remove the screw above the trigger and push up the trigger plate and trigger to remove them. The barrel unit with the toggle can now be slid forward on the frame and removed, and the toggle and breech block can be taken from the barrel assembly by sliding them rearwards. The breech block is closed at the rear by a screw-head; give this half a turn and it, together with the firing pin and firing-pin spring, can be removed.

Reassembly is the reverse of the above procedure, but care should be taken when hooking the recoil spring on to the toggle and replacing the recoil spring housing in position.

The Borchardt was provided with a shoulder stock in order to convert it into a carbine; this—the earliest of such attachments—is undoubtedly also the best, since it is fitted by sliding it across a dovetail section on the recoil spring housing and then tightening up a thumbscrew in the stock to draw pistol and stock tightly together. This results in an absolutely rigid assembly, far better than the later Mauser or Luger designs, and it is possible to make good target shooting with a stocked Borchardt at two hundred yards or more.

Borchardt later patented an improved model of this pistol (American Patent 987,543 of 21 March 1911), but there is no evidence that one was ever made. The pistol was first made by Ludwig Loewe, but in 1896 this company amalgamated with Deutsche Metallpatronenfabrik, Karlsruhe, to become Deutsche Waffen- und Munitionsfabrik (DWM) and the pistols manu-

Borchardt 1894

Calibre	7.65mm Borchardt
Method of operation	Recoil, toggle-locked, striker-fired
Safety devices	Manual catch on left side of frame above butt
Magazine type	Single-column detachable box in butt
Position of catch	On left side of butt behind trigger
Magazine capacity	8 rounds
Front sight	Fixed blade
Rear sight	Tangent V-notch graduated 100–700m
Overall length	10.98in (279mm)
Barrel length	6.5in(165mm)
Number of grooves	4
Direction of twist	Right-hand
Empty weight	41.6oz (1,160g)
Markings	On top of breech: 'WAFFENFABRIK LÖWE BERLIN'; on toggle: 'DRP Nr. 75837'; on right side of frame: 'SYSTEM BORCHARDT PATENT'
Serial number	On bottom of butt, bottom of magazine and trigger

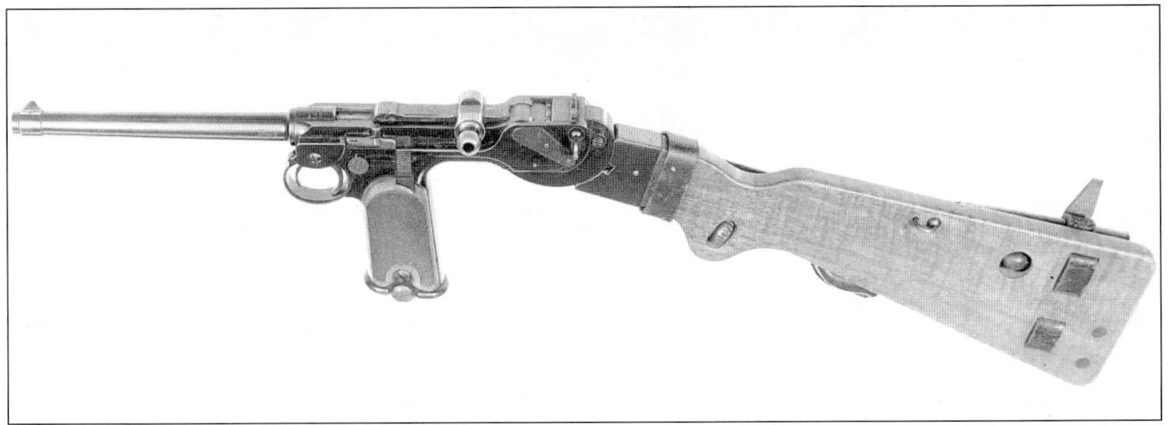

Above: A Borchardt with its shoulder stock fitted. The stock forms a backing board for the leather holster on the other side.

factured after 1 January 1897 bear the DWM monogram on the toggle in a similar fashion to the later Luger pistols. The version examined here, serial number 107, was manufactured by Loewe.

Later pistols (after January 1897) carry the DWM script monogram on the toggle, and on the right side of the frame 'SYSTEM BORCHARDT PATENT DEUTSCHE WAFFEN- UND MUNITIONSFABRIK BERLIN'.

BUCHEL

Ernst Friedrich Buchel was a gunsmith of Zella Mehlis, running a business which dated from some time in the early 1880s. He became best known for his target rifles and pistols sold under the names of Luna and Tell. These were single-shot weapons in the common target calibres of the time—ca. 1900 to 1939—using a falling block breech operated either by a lever running down the backstrap of the butt (the Tell pattern) or by an unusual ring protruding from the bottom of the grip (the Luna pattern). This was pulled forward by the free hand to open the breech so that the marksman's grip on the pistol did not have to be released in order to reload. Virtually all Buchel's pistols were 'made to measure', the only near-standard dimension being the 300mm barrel; the rest of the weapon depended upon the whims of the purchaser. In general, they weighed about 1,150g.

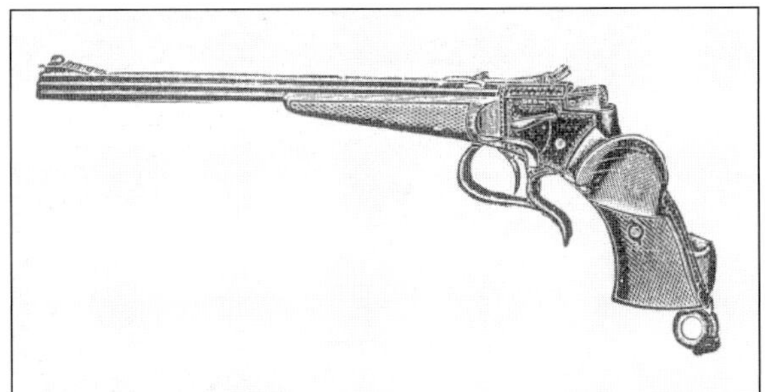

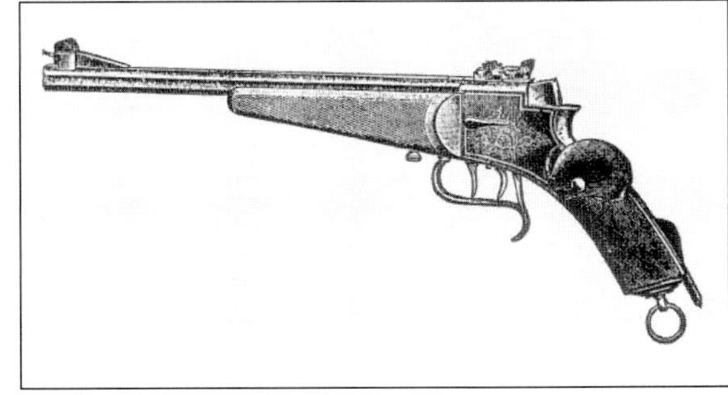

Right, upper: Buchel's Luna target pistol, showing the actuating ring for the breech block beneath the butt.
Right, lower: The Buchel Tell pistol, showing the backstrap lever which operated the falling-block breech. (John Walter)

BUHAG

Buchsenmacher Handwerkgenossenschaft AG, Suhl, GDR

In the days of East Germany the Buhag concern was one of the few companies maintaining the gunmaking tradition of Suhl outside a state cooperative. Their only product was a .22 Short RF target pistol, the Olimpiamodell, which appears to be based upon the pre-war Walther Olympia, using a fixed long barrel, open-topped slide and internal hammer. Target sights and a muzzle counterweight were available, as were grips of varying contour to suit the user. These pistols were rarely seen in the West, though they appear to be a serviceable and accurate product.

CONTINENTAL

The two pistols bearing the name 'Continental' and purporting to be of German origin (since there are several non-German Continental pistols as well) both bear the name of the Rheinische Waffen- und Munitionsfabrik (RWM) of Köln (Cologne). Whether such a company ever existed is open to some doubt; if it did exist, whether it actually made its own pistols is in even greater doubt.

The first model was certainly not made in Germany: it bears all the hallmarks of the cheap

Below: This 6.35mm Continental bears all the signs of cheap Spanish manufacture. The grips are of translucent plastic material, added by an amateur handyman, and are not original.

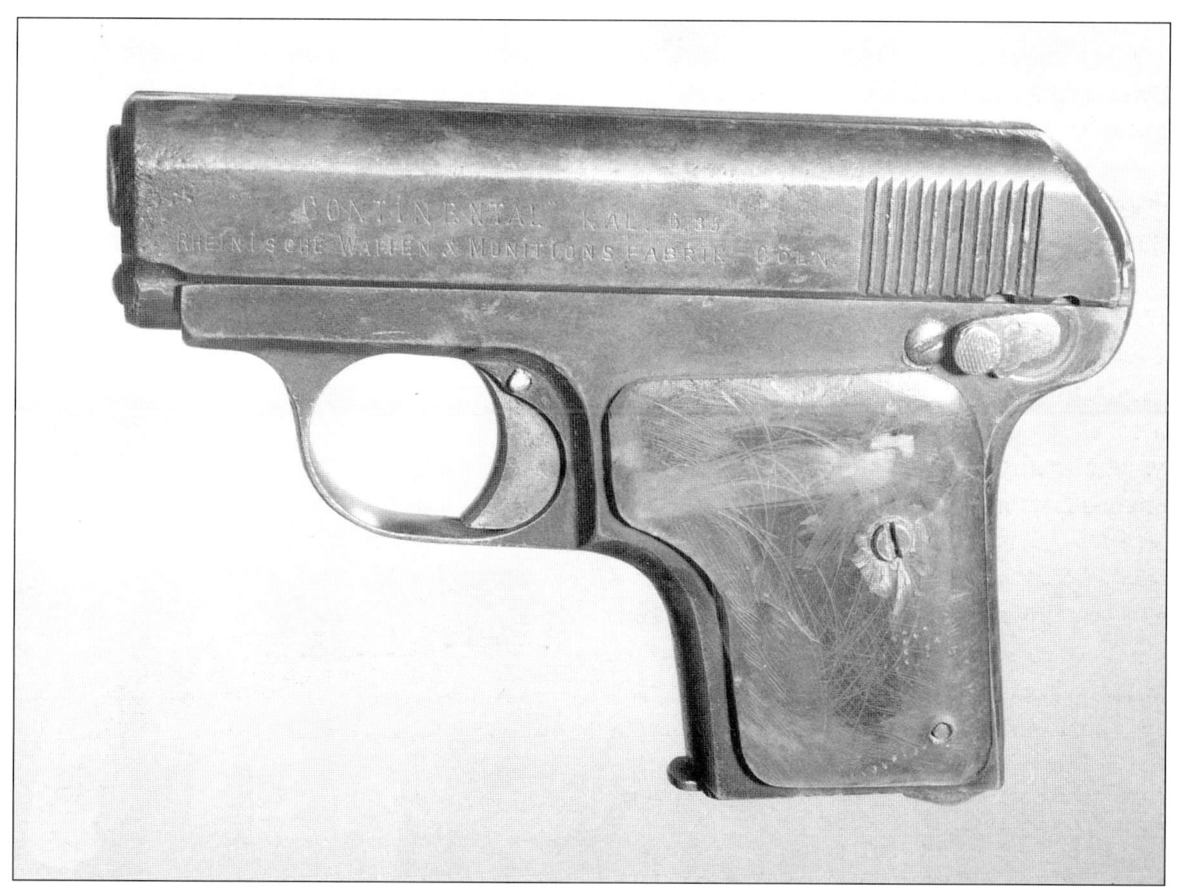

Continental

Calibre	6.35mm Browning
Method of operation	Blowback, hammer-fired
Safety devices	Manual catch on left side of frame above butt
Magazine type	Detachable box
Position of catch	At heel of butt
Magazine capacity	7 rounds
Front sight	Fixed blade
Rear sight	Groove in slide top
Overall length	4.76in (121mm)
Barrel length	2.08in (53mm)
Number of grooves	4
Direction of twist	Right-hand
Empty weight	14.1oz (400g)
Markings	On left side of slide: 'CONTINENTAL KAL 6,35 RHEINISCHE WAFFEN UND MUNITIONSFABRIK CÖLN'
Serial number	None

Spanish Eibar pistol design, pirated from the Browning M1903 and M1906 models and produced by the million between 1906 and 1936. Some were good; many more were badly made of poor material, and this Continental is one of the latter class.

The design has been copied from the original Browning 1906 pattern and altered to make it a little easier to manufacture: instead of being striker-fired it has an internal hammer, which at least carries the asset of allowing a good safety catch to be fitted which both positively locks the hammer in the 'safe' position and disconnects the lockwork to permit the trigger to move without placing any strain on the linkage. It is unfortunate that the only specimen I have been able to find has lost its original butt grips and has been fitted at some time with a poorly made set of plastic grips which do nothing for the appearance. The pistol carries a full set of genuine German proof marks, and after much investigation I have concluded that the RWM of Cologne was actually a sales agency and the pistol was made by Francisco Arizmendi of Eibar, who manufactured it for sale in Germany in the early 1920s.

Stripping the Continental is in the usual manner of Browning designs, since the barrel is held in the frame by two ribs on its underside engaging in grooves in the frame. But stripping is at least made easier by the provision of a special notch on the slide, enabling the slide to be positioned correctly to permit the barrel to be rotated for unlocking. On most Browning designs one has to hold the slide in just the right position—against the pressure of the recoil spring—to unlock the barrel; this takes a certain amount of practice and a good deal of patience.

To dismantle the Continental, first remove the magazine and clear the gun, then push the slide back slightly until the safety catch can be turned up into the foremost of the two notches on the slide's lower edge. With the slide so locked it should now be possible to rotate the barrel and unlock the ribs from their grooves. Once this is done the slide is gripped to take the pressure off the recoil spring and the safety catch is turned down. The slide will now go forward and can be removed complete with

Below: The Continental dismantled, showing the simplicity of the design.

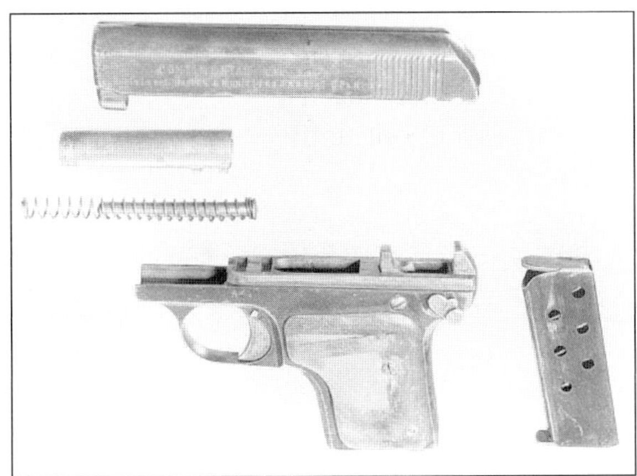

barrel, recoil spring and guide rod. There is no reason to proceed further.

Difficulty may be experienced in rotating the barrel, since the safety catch is usually of soft metal and after many years' use will have worn to the point where the slide is allowed to stop slightly forward of the proper unlocking point. Once the slide and barrel unit are removed, the barrel can be rotated inside the slide until the lugs are visible, when the barrel is free to be lifted from the slide. It cannot be taken out forwards. It will be noted that the muzzle is surrounded by an ornamental band of flora engraving which acts as a convenient finger grip for dismantling.

To reassemble, place the barrel in the slide and position it so that the two lugs match the two cut-out slots at the bottom of the ejection opening. Now rotate the barrel through 90°. Place the recoil spring in the housing hole in the slide and put the guide rod into the rear end of the spring. With the slide and barrel unit held upside down, offer it up to the frame and slide it back until the safety catch can be relocated in the stripping notch. Now the barrel can be rotated through 90°, watched through the ejection port, until it engages with the frame. Release the safety catch and allow the slide to go forward. Occasionally the recoil spring guide rod does not seat in its locating hole in the frame and, after the slide has gone forward, about an inch of rod protrudes beneath the barrel, which is disconcerting. If this happens, grasp the rod and waggle it about until it drops into its correct location.

CONTINENTAL (2)

The second weapon attributed to the Rheinische Waffen und Munitionsfabrik is, however, an entirely different weapon and one which suggests German origin. It appears to be based upon the Webley & Scott Police Model automatic of 1906 and is in 7.65 ACP calibre. The left side of the slide is marked 'Continental Automatic Pistol 7,65 m/m System Castenholz'. I have been unable to trace any details of this 'system' and cannot offer any suggestion as to its features. One thing we can be fairly certain of is that this pistol was not made by Arizmendi like the other model; had he done so he would undoubtedly have marketed it elsewhere under some other name, and this design has never appeared in Spain to the best of my knowledge. The pistol is said to bear German proof marks, and it may be that it was made by some small factory in Belgium or Germany and marketed by RWM, probably before 1914.

Since no actual specimen of this pistol has been found, and the only illustration we have is a poor one from an old catalogue. We cannot be certain of some details: for example, this Continental does not appear to have any form

Continental (2)

Calibre	7.65mm Browning
Method of operation	Blowback, hammer-fired
Safety devices	Not known
Magazine type	Detachable box
Position of catch	At heel of butt
Magazine capacity	8 rounds
Front sight	Fixed blade
Rear sight	U-notch in slide
Overall length	6.40in (167mm)
Barrel length	3.93in (100mm)
Number of grooves	6
Direction of twist	Right-hand
Empty weight	20.10oz (570g)
Markings	On left side of slide: '*CONTINENTAL* AUTOMATIC PISTOL CAL. 7,65m/m SYSTEM CASTENHOLZ'; on right side of slide:'RHEINISCHE WAFFEN UND MUNITIONSFABRIK KÖLN'
Serial number	Not known

Above: The System Castenholz Continental in 7.65mm calibre.

of safety catch, which, on the original Webley & Scott, was alongside the hammer very much in the same way as that of the 1912 Mauser c/96 pistols. I feel it safe to assume that such an otherwise accurate copy will dismantle in the same manner as the original.

Remove the magazine and draw back the slide to eject any round in the chamber. Allow the slide to go forward but do not press the trigger. Dismantling is effected by springing the trigger guard from its lower seating and swinging it down and forwards. This allows the slide and barrel to be drawn off forward. The barrel can then be removed from the slide, and that is all the dismantling necessary. Reassembly is simply the reverse: insert the barrel into the slide, fit the slide back on to the frame and replace the trigger guard.

DECKER

Wilhelm Decker, Zella Mehlis

Wilhelm Decker of Zella Mehlis took out patents in 1912 covering a remarkable pocket revolver and put it into production in the same year. Had it not been for the outbreak of war in 1914 it might have become better known, but the war drove such novelties from the market and it never returned.

The Decker revolver was a six-shot solid frame model in 6.35mm Browning chambering. It was a hammerless design in the strictest sense of the phrase: most revolvers described as hammerless actually use a concealed hammer, but the Decker used an axial striker, cocked and released by a long pull on the trigger. It was thus a self-cocking lock, or, in the modern idiom 'double-action only'. The trigger was attached to a long bar running beneath the cylinder which, when drawn back, rotated the cylinder by means of a pawl, then locked the cylinder in place, and finally cocked and released the firing pin.

Loading was done through a gate on the left side, ejection of spent cases being through the same gate, thrusting them out by means of a pin carried inside the cylinder arbor. On the right side of the frame was a thin sheet metal cover concealing the rear of the cylinder and preventing the cartridges falling out and also making a smoother contour to the revolver so that it was less likely to snag inside a pocket

Below: The Decker revolver. Note the position of the loading gate and the safety catch: the pistol can only be loaded or unloaded when set to 'safe'.

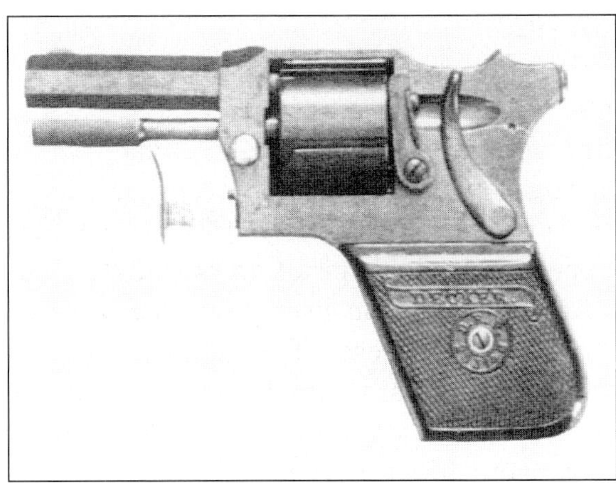

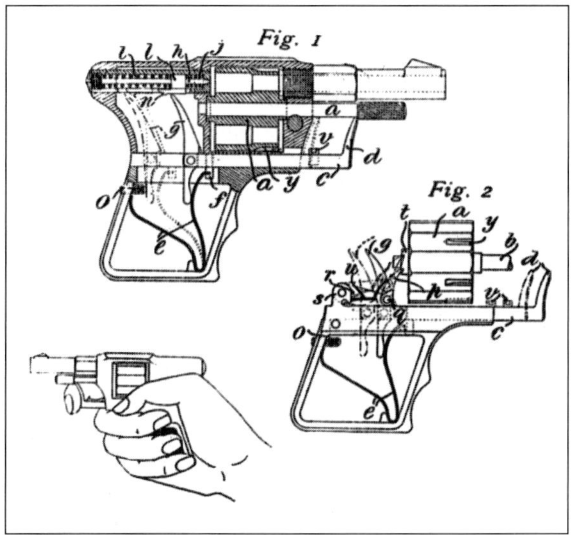

Above: The patent drawings of the Decker revolver.

when it was being drawn. There was a large safety lever on the left side of the frame, so placed that it had to be drawn back into the 'safe' position before the loading gate could be opened, thus preventing accidental discharges whilst loading.

Decker revolvers are rare today, for it is doubtful if more than a few hundred were made. Decker himself makes later appearances in the patent files between 1919 and 1922 with various automatic pistol mechanisms and details, none of which ever bore fruit, and he appears to have abandoned the pistol field by the middle 1920s.

It seems likely that the Decker revolver was also marketed for a short time as the Müller Special revolver by one R. H. Müller. In the spring of 1914 announcements appeared in the trade press in Britain referring to the imminent appearance of this pistol on the market, and from the description given it is virtually certain that it was the Decker. This would also appear to have been a war victim: no specimen has ever been found, and it is probable that the venture never got under way at all.

DREYSE

Rheinische Metallwaren und Maschinenfabrik, Sommerda

The name of Johann-Niklaus von Dreyse is more generally associated with the famous Dreyse Needle-Gun, the first practical bolt-action breech-loading military rifle, but there are also three twentieth-century pistols bearing his name, even though he died in 1867. After his death the Dreyse gunmaking business was continued by his son Franz, though in a somewhat reduced form, and after the death of Franz in 1894 the company almost collapsed, eventually being bought by the Rheinische Metallwaren und Maschinenfabrik in 1901. As well as the factory and patents, they also acquired the name, and proceeded to use it as a brand name on a number of weapons, including the following three pistols.

6.35mm Model 1907

The 6.35mm Pocket Pistol is constructed according to a patent taken out by Louis Schmeisser in 1909 (British Patent 20,660) which covers the peculiar method of holding everything together. So far as its operation is concerned, it is a simple blowback pistol, soundly enough made but of no particular excellence. When the slide is pulled back in the usual way to load the chamber and cock the action, an unusual construction is immediately apparent, as the breech section of the slide carries a top rib which also moves, making ejection of the spent case a more than usually precise operation. Both the front and rear sights are attached to this rib, and to strip the gun, after the usual safety precautions have been taken, the rear sight is grasped and pulled up against the spring of this rib; it is then pulled backwards to withdraw the rib entirely from the

Above: Another design from the drawing board of Louis Schmeisser, the Dreyse 6.35mm pistol has some unique features.

slide. The pistol should now be held upside down by the butt, in the right hand, while the left fingers grip the serrated portion of the slide and push back against the recoil spring. If this is done correctly, the barrel drops out into the left palm. It is located in the gun simply enough (by a peg passing down into the frame) and is anchored in place by the top rib alone. After the barrel drops clear the slide can be taken off in a forward direction and the recoil spring and guide rod can be taken from the frame anchorage. The firing pin and spring, which normally abut against the upstanding portion of the frame, can be slipped from their tunnel in the slide. No further stripping is advisable.

Dreyse 6.35mm Model 1907

Calibre	6.35mm Browning
Method of operation	Blowback, striker-fired
Safety devices	Manual catch on left grip
Magazine type	Single-column detachable box in butt
Position of catch	At heel of butt
Magazine capacity	6 rounds
Front sight	Fixed blade
Rear sight	Fixed V-notch
Overall length	4.48in (114mm)
Barrel length	2.05in (52mm)
Number of grooves	4
Direction of twist	Right-hand
Empty weight	14.1oz (400g)
Markings	Left side of slide: 'DREYSE'; on top of grips, moulded, a monogram 'RMF'
Serial number	Beneath the barrel, beneath the breech section of the slide and on the right side of the frame

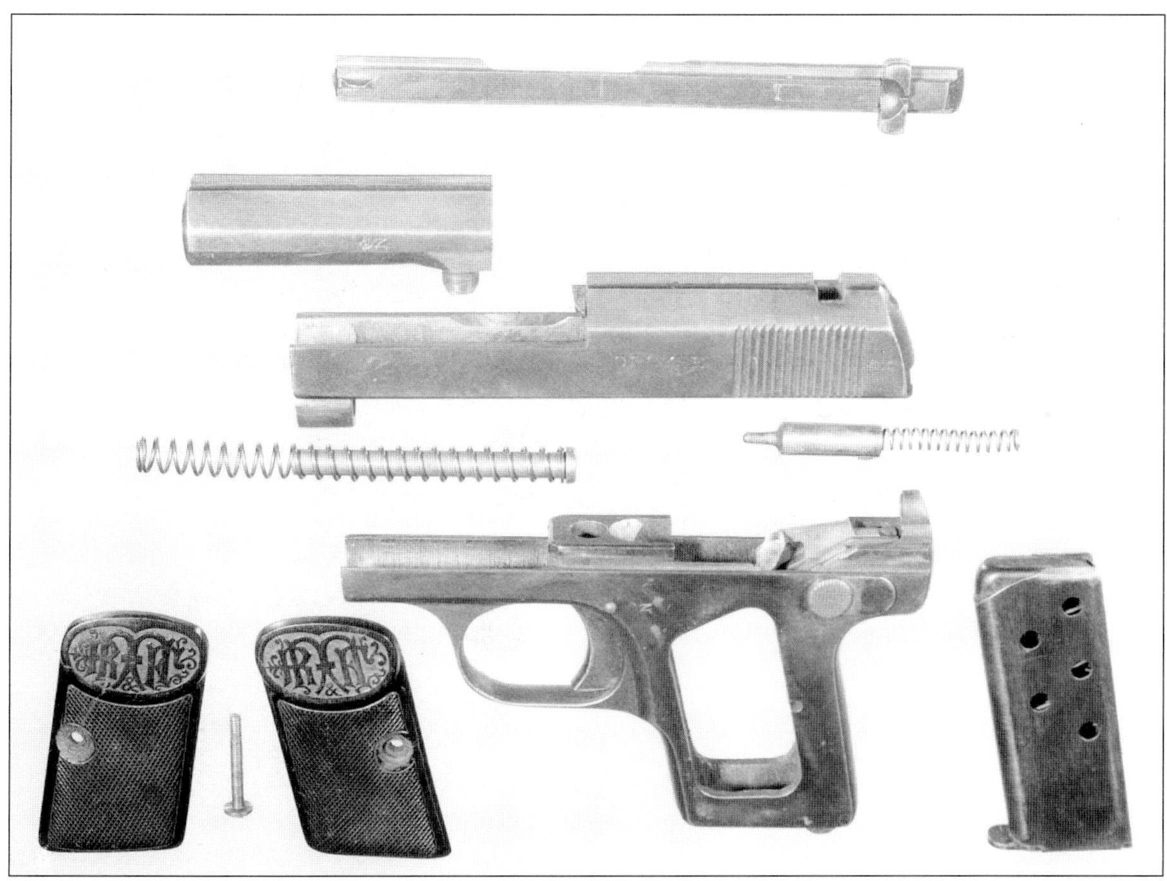

Above: The 6.35mm Dreyse dismantled. Note the locking strip at the top, which fits into the top of the slide and holds the barrel in place.

Reassembly is in the reverse order. To replace the barrel, it is best to hold the pistol the correct way up, with the fingers round the grip, and, pushing the slide back an inch or so, trap it there with the thumb. Then the barrel can simply be dropped in place, the slide allowed to go forward and the top rib slid into place and locked by springing the rear sight into its slot.

7.65mm Model 1907

The next larger Dreyse pistol, the 7.65mm, was originally developed for civil sale just before World War I but was taken into military service in 1917 in some numbers as a substitute standard weapon, notably for use by staff officers and rear-area troops. It possesses many interesting constructional features and evidence of much original thought in its design; these various features can best be examined in the course of dismantling.

To ensure that the gun is safe, having removed the magazine by pressing the catch in the bottom of the butt, it is necessary to pull the slide back. However, the slide in this pistol is not simply 'everything above the butt': above the barrel is a grooved section, and, by gripping this and pulling back, it will be seen that the slide is only the top half of what appears to be the barrel casing, and that it goes on to form a breech block which retracts from the fixed casing above the butt. When the slide is released the firing pin protrudes through the back of the breech block to show that the gun is cocked.

Dreyse 7.65mm Model 1907	
Calibre	7.65mm Browning
Method of operation	Blowback, striker-fired
Safety devices	Manual catch left rear of frame
Magazine type	Detachable box in butt
Position of catch	At heel of butt
Magazine capacity	7 rounds
Front sight	Fixed blade
Rear sight	Fixed V-notch
Overall length	6.29in (160mm)
Barrel length	3.66in (93mm)
Number of grooves	4
Direction of twist	Right-hand
Empty weight	25oz (710g)
Markings	On left of breech block cover plate: 'DREYSE RHEINMETALL ABT. SOMMERDA'; at the top of the grips a monogram, moulded, of 'RMF'
Serial number	On top of frame, just in front of magazine well; on bottom of barrel housing below breech; and on top of breech block

To strip the gun a screwdriver or similar thin implement is desirable; the end of the barrel is surrounded by a thin collar and this must be pressed in 0.25in (6mm) in order to allow a stud formed in this collar to free itself from a groove in the slide. Once free, the slide can be lifted up, but great care must be taken at this point since the barrel collar and recoil spring are liable to fly out violently. They should be released under control and the slide may then be lifted.

By pulling the slide right back in the barrel housing and then lifting its nose, it can be pulled clear together with the breech block section which forms the rear end. The extractor can be lifted from its groove in the block, and the firing pin and spring can be removed by unscrewing the large slotted plug through which the rear of the firing pin protrudes when cocked. No further stripping is really necessary. To re-assemble, the reverse order is followed, the barrel sleeve being pushed down with the screwdriver until the slide can be dropped into place over the lug.

There are two further items of interest in this weapon. Below the rear end of the breech block, on the frame, is a thumb catch which can be pressed to the right to release the whole barrel and slide assembly, which then hinges about a pivot just forward of the trigger guard. It is, frankly, difficult to see what benefit this bestows on the design other than making it slightly easier to clean. Secondly, a screw in the barrel housing, on the left of the breech, locks the barrel in place. By removing this screw the barrel is unlocked and can be unscrewed and withdrawn by a suitable tool which engages recesses in the barrel forging just in front of the breech.

The firing mechanism of this particular weapon is commonplace, but some of the wartime manufactured pistols have a slightly modified system which, when the trigger is pulled, causes the striker to be first driven back—further compressing the striker spring—before being released. This system, also used on the 9mm Dreyse, is probably a reflection on the quality of wartime ammunition and an insurance against poor-quality springs, faulty main-

Below: The 7.65mm Dreyse is another original and unique design. Notice that the finger grips are at the front of the slide.

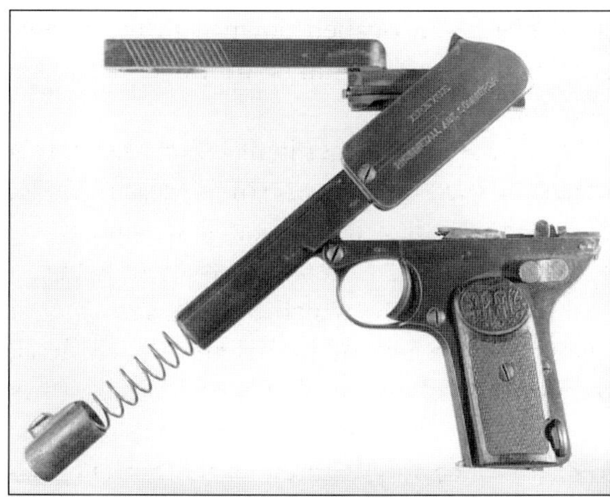

Above: Dismantling the Dreyse. A minor item of interest is the very positive form of magazine catch at the heel of the butt.

tenance, mud and similar evils, all of which could weaken the blow of the striker if the usual system were in use. Another wartime expedient was the forming of the front end of the slide with a small finger-recess in the top surface, through which it was possible to pull back the barrel sleeve with the fingernail without recourse to tools.

9mm Model

The 9mm Dreyse, while resembling an enlarged version of the 7.65mm in general appearance, has one or two features which make it considerably different in construction. The weapon appears to have been designed just prior to World War I for private sale and, being chambered for the 9mm Parabellum cartridge, was frequently used by soldiers although it does not appear to have been honoured by official adoption or approval. It is of the blowback pattern and ranks as one of the earliest weapons to attempt to adapt this system for a cartridge as powerful as the Parabellum. Application of blowback with a round of this power demands either a heavy recoiling mass or a strong recoil spring, and, since the construction of the breech block is the same as that seen in the 7.65mm pistol (giving a fairly light recoiling mass), a strong recoil spring it has to be. This, in turn, leads to difficulty in cocking: anyone doubting this is invited to try his hand at cocking a 9mm Spanish Astra, particularly when it has been lightly oiled. So, in order to relieve the user of this problem, the Dreyse is designed to disconnect the recoil spring from the slide during the hand-cocking action.

The basic configuration of the 9mm pistol is much the same as that of the 7.65mm version: the recoil spring surrounds the barrel and is held by a bush as before. Instead of the recoiling portion anchoring to the bush at the muzzle, the portion of the slide extending over the barrel is furnished with a cocking piece, a steel arm

Dreyse 9mm Model

Calibre	9mm Parabellum
Method of operation	Blowback, striker-fired
Safety devices	Manual catch left rear of frame
Magazine type	Single-column detachable box in butt
Position of catch	At heel of butt
Magazine capacity	8 rounds
Front sight	Fixed blade
Rear sight	Fixed V-notch
Overall length	8.11in (206mm)
Barrel length	4.96in (126mm)
Number of grooves	6
Direction of twist	Right-hand
Empty weight	37oz (1,050g)
Markings	On left of breech block cover plate: 'DREYSE RHEINMETALL ABT. SÖMMERDA.' or 'RHEINISCHE METALLWAREN UND MASCHINENFABRIK SÖMMERDA'; at the top of the grips a monogram, moulded, of 'RMF'.
Serial number	On top of frame, just in front of magazine well; on bottom of barrel housing below breech; and on top of breech block

Above: The 9mm Dreyse is an enlargement of the 7.65mm model, but there are some changes in the method of construction.

hinged at the muzzle to the slide and provided with thumb and finger grips at the rear, above the rear of the breech block. This cocking piece forms a cover to the whole top of the pistol; it is also provided with a lug which engages, when the cocking piece is down, with a lug formed on the recoil spring bush—which in this weapon extends well back, to a point about half way down the barrel. It will be observed that the barrel seems disproportionately long for such a pistol, and the probable reason is to permit sufficient travel of the bush before coming up against the breech end of the barrel.

To load the pistol, a magazine is first inserted in the butt, then the grips at the rear end of the cocking piece are grasped and the whole piece is lifted slightly so as to disengage the two lugs. Then the cocking piece (and with it the slide and breech block) is pulled to the rear and then pushed back—loading the first round into the chamber—with no more exertion than that needed to overcome the slight resistance of the striker spring being partially compressed as the striker engages with the sear. Once the breech is firmly closed, the cocking piece is pressed down once more so that the lugs engage. On firing, the recoiling breech block carries with it the slide and cocking piece, and due to the engagement of the two lugs the cocking piece pulls back the recoil spring bush and compresses the recoil spring.

While this is all very well in theory—and all very well in practice in a brand new gun of good material—it tends to fall down with use. The principal drawback seems to be that the lugs, and particularly the upper one on the cocking piece, were not particularly well hardened and after some years of use they tend to wear, to the point where engagement with the recoil spring collar lug is doubtful. Once this point is reached, firing the pistol causes the lugs to jump out of contact, the cocking piece flies up and the slide and breech block recoil violently and remain open. This is almost always the case with those Dreyse 9mm pistols which make their appearance from time to time today. I have fired one once, but I have no desire to repeat the performance.

As mentioned in the previous section on the 7.65mm, the firing mechanism is designed so as to throw additional compression on the striker spring when the trigger is pulled.

Stripping this pistol is much the same as stripping the 7.65mm version. The cocking piece should be pulled up and retracted, whereupon a spring catch holding the recoil spring collar is revealed at the muzzle. With this catch depressed, the bushing and spring can be removed. The axis pin hinging the cocking piece to the slide can be pushed out to disconnect the two items and allow the slide and breech block to be drawn to the rear. Instead of the thumb piece of the 7.65mm pistol, which allowed the weapon to be 'broken open', the 9mm model has a much stronger and more positive spring-loaded pin passing through the frame and breech casing; by depressing the spring with a fine drift or screwdriver, the pin can be pushed out to the right and the barrel tilted about the frame to facilitate cleaning.

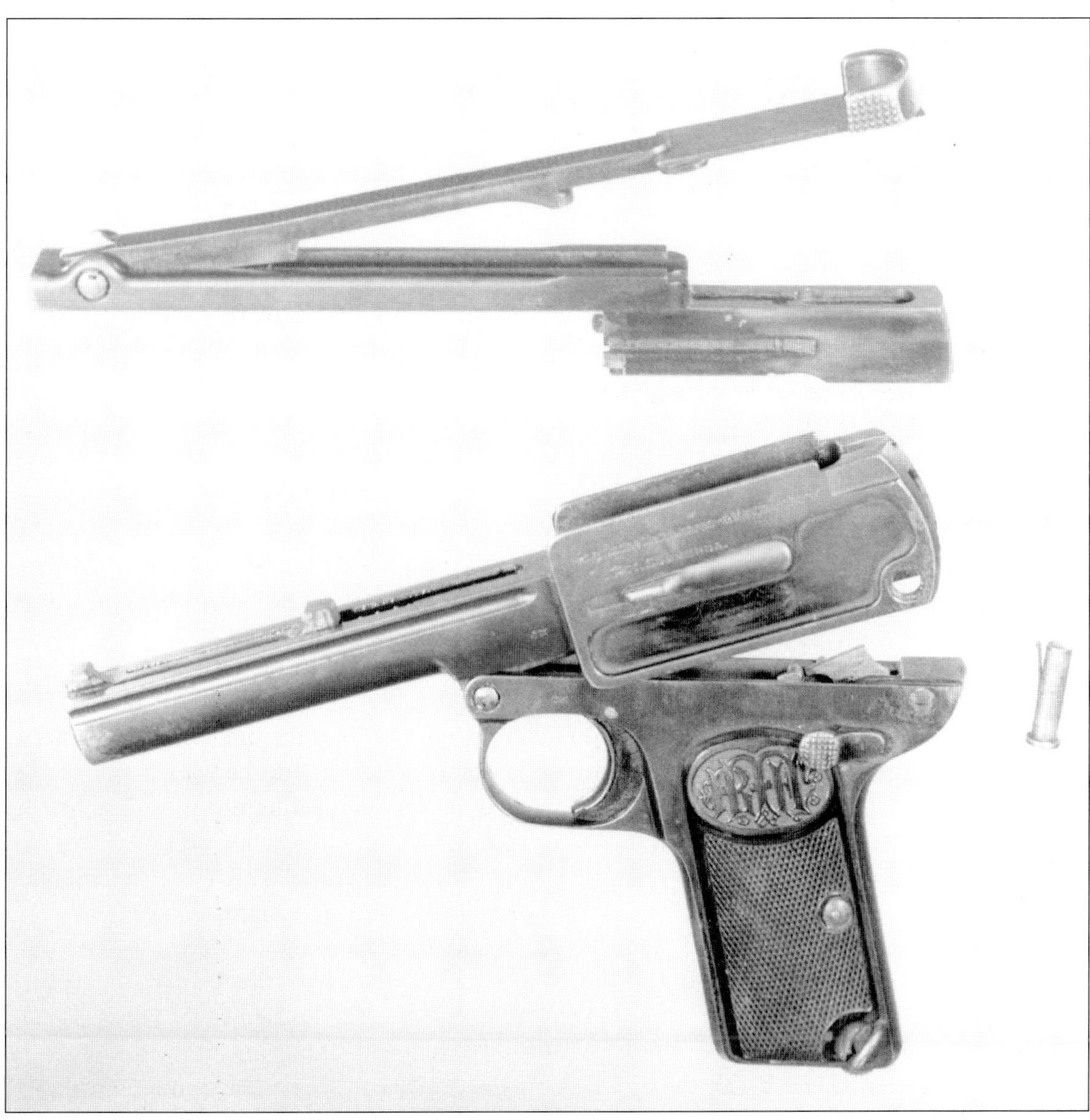

Above: Dismantling the 9mm Dreyse. Notice the upstanding lug in the top of the frame, ahead of the trigger. This engages with the hook on the topmost section of the slide when firing, but is disengaged in order to cock the pistol.

The 9mm Dreyse was made in relatively small numbers; manufacture stopped sometime during the First World War—available evidence points to mid-1916 or thereabouts—and it was never revived, though some dealers who had bought stocks before the war were still advertising the pistol in the early 1920s. It is quite rare today.

DWM

Deutsche Waffen- und Munitionsfabrik, Berlin

The origins of Deutsche Waffen- und Munitionsfabrik of Berlin lay with the formation in 1872 of Heinrich Ehrmann & Company to manufacture brass cartridges. Ehrmann & Co. became Deutsche Metallpatronenfabrik Lorenz in 1878, but was sold in 1889 to Ludwig Loewe of Berlin. Loewe, one of Germany's leading firearms and machine tool manufacturers, dropped the 'Lorenz' part of the title and subsequently formed prosperous alliances with other ammunition firms. Deutsche Metallpatronenfabrik became Deutsche Waffen- und Munitionsfabrik in 1896, absorbing Loewe's arms manufactory. The company expanded steadily and prospered during 1914–18, but the post-war slump and Versailles Treaty provisions hit the company hard; by 1922 it was no more than a holding company, calling itself the Berlin-Karlsruhe Industriewerk (BKIW). Rearmament in the 1930s revitalised BKIW, which reverted to the DWM title in 1936. War once more led to expansion followed by desperate contraction: the rump of DWM became Industriewerke Karlsruhe (IWK) in 1949, a title revised in the 1970s to become IWKA Industrieanlagen GmbH.

DWM 7.65mm

Calibre	7.65mm Browning
Method of operation	Blowback, striker-fired
Safety devices	Manual catch left rear of frame, grip safety in rear of butt
Magazine type	Detachable box in butt
Position of catch	At heel of butt
Magazine capacity	7 rounds
Front sight	None
Rear sight	Groove in slide top
Overall length	6.00in (152mm)
Barrel length	3.46in (88mm)
Number of grooves	6
Direction of twist	Right-hand
Empty weight	20.1oz (570g)
Markings	Left side of slide: 'DWM' flowing script monogram (if plastic grips are fitted, then the 'DWM' monogram is moulded in)
Serial number	On right side of frame

Above: The DWM 7.65mm pistol was closely modelled on the Browning 1910.

DWM manufactured a wide range of firearms during its life, including Borchardt, Parabellum (Luger) and DWM pistols. Details of the Borchardt and the Parabellum will be found in the relevant sections.

In the aftermath of World War I, DWM found themselves in a quandary: they had a skilled workforce and splendid machinery, but they were forbidden, under the terms of the Versailles Treaty, to manufacture military pistols. They therefore decided to manufacture a pocket pistol for the commercial market.

Instead of employing a designer to come up with something completely novel, DWM took the easy way out and produced a closet copy of the 1910 Belgian Browning, the weapon which made the word 'Browning' synonymous with 'automatic pistol' on the Continent. Its principal features are the placing of the recoil spring around the barrel and the provision of a simple grip safety. In fact they made such a good job of copying that Fabrique Nationale of Belgium, who had designed and produced the original, threatened legal action, even though the Browning patents were on the point of expiry. This, together with declining sales in the later 1920s, led DWM to cease production in 1928, after about 50,000 had been made.

DWM marketed its gun initially as the Model 22. The original version had walnut grips, but these were soon changed to black plastic and the pistol became the Model 23, though this was purely company inventory nomenclature and never appeared on the pistols. The sole marking is the DWM monogram on the left side of the slide and on the black plastic grips.

To strip the DWM, first remove the magazine and clear the gun. Then pull the slide back until the safety catch can be turned up into a notch on the slide to lock it back. Grasp the barrel and rotate it through about 90° until the barrel lugs are unlocked from the frame grooves. Then take the strain on the slide and release the safety catch, allowing the slide to move forward and off the frame. Now depress the bush around the muzzle and turn it until it is freed and forced off by the pressure of the recoil spring; remove the bush and spring and draw out the barrel through the front of the slide. The striker and its spring can be removed from the rear of the slide. Removing a single screw in the right-hand grip will permit both butt grips to be removed, when the lockwork and grip safety mechanism can clearly be seen.

Reassembly is the reverse of stripping, assembling barrel and recoil spring into the slide first.

EM-GE

Em-Ge was the trademark of Moritz & Gerstenberger of Zella Mehlis, who operated from 1922 to 1945 making and selling a wide range of starting pistols, personal defence gas pistols, sporting shotguns and air guns. During the war, using the code identifier 'ghk', they manufactured various types of signal pistol. The company expired in 1945, but in the 1950s, in Gerstetten-Gussenstadt, West Germany, it was reconstituted as Gerstenberger & Eberwein, trading as Em-Ge Sportgeräte GmbH & Co KG. Starting and gas pistols and air weapons still form the greater part of their business, but in the 1960s they began manufacturing three cartridge revolvers.

Model 220

This was a .22 calibre solid-frame double-action revolver of simple construction. Loading and unloading were done by removing the cylinder axis pin and removing the cylinder completely.

Model 220KS

This was a superior version of the Model 220, having a loading gate on the right side and a sliding ejector rod mounted in front of it, alongside the barrel and guided by a rod underneath the barrel.

Model 32

As the title suggests, this is in .32 Smith & Wesson calibre and comes in two versions. The

Em-Ge Model 220KS

Calibre	.22 Long Rifle rimfire
Method of operation	Double-action revolver
Safety devices	None
Magazine type	Rotating cylinder
Position of catch	None
Magazine capacity	6 rounds
Front sight	Fixed blade
Rear sight	Fixed V-notch
Overall length	6.69in (170mm)
Barrel length	2.48in (63mm)
Number of grooves	6
Direction of twist	Right-hand
Empty weight	15.9oz (450g)
Markings	Left side of frame, below hammer: 'Gerstenberger & Eberwein Gussenstadt'; right side of barrel: 'MADE IN GERMANY'; 'EM-GE' medallions on grips
Serial number	On right side of frame

Top: This Em-Ge Model 220KS is a good representative of the company's solid-frame, gate-loaded, rod-ejecting models in .22 or .32 calibres. (John Walter)
Above: The Em-Ge Model 323 uses a simple but effective side-opening cylinder for loading and ejection.

Em-Ge Model 300

Calibre	.32 S&W Long
Method of operation	Double-action revolver
Safety devices	None
Magazine type	6-shot revolving cylinder
Position of catch	On recoil shield, right side of frame
Magazine capacity	6 rounds
Front sight	Fixed blade
Rear sight	Adjustable U-notch
Overall length	10.63in (270mm)
Barrel length	5.90in (150mm)
Number of grooves	6
Direction of twist	Right-hand
Empty weight	32.8oz (930g)
Markings	Left side of frame, below cylinder: 'Gerstenberger & Eberwein Gussenstadt'; left side of top strap, above cylinder: 'MADE IN GERMANY' (or 'MADE IN WEST GERMANY'); left side of barrel: 'CAL 32 S&W Lg'
Serial number	On bottom of butt frame

earlier, from the 1960s, is simply an enlarged Model 220, a solid-frame revolver with removable cylinder for loading and unloading. It came with either 50mm or 75mm barrels and had a six-shot cylinder.

Some time in the late 1970s the design changed subtly to become the Model 323, reflecting, perhaps, the more sophisticated demands of newer shooters. While still a solid-frame pistol, it now had a cylinder crane which was released by pulling a sleeve surrounding the ejector rod. The cylinder then swung out to the left and the contents could be ejected in the usual manner by pushing back on the ejector rod. The front sight was on a ramp and the barrel had a slight upper rib, and in general it was finished to a higher standard.

Model 300

This was intended as an inexpensive target revolver and was a very superior product. It embodied the same swing-out cylinder as the Model 32 but was more robust in all dimen-

Below: Representing the top of the Em-Ge line is this Model 300 with target sights and hand-filling grips.

sions, had a longer and heavier barrel with a ventilated rib, micrometer-adjustable back sight, a very smooth double-action lock and anatomically shaped grips.

ERMA

Erma-Werke B. Geipel GmbH, Erfurt (1919-1945)
Erma-Werke, München-Dachau (1949–)

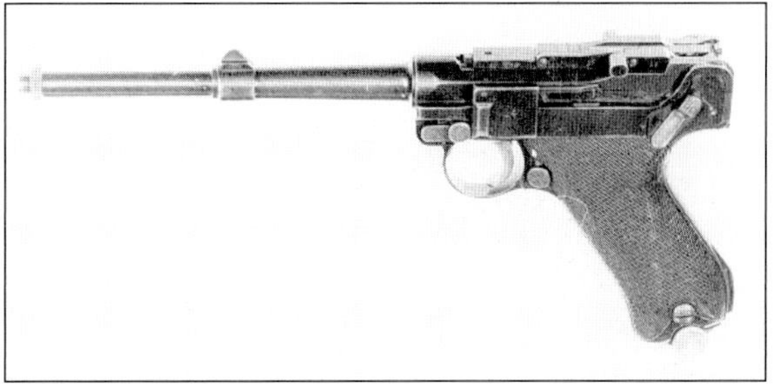

Above: A service Pistole '08 fitted with the Erma conversion unit to permit indoor target practice in .22 calibre.

The Erma-Werke (an acronym derived from Erfurter Maschinen und Werkzeugfabrik, the firm's original name) are probably better known for the range of submachine guns, based upon Vollmer's patents, which they produced in the 1930s, culminating in the immortal MP38 and MP40 designs. They were also, and still are, involved in the pistol business—an involvement which was born in a rather roundabout manner.

In 1933 the German Army began to re-equip, and among other things they needed a convenient system for pistol practice without using a full-sized range. Ermawerke produced the answer with a conversion unit (originally patented in 1927) which turned a standard 7.65mm or 9mm Parabellum pistol into a .22 automatic. This conversion unit included an insert barrel, a breech block and toggle unit, and a magazine. The replacement toggle carried its own recoil spring, since the normal spring (which remained in place in the butt when the pistol was converted) was far too strong to be operated by a .22 cartridge. There were a variety of

Below: The converted P '08 in pieces, showing the special toggle unit and the barrel insert.

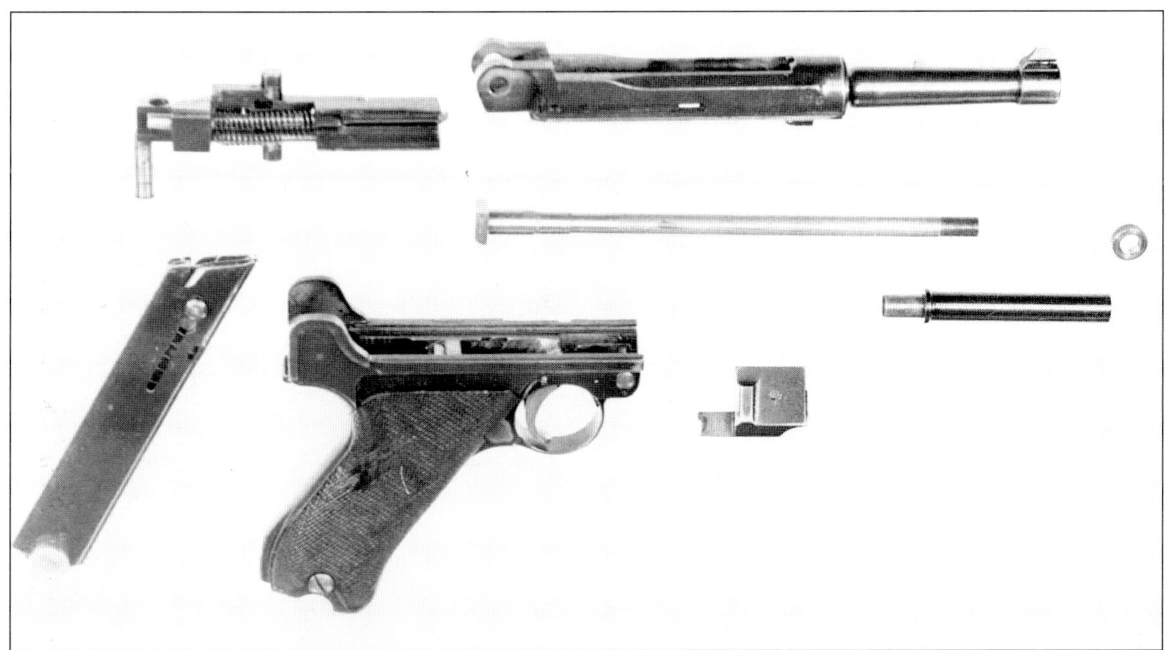

these conversion units for pistols of different calibres and barrel lengths, but the principle remained the same for all. The units were standardised by the German Army in November 1934, and shortly thereafter they were placed on the commercial market. The design was revived in post-war years and remained on sale until the 1950s, when the declining numbers of Parabellum pistols made it no longer worth producing.

From the success of this device, Erma concluded that there could be a market for inexpensive target and practice pistols, and in 1936 they introduced a .22LR blowback automatic, later to be known as the Old Model. This was a fixed-barrel model with an open-topped slide, die-cast zinc frame and external hammer. It was made in two barrel lengths, 110 and 200mm, and was fitted with an adjustable target-type rear sight, and balance weights were made available. Dismantling can be accomplished by drawing back the slide and locking it back with the safety catch, then rotating the dismantling lever on the left front of the frame, after which releasing the safety catch allows the slide to be slipped forward, lifted at the rear, and passed over the barrel to remove it.

Erma Old Model

Calibre	.22 Long Rifle rimfire
Method of operation	Blowback
Safety devices	Manual safety catch on left side of frame
Magazine type	Single-column detachable box in butt
Position of catch	Left side of butt
Magazine capacity	10 rounds
Front sight	Fixed blade
Rear sight	Adjustable V-notch
Overall length	9.05in (230mm)
Barrel length	4.33in (110mm)
Number of grooves	6
Direction of twist	Right-hand
Empty weight	35.1oz (992g)
Markings	Left side of slide: 'Erma Waffenfabrik Erfurt'; left side of frame 'MADE IN GERMANY'; left side of barrel: '.22 Long Rifle'
Serial number	On right side of frame

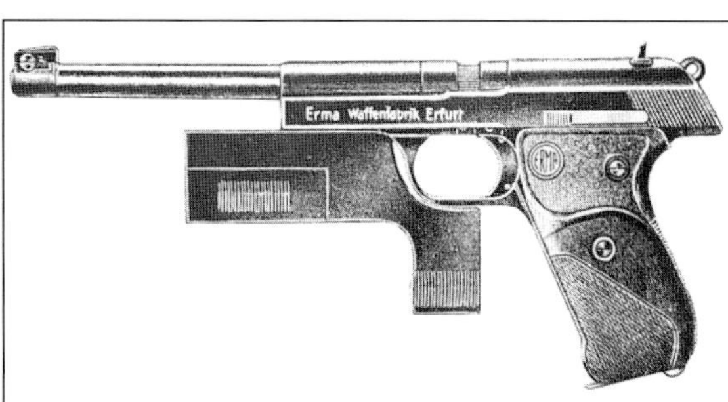

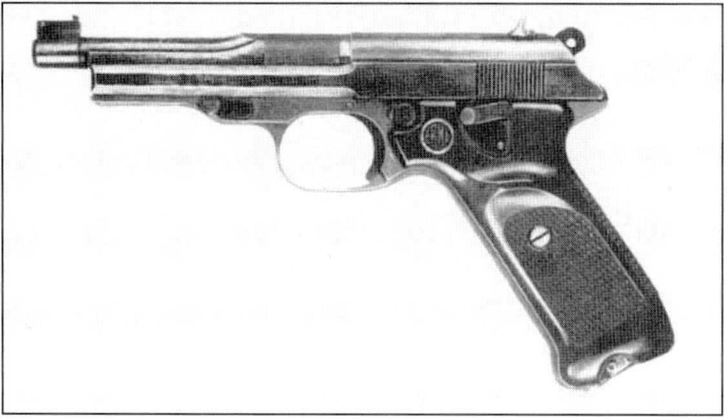

In 1937 an improved version, the New Model, appeared. The grip was at a sharper angle, the magazine was based on that of the Parabellum, and a Parabellum-style stripping catch was mounted on the forward end of the frame. The barrels were interchangeable, and there were slight differences in the barrel contour among the styles available. The Master was supplied with a 300mm barrel as standard, the Sport with a 210mm barrel and the Hunter with a 100mm barrel. Production of all these designs stopped in 1940, since Erma-Werke was by then fully occupied with war production.

In 1945 Erfurt fell within the Soviet Occupation Zone and the company was reconstituted in Munich-Dachau in the late 1940s. In the 1950s they resumed development of sub-

Left, upper: The Old Model Erma .22 target pistol, complete with barrel weights.
Left, lower: The New Model Erma—a somewhat more rakish weapon.

Erma New Model – Master Model

Calibre	.22 Long Rifle rimfire
Method of operation	Blowback
Safety devices	Manual safety catch on left side of frame
Magazine type	Single-column detachable box in butt
Position of catch	Left side of butt
Magazine capacity	10 rounds
Front sight	Fixed blade
Rear sight	Adjustable V-notch
Overall length	15.35in (390mm)
Barrel length	11.80in (300mm)
Number of grooves	6
Direction of twist	Right-hand
Empty weight	38.8oz (1,100g)
Markings	Left side of slide: 'Erma Waffenfabrik Erfurt DRGM'; left side of barrel: '.22 Long Rifle'
Serial number	On right side of frame, on right side of slide

Erma EP22

Calibre	.22 Long Rifle
Method of operation	Blowback, toggle action, striker-fired
Safety devices	Manual safety
Magazine type	Single-column detachable box in butt
Position of catch	Left side of butt
Magazine capacity	8 rounds
Front sight	Fixed blade
Rear sight	Fixed V-notch
Overall length	7.20in (183mm)
Barrel length	3.26in (83mm)
Number of grooves	6
Direction of twist	Right-hand
Empty weight	35.6oz (1,010g)
Markings	Left side of frame: 'ERMA EP .22'; right side of frame: 'MADE IN GERMANY Cal .22 L.R.'
Serial number	On left side of frame

machine guns, and returned to the pistol business in 1964 with the EP22, a blowback .22RF resembling the Parabellum. They used the toggle system developed for the 1934 conversion kit, though with the recoil spring in the rear of the frame and with a trigger system which was more conventional than that of the 9mm pistol. As well as being of a size comparable with the standard 9mm Pistole '08, the EP22 was also

Below: A sectioned drawing of the Erma EP22, a Parabellum lookalike but in rimfire calibre.

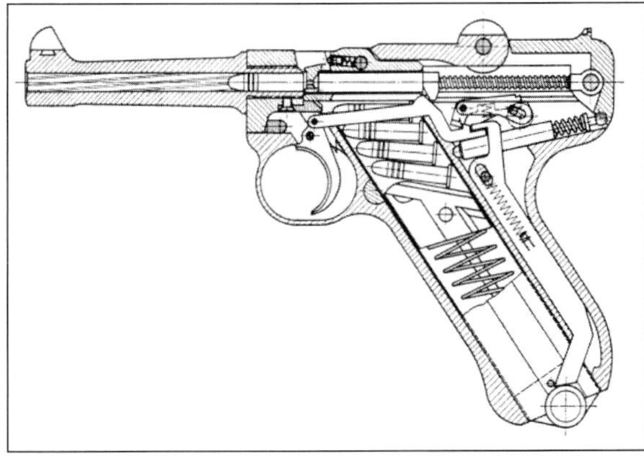

available as a long-barrelled Navy model, and as a carbine with wooden fore end and detachable stock. The EP22 continued in production until the early 1970s.

In 1968 came a second model, the KGP68, which was an improved EP22 but chambered for the 7.65mm ACP or 9mm Short cartridges. Modifications to the design of the toggle system turned these into delayed blowback weapons, and there were minor improvements in the trigger mechanism. The US Gun Control Act of 1968 raised some problems, which were met by developing the KGP68A; this added a magazine safety system which prevented firing if the magazine was not fully engaged. Finally, for those who wanted to fire the .22 cartridge, the KGP69 was produced, incorporating most of the 68 improvements but reverting to a pure blowback system.

In 1984 a further step was taken by the production of a series of blowback automatics more or less derived from the series of starting and tear gas pistols which the company had been

Erma KGP68A

Calibre	7.65mm Browning (or 9mm Short/.380 Auto)
Method of operation	Recoil, toggle-locked
Safety devices	Manual safety catch on left side of frame; magazine safety
Magazine type	Single-column detachable box in butt
Position of catch	Left side of butt
Magazine capacity	6 rounds (7.65mm) or 5 rounds (9mm)
Front sight	Fixed blade
Rear sight	Fixed V-notch
Overall length	7.36in (187mm)
Barrel length	3.46in (88mm)
Number of grooves	6
Direction of twist	Right-hand
Empty weight	22.6oz (640g)
Markings	Left side of frame: 'Kal 7.65 ERMA WERKE Mod KGP68'; right side of frame: 'Made in Germany'
Serial number	On left side of frame above trigger

Erma KGP69

Calibre	.22 Long Rifle
Method of operation	Blowback, striker-fired
Safety devices	Manual safety catch left rear of slide; magazine safety
Magazine type	Single-column detachable box in butt
Position of catch	Left side of butt
Magazine capacity	8 rounds
Front sight	Fixed blade
Rear sight	Fixed V-notch
Overall length	7.72in (196mm)
Barrel length	3.93in (100mm)
Number of grooves	6
Direction of twist	Right-hand
Empty weight	29.6oz (840g)
Markings	Left side of frame: 'Kal 22 l.r. ERMA-WERKE Mod KGP69'
Serial number	On left side of frame

Below: The Erma EP457 moved up to the 7.65mm centrefire cartridge and abandoned the Parabellum pattern for a more conventional shape. (John Walters)

Above left: The Erma KGP69 followed the Parabellum lines, improved on the EP22 but still fired the .22 cartridge. Above right: In 7.35mm calibre, the Erma 655 is a double-action pistol on similar lines to the Walther PPK.

making since the late 1960s. The pistols had double-action lockwork, slide-mounted safety catches and external ring hammers. The EP452 resembles a scaled-down Colt M1911A1 and fires the .22LR cartridge; the EP457 and 459 were similar, but chambered for the 7.65mm ACP and 9mm Short cartridges respectively. The 452 was of blackened alloy, the others of stainless steel.

Erma EP457

Calibre	7.65mm Browning
Method of operation	Blowback, hammer-fired
Safety devices	Manual catch left rear of slide
Magazine type	Single-column detachable box in butt
Position of catch	At heel of butt
Magazine capacity	8 rounds
Front sight	Fixed blade
Rear sight	Fixed V-notch
Overall length	6.30in (160mm)
Barrel length	3.22in (82mm)
Number of grooves	6
Direction of twist	Right-hand
Empty weight	21.9oz (620g)
Markings	Left side of slide: 'ERMA-WERKE Mod EP457 Kal. 7,65mm'
Serial number	On left side of frame behind trigger

The EP552 was based on the appearance of the Walther PPK and fired the .22LR cartridge; the EP555 was similar but fired the 6.35mm ACP cartridge. The EP652 and 655 were similar again but with a squarer outline to the slide.

The EP25 is a 6.35mm pistol which resembles the Browning 1910, but with the dismantling catch of the Sauer 38H added. It is a blowback pistol with a fixed barrel, and the return spring is concentric with the barrel and the slide as tapered up at the muzzle end. The grip is quite large for this calibre, and the dismantling catch is inset into the upper edge of

Erma EP522

Calibre	.22 Long Rifle
Method of operation	Blowback, hammer-fired
Safety devices	Manual safety/de-cocking lever on left rear of slide
Magazine type	Single-column detachable box in butt
Position of catch	At heel of butt
Magazine capacity	7 rounds
Front sight	Fixed blade
Rear sight	Fixed U-notch
Overall length	5.39in (137mm)
Barrel length	2.85in (72.5mm)
Number of grooves	6
Direction of twist	Right-hand
Empty weight	14.46oz (410g)
Markings	Left side of slide: 'ERMA-WERKE Mod EP552 Kal. .22 long rifle'
Serial number	Left side of frame, behind trigger

Erma EP25

Calibre	6.35mm Browning
Method of operation	Blowback, striker-fired
Safety devices	Manual safety catch above trigger on left side
Magazine type	Single-column detachable box in butt
Position of catch	At heel of butt
Magazine capacity	7 rounds
Front sight	Fixed blade
Rear sight	Fixed V-notch
Overall length	5.31in (135mm)
Barrel length	2.75in (70mm)
Number of grooves	6
Direction of twist	Right-hand
Empty weight	18.3oz (570g)
Markings	Left side of slide: 'Made in Germany ERMA WERKE EP25 Kal. 6,35/.25'
Serial number	On left side of slide

the trigger aperture. Pulling this down allows the slide to be pulled back beyond its normal stop and then lifted so that it can be slipped forward and off the barrel.

In the mid-1980s the EP85A pistol appeared, a completely different design from any other Erma offering. This was intended for international competitive use in either .22LR or .32 centrefire calibres, and could be converted between these calibres as required. A conventional blowback, it used a fixed barrel with a short slide having arms beneath the barrel to compress the return spring. Both the fore and rear sights were fully adjustable and could be changed for different sizes of aperture or height of blade. A pair of barrel weights, one of 180g and the other of 100g, were supplied with each barrel, as well as alternative sight pieces, loading aid, spare magazines and Allen keys for dismantling and adjusting. The trigger can be adjusted for position, pull weight and distance, and the sear can also be adjusted.

Dismantling, or changing the barrel, is a simple business. After clearing the gun, pull back the slide and lock it open. Then unscrew the

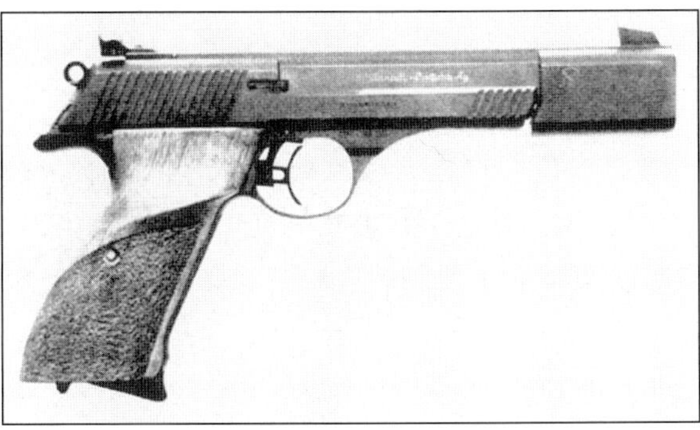

Above: For the target shooter, the Erma 85A has a long barrel and balance weights.

hexagonal screw in front of the trigger guard, so releasing the barrel. The barrel can then be lifted off the frame. The slide is then released under control and taken off the front of the frame, together with the return spring. Removal of a single screw allows the grips to be removed. No further dismantling is recommended.

The company had also produced revolver-type starting pistols and in the 1970s began making cartridge-firing models. These were based broadly upon the Smith & Wesson shape

Erma EP85A

Calibre	.22 Long Rifle or .32 S&W Long
Method of operation	Blowback, hammer-fired
Safety devices	Manual safety catch on left side
Magazine type	Single-column detachable box in butt
Position of catch	At heel of butt
Magazine capacity	8 rounds (.22); 5 rounds (.32)
Front sight	Adjustable and replaceable blade
Rear sight	Adjustable and replaceable aperture
Overall length	10.00in (254mm)
Barrel length	6.00in (152mm)
Number of grooves	6
Direction of twist	Right-hand
Empty weight	41.0oz (1,163g)
Markings	Right side of slide: 'Made in Germany ERMA WERKE ESP'
Serial number	On right side of frame

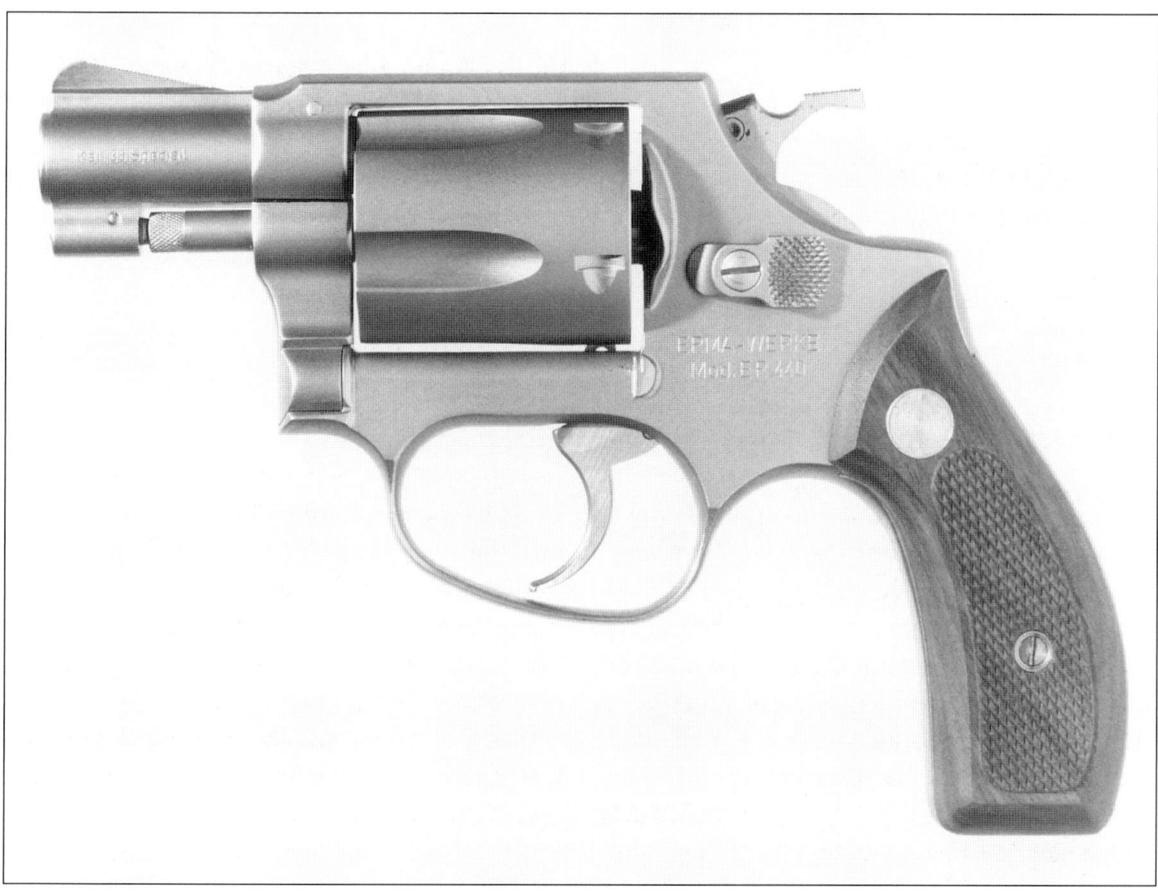

Above: This well-engineered revolver is the Erma ER440 in .38 Special chambering. (John Walters)

Erma ER440

Calibre	.38 Special
Method of operation	Double-action revolver
Safety devices	None
Magazine type	5-shot cylinder
Position of catch	Left side of frame, behind cylinder
Front sight	Fixed blade
Rear sight	Fixed U-notch
Overall length	6.30in (160mm)
Barrel length	3.00in (76mm)
Number of grooves	6
Direction of twist	Right-hand
Empty weight	21.9oz (620g)
Markings	Left side of frame: 'ERMA-WERKE Mod. ER 440'
Serial number	On right side of frame above trigger

and are solid-frame, side-opening models with transfer-bar firing locks. The ER422 and ER423 were chambered for the .22 Long Rifle and .22 WMRF cartridges and were available with various barrel lengths. The ER432 was a short-barrelled revolver for the .32 S&W cartridge, the ER440 was for the .38 Special round and had a five-chambered cylinder, and the ER442 was in either .22LR or .22 Magnum RF with a six-chambered cylinder.

FREMDENGERÄTE

Fremdengeräte (foreign equipments) was the German Army term for weapons acquired from conquered or assimilated countries and taken into military service, Each foreign weapon was given an identity number and letter, the letter indicating the country of origin. However, the fact that a piece of equipment was given a Fremdengerät number should not be taken as *prima facie* evidence that the weapon was actually used by the German Army or that they ever even saw one. The methodical German quartermasters carefully listed every foreign weapon of which they were aware and gave it a number against the day that they might actually acquire one. So, for example, the US 14in railway gun M1920, of which there were two, one in California and one in the Panama Canal Zone, was listed as the 35.5cm Kanone (E) 681(u). In similar vein, virtually every foreign military pistol was given a number, even though it is fairly certain that pistols such as the French M1935 (625(f)), the Belgian Browning M1900 (620(b)) or the Soviet Nagant M1985 revolver (612(r)) were never used on an official basis. We have, therefore, restricted out review of the Fremdengerät pistols to the more important or interesting ones.

Pistole Modell 12(ö)

Österreichische Waffenfabrik Gesellschaft m.b.H Steyr, Steyr, Austria.

The (ö) stands for *österreichisch*, or Austrian, and the weapon in question is probably better known as the Steyr Model 1912, or Steyr-Hahn (Steyr with hammer). This was the official pistol of the Austro-Hungarian and Romanian Armies during World War I, and during World War II it was slightly modified and taken into German Army service.

As originally designed, it had a feature not entirely uncommon in the early years of this century—a unique cartridge designed with, and intended for, this gun alone. The 9mm Steyr cartridge is longer than the 9mm Parabellum, the bullet is more pointed and usually steel-jacketed, and the propelling charge is more powerful. All this gives the Steyr round a respectable reputation for power and penetration, but for reasons concealed in history no other gunmaker took it to his bosom, and consequently the 1912 models have tended to stay in the area of their birth, where ammunition was freely available. (Webley & Scott of Birmingham manufactured one of their automatic pistols chambered for this round in the early 1920s, but this was against a contract for the Romanian Army and was never offered commercially in this calibre.)

When Austrian military units were assimilated into the Wehrmacht in 1938, a weapon demanding a special cartridge was felt to be an unwarranted strain on the supply system. A fresh issue of P '08 or P38 pistols would have been one solution, but these were not readily available in quantity at the time, and the independently minded Austrians preferred their Steyr—rightly so, in my opinion. So the next most obvious solution was adopted—rechamber the 1912 models to accept the 9mm Parabellum cartridge. The base dimensions were so close as to obviate any alterations to the bolt face or extractor, and the shorter length made no difference to the magazine, only the barrel feed ramp having to be redesigned to work more smoothly with the shorter and more blunt tip of the Parabellum bullet. Once converted, the slide was stamped '08' or 'P-08' on the left side and the weapon was taken into German service as the Pistole Model 12 (ö).

The 1912 Steyr is a locked-breech pistol, and one of the most robust and reliable weapons ever made. Although theoretically impossible, it can be made to fire 9mm Parabellum ammunition without modification, albeit with some difficulty in feeding. But with the proper ammunition it is a powerful and accurate pistol. The designer of the pistol is not known, but

Above: Pistole Mod 12(ö), or the Steyr M1912 of the Austro-Hungarian Army.

there are several features which suggest familiarity with the Mannlicher pistols made by Steyr, whilst the system of operation owes much to the Roth-Steyr pistol of 1908. The locking system is based on barrel rotation: the barrel is provided with four lugs, two at the top which engage in transverse slots in the slide, one transverse at the bottom which rides in a slot in the frame and limits forward and backward movement, and one helical lug under the barrel, which, riding in a groove in the frame, governs the rotation of the barrel.

On firing, the barrel and slide, locked together by the engagement of the top lugs, recoil about 0.32in (8mm). During this movement the helical lug is drawn through the fixed groove on the frame and rotates the barrel about 20°, withdrawing the top lugs from engagement with the slide. As these reach the disengaged point the fourth lug, on the bottom of the barrel, strikes the rear end of its slot and halts the barrel. The slide continues to recoil, compressing the recoil spring under the barrel. The empty case is extracted from the chamber and ejected and the hammer is re-cocked. The return stroke of the slide collects the next round from the magazine and chambers it, and as this happens the slide begins to push the barrel forward. The helical lug now rotates the barrel back to bring the transverse lugs into engagement with the slide, and movement is stopped when the limiting lug strikes the front edge of its slot in the frame. The pistol is now ready to fire once more.

As with most designs emanating from Steyr, the magazine is integral with the butt and is loaded from a special 8-round charger. To load, the slide is pulled back until the safety catch can be turned up so that the hook-like projection on its front end engages in a notch in the slide. The charger is then placed in the charger guides in the slide and the rounds are pressed into the magazine. The charger is removed, the safety catch is disengaged and the slide runs forward to load the chamber. To empty the magazine, the slide is pulled back and locked, and the milled catch above the left butt grip is pressed. This releases a keeper spring in the magazine and allows the magazine spring to eject the entire contents so forcibly that they land about fifteen feet away.

Possibly the only fault that can be found with this pistol is that the butt is built too squarely to the rest of the frame, which means that when trying to shoot instinctively one tends to shoot too low. Had there been another ten or fifteen degrees of rake to the butt, and had it been chambered for a more popular cartridge, the 1912 Steyr might have been a more successful pistol and would have had a longer manufacturing life. A few pistols were marketed commercially just before World War I; these were beautifully finished and were marked 'WAFFEN-FABRIK, STEYR' on the slide and bore Austrian civil proof marks. They are very rare today.

An interesting variation of this pistol in the possession of the Imperial War Museum is one having a long magazine extension to give a 20-

Below: The Steyr 1912 stripped to show the barrel rotating lugs and the return spring lying in the frame. Note also that the magazine is a permanent part of the weapon.

Pistole Modell 12(ö)

Calibre	9mm Parabellum
Method of operation	Short recoil, hammer-fired, rotating barrel lock, single-action
Safety devices	Manual safety catch at left rear of frame
Magazine type	Single-column integral inside butt
Position of catch	None; cartridge release catch on top of left grip
Magazine capacity	8 rounds
Front sight	Adjustable blade
Rear sight	Fixed V-notch
Overall length	8.60in (216mm)
Barrel length	5.10in (128mm)
Number of grooves	4
Direction of twist	Right-hand
Empty weight	35.0oz (992g)
Markings	Left side of slide: 'P '08 STEYR 1916' (or other 1912–1918 date)
Serial number	Full number on left of slide and left of frame, above trigger

shot capacity and a switch on the right side to disengage the disconnector and permit full automatic fire. It is chambered for 9mm Steyr, and there is no apparent provision for a shoulder stock. In the absence of any official record of the modification, it is believed to have been produced for use by pilots of early military aircraft—a similar modification was carried out by the US Army to their Colt .45 M1911 pistol. Whatever its use, firing such a powerful cartridge at full automatic with one hand while attempting to fly an aeroplane with the other must have been quite a stimulating experience.

To strip the Steyr pistol, after pulling the slide back and emptying the magazine if necessary, let the slide forward and press the trigger. At the front end of the gun, just below the muzzle, a spring clip will be seen passing through the slide and frame. With a suitable soft tool, such as a screwdriver handle, tap this pin through from left to right. It will slip out on the right side and be held in the slide by the spring leaf which forms the locking system holding the pin in place. One is tempted to feel that this is sufficient and the gun should now come to pieces, but it is necessary to remove the cross-pin by using a screwdriver blade inserted from the left of the slide to lift the spring leaf and allow the pin to be pulled out completely. Once this is done, pull the slide back to the full extent of its travel and lift it from the frame. Examination will show that the slide is formed with lugs at the front which must go all the way back to where the frame is cut out to release them; and the slide cannot come forward because of the guide rails and grooves at the rear end which terminate just behind the magazine. The barrel can be lifted from its seating in the frame, and this really is all that needs to be done. By removing the grips it is possible to dismantle the magazine, but this is not recommended.

To reassemble the pistol, place the barrel back on to the frame, ensuring that the rotation lug engages in its groove in the frame, and then ease the barrel back to the fully recoiled position, with the limiting lug hard against the rear of its slot. Then drop the slide on, seeing that the lug adjacent to the pin slot drops into the cutaway portions of the frame near the breech of the barrel. Push the slide forward, depressing the magazine platform to allow it to move, and then insert the cross-pin so that it passes in front of the recoil spring. Ensure that the pin passes right through the frame and the spring leaf snaps into place on the left-hand side. Note, when reassembling the pin, that it has an arrow engraved upon it: this arrow should be uppermost and pointing from right to left when replacing.

Pistole Modell 27(t)

Ceska Zbrojovka a.s., Prague, Czechoslovakia

This weapon began life as the Model 27, manufactured by the Czechoslovakian company

Ceska Zbrojovka, but, after the annexation of that country in 1939, large numbers of the model were taken into use by the German Army under the title 'Pistole Modell 27(t)', the (t) standing for *tchechoslowakisch*.

The Model 27 is the lineal descendant of two very similar CZ designs, the Models 22 and 24; telling all these apart from their exterior appearance is quite difficult. The earlier models use a locked breech relying on the rotation of the barrel through about 20° to unlock it from the slide, and the Model 24 incorporates a magazine safety. The Model 27, however, differs considerably in its internal arrangements, being a simple blowback design. The story behind all this is not without interest. When the CZ factory was established in the newly formed state of Czechoslovakia in 1920, a licence was obtained to manufacture a Mauser rifle for the Czech Army, and Mauser sent Josef Nickl, their engineer, to oversee the setting-up of production. When the company happened to mention to Nickl that they needed a pistol design for the Czech Army, Nickl was happy to oblige—he had designed a few pistols for Mauser but only one had ever got as far as a prototype. He produced what was virtually a cut-down Mauser of 1908, complete with rotating-barrel breech lock, in 9mm Short calibre, which became the CZ1922 pistol. After Nickl had returned to Germany, the CZ engineers made some small,

Below: Pistole Mod 27(t), or the CZ27. Compare this with the Nickl pistol shown on page 131.

generally cosmetic changes to turn it into the CZ1924 model, but the Czech Army complained that it was too expensive and complicated, so the CZ engineers took a harder look at it and did away with the breech lock, turning the weapon into a simple blowback design. This became the CZ27 and was also produced in 7.65mm calibre. The quick and easy way to distinguish the CZ27 from its forebears is to look at the finger grip serrations on the slide: on the CZ27 they are vertical, but on the 22 and 24 they are sloping.

Stripping the Model 27 is relatively simple. Having removed the magazine and cleared the gun, pull back and release the slide to cock the hammer. Holding the pistol in the right hand in the normal fashion, with the tip of the right forefinger press in the end of the transverse pin just above the trigger guard. At the same time, with the left thumb, pull down the milled catch on the opposite end of the pin. This catch will drop about 0.4in (9mm) until a rebate comes free from a slot in the frame. Now pass the first two fingers of the right hand over the top of the slide, push the slide back slightly, and grip it against the spring pressure. This releases the pressure on the transverse pin and it can now be withdrawn to the left. Slacken the grip of the slide and it will go forward, propelled by the spring, and can be pulled clear of the frame. Then lift the recoil spring, guide rod and stop block away from the barrel. Turn the bush at the muzzle until it can be pulled free from the slide. Withdraw the barrel forward until the three milled ribs are aligned with the slot milled on the inside of the slide, then rotate the barrel through 180° and remove it completely. The firing pin can be removed from the slide by pressing in its rear end with a small screwdriver or drift and sliding up the dovetailed retaining block. Removing one screw on each side of the grip allows the plastic moulding to be slid off

Pistole Modell 27(t)

Calibre	7.65mm Browning
Method of operation	Blowback, hammer-fired
Safety devices	Manual catch at left front of butt, spring retention to 'safe'
Magazine type	Single-column detachable box in butt
Position of catch	Bottom rear of butt
Magazine capacity	8 rounds
Front sight	Fixed blade
Rear sight	Fixed U-notch
Overall length	6.50in (165mm)
Barrel length	3.82in (97mm)
Number of grooves	6
Direction of twist	Right-hand
Empty weight	25.0oz (710g)
Markings	See text
Serial number	On slide top, lock cover plate, front right of frame and underside of barrel

backwards. A small screw just above the safety catch retains the lock cover plate in place. The stripping of the lockwork, while fairly self-evident upon inspection, is not recommended.

To reassemble, the reverse procedure is followed. When replacing the slide assembly the stop block should be placed on the barrel ribs—it can be fitted either way—and the recoil spring should be threaded through the block and into the recess at the front of the slide. Then insert the guide rod into the spring. At this point it is as well to ensure that the muzzle bush has been fitted properly in the front of the slide. Then, with the barrel upside down, slip the receiver on to the slide, making sure the stop block is not displaced. When the slide and receiver are correctly fitted, pushing the slide back a fraction of an inch will relieve pressure on the stop block and permit the transverse pin to be pushed home and locked.

The markings depend on whether or not the weapon was made under German Army control. Czech models are engraved 'CESKA

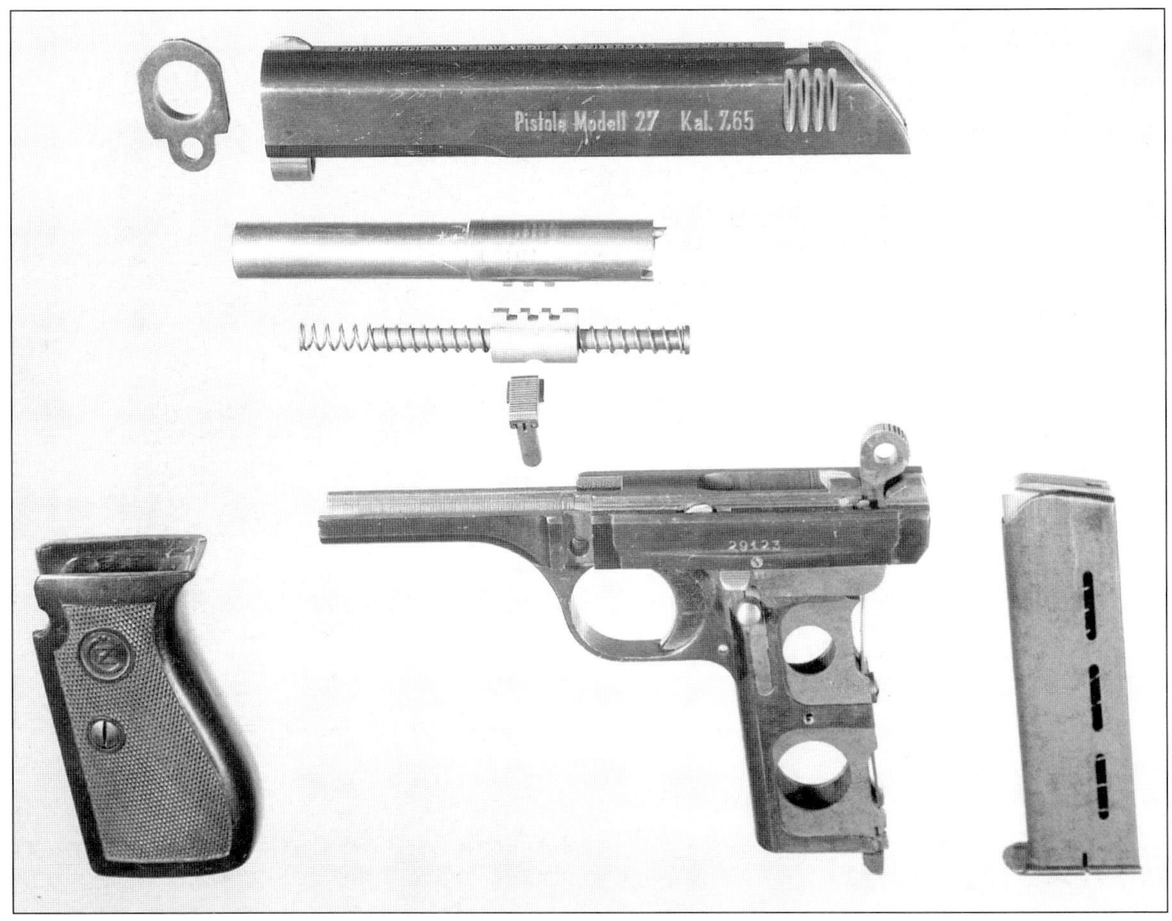

Above: The P Mod 27(t) stripped, showing the unusual method of retaining the barrel.

ZBROJOVKA A. S. v PRAZE' on the top of the slide, while those made for the German Army are marked 'BÖHMISCHE WAFFENFABRIK A. G. IN PRAG' on the slide top and 'Pistole Modell 27 Kal. 7,65' on the left side of the slide. They also have 'P Mod 27' marked on the bottom of the magazine. Civilian models, moreover, have 'CZ' and an arrow on the underside of the barrel; on the left rear of the slide together with the last two digits of the year of manufacture; on the bottom of the magazine; and on the left of the frame above the butt grip alongside the serial number. German Army models have Waffenamt acceptance marks ('WaA 78') on the frame and also on the undersurfaces of the barrel.

A point to watch with the commercial and Czech service versions of the 22, 24 and 27 pistols is that they are marked with the year of manufacture, and it is therefore possible to find. for example, a CZ24 pistol marked '27'—which is, to say the very least, confusing.

Pistole Modell 35(p)

Although generally referred to as the Radom, the Polish name for this pistol is VIS, said to be derived from the Latin word for 'power'. Made only in 9mm Parabellum calibre, it was developed for the Polish Army and earns its place here, like the other *Fremdengeräte*, by virtue of its use by the German Army, in which it was

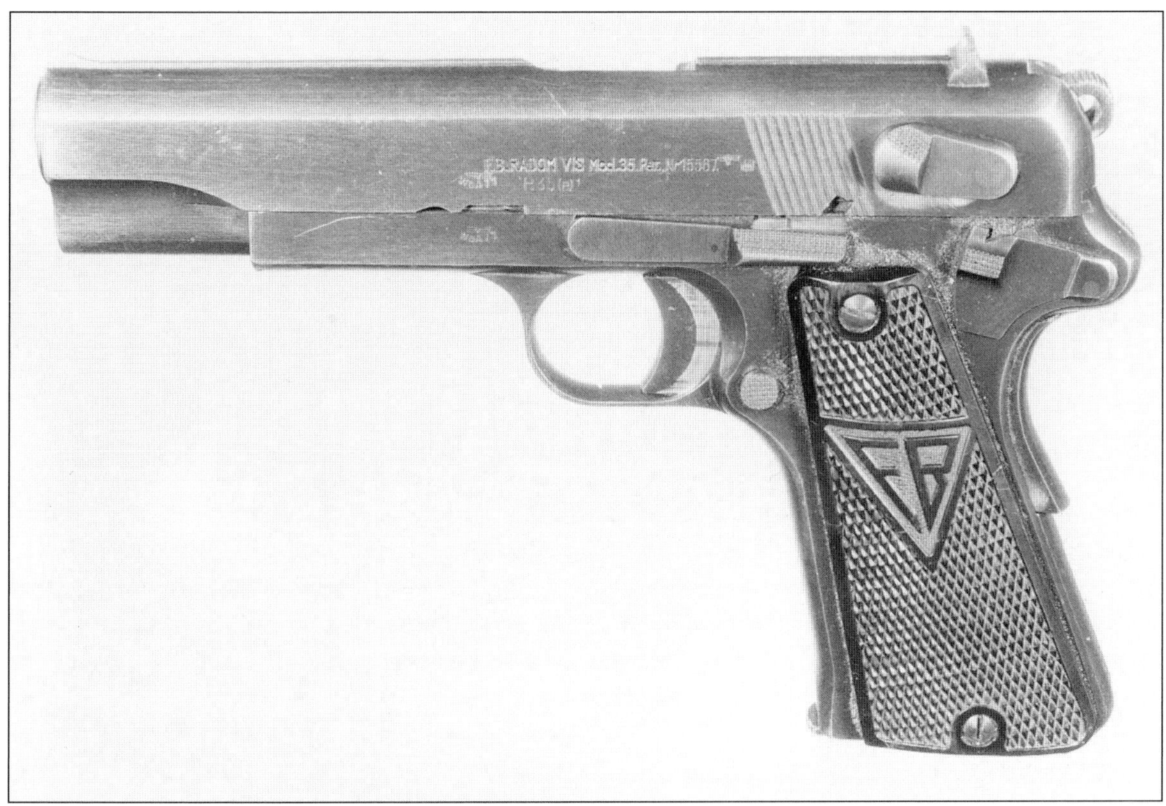

known as the Pistole Modell 35(p), the (p) standing for *polnisch*.

Above: The Pistole 35(p), or the Polish Radom or VIS, was one of the best 9mm pistols of the war years.

During the 1920s and the 1930s the Polish Army had been armed with a random collection of handguns, including Browning, Colt, Steyr, Parabellum and Mauser pistols and Nagant revolvers. In order to standardise on one design, gunmakers were invited to enter pistols for a competitive trial held in 1935. Among the entrants were Breda of Italy, Mauser, Skoda, and two Polish engineers named Wilniewczyc and Skrzypinski with the VIS pistol. The competition was a draw between the Skoda pistol and the VIS model and, being patriotic, the Polish Ministry of Military Affairs bought the license to manufacture the VIS. Production was entrusted to the Government Small Arms Factory at Radom, the Fabryka Broni w Radomu, whence the name 'Radom' springs. The prototype was extensively tested and the pistol was put into production in 1936. Only one model was made, and production continued until Poland's defeat in 1939. Shortly after this the factory was reopened under German control and the Model 35 continued to be made until 1944, the entire output going to the German Army.

The pistol resembles the Colt M1911A1 model and is largely based upon that weapon, with the addition of the Browning variation developed for the Belgian Model 35 (notably the substitution of a forged cam under the barrel instead of a swinging link, which serves to pull the barrel down and free from engagement with the slide during recoil). Further design changes introduced by the Poles included the provision of a recoil spring guide rod under the barrel, thus doing away with the removable bushing of the Colt design and giving rise to alterations in the stripping procedure. The external view of the pistol shows what appears to be a normal safety catch on the frame, above and to the rear of the left butt grip, plus another catch on the slide. In fact neither of these are safety catches in the strict sense, the only safety device being a grip safety. The thumb catch on the slide, when pressed down, first retracts the firing pin inside its housing in the slide and then trips the sear to drop the hammer, allowing the hammer to be lowered safely on to a loaded chamber. The pistol can then be quickly readied for firing by simply thumbing back the hammer. The catch on the frame is purely to aid stripping. Another addition was the provision of a groove in the rear of the butt for attachment of a wooden holster stock to convert the pistol into a short carbine for use by mounted troops.

Pistole Modell 35(p)

Make	Fabryka Broni w Radomu
Calibre	9mm Parabellum
Method of operation	Recoil, locked breech, hammer-fired
Safety devices	Grip safety in rear of butt; hammer-lowering catch on slide
Magazine type	Single-column detachable box in butt
Position of catch	Left of butt, behind trigger guard
Magazine capacity	8 rounds
Front sight	Fixed blade
Rear sight	Fixed V-notch
Overall length	8.31in (211mm)
Barrel length	4.53in (115mm)
Number of grooves	6
Direction of twist	Right-hand
Empty weight	37.0oz (1,050g)
Markings	See text
Serial number	On right side of frame above trigger; on underside of slide alongside breech block section; last three digits on barrel lug

The later models produced under German control may be found to depart from the original Radom pattern in respect of the hammer release catch, which may be missing entirely, and the butt grips, which may be plain slabs of wood. This was simply due to the problem of matching supply with demand as materials got more scarce and the war increased in ferocity.

It should be noted that the Radom factory put the VIS pistol back into production, not for military use but for commercial sale, in the late 1980s. It is absolutely identical with the prewar model, with the same markings, but is distinguished by the more recent date of manufacture marked on the slide.

The Model 35 is a locked-breech pistol working on the Browning principle of locking barrel and breech together by lugs. The inside of the top surface of the slide is furnished with lateral grooves and the top of the breech section of the barrel is provided with lateral lugs. Below the barrel is a shaped lug which incorporates a cam surface and which, when the gun is loaded and ready, is located just ahead of a lateral pin in the gun frame. In this position the barrel lugs are tightly locked into the slide grooves and the barrel and slide are efficiently locked together. When the weapon is fired, the recoil drives the two components back together, retaining the locked breech situation until pressure has dropped in the barrel. As the unit recoils, the toe of the shaped lug beneath the barrel engages with the transverse pin, and the cam contour is such that, as recoil continues, the barrel is pulled down and freed from the lug/groove interlock. Once the barrel is far enough down for the lock to be entirely free, then the slide is allowed to recoil by itself, extracting the spent case, while the barrel is held by the cam and cross pin. The recoil spring drives the slide back, feeding a new round into the chamber, and the pushing action of the slide eases the barrel away from the

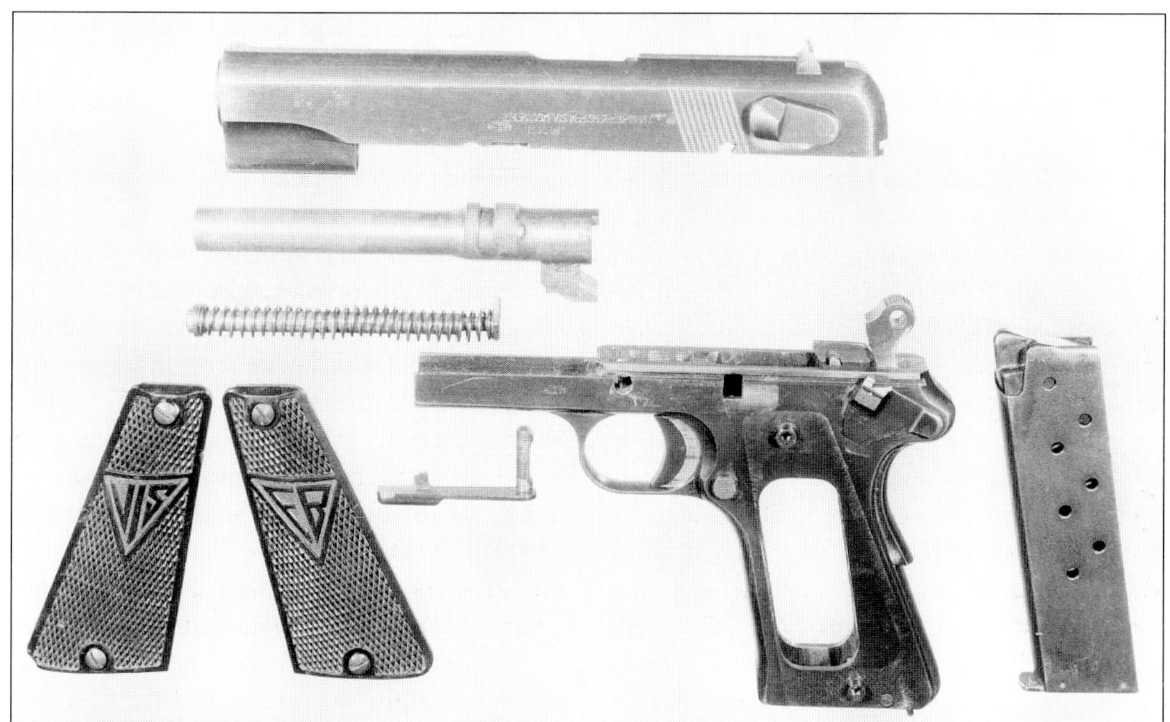

Above: The P Mod 35(p) stripped reveals itself as almost entirely Browning in its mechanical features.

cross pin and allows it to be cammed up again into engagement with the slide.

To dismantle the 35, after removing the magazine and clearing the gun pull back the slide about 1in (25mm) until the thumb catch on the frame can be turned up to engage in the slot in the under surface of the slide. This will expose the recoil spring guide rod at the front of the pistol; grasp this rod and pull forward, while withdrawing the slide stop pin from the frame. Now depress the thumb catch and the slide can be eased forward under control and slipped off the frame to the front. The end of the recoil spring guide rod nearest the breech is formed into a saddle; by turning this through 90° the rod and spring can be lifted clear of the barrel lug and slipped out of their housing. The barrel can now be lifted and pulled clear of the slide. Pressing in the end of the firing pin will permit the retaining plate to be slid off downwards and, with this removed, the extractor can be withdrawn with any suitable tool. By unscrewing the screws at the top and bottom of each grip, the grips can be removed, but this does not give access to the lockwork and there is little point to it. All the lockwork is pinned into the frame.

To reassemble the weapon, the stripping procedure is reversed. It is advisable to assemble the barrel and recoil spring unit into the slide and then connect the slide and the frame with both units upside down; this prevents the barrel from dropping free from its locking grooves in the slide. Correct assembly can be checked by looking into the hole for the slide stop pin, where the square edge of the guide rod saddle should be visible in the front edge of the hole. Place the pin in position, pull on the guide rod, and the pin will simply drop into place.

Original Polish Army pistols carry this inscription on the left side of the slide: 'F. B.

RADOM 1938' (or other date)/engraved Polish Eagle/ 'VIS Mo 35 Pat Nr 1 5567'. The right butt grip has 'VIS' and the left 'FB' moulded in. The weapons made for the German Army are similarly engraved except that the Polish Eagle is omitted, and beneath, less heavily engraved, is 'P.35(p)'.

Pistole Modell 37(u)

Fegyver es Gepgyar Reszvenytarsasag, Budapest, Hungary

The (u) meaning 'ungarisch' or Hungarian, it follows that this is another one of the pistols taken over by the German Army during the course of the 1939–45 war. Originally the Hungarian Army Model 37, it underwent slight modification when adopted by the Wehrmacht by the addition of a thumb-operated safety catch and a change in markings.

The Model 37 is a sturdy, reliable and simple blowback pistol of conventional design, with the added refinements of a slide stop and a grip safety, plus the manual safety added by the German specification. It shoots well, but the 7.65mm calibre can only be considered marginal for combat use. The original Hungarian model was also made in 9mm Short/.380in calibre, though this is but a small improvement.

To strip the Model 37, first remove the magazine and clear the gun. Then pull back the slide until the slide stop on the left of the frame can be pushed up into the rearmost of the two

Below: Frommer's last design, the Hungarian Model 1937, in its German guise as the P Mod 37(u). It differs from the original Hungarian pattern in having a safety catch and being in 7.65mm calibre instead of 9mm Short.

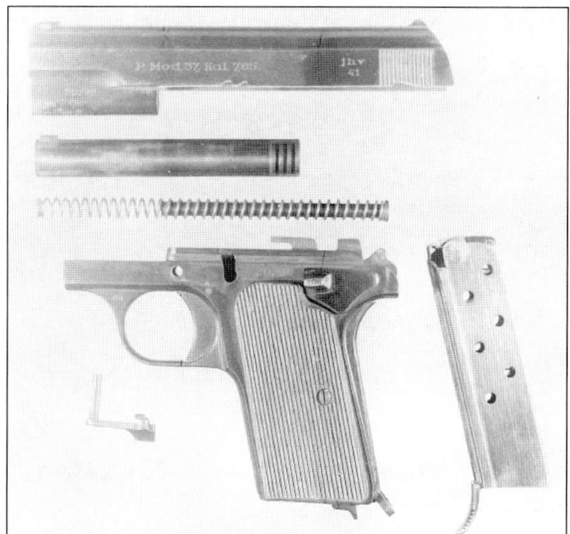

Right: The Hungarian 36 stripped.

notches on the lower edge of the slide. Now grasp the exposed muzzle and rotate the barrel anti-clockwise about 120° until it can be pulled free from the slide. Hold the slide against the pressure of the recoil spring and release the slide stop; the slide can now be eased forward off the frame together with the recoil spring and its guide rod. Remove the slide stop (before it falls out) and remove the grips—by unscrewing the usual screws—to expose the lockwork. Examination of the parts will show that the barrel is held in place in the gun by four milled ribs on the underside engaging with matching grooves on the frame.

To reassemble, the procedure is simply reversed. If the barrel refuses to turn into the locked position, check that the slide stop is engaged in the correct notch; if it is engaged in the front notch, there will be insufficient clearance for the lugs to engage properly.

Pistole Modell 37(u)

Calibre	7.65mm Browning
Method of operation	Blowback, hammer-fired
Safety devices	Manual catch at left rear of frame
Magazine type	Single-column detachable box in butt
Position of catch	Bottom rear of butt
Magazine capacity	7 rounds
Front sight	Fixed blade
Rear sight	Fixed V-notch
Overall length	7.17in (182mm)
Barrel length	4.33in (110mm)
Number of grooves	6
Direction of twist	Right-hand
Empty weight	27.0oz (765g)
Markings	Hungarian models: on left of slide: 'FEMARU FEGYVER ES GEPGYAR R.T. 37M'; German models: 'P. Mod 37, Kal 7,65', manufacturer's code 'jhv' and last two digits of year of make; 'P. MOD 37' on bottom of magazine
Serial number	On left rear of frame, on left front of slide and on barrel

Pistole Modell 39(t)

Like the Model 27(t), this is another Ceská Zbrojovka design, but it bears no resemblance to the earlier Models 22, 24 or 27. There appear to have been one or two slight variant models produced by way of exercises before the design settled down to the final production Model 39 described here, but these are probably no longer in existence.

From the shooting point of view, the notable feature of this pistol is that it is a pure self-cocker—one can never cock the hammer. When the slide is pulled back in the usual way to chamber the first round, the hammer drops back as the slide returns, stopping clear of the firing pin. Pulling the trigger cocks the hammer, moves aside the blocking bar which had prevented hammer-to-firing pin contact and then releases the hammer to drop and hit the firing pin. As the slide recoils so the disconnector, in addition to its usual function, brings the locking bar back into play to hold the hammer off the striker as the slide reloads the chamber. Furthermore,

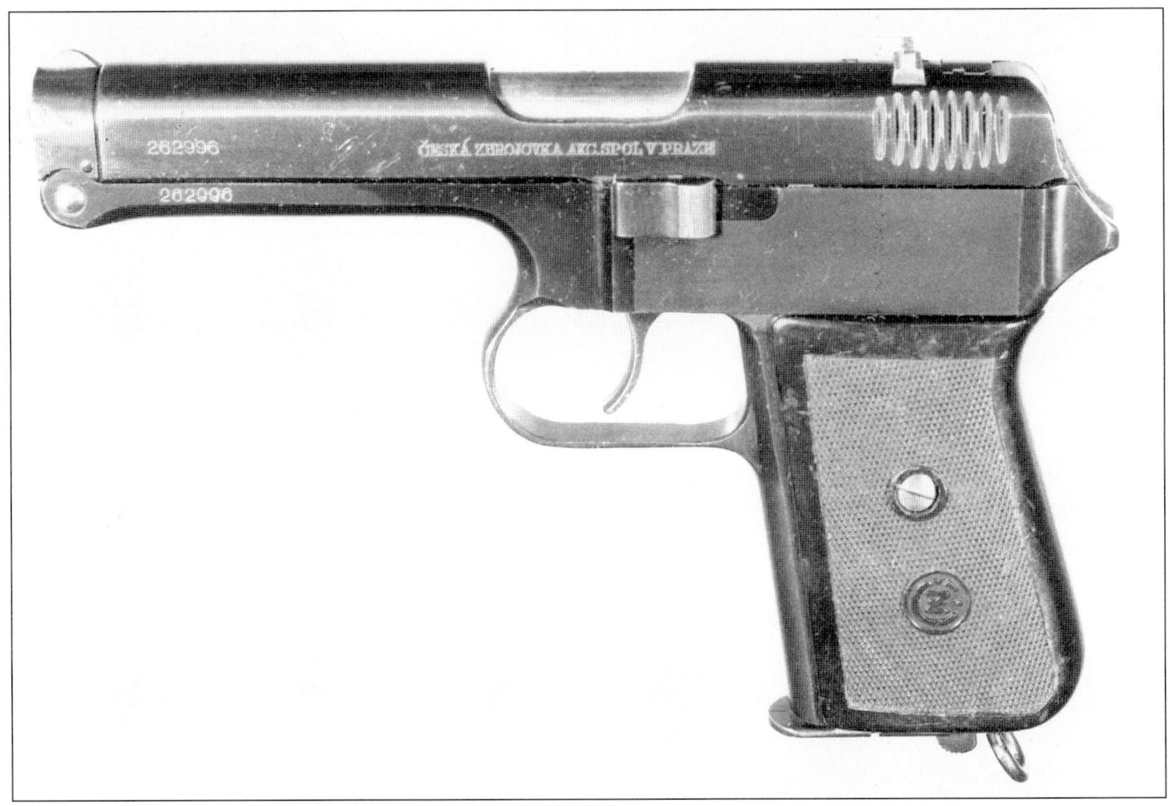

Above: The Pistole 39(t) was the Czech Model 38, a peculiar self-cocking design. Although the Germans gave it an equipment number, it appears doubtful whether they ever adopted it in quantity.

since the pistol cannot be fired except by a conscious operation of the trigger, and cannot possibly fire if dropped or knocked, there are no safety devices.

The weapon was taken into use by the German Army, and it seems that the entire production was by CZ of Prague: no examples of other contractors' manufacture are known. According to some authorities, this weapon is chambered for a peculiar Czech version of the 9mm Short round which is a fraction shorter in the cartridge case than the standard round. It is alleged that this round was produced for Czech Army use in the mid-1930s. This may be so, but I have never yet seen one of these short Czech cartridges, nor any documentary evidence of their existence; furthermore, every Model 39(t) which I have met seems to work quite happily on standard 0.380in Auto ammunition.

The Model 39 is one of the easiest pistols to strip. After removing the magazine and clearing the gun, hold the butt in the right hand, and with the left hand grip the top of the slide. Press forward the milled catch on the left side of the slide with either thumb and pull up on the slide. It will pivot about the muzzle and will then slide free of the barrel, leaving the barrel hinged to the frame. The firing pin and the one-piece plastic grip can be removed in the same way as for the Model 27. The lock cover plate is above the side of the butt and can be slid down and removed, after which the dismantling of the lockwork becomes apparent. If it is necessary to remove the barrel or recoil spring (which is recessed into the frame top), the hinge pin at

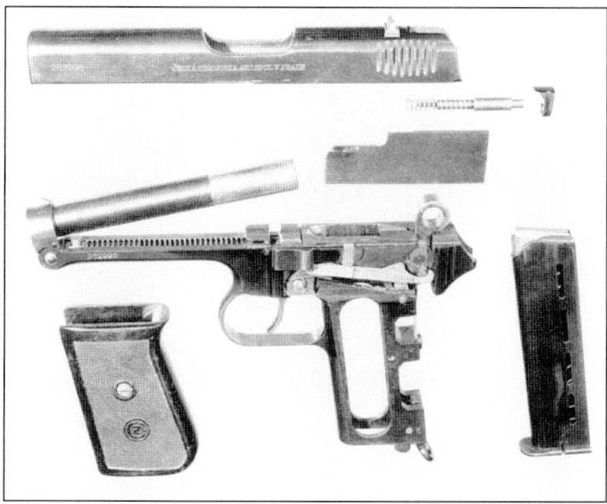

Above: Perhaps the greatest feature of the P Mod 39(t) was its ease of stripping for routine maintenance.

Pistole Modell 39(t)	
Calibre	9mm Short/0.380in Auto Pistol
Method of operation	Blowback, hammer-fired, double-action only
Safety devices	None
Magazine type	Single-column detachable box in butt
Position of catch	Bottom rear of butt
Magazine capacity	8 rounds
Front sight	Fixed blade
Rear sight	Fixed V-notch
Overall length	8.11in (206mm)
Barrel length	4.65in (118mm)
Number of grooves	6
Direction of twist	Right-hand
Empty weight	33.0oz (935g)
Markings	Left of slide: 'CESKA ZBROJOVKA AKC SPOL V PRAZE'; right of frame: Bohemian lion, year of manufacture and inspector's mark
Serial number	On left front of slide, and left front of frame (it is unusual in not having a number on the barrel, which was probably due to the fact that the barrel is more or less permanently attached)

the barrel front end should be gently driven out, but beware of the recoil spring when doing this. To reassemble, the reverse procedure is carried out. Note that at the bottom front of the slide is a hole which engages with a stud on the recoil spring follower on the frame. Make sure that the slide is absolutely square to the frame before closing it, so that hole and stud mate up correctly; the slide generally needs a firm slam to latch it.

Although this pistol was given a Fremdengerät number, it is believed that few were actually taken into service by the German Army, and specimens carrying the usual Wehrmacht acceptance stamp and the German inscription 'P Mod 39(t)' are exceptionally rare. The Germans, understandably, do not appear to have been particularly impressed by this pistol and terminated its production in the early summer of 1939.

Pistol Model 615(r)

State Rifle Factories, Tula and Izhevsk, USSR

In 1941 the German Army captured so much Soviet equipment that it was worth their while to convert factories to the manufacture of Soviet-calibre artillery ammunition, and they continued to use captured Soviet guns throughout the war. The quantity of small arms captured was immense, but very little was ever employed by the Germans since the ammunition was not to German standard calibres and the weapons were not so outstandingly good that it would be worth manufacturing ammunition for them. There was one exception to this, and that was the Tokarev TT-33 pistol; this was chambered for the Soviet 7.62mm pistol cartridge, which was, in fact, dimensionally the same as the standard German 7.63mm Mauser pistol cartridge, so that supplies could be easily obtained. As a result, the Tokarev was widely carried, notably on the Eastern Front, and became the Pistol 615(r).

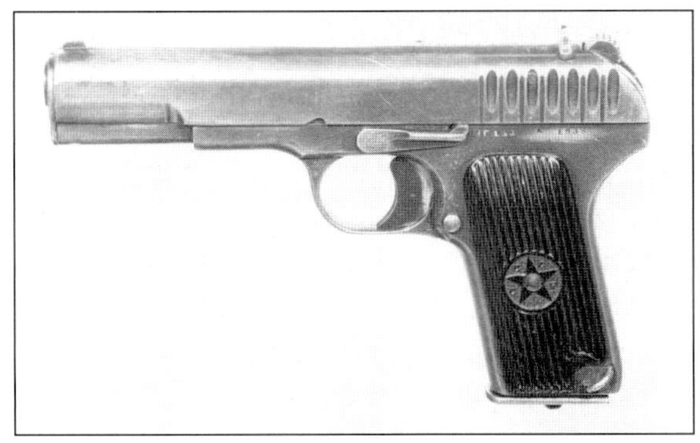

Above: The P Mod 615(r) was the Soviet TT-33/34 Tokarev, which, conveniently, fired the 7.63mm Mauser cartridge. Below: The Tokarev in pieces. Note that the barrel locking lugs encircle the barrel, indicating that this is a TT-34 pistol; note also the hammer unit in a removable module.

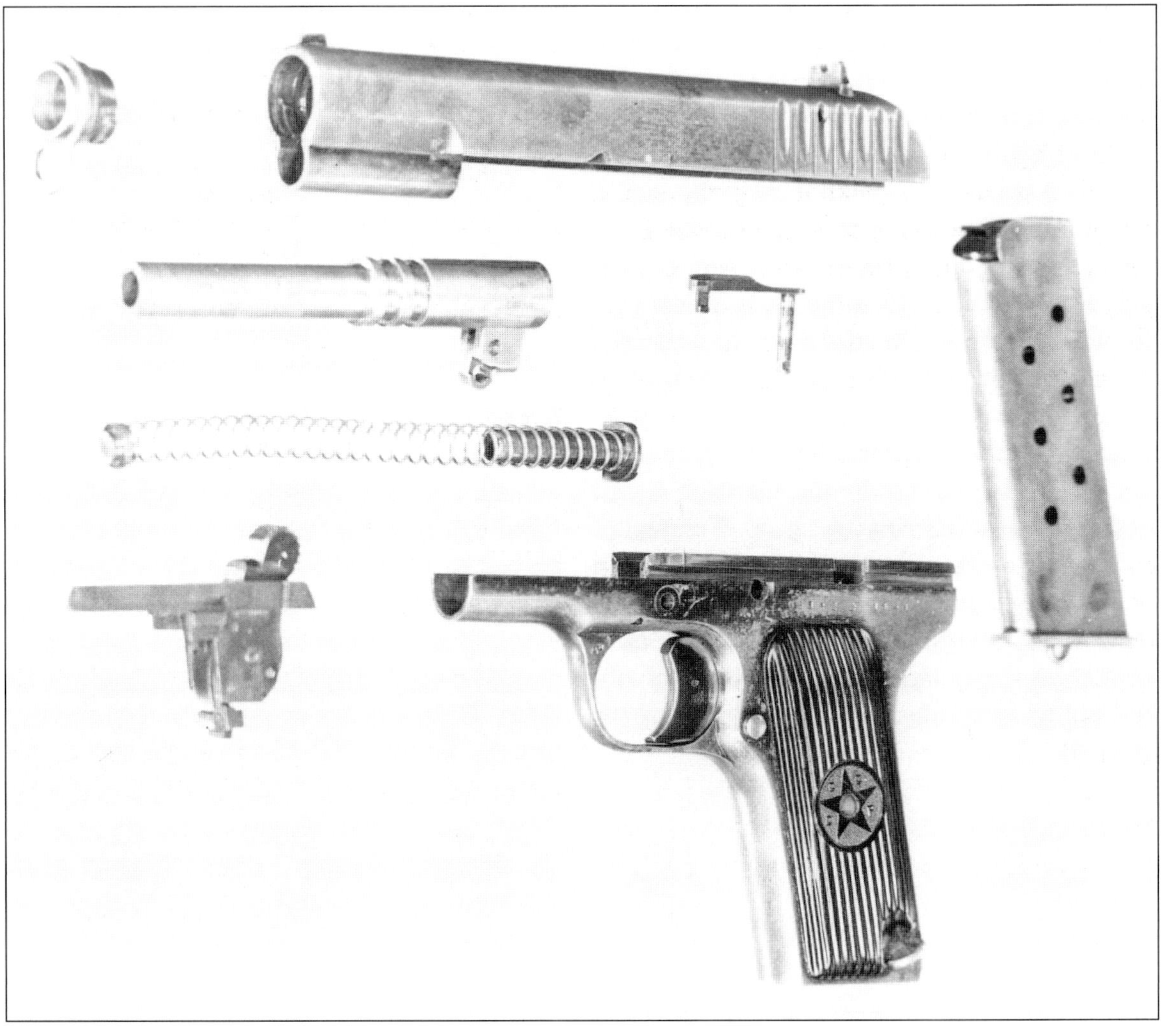

The Tokarev is another of the 'Colt cousins' which appeared in various countries in the 1930s, pistols which adopted the Colt dropping barrel method of recoil operation. Being a Soviet product, though, it had some peculiarities of its own which mark it out from the rest of the clan. The hammer mechanism and mainspring, for example, are in a separate module which can be removed from the frame for cleaning or repair, rather then having to delve inside the depths of the frame. There are actually two models of the Tokarev, externally identical, the TT-33 and the TT-34; the difference lies in the forming of the barrel. In the TT-33 the barrel is machined with two ribs on its upper surface, over the chamber area, which mate with two grooves inside the slide top, in the same manner as the Colt, Browning and many other pistols using the dropping barrel. But machining these two lugs on top of the barrel means an additional manufacturing process, and some ingenious Soviet engineer pointed out that by making these lugs into raised rings around the entire barrel, they could be cut during the shaping of the barrel on the lathe and would thus not require the attention of a milling machine and a second operation. The idea was adopted and the pistol became the TT-34.

Another unusual feature is the forming of the feedway magazine lips in the frame of the pistol instead of on the mouth of the magazine; this means some extra work on the frame, but it also means that the Tokarev magazine can absorb a great deal of knocking about and minor damage without causing feedway jams. Finally, there is no form of safety device: people who were issued with this pistol were assumed to have sufficient sense not to shoot themselves in the foot or be a danger to their own side.

Stripping the Tokarev follows the usual pattern of Browning designs. After removing the magazine and clearing the gun, press in the recoil spring plunger beneath the muzzle (the point of a bullet or some similar instrument is required). This frees the barrel bush, which can be rotated to one side so that the recoil spring and plunger pop out from the slide and can be grasped and withdrawn completely.

Using the magazine bottom plate, press back on the slide stop retaining clip on the right side of the frame, so that the slide stop pin can be withdrawn to the left. Now turn the pistol upside down and the slide can be pulled forward off the frame. Be careful to catch the hammer mechanism unit since this will probably drop out of the frame as the slide goes forward. The return spring guide rod will be found lying on the barrel, and can be removed, after which fold the barrel link forward, lift the breech end of the barrel to disengage the locking lugs, and move it forward and out of the slide. If the hammer mechanism has not fallen out by this time, it can be pulled out of its housing.

Reassembly is simply a reversal of the stripping procedure and is begun by inserting the hammer mechanism. The only difficult part is preparing the barrel and return spring for refitting. Slide the barrel back into the slide, fold the link to the rear, and ensure that the barrel lugs are engaged with the slide. Now lay the return spring guide rod on top of the barrel,

Tokarev TT-33 or TT-34

Calibre	7.62mm Soviet Pistol or 7.63mm Mauser
Method of operation	Short recoil, dropping barrel, single-action
Safety devices	None
Magazine type	Single-column detachable box in butt
Position of catch	Left front of butt
Magazine capacity	8 rounds
Front sight	Fixed blade
Rear sight	Fixed U-notch
Overall length	7.72in (196mm)
Barrel length	4.57in (116mm)
Number of grooves	4
Direction of twist	Right-hand
Empty weight	30.0oz (850g)
Markings	On left side of frame, above grips: 'TT-33' : factory identifying mark : year of manufacture
Serial number	On left side of frame, top of slide and on barrel, visible through ejection port (this is not immutable: inspection of a number of pistols suggests that provided the register number was on all three basic components, nobody was particularly worried about exactly where they went)

with the rounded side upward and the shank towards the muzzle, just in front of the link. Hold the slide inverted, invert the frame (holding it so that the hammer mechanism does not fall out) and slide the two together. When the slide has gone back as far as it can, turn the pistol the right way up and peer through the hole in the frame for the slide stop pin. The link should be visible, and, by moving the slide relative to the frame, line it up with the hole, and then insert the slide stop. Using the magazine floor plate again, slide the spring retainer over the end of the pin.

Now slip the return spring into the front of the slide and around the return spring rod. Insert the muzzle bush, press in the spring and plunger, and rotate the barrel bush into place, allowing the plunger to engage with it. Insert the magazine, cock the hammer and pull the trigger to check that everything is working properly.

Pistole Modell 640(b)

Fabrique Nationale d'Armes de Guerre, Herstal-lez-Liège, Belgium

When the Germans occupied Belgium in 1940, they moved very quickly to take over the Fabrique Nationale factory in Liège, having had a great deal of trouble with the same firm in 1914. (Indeed, they had so little success in trying to make the Belgians manufacture arms for them that they eventually turned the factory into an automobile workshop for the duration of World War I.) Among the various weapons in production was the FN High-Power Model 1935 pistol, often called 'John Browning's last design'. This was so good that the production line was kept going, the pistols being taken into the German Army as the Pistol Model 640(b)—the (b) for *belgisch*—and over 315,000 were manufactured under the German regime.

The FN High-Power was a further development of Browning's design which had produced the Colt M1011 pistol for the US Army. Even before World War I Browning had decided to drop his swinging link connection, which withdrew the barrel from its lock with the slide, and substitute a shaped cam acting against the slide stop pin across the frame. In the early 1920s he took the design to FN in Belgium, where work began developing it, and after his death in 1926 it was continued by Saive, the Belgian designer, who modified it to use an external hammer (Browning's original idea was to use a striker) and converted it to 9mm (instead of .45) so as to provide a much larger magazine capacity that had hitherto been thought possible. The pistol was ready for production in 1928, but the 1929 economic collapse caused it to be shelved, and it was not until 1935 that it was finally announced. It was immediately adopted by Belgium, Latvia, Lithuania, China and Peru, though in fact relatively few were delivered before war broke out in 1939. After 1945 FN were in a position to resume production very quickly, and ultimately it became the service weapon in about 55 countries.

Right: A Pistole Mod 640(b), or Browning High-Power. This is a specimen built in Liège under German supervision; there is a Wehrmacht acceptance stamp at the end of the lower line of inscription on the slide. (Photo by G. Z. Trebinski)

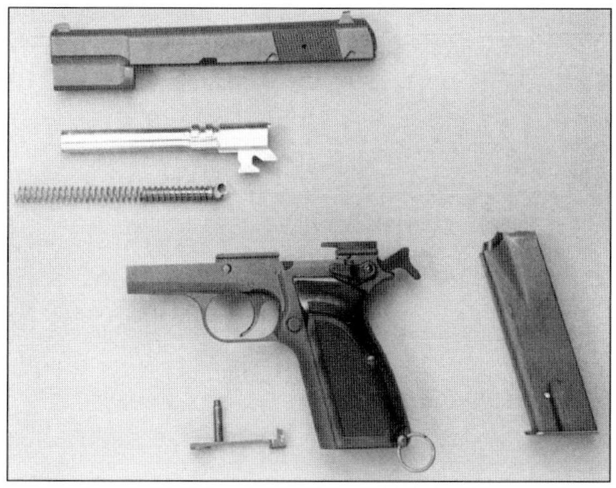

Above: A modern High-Power stripped. It is identical to the wartime model except for the more luxurious grips. Note that the barrel locking lugs only appear on the upper surface of the barrel; compare this with the Tokarev.

High-Power Model 35

Calibre	9mm Parabellum
Method of operation	Short-recoil, Browning link, single-action
Safety devices	Manual safety catch left rear of frame; magazine safety
Magazine type	Double-column detachable box in butt
Position of catch	Left front edge of butt
Magazine capacity	13 rounds
Front sight	Fixed blade
Rear sight	Fixed U-notch or adjustable tangent sight
Overall length	7.72in (196mm)
Barrel length	4.40in (112mm)
Number of grooves	6
Direction of twist	Right-hand
Empty weight	34.0oz (965g)
Markings	Left side of slide: 'FABRIQUE NATIONALE D'ARMES DE GUERRE. HERSTAL-BELGIQUE BROWNING'S PATENT DEPOSE' (German Waffenamt acceptance marks will be found stamped, possibly more than once, alongside this; in addition, the pistol is usually marked on the left side with 'P640(b)', but this is not always present)
Serial number	On right side of frame, slide and barrel

Dismantling the High-Power is relatively simple, because the awkward muzzle bush of the Colt .45 is dispensed with. After removing the magazine, pull back the slide to eject any round in the chamber, then release the slide and pull the trigger. Pull back the slide again a short distance and turn up the safety catch into a recess in the underside of the slide, so as to hold the slide back. Press up the slide stop lever and withdraw the pin from the slide. Holding the slide firmly, press down the safety catch and allow the slide to come forward and off the frame. Press the recoil spring guide towards the muzzle so as to disengage it from the barrel, and remove it. Lift the breech end of the barrel and remove it from the slide. The grip plates can be removed by taking out the usual screws, so exposing the lockwork for cleaning.

Reassembly is simply the reverse of the dismantling procedure, and there are no hidden traps.

Pistole Modell 641(b)

Fabrique Nationale d'Armes de Guerre, Herstal-lez-Liège, Belgium

The Browning Model 1910 pistol was one of the most graceful and elegant designs ever to be produced, and it became immensely popular both as a military/police pistol and as a commercial product for home defence and sport shooting. Its principal novelty, at the time of its introduction, was the wrapping of the return spring around the barrel, and the consequent tubular appearance of the slide.

In 1923 the government of the new state of Yugoslavia came to Browning with an order for several thousand Model 1910—but please could they have a longer barrel and a bigger magazine? Extending the butt frame and making a larger magazine was a relatively simple task; making a larger barrel was easy; but making a

Above: The Pistole 641(b) was popular with German staff officers, being simply the Browning 1910/22 pistol and a very elegant piece of workmanship.

longer slide meant a new and complex forging and a major machining operation. So the FN engineers adopted the same trick that Walther had to extend his slide on the Walther Model 7 (q.v.). The slide already ended in a screw-threaded section, and now the engineers simply designed an extended nose to screw into this and thus lengthen the slide to cover the new barrel and, of course, a longer return spring. The Yugoslavs were pleased with the result, and FN put it on the market as the Model 1910/22, often called the Model 1922. It was made in both 7.65mm and 9mm Short calibres.

In 1940 the Germans retained it in production and adopted the pistol for military use; the 7.65mm version was known as the Pistole Modell 626(b) and the 9mm model was the Modell 641(b). The 9mm version was very popular with staff officers who required a self-defence weapon firing a reasonable size of bullet but had no need for a heavy service pistol.

Dismantling the Model 1910/22 is quite simple. After having removed the magazine and

Below: A sectional drawing of the Browning 1910/22.

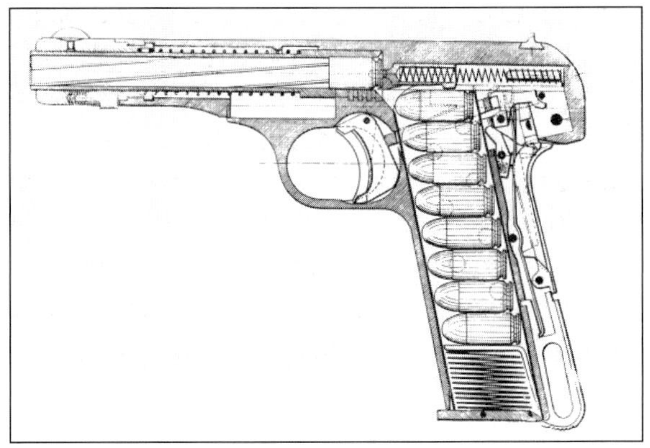

Browning 1910/22

Calibre	9 × 17mm Short/.380 Auto
Method of operation	Blowback, striker-fired, single-action
Safety devices	Manual safety catch left side of frame; grip safety
Magazine type	Single-column detachable box in butt
Position of catch	At heel of butt
Magazine capacity	9 rounds
Front sight	Fixed blade
Rear sight	Fixed U-notch
Overall length	7.00in (178mm)
Barrel length	4.50in (114mm)
Number of grooves	4
Direction of twist	Left-hand
Empty weight	25.0oz (708g)
Markings	Left of slide: 'FABRIQUE NATIONALE D'ARMES DE GUERRE HERSTAL BELGIUM BROWNING'S PATENT DEPOSE' and Waffenamt acceptance marks; grips of early wartime production retained the usual FN monogram, but later were plain wood with no markings
Serial number	On left side of slide and on front extension; on left side of frame, above trigger; and on barrel, visible through ejection opening

ensured that the chamber is empty, press in the spring catch which locks the nose of the slide in place and unscrew the nose piece, taking care as it comes loose not to let the return spring take charge of affairs. Remove the nose piece and return spring, then draw the slide back and lift it completely off the frame. The firing pin can be removed by pressing in the rear end and sliding the keeper plate out of its housing. Reassembling the weapon means simply running the slide back on the frame, replacing the return spring round the barrel and then screwing the nose piece back into the slide until it is fully home and the spring catch engages in its slot.

GECADO

G. C. Dornheim GmbH, Suhl

Founded in 1863, Dornheim was principally a sales agency, though it had a small ammunition-making capacity, manufacturing sporting calibres and head-stamping them 'Gecado', its registered tradename. The company appears to have traded quite successfully until 1940, when it was taken over by the Gustav Genschow company, who continued to produce the Gecado ammunition in limited quantities until 1945.

Two automatic pistols called Gecado were sold during the period 1925–35 and were actually made for them in Spain by SEAM (the Sociedade Español de Armas y Municiones of Eibar). The 6.35mm model was a pirated copy of the Browning 1906, while the 7.65mm model was another pirated design based on the Browning 1903 pistol. Both were very much in the 'Eibar' style, of average finish and quality, and marked by the word 'GECADO' inside a diamond stamped on the slide, together with 'KAL. 6,35' or 'KAL. 7,65' and Spanish proof marks. (The 6.35mm model was sold in Spain as the

Below: The pre-1939 Gecado 6.35mm pistol manufactured by the Spanish SEAM company.

Gecado	
Calibre	7.65mm Browning
Method of operation	Blowback, hammer-fired
Safety devices	Manual safety catch on left side
Magazine type	Single-column detachable box in butt
Position of catch	Heel of butt
Magazine capacity	7 rounds
Front sight	None
Rear sight	Groove in slide top
Overall length	5.19in (132mm)
Barrel length	2.57in (65mm)
Number of grooves	4
Direction of twist	Right-hand
Empty weight	20.7oz (587g)
Markings	Left of slide: 'GECADO' in elongated diamond frame, 'CAL 7,65'
Serial number	On right side of frame

Union 1 and the 7.65mm as the Silesia during the same period.)

The name reappeared briefly in the period 1955–65 on the Reck P-8 6.35mm pistol, apparently marketed under the auspices of Dynamit Nobel, who by then had acquired rights to the brand name.

Gecado Model 11	
Calibre	6.35mm Browning
Method of operation	Blowback, striker-fired
Safety devices	Manual safety catch on left side above trigger
Magazine type	Single-column detachable box in butt
Position of catch	Heel of butt
Magazine capacity	6 rounds
Front sight	Fixed blade
Rear sight	Fixed V-notch
Overall length	4.57in (116mm)
Barrel length	2.24in (57mm)
Number of grooves	6
Direction of twist	Right hand
Empty weight	15.0oz (425g)
Markings	Left side of slide: 'GECADO' in elongated diamond frame, 'MOD. 11 KAL. 6,35 (.25) MADE IN GERMANY'; left grip carries a round medallion with 'GECADO' in the centre
Serial number	On left side of slide

Above: The post-1950 Gecado was a very different weapon—actually the Reck 8 pistol under a different name.

The name Gecado will also be found on a revolver, the Weirauch HW3 (see entry under Weirauch for details) of the 1960s, presumably being sold byDynamit Nobel agents.

GUSTLOFF

Gustloffwerke, Waggenwerk Suhl, Suhl.

The Wilhelm Gustloff Stiftung (foundation) was an institution set up by the National Socialist German Worker's Party (NSDAP) to operate various companies which were taken over by the state, their original owners having been decreed enemies of the state. It was originally established as the Berlin-Sühler Waffen- und Fahrzeugfabrik (BSW) and swallowed up, among others, the Simson company (q.v.) in 1936.

In 1940 it was renamed Gustloffwerke and was extensively involved in the production of military small arms in three factories, Suhl (code 'dfb'), Weimar (code 'bed') and Meiningen (code 'nyw'). From 1938 to 1939, the company had worked on the design of a 7.65mm automatic pistol in the hope of landing a military contract. It was a blowback model with coaxial recoil spring and an internal hammer; a unique hammer spring tensioning lever was fitted in the top of the left butt grip and worked in conjunction with the double-action lock—reminiscent of the mechanism of the better-known Sauer 38H. If the hammer was cocked, tension could be removed from its spring by using the lever. If it was lowered, the pistol could be fired double-action by pulling the trigger through. The slide was engraved 'Gustloffwerke Waffenfabrik Suhl', and the grips carried a 'G' medallion.

In January 1940 a specimen pistol was presented to Hitler, together with the suggestion that it might be adopted for use by the various police services in Germany. Arrangements were made for production to take place in the Weimar factory, using, it is alleged, inmates from the nearby Buchenwald concentration camp, and Gauleiter Sauckel of Weimar, Reichs General Trustee for Labour, made several applications to Hitler for a prototype order. However, no order ever eventuated and the project was abandoned. Apart from details of correspondence by Sauckel, which are in the Federal German State Archives, no records or drawings of this project remain. A few Gustloff pistols, with both steel and die-cast zinc frames, are in the hands of collectors.

Above: One of the hand-made prototype models of the Gustloff, which never got into production.

Gustloff

Calibre	7.65mm Browning
Method of operation	Blowback, hammer-fired
Safety devices	Manual safety/de-cocking lever at top of left grip
Magazine type	Single-column detachable box in butt
Position of catch	Left side of butt
Magazine capacity	8 rounds
Front sight	Fixed blade
Rear sight	Fixed V-notch
Overall length	6.61in (168mm)
Barrel length	3.74in (95mm)
Number of grooves	6
Direction of twist	Right-hand
Empty weight	25.9oz (735g)
Markings	On left side of slide: 'GUSTLOFF-WERKE WAFFENWERK SUHL'; on barrel, visible through ejection port: 'Kal 7,65mm'
Serial number	On bottom of butt frame

For the Gustloff involvement in the Volkspistole programme, see under Volkspistole.

HAENEL

C.G.Haenel Gewehr- und Fahrradfabrik, Suhl

Model I

Inscribed 'Schmeisser's Patent', the Haenel is largely the design of Hugo Schmeisser, being based on his 1921 patents for attachment of the barrel and for linking the safety catch and magazine catch together. While this is a relatively commonplace pistol of the pocket blowback class, these patent features lead to a unique dismantling method, and one liable to lead to considerable headscratching among the uninitiated.

The safety catch is the key to much of the mystery. In the first place, the weapon cannot

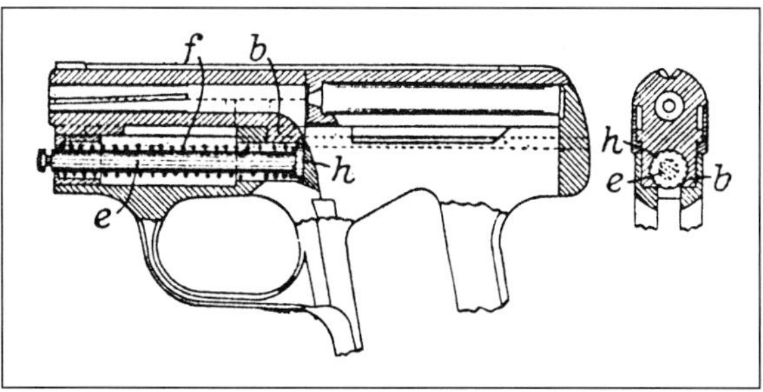

Top: A 1923 advertisement for the Haenel pistol.
Above: Patent 167,724, 19 February 1921, Hugo Schmeisser: a brief patent relating to the method of attaching the barrel that was used on the Haenel pistol.

be cocked unless the catch is set to 'fire'; in the second place, the magazine cannot be withdrawn or replaced unless the catch is set to 'safe'; and, in the third place, once the magazine is withdrawn the safety catch cannot be moved. All this leads to the need for a definite programme when clearing the gun and preparing to strip it. First, with the safety catch at 'fire', pull back the slide, check that the gun and magazine are empty, release the slide and press the trigger. Then turn the safety catch backwards to 'safe' and remove the magazine. One can check the state of the striker, since there is a signal pin which protrudes from the rear of the slide when the action is cocked. Now push the slide back about 0.5in (12mm) and press up the safety catch until it locks into a small notch on the lower edge of the slide. Examining the front end of the weapon will show that the recoil spring guide rod has a groove turned in it near its front end. Using the lip on the magazine bottom plate as a tool, hook this under the guide rod groove, lever the rod out about 0.5in (12mm), then push it sideways and release it so that it remains out, about one inch (25mm) in front of the frame. This operation has pulled the guide rod out of engagement with a hole in the barrel lug. The barrel can now be lifted straight up out of the frame.

Looking into the frame will show the position of the guide rod, and this should now be gripped, pulled and released so that it will spring back into its seating. Taking the strain on the slide, release the safety catch from engagement and ease the slide forward and off the frame. Finally pull out the recoil spring and guide rod. The removal of one screw in the right grip will permit both grips to be lifted from the frame, revealing the manifold workings of the safety catch; just above the magazine-well entrance is a small pressure plate which controls the movement of the catch, and when this is depressed

Below: The Haenel pistol looks commonplace, but, being designed by Hugo Schmeisser, it has a few hidden tricks.

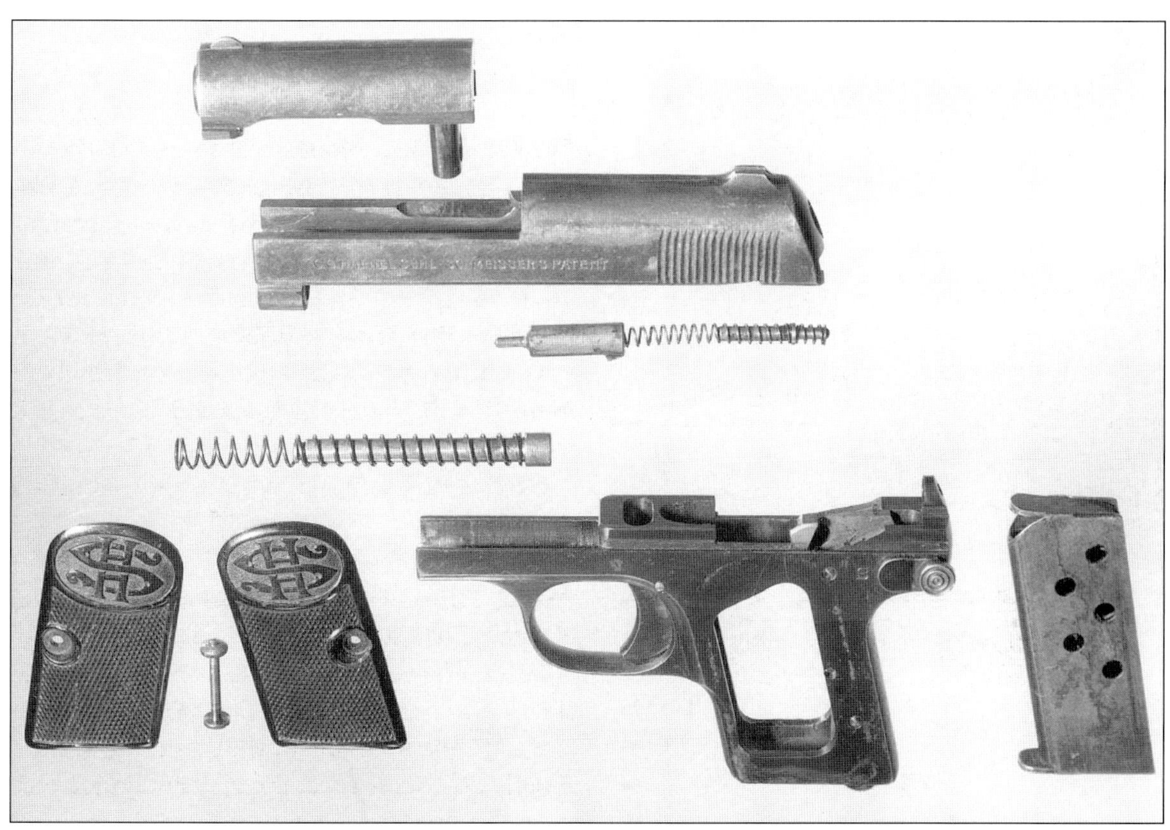

Above: The Haenel-Schmeisser dismantled, revealing the method of attaching the barrel to the frame.

Heinel Pistol

Calibre	6.35mm Browning
Method of operation	Blowback, striker-fired
Safety devices	Manual catch on left rear of grip
Magazine type	Single-column detachable box in butt
Position of catch	Bottom rear of butt
Magazine capacity	6 rounds
Front sight	Fixed blade
Rear sight	Fixed V-notch
Overall length	4.72in (120mm)
Barrel length	2.48in (63mm)
Number of grooves	6
Direction of twist	Right-hand
Empty weight	13.5oz (383g)
Markings	Left of slide: 'C. G. HAENEL SUHL - SCHMEISSER'S PATENT'; at top of each grip, a monogram 'HS' in an oval
Serial number	On right of frame; last two digits under breech block and barrel lug

by the magazine the catch is free to move. Moreover, as the catch is moved, a rod passes down behind the magazine latch itself and prevents its movement and thus the entry or release of the magazine when the safety catch is not at 'safe'. Altogether this is a most involved little weapon.

Model 2

The Model 1 was originally known simply as the Schmeisser-Pistole, but in 1927 this second model appeared as the Model 2, whereupon the original design became the Model 1.

The Model 2 is to the same mechanical design so far as the method of barrel assembly and the operation of the safety catch are concerned, but the whole pistol is now to a more

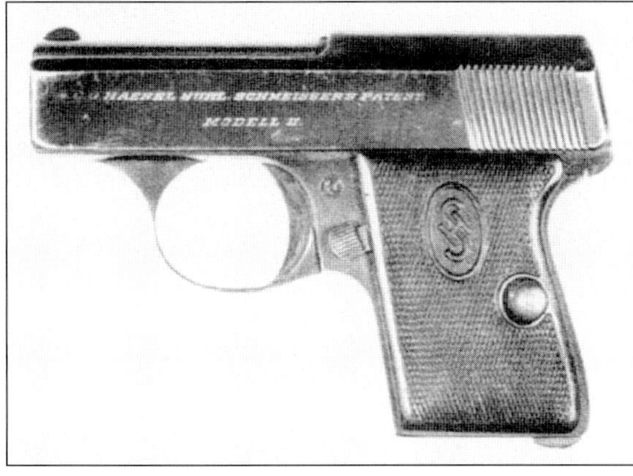

Above: The Schmeisser Model 2, by Haenel, is less common and had a few design changes.

severely square shape, apparently following the style set by the contemporary Mauser WTP and Walther Model 9. The safety catch is repositioned to the front edge of the left grip, and most of it is concealed by the grip plate. Operation and dismantling of the Model 2 is exactly as for the Model 1.

Schmeisser Model 2	
Calibre	6.35mm Browning
Method of operation	Blowback, single-action, striker-fired
Safety devices	Manual safety catch on left grip
Magazine type	Single-column detachable box in butt
Position of catch	At heel of butt
Magazine capacity	6 rounds
Front sight	Fixed blade
Rear sight	Groove in slide top
Overall length	3.94in (100mm)
Barrel length	2.05in (52mm)
Number of grooves	8
Direction of twist	Right-hand
Empty weight	11.8oz (335g)
Markings	Left side of slide: 'C. G. HAENEL SUHL. CAL 6.35 SCHMEISSER'S PATENT. MODELL II'; top of each grip: 'SCHMEISSER' or a monogram 'HS'
Serial number	On right side of frame

HECKLER & KOCH

Heckler & Koch was established in 1949 in an old Mauser factory in Oberndorf and began making machine tools. In the early 1950s they were asked by the Federal Government to examine and develop a military rifle design which had been submitted from Spain. This was successfully performed, the rifle becoming the Federal German Army standard Gewehr 3, and the company was then launched into the firearms business. It has produced several highly successful designs of rifles, pistols, submachine guns and machine guns but ran into financial difficulties in 1990 due to the cancellation of a long-promised military contract. The company was purchased by British Aerospace/Royal Ordnance and has continued to produce competitive designs.

HK4

Their first pistol venture was the HK4, which was more or less based upon the pre-war Mauser HSc design, a simple but high-quality double-action blowback weapon. It was available in four calibres—.22 rimfire, 6.35mm, 7.65mm and 9mm Short—and the basic frame and slide are the same for all of them. Whatever calibre the gun was purchased in, it was merely a matter of buying a conversion kit—a new barrel and return spring—to change it to any of the other calibres. The change from centrefire to rimfire or vice-versa was simply a matter of removing the breech block faceplate from the slide, reversing it, and replacing it, so changing the point of strike of the firing pin.

In fact, although described as being a blowback weapon, the HK4 in 7.65mm and 9mm versions is almost a delayed blowback and certainly could be called a 'braked blowback'. Since the slide is light, plain blowback action would

Top: The Heckler & Koch HK4 marked the company's first venture into the pistol field and was little more than an up-to-date version of the pre-war Mauser HSc.
Above: A sectioned view of the HK4 pistol.

Heckler & Koch HK4

Calibre	.22, 6.35mm, 7.65mm, 9mm Short (see text)
Method of operation	Blowback, hammer-fired (but see text)
Safety devices	Manual safety catch on left rear of slide
Magazine type	Single-column detachable box in butt
Position of catch	At heel of butt
Magazine capacity	Originally 8 rounds (.22, 6.35mm, 7.65mm) or 7 (9mm Short); later 10 rounds (.22, 6.35mm), 9 (7.65mm) or 8 (9mm Short)
Front sight	Fixed blade
Rear sight	Fixed U-notch
Overall length	6.18in (157mm)
Barrel length	3.34in (85mm)
Number of grooves	6
Direction of twist	Left-hand
Empty weight	18.34oz (520g)
Markings	Left side of slide: 'HECKLER & KOCH GMBH OBERNDORF/N MADE IN GERMANY Mod HK 4'; right side of slide: 'Cal XXX' (as appropriate)
Serial number	Beneath frame in front of trigger guard (a factory process number is also stamped on the frame beneath the left grip)

be rather violent when firing these two larger cartridges, so their chambers have four short flutes cut into the wall. These are not the normal sort of flutes which extend forward into the leed, or forcing cone, nor do they extend back to the chamber mouth. As a result, when the pistol is fired, the cartridge case expands slightly into these flutes and thus the metal must contract back to normal dimensions before the empty case will move backwards and apply pressure to the breech block face. There is, therefore, a very slight delaying action which is sufficient to allow the bullet to leave the muzzle and the chamber pressure to drop to a safe level before the case begins to leave the chamber.

Dismantling the HK4 presents no problems. Set the safety catch to 'safe', remove the magazine and pull back the slide to eject any round which may be in the chamber. Release the slide and pull the trigger. Push forward the barrel catch, which is in the rear surface of the trigger-guard, ease the slide forward to its stop and then lift it off the frame. Using the magazine floor plate as a tool, pull the barrel forward in the slide until the extractor clears its groove in the slide and then lift the barrel and return

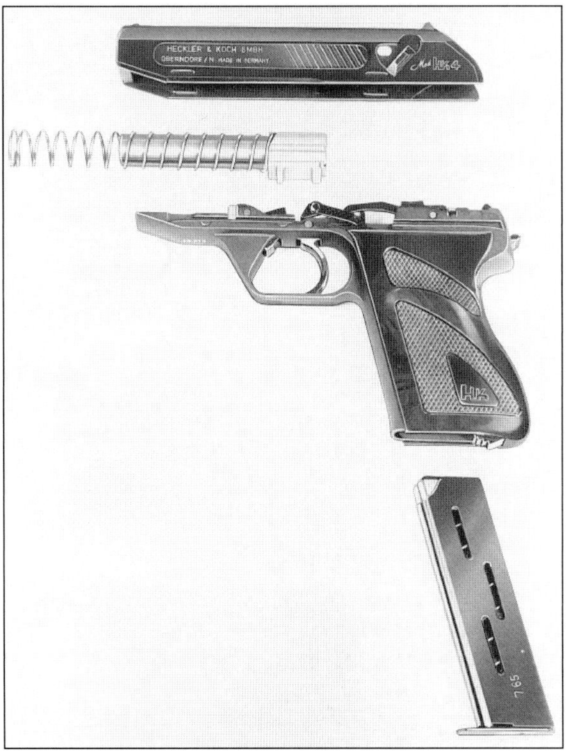

Above: The HK4 dismantled into its principal components.

spring out. Reassembly is simply the reverse process.

To change calibres is simply a process of dismantling the gun as described above, then reassembling it with the appropriate barrel and return spring. The only added complication comes when changing from centrefire to rimfire. In this case, hold the extractor clear of the breech faceplate with a pin or small nail, and slide off the faceplate. When changing to rimfire, turn the plate so that the letter 'R' is showing and the firing pin is visible in the top hole. For centrefire the side marked 'Z' is showing and the firing pin protrudes through the central hole.

P9, P9S

Having successfully placed a pocket pistol on the market, H&K now aimed for the military and police user with a locked-breech pistol in 9mm Parabellum calibre. These are delayed blowback pistols, originally made in 9mm and 7.65mm Parabellum calibres; the difference between the two is that the P9 was single-action, the P9S double-action.

The delayed blowback system is derived from that of the G3 rifle which uses a roller-locked breech block. In the pistol, the slide carries a two-part bolt, the front part of which carries two rollers which engage in recesses in the barrel extension. As the slide closes on loading, the heavy rear section of the bolt forces the rollers out into the recesses. On firing, the chamber pressure forces the case against the bolt face; this tries to force the rollers back, and the shape of the recesses turns this into an inward thrust. But the rollers cannot move in until they force the heavy section of the bolt backwards by pressing upon an angled tongue. Once the inertia of the bolt (and the slide) is overcome, the rollers move in and the entire slide and bolt run back to complete the reloading cycle.

The P9 had an internal hammer, with a thumb-operated de-cocking lever on the left

Below: The H&K P9S—one of the first modern double-action 9mm pistols.
Right: The component parts of the P9S, showing, among other things, the intricacies of the roller-delayed breech block.

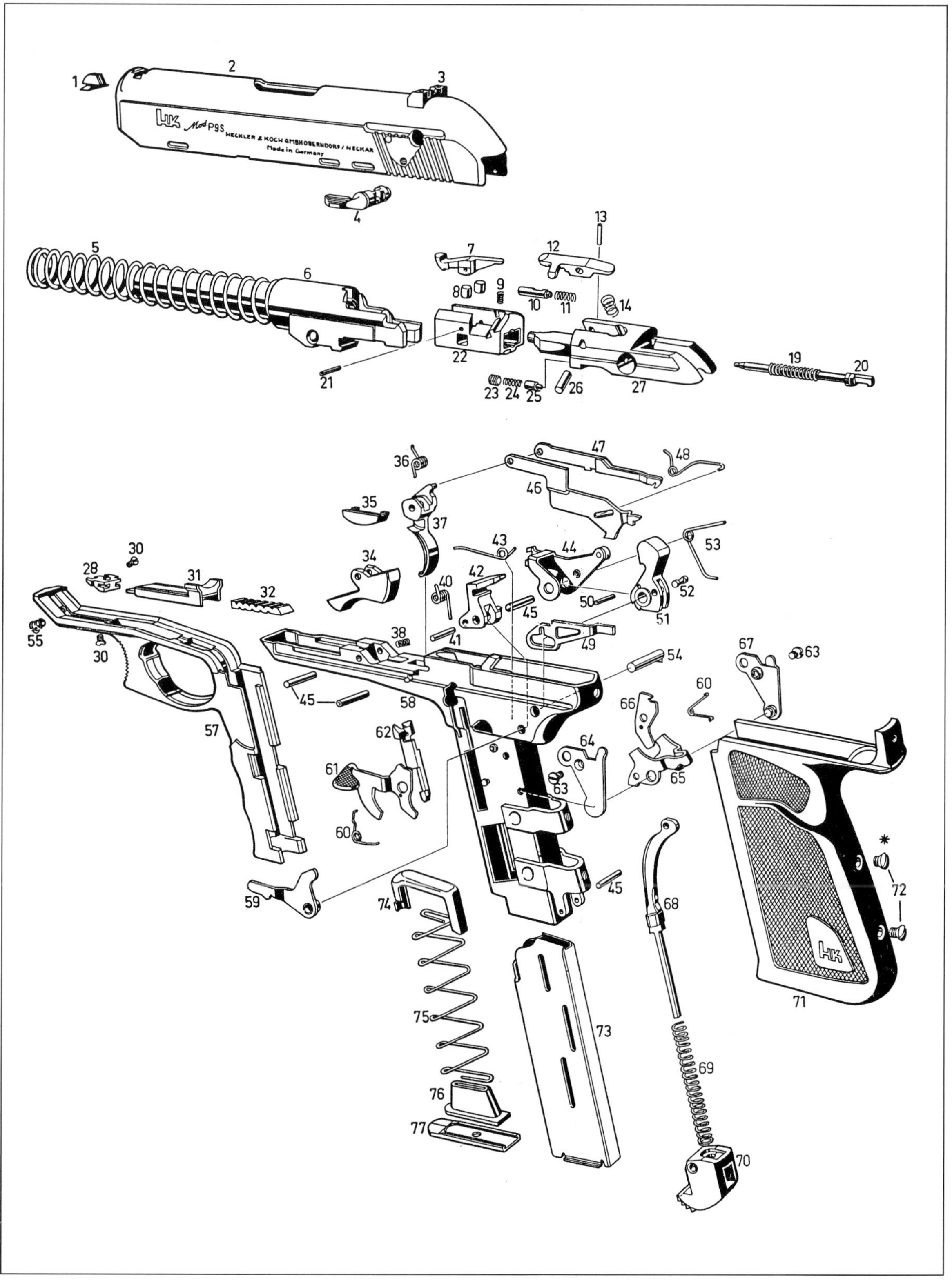
1
2
3
HK Mod P9S HECKLER & KOCH GMBH OBERNDORF / NECKAR
Made in Germany
4
5
6
7
8
9
10
11
12
13
14
19
20
21
22
23
24
25
26
27
28
30
31
32
34
35
36
37
38
40
41
42
43
44
45
46
47
48
49
50
51
52
53
54
55
57
58
59
60
61
62
63
64
65
66
67
68
69
70
71
72
73
74
75
76
77
*

side. This lever allowed the hammer to be lowered under control or cocked from the 'down' position. There was a manual safety catch on the slide and a chamber-loaded indicator pin. The bore was 'polygonally rifled', a system originated by H&K in which the rifling grooves are merged into the bore diameter so that the bore looks like a flattened circle. This reduces friction on the bullet and allows a rather higher velocity than might be expected. Another innovation was the plastic coating of the exterior surfaces of the frame.

The P9 was discontinued in the late 1970s but the P9S continued in production. This differed only in having a double-action lock and a suitably shaped trigger guard; at first this was merely larger, but in the mid-1970s the front of it was reverse-curved to suit it to the fashionable two-handed grip. In 1977 a version in .45 ACP was marketed. The Model P9 Sport is a competition version of the P9S, with an extended barrel carrying a muzzle weight which blends in with the slide contours.

Dismantling the P9 or P9S is not difficult. After removing the magazine, pull back the slide and verify that the chamber and feedway are empty. Release the slide. Press the barrel catch in the trigger guard forward and upward. Move the slide as far forward as it will go, and then lift it from the frame. Invert the slide and remove the barrel and return spring by pushing the barrel forward until it can be lifted out. Using one edge of the barrel extension as a tool, push it between the bolt head and the slide, pressing against the locking lever in the slide until the bolt head springs forward and can be removed. It is not necessary to go further than this.

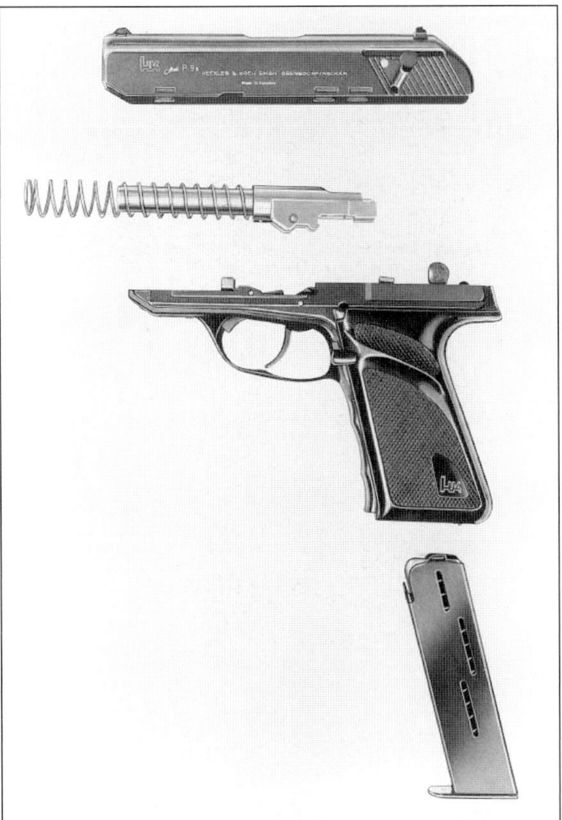

Left: The P9S dismantled

Heckler & Koch P9S

Calibre	9mm Parabellum
Method of operation	Delayed blowback, roller-locked, hammer-fired
Safety devices	Manual safety catch on left rear of slide
Magazine type	Single-column detachable box in butt
Position of catch	At heel of butt
Magazine capacity	9 rounds
Front sight	Fixed blade
Rear sight	Fixed U-notch
Overall length	7.60in (192mm)
Barrel length	4.00in (102mm)
Number of grooves	Polygonal
Direction of twist	Right-hand
Empty weight	31.0oz (875g) without magazine
Markings	Left of slide: 'HK Mod P9S HECKLER & KOCH GMBH OBERNDORF/NECKAR Made in Germany'
Serial number	On left side of frame and on barrel, visible through ejection opening

To reassemble the gun, insert the bolt head into the slide by placing its rectangular opening over the locking piece, with the extractor towards the ejection opening, press the locking lever down with one shank of the barrel extension and at the same time push the bolt in until it engages. Place the barrel and return spring into the slide, with the large diameter of the spring at the muzzle end; push the barrel forward against the spring, press it into the slide and allow it to run back so that the barrel extension pieces engage with the locking rollers. Place the slide on the frame so that the lugs engage, pull the slide back and release it; decock the pistol and insert the magazine.

VP '70

This was a highly innovative design which failed to gain the acceptance it merited. It was a blowback, firing the 9mm Parabellum cartridge from a fixed barrel. The magazine carried 18 rounds, and the pistol was double-action only, using a self-cocking striker mechanism; pulling the trigger fist cocked the striker and then released it, and the trigger movement gave a distinct 'first pressure' as the cocking took place, after which a further pressure released the striker. Since this system allows a pistol to be carried safely when loaded, no manual safety was fitted, though a push-button safety catch could be provided as an optional fitting.

A plastic holster-stock was provided; when this was clipped to the butt and frame, a connection was made with the firing mechanism which allowed the firing of single shots, or, when

Below: the H&K VP '70 was one of the first pistols to employ synthetic materials in its basic construction.

Heckler & Koch VP '70Z

Calibre	9mm Parabellum
Method of operation	Blowback, self-cocking, striker-fired
Safety devices	No applied safety
Magazine type	Double-column detachable box in butt
Position of catch	Left front edge of butt
Magazine capacity	18 rounds
Front sight	Fixed blade
Rear sight	Fixed square notch
Overall length	8.01in (204mm)
Barrel length	4.556in (116mm)
Number of grooves	Polygonal
Direction of twist	Right-hand
Empty weight	29.0oz (820g) without magazine
Markings	Left of slide: 'HECKLER & KOCH GMBH OBERNDORF/N Made in Germany'; bottom of butt grips: 'HK VP '70Z'
Serial number	On right side of frame

a change lever on the butt was moved, allowed the weapon to be fired in three-round bursts for each pressure of the trigger, turning it into a species of submachine gun.

This original version was introduced in 1970; shortly afterwards it was renamed the VP '70M (for Militärische) and a second version, the VP '70Z (for Zivil) was introduced. This did away with the three-round burst mechanism and the holster-stock, so that it could be sold as a simple semi-automatic pistol. The VP '70M was bought by a few African military forces and the VP '70Z by some police forces, but in general sales were disappointing and manufacture was terminated in the mid-1980s.

Dismantling the VP '70 (either model) is simplicity itself. Apply the safety catch, remove the magazine, and pull back the slide to clear the gun, then release the slide. Pull down the dismantling catch in the top of the trigger guard, pull back the slide to its fullest extent, lift the rear end, and then pass the slide forward over the barrel. Remove the return spring from around the barrel. To remove the firing pin, turn the cap at the rear of the slide through 90° and allow the cap, firing pin and spring to come out. Reassembly is the reverse process; the only point to watch is that, when replacing the firing pin, the wings must be located in the two grooves in the firing pin housing.

The P7 Family

The P7 originated as the 'PSP' (Polizei Selbstlade Pistole) in response to a late 1970s demand from the Federal German Police for a pistol with adequate performance but with the minimum of handling required to bring it into action quickly. The VP '70 had shown that 9mm Parabellum blowback designs were still regarded with some distrust, so this model went back to delayed blowback but used a totally new system of achieving the desired delay. In the frame, beneath the barrel, is a cylinder with a port to the barrel. Attached to the inner front of the slide is a piston rod, surrounded by a return

Below: The VP '70 partly dismantled, revealing the fixed barrel.

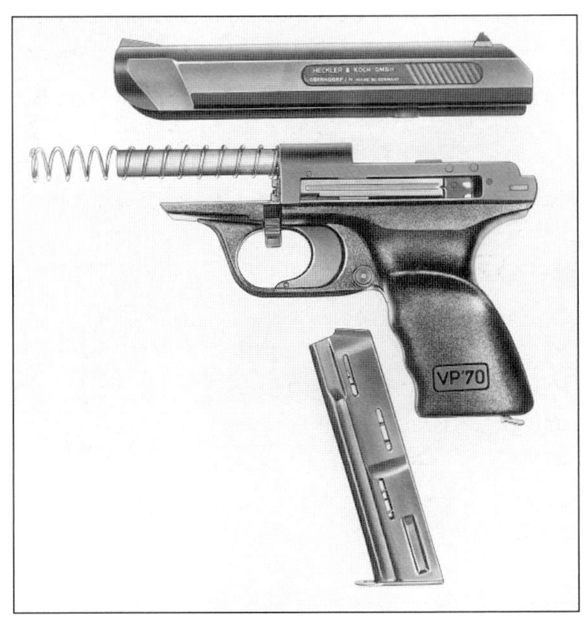

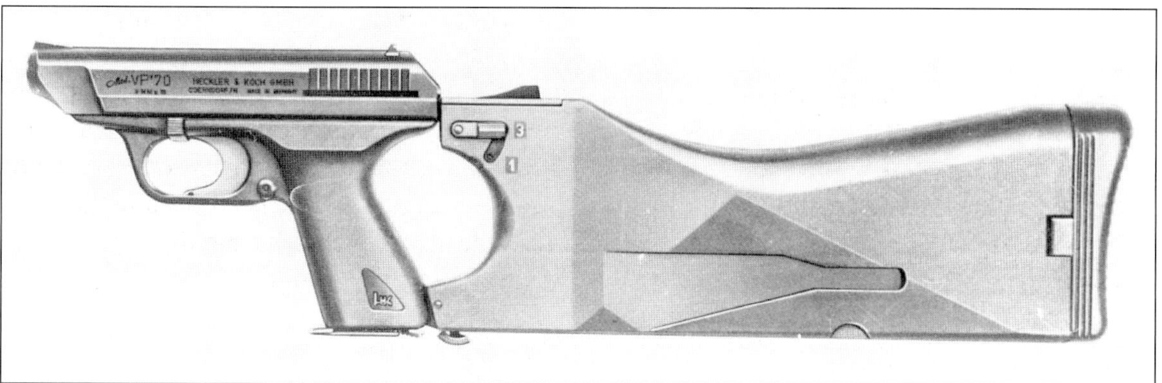

Above: When fitted with this butt, the VP '70 became a form of submachine gun. Note the change lever selecting either single shots or three-round bursts.

spring, which enters the cylinder. As the pistol is fired, gas under high pressure enters the cylinder; as the slide moves back, so the piston rod is driven into the cylinder, where its movement is resisted by the high-pressure gas. This delays the opening of the breech until the bullet is clear of the barrel and the gas pressure in the barrel falls, allowing the slide to move back and the piston to force the gas out of the cylinder and into the barrel, there to escape from the muzzle and breech during the reloading cycle.

To give an additional element of delay—since otherwise there could be a slight opening movement of the breech before sufficient gas pressure in the cylinder arrests the movement—the chamber has blind flutes, as described above for the HK4 pistol, which allow expansion of the case metal and act as a brake on the initial extraction.

To allow the pistol to be brought into action quickly, the firing mechanism is also unique. There is a moving grip device at the front of the butt, resembling a grip safety. As the pistol is brought to the firing position, the hand naturally squeezes this grip inwards, and this cocks the firing pin ready for the first shot, made by simply squeezing the trigger. So long as the grip is kept squeezed, the cycling of the action results in the striker being automatically cocked as the slide closes, ready for the next shot. Should the pressure be released, the striker is uncocked and the pistol is safe; if, for example, the pistol is dropped, it is in a safe condition as soon as it leaves the hand and cannot fire when it hits the ground. Should a misfire occur, the firer merely releases and re-squeezes the grip to make a second attempt at firing. The pistol can also be silently de-cocked by pulling back the slide a short distance and releasing the cocking grip.

Dismantling the P7 family is very easy. Remove the magazine, pull back the slide, check that the chamber and feedway are empty and

Below: The H&K PSP (Polizei Selbstlade Pistole) was designed to meet the demands of the German Federal Police.

Heckler & Koch P7 M8	
Calibre	9mm Parabellum
Method of operation	Delayed blowback, self-cocking, striker-fired
Safety devices	No form of applied safety
Magazine type	Single-column detachable box in butt
Position of catch	Junction of front edge of butt and trigger guard
Magazine capacity	8 rounds
Front sight	Fixed blade
Rear sight	Fixed square notch
Overall length	6.73in (171mm)
Barrel length	4.13in (105mm)
Number of grooves	Polygonal
Direction of twist	Right-hand
Empty weight	29.9oz (855g)
Markings	Left side of slide: 'HECKLER & KOCH GMBH OBERNDORF/N MADE IN GERMANY 9mm × 19'; bottom of butt, both sides: 'HK P7 M8'
Serial number	On right side of frame

Heckler & Koch P7 M13	
Calibre	9mm Parabellum
Method of operation	Delayed blowback, self-cocking, striker-fired
Safety devices	No form of applied safety
Magazine type	Double-column detachable box in butt
Position of catch	Junction of front edge of butt and trigger guard
Magazine capacity	13 rounds
Front sight	Fixed blade
Rear sight	Fixed square notch
Overall length	6.65in (169mm)
Barrel length	4.13in (105mm)
Number of grooves	Polygonal
Direction of twist	Right-hand
Empty weight	34.4oz (975g)
Markings	Left side of slide: 'HECKLER & KOCH GMBH OBERNDORF/N MADE IN GERMANY 9mm × 19'; bottom of butt, both sides: 'HK P7 M13'
Serial number	On right side of frame

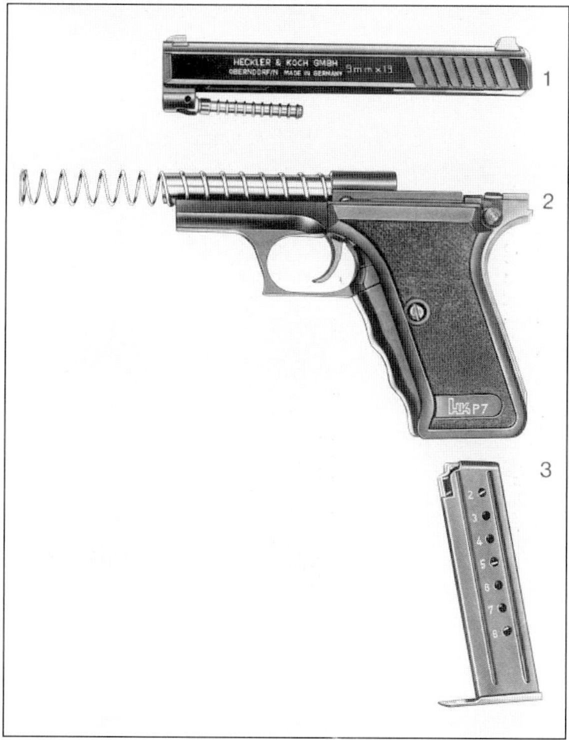

Left: After some modifications and practical tests, the PSP became the P7. This is the P7 M13 in nickel finish.
Above: The fundamental parts of the P7 pistol. Note the delayed blowback piston under the slide.

release the slide. Press in the dismantling button at the left rear of the frame. Pull the slide all the way back and lift off, removing it to the front, over the barrel. Unscrew the grip screws, lift the grip plates slightly at their front, push forward and lift them clear. To remove the firing pin and spring (do this with the pistol assembled, before dismantling), squeeze the grip until the firing pin is flush with the rear end of the slide. Then, using the magazine floor plate extension as a screwdriver, push in and rotate the firing pin retainer through 90° clockwise. Squeeze the grip all the way in and the firing pin can be withdrawn. To replace the firing pin simply insert pin, spring and retainer into their hole, press the retainer about a millimetre inwards and rotate to the left to lock. Reassembling the pistol is simply the reverse of dismantling, but be careful to insert the recoil piston into its cylinder as the slide is being replaced.

There are two distinct models of the P7; the P7 M8 which has an 8-shot magazine, and the P7 M13 with a 13-shot magazine.

Model P7 K3

Although this resembles the P7 models described above in outward appearance, internally it differs considerably by being a pure blowback and having no gas piston and cylinder. This is simply because it uses the 7.65mm ACP or 9mm Short cartridges, neither of which demands a locked breech. The squeeze-cocking mechanism remains the same. There are also conversion kits to change either calibre into .22LR chambering.

Heckler & Koch P7 K3

Calibre	.22 Long Rifle or 7.65mm Browning or 9mm Short/.380 Auto
Method of operation	Blowback, self-cocking, striker-fired
Safety devices	No form of applied safety
Magazine type	Single-column detachable box in butt
Position of catch	Junction of front edge of butt and trigger guard
Magazine capacity	8 rounds
Front sight	Fixed blade
Rear sight	Fixed square notch
Overall length	6.30in (160mm)
Barrel length	3.80in (96,5mm)
Number of grooves	Polygonal
Direction of twist	Right-hand
Empty weight	27.3oz (775g); .22: 26.8oz (760g) 7.65mm: 26.4oz (750g) 9mm Short
Markings	Left side of slide: 'HECKLER & KOCH GMBH OBERNDORF/N MADE IN GERMANY 9mm K' (or '.22 LR', or '7.65 × 17'); bottom of butt, both sides: 'HK P7 K3'
Serial number	On right side of frame

Above: The P7 K3 in 7.65mm calibre does away with the delaying system and is a simple blowback pistol.

Heckler & Koch P7 M10

Calibre	.40 S&W
Method of operation	Gas-delayed blowback, self-cocking, striker-fired
Safety devices	No form of applied safety
Magazine type	Detachable box in butt
Position of catch	Forward edge of butt, both sides
Magazine capacity	10 rounds
Front sight	Fixed blade
Rear sight	Fixed square notch
Overall length	6.88in (175mm)
Barrel length	4.13in (105mm)
Number of grooves	Polygonal
Direction of twist	Right-hand
Empty weight	30.0oz (850g) without magazine
Markings	Right of slide: 'M10 HK Inc Sterling VA'; bottom of butt, both sides: 'HK P7 M10'
Serial number	On right side of frame, right side of slide

Model P7 M45

This model was developed in 1987 for possible sale in the United States and was a somewhat modified version of the P7 M8 in .45ACP calibre. Due to the extra power of the .45 cartridge, the gas cylinder system of delaying the slide opening was changed to an oil-filled cylinder with a port in the piston head. As the slide moved back, the piston head was forced through the oil, and the oil, being incompressible, was forced to pass from one side of the piston to the other via the restrictive port. This system, analogous to the recoil system of an artillery weapon, both delayed the slide opening and also damped the recoil blow, so that it was a very comfortable pistol to fire. However the complex arrangements of valving (to allow the oil to pass back easily as the slide closed) made the mechanism too expensive to be practical, and after a small number of prototypes the P7 M45 project was closed.

Model P7 M10

This was little more than the P7 M13 modified to handle the .40 Smith & Wesson cartridge. The frame was identical with that of the 9mm P7 M13 but the slide was somewhat heavier in order to support the heavier cartridge. The same gas delayed blowback system was used, though with a stronger return spring. The outward appearance was the same but the ballistic per-

Below: The most recent variation of the P7 tribe is this P7 M10, chambered for the .40 Smith & Wesson cartridge and with a ten-round magazine capacity.

formance was superior to that of the 9mm weapons. However, it apparently failed to attract sufficient customers and manufacture was confined to the period 1992–94.

Model P7 PT8

This was a special version of the P7 pistol designed solely for firing the 9mm PT Plastic Training cartridge. The design is that of the P7 M8 except that there is a heat-absorbing insert in the top front of the trigger guard and a lanyard loop on the bottom of the butt, and the rear sight is screwed in place. In order positively to distinguish this pistol from the remainder of the P7 family, the slide was marked with a prominent blue spot on each side. The slide is some 50 per cent lighter than that of the normal pistol and there is no gas retarding system; there is also a different return spring, and the chamber is floating, so that additional recoil force is delivered to the slide to ensure semi-automatic operation. In this system the chamber has a loose liner, such that when the cartridge is fired some of the gas goes between the front edge of the liner and the rear edge of the barrel, which thereby produces an increase in the area against which the gas can work, so increasing the force of the rearward thrust.

The manufacturers were at pains to state that the P7 PT8 must never be used with service ball ammunition. However, if this ammunition were to be inadvertently fired, damage would be suffered by the pistol but the design is such that no injury would result to the firer. Firing the correct plastic training ammunition, the pistol would deliver a 10cm group at a range of 8m; at 25m the bullet's energy was less the 10 Joules (7.5ft-lb); and the absolute maximum range was about 125m.

Dismantling the P7 PT8 was exactly the same as for the P7 K3 described above.

Heckler & Koch P7 PT8

Calibre	9mm PT Ammunition only
Method of operation	Amplified blowback, self-cocking, striker-fired
Safety devices	No form of applied safety
Magazine type	Single-column detachable box in butt
Position of catch	Front edge of butt, both sides
Magazine capacity	8 rounds
Front sight	Fixed blade
Rear sight	Fixed square notch
Overall length	6.70in (170mm)
Barrel length	4.13in (105mm)
Number of grooves	Polygonal
Direction of twist	Right-hand
Empty weight	27.9oz (790g)
Markings	Left side of slide: 'HECKLER & KOCH GMBH OBERNDORF/N MADE IN GERMANY 9mm PT'; bottom of butt, both sides: 'HK P7 PT8'
Serial number:	On right side of slide, right side of frame

P11 ZUB

This is an unusual weapon which is unlikely to be encountered in collections or sales for many years to come. It is a special weapon for underwater use by frogmen and similar operators, and it is reputed to be used by the German GSG9, British SBS and US SEALs among others, though none of them will actually confirm this. There is a strong suspicion that a similar Soviet weapon was actually based upon this German design, development of which began in the mid-1970s. The existence of this pistol had been known since the early 1980s, but it was not until 1997 that it was formally acknowledged and some details made public.

The pistol is actually little more than a butt, trigger and socket-like frame. A pre-loaded five-barrel module is slipped into the socket, thus completing the weapon. The five barrels are loaded with a special cartridge which uses an electric primer activated by a battery in the grip and is itself loaded with a slender, dart-like,

Left: This regrettably poor picture is the only one available of the P11 underwater pistol.
Right: The USP reduced to its lowest common denominator.

Heckler & Koch P11 ZUB

Method of operation	Electric ignition, multiple barrels
Magazine type	5-round detachable module
Front sight	Fixed blade
Rear sight	Fixed U-notch
Overall length	7.87in (200mm)
Barrel length	Not known, but said to be rifled
Loaded weight:	42.0oz (1,200g)
Markings:	Right side of butt: 'HK P11 ZUB'

finned projectile. Pulling the trigger fires the barrels in sequence, launching the darts. When the last of the five barrels has been fired, the entire empty module is removed and discarded and a fresh module loaded.

For obvious reasons, full details of construction, dismantling, markings and performance are not available; such details as have been made public are given in the accompanying panel.

USP

The USP (Universal Self-loading Pistol) appeared in 1994 and introduced the first locked breech pistol from Heckler & Koch. The weapon is recoil-operated, using a form of Browning dropping barrel lock; instead of the usual hinged link or cam, there is a shaped claw beneath the breech, which, as the slide and barrel move rearwards, hooks into a cam surface to withdraw the barrel from engagement with the slide. Locking is performed by the currently popular method of forming the chamber area of the barrel into a rectangular lump and forcing this into a rectangular ejection opening in the slide.

The design also incorporates a patented recoil damping system. The return spring rod carries two springs, a buffer spring and the normal return spring. On firing, as the barrel moves back so it pulls on the guide rod and compresses the short buffer spring, absorbing some of the recoil. As the barrel disconnects from the slide and the slide is free to move independently, it then places the return spring under compression in the usual way, and at the same time the buffer spring is relieved of the pull and reasserts itself, moving forward. As the slide comes to the end of the recoil stroke, so it also begins to compress the buffer spring once more, giving

Below: The current H&K heavyweight is the USP, here in .40 S&W calibre. Note the grooving at the front end of the frame for the attachment of a laser target spot projector.

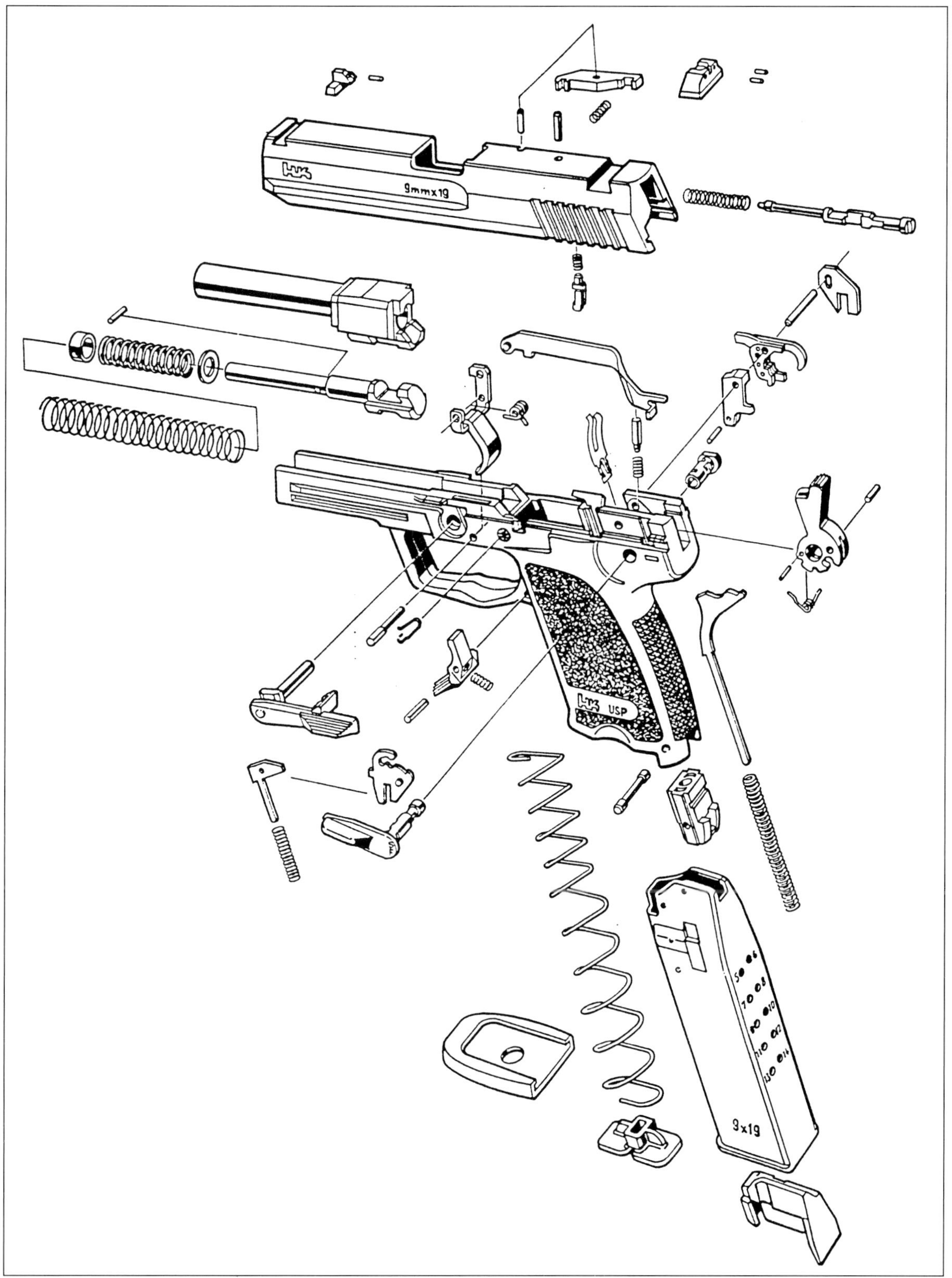
9mm x 19
USP
9x19

Right: A phantom view of the interior of the USP.

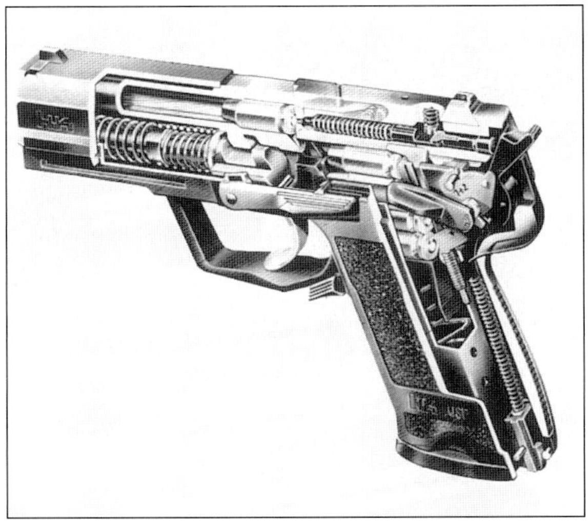

an additional brake to the recoil movement and stopping it. Both the springs then reassert themselves and the slide goes forward, loading the fresh round and returning the barrel to battery.

The slide and barrel are of steel, as might be expected, but the frame is of polymer plastic, exceptionally tough and dimensionally stable The sights are provided with white luminous dots for aiming in poor light, and all the controls are ambidextrous.

The USP can be had in no fewer than nine versions, largely because the trigger and firing mechanisms are modular and can be readily changed. Thus the action can be double-action or self-cocking only, and the safety systems can be varied, leading to the following options:

1. Double-action with manual safety/de-cocking lever on left side of frame.
2. Double-action with manual safety/de-cocking lever on right side of frame.
3. Double-action, no safety, de-cocking lever on left side of frame.
4. Double-action, no safety, de-cocking lever on right side of frame.
5. Self-cocking only, with manual safety catch on left side of frame.
6. Self-cocking only, with manual safety catch on right side of frame.
7. Self-cocking only, no safety catch, no de-cocking lever.

Below: Another view of the USP.

Heckler & Koch USP

Calibre	9mm Parabellum or .40 Smith & Wesson or .45ACP
Method of operation	Recoil, double-action, hammer-fired (but see text)
Safety devices	Manual safety and/or de-cocking lever on left of frame
Magazine type	Double-column detachable box in butt
Position of catch	Junction front edge of butt and trigger guard
Magazine capacity	15 (9mm) or 13 (.40) or 12 (.45) rounds
Front sight	Fixed blade
Rear sight	Fixed square notch
Overall length	7.64in (194mm) 9mm & .40; 7.87in (200mm) .45
Barrel length	4.25in (108mm) 9mm & .40; 4.40in (112mm) .45
Number of grooves	Polygonal
Direction of twist	Right-hand
Empty weight	27.2oz (770g) 9mm; 29.2oz (830g) .40; 31.2oz (887g) .45
Markings	Left side of slide: 'HK USP 9mm × 19' (or as appropriate); right side of frame: 'Heckler & Koch Made in Germany'
Serial number	On left side of slide

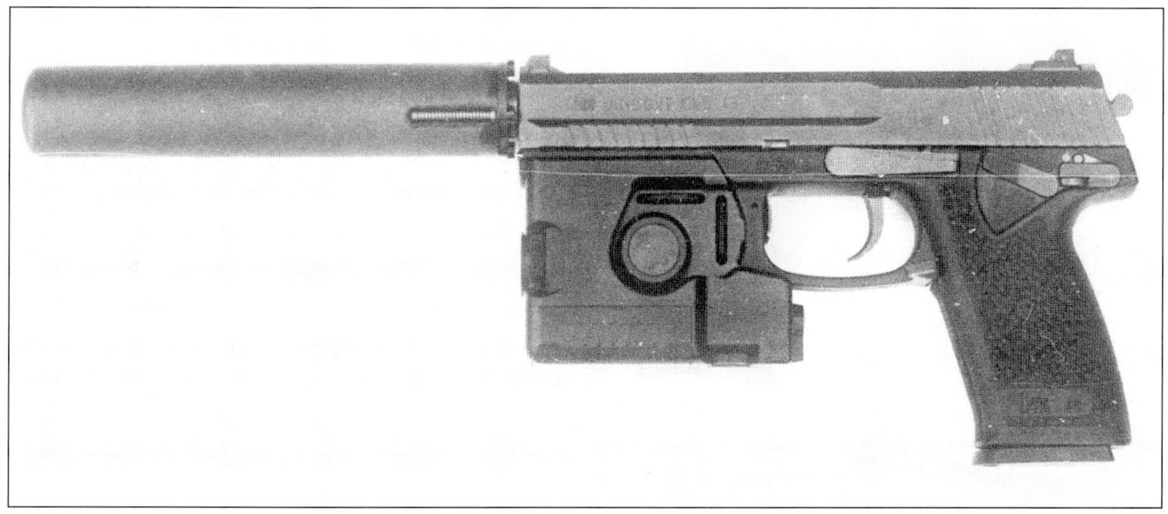

Above: The Mark 23 Mod 0 is the US Special Forces' version of the USP, chambered for the .45 ACP cartridge and provided with a sound suppressor and a laser spot projector as standard accessories.

8. Double-action, manual safety catch on left side of frame.
9. Double-action, manual safety catch on right side of frame.

Dismantling the USP is much the same as with any Browning-derived system. Withdrawing the slide stop pin allows the slide and barrel, complete with buffer and return springs and guide rod, to be slipped forward off the frame, and the barrel and springs can then be lifted from the slide. No further dismantling is really necessary.

Heckler & Koch Mark 23 Mod 0

Calibre	.45 ACP
Method of operation	Recoil, double-action, hammer-fired
Safety devices	Manual safety, manual de-cocking lever on left of frame
Magazine type	Double-column detachable box in butt
Position of catch	Forward edge of butt behind trigger
Magazine capacity	12 rounds
Front sight	Fixed blade with tritium dot
Rear sight	Fixed square notch with two tritium dots
Overall length	9.65in (245mm); with suppressor 16.57in (421mm)
Barrel length	5.87in (149mm)
Number of grooves	Polygonal
Direction of twist	Right-hand
Empty weight	42.7oz (1,210g):

Mark 23 Mod 0

This is a highly specialised version of the USP which was developed for the US Special Forces. It is, in effect, a USP in .45 ACP calibre and with provision for a silencer and a laser aiming spot module to be fitted. A total of 7,500 pistols were supplied to USSOCOM (Special Operations Command) by 1997 and it is unlikely that any more will ever be made.

HEGE

Hege Waffen (Hebsacker Gesellschaft), Schwabisch Hall, are a distributor rather than a manufacturer, and in the 1960s and 1970s sold numbers of pistols in Western Europe under their Hege tradename. By the late 1970s there were at least three pistols on sale under the title 'Hege AP66': one was a Hungarian copy of the Walther PP, made by FEG; one was a similar

Left, upper: The 7.54mm Hege AP 66 is actually a Hungarian copy of the Walther PP double-action pistol.
Left, lower: Another Hege pistol from Hungary, this time the Tokagypt, a 9mm Parabellum version of the Russian Tokarev, sold as the AP66 Firebird.

copy but made by an unknown German firm; and the third was the Spanish Astra Constable automatic. The Tokagypt pistol (basically a Soviet Tokarev but in 9mm Parabellum calibre and made in Hungary) was also sold as the AP66 Firebird between 1967 and 1975. After 1980 this part of the business was run down and the company has subsequently specialised in black-powder replica weapons.

HEIM

C.E. Heinzelmann, Plochingen-am-Neckar

This firm made the Heim pistol, a 6.35mm blowback automatic which externally resembles the Mauser WTP but internally is closer to the Browning 1910, with a fixed barrel and coaxial recoil spring secured by a muzzle bush. It carries the company's name on the slide and appears to have been made for a short time in the early 1930s. The weapons are therefore un-

Heim	
Calibre	6.35mm Browning
Method of operation	Blowback, striker-fired
Safety devices	Manual safety in front edge of left grip
Magazine type	Single-column detachable box in butt
Position of catch	Bottom rear of butt
Magazine capacity	6 rounds
Front sight	None
Rear sight	Groove in top of slide
Overall length	4.25in (108mm)
Barrel length	2.17in (55mm)
Number of grooves	6
Direction of twist	Right hand
Empty weight	10.93oz (310g)
Markings	Left side of slide: 'C. E. HEINZELMANN PLOCHINGEN A.N. PATENT HEIM - 6,35'
Serial number	On right of frame

Below: The 6.35mm Heim, a neat design of which little is known and few are ever seen.

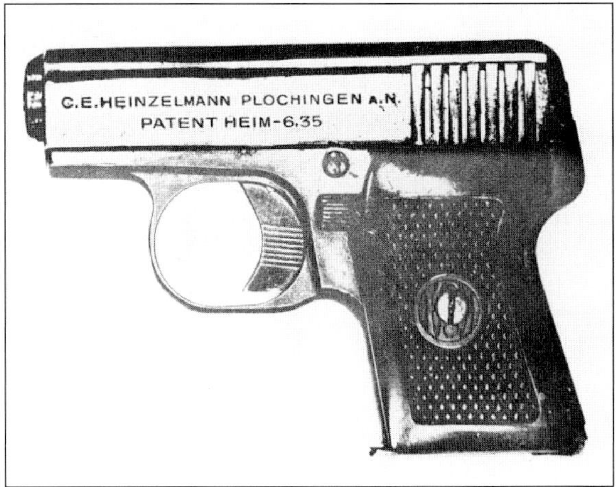

common, and I have been unable to locate a specimen for detailed examination.

HELFRICHT

Alfred Krauser, Zella Mehlis

The Helfricht pistol is, at first appearance, a fairly run-of-the-mill 6.35mm pocket pistol of the blowback variety. However, closer examination shows a couple of interesting features which lift it out of the general trend of this class. The method of assembly is quite unique, and the design also leads to a peculiar ejection port, which, more than any other, combines the essentials of simplicity and protection from dust and dirt for the inside of the pistol.

Examination of the weapon will show that the ejection port on the right side is in fact split longitudinally, and when the gun is at rest the top and bottom halves are displaced. The lower half is closed by the breech block while the top half is closed by a section of the frame locking system. The barrel is at the bottom of the frame, immediately above the trigger. The rear of the weapon shows a slotted boss in the back of the slide, and this boss controls the dismantling.

With the magazine removed and the gun cleared in the usual way, apply a screwdriver to the slot in this boss and, pressing in, rotate the boss through about 120° clockwise. On releas-

Below: The Helfricht Model 4, a neat design concealing some odd features.

Left: Dismantling the Helfricht shows the details of the locking system.

ing screwdriver pressure, the boss will be forced out of the frame about 0.33in (8.5mm) by spring pressure. The slide can now be grasped and pulled off the pistol backwards. It will then be seen that the slide also forms the breech block (which carries the usual extractor, striker and spring) and that through the upper part of the slide runs a rod, the rear part of which is the boss just turned and the front end of which carries upon it two key-like lugs. On the frame, above the barrel, are two mating lugs, slightly hook-shaped at their front end. If the locking rod is rotated so that the key lugs are pointing up, the slide can be replaced on the frame and the keys will slide through the gaps at the top of the frame lugs until they are almost matching the front edges. Pressure on the slotted boss at the rear of the rod, overcoming a spring, will push the keys forward far enough to pass the hooked portion of the frame lugs, when the rod and keys can be rotated anti-clockwise to lock firmly in front of the frame lugs. The spring, which is wrapped around the locking rod, also acts as the recoil spring, so that, upon firing, the breech block and slide are blown back and, since the keys and lugs are firmly engaged, the locking rod—which now functions as a recoil

Helfricht Model 3

Calibre	6.35mm Browning
Method of operation	Blowback, striker-fired
Safety devices	Manual catch at left front of butt
Magazine type	Single-column detachable box in butt
Position of catch	At heel of butt
Magazine capacity	6 rounds
Front sight	Fixed blade
Rear sight	Groove in top of slide
Overall length	4.72in (120mm)
Barrel length	2.00in (51mm)
Number of grooves	6
Direction of twist	Right-hand
Empty weight	11.4oz (323g)
Markings	Left of slide: 'GERMANY PATENT (HELFRICHT)'
Serial number	On underside of breech block

Helfricht Model 4

Calibre	6.35mm Browning
Method of operation	Blowback, striker-fired
Safety devices	Manual safety catch left side of butt
Magazine type	Single-column detachable box in butt
Position of catch	At heel of butt
Magazine capacity	6 rounds
Front sight	Fixed blade
Rear sight	Groove in slide top
Overall length	4.50in (109mm)
Barrel length	1.80in (46mm)
Number of grooves	6
Direction of twist	Right-hand
Empty weight	12.0oz (340g)
Markings	Left of slide: 'Helfricht's Patent Mod. 4'; left grip: 'KH' monogram; right grip: 'Caliber 6,35'
Serial number	On underside of breech block

Above: A Helfricht Model 3, showing the split ejection port used with all models.

spring guide rod—permits the slide to move back and compress the recoil spring. When recoil is finished the spring forces the slide home again, reloading the pistol in the process.

The pistol described here is the Model 4; the Models 2 and 3 are identical, but have the slide shortened and ending just in front of the trigger guard and a short length of the barrel exposed. The only difference between the two lies in the safety catch, which, in the Model 2, extends beneath the left grip to appear at the rear edge formed into a hook which locks into a small recess in the slide when the catch is set to 'safe'. The Model 3 has the safety catch in the same place, in the left grip, but does not have the extended tail and relies entirely upon locking the trigger internally.

The same pistol was also sold as the Helkra, presumably through some specific dealership.

Below: The Detective 22 revolver by Heym, as sold in the United States.

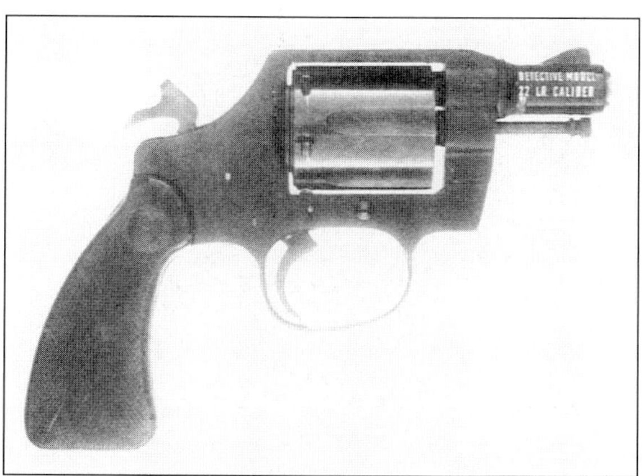

HEYM

F. W. Heym GmbH & Co KG Jagdwaffen und Wehrtechnik, Münnerstadt, Germany

This firm was established in Suhl in 1865 and moved into the Western zone after 1945. It has primarily been a maker of very high quality shotguns and rifles, but for a brief period in the 1960s made a short-barrelled revolver in .22LR calibre. This was a solid-frame, double-action weapon of good quality and was sold in the United States by Hunter of Hollywood as the Detective model. The only point of interest in the design was the apparent presence of a hard-

Heym Detective

Calibre	.22 Long Rifle rimfire
Method of operation	Double-action revolver
Safety devices	None
Magazine type	6-shot cylinder
Position of catch	Left side of frame
Front sight	Fixed blade
Rear sight	Groove in top strap
Overall length	7.87in (200mm)
Barrel length	2.00in (51mm)
Number of grooves	6
Direction of twist	Right-hand
Empty weight	24.0oz (680g)
Markings	Left side of barrel: 'H Y HUNTER INC. FIREARMS MFG CO HOLLYWOOD CALIF. MFG. IN WEST GERMANY'; right side of barrel: 'DETECTIVE MODELL 22 LR CALIBER'
Serial number	Right side of frame, rear face of cylinder

ened steel liner in the barrel and a hardened steel cylinder, with the frame and barrel jacket being made of softer steel. The cylinder opened to the left, on the usual sort of crane locked by a latch on the left side, and pressure on the central rod gave simultaneous ejection of all chambers. There was a floating firing pin in the standing breech and a flat-faced hammer.

JÄGER

F. Jäger & Co Waffenfabrik., Suhl.

This weapon is of particular interest as it represents an attempt to design a pistol which could be produced with the simplest possible machinery. Most of the parts are metal pressings, the only forging being the barrel block. The antecedents of this weapon are clouded, but it would appear to have been an early exploration of a mass-production technique which, applied to heavier weapons, has since become relatively commonplace.

Disassembling the Jäger is not a task to be undertaken lightly, but it is the best way of examining the system of construction. After removing the magazine and clearing the gun in the usual manner, remove the screw just above the trigger. This unlocks the front rib of the entire weapon and, by depressing the catch beneath the muzzle, all this front rib and trigger guard—complete with trigger—can be swung open, pivoting about a pin at the toe of the butt. By depressing another spring catch under the breech the rear rib can be similarly swung down, and by removing the screws in the butt the side

Below: The 7.65mm Jäger pistol was among the first—if not actually *the* first—to use stamped sheet steel for its construction.

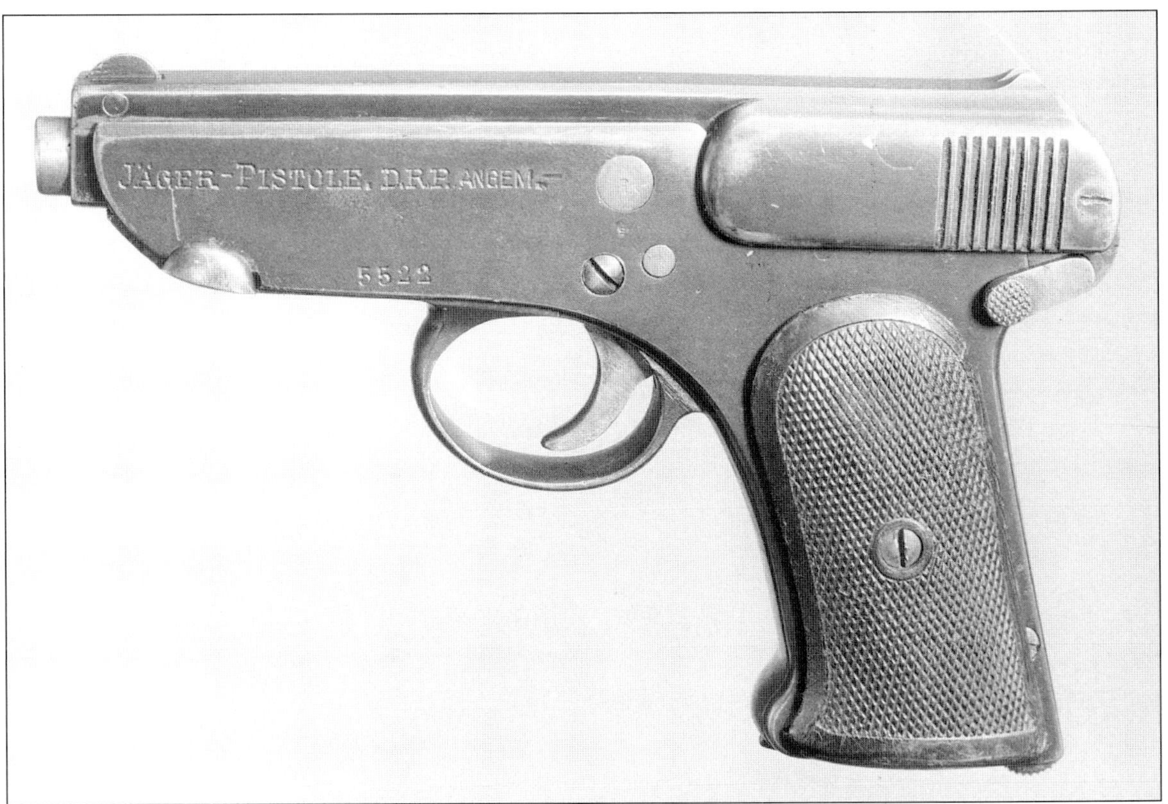

Jäger

Calibre	7.65mm Browning
Method of operation	Blowback, striker-fired
Safety devices	Manual safety catch left rear of frame
Magazine type	Single-column detachable box in butt
Position of catch	At heel of butt
Magazine capacity	7 rounds
Front sight	Fixed blade
Rear sight	Fixed V-notch
Overall length	6.10in (155mm)
Barrel length	3.11in (79mm)
Number of grooves	4
Direction of twist	Right-hand
Empty weight	22.8oz (646g)
Markings	Left of frame: 'JÄGER-PISTOLE. D.R.P.ANGEM.'
Serial number	On left side of frame above trigger guard

plates can be separated, allowing the slide and barrel to fall free of the wreckage. It can now be seen that the slide is a pressing carrying the striker and spring; the barrel is a forging with two substantial lugs at each side of the breech anchoring it to the frame side plates; a simple trigger bar lies in a rebate in the right side frame and connects the trigger to the striker; and the recoil spring encircling the barrel is retained by the bushing formed by the front end of the slide pressing.

To reassemble the weapon, place the recoil spring round the barrel and engage this with the slide unit. Hook the side frames over the barrel lugs, working them into place under the slide, and remember to install the trigger bar. Insert the front and rear ribs and the screws. Close the ribs, engaging the spring catches, and place the lock screw in position above the trigger.

Although a little daunting to a traditionally minded observer, the Jäger is quite robust and safe in operation. However, it is insufficiently robust and simple to be acceptable as a combat weapon. In spite of this it is a desirable weapon from the collector's point of view, since relatively few pistols have been made in this fashion, and of those the Jäger was the only one to attain commercial sale. It was patented just prior to World War I, and about 6,000 were made in 1915–18.

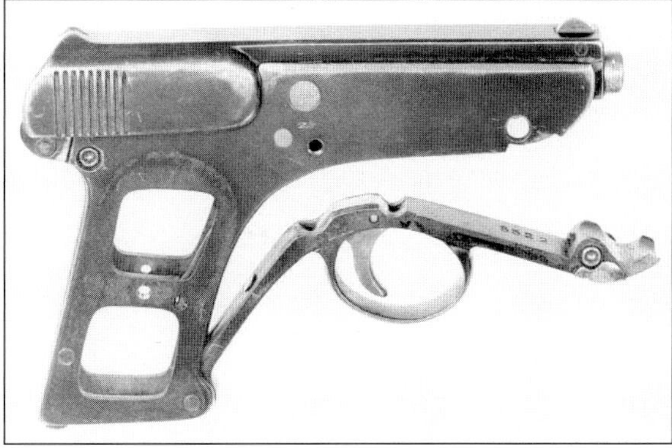

Above: Dismantling the Jäger pistol.

KESSLER

F. W. Kessler, Suhl

This is a somewhat mysterious 7.65mm automatic pistol, sold by Kessler but probably made

Below: The Kessler—an unusual design and rarely seen.

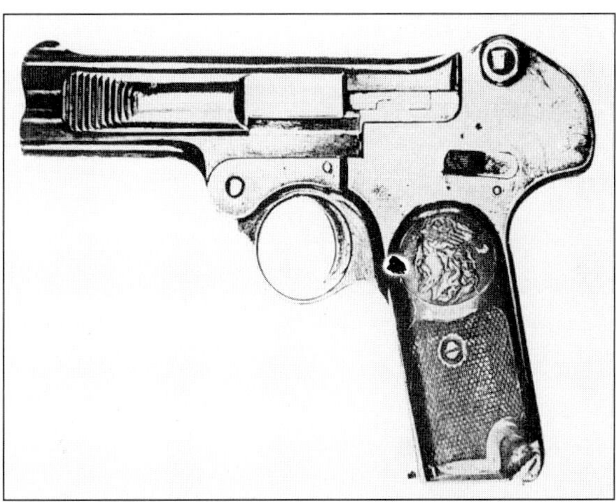

Kessler	
Calibre	7.65mm Browning
Method of operation	Blowback, striker-fired
Safety devices	Manual safety catch left side of frame
Magazine type	Single-column detachable box in butt
Position of catch	At heel of butt
Magazine capacity	7 rounds
Front sight	Fixed blade
Rear sight	Fixed U-notch
Overall length	6.46in (164mm)
Barrel length	3.74in (95mm)
Number of grooves	4
Direction of twist	Right-hand
Empty weight	22.8oz (646g)
Markings	Not known
Serial number	Not known

by Pickert since it carries the Pickert Arminius badge on the grip plate. The shape is reminiscent of the Browning 1900 model, with a hump at the rear of the frame, which might be thought to carry an inverted hammer, but the mechanism uses a bolt moving within a fixed receiver, cocked by finger grips in front of the bolt. Only photographic evidence is available, a specimen never having been encountered. It probably dates from just before 1914 and could not have been made in any quantity.

KLESESEWSKI

The name 'Klesesewski, Berlin' appears on a 6.35mm automatic pistol which is also marked 'American Automatic Pistol Cal. 6.35' and has a butt motif of a bird resembling a vulture. The same butt motif appears on an identical pistol marked 'Cal. 6,35 Model 1911 Automatic Pistol Original Model Victoria Arms Co.'. The pistol is undoubtedly Spanish in origin but bears no point of resemblance to any of the Victoria designs produced by Esperanza y Unceta and must be ascribed to some unknown Eibar maker of the late 1900s. Since the only specimen seen showed no signs of German proof marks, it must be assumed that the name is fictitious and part of a clumsy attempt to pass off a cheap Spanish pistol as a German product.

KOMMER

Theodor Kommer Waffenfabrik GmbH, Zella Mehlis

Models 1 and 2

By and large these are no more than workmanlike copies of the Browning 1906 design, though well made and by no means to be written off as cheap 'suicide specials'. Of normal blowback pattern, they incorporate the common German refinement over Browning's original Baby by having a means of positively locating the slide to aid barrel removal and a non-slip surface on the barrel to help oily fingers to get a grip.

Stripping is simplicity itself. After clearing the gun, the slide is pushed back about half an inch (12mm) until the safety catch can be turned up into a notch in the lower edge of the slide. Then the milled collar round the muzzle

Below: The Kommer Model 2—a simple and robust 6.35mm design.

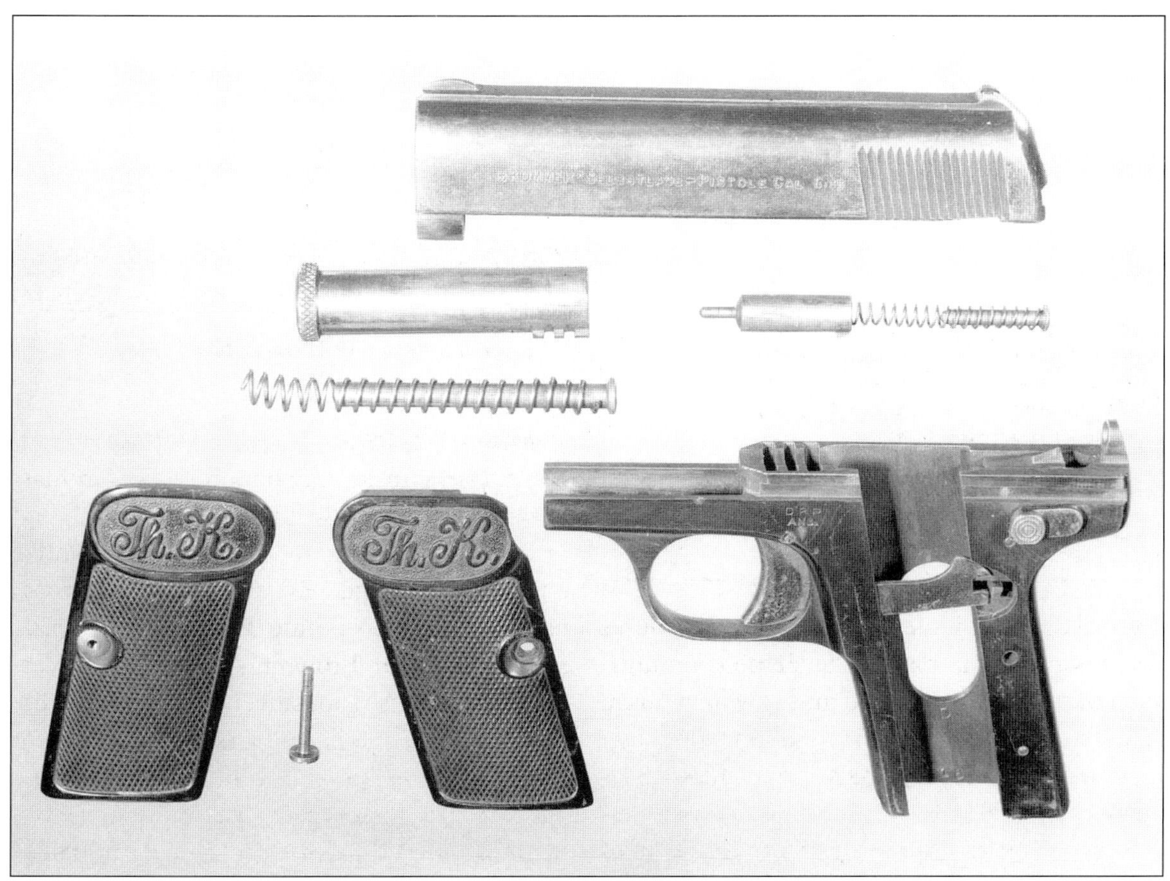

Above: Dismantling the Kommer is easier than most, thanks to the knurled collar around the muzzle, allowing a good grip to rotate the barrel.

is gripped and the barrel turned about 90° clockwise to rotate the locking lugs out of engagement with the frame; this can be checked by looking through the ejection port. Once freed, the safety catch can be released and the slide, barrel and firing pin with its spring can be slid from the front of the frame. Turning the barrel once again will permit its removal through the front of the slide. One appealing point of this pistol is that its butt is of a respectable size—larger than the general run of 6.35mm weapons—which gives, firstly, a good magazine capacity and, secondly, the possibility of a decent grasp by the average hand for more accurate shooting.

Model 3

The Model 3 was a Model 2 but with a deeper frame to increase the magazine capacity to 9 rounds.

Model 4

The 7.65mm Kommer Model 4 is almost an exact copy of the Belgian Browning as far as mechanical arrangements go and has no outstanding feature. It is well made, however, and is above average both in its fit in the hand and in general handiness for shooting. It is not common and is believed to have gone into production in 1939 and ceased in 1940 with only a few hundred made.

Stripping is based on the Browning design. After clearing the gun in the usual way, pull the slide back a short way until the safety catch can

Kommer Model 2

Calibre	6.35mm Browning
Method of operation	Blowback, striker-fired
Safety devices	Manual catch left rear of frame
Magazine type	Single-column detachable box in butt
Position of catch	At heel of butt
Magazine capacity	7 rounds
Front sight	Fixed blade
Rear sight	Fixed U-notch
Overall length	4.25in (108mm)
Barrel length	2.00in (51mm)
Number of grooves	6
Direction of twist	Right-hand
Empty weight	13.0oz (368g)
Markings	Top rib of slide: 'T. H. KOMMER WAFFENFABRIK ZELLA MEHLIS II'; left side of slide: 'KOMMER SELBSTLADE-PISTOLE CAL 6,35'; left side of frame: 'DRP ANGEM'
Serial number	No serial number as such, but factory assembly numbers will be found on the barrel, under the slide and inside the magazine well

be turned up into a notch on the slide. Then grasp the barrel and turn it through 90° to unlock it from the frame; releasing the safety catch allows the slide to go forward off the frame. To remove the barrel and recoil spring from the slide, press in the milled bush surrounding the muzzle and give it a half-turn to unlock, allowing it to be forced out by the recoil spring. Bush, spring and barrel can then be removed. Reassembly is the reverse, first assembling barrel, spring and bush into the slide and then placing this on the frame as a complete unit.

Below: The 7.65mm Kommer Model 4—a rare and well-made pistol.

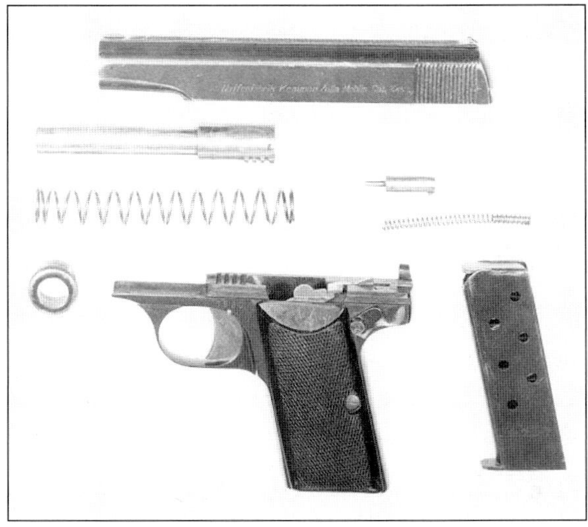

Above: Dismantled, the Kommer 4 is seen to be the usual Browning copy.

Kommer Model 4

Calibre	7.65mm Browning
Method of operation	Blowback, striker-fired
Safety devices	Manual catch left rear of frame
Magazine type	Single-column detachable box in butt
Position of catch	At heel of butt
Magazine capacity	7 rounds
Front sight	Fixed blade
Rear sight	Fixed U-notch
Overall length	5.50in (140mm)
Barrel length	3.00in (76mm)
Number of grooves	6
Direction of twist	Right-hand
Empty weight	20.0oz (567g)
Markings	Left of slide: 'Waffenfabrik Kommer Zella Mehlis Kal 7,65.'
Serial number	On left side of frame

KORRIPHILA

Korriphila GmbH, Ulm/Donau, Germany; later Franconia Jagdwaffen, Wurzburg, Germany

This company appeared in the 1960s, producing a small 6.35mm blowback automatic of high quality known as the TP-70. It used a double-action lock but was otherwise a quite commonplace design with a slide-mounted safety catch. It was sold in the United States in the 1970s as the 'Budischowsky', this being the name of the designer.

In the early 1980s the company announced the Model HSP 701, a delayed-blowback automatic which was to be made in various calibres from 9 × 18mm Police to .45ACP. The breech

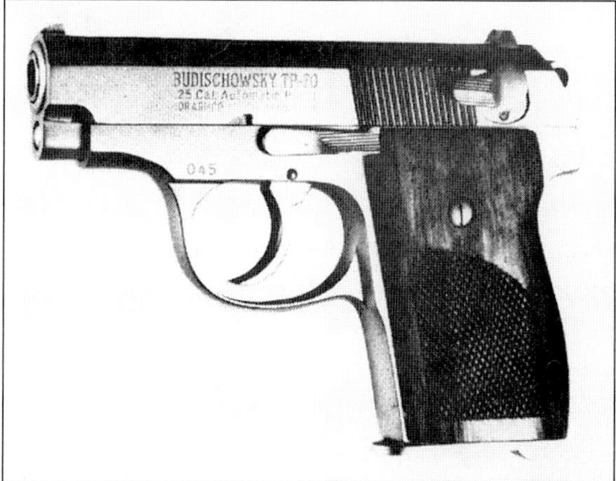

Left: The Korriphila, sold as the Budischowsky TP-70 in the United States.

Korriphila TP-70

Calibre	6.35mm Browning
Method of operation	Blowback, double-action, hammer-fired
Safety devices	Manual safety catch on left rear of slide
Magazine type	Single-column detachable box in butt
Position of catch	At heel of butt
Magazine capacity	6 rounds
Front sight	Fixed blade
Rear sight	Fixed U-notch
Overall length	4.60in (117mm)
Barrel length	2.60in (66mm)
Number of grooves	6
Direction of twist	Right-hand
Empty weight	12.3oz (348g)
Markings	Left of slide: 'BUDISCHOWSKY TP-70 .22 Cal Automatic Pistol'
Serial number	On left side of frame

Korriphila HSP 701

Calibre	9mm Parabellum and others
Method of operation	Delayed-blowback, roller-locked, hammer-fired, double-action
Safety devices	Manual safety catch at left rear of slide
Magazine type	Single-column deatchable box in butt
Position of catch	Left front edge of butt behind trigger guard
Magazine capacity	9 rounds
Front sight	Fixed blade
Rear sight	Adjustable square notch
Overall length	7.20in (183mm)
Barrel length	4.00in (102mm)
Number of grooves	6
Direction of twist	Right-hand
Empty weight	34.9oz (990g)
Markings	Left side of slide: 'KORRIPHILA HSP 701 Cal 9mm Para [or as appropri ate] Made in Germany'
Serial number	On left side of frame above trigger

Below: The Korriphila HSP 701 was intended to be a serious locked-breech police and combat pistol but few were made.

delay was achieved by a separate breech block and a transverse roller which dropped into a recess in the frame and prevented the block moving backwards until an operating finger on the slide forced the roller out of its seat. However, little seems to have been heard of this weapon since the initial announcements. I have been unable to obtain specimens of either for closer examination.

KORTH

Korth Vertriebsges mbH, Ratzeburg, Germany

This firm began as a private company but is now part of the Dynamit Nobel group. It commenced making revolvers in the 1970s and rapidly made a reputation for the highest quality weapons for sport and target shooting. The basic design is a conventional solid-frame, swing cylinder, double-action weapon with full ejector shroud, ventilated rib, automatic ejection after the cylinder opens, adjustable firing pin strike and adjustable trigger pull. A unique feature is the positioning of the cylinder release catch alongside the hammer.

Within this basic description are two different weapons:

Sport Revolver

A 6-shot revolver with 6in barrel, this comes in a variety of calibres from .22LR to .357 Magnum. Since the .357, .38 and 9mm versions fire virtually the same bullets, interchangeable cylinders are provided to suit the different chamber dimensions of these three rounds. The pistol may be found in blued carbon steel or stainless steel.

Combat Revolver

This is very much the same as the Sport model and in the same range of calibres, but with options of a 3in or 4in barrel, and with a more

Below: The Korth Sport revolver is a Smith & Wesson type of superlative build-quality and accuracy.

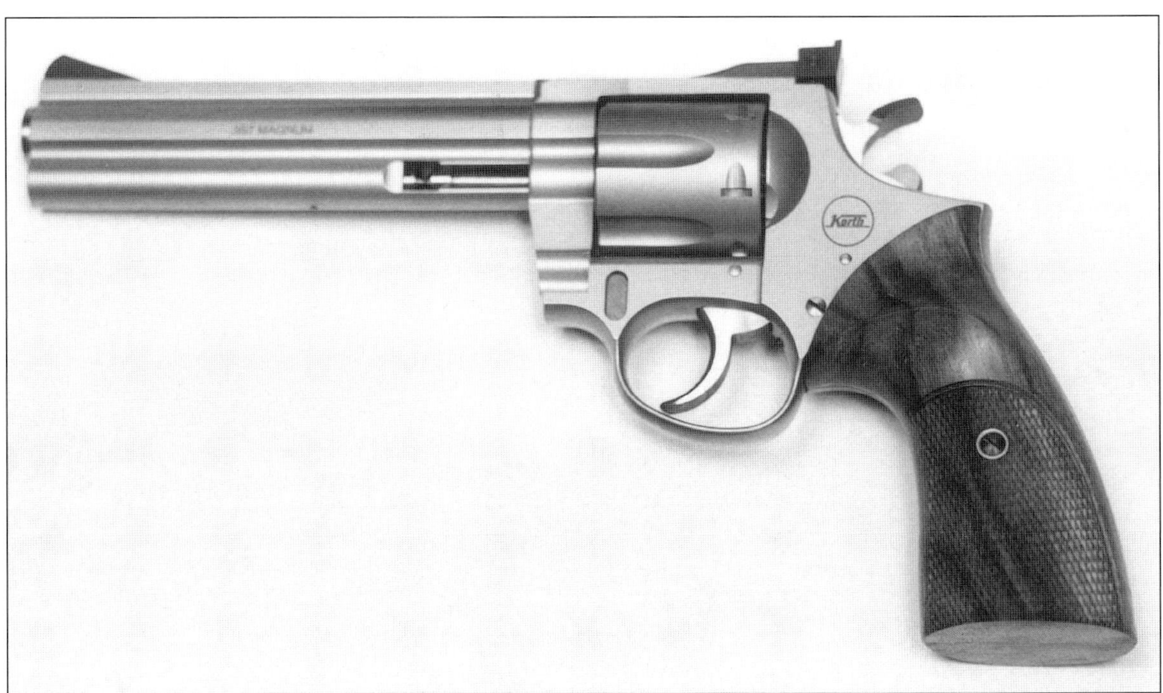

Korth Sport

Calibre	.357 Magnum and others (see text)
Method of operation	Double-action revolver
Safety devices	None
Magazine type	6-shot cylinder
Position of catch	Alongside hammer
Front sight	Fixed ramp blade
Rear sight	Adjustable square notch
Overall length	11.14in (283mm)
Barrel length	5.90in (150mm)
Number of grooves	6
Direction of twist	Right-hand
Empty weight	40.9oz (1160g)
Markings	Left side of frame: 'KORTH' in circle; calibre will be marked on left side of barrel
Serial number	On bottom of grip frame

Korth Combat

Calibre	.357 Magnum and others (see text)
Method of operation	Double-action revolver
Safety devices	None
Magazine type	6-shot cylinder
Position of catch	Alongside hammer
Front sight	Fixed ramp blade
Rear sight	Adjustable square notch
Overall length	8.26in (210mm)
Barrel length	3.00in (76mm)
Number of grooves	6
Direction of twist	Right-hand
Empty weight	33.5oz (950g)
Markings	Left side of frame: 'KORTH' in circle; calibre is marked on left side of barrel
Serial number	On bottom of grip frame

combat-oriented rear sight. Like the Sport, it is built from the finest quality materials and immaculately finished in either blued carbon steel or stainless steel.

Automatic

In 1985 the company announced an automatic pistol, though it was not until 1987 that it became available. The design shows little or no mechanical surprises, being a double-action weapon using the Browning dropping-barrel method of breech-locking, but the quality is superlative and the accuracy formidable. Disassembly is performed by a dismantling catch on the left side of the frame; pull back the slide and lock it by means of the safety catch and a

Below: For more utilitarian purposes, the Korth Combat model in .38 Special is another high-quality product.

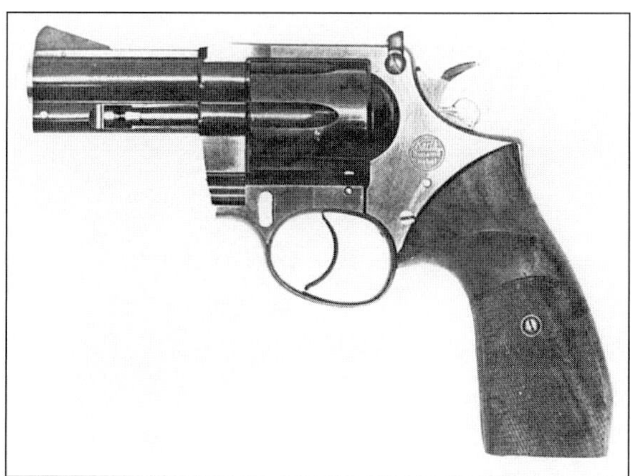

Korth Automatic

Calibre	9mm Parabellum or 9mm IMI or 7.65mm Parabellum
Method of operation	Recoil, double-action
Safety devices	Manual safety on left side of frame
Magazine type	Double-column detachable box in butt
Position of catch	Left side of frame above trigger
Magazine capacity	10 rounds
Front sight	Fixed blade
Rear sight	Adjustable square notch
Overall length	9.10in (231mm)
Barrel length	5.00in (127mm)
Number of grooves	6
Direction of twist	Right-hand
Empty weight	43.7oz (1,240g)
Markings	Left of slide: 'KORTH' in frame; 'MADE IN W. GERMANY WAFFENFABRIK W. KORTH RATZENBURG Cal. 9mm Para [or as appropriate]'
Serial number	On right side of frame

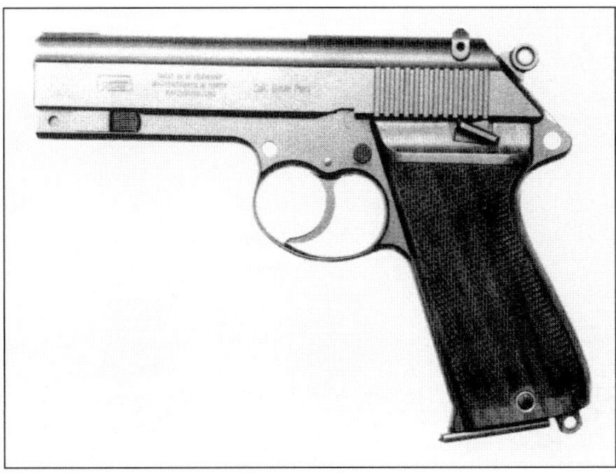

Above: The Korth Automatic pistol does not seem to have made the same impression on the market as have the company's revolvers, although it is of the same immaculate quality.

notch in the underside, then rotate the stripping catch, release the safety and allow the slide to run forward off the frame.

LANGENHAN

Friedrich Langenhan Waffen- und Fahrradfabrik, , Zella Mehlis

Fritz Langenhan of Suhl turned out three pistols of unusual design, one of which was taken into use during World War I as a substitute standard military weapon. They are all three of first-class material, and the commercial models exhibit an excellent finish, but their breech design causes many people to view them with reserve. The two small models are inherently safe enough, but the Military Model is liable to be dangerous when worn. This stricture applies, of course, to any pistol, but there can be no doubt about the danger which lies in the particular system of construction adopted by Langenhan if the degree of wear is at all noticeable.

Right: The Langenhan 6.35mm pistol—less commonly seen than its larger brother.

6.35mm Models 2 and 3

These two commercial pistols are virtually the same, except that the Model 2 is slightly larger, with a longer barrel and larger frame and magazine. They are simple blowback pistols, hammer-fired, with the breech block a separate component held to the slide by a heavy crossbolt secured by a screw. (An aberrant model has been seen in which this screw is replaced by a stripping catch on the right-hand side and with the letter V and an arrow pointing towards the muzzle.) The recoil spring is mounted in a boring above the barrel and retained by a screw at the front end of the slide, at the muzzle. These recoil springs are unusual in that they are of flat riband section instead of the more usual spirally wound wire type. There is a thumb-operated safety catch on the slide just behind the left grip and, almost invariably at this remove of time, they are so worn that they are quite useless when set at 'safe': strong pressure on the trigger will override them, cause them to slip and allow the pistol to fire.

To strip either of these weapons the procedure is the same and is liable to be difficult—though theoretically it should be easy. After one has cleared the gun and removed the magazine, the large screw on the right side of the slide must be removed. It should now be possible to push the crossbolt through and release the slide from

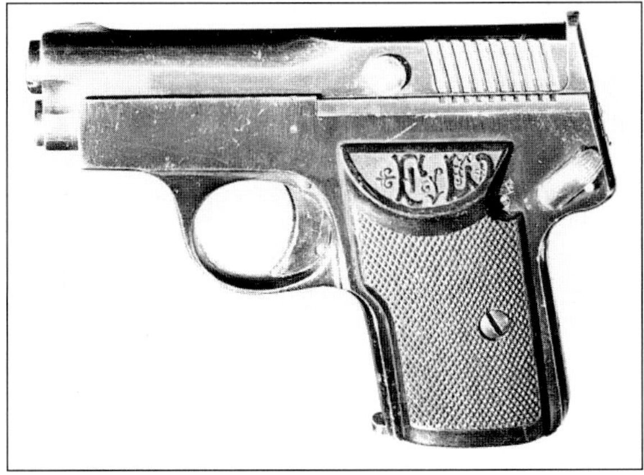

Above: Dismantled, the 6.35mm Langenhan shows the same separate breech block as the 7.65mm model, but secured in a different (and safer) manner.

the breech block, when the slide will move forward about half an inch (12mm) under the pressure of the recoil spring. What usually happens is that the crossbolt shows not the slightest inclination to move, and it is therefore necessary to swamp it with penetrating oil and then find a well-fitting drift and drive it out on the bench.

In the case of the model with the stripping catch, the catch should be turned up and forward—as directed by the arrow—and the crossbolt can then be withdrawn to the right, though if the gun has not been dismantled for some time it might require some assistance by tapping the left end of the crossbolt.

Once the two components are separated the slide will go forward and can be removed over the barrel, while the breech block can be pulled straight back from the frame. Once this is done, the peculiar construction of the breech block can be seen: only the left side is retained by frame ribs, the right side simply sliding back and forth on top of the frame side which is lower on the right than on the left. This appears frail, but, provided the slide is properly attached, there is no reason why the block should lift under the firing stress. The reason for this construction is so that there is an ejection opening provided as the breech block slides back on recoil.

The great danger in this method of construction is, of course, that the crossbolt might shear. If this were to happen the breech block will come straight out of the frame on recoil and undoubtedly hit the firer in the face. The other unfortunate feature of the small Langenhans is the uniformly vile trigger pull, quite the heaviest I have ever met in a pistol. The specimen shown here, when tested with the usual apparatus, gave the appalling figure of 18lb (7.8kg)—considerably more than the heaviest rifle pull and quite out of proportion to the size of the weapon, more particularly as this class of pistol is generally considered a lady's gun.

Langenhan Model 2	
Calibre	6.35mm Browning
Method of operation	Blowback, hammer-fired
Safety devices	Manual catch at left rear of frame
Magazine type	Single-column detachable box in butt
Position of catch	At heel of butt
Magazine capacity	7 rounds
Front sight	Fixed blade
Rear sight	Fixed V-notch
Overall length	5.71in (145mm)
Barrel length	3.15in (80mm)
Number of grooves	6
Direction of twist	Right-hand
Empty weight	17.7oz (502g)
Markings	Right side of breech block: 'Langenhan 6,35'; top of grips: 'FL' monogram
Serial number	On bottom of butt frame

Langenhan Model 3	
Calibre	6.35mm Browning
Method of operation	Blowback, hammer-fired
Safety devices	Manual catch at left rear of frame
Magazine type	Single-column detachable box in butt
Position of catch	At heel of butt
Magazine capacity	5 rounds
Front sight	Fixed blade
Rear sight	Fixed V-notch
Overall length	4.75in (121mm)
Barrel length	2.28in (58mm)
Number of grooves	4
Direction of twist	Right-hand
Empty weight	16.5oz (468g)
Markings	Right side of breech block: 'Langenhan 6,35' (some early models may have 'Mod. III' in addition)
Serial number	On bottom of butt frame

Reassembly of the pistol is the reverse of stripping: slide the breech block on from the rear and the slide from the front, and connect the two with the crossbolt.

7.65mm Model

This model, frequently referred to as the F. L. Selbstlader, was only produced for military use during World War I and was never placed on sale in the commercial market in spite of having been originally designed as a commercial venture; every known example has the Prussian War Office stamp on the frame, a gothic 'W' surmounted by a crown. There are slight variations in manufacture to be found, some models having grips of wood and some of hard moulded rubber, and the safety catch may exhibit small changes in shape; but these were purely manufacturing expedients carried out during the production life and do not constitute a change in model. The peculiar Langenhan design of separate breech block is also present in this pistol, but with a very different connection between slide and block. This connection is best explored during the course of stripping.

After taking the normal safety precautions, loosen the large screw at the rear of the slide; this is slotted for a screwdriver and is also milled at the edge to form a grip for the fingers. It is best tightened by screwdriver and loosened the same way, but for emergency use finger-tightness suffices. After loosening this screw a few turns, it will be possible to hinge up the milled stirrup which forms the finger grip for slide retraction, and, as this comes free from the breech block, so the slide will move forward under pressure of the recoil spring, about one inch, after which it can be completely removed to the front. The breech block can now be pulled off the frame backwards to disclose the same lopsided construction as was seen in the 6.35mm models. The grips can be removed, by loosening the obvious screws, to expose the exceptionally simple lockwork. Under the breech block can be found the two screws holding extractor and firing pin in place, and at the rear of the block is a small screw which, when

Above: The Langenhan Armee Pistole in 7.65mm calibre

removed, leaves a hole in the rear through which the firing pin can be extracted.

The suspect feature of this weapon is the means of attaching the breech block to the slide: if the screw comes loose while firing, recoil shock is liable to flip up the stirrup, and the next shot fired will propel the breech block to the rear, straight out of the slide and at the firer. For this reason it behoves anyone firing one of these weapons to ensure that the mating surfaces of slide and breech block are not worn, and secondly to ensure that the lock screw is tightened with a screwdriver and not reliant on finger pressure. While the screw may come loose, the recessed seating on the stirrup ensures that there is no danger of disconnection until it has made at least seven complete turns in the direction of unscrewing—and this should be spotted soon enough. In the interests of science I fired one of these pistols recently, first with the screw tightened by screwdriver and then with it tightened as far as I could with my fingers—and I do not lay claim to any super grip. Screwed hard down, the screw survived

Below: Detail of the breech block retaining system on the 7.65mm Langenhan.

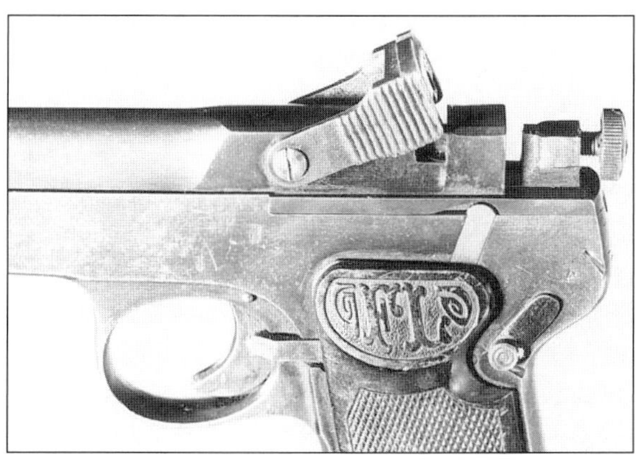

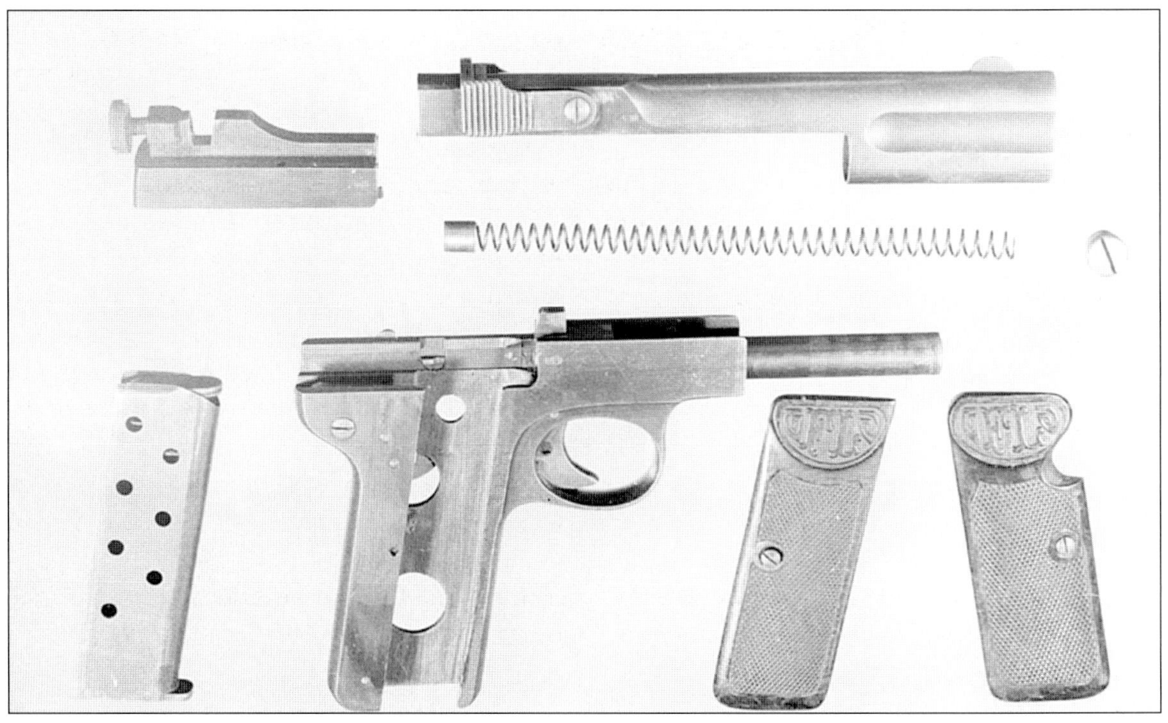

Above: The 7.65mm model dismantled to show the separate breech block.

Langenhan Armee-Modell

Calibre	7.65mm Browning
Method of operation	Blowback, hammer-fired
Safety devices	Manual safety catch at left rear of slide
Magazine type	Single-column detachable box in butt
Position of catch	At heel of butt
Magazine capacity	8 rounds
Front sight	Fixed blade
Rear sight	Fixed V-notch
Overall length	6.60in (168mm)
Barrel length	4.13in (105mm)
Number of grooves	4
Direction of twist	Right-hand
Empty weight	23.5oz (666g)
Markings	Right side of breech block: 'F. L. SELBSTLADER DRGM 625263-683251'; if rubber grips are fitted, then an 'FL' monogram is moulded into the top
Serial number	Full number on right side of frame behind trigger guard; last three digits under slide and on top spur of breech block

27 rounds before showing signs of looseness; with the screw turned finger-tight, fifteen rounds was enough to loosen it. This is rather a pity, because the Army model shoots well, it fits well in the hand and it has a remarkably good trigger pull—more remarkably when one recalls the terrible trigger pull of the smaller weapons.

To reassemble, reverse the stripping procedure. Do not be tempted, at any time, to unscrew the spring retaining screw from the front of the slide. Due to the heavier recoil of this pistol, the spring is much stronger than that on the 6.35mm models and it can prove very difficult to replace. It is of interest to see that these springs are invariably the usual coiled-wire type, and not the more elegant—and doubtless more expensive—coiled riband seen in the 6.35mm pistols.

LIGNOSE

Aktiengesellschaft Lignose, Berlin

The Aktiengesellschaft Lignose was an old-established explosives and ammunition company which began a post-war programme of expansion by purchasing the moribund Bergmann company in 1921 and took over their factory in Suhl. Among the acquisitions was the Chylewski one-hand pistol which Bergmann had acquired and redesigned as the Einhand Pistole, and Lignose put it into production as the Lignose Einhand. Another was the Bergmann Taschenpistole, which also had its name changed to Lignose. Both were given distinctive numbers, as had been the Bergmann practice: the Taschen models became the 2 and 3, while the Einhand became the 2A and 3A, the number 1 being reserved for a prospective Einhand in 7.65mm which, together with a 9mm Short version, never appeared. Apart from the change in number and the markings, there was no significant difference between these and the previous Bergmann products.

Model 2

The Model 2 Bergmann/Lignose is a conventional blowback, the usual adaptation of the Browning design. It is notably well-made and finished, and certainly one of the more desirable pocket pistols.

To strip the Model 2, after the magazine has been removed and the slide operated to clear the gun, do not press the trigger; this is a hammer-fired pistol and, if the trigger is pressed, the hammer will rise into the slide and prevent

Below: The Lignose Model 2 was a straightforward blowback design, from the Bergmann stable.

its removal. Push back the slide almost to its full stroke and turn the safety catch up into the usual notch. The knurled section of the barrel at the muzzle can be grasped and the barrel turned through 180° to unlock it from the frame. Now release the safety catch and ease the slide forward; it is not necessary to take the slide completely to the end of the frame. The locking surfaces are cut away and, once the rear end of the slide has travelled forward as far as the top of the safety catch, the whole slide can be lifted off the frame. The barrel can now be rotated to free it and the recoil spring and rod lifted clear. The extractor and firing pin are secured in place by pins driven through the slide and should not be disturbed except when replacing broken units. Owing to the cutaway sections of the slide and frame mating surfaces, reassembly is much easier than normal, since the recoil spring and rod can be assembled to the slide and positively located in the frame before the slide is lowered and pushed back—which is an improvement on the usual method of 'grope and hope'.

The Model 3 was a variation of the Model 2 which differed only in having a larger butt and a magazine capacity of nine rounds.

Lignose Model 2

Calibre	6.35mm Browning
Method of operation	Blowback, hammer-fired
Safety devices	Manual safety catch at left rear of frame
Magazine type	Single-column detachable box in butt
Position of catch	At heel of butt
Magazine capacity	6 or 9 rounds
Front sight	Fixed blade
Rear sight	Groove in slide top
Overall length	4.50in (114mm)
Barrel length	2.09in (53mm)
Number of grooves	6
Direction of twist	Right-hand
Empty weight	14.3oz (405g)
Markings	Left side of slide: 'AKT.-GES. LIGNOSE, BERLIN ABTEILUNG SUHL CAL 6,35 - D.R.P'.; or on right side of slide: 'THEODOR BERGMANN GAGGENAU SUHL CAL. 6,35 D.R.Pa.'; on both grips the word 'LIGNOSE' or the word 'BERGMANN' moulded in
Serial number	On right side of slide, barrel and mouth of magazine opening

Models 4 and 5

The Model 4 was simply a larger version of the Model 2, dimensioned for the 7.65mm Browning cartridge, while the Model 5 was the same pistol but with a barrel chambered for the 9mm Browning Short (.380 Auto) cartridge.

Left: Stripped, the Lignose Model 2 shows its Browning ancestry.

Einhand Models 2A and 3A

These models were produced by Lignose in 6.35mm during the 1920s and remained popular up to 1939, when they ceased production. There were plans to manufacture them in 7.65mm and 9mm Short calibres in 1925, but these seem not to have materialised. The weapons are oddities in that they attempted to solve a long-standing problem—how to prepare an

Lignose Models 4 and 5

Calibre	7.65mm Browning (Model 4); 9mm Short (Model 5)
Method of operation	Blowback, single-action, hammer-fired
Safety devices	Manual safety catch left side of frame
Magazine type	Single-column detachable box in butt
Position of catch	At heel of butt
Magazine capacity	8 rounds (7 in Model 5)
Front sight	Fixed blade
Rear sight	Fixed U-notch
Overall length	4.96in (126mm)
Barrel length	3.15in (60mm)
Number of grooves	6
Direction of twist	Right-hand
Empty weight	18.8 oz (535g)
Markings	Left side of slide: 'AKT.-GES. LIGNOSE BERLIN ABTEILUNG SUHL CAL. 7.65 D.R.P.'; or on right side of slide: 'THEODOR BERGMANN GAGGENAU SUHL CAL. 7.65 D.R.Pa.'; on both grips the word 'LIGNOSE' or the word 'BERGMANN' moulded in
Serial number	On right side of slide, barrel and mouth of magazine opening

Lignose Model 2A

Calibre	6.35mm Browning
Method of operation	Blowback, hammer-fired
Safety devices	Manual safety catch left rear of frame
Magazine type	Single-column detachable box in butt
Position of catch	Heel of butt
Magazine capacity	6 rounds; 9 rounds in Model 3A
Front sight	Fixed blade
Rear sight	Groove in slide top
Overall length	4.75in (121mm)
Barrel length	2.15in (55mm)
Number of grooves	6
Direction of twist	Right-hand
Empty weight	13.5oz (385g); Model 3A 14.5oz (425g)
Markings	Left side of slide: 'AKT.-GES. LIGNOSE BERLIN ABTEILUNG SUHL CAL. 6,35 D.R.P.'; or on right side of slide: 'THEODOR BERGMANN GAGGENAU SUHL CAL. 6,35 D.R.Pa.'; on both grips the word 'LIGNOSE' or the word 'BERGMANN' moulded in
Serial number	On right side of slide

automatic pistol for firing with one hand. Almost every pistol demands two hands, one to hold it steady while the other hand retracts the bolt or the slide in order to cock the mechanism and place a cartridge in the chamber. A number of inventors have proposed various systems of levers whereby one-handed operation can be achieved, but only this design has prospered.

The design is due to Witold Chylewski, a Pole resident in Hungary who obtained a patent in 1919 covering a one-handed cocking system in which the front edge of the trigger guard forms part of a sliding unit with a connection to the slide of the pistol. By grasping the pistol, curling the finger around the front of the trigger

Below: An advertisement from 1923 for the Lignose Einhand pistol.

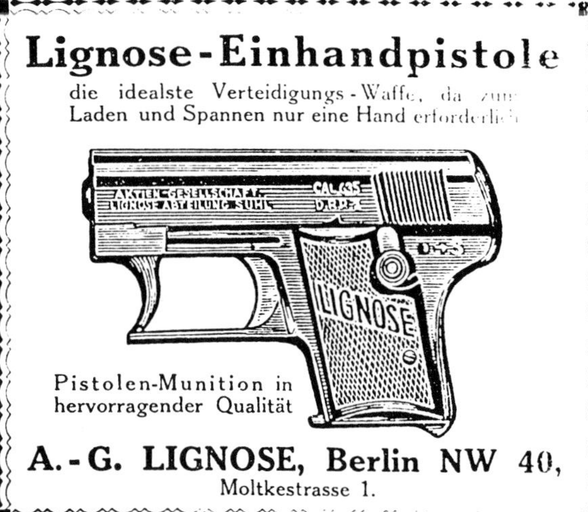

Right, upper: Cocking the Lignose Model 31. In this photograph the trigger guard has been pulled back to retract the slide.
Right, lower: Release the trigger guard and the pistol is now ready to fire.

guard and pulling it back, the slide is retracted. If the trigger guard is then released, the slide runs forward, propelled by the usual type of return spring, and loads a round into the chamber, leaving the pistol cocked. The firer now transfers his finger to the trigger to fire in the normal way. The pistol reloads itself, but, of course, the trigger guard stays in one place during the recoil stroke. Quite obviously, the pistol has to be a small-calibre blowback: anything large would require such a strong return spring as to be beyond the power of a single finger to cock.

Chylewski took his patent to Switzerland and about one thousand pistols were made by SIG in 1920. The next step is unknown, but the design was quickly acquired by the Bergmann company, which began producing it as the Einhand pistol early in 1921. However, no sooner had this begun than the firm was bought up by AG Lignose, who continued to manufacture the design for several years.

Apart from this cocking system, the Einhand models are simple enough 6.35mm blowback pistols; they are, in fact, the Bergmann/Lignose Model 2 and Model 3 but with the one-hand cocking modification. There are two versions, the Model 2A and the Model 3A, which differ only in the dimensions of the butt, the 2A having a magazine containing six rounds and the Model 3A one containing nine.

To dismantle either model, after removing the magazine, clearing and pulling the trigger, pull the slide back and rotate the safety catch so as to engage in the usual notch in the lower edge of the slide. Press the spring catch which is now revealed ahead of the trigger guard, and slide the trigger guard and cocking piece forward off the frame. Then rotate the barrel to free its breech ribs from engagement in the frame. Holding the slide, release the safety catch and allow the slide and barrel to go forward off the frame; rotate the barrel to release it from the slide and lift it clear. The striker and its spring can now be lifted from the slide, while withdrawal of the usual screws will allow the grips to be removed to give access to the simple lockwork.

Reassembly is the opposite of the above—there are no complications.

In the cases of both the Taschen and Einhand pistols, those with Bergmann markings are much less common than those with Lignose markings.

MANN

Fritz Mann Werkzeugfabrik, Suhl

Westen Taschen Modell (Vest-Pocket Model)

This peculiar little weapon is the product of Fritz Mann of Suhl and exhibits an originality of mind not usually seen in the pocket pistol field. Most makers seem to be quite happy to base their designs on Browning's well-tried 6.35mm automatic of 1906, but the Mann is unusual in having a solid-top frame with an independent breech bolt working in it. A boring in the top of the frame above the barrel carries a spring surrounding a rod attached to the finger grip at the rear of the pistol. The lower section of this grip is attached to the bolt. Thus recoil of the bolt carries with it the rod in the boring above, which compresses the recoil spring. The bolt carries within it the striker and spring.

Complete stripping is impossible without proper tools, as the sear rides in a slot under the bolt and complete removal of the bolt cannot be achieved until the sear axis pin is driven out with a suitable drift. However, sufficient stripping for routine cleaning can be managed without this step, though a fine screwdriver is needed. Having cleared the gun in the normal way, unscrew carefully the screw in the boring above the muzzle. This will unscrew the recoil rod from the finger grip and, since the recoil spring is wrapped around the rod, it will push out with some force when finally undone. Withdraw the rod and spring. Now the thumb piece and bolt can be pulled back and the thumb piece removed from the bolt by rotating it. The barrel can now be removed by gripping the ornamental collar at the muzzle, rotating it through 90° and withdrawing it. Removal of the grips exposes the sear pin, which, as mentioned above, should be drifted out to let the sear fall clear of the bolt and permit the bolt to be pushed forward through the frame to remove it. In order to let the bolt through, the ejector will have to be released, and this can be done by pushing in the stud which normally locks the safety catch in the 'safe' position—i.e., the small stud showing alongside the letter 'F'. Once released, the ejector can be slipped forward and hooked out through the barrel aperture of the frame with a thin screwdriver.

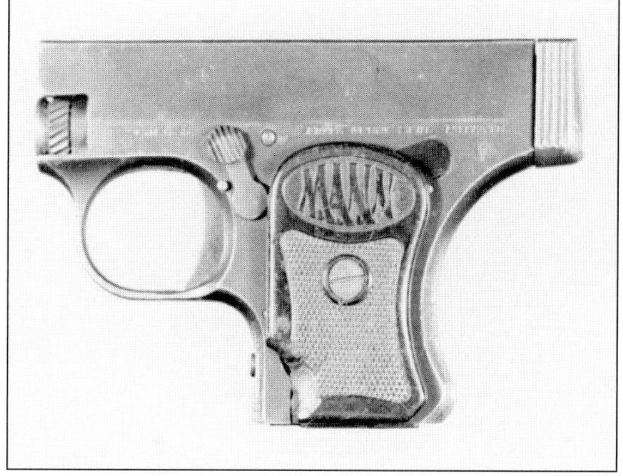

Above: The diminutive Mann 6.35mm Vest-Pocket pistol—a unique design.

To reassemble the weapon, get the bolt in first and replace the sear and its axis pin. Then slip the extractor into place and hold it in position with the stud in its hole, using a screwdriver, until the barrel is slid in and rotated to lock. This ensures that the ejector drops into its proper place into a cutaway in the barrel and is not forced from its seat during the barrel locking movement. Then pull the bolt back, insert the striker and spring and screw on the finger grip. Push the bolt home, insert the recoil spring and rod into the boring, force home against the finger grip with a screwdriver and screw firmly home. Taking one consideration with another, this is not a design to be commended.

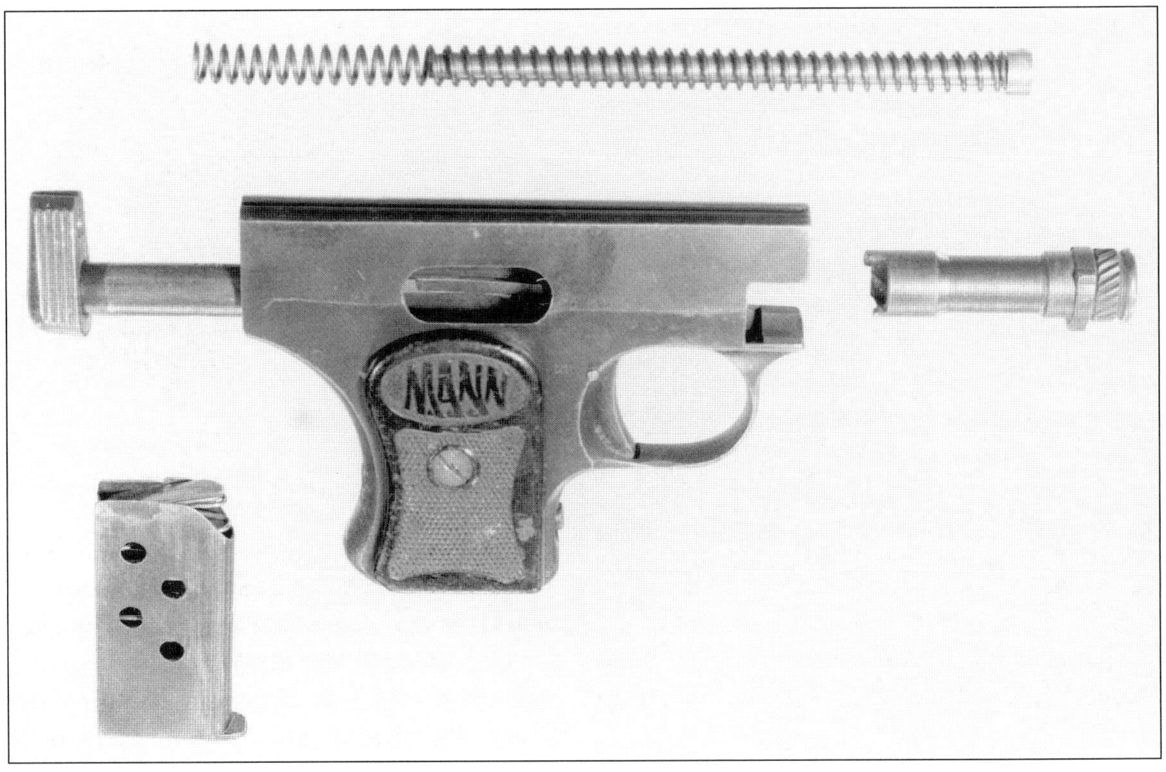

Above: Stripping the Mann VP shows some of the peculiarities of the weapon.

The pistol went into production early in 1920 but was out of production by 1924. Serial numbers suggest that about 18,000 were made.

Mann VP

Calibre	6.35mm Browning
Method of operation	Blowback, striker-fired
Safety devices	Manual safety catch left side of frame
Magazine type	Single-column detachable box in butt
Position of catch	Bottom front of butt
Magazine capacity	5 rounds
Front sight	None
Rear sight	Groove in top surface of frame
Overall length	4.13in (105mm)
Barrel length	1.65in (42mm)
Number of grooves	6
Direction of twist	Right-hand
Empty weight	9.0oz (255g)
Markings	Left side of frame: 'CAL. 6,35 FRITZ MANN SUHL'
Serial number	On front edge of butt below magazine catch; last three digits on trigger

Taschen Modell

The Pocket Model Mann is an entirely different weapon from the 6.35mm. It would seem that Mann's original intention was to produce a 7.65mm pistol to the same design as the Vest-Pocket Model, but the extra power of the 7.65mm cartridge led him to abandon the idea and fall into line with his competitors, basing his design on the usual Browning model. In 1924 the Pocket Model went on sale in 7.65mm Browning and 9mm Short versions; about 45,000 of the two models were made before manufacture ended in 1928.

The only unusual feature of this pistol is the operation of the magazine catch: it is a function of the safety catch. The safety catch is in the front edge of the left butt grip and has three positions. Pushed towards the slide it is at 'fire'; brought down to its mid position it is at 'safe'; and forcing it still further down, against a spring, releases the magazine. Presumably this is the feature referred to in the slide inscription 'Mann's Patent'.

The Pocket Model is stripped in the usual fashion of Browning copies. After removing the magazine and clearing the gun, the slide is pulled back and held there while the muzzle is grasped and rotated to unlock the ribs from their anchorage in the frame. The barrel and slide can then be pushed forward off the frame. The recoil spring and barrel can then be removed from the slide, and the firing pin and spring can be slid from their recess. Withdrawal of the usual screws allows the grips to be removed, when the working of the safety catch and lockwork can be seen. Reassembly is the reverse of stripping.

Mann Taschen Modell

Calibre	7.65mm Browning or 9mm Short
Method of operation	Blowback, striker-fired
Safety devices	Manual safety catch left side of frame
Magazine type	Single-column detachable box in butt
Position of catch	Forms part of safety catch
Magazine capacity	5 rounds
Front sight	None
Rear sight	Groove on top of slide
Overall length	4.75in (121mm)
Barrel length	2.35in (60mm)
Number of grooves	4
Direction of twist	Right-hand
Empty weight	12.5oz (354g); 9mm model 13.3oz (378g)
Markings	Left side of slide: 'CAL. XX MANN-WERKE A.G. SUHL MANN'S PATENT'; moulded into the grips: 'MANN'; magazine bottom plate: 'MANN PISTOLE 7.65 [or 9mm] and two 'MW' monograms
Serial number	On right side of frame

Above: In contrast to the 6.35mm VP, the 7.65mm Vest-Pocket pistol was a model of conservative design.

In about 1930 Mann advertised that the Taschen Modell would be available to special order chambered for a new bottlenecked 6.33mm cartridge developing a 320m/sec muzzle velocity with a 4.0g bullet (1,050ft/sec with 62gr). Whether, in fact, this cartridge and the associated pistol ever existed is doubtful; certainly, nobody appears ever to have actually seen one of these cartridges or one of the pistols, and it is hard to understand why Mann should have gone to the trouble of reducing the calibre of the pistol, and reducing the performance, when he had already ceased to manufacture a perfectly serviceable design. The whole affair sounds most unlikely, and was probably no more than a trial balloon to see if there might be a market for the idea—and apparently there was not.

MAUSER

Gebrüder Mauser & Cie, Oberndorf-am-Neckar (1874–84)
Waffenfabrik Mauser (1884–1922)
Mauserwerke AG (1922–45)
Mauserwerke Oberndorf AG (1950–)

Peter-Paul Mauser came of a gunmaking family and is famed principally for his rifle designs:

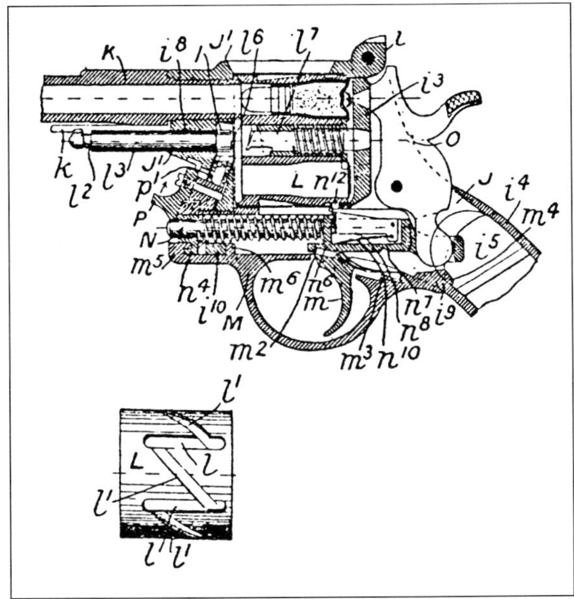

Right: Patent 722, 7 March 1878, Peter-Paul Mauser. This shows the basic features of the Mauser 'Zig-Zag' pistol, notably the method of cylinder rotation. The actual production pistols exhibited several minor changes which had doubtless been found necessary during the development of the prototype.

from 1872 onwards, he was concerned with manufacturing military rifles both for the German Army and for overseas sale. The firm of Gebrüder Mauser & Co was formed in 1874, replacing the earlier partnership of Gebrüder Mauser, and about this time he began to take an interest in pistol design. The German Army were casting about for a repeating pistol of some type with which to re-equip, and Mauser bent his talents to the design of a revolver.

'Zig-Zag' Revolver M78

The Mauser revolver, commonly called the 'Zig-Zag' for reasons which will become apparent, was a remarkable weapon, distinctly original in design and impeccably made and finished. The principal originality lies in the method adopted to revolve the cylinder and index it for each shot. The circumference of the cylinder is grooved in a zig-zag fashion; the trigger operates the hammer in either the single or double-

Below: The Mauser revolver with the hammer cocked and the cylinder operating rod showing at the front of the frame.

Mauser M78 'Zig-Zag' Revolver

Calibre	9mm Mauser
Method of operation	Six-chambered, double-action revolver
Safety devices	None
Magazine type	Rotating cylinder
Magazine capacity	6 rounds
Front sight	Fixed blade
Rear sight	Fixed V-notch
Overall length	10.60in (269mm)
Barrel length	5.40in (136mm)
Empty weight	26.5oz (750g)
Markings	Barrel rib: 'GEBR. MAUSER & CIE OBERNDORF A/N WURTTEMBERG 1878 PATENT'
Serial number	On rear of butt strap, on rear face of cylinder and on frame below cylinder

action mode and the lockwork actuates a rod lying in the frame beneath the cylinder. When the hammer is cocked, the rod is thrust forward and a stud in its top surface, engaging in a cylinder groove, enters an oblique groove and rotates the cylinder through one-sixth of a turn to present a fresh chamber in front of the hammer. As the hammer falls to fire, the rod is retracted, but this time the stud travels straight down a groove without moving the cylinder. In this respect it differs from the Fosbery patent of 1896 used on the Webley-Fosbery and Union Arms revolvers: Fosbery's zig-zag moved the cylinder one-twelfth of a turn on recoil and again on run-out.

The system of loading is another unusual aspect of the Mauser revolver. The early models were solid-framed and used the normal gate loading system, with the hammer having to be cocked and lowered in order to move the cylinder round chamber by chamber. This was slow and hazardous, and the next step was the introduction of the bottom-break design, which is the most common pattern of Mauser revolver found today. The barrel and cylinder assembly is hinged to the frame above the standing breech and double-locked by a spring catch and a posi-

Below: The Mauser revolver opened for loading.

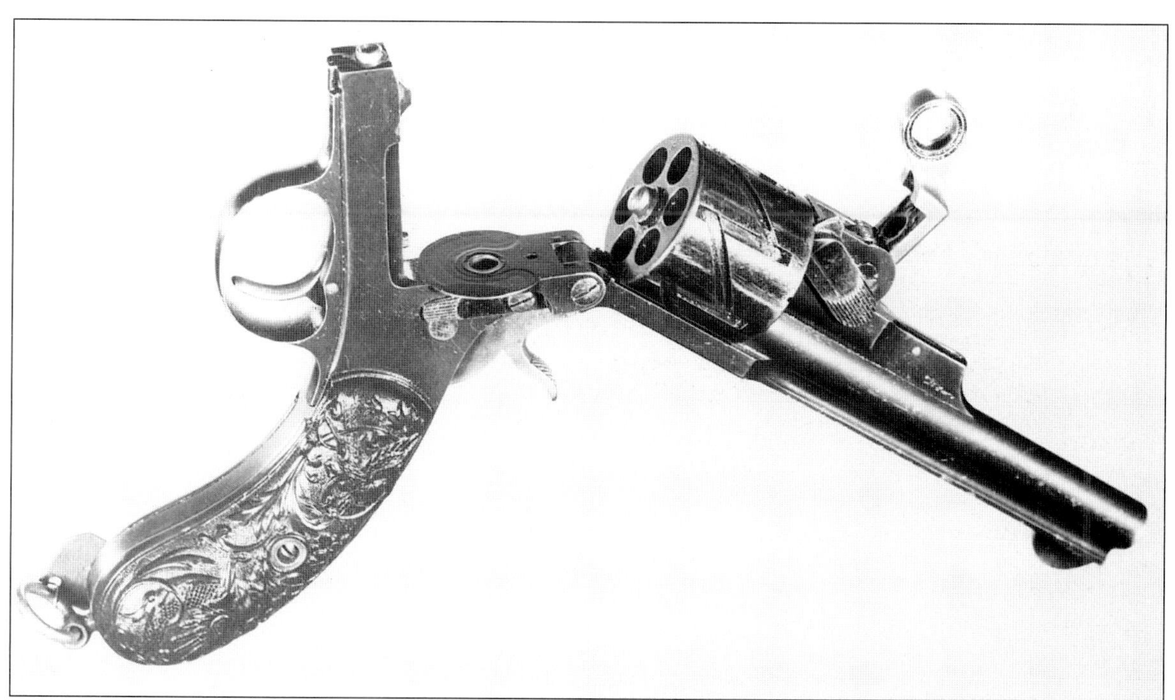

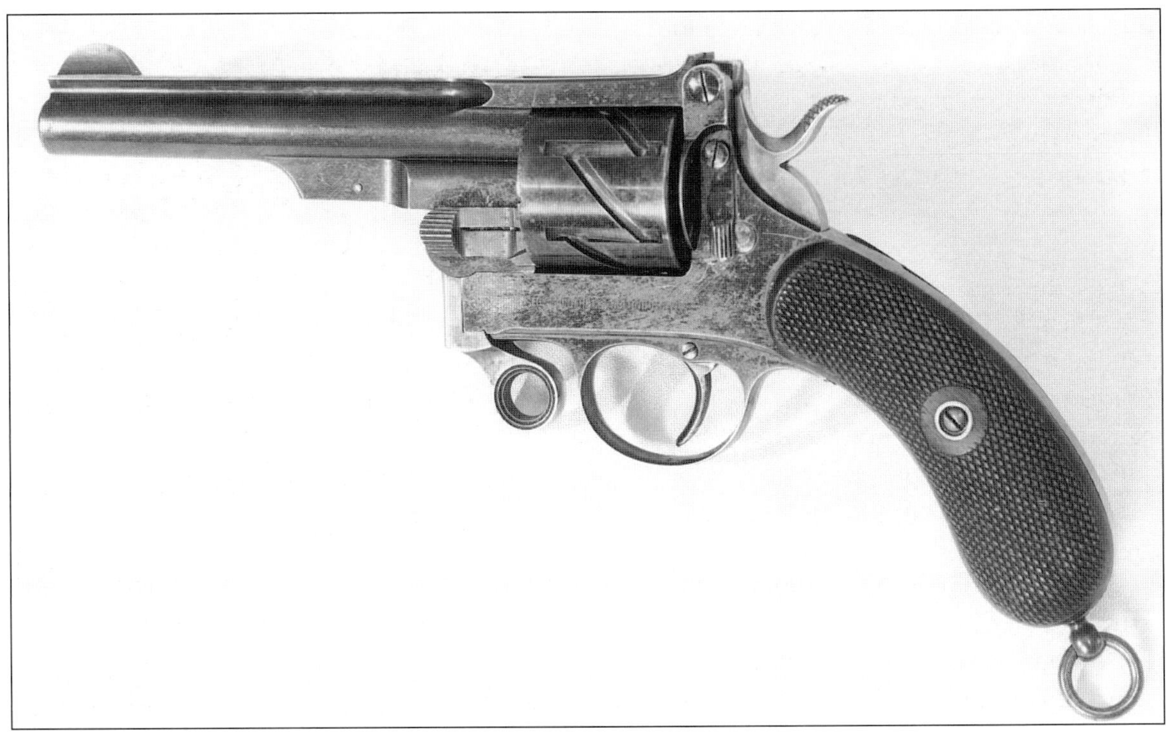

Above: Left side of the Mauser 'Zig-Zag' revolver, with a different butt.

tive latch. The positive latch, with a milled finger grip, is just in front of the cylinder, while the spring catch is operated by the ring which can be seen ahead of the trigger guard. To open the pistol after firing, the milled latch is moved and the ring grip pushed down and forward to release. The entire barrel and cylinder unit can now be swung through about 80°; at this point the barrel stops and further pressure on the ring grip operates a cam which forces the central extractor plate out of the cylinder to eject the empty cartridge cases. Releasing the ring grip allows the extractor to reseat in the cylinder and the gun can now be reloaded.

Once the weapon is loaded—and the wise man holds the pistol upside down during this part of the proceedings, so as not inadvertently to shake all the rounds from the cylinder—grasping the barrel and closing the gun allows the spring catch to re-engage, whereupon it can be secured by the finger latch.

The Mauser revolver was produced in three standard calibres, 7.6mm, 9mm and 10.6mm. The 10.6mm was primarily intended as a military weapon, but it was not accepted by the Army on the grounds of expense and complication, and the Commission Revolver (or Reichsrevolver) was issued in its stead. Thus relatively small numbers were made, and the commonest version today is the 9mm type. But even this is fairly scarce, since the failure to obtain a military contract caused Mauser to lose interest in the design. Moreover, since it was a good deal more expensive than most of its competitors, sales were not large, and manufacture ceased in the mid-1880s.

c/96 Automatic Pistol

Although production of the 1878 revolver continued for some years, and Mauser drew up, and patented, various improvements, he apparently never felt impelled to put an improved version into production, and his next step was to design a mechanical repeating pistol, a type of weapon which had a brief career in the 1885–95 period. However, he was astute enough to realise the drawbacks of this type of weapon, and, looking forward, decided that the future lay with the application of the automatic principle which Maxim had unveiled in 1884. If this idea could be applied to a hand weapon, then the mechanical repeater would be killed stone dead overnight and the revolver would have its foundations severely shaken. Mauser thus started on the road which led to the famous Military Model automatic. This was developed in 1893 by the General Superintendent of the Mauser factory, one Herr Federle (or Feederle), with assistance from his two brothers.

It would appear that this development originated simply as a private amusement of the Federle brothers and was not a Mauser company project. However, when, in 1894, Mauser himself decided to investigate automatic pistols, he apparently called on the Federles to implement their design, and the first prototype was completed in March 1895. The basic features were patented under Mauser's name in German 90,430, 11 December 1895, and British 959, 14 January 1896. It should be pointed out that this was standard commercial practice in those days: the logic was simple and irrefutable—if you develop an invention in my workshop, using my facilities, in my time, when paid by me, then the invention is my property.

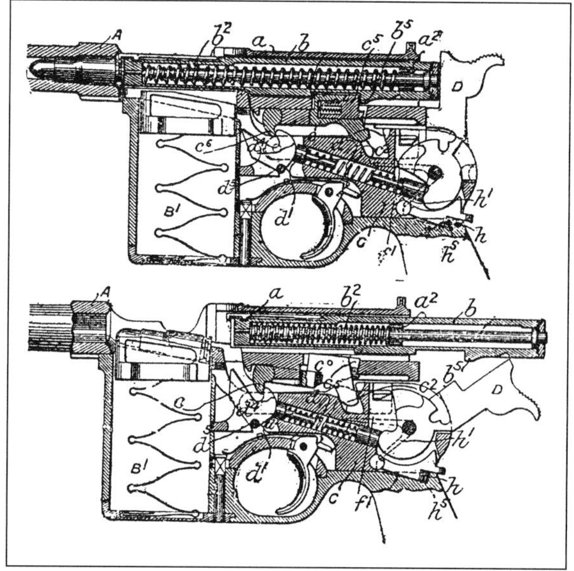

Above: Patent 95, 14 January 1896, Peter-Paul Mauser. This was the definitive 'Broomhandle' patent, setting forth the various unique features of the Mauser c/96 pistol. It shows, among other things, the early form of breech lock with a single lug engaging the bolt, and the hammer is of a shape never seen on a production pistol, but the remainder of the drawings show that there was little or no significant change throughout its long career. It is also noteworthy that the ability to dismantle the pistol without the use of tools was claimed as a novelty in the patent.

Below: Patent drawing of Mauser's projected repeating pistol, with tubular magazine under the barrel. It never got past the prototype stage.

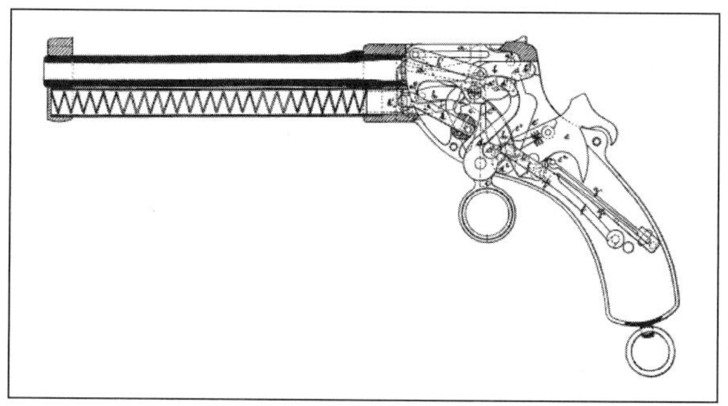

Between the making of the prototype and the start of production there were the usual number of provisional designs exploring the effects of various modifications, with magazines of 6-, 10- and 20-round capacity and in a variety of calibres. It seems that the only reliable cartridge which was adaptable to Mauser's system at that time was the 7.65mm Borchardt; Mauser adopted this as his standard round with a few slight changes in dimensional tolerances and a heavier propelling charge and rechristened it 7.63mm Mauser. By mid-1896 the design was finalised and the seal of approval was virtually set upon the pistol when Kaiser Wilhelm himself attended a demonstration at Potsdam in August 1896 and personally fired a few rounds from a specimen.

Production was slow for the first few months until the necessary facilities were organised, and full production finally began about the middle of 1897. Within a short time a number of minor modifications were incorporated, some to improve the functioning and some to facilitate manufacture. One of the most important changes, and one which is readily visible, was the provision of a double locking notch beneath the bolt in place of the original single notch; this was introduced early in 1897 and before volume production began. By serial number 360 all the minor changes had been incorporated and from then on the design remained unaltered in its essentials throughout its life. The early models can be identified by the engraving 'SYSTEM MAUSER' over the chamber; in August 1897 this was changed to 'WAFFENFABRIK MAUSER OBERNDORF A.N.'

In order to avoid too much repetition, the 1896 model will now be described in detail; subsequent models can then be dealt with briefly by noting their points of difference from the 1896.

The Mauser Military Model 1896 is a locked-breech pistol using a fixed magazine located ahead of the trigger. It is loaded from a charger by pulling back the bolt until it is held to the rear by the raised magazine platform, inserting the charger into grooves in the barrel extension and forcing the rounds down into the magazine by thumb pressure; one side of the barrel extension is recessed in order to facilitate the thumb's pressing the last round home. Removing the charger then allows the bolt to run forward and chamber the first round. The barrel is forged in one piece with a barrel extension in the form of two arms finishing in a square-section tunnel at the rear, in which the bolt moves. Beneath the boltway and attached to the barrel extension is the breech locking block, which has two square lugs on its top surface and which is recessed into the top of the frame. The barrel unit moves in milled grooves on top of the frame, which is merely a shell carrying the grip and magazine and with the firing mechanism block fitted inside. This latter unit is entirely self-contained, it can easily be removed in one piece and it also forms the attachment between the trigger pinned to the frame and the hammer hinged to the firing mechanism block.

At the instant of firing, the breech locking block is raised so that the lugs on its top surface engage in two matching grooves on the underside of the bolt, thus locking bolt and barrel ex-

Mauser 1896 Military

Calibre	7.63mm Mauser
Method of operation	Recoil, locked breech, hammer-fired
Safety devices	Manual safety catch alongside hammer
Magazine type	Integral, single-column, in front of trigger guard
Magazine capacity	10 rounds
Front sight	Fixed blade
Rear sight	Adjustable U-notch, graduated to 500m
Overall length	11.61in (295mm)
Barrel length	5.51in (140mm)
Number of grooves	4
Direction of twist	Right-hand
Empty weight	39.5oz (1,120g)
Markings	Over chamber: 'SYSTEM MAUSER' on early models, or 'WAFFENFABRIK MAUSER OBERNDORF A.N.' on later models; right rear of frame: 'WAFFENFABRIK MAUSER OBERNDORF A.N.'
Serial number	Full number on left side of breech and rear of bolt; last two digits on almost every removable part.

tension securely together. The locking block itself is securely held up by its lower end resting on a steel spur in the firing mechanism block. When the trigger is pressed, the lockwork transmits the movement to the cocked hammer, releasing it to fall against the firing pin in the bolt, which is driven forward to fire the cartridge. Recoil drives the barrel, barrel extension and bolt backwards for 0.094in (2.4mm). The rearward movement of the breech locking block is transmitted through a bell-crank to the firing mechanism mainspring, further compressing it. At the end of this recoil movement, the lower edge of the locking block slips from the spur in the firing mechanism block and, owing to the pressure of the mainspring, the locking block is pulled down and out of engagement with the bolt. The locking block then comes hard against a bearing surface in the gun frame and prevents any further rearward movement of the barrel or barrel extension. The bolt, however, is free to move and continues to travel back inside the barrel extension, cocking the hammer and compressing the recoil spring which is inside the bolt. When the movement of the bolt stops, the compressed spring drives the bolt back, stripping the top round from the magazine and entering it into the chamber. As the round seats in the chamber, so the bolt forces the barrel and barrel extension forward and the breech locking block is pulled back up on to the spur in the firing mechanism block, lifting the lugs back into engagement with the bolt and locking the breech once more ready for firing. When the last round in the magazine has been fired, the magazine platform rises and holds the bolt open ready for reloading.

The applied safety on this pistol is in the form of a vertically rocking bar incorporated in the firing mechanism assembly and alongside the hammer. To make the gun safe the bar is pulled down, locking the hammer, and it is pushed up to prepare the gun for firing. There is no half-

Below: An early Mauser c/96 pistol with large ring hammer and six-shot magazine.

cock position on the hammer, but there is an interesting form of safety indicator in that the head of the hammer is formed so as to obscure the rear sight when it is not cocked, which acts as a reminder should the firer attempt to take aim without having loaded and cocked the pistol first. The rear sight is a fixed U-notch and there is no provision for a shoulder stock.

The 1896 Model can thus be seen to be a definite one-hand gun, with a ten-shot magazine and a 5.51in (140mm) barrel; a small number with a six-shot magazine and 4.72in (120mm) barrel were made early in 1897. This model, in either barrel length, is rarely seen outside museums and collections today. It is also said that a small number—perhaps two or three hundred—were chambered for the 7.65mm Parabellum cartridge and supplied to Turkey in the early 1900s, but I can find no confirmation of this and have certainly never seen a Mauser in this chambering.

Below: A flush-sided Mauser c/96, as supplied to the Italian Navy in 1899.

Military Models c/98, c/03 and c/06

In 1898 came the model which is the most common today. It was on the same general lines as the 1896 but with the following detail differences:

1. The barrel is 5.51in (140mm) long.
2. The head of the hammer is now a ring instead of a cone and no longer obscures the backsight when down.
3. The backsight is an adjustable tangent type, with V-notch, graduated from 50 to 700m.
4. The rear of the butt is grooved to take a holster stock.
5. The pitch of rifling is increased to one turn in 18 calibres, in order to improve the stability and accuracy of the bullet.

Shortly after the introduction of this model, the whole appearance of the pistol was subtly changed by making the frame sides smooth instead of recessed and panelled. The change did not last long, and by 1906 the panelled sides were back to stay.

The 1903 model appeared next, and the differences were as follows:

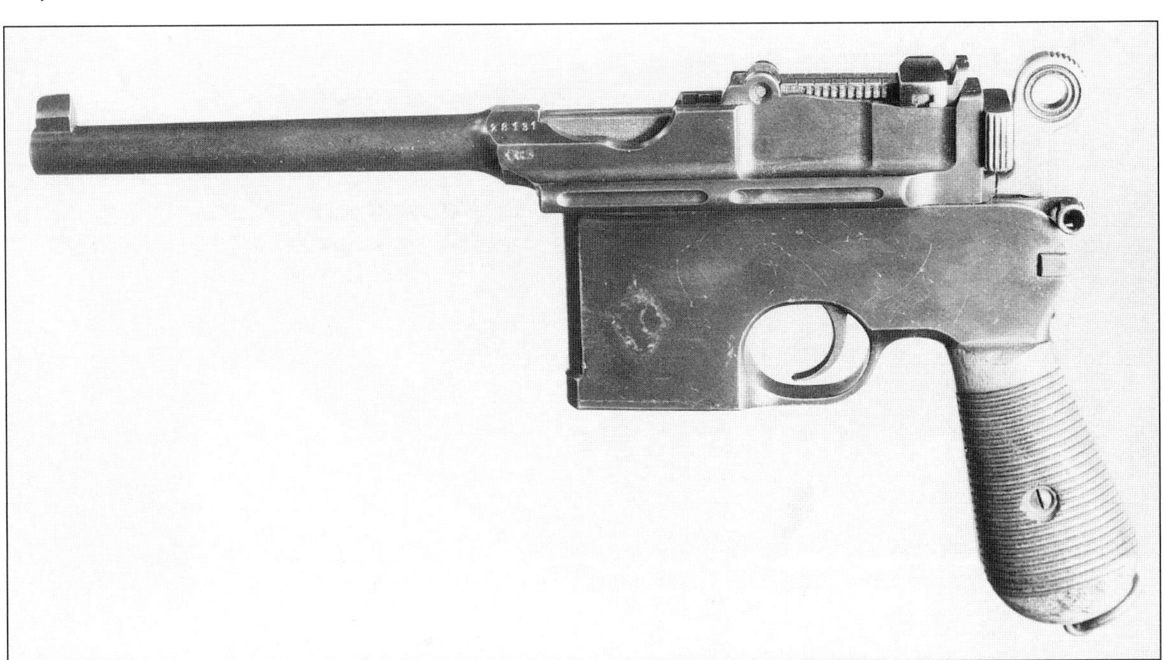

1. A more positive form of disconnector was built into the firing mechanism.
2. Slight changes in the contour of the trigger and the method of mounting it in the frame improved the trigger pull.
3. The back sight was graduated to 1,000m.
4. The firing pin was no longer retained by a sliding plate in the bolt but was formed with two lugs. By pressing in and rotating the pin through half a turn it can be withdrawn.

The 1905 Model saw a return to the original handgun concept:

1. 4in (101mm) barrel.
2. 6-shot magazine.
3. There is a very large ring hammer, obscuring the back sight when down.
4. Shorter butt, without groove for holster stock.

This model weighs 33oz (1,020g) and is only 10.0in (254mm) long.

In 1907 it looked as if Mauser was about to abandon the design for something more modern when he patented a considerably changed design utilising a removable magazine in the butt and a totally different mechanism; but the matter was allowed to drop, although some of the features of this patent showed up in Mauser pocket pistol designs of later years. The year 1907 also saw the inception of the 9mm Mauser cartridge, which was virtually a straightened-out 7.63mm Mauser case with a 9mm bullet in it, probably inspired by Luger's development of the 9mm Parabellum. The result gave exceptionally powerful ballistics, and is generally referred to as the 9mm Mauser Export cartridge. A pistol was designed to accept it which was simply the 1903 model suitably chambered and strengthened. It appears to have been principally developed for the South American market as a hunting weapon and was not generally available in Europe; it is certainly quite rare today. The basic characteristics are as for the 1903 model except that the weight is 46.5oz (1,320g), and the length 12.25in (318mm). The 5.5in (140mm) barrel is rifled with six grooves, right-hand twist, one turn in 30 calibres.

Model 1912

The next change in the Military Model came in 1912 with a return to the shoulder carbine concept:

1. Rifling changed to six grooves, right-hand, one turn in 24 calibres.
2. A broader and shorter extractor is fitted, the bolt is heavier and the recoil spring slightly stronger.
3. The hammer is smaller and lighter.
4. The operation of the safety catch is completely reversed, being pulled down to fire and pushed up to make safe.
5. Weight 40.2oz (1,140g), length 11.65in (298mm).
6. Butt grooved for holster stock.
7. Adjustable rear sight graduated to 1,000m.

This is probably as common as the c/98, thousands being made between 1912 and 1918.

9mm Model 1916

In 1916 a contract was placed by the German Army for a quantity of these pistols to be chambered for the 9mm Parabellum cartridge. It was realised that it would be quicker to adopt this method of supplementing the supply of 9mm pistols to the front than to retool Mauser's factory to build the Pistole '08, since the only changes to the 1912 Model would be the barrel bolt face and magazine. The magazine had to be altered to take the shorter cartridge, but otherwise it is basically a reworked 1912 Model. The butt grips are distinctively marked with a large figure '9' cut into the wood and coloured red. A few were made up after the war from spare parts and have the '9' black instead of red or, in some cases, do not have the butt carved at all. They also display commercial proof marks instead of the Government acceptance marks found on the 'red 9' models. These, needless to say, are exceptionally rare today.

Bolo Mauser

After the first World War the Versailles Treaty forbade the manufacture of 9mm pistols and also of weapons with barrels more than 4in (101mm) long or weapons having the provision for attaching a shoulder stock. Thus in 1920 a new Mauser made its appearance; this was similar in design to the previous types but, in deference to the treaty, had a barrel of 3.88in (99mm). The butt was still grooved for the holster, though it is averred that no holster stocks were made or supplied for this model. The whole production was aimed at the Russian

Mauser M1916

Calibre	9mm Parabellum
Method of operation	Recoil, single-action
Safety devices	Manual safety at rear of receiver
Magazine type	Integral box, charger-loaded
Magazine capacity	10 rounds
Front sight	Fixed blade
Rear sight	Tangent U-notch, graduated to 500m
Overall length	11.66in (296mm)
Barrel length	5.51in (140mm)
Number of grooves	6
Direction of twist	Right-hand
Empty weight	39.5oz (1,120g)
Markings	Right side of frame: 'WAFFENFABRIK MAUSER OBERNDORF/NECKAR'
Serial number	On left side of breech

Below: A 9mm M1916, showing the method of loading by using a charger.

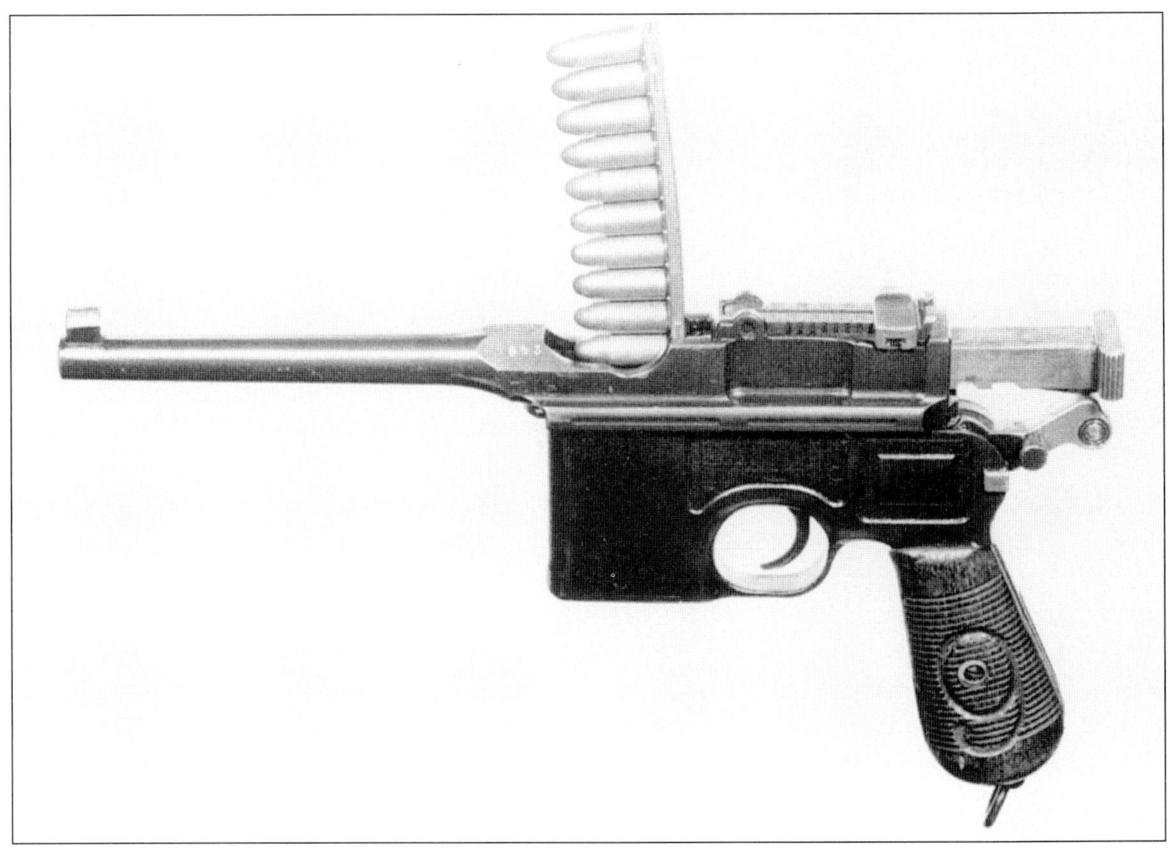

market, which at this time was avidly seeking pistols of any sort, and from this principal user came the designation Bolo Mauser, 'Bolo' being the contemporary slang term for Bolshevik. Irrespective of the availability or otherwise of the holster stock, the Bolo is still fitted with the tangent back sight graduated to 1,000m, and it is interesting to observe that the Russians adopted their own variation of the 7.63mm Mauser cartridge, having very slight dimensional differences from the original, as their service small-arms round, chambering their Tokarev automatic pistol and a number of submachine guns to take it.

Mauser Bolo or M1920

Calibre	7.63mm Mauser
Method of operation	Recoil, single-action
Safety devices	Manual safety catch at rear of receiver
Magazine type	Integral box, charger-loaded
Magazine capacity	10 rounds
Front sight	Fixed blade
Rear sight	Tangent adjustable V-notch, graduated to 1,000m
Overall length	9.88in (251mm)
Barrel length	3.89in (99mm)
Number of grooves	6
Direction of twist	Right-hand
Empty weight	36.9oz (1,045g)
Markings	Right side of frame: 'WAFFENFABRIK MAUSER, OBERNDORF/NECKAR'
Serial number	On left side of breech

Military M30

In 1922 came a major organisational upheaval, the result of which was that Waffenfabrik Mauser now became Mauser-Werke AG, and

Below: A 7.63mm Bolo Mauser, built to stay within the limitations of the Versailles Treaty and supplied to Soviet Russia.

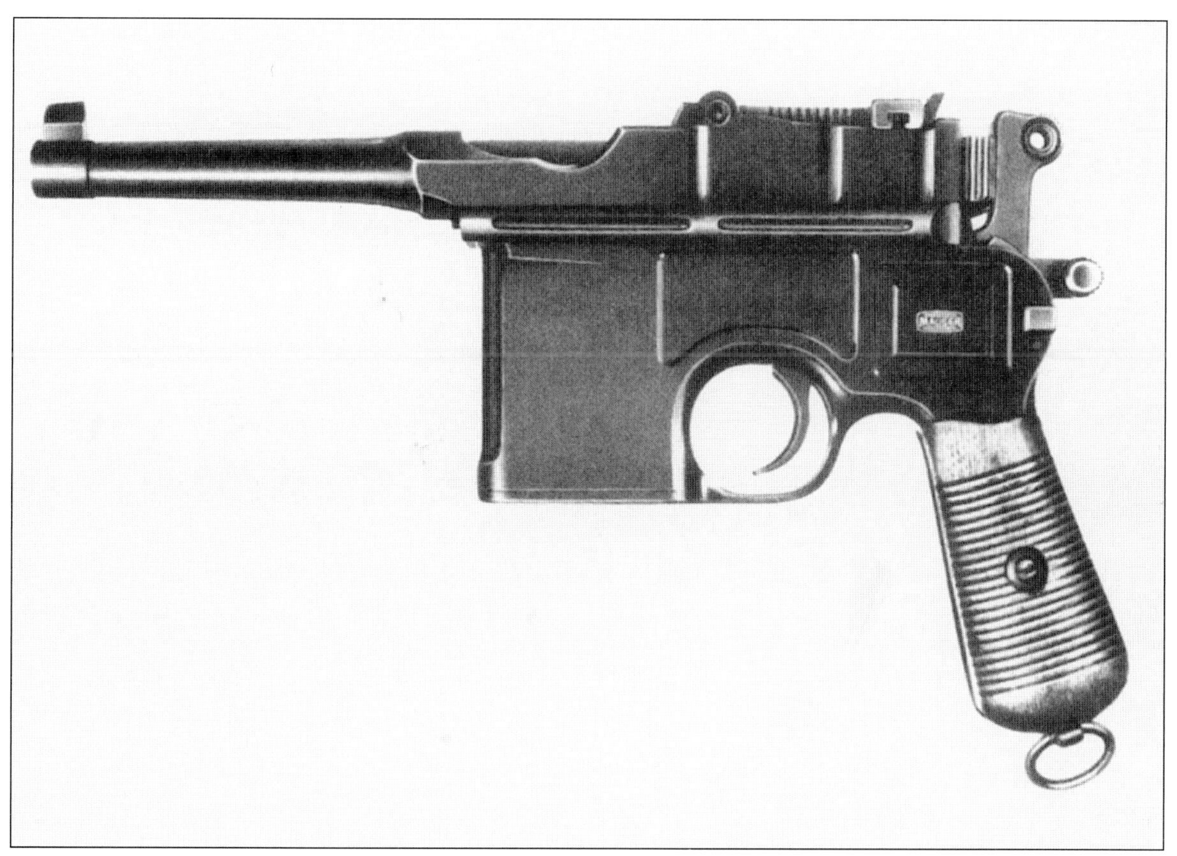

the markings on the pistols changed accordingly. By the end of the decade the minor provisions of the Versailles Treaty were becoming more honoured in the breach than in the observance as far as small arms were concerned. By this time, too, world markets were once again asking for Mauser pistols, and in default of the genuine article were purchasing Spanish copies. Mauser had to move or lose their market, and thus the 1930 Military was produced. This was virtually the 1912 model but with a barrel of 5.23in (133mm), holster stock and 1,000m sights. The principal change in this model was the adoption of the Mauser Universal Safety, a redesign of the safety catch. For the first time an inscription makes its appearance, and, quite uniquely, the safety catch has three positions. Pulled right back alongside the hammer, so that the letter 'F' is exposed, the pistol is ready for firing. Pushed right forward so that the letter 'S' is exposed, the hammer is blocked from touching the striker, though nothing else is locked. In this position the bolt can be retracted and the hammer cocked, and pressing the trigger will cause the hammer to fall, although due to the blocking arrangement the striker will not be touched and the gun will not fire. The third position of the lever is midway between the other two, so that both the 'F' and the 'S' are visible. In this position the whole mechanism is locked solidly, and it was recommended that this position—with the hammer cocked and the bolt open—be used for reloading the magazine.

Mauser 1930

Calibre	7.63mm Mauser
Method of operation	Recoil, single action
Safety devices	Universal Safety at rear of receiver (see text)
Magazine type	Integral box, charger-loaded
Magazine capacity	10 rounds
Front sight	Fixed blade
Rear sight	Tangent V-notch graduated to 1,000m
Overall length	11.25in (286mm)
Barrel length	5.24in (133mm)
Number of grooves	6
Direction of twist	Right-hand
Empty weight	40.6oz (1,150g)
Markings	Left of frame: 'WAFFENFABRIK MAUSER OBERNDORF NECKAR D.R.P. U.A.P.'
Serial number	On left side of breech

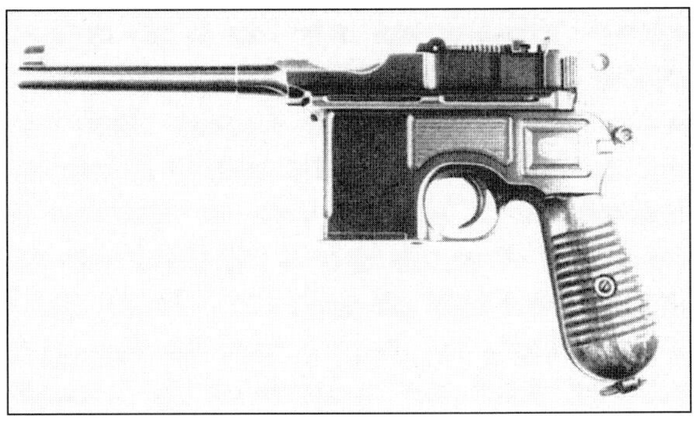

Above: A 7.63mm Model 1930, still basically the same as the 1896 version.

This model also saw the introduction of the Mauser badge, an oval with 'MAUSER' inside it, engraved on both sides of the pistol frame. The 1930 model is invariably beautifully made of the finest material; the majority of them were exported to China and South America but in the early 1930s these countries were deluged with large quantities of Spanish and Chinese imitations (retailing at much lower prices) and, once these weapons gained a foothold, sales of the Mauser gradually dwindled.

Concurrently with the 1930 Military a second Bolo model was produced, reputedly to the special order of the Soviet Government. These were made with a barrel length of 3.7in (94mm) but were otherwise identical with the 1930 Military, having the Universal Safety feature. The butts were grooved for the holster stock, but holster stocks were not supplied with them. They are, of course, exceptionally rare outside Russia.

Model 711 and 'Schnellfeuerpistole'

Spanish imitations of the Mauser were gaining a foothold among the less discerning customers in the 1930s, notably a version with a detachable magazine which allowed the use of magazines of larger capacity, up to 20 rounds being common. Another Spanish weapon that was making an impression, particularly among Chinese warlords, was an imitation of the 1912 Military but with the sear modified so that full automatic fire was possible. This also used a removable box magazine to hold 20 or 30 rounds, thus giving the owner a submachine gun on the cheap. This type of weapon is a snare and a delusion: owing to the short bolt travel, light reciprocating parts and powerful cartridge, the rate of fire is astronomical and controlling the weapon is out of the question.

Mauser appreciated this, but, since there seemed to be a demand for this sort of weapon, and since competitors were making inroads into their profits, in the interest of the shareholders they felt that they ought to do something about satisfying it, so they first produced the Model 711, which was simply a Model 1930 but with a removable magazine. They followed this fairly quickly with the Schnellfeuerpistole or Model 712 of 1932. This model was produced to a design by Josef Nickl, a Mauser engineer who had been largely responsible for the 1907 design and for the 1910 pocket pistol. It is basically the Model 711 but with the sear altered and a selective fire switch added to the left side. The magazine can be found in 10- or 20-round sizes. When the switch is pushed to 'R' (for Repetition) the rate of fire is about 850 rounds per minute, far too high to be of any practical use. With the selector at 'N' (Normal), the mechanism functions in the normal single-shot fashion.

In about 1936 a second version of the Schnellfeuer- or Reihenfeuerpistole was made in small numbers, the selector mechanism being based on patents granted to Karl Westinger, another Mauser engineer. The changes internally are very slight, having more effect on ease of production than on operation, and the selector switch is a pointed oval shape instead of the plain rectangular switch of the Nickl type. Both variations were supplied to the Chinese, Yugoslavian and German Armies (to the last in small numbers only on a trial basis). While the weapon was as well made as any other Mauser, it has one overriding drawback as a machine-carbine in that it fires from a closed breech. Consequently, when the trigger is released after a burst of fire a round is loaded ready for firing. This, when the gun has become heated from continuous bursts of fire, is liable to lead to 'cooking off' the round in the breech due to ignition of the cartridge from heat soaked up from the surrounding hot metal. Three 10-round bursts are enough to warm up the cham-

Mauser 712 or 'Schnellfeuerpistole'

Calibre	7.63mm Mauser
Method of operation	Recoil, single-action
Safety devices	Universal Safety at rear of receiver
Magazine type	Single-column removable box
Position of catch	Right side, rear of magazine housing
Magazine capacity	10 or 20 rounds
Cyclic rate of fire	900rds/min
Front sight	Fixed blade
Rear sight	Tangent V-notch graduated to 1,000m
Overall length	11.25in (286mm) without butt stock
Barrel length	5.25in (133mm)
Number of grooves	6
Direction of twist	Right-hand
Empty weight	42.5oz (1,206g)
Markings	Left of frame: 'WAFFENFABRIK MAUSER OBERNDORF A. NECKAR D.R.P. U.A.P.'; right of frame: Mauser badge
Serial number	On left side of chamber

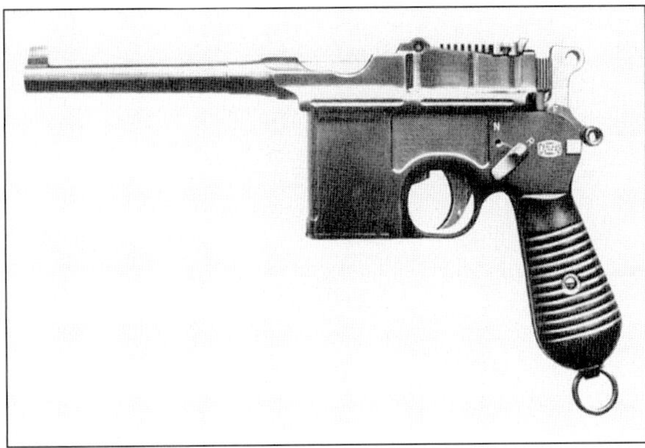

Above: A Model 712 selective-fire pistol, Nickl design.

ber to the point where the next round will self-ignite ('cook off') within twenty seconds without fail.

In 1936, with contracts for Parabellum P '08 pistols occupying most of their pistol machinery, Mauser finally ceased production of the Military Model, though assembly of pistols from the remaining stock of parts continued into 1938. It was never revived, since the design is too complex for modern mass-production techniques and it was no longer a serious contender as a military weapon. Exact figures are not available, but it has been reliably estimated, basing the calculations on known production runs and serial numbers, that total production of this pistol ran to about 1.2 million. Of that total, some 100,000 were Model 712s and 150,000 were the 9mm Parabellum Model 1916.

To strip the Military Models proceed as follows. After checking that the gun is empty, press in the magazine stud which protrudes below the magazine bottom plate and slide the plate off forwards. Remove the magazine spring and platform. With the hammer cocked, rest the muzzle on some suitable support and press up the locking catch in the frame just below the hammer. Press the butt down and the barrel group will slide off the frame backwards, carrying with it the firing mechanism block. Grasp the barrel with one hand and the firing mechanism block with the other and pull the two apart, the block moving down and to the rear. Dis-

Below: The Westinger design of Model 712, with the oval selector switch.

mantling the firing mechanism unnecessarily is not recommended. Insert the blade of a screwdriver into the slot in the rear of the firing pin, press in and give a quarter turn to release it, when it will be free to come out of the bolt. By pushing a suitable drift—or even a pencil—into the bolt to compress the recoil spring, it will be possible to remove the bolt retaining plate through the frame, whereupon the bolt and frame can be slid back out of the barrel extension and the recoil spring removed from the bolt.

Reassembly is the reverse of the stripping operation. It will be necessary to compress the recoil spring with the drift so as to be able to insert the cross piece. The firing mechanism block can be engaged with the barrel unit quite easily upon inspection, but make sure that the frame retaining latch below the hammer falls into the locked position after replacing the barrel assembly to the frame.

Having discussed the Military Mauser at some length, it is now time to turn and examine the other models of Mauser pistol which have been produced.

Model 1906/08

Although this model was superficially similar to the Military Model (insofar as it had the magazine in front of the trigger guard), it used a vastly different operating system which was derived from an experimental Mauser self-loading rifle which, in turn, had been derived from the Friberg locking system patented in 1887. The bolt, carried in a barrel extension, was locked in the closed position by two swinging flaps which were hinged at their rear end. The front ends moved in as the bolt closed, so as to prop behind recesses on the sides of the bolt. On firing, barrel, extension and bolt all moved backwards until cams in the frame swung the two flaps open and then halted the movement of the barrel and extension. This allowed the bolt to go to the rear, compressing the usual sort of spring, and then run forward to chamber a fresh round, after which barrel, bolt and extension ran forward again and the flaps were swung into place to lock the bolt once more.

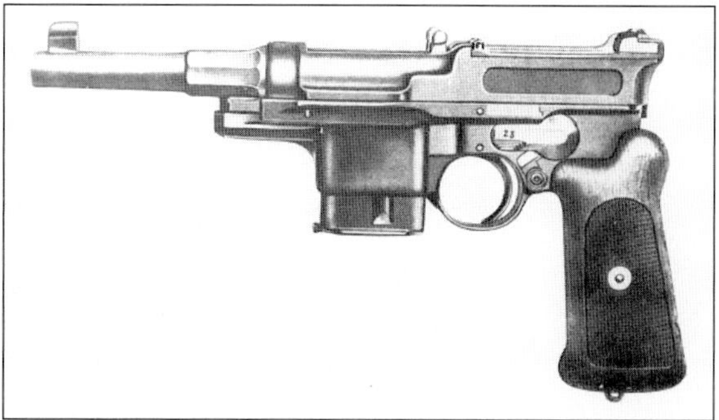

Above: The prototype Mauser Model 1908, which never went into production

This was all very fine on a rifle with a long receiver into which the flaps could fit, but when translated into a pistol design it became impossibly top-heavy; Mauser had, in effect, moved the locking apparatus out of the frame and into the barrel extension, and it led to a heavy concentration of mechanical goings-on above the frame, and a distinctly muzzle-heavy handful. One innovation in this pistol was the use of a hold-open stop operated by the magazine follower: as the last round was loaded, so the magazine follower rose into contact with the underside of the bolt, and when that shot was fired and the bolt recoiled, on its return it was held open by a lug which has been raised into the bolt's path by the follower. So far so good, but the innovative part of the patent was that as a freshly loaded magazine was inserted this freed the lug and the bolt ran forward as soon as the magazine locked into place, loading the first round. This has been seen on countless automatic pistols since then, but in 1906 it was quite a novelty.

Novelties, however, do not sell pistols, nor do they turn bad designs into good ones: the Mauser 06/08 never got much further than prototypes because nobody who saw it was impressed by its appearance (and, after all, whether one likes the Military Model or not, one has to admit that it is an elegant-looking weapon, whereas the 06/08 certainly is not); and, from various reports, it would appear that those who tried it were far from impressed by its lack of reliability and its tendency to dream up new and improbable ways of jamming. It was quietly taken outside in about 1910 and knocked on the head.

Below: The Model 1912/14 was produced in limited numbers but had its career abruptly terminated in 1914 by the war.

Blowback Pistols

Mauser appears to have begun examining the blowback idea in about 1907, with the intention of producing a simpler military pistol, and one of his first attempts was the 9mm Parabellum Model of 1909. But the military would never accept a blowback pistol with a cartridge as powerful as the 9mm Parabellum, and very few were ever made. Photographs indicate that this pistol was very similar to the later Model 1910 (described below) and probably acted as the test-bed for some of the weapon's mechanical features.

The company returned to this idea in 1912, when it produced what was virtually an enlarged Model 1910 pistol, modified so as to operate on the delayed blowback principle and chambered for a new 9mm cartridge, which was of similar dimensions to the 9mm Parabellum but which had a streamlined lightweight bullet and a reduced charge, making it suitable for a blowback design. The pistol was accepted by the Brazilian Navy in 1913 and an order was placed; Mauser, though, had to do some fine-tuning to the design before they were satisfied, and the pistol was then designated the Model 1912/14.

Early in 1914 a quantity of these pistols, together with a stock of ammunition, was sent to Britain to form part of the equipment for a number of warships which were being built for the Brazilian Navy. Upon the outbreak of war in 1914 all these warships were immediately commandeered into British service and were taken over, complete with their equipment, by the Royal Navy. Among this equipment were, according to an Admiralty document, '800 Mauser 9mm carbines' which, fairly certainly, were M1912/14 pistols with their shoulder stocks. What eventually became of them is a mystery: the supposition is that the Royal Navy used them until such time as the supply of special ammunition ran out and then threw the pistols overboard. There is no record of their disposal, nor of any specimen remaining in any military or naval museum.

Nickl-Pistole

The last venture in this period came in 1916 when Josef Nickl, a Mauser engineer, took the frame of the 1912 pistol and allied it to a rotating barrel breech locking system similar to that of the Steyr 1912 design. Chambered for the 9mm Parabellum, it was put forward as a potential military pistol, but in 1916 the German Army was in no mood to think about new types of pistol and the idea got no further in that direction. Nevertheless, Nickl continued to fiddle with the design, and when, after 1919, he was attached to the Czechoslovakian arms factory Ceska Zbrojovka, he successfully persuaded them to adopt a version of this design in 9mm Short chambering known as the CZ22. On returning to Germany Nickl resumed his development, and examples of this pistol have been seen in virtually every common pistol calibre, though none was ever produced in quantity or for sale. However, when the design was again turned down by the military, in the mid-1930s, Nickl finally gave up on it and retired.

Above: The Nickl-Pistole as made by Ceska Zbrojovka or Brno for the Czech Army in 1922.

Beautifully made, the Nickl pistol has an odd appearance since there is no overhang at the rear, the back of the slide being flush with the butt backstrap. The slide swells into a tubular upper part, and the retracting grip is made of diagonal ribs. The marking '9mm N Cs st Zbrojovka Brno' is on the lock cover plate above the left grip.

The mechanism is somewhat complicated for a 9mm Short cartridge. The barrel is locked to the slide by two lugs at the sides, engaging in slots in the slide walls. A third, helical lug

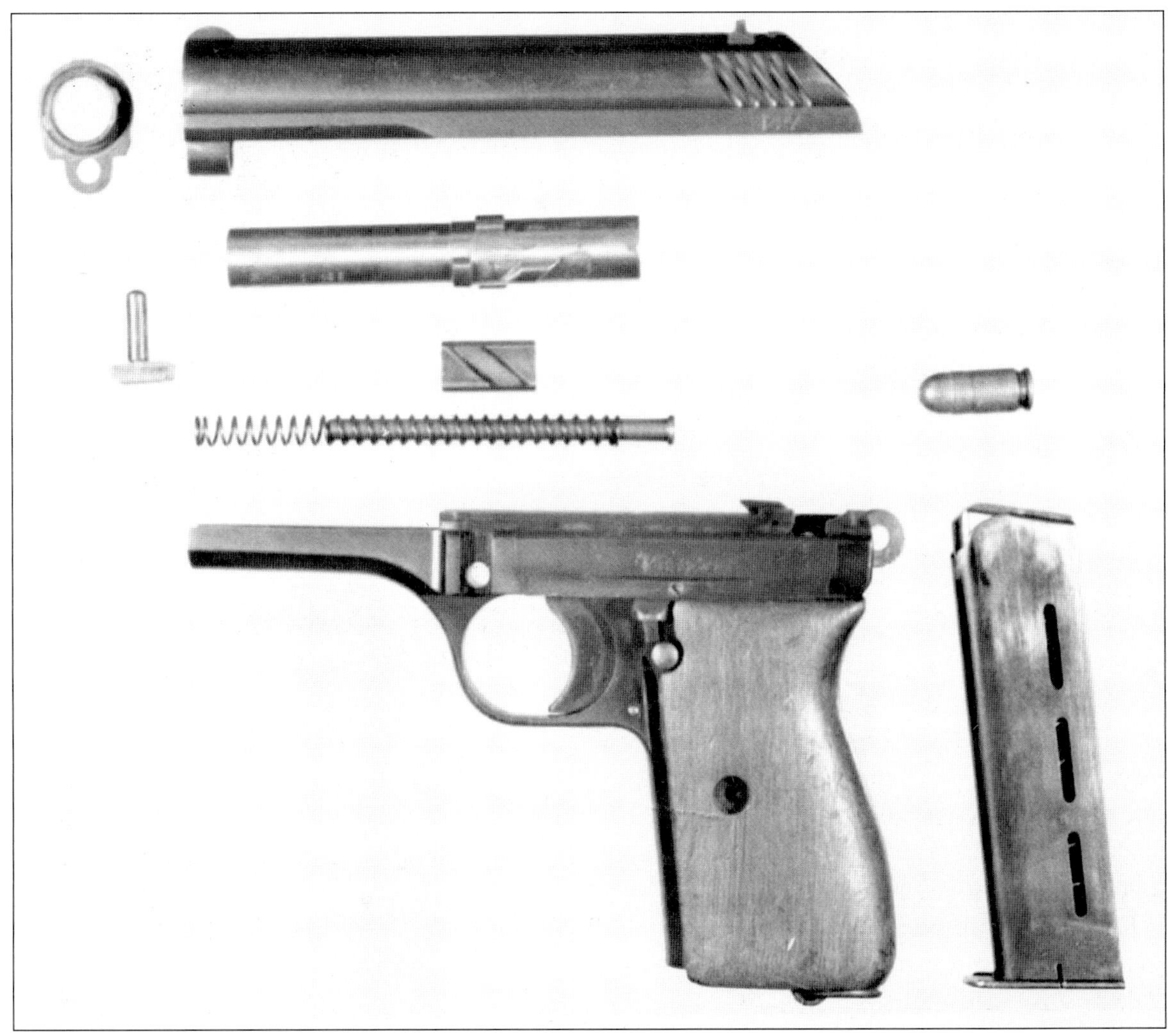

Above: The Nickl pistol dismantled, showing the rotating barrel lugs.

under the barrel engages in a groove in the frame. On firing, barrel and slide move back, and as the helical lug is pulled through the fixed groove, so it causes the barrel to turn about 20° until the side lugs disengage. The barrel then stops and the slide is free to run back and complete the extraction and reloading cycle. On the closing movement of the slide the barrel is driven back, the helical lug turns it back and the side lugs re-engage with the slide. There is an external hammer.

Production of this pistol was passed across to the Strakonitz factory in 1923; if any were made there, they retained the Brno marking, since a 1922 with a Strakonitz marking has never been recorded. On receiving the pistol, Myska, the Strakonitz factory designer, set about redesigning it to make production easier. (One reason for the shift of manufacture was the Brno factory's inability to meet production schedules.) This became known as the CZ 1924 and the changes were principally concerned with minor details; the only user-significant change was the addition of a magazine safety and the adoption of hard rubber grips instead

Mauser CZ 22 or Nickl-Pistole

Calibre	9mm Browning Short
Method of operation	Recoil, rotating barrel, hammer-fired, single-action
Safety devices	Manual safety catch left side of frame
Magazine type	Single-column detachable box in butt
Position of catch	Heel of butt
Magazine capacity	8 rounds
Front sight	Fixed blade
Rear sight	Fixed U-notch
Overall length	6.00in (152mm)
Barrel length	3.55in (91mm)
Number of grooves	6
Direction of twist	Right-hand
Empty weight	24oz (700g)
Markings	See text
Serial number	On right side of frame

of wooden ones. The marking was changed to 'Ceska Zbrojovka A.S. v Praze' and engraved on the top rib of the slide. According to Czech records, a version in 9mm Parabellum calibre, fitted for a shoulder stock, was made by them for the Turkish Army, but no specimen of this model is known to exist.

Eventually, this pistol became modified and re-modified and transposed until it became the CZ27, which, during the period 1938–45, was adopted by the German Army as the Pistole Mod. 27(t) and is described elsewhere under that heading.

Pocket Models of 1910, 1914 and 1934

In 1910 the first Pocket Model was introduced in 6.35mm calibre. This is in marked contrast to the Military Model and is a commonplace blowback weapon. It is based, so far as shape and appearance go, on the 1907 patents, but it was considerably modified by Nickl before it appeared on the market. The most notable change was the blowback action, since the 1907 patent had been for a locked breech weapon. It

Above: The three Mauser pocket pistols based on the 1912/14 shape but built as pure blowbacks. Top to bottom: the 7.65mm M1934, with German Navy markings; the 7.65mm M1914; and the 6.35mm M1910.

Above: The Model 1934 pistol, showing the wrap-around wooden butt.

is exceptionally well made and, being somewhat heavier and with a longer barrel than the average 6.35mm weapon, is a much more accurate and reliable proposition than most of its contemporaries in that calibre.

In 1914 the same design was used to produce a similar weapon in 7.65mm calibre, the only differences being in the dimensions to accept the larger cartridge. Finally, in 1934, another improvement was made in the shape of the butt, which was made to fit the hand better. All three models are mechanically identical—indeed, parts from a 1914 will interchange happily with a 1934—but there were a small number of minor changes to special order, such as longer barrels, introduced at various times. Since all the standard models are identical, the following description can be taken as representative of all three.

The pistol consists of three principal units, the barrel, the slide and the frame with an integral butt grip. The magazine is inserted in the butt in the conventional manner and released by a spring catch at the rear edge of the butt. The magazine floor plate of the 1910 and 1914 models has a square front edge, while that of the 1934 model is rounded and carries the

Mauser badge. The weapon is striker-fired, and the striker has an extended tail rod which protrudes through a hole at the rear of the slide when the action is cocked. A hold-open device keeps the slide back when the last round has been fired, and it can only be released by inserting a fresh magazine—full or empty—which then allows the slide to go forward. In addition, a magazine safety device is incorporated to prevent the striker from being released unless there is a magazine in the butt. The remaining features of interest are best examined during the course of dismantling the weapon.

To strip the pistol, after taking the usual precautions pull the slide back until it locks to the rear. At the front of the frame, underneath the muzzle, is a small catch retaining a plate at the front of the barrel locking pin. In the 1910 and 1914 models this is a neat piece of knurled steel, spring-loaded, but in the 1934 model it is simply a folded piece of spring steel—less elegant but equally functional. Pressing in this catch allows the locking pin plate to be rotated through 90° (in either direction) and pulled forward to remove the pin. The barrel can now be lifted straight up and removed from the gun. It will be seen that the barrel is formed with two lugs, one light and near the muzzle and one heavy and at the breech. Both of these are pierced, the front one for the recoil spring guide tube and the rear one for the locking pin. This method secures the barrel quite firmly to the gun frame but allows it to be removed very easily for cleaning.

Having removed the barrel, release the magazine and pull it out about half way. Then push it back in, keeping a restraining grip on the slide. As the magazine goes home, the slide will move forward until stopped by the magazine platform.

Mauser Models 1910, 1914, 1934

Calibre	6.35mm 1910; 7.65mm 1914, 1934
Method of operation	Blowback, striker fired
Safety devices	Manual safety catch front left of butt
Magazine type	Single-column detachable box in butt
Position of catch	Heel of butt
Magazine capacity	9 rounds 1910; 8 rounds 1914, 1934
Front sight	Fixed blade
Rear sight	Adjustable U-notch
Overall length	5.25in (116mm) 1910; 6.0in (152mm) 1914, 1934
Barrel length	3.15in (80mm) 1910; 3.42in (87mm) 1914, 1934
Number of grooves	6
Direction of twist	Right-hand
Empty weight	15.0oz (425g) 1910; 21.0oz (595g) 1914, 1934
Markings	1910, 1914: Right side of slide: 'WAFFENFABRIK MAUSER A.-G. OBERNDORF A.N. MAUSER'S PATENT'; left side of frame: Mauser badge; both grips: 'MW' monogram. 1934: right side of slide: 'MAUSER-WERKE A.G. OBERNDORF A.N.'; left side of slide 'CAL. 7,65 D.R.P. U.A.P.'; left side of frame: Mauser badge
Serial number	On left front of slide and rear of frame; last three digits on front barrel support

Below: The 6.35mm Model 1910, which was gradually enlarged to produce the 7.65mm M1914 and M1934.

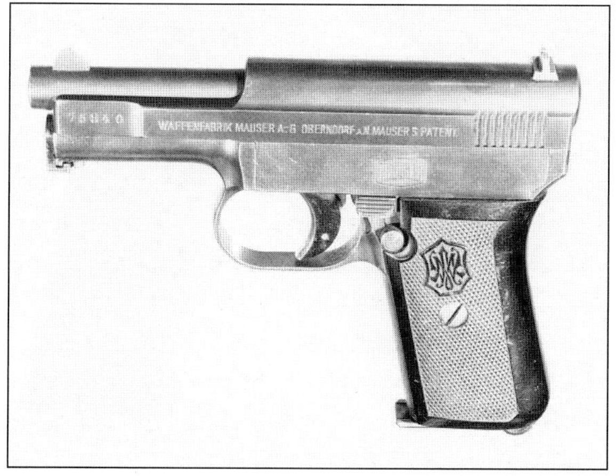

Push the slide back slightly until the interlocking faces of frame and slide, at the rear end of the slide, are matching and pull the trigger to release the striker. Then remove the magazine and allow the slide to go forward, removing it at the front of the frame. The recoil spring and its guide tube can be removed, as can the striker and its spring from their hole in the slide. Then remove the grip screws on each side of the butt and pull the grip straight to the rear; the interior surface is shaped to fit round ribs in the frame, and it can only come off in the one direction. Do not attempt to twist or prise it off with any instrument, or the material will split. If the grip is stiff to move, try tapping the front edges gently with a wooden block. With the grip removed it will be seen how the hand-filling grip is entirely due to the shaping of the woodwork and owes nothing to the shape of the frame. At the top of the left-hand butt frame is a dovetailed plate which conceals the lock mechanism, and this can now be removed by pushing it upwards and sliding it out of the frame. Individual components of the lockwork are now accessible, but it is not recommended that they be removed except for repair.

Below: The Model 1934 stripped, showing the method of retaining the barrel.

WTP

In 1918, as the war ended, Mauser saw the considerable potential that lay in producing a really small pocket pistol; it seemed that everyone else in Germany was doing so, so they might as well join in and produce a quality article. The result was the Westentaschenpistole, or Vest-Pocket Pistol, in 6.35mm calibre. Typically Mauser in that it was a completely original concept and not, as was generally the case in that era, a copy of the Browning 1906 model, it is also completely different from any other Mauser product. It is a simple blowback of small dimensions but, as usual, well made and robust for its class. About 57,000 were produced.

To strip the WTP 1, clear the gun, press the trigger and remove the magazine. Remove the grip screws and slide the entire plastic one-piece grip off to the rear. Now press in the spring catch and pull down the plunger in the base of the trigger guard and accessible from the right side. It travels only about 0.25in, but this is sufficient to unlock the barrel from the frame. Now push the slide forward, and the slide and barrel will come off the front of the frame in one piece. Turn this unit upside down, press the barrel forward and lift its rear end, allowing it to be withdrawn rearwards from the slide together with the recoil spring and guide rod. Press in the firing pin follower with a drift or pencil, and slide the retaining plate down and free of the slide; the striker, spring and follower can be removed. The magazine catch-cum-mainspring can be removed by rotating it through 90° and lifting it from its stud at the rear of the butt frame.

The reason for removing the butt grip first is that the ejector is controlled by the mainspring—this can be seen when the weapon is stripped—but there is not sufficient clearance within the butt moulding to allow this spring to move back far enough to permit the ejector to

Below: The Mauser WTP 1 vest-pocket pistol.

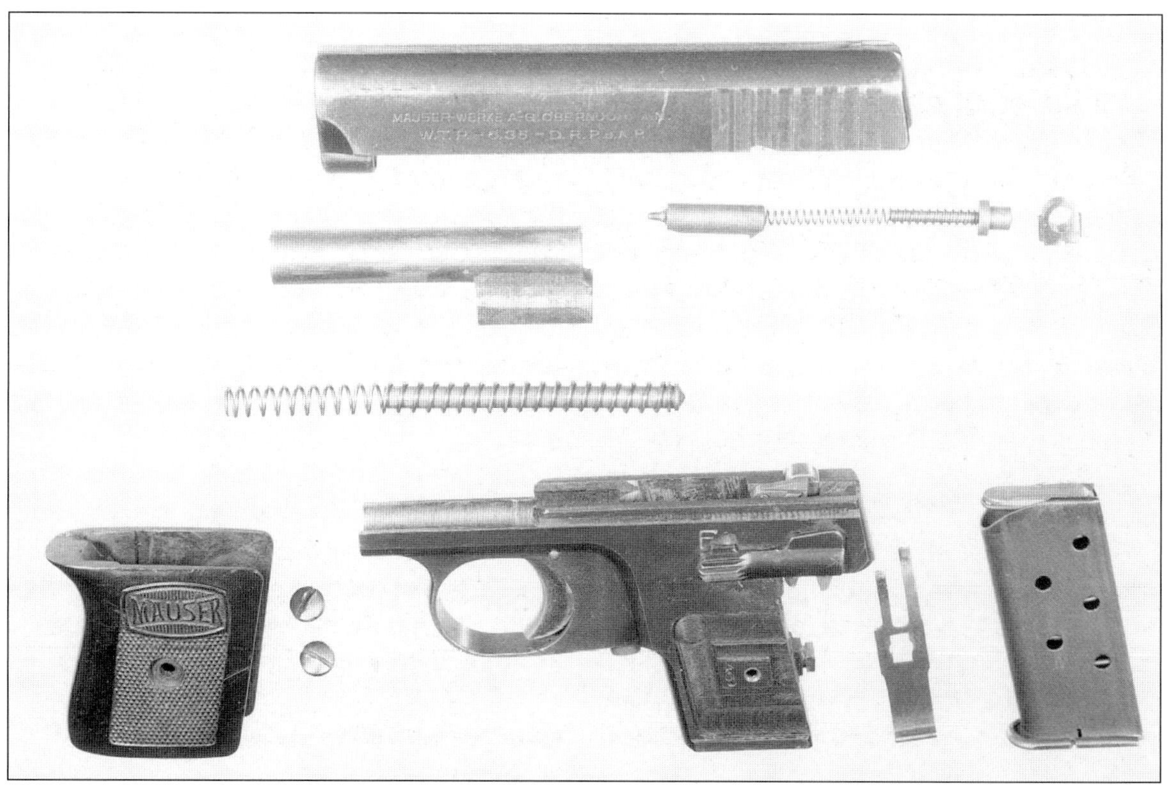

Above: The WTP 1 dismantled.

Mauser Model WTP 1

Calibre	6.35mm Browning
Method of operation	Blowback, striker-fired
Safety devices	Manual safety catch left rear of frame
Magazine type	Single-column detachable box in butt
Position of catch	Heel of butt
Magazine capacity	6 rounds
Front sight	None
Rear sight	Groove in slide top
Overall length	4.50in (114mm)
Barrel length	2.36in (60mm)
Number of grooves	6
Direction of twist	Right-hand
Empty weight	11.5oz (326g)
Markings	Left side of slide: 'MAUSER-WERKE A.G. OBERNDORF A.N. W.T.P. - 6,35 - D.R.P. U.A.P.'; both grips: Mauser badge
Serial number	Full number top left front of slide; last four digits on butt frame, beneath grips; last three digits on barrel below chamber

be depressed below the level of the frame and allow the slide to be slipped off and on during stripping or assembly. One can get the slide off, overcoming the obstruction by force, but putting it back on again is a different matter.

WTP 2

The year 1938 saw the introduction of the Westentaschenpistole 2, an improved version of the previous model. It is smaller and lighter than the Model 1, has a different safety catch, has the tail of the striker thinned down to protrude through the frame to act as a cocking indicator, and is fitted with a magazine safety. The more familiar one-piece butt grip of the Mauser designs has been abandoned in this model in favour of a more conventional two-piece pattern each side of a shaped butt frame. Owing to this the lockwork is slightly changed and there

Mauser Model WTP 2

Calibre	6.35mm Browning
Method of operation	Blowback, striker-fired
Safety devices	Manual safety catch left side of frame
Magazine type	Single-column, detachable box in butt
Position of catch	Heel of butt
Magazine capacity	6 rounds
Front sight	None
Rear sight	Groove in top surface of slide
Overall length	4.00in (102mm)
Barrel length	2.16in (55mm)
Number of grooves	6
Direction of twist	Right-hand
Empty weight	10.5oz (298g)
Markings	Left side of slide: 'Mauser-Werke A.G. Obendorf a.N.' (in cursive script) and Mauser badge; right side of slide: 'W.T.P. - 6.35 - D.R.P.'; Mauser badge on both grips
Serial number	On right rear of slide

Above: The WTP 2 of 1934 was a rather more robust pocket pistol.
Below: The WTP 2 in pieces, showing the different frame and butt construction.

is no longer any need to remove the grips from the frame before starting to strip the gun. Apart from this, stripping is identical with the WTP 1, the same trigger guard plunger locking barrel and frame together. Note also that in this model there is no retaining plate for the striker and

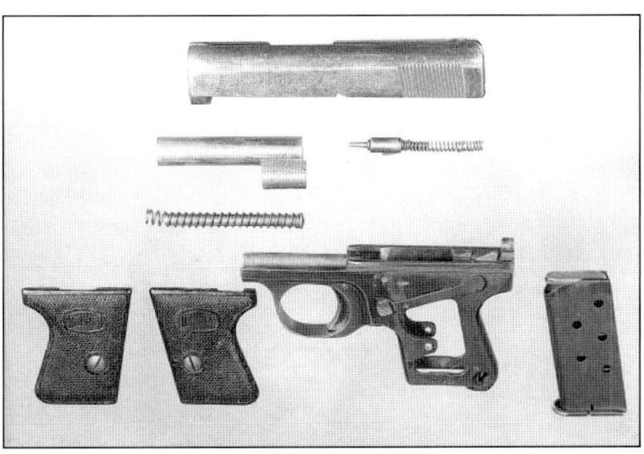

spring: they can be slipped straight out of the slide once it has been removed.

About 17,000 WTP 2s were produced before the demands of war closed the assembly line; sufficient parts were on hand to permit another thousand to be manufactured under French control in 1945–46.

HSc

In 1937 Mauser developed a double-action pistol, possibly to compete with Walther's PP and PPK models. This is the Model HSc, 'HS' standing for 'Hahn Selbstspanne' (Hammer, Self-Cocking) and the 'c' indicating the third development model. Although the weapons were intended as a commercial venture, most

Mauser HSc

Calibre	7.65mm Browning
Method of operation	Blowback, hammer-fired, double-action
Safety devices	Manual safety catch left rear of slide
Magazine type	Single-column detachable box in butt
Position of catch	Heel of butt
Magazine capacity	8 rounds
Front sight	Fixed blade
Rear sight	Fixed V-notch
Overall length	6.00in (152mm)
Barrel length	3.38in (86mm)
Number of grooves	6
Direction of twist	Right-hand
Empty weight	21.0oz (595g)
Markings	Left side of slide: Mauser badge, 'Mauser-Werke A.G. Oberndorf a.N. Mod. HSc Kal. 7,65mm'
Serial number	On front edge of butt; last three digits on barrel and beneath slide (note that post-war 7.65mm pistols have a serial number prefixed '00', while 9mm Short models are prefixed '01')

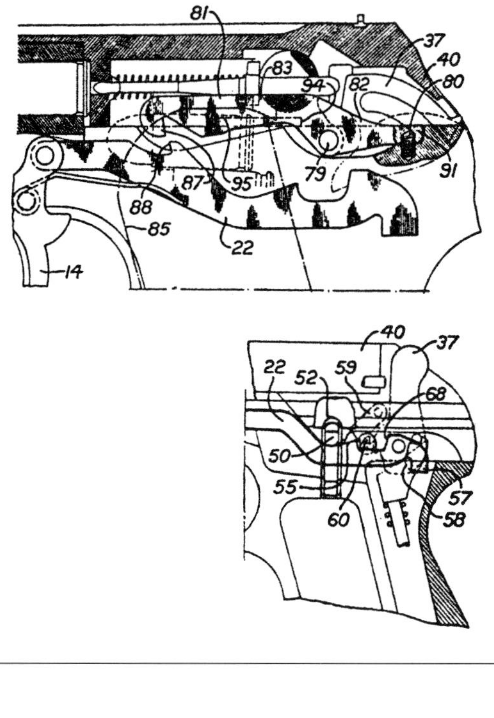

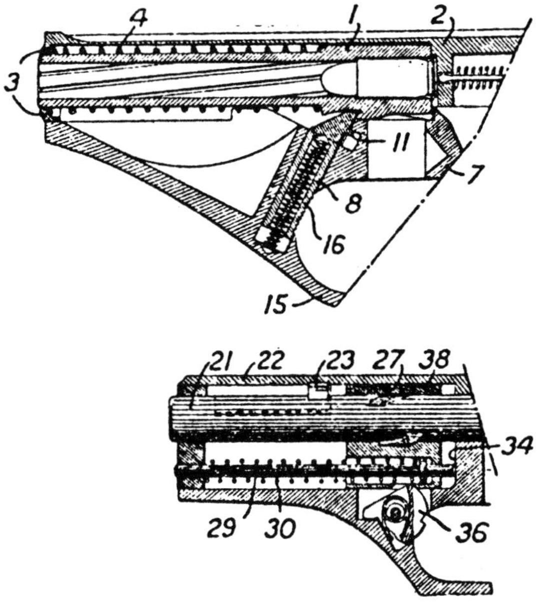

Below left: Patent 461,961, 20 August 1935, Mauserwerke AG. This protects the double-action lock and firing-pin safety system of the Mauser HSc pistol.
Below right: Patent 465,041, 23 October 1935, Mauserwerke AG. This covers the stripping catch used on the Mauser HSc and thus, with the previous patent, fairly covers that weapon. Note that this patent also threw in an alternative method of stripping catch for good measure.

Above: A post-1950 commercial model of the Mauser HSc.

of them were inducted into military service on the outbreak of war in 1939; it appears that the majority of the Mauser 7.65mm pistols employed by the German forces during the war years were used by the Kriegsmarine (Navy) or the Luftwaffe (Air Force) rather than the Army.

The HSc is a most advanced design, and production was resumed after the war and continued until the 1980s (after which the rights were sold to Renato Gamba of Italy and the gun was marketed by them, as the RGP 81, for some years). It has a streamlined appearance and is of first-class material and workmanship throughout. The pitch of the grip and the general fit of the pistol in the hand make it an exceptionally good weapon for instinctive shooting. Most models of this pistol are seen with wooden one-piece grips, but in 1944 moulded plastic grips were adopted in order to simplify production and some of the last of the wartime production show the use of one or two of the smaller components of stamped metal rather than the milled units of the original design. In addition to being made in 7.65mm calibre, very small numbers were made in 0.22in Long Rifle and in 9mm Short. The hammer is largely concealed within the wings of the slide, with a short spur to enable it to be cocked by the thumb. A few of the guns are reputed to have been made completely 'hammerless' in appearance, with the slide totally concealing the hammer. The safety catch on the slide is arranged to move the firing pin bodily out of the path of the hammer when set to 'safe'.

To dismantle the HSc, remove the magazine and clear the gun. Leave the hammer cocked

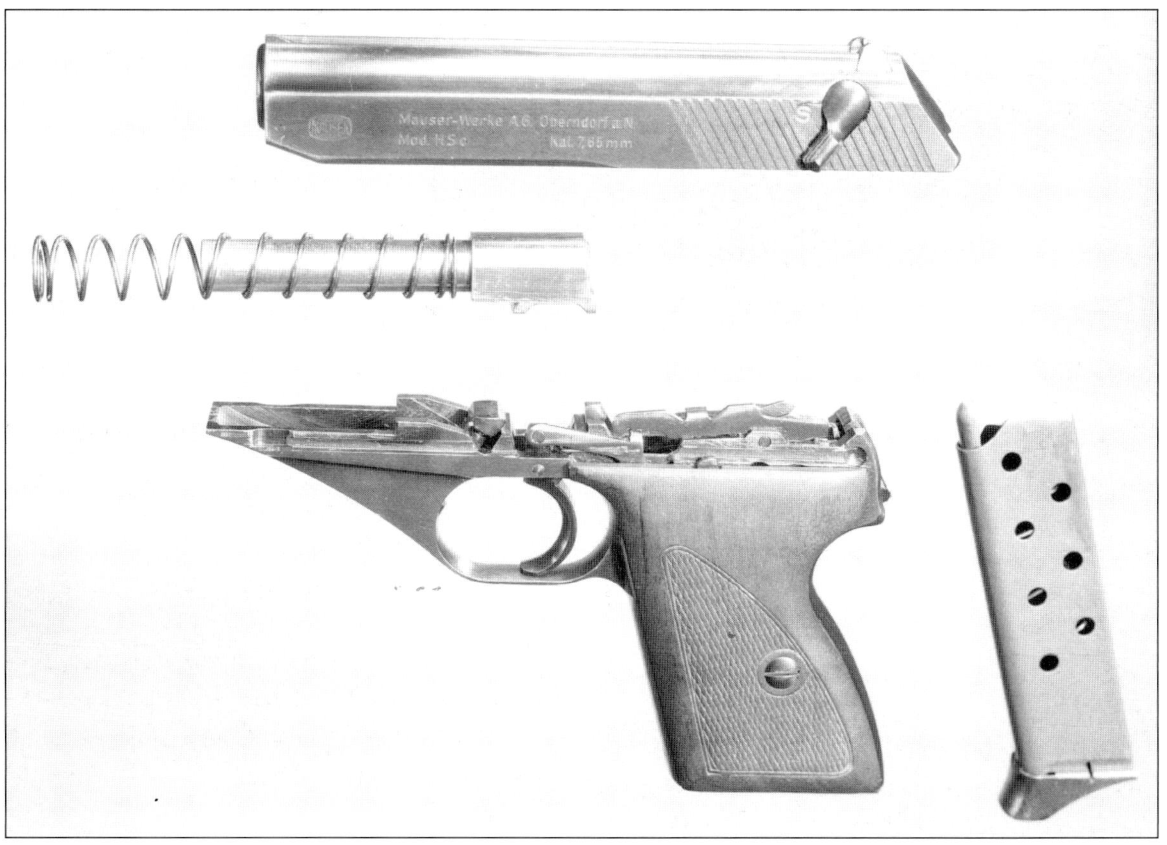

Above: This stripped HSc is a pre-1939 model: it is mechanically the same but has a different finish and different markings.

and set the safety catch to 'safe'. Then press in the stud or catch in the front edge of the trigger guard and pull the slide back and up to clear the frame rails. Once free, the slide can then be slipped forward over the barrel and removed. The recoil spring can then be slipped from the barrel; removing the usual screws allows the grip to be removed to the rear of the frame to give access to the lockwork. Reassembly is simply the reverse process.

Approximately 251,000 HSc pistols were made between their introduction in 1940 and the end of the war in 1945. Immediately after the war a further 16,000 were assembled under French control.

HsP

In the latter 1970s the German Federal Police published a stringent specification for an automatic pistol, which, among many other things, demanded that it should be possible to carry the weapon in a perfectly safe condition but draw it and fire it without any unnecessary manipulation of safety devices, cocking levers or anything other than the trigger. Mauser's entry in this contest was the HsP (for 'Hahn sicherung Polizei'—'Hammer Safety, Police'). A recoil-operated double-action pistol, it relied upon a swinging wedge beneath the barrel to lock the breech, which was unlocked by a cam track in the frame. A combined safety catch and de-cocking lever was fitted into the left grip, and there was a dismantling latch similar to that of the Parabellum pistol on the front left side of the frame.

Above: The HsP was virtually a Mauser HSc but with a locked breech and chambering 9mm Parabellum ammunition. Designed to meet a Federal Police specification, it was not selected for further development.

In the event, the Police expressed a preference for the competing Heckler & Koch design (which became the P7) and Mauser therefore abandoned the project. It is doubtful if more than a handful of HsP pistols were made.

Mauser Model HsP

Calibre	9 × 19mm Parabellum
Method of operation	Recoil, wedge-locking, double-action, hammer-fired
Safety devices	Manual safety, de-cocking lever left side of butt
Magazine type	Single-column detachable box in butt
Position of catch	Front left side of butt
Magazine capacity	8 rounds
Front sight	Fixed blade
Rear sight	Fixed U-notch
Overall length	6.50in (165mm)
Barrel length	3.30in (85mm)
Number of grooves	4
Direction of twist	Right-hand
Empty weight	26.5oz (750g)
Markings	Right side of slide: 'Mauser-Werke Oberndorf GmbH'; left side of slide: 'Modell HSP 9mm Para'
Serial number	On right side of frame above trigger

Models 80 and 90

These pistols, the first of which (the M80.SA) appeared in 1992, are actually made by Fegyver es Gazkeszuelekgyara NV of Budapest, Hungary, and are supplied to Mauser 'in the white' for Mauser to put their markings on and finished to their usual high standard of colour and polish.

The pistol, as might be guessed from the illustration, is simply a copy of the FN-Browning Mle 1935 High-Power and had been manufactured in Hungary as the FEG Model P9R since the early 1980s. It is a straightforward single-action, recoil-operated pistol, using the Browning dropping barrel method of locking the breech by means of lugs engaging in the slide.

Dismantling follows the usual Browning procedure. After removing the magazine and clearing the gun, pull the slide to the rear and lock it there by turning up the safety catch into the front notch on the slide. Now pivot the slide stop lever upwards, press the stub end of the pin which protrudes on the right side of the frame and draw out the slide stop pin to the

Below: The Mauser 80.SA is simply the FEG (Hungary) copy of the Browning High-Power, delivered to Mauser 'in the white' and finished to Mauser standards with Mauser markings.

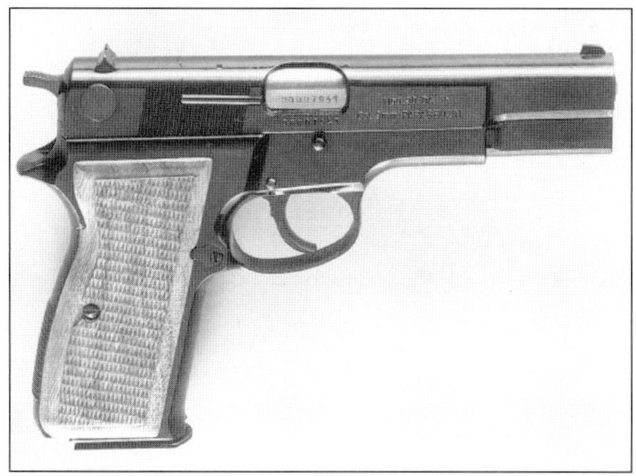

Left, upper: The 90.DA is the double-action version of the 80.SA . . .
Left, lower: . . . and the Compact DA is a shortened version of the 90.DA.

left. Hold the slide securely and press down the safety catch; this will allow the slide to come forward and be removed from the frame complete with barrel and return spring. Invert the slide and remove the spring and barrel. No further dismantling is necessary or advisable. Reassembly is simply a reversal of the stripping procedure.

The M80.SA was followed in the early 1990s by the M90.DA, which was the same pistol but with a double-action lock and a somewhat modified contour to the trigger-guard; and then by the M90.DA Compact, a smaller version of the double-action model. Operation and stripping of these two are exactly the same as for the basic M80.SA model, except for the addition of a safety/de-cocking lever on the left rear of the slide. When applied, this locks the firing pin and lowers the hammer, so that the pistol can be carried safely with a round in the chamber and fired simply by pulling through on the trigger to raise and drop the hammer.

.38 Revolver

Introduced in 1980, this was the Italian 'Trident' revolver made by Renato Gamba and marketed under the Mauser name in a reciprocal agreement whereby Gamba made and mar-

Mauser 80.SA, 9.0DA, 90.DAC

Calibre	9 × 19mm Parabellum
Method of operation	Recoil, Browning dropping barrel, hammer-fired
Safety devices	80.SA: catch of frame; 90.DA, 90.DAC: de-cocking lever on slide
Magazine type	Double-column detachable box in butt
Position of catch	Front edge of butt
Magazine capacity	14 rounds 80.SA, 90.DA; 13 rounds 90.DAC
Front sight	Fixed blade
Rear sight	Fixed U-notch
Overall length	8.00in (203mm) 80.SA, 90.DA; 7.40in(188mm) 90.DAC
Barrel length	4.64in (118mm) 80.SA, 90.DA; 4.13in (105mm) 90.DAC
Number of grooves	6
Direction of twist	Right-hand
Empty weight	31.7oz (900g) 80.SA; 35.2oz (1,000g) 90.DA; 33.5oz (950g) 90.DAC
Markings	Right side of slide, all models: 'MAUSER Model 80.SA [or DA or Compact DA] CAL 9mm PARABELLUM'
Serial number	On right side of slide; on barrel, visible through ejection port

Mauser Trident 38SP

Calibre	.38 Special
Method of operation	Double-action revolver
Safety devices	None, but available as an optional extra
Magazine type	6-shot cylinder
Position of catch	Left side of frame, on recoil shield
Front sight	Fixed blade
Rear sight	Fixed U-notch
Overall length	6.89in (175mm)
Barrel length	2.50in (63.5mm)
Number of grooves	6
Direction of twist	Right-hand
Empty weight	23.2oz (660g)
Markings	On left side of barrel: 'CALIBER 38SP'; on right side of barrel: 'MAUSER'
Serial number	At bottom of pistol grip frame

keted the HSc pistol under licence (as described above).

The revolver was a conventional solid-frame, side-opening model, based upon Colt practice (the cylinder was released by pulling back on the thumb-catch on the left side of the frame) with a six-chambered cylinder and short barrel. The front sight was mounted on a prominent ramp which extended for the full length of the barrel, falling to meet the barrel/frame junction. It was chambered for the .38 Special cartridge, and it was hoped that it would find a market 'as an ideal companion for every Mauser

Below: Not many people know that Mauser marketed this .38 Special revolver in the 1970s. It was part of a deal whereby Renato Gamba sold the HSc in Italy and Mauser sold the Gamba revolver in Germany.

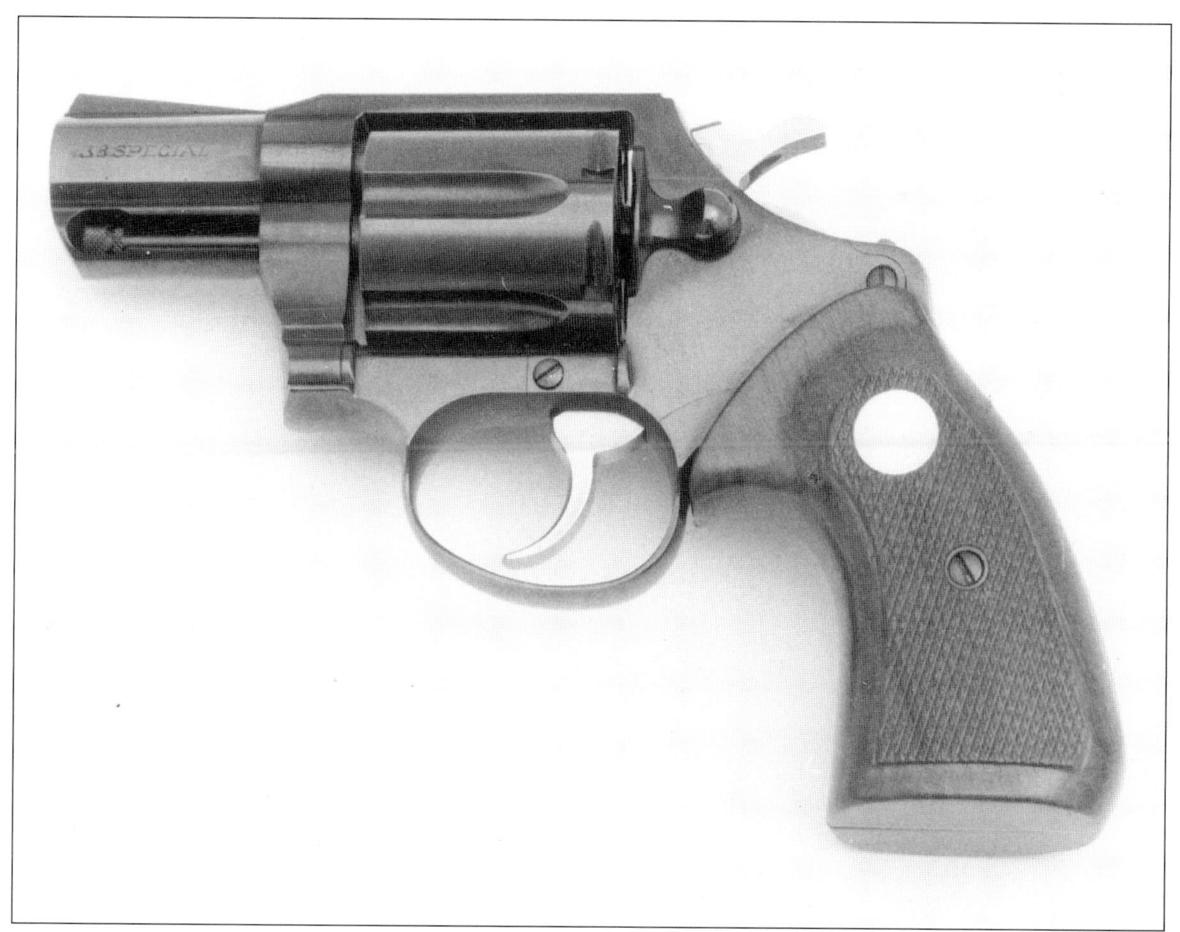

rifle', but European hunters are less likely to carry a revolver than are American hunters, and sales were not good. Renato Gamba got into difficulties in 1984, and the revolver was withdrawn from the Mauser list in 1985.

Parabellum Pistols

As related in the entry on the Parabellum pistol, Mauser obtained the DWM production machinery and took over the manufacture of Parabellum pistols in 1934, becoming the principal contractor until the pistol went out of production ten years later.

The Parabellum pistol will always carry an aura of glamour, and in the late 1970s, as a result of insistent demands from the United States, Mauser decided to return to the Parabellum and make it as a 'collector's item'; they could do this because they were able to obtain the production machinery originally used by the Swiss for their version of the Parabellum. The design was therefore based upon the Swiss 06/29, and the first example to appear was known as the Model 29/70. This was replaced by the Model 06/73, with a grip shaped in the German manner rather than in the Swiss. Later came the Mauser-Parabellum-Sport with a heavy barrel, sometimes a slab-sided barrel, and a fully adjustable back sight.

The final venture was a series of 'commemorative' models, with markings based upon the original Bulgarian, Swiss, Russian or German Navy models. All these pistols were extremely well finished, many being engraved and inscribed to order, and were expensive products

Below: Having acquired the original machine tools from the Swiss, Mauser put the Swiss Parabellum pistol back into production as the Mauser-Parabellum 29/70. Made to a superlative standard of fit and finish, it was aimed squarely at the collectors' market.

Mauser-Parabellum 29/70	
Calibre	7.65mm or 9mm Parabellum
Method of operation	Recoil, toggle-locked, single-action
Safety devices	Manual safety catch left rear of frame
Magazine type	Single-column detachable box in butt
Position of catch	Left side of butt behind trigger
Magazine capacity	8 rounds
Front sight	Fixed blade
Rear sight	Fixed V-notch
Overall length	8.46in (215mm)
Barrel length	3.00in (100mm)
Number of grooves	4 or 6
Direction of twist	Right-hand
Empty weight	32.0oz (907g)
Markings	Mauser badge on front toggle; commemorative models had markings replicating the original, e.g. 'DWM' monogram, Swiss cross, Bulgarian lion
Serial number	On right side of frame

aimed squarely at the collectors' market. Once that appeared to have been satisfied, in the middle 1980s, Mauser closed down the line, and it is unlikely that the Parabellum will ever reappear.

Below: Mauser also produced a limited number of 'commemorative' Parabellum models. The example featured here celebrated seventy-five years of the Parabellum in 1975.

MAYER

Mayer & Söhne, Neheim-Hüsten and Arnsberg

This company—which was originally in Hüsten but then moved to Arnsberg in the early 1980s—manufactures a variety of blank and starting pistols but also makes what is perhaps the last hinged-frame revolver in Europe. Sometimes sold under the tradename Perfecta, this is an inexpensive pistol, largely manufactured from light alloy, and chambered for the .22 Long Rifle or .32 S&W Long cartridge. The frame and barrel are hinged together, with a cam operating the usual sort of collective ejector in the centre of the cylinder. Locking is done by a square catch, hinged to the top strap so that it snaps down over the standing breech and is retained by a spring clip. There are knurled buttons on each side to offer a good grip to lift the catch and open the pistol.

With the pistol opened, withdrawal of a screw in the top strap allows the removal of a catch which holds the cylinder in place, and the cylinder itself can then be removed. Removal of

Mayer Model 22 and Model 32	
Calibre	.22 LR rimfire or .32 S&W Long centrefire
Method of operation	Revolver, double-action
Safety devices	None
Magazine type	Revolving cylinder
Position of catch	Top strap
Magazine capacity	6 (.22) or 5 (.32) rounds
Front sight	Fixed blade
Rear sight	Fixed U-notch
Overall length	7.68in (195mm)
Barrel length	3.00in (76mm); 2, 4 and 5in barrels also available
Number of grooves	6
Direction of twist	Right-hand
Empty weight	20.7oz (585g)
Markings	Left side of barrel: 'MAYER & SÖHNE'
Serial number	On frame beneath cylinder

Above: A representative Mayer .32 S&W revolver.

the grips, by means of the usual central screw, reveals screws which retain the left side cover plate; with this removed there is full access to the simple lockwork.

MENZ

Waffenfabrik August Menz, Suhl

August Menz came into the pistol business by way of a contract to manufacture the Beholla (q.v.) pistol for the German Army in 1916–18, producing it under the name Menta. When the war ended he retained the machinery and continued to make the pistol for commercial sale, and also produced a scaled-down version in 6.35mm calibre. From this beginning he went on to produce a number of pistols of his own design, for sale by his own firm and through dealers until he was bought out by the AG Lignose in 1937.

Menta

The 7.65mm version of the Menta was exactly the same as the Beholla, and the description and data given in that entry should be referred to. The 6.35mm Menta was unique to Menz and was produced for a short time in the early 1920s. It is exactly the same as the 7.65mm model as far as construction and appearance go, differing only in dimensions.

VP 6.35mm

This 6.35mm Vestpocket model was made in small numbers and is rarely seen today. It appears to have taken the Menta as its starting point and added a few improvements. The firing pin acts as a cocked indicator, protruding

Menz Menta	
Calibre	6.35mm Browning
Method of operation	Blowback, single-action, striker-fired
Safety devices	Manual safety catch left side of frame
Magazine type	Single-column detachable box in butt
Position of catch	Heel of butt
Magazine capacity	6 rounds
Front sight	Fixed blade
Rear sight	Fixed V-notch
Overall length	4.65in (118mm)
Barrel length	2.48in (63mm)
Number of grooves	6
Direction of twist	Right-hand
Empty weight	13.5oz (384g)
Markings	Left of slide: 'MENTA KAL. 6.35'
Serial number	On left side of frame

Menz VP	
Calibre	6.35mm Browning
Method of operation	Blowback, striker-fired
Safety devices	Manual catch on left rear of frame
Magazine type	Single-column detachable box in butt
Position of catch	Bottom rear of butt
Magazine capacity	6 rounds
Front sight	Fixed blade
Rear sight	Fixed V-notch
Overall length	4.65in (118mm)
Barrel length	2.35in (60mm)
Number of grooves	6
Direction of twist	Right-hand
Empty weight	15.0oz (425g)
Markings	On left of slide: 'MENZ 6,35'
Serial number	On front edge of butt

Above: A Menz Liliput pistol in 6.35mm calibre.

through the rear of the slide; the barrel is retained by a pin passing through the frame *below* the slide; and the barrel has a secondary anchor in the recoil spring guide rod which protrudes from the front of the frame and has a groove around the end to allow it to be gripped and pulled out to free the barrel. Another change is that the top of the slide is perfectly flat and does not rise at the rear as it does on the Beholla/Menta.

Liliput

The Liliput models are of much greater interest. Menz's original development in this pattern was in 1920 when he produced a pistol in the little-known calibre of 4.25mm. Just what possessed him to do this is unknown; the cartridge had been developed in pre-war years by an Austrian company for a 'lady's garter' gun called the Erika, and was more in the nature of an irritant than a lethal device—although of course it could inflict serious injury if it struck a vital organ. The 1920 model Liliput was a tiny blowback pistol only 3.5in long and carrying six rounds in the magazine. Since the ammunition was scarce and not to be found in many places other than the principal cities, Menz was smart enough to cut his losses by redesigning the pistol to take the standard 6.35mm cartridge. This became the 1925 Model and is identical with the 1920 except for larger dimensions. Generally speaking these pistols do not wear well, the material being soft and the fitting less than precise; every one I have seen displays dangerous slop in the fit of the slide to the frame and I have never found one in a condition which I would consider fit to fire. There may be exceptions to this, but on the whole the Liliput should be considered as a 'collection for looking at' pistol rather than a 'collection for shooting' one.

Stripping the Liliput, like so many other things, is simple once one knows the trick. Indeed, given half a chance it will fall to pieces in the hand if given a violent blow, but this fails to reveal the correct system of disassembly. It will be seen on examination that the rear end of the frame terminates in an upstanding portion which engages in the slide and has a bifurcated metal block around it. This block, the firing pin spring anchorage, also serves to hold the whole pistol together. After clearing the gun and removing the magazine, push this bifurcated block in with a thin screwdriver for about 0.25in (6mm). Then pull the slide back and up and the rear end will come free from the frame. The slide can then be pushed forward to be removed completely. It is now revealed that the barrel and frame are a one-piece forging, with simple lockwork inletted; the latter assembly may be observed by removing the left-hand butt grip after undoing the usual screw.

Menz Liliput 1925

Calibre	6.35mm Browning
Method of operation	Blowback, striker-fired
Safety devices	Manual catch at left rear of frame
Magazine type	Single-column detachable box in butt
Position of catch	Bottom rear of butt
Magazine capacity	6 rounds
Front sight	Fixed blade
Rear sight	Groove in slide top
Overall length	4.00in (102mm)
Barrel length	2.00in (51mm)
Number of grooves	6
Direction of twist	Right-hand
Empty weight	10.0oz (284g)
Markings	Left side of slide '"LILIPUT" KAL. 6,35 Model 1925'; left grip: gold medallion, a wreath surrounding an allegorical head; right grip: '6,35' surrounded by a gold wreath
Serial number	On left front of trigger guard

Below: The Menz Liliput dismantled.

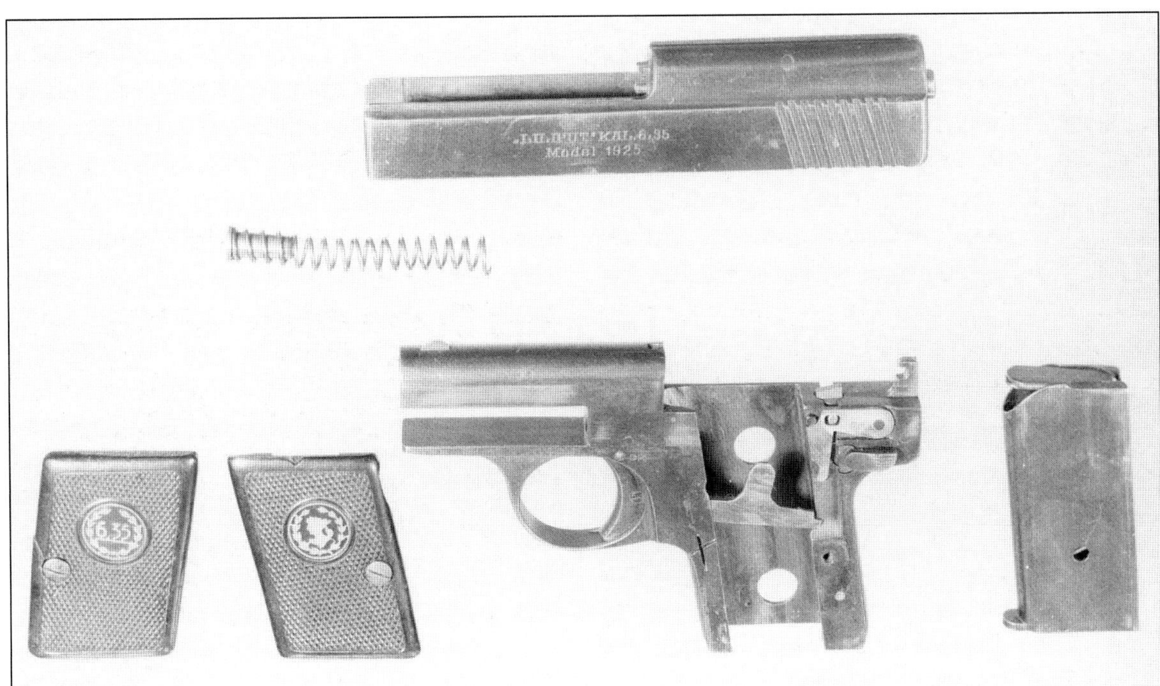

Menz Model 2

Calibre	7.65mm Browning
Method of operation	Blowback, striker-fired
Safety devices	Manual catch at left rear of frame
Magazine type	Single-column detachable box in butt
Position of catch	Bottom rear of butt
Magazine capacity	6 rounds
Front sight	Fixed blade
Rear sight	Groove in slide top
Overall length	5.12in (130mm)
Barrel length	2.67in (68mm)
Number of grooves	6
Direction of twist	Right-hand
Empty weight	15.34oz (435g)
Markings	Left side of slide: 'MENZ Kal. 7,65 Modell II'; both grips: gold medallion, a wreath surrounding either a monogram 'AM' or the figures '7,65'
Serial number	On left front of trigger guard

Reassembly is simply a reversal of the above procedure: engage the slide with the recoil spring rod, draw it back and down until it is almost engaged with the upstanding locking bar, then press in the firing spring housing and lower the slide into engagement. Note that the firing pin housing must be treated with care and not burred or damaged in any way, since the free movement of this component in its housing in the slide is vital to the correct assembly of the pistol. Should it fail to engage properly, the first round fired will either force it into proper engagement or disengage it completely; one is consoled by the thought that, owing to the design, it is impossible for the slide to come off backwards.

For all its defects, the Liliput was no doubt a serviceable enough pocket pistol when it was new, and it appears to have been sold through a variety of outlets under different names: the Bijou, Kaba, Kaba Spezial and Okzet were all the 6.35mm Liliput in disguise.

Model 2

This is simply a Liliput in 7.65mm calibre, and, apart from a slight difference in the cutting of the finger grips on the slide, the early 7.65mm models are identical but for size. However, after about serial number 500, the front end of the frame and slide were tapered—an effect rather similar to the front end of the Browning 1910 model.

Operation and dismantling are exactly the same as for the smaller weapon.

P&B Model 3

This was a very different design from anything that Menz had done before, and it was also of considerably better quality that the Liliput designs. The term 'P&B' stands for 'Polizei und Behorden', or 'Police and Authority', indicating the market that Menz was attempting to enter. The Model 3 was a fixed-barrel blowback with the return spring wrapped around the barrel in Browning 1910 style, a well-raked butt and an external hammer, and, in general, suggests that he was competing against the contemporary Walther PP and PPK. There was a prominent collar, retaining the return spring, around the muzzle, and the front edge of the grip was shaped into a 'toe' at the bottom of

Below: A Menz Polizei und Behorden Model 3 pistol.

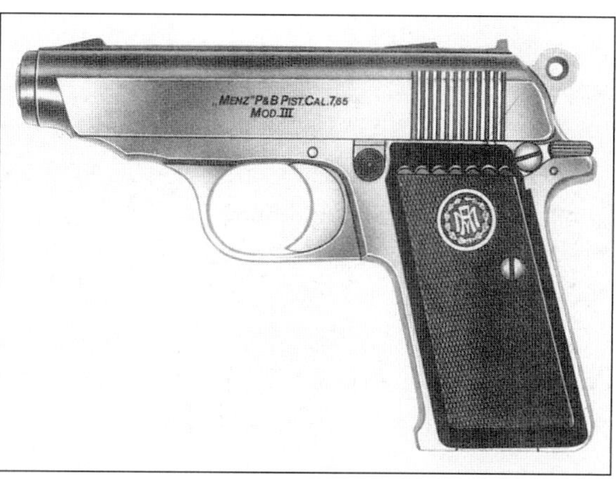

Menz P&B Model 3

Calibre	7.65mm Browning
Method of operation	Blowback, single-action, external hammer-fired
Safety devices	Manual safety catch left rear of frame, behind grip
Magazine type	Single-column detachable box in butt
Position of catch	Push-button left of frame behind trigger
Magazine capacity	8 rounds
Front sight	Fixed blade
Rear sight	Fixed U-notch
Overall length	6.18in (157mm)
Barrel length	3.48in (88,5mm)
Number of grooves	6
Direction of twist	Right-hand
Empty weight	24.7oz (700g)
Markings	Left side of slide: '"MENZ" P&B PIST. CAL. 7,65 MOD. III'; both grips: gold medallion with wreath surrounding monogram 'AM'
Serial number	On left side of frame

the butt so as to improve the grip. Dismantling is simply a matter of pressing in, turning a half-turn and removing the collar from around the muzzle so as to release the spring tension, then pulling the slide back and lifting the rear end so as to pass it forward over the barrel.

P&B Model 3A

Information about this model is conflicting, and this seems to be because it was produced in very small numbers with various changes in details. Broadly it was the same as the Model 3 but without the external hammer and using a striker, but versions with the trigger at the rear of the trigger-guard aperture or with the trigger in the centre of the aperture, and with varying numbers of finger-grip grooves on the slide, have been mentioned by various authorities.

It seems fairly certain that the Model 3 and Model 3A were by way of being development models en route to the final P&B Special, described below. They do not appear to have been sold in large numbers and are relatively uncommon today.

The basic dimensions of the Model 3A can be taken as being the same as those of the Model 3.

P&B Special

This was the final product in the Menz line, and by this time he had perfected his design and brought it very close to that of the Walther PP—probably as close as he could get without treading on Walther's patent rights. The exact date is in some doubt but it was probably in 1936, since the number manufactured before Menz ceased operations in 1937 was no more than about 3,500

The P&B Special was broadly the same as the earlier Model 3 in that it was a fixed-barrel blowback with the return spring around the barrel, but it was a considerable advance on the Model 3 in its details. The muzzle collar re-

Menz P&B Special

Calibre	7.65mm Browning
Method of operation	Blowback, double-action, hammer-fired
Safety devices	Manual safety catch on top left of slide
Magazine type	Single-column detchable box in butt
Position of catch	Heel of butt
Magazine capacity	8 rounds
Front sight	Fixed blade
Rear sight	Fixed U-notch
Overall length	6.22in (158mm)
Barrel length	3.35in (85mm)
Number of grooves	6
Direction of twist	Right-hand
Empty weight	26.2oz (745g)
Markings	Left of slide: 'AUGUST MENZ WAFFENFABRIK SUHL PB SPEZIAL KAL. 7,65'; both grips: gold medallion bearing wreath surrounding 'AM' monogram
Serial number	On right side of frame

taining the spring was dropped, and the method of slide removal was similar to that of the Walther—by pulling down the front end of the trigger guard. There was an external hammer and double-action lockwork, and the safety catch was on the slide, not a rotating lever like the Walther but a vertically sliding catch on the left side of the slide just in front of the rearsight. The pistol was available as a 7.65mm weapon, or it could be bought complete with a conversion kit with two replacement barrels, one in 9mm Browning Short and the other in 4mm Geco chambering for target practice.

To dismantle the P&B Special, after removing the magazine and clearing the gun pull back the slide until a catch on the left side of the frame can be engaged with a notch in the underside of the frame edge. Now squeeze the serrated catch on the front of the trigger guard and unlock it from the frame, pivoting it down about its rear end. Note that this differs from the Walther pattern in not being sprung and thus requiring a positive catch to hold it in the frame. Once this is free, the slide can be pulled further back, lifted and passed forward over the barrel and removed. The spring around the barrel can now be removed. The barrel is screwed into a lump on the frame, but is only removed in order to change calibres.

Reassembly is the reverse; the only point to watch is that when the slide is pulled back on to the frame, lowered and run forward it can be held by the catch. The trigger guard is then pushed back up into engagement with the frame and the slide must then be pulled back slightly to allow the catch to be pressed with a finger so as to permit the slide to run forward.

In 1937 the AG Lignose-Berlin company acquired the Menz business and operated it until some time during the 1939–45 war under the name Th. Bergmanns Erben GmbH (i.e. the 'heirs of Theodor Bergmann') and continued the manufacture of Menz and other pistols. For details see the entry under Bergmann Erben.

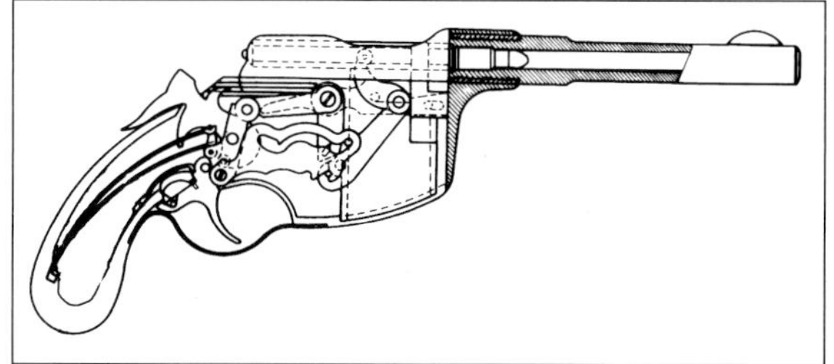

Above: Patent drawing of the Mieg semi-automatic pistol, modified from his earlier mechanical repeater. Neither weapon, so far as can be discovered, got beyond the drawing board.

MIEG

Armand Mieg, Heidelberg, Germany

Mieg was the patentee (in 1890) of a complicated mechanical repeating pistol which used the usual system of finger-operated levers to operate a turnbolt mechanism. This was predicated for a 6.65mm bottle-necked cartridge identified by documents as DWM No 396, but it seems unlikely that the pistols ever went beyond the prototype stage. In 1893 a fresh patent modified the design into a delayed blowback automatic, still using a reciprocating bolt and relying upon a system of levers for its delay operation, broadly similar to the better-known Austrian Schönberger pistol. It used an 8mm bottle-necked round, DWM No 372, but this, too, got no further than a few hand-made models, and no specimen is known to exist today.

NORDHEIM

Gotthilf von Nordheim, Zella Mehlis, Germany

The Nordheim was a 7.65mm blowback automatic which appears to have been manufactured for a brief period immediately before the out-

Nordheim	
Calibre	7.65mm Browning
Method of operation	Blowback, striker-fired
Safety devices	Manual safety catch left rear of frame
Magazine type	Single-column detachable box in butt
Position of catch	Rear edge of butt
Magazine capacity	7 rounds
Front sight	Fixed blade
Rear sight	Fixed U-notch
Overall length	6.14in (156mm)
Barrel length	3.62in (92mm)
Number of grooves	6
Direction of twist	Right-hand
Empty weight	21.0oz (595g)
Markings	Left of slide: 'DEUTSCHE SELBSTLADE-PISTOLE CAL. 7,65 ZUM PATENT ANGEM.'
Serial number	On left side of frame

break of war in 1914. It was, fairly obviously, inspired by the Browning 1910 design insofar as the recoil spring was wrapped around the fixed barrel and retained by a screwed-in bush at the muzzle. The bush, though, is ribbed and quite large, extending some distance in front of the slide, and the barrel protrudes through it for a further 10mm or so. The slide is rather more severely rectangular than that of the Browning, though it merges into a cylindrical form to receive the screwed bush. The quality of finish is also rather inferior to that of the Browning.

Below: This square-looking pistol is the 7.65mm Nordheim, and, irrespective of its appearance, it is pure Browning 1910 under the skin.

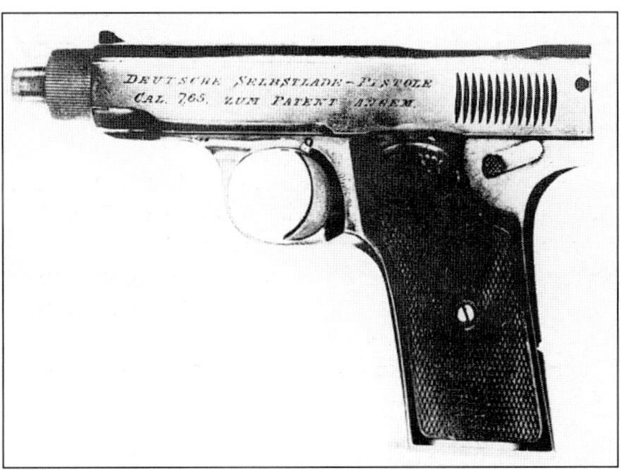

Dismantling is accomplished in the same manner as for the Browning 1910. After clearing the gun, carefully unscrew the muzzle bush to release the pressure on the return spring, draw back the slide to its maximum point, lift, and slip forward over the barrel to remove slide and spring. The grips can be removed by means of the usual screws, revealing the simple lockwork. The striker is held in position by a cap which is retained by a pin driven through the rear of the slide; removal is not recommended except to replace either striker or spring in the event of breakage.

ORTGIES

Ortgies & Co., Erfurt
Deutsche Werke AG, Berlin

Heinrich Ortgies was a German who lived in Liège for several years and there designed an automatic pistol which he patented in 1918. He then returned to Germany, set up a factory in Erfurt and began making the Ortgies pistol in 7.65mm calibre. Within a few months, however, Herr Ortgies died and the company (Ortgies & Co) was taken over by Deutsche Werke AG, a Berlin company which had previously shown no interest in firearms. They continued to operate the Erfurt factory with considerable success, so much so that they eventually transferred their headquarters from Berlin to Erfurt.

At that time only the 7.65mm Ortgies pistol had been made and sold, though Ortgies had prepared designs for 6.35mm and 9mm Short models. Under Deutsche Werke, all three calibres were put into production by 1922, the 6.35mm first. While this model is identical, except for size, to the 7.65mm model, the 9mm model sometimes exhibits minor variations. Some examples, in both 7.65mm and 9mm, can be found with a manual safety catch on the left side of the frame at the top centre of the butt grip; another variation is the use of screws to hold the grip plates instead of the Ortgies 'invisible' attachment originally used. It has been estimated—basing the estimation upon known serial numbers—that some 250,000 Ortgies pistols were manufactured before production ended in 1929, though manufacture of the 9mm model, which was apparently less popular, is said to have stopped in about 1925.

The Ortgies pistols are well-made weapons of exceptionally neat and tidy appearance and were widely exported in the 1920s and 1930s, notably to the United States. All three calibres—6.35mm, 7.65mm and 9mm Short/0.380in—are identical in appearance except for their differing sizes. The design is that of a fairly normal blowback weapon but has three patented features—the barrel mounting, the method of attaching the grips, and the disconnector (or method of ensuring that only one shot is fired at a time). These features were patented at various dates in 1916 and 1918 by Ortgies and do not appear to have been adopted by any other manufacturer. They can best be explored and described in the process of stripping the weapon.

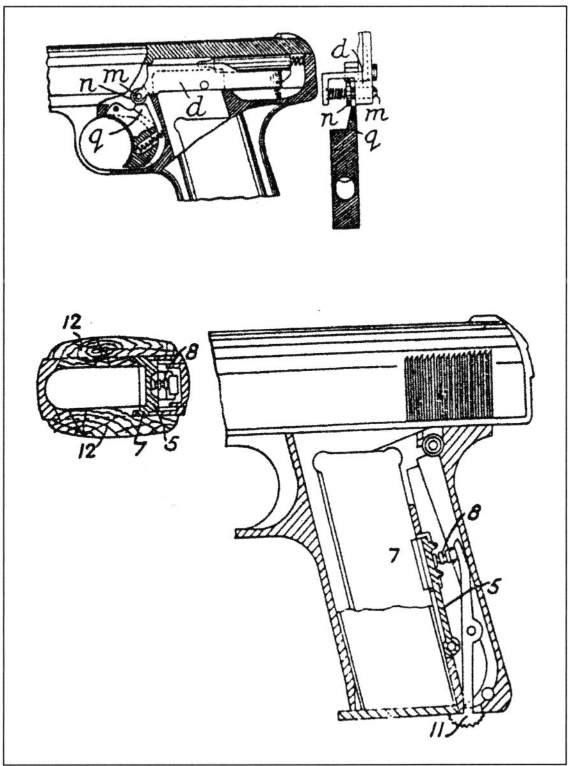

The Ortgies is renowned for being one of the 'puzzle' guns: encountered for the first time, it can be examined for quite a while without giving any hint of where to start on the process of dismantling. After clearing the gun, press in the button at the top rear of the left butt grip (in the case of some 7.65mm and 9mm models, the rearmost of the two buttons). This operates a latch under the slide which engages in a groove to hold the slide in place on the frame. With the button depressed the slide can be pulled back a short distance, lifted straight upwards and finally eased forward to slide the recoil spring off the barrel. The striker, spring and follower pin can be slipped from their groove in the breech block section of the slide.

Grasp the frame in the right hand, holding the butt in the usual way. Then grip the barrel and twist it about its mounting stud, moving the muzzle to the left of the frame. It will swing round through 90°, unlocking a form of bayonet catch which holds it to the frame, and can then be lifted clear. Just below the barrel mounting point, a hole in the frame allows a spring-

Left: Patents 146,422, 3 July 1916; 146,423, 18 June 1918; and 146,424, 20 September 1918—Heinrich Ortgies. These three patents had originally been granted in Germany during the war years, and they were therefore granted their original dates when submitted to the British and US Patent Offices after the war—which accounts for three consecutive numbers having dates well apart. These three patents cover all the unique features of the Ortgies pistols, notably the method of attaching the barrel, the disconnector and the grip retention.

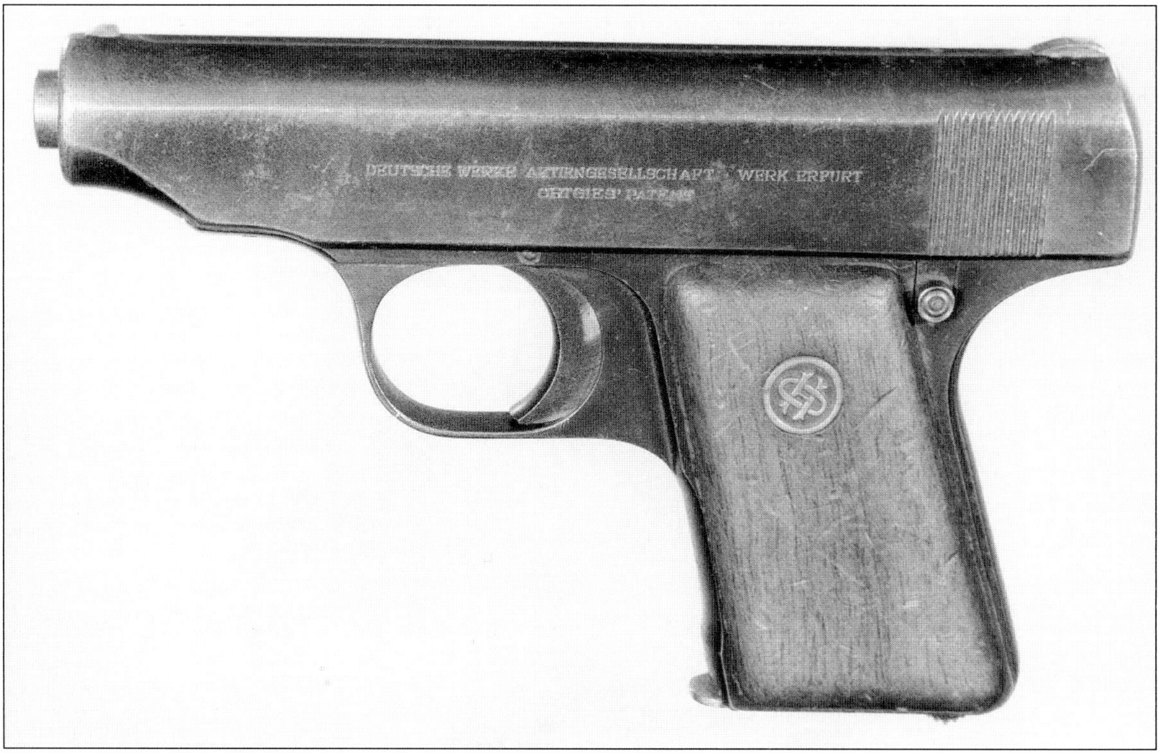

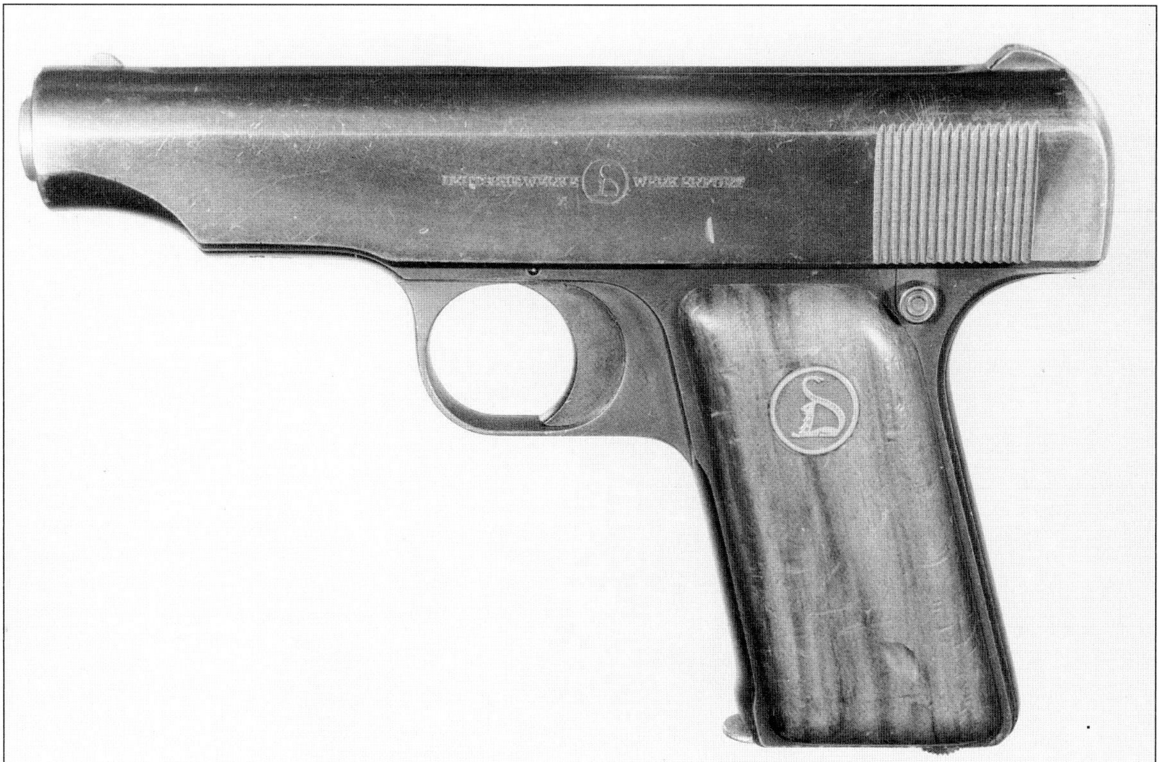

Left, upper: This 6.35mm Ortgies bears the name of the Deutsche Werke but still has Heinrich Ortgies' monogram on the grips.
Left, lower: This Deutsche Werke Ortgies pistol in 7.65mm calibre has the company's symbolic animal on the grip medallions.

loaded button to protrude. This, when the gun is at rest, lies in the groove in the inside of the slide. As soon as the gun is fired and the slide recoils, the groove moves back and the stud is forced, by the contour of the interior surface of the slide, to move inwards to disconnect the trigger from the sear. They remain disconnected until the slide has come back into the loaded position; meanwhile the sear has sprung back into place and is holding the firing pin ready for the next round. This pin thus serves two purposes: it acts as a disconnector to prevent more than one shot being fired for each pressure of the trigger, and it also acts as an automatic safety device which prevents the gun being fired until the slide is fully closed. The action of this mechanism can be checked and studied very easily when the gun is stripped by pulling the trigger and then pushing in the button with the thumbnail.

The next interesting feature of the Ortgies design is the grip safety. This protrudes from the back of the butt in the normal way and, with the gun in its stripped condition, can be seen to terminate in a sort of hook at the rear of the frame. By pushing in the stripping button and pulling on the hook, the grip safety will move out. With the gun assembled the firing pin spring provides the motive power to press the grip safety out whenever the button is pressed. Thus gripping the gun automatically removes the safety and the button must be pressed to bring it back into operation. When the grip safety is out, in the 'safe' position, it engages with the sear and prevents movement. Another interesting feature of this arrangement is that when the grip is out, the firing pin spring is less compressed; when the grip is squeezed in, ready to fire, more pressure is placed on the firing pin spring. This is an ingenious method of making sure the spring is not kept at full tension if the gun is laid away while cocked.

The magazine of some early models exhibits a peculiar feature: the left side is perforated with six holes, through which the cartridges may be inspected, and is marked '9mm'. The right side is perforated with seven holes and is marked '7.65mm'. The magazine will load either type of ammunition, 7.65mm Browning or 9mm Short, and this appears to be a legacy of Ortgies' original idea of providing a replacement barrel conversion kit which would allow the buyer of a 7.65mm pistol to convert it to fire 9mm Short (or vice-versa) by simply buying a new barrel. So far as I am aware, this idea never got off the ground, being dropped after Ortgies' death, but the early magazines that had been prepared for this conversion were used up in normal 7.65mm production.

Ortgies 6.35mm

Calibre	6.35mm Browning
Method of operation	Blowback, striker-fired
Safety devices	Grip safety at rear of butt
Magazine type	Single-column detachable box in butt
Position of catch	Bottom rear of butt
Magazine capacity	7 rounds
Front sight	Fixed blade
Rear sight	Fixed V-notch
Overall length	5.25in (133mm)
Barrel length	2.72in (69mm)
Number of grooves	6
Direction of twist	Right-hand
Empty weight	14.0oz (396g)
Markings	See text
Serial number	Full number under frame in front of trigger guard, on barrel alongside breech and on frame under breech block section of slide; last four digits on inside surface of sear

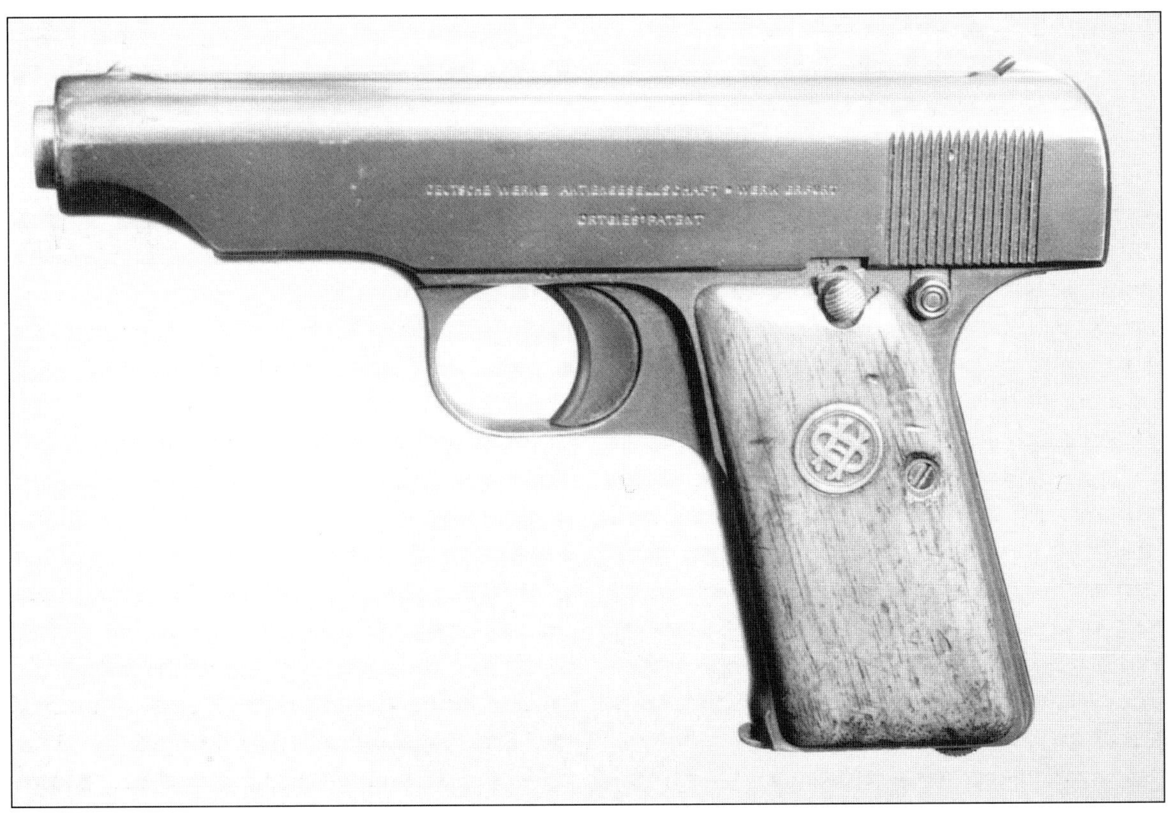

Above: The 9mm Ortgies pistol was the only one to have a manual safety catch.

Finally comes the method of attachment of the grips. There is a simple spring catch inside the magazine cavity, about half way up on the rear edge. By placing a screwdriver inside the cavity and pressing against the spring, the grips are freed and can be lifted off. Notice that the magazine catch spring is the motive power for this device, so that when the magazine is in place greater tension is exerted on the grip catches and the grips are even more firmly held. Herr Ortgies was a firm believer in killing two birds with every stone he threw.

A word deserves to be said in praise of the finish of these guns, which is particularly apparent when the weapons are dismantled. All the metal surfaces are highly polished with the frame and slide blued, and the fit of the wooden grips is immaculate.

A number of 7.65mm and 9mm/0.380in models have two minor differences from the usual versions in that they are fitted with a manual safety catch just above the left grip and the butt grips are held by a screw. This addition first appears on a series of 9mm pistols manufactured for a military contract to Czechoslovakia, and it would seem that it was thereafter offered as an option on commercial models. The safety catch merely locks the grip safety in the 'safe' or 'out' position, so that it cannot be squeezed in.

Reassembling the Ortgies demands that another trick be mastered. The grips should be fitted on to the frame with their forward edges engaged in the aperture; then, while squeezing the rear edges together, press in the spring catch and the grips will snap into place. To replace the barrel drop it into the socket and turn until the muzzle points in the generally accepted direction. Take care to align the barrel as precisely as possible with the frame—the two should lock perfectly into alignment, but a little wear might have taken place. Now comes the tricky bit: the firing pin, spring, and follower should be slipped into position in the slide. Examination will soon reveal that, since these items protrude at the rear a fair distance, assembly is going to be impossible. But a short distance behind the firing pin mounting, in the groove in the slide, is a small semicircular lateral groove. Using a fine screwdriver, push the follower pin and spring in towards the firing pin until the rim of the follower pin can be pressed down into this lateral groove; but beware, for it takes very little disturbance to loosen this lodgement, and if this happens the pins and spring will be flung a considerable distance. To guard against this, grip the slide with one finger extending around the open end so as to catch the spring if it comes adrift. With the other hand take up the frame, enter the barrel into the recoil spring which descends from the slide and insert so that the barrel enters the slide muzzle port. Then press the rear end of the slide down and it will snap over the catch and into place.

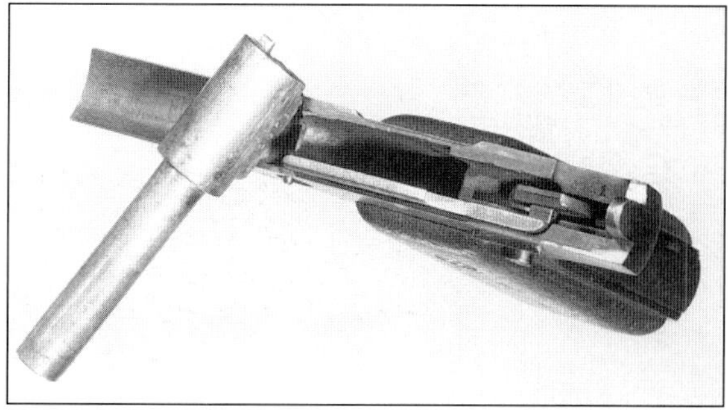

Above: How to remove the barrel from an Ortgies pistol,

The maker's marks come in several forms. The original Ortgies-made models are marked 'ORTGIES & CO ERFURT ORTGIES PATENT' on the slide, and the grips carry a bronze me-

Ortgies 7.65mm

Calibre	7.65mm Browning
Method of operation	Blowback, striker-fired
Safety devices	Grip safety at rear of butt; may have locking button
Magazine type	Single-column detachable box in butt
Position of catch	Bottom rear of butt
Magazine capacity	8 rounds
Front sight	Fixed blade
Rear sight	Fixed U-notch
Overall length	6.50in (165mm)
Barrel length	3.42in (87mm)
Number of grooves	6
Direction of twist	Right-hand
Empty weight	22.5oz (638g)
Markings	See text
Serial number	Full number under frame in front of trigger guard, on barrel alongside breech and on frame under breech block section of slide; last four digits on inside surface of sear

Ortgies 9mm

Calibre	9mm Short/.380 Auto Pistol
Method of operation	Blowback, striker-fired
Safety devices	Grip safety; manual catch left side of frame
Magazine type	Detachable box
Position of catch	Bottom rear of butt
Magazine capacity	7 rounds
Front sight	Fixed blade
Rear sight	Fixed V-notch
Overall length	6.50in (165mm)
Barrel length	3.45in (87mm)
Number of grooves	6
Direction of twist	Right-hand
Empty weight	21.0oz (595g)
Markings	See text
Serial number	Full number under frame in front of trigger guard, on barrel alongside breech and on frame under breech block section of slide; last four digits on inside surface of sear

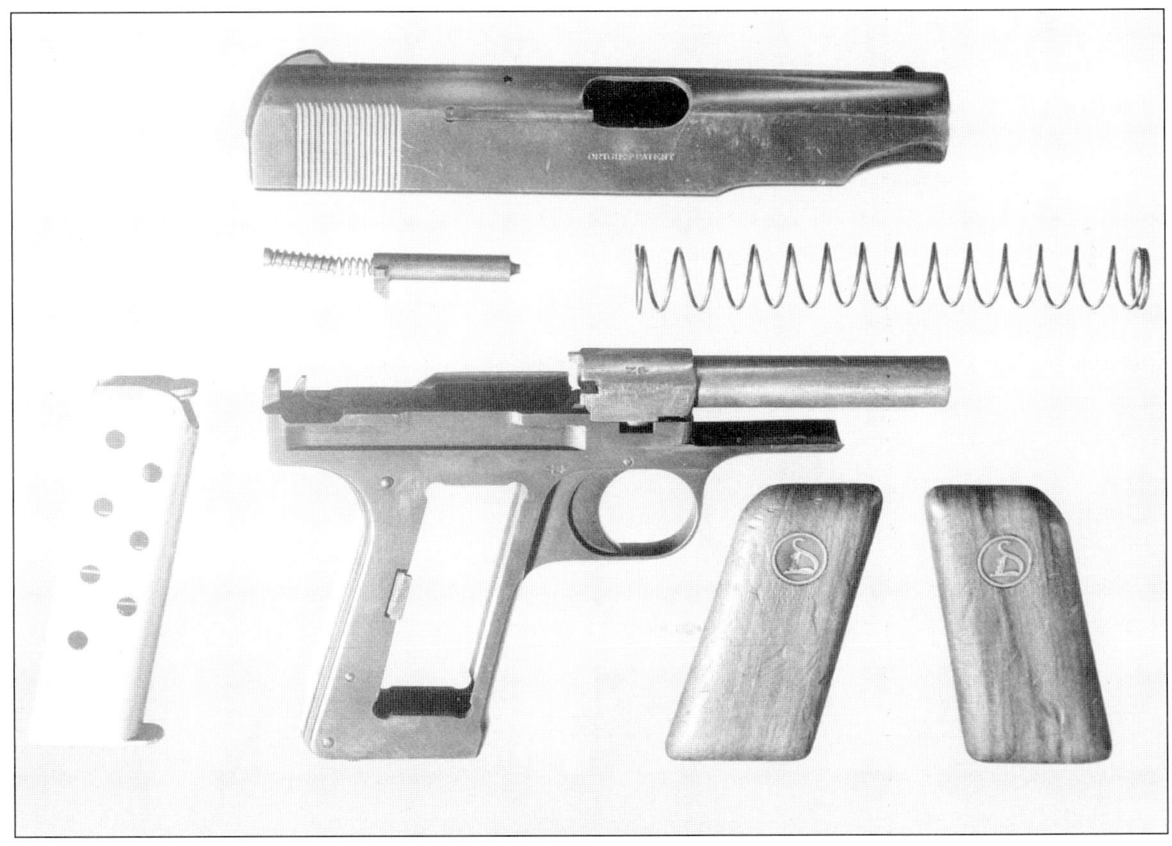

Above: A 7.65mm Ortgies stripped but with the barrel left in place on the frame.

dallion with the intertwined initials 'HO'. This system of marking was continued for some time after the business was taken over by Deutsche Werke, and was then changed to 'ORTGIES PATENT DEUTSCHE WERKE AKTIENGESELLSCHAFT BERLIN'. This will only be found on a small number of 7.65mm pistols. It has been stated that some few were marked simply 'D. W. A. BERLIN', though I have never seen any with this marking.

Once the company had established itself in Erfurt the marking changed to 'DEUTSCHE WERKE AKTIENGESELLSCHAFT WERK ERFURT. ORTGIES PATENT'. On the barrel, visible through the ejection port, is 'CAL. 6,35m/m [or 7,65 etc]'. On the grips is the same bronze medallion with a monogram of 'HO'. These markings appeared on the early Deutsche Werk production using up components purchased from Ortgies.

Next, just after the 71,000 serial number, came a new system. On the left of the slide was 'DEUTSCHE WERKE [monogram] WERK ERFURT' and on the right of the slide 'ORTGIES PATENT'. On the barrel, visible through the ejection port, was 'CAL. 7,65m/m [or 6,35 etc]'. On each grip, inletted in a metal stud, was a monogram in the form of an ornamental letter 'D' formed by a mythical animal (some people say a cat, others a lion) with a long tail curling over its head. The same monogram divides the slide inscription. Finally came a marking which was the same but omitted the words 'Ortgies Patent', and it is assumed that this marked the expiry of Ortgies' original patent.

PARABELLUM (LUGER)

The Parabellum pistol, more commonly known as the Luger, is undoubtedly the most widely known of all German designs and is probably the most coveted mass-produced pistol in the world today: its ownership and study have reached the status of a minor religion, it has been the subject of innumerable articles and books and, generally speaking, it has assumed an importance which is far from justified.

The Parabellum is a good, sound, well-made weapon, but not as good or sound as several other and more combat-worthy designs adopted by other nations. Its ascendancy is surely due to the fact that it was the right pistol in the right place at the right time: when the German Army decided that it needed an automatic pistol, the Parabellum was ready and, what is more, it was a native product. In the early years of the twentieth century it was unthinkable for a major nation to outfit its army with a weapon developed in a foreign country, which left Germany the choice between the Mauser and the Parabellum. The latter being the handier to use and, moreover, readily available in the desired calibre, it won the day; from then on, Germany's military progress being what it was, the Parabellum's future was assured. Moreover, the smaller nations who looked to Germany for their lead in military matters also took to the weapon in quantity. When World War I was fought, the revolver-armed soldiers of the Allies prized any automatic pistol they could capture as a useful addition to their trench-fighting armoury, and the Parabellum was the best of those available. It all helped to build up the mystique. Reading some of the American magazines of the 1930s, I used to wonder if the German Army had ever been equipped with any other weapon.

So much for the legends—now let us study the facts and trace the history of this weapon. Georg Luger, the man who gave his name to the pistol (which was originally called the Parabellum-Pistole, System Borchardt-Luger), was an engineer employed by the Berlin firm of Ludwig Loewe & Co and also acted as their representative in dealings with various governments. His great passion, it would appear from his various patents, was the development of an automatic rifle. The Borchardt pistol was being made by Loewe in the 1890s and Luger, in his capacity as representative, demonstrated this weapon in the United States in 1894. It would seem that he approved of Borchardt's conception but disapproved of its execution and so he set himself the task of cleaning up the design

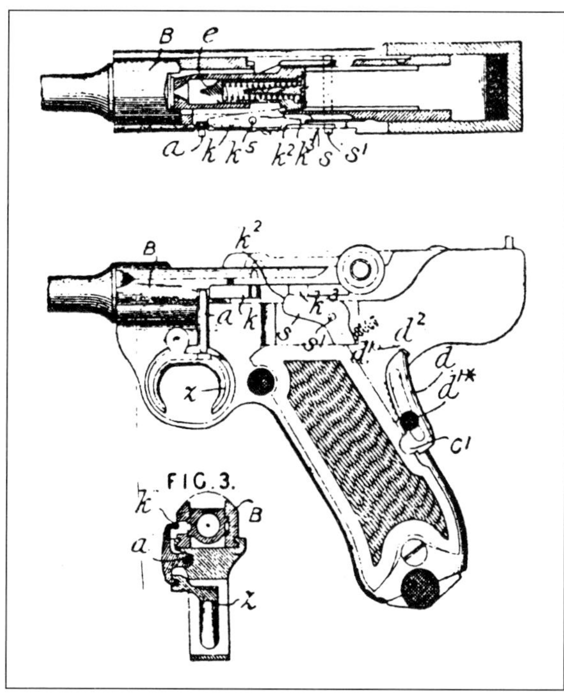

Right: Patent 9040, 29 April 1899, Georg Luger. Although Luger had obtained previous patents for various features of automatic rifles, this was his first pistol patent, and it is obviously part of the transition from Borchardt to Luger design. The patent specifically protects the trigger and firing mechanism, and the grip safety device, both of which became prime features of the 'pure' Luger pistol.

and producing a handier and more reliable weapon. The fruits of his labours are enshrined in British Patent 4399 of 7 March 1900, a voluminous document which goes into the most meticulous detail of every feature of the pistol; indeed, it is a model of how a watertight patent should be drawn up.

In essence, while keeping the rising toggle action of the Borchardt, Luger had improved the system of springing the toggle and had managed to rake the butt so as to make aiming more instinctive. Several other minor points were covered—a change in operation of the sear, an improved safety catch, an alteration to the extractor, and so on. Luger had already made one or two models forming intermediary stages between the Borchardt and his own pistol, and, while several of these reached the hardware stage, none was ever produced in volume or for sale.

The 1900 model is the archetypal Parabellum from which every variation stems, although, as will be seen, the differences between the models are relatively small. The more advanced Luger collectors and aficionados make innumerable distinctions between models, even declaring that two identical models made on contract for two different governments—and thus distinctively marked—are distinctive models. I would not dispute their erudition, but for our purposes here I intend to keep it simple, and note only those models which show a design difference.

Like every other Parabellum which came after it, the 1900 consists of three basic units—the frame, the barrel and barrel extension, and the bolt group. The frame carries the magazine within the butt, is grooved at the top to guide the movement of the barrel and extension, and terminates at the rear in two upswept 'ears' which form cam surfaces at their front. The frame also carries the trigger, the locking pin

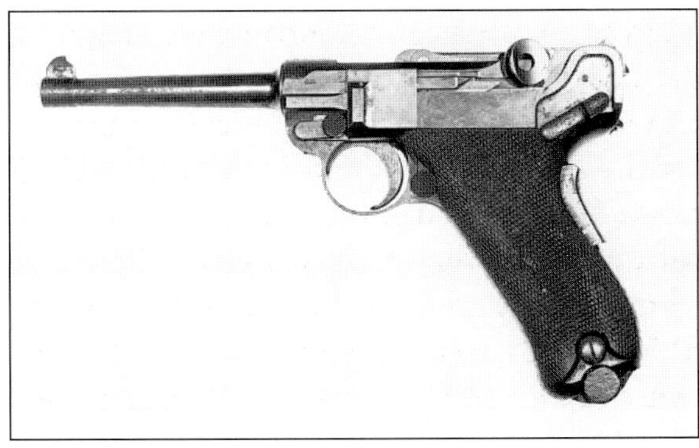

Above: A 7.65m Parabellum pistol of the 1900 pattern.

and the safety catch, together with a grip safety device in the rear edge of the grip. The barrel, tapered and with a reinforced muzzle, is screwed into the front of the extension, which extends rearward in the form of two arms. The left-hand arm carries the sear and the right-hand arm the ejector; both are machined on their inner surfaces to form guides for the reception of the bolt.

The bolt unit comprises the bolt proper, carrying within it the firing pin and spring, and having in its upper surface the extractor. Attached to the bolt is the toggle unit. This is formed from two arms, hinged together in the middle and hinged to the bolt at the front end, and with a hole for an axis pin at the rear end. The joint of the toggle is furnished with distinctive finger grips at each side, the right-hand grip carrying a retaining catch and being cut away at the rear.

The features which distinguish the 1900 model from later types are as follows. The recoil spring concealed within the butt is a convoluted leaf spring and not a coil spring; the toggle joint grips are cut away and carry the retaining catch; the top of the bolt is perfectly flat; there is no form of inscription either upon the side of the extractor nor upon the frame beneath the safety catch; the thumb-operated surface of the safety catch is longitudinally grooved for about two-thirds of the length of the catch lever instead of being knurled; a grip safety is fitted; there is no lug on the butt to take a shoulder stock; and the safety catch is pushed upwards to make the pistol safe. The barrel is 4.5in long; models for the European market had the top surface of the chamber plain, while models made for export to the United States had an ornate American Eagle engraved over the chamber. All were made by Deutsches Waffen- und Munitionsfabrik of Berlin and have a flowing DWM monogram engraved on the front link of the toggle.

The mechanism of this model really owes more to Hugo Borchardt than to Georg Luger, since it differs in one important respect from the mechanism used on later models. To open the breech of the 1900 model it is necessary to grasp the toggle and pull the unit straight to the rear before attempting to lift and break the joint. The reason for this can be seen on examination of the right-hand toggle joint. This contains a thin spring retaining catch which, when the action is closed, engages with a groove formed in the upper right side of the frame; the top of this groove is cut away in the rear of the catch, with the effect that the toggle joint cannot rise until it has moved back far enough to align with the cut-out section. In other words, it is necessary to retract the barrel, simulating recoil, before the action will open—a state of affairs which is also found on the Mauser Military pistol. While this feature is shown in the patents, its purpose is not specified directly, but it is a form of anti-bounce lock. This type of fitting is relatively common in light machine guns using a reciprocating bolt and is provided so that the rapidly moving bolt does not bounce back from the breech face on closing and before the mechanical locking system can take effect. The Parabellum is the only pistol ever to use an anti-bounce lock and it is probably due to Borchardt's preoccupation with automatic rifles, in which relatively strong return springs and lightweight bolts gave rise to bounce. In most pistol designs the weight of the recoiling mass accounts for so high a proportion of the total weight that bounce is virtually impossible, but with the Parabellum and Borchardt bolts being so light an anti-bounce lock seems to be a reasonable form of insurance. The device was soon found to be superfluous: obviously, once the breech has closed in a toggle joint design, the over-centre mechanical lock has taken place and bounce cannot occur. Practical experience bore out this contention and the anti-bounce lock

Below: The toggle action of the Parabellum pistol. Top: the breech is locked because the toggle joint is below a line between the other two joints, and any rearward movement will thrust the centre joint down, against the solid frame. Centre: the joint strikes the curved surface of the frame as the barrel and extension move back, and is thus broken. Bottom: the breech is fully open for reloading.

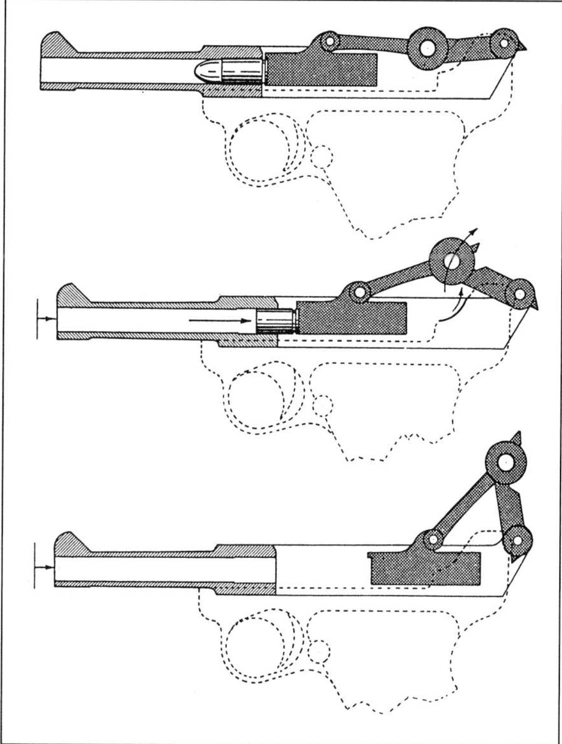

was deleted from those later models which were Luger's refinement over the original.

It might be as well now to examine the 1900 model in some detail as regards mechanism and stripping, so as to lay a foundation, after which subsequent models can be briefly noted with their points of difference from the 1900 type.

The breech mechanism of the Parabellum and that of its forerunner, the Borchardt, have never been copied in any other pistol. It is more or less based on Maxim's original toggle lock, introduced in his well-known machine gun in 1884, with the vital difference that Maxim's toggle dropped while Borchardt's rose. In the refinements of the Luger design the toggle lock consists of three basic elements: the bolt, which reciprocates in slides in the barrel extension; and the forward toggle link, which is pinned to the bolt at its forward end and pinned in turn at its rear end to the third element, the rear toggle link. The joint of the two links is formed into two prominent grips which are used for operating the toggle and bolt by hand when loading, and which also form an operating surface which engages with the cam surface formed by the upswept shoulders of the frame. The rear toggle link is hinged to the rear end of the barrel extension in such a fashion that, when the bolt is closed with a round in the chamber, the two toggle links lie perfectly flat and form a rigid strut between the face of the bolt and the pin locking the rear link to the extension. In fact, if the weapon is closely examined, it can be seen that the axis of the central toggle joint is slightly lower than the axes of the bolt and frame pins, so that any compression of the struts tends to force the central joint down and make the lock even more secure.

When the pistol is fired, the recoil drives the barrel and its attached extension—complete with bolt and toggle—to the rear. The toggle still forms a rigid strut and thus securely locks the breech while the chamber pressure is high. This recoil continues for about 0.25in (6.5mm) against the pressure of the recoil spring. The latter, a leaf spring running down the rear of the butt grip, is engaged by a hook depending from the rear toggle link and, as soon as recoil commences, this hook exerts more and more pressure on the spring. At the end of the recoil stroke the toggle joint pieces strike the cam surfaces of the frame and the joint is forced upwards so as to break the over-centre strut type mechanical lock previously obtained. At the same time the recoil movement is stopped by a lug on the barrel extension meeting a stop surface on the frame, and hence the recoil force is now concentrated in the bolt and toggle. Momentum throws the bolt to the rear, causing the toggle to continue rising and 'fold' upon itself. The rising of the rear link pulls more on the pendant hook and places more pressure on the recoil spring. When the rear link has risen to the vertical, a flange formed on its upper surface is brought into contact with a stop surface on the frame and halts the movement of toggle and bolt. The recoil spring now pulls down on the hook and, through this, on the rear link. The toggle moves down—unfolds—and the bolt is driven forward, picking up a cartridge from the magazine en route and chambering it as the toggle straightens out and once more forms the rigid strut. As the toggle takes up its final position, so the anti-bounce catch locks over the groove in the frame and the barrel and extension complete their forward movement into battery, ready for the next round to be fired.

Right: Patent 4399, 7 March 1900, Georg Luger. This was Luger's master patent, which covered all the essential features of his reconstruction of the Borchardt pistol which Luger was seeking to protect. It shows the leaf recoil spring and the grip safety, and it includes a hold-open device which did not actually appear on Luger pistols for some years. It also shows the knurling on the safety catch—a quick identification feature of the early Lugers.

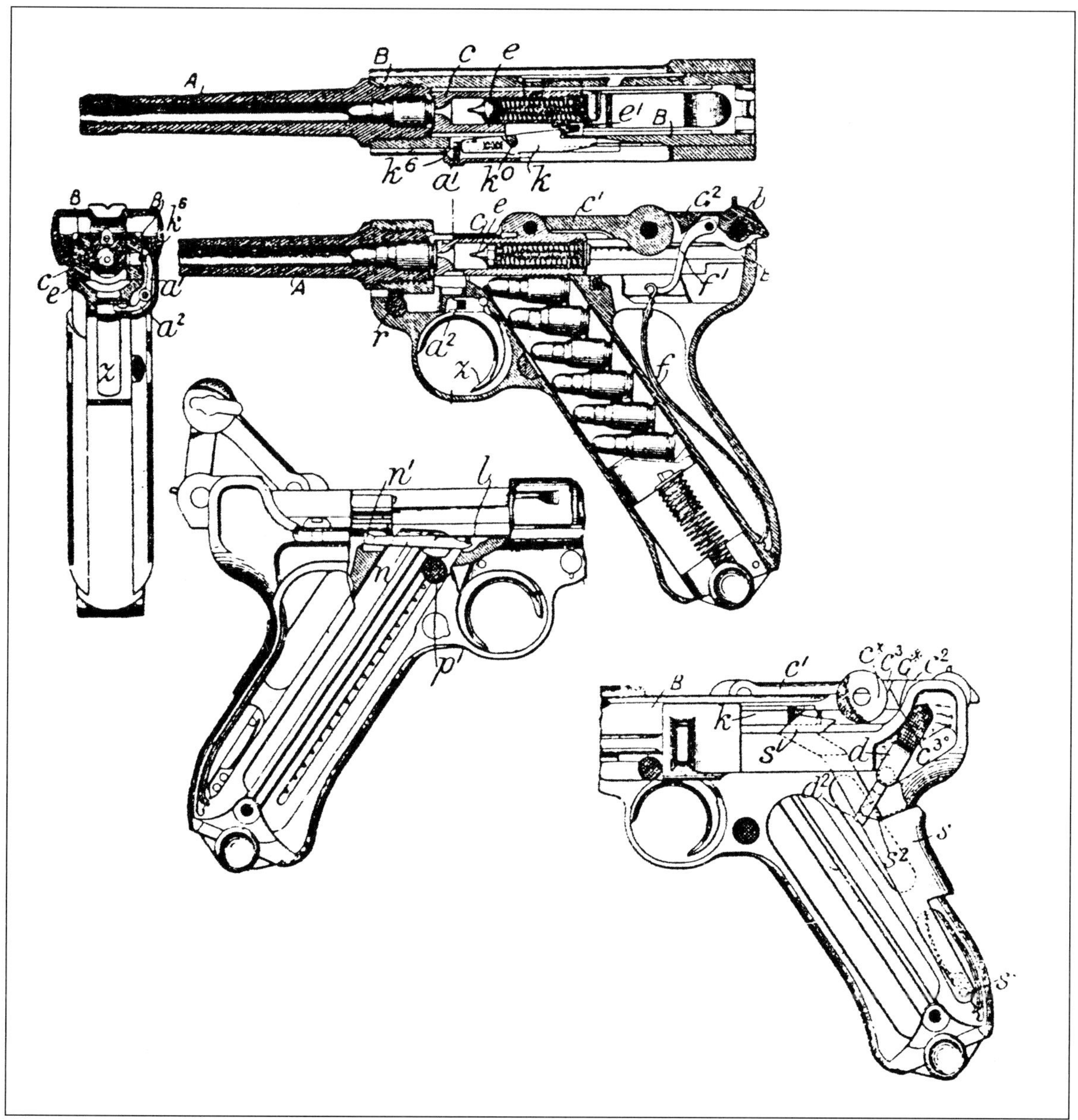

The firing mechanism of the Parabellum is another distinct oddity never copied elsewhere and it is probably the worst feature of the design from the shooting point of view (though an elegant solution from the engineering aspect). The pistol is striker-fired, the striker being carried inside the bolt together with its operating spring and a bayonet cap to retain it in place. The bent, or operating catch of the striker, protrudes from the side of the bolt in a position to engage the sear, which lies in the side of the barrel extension and is retained by a vertical pivot which allows the sear to rock laterally. The problem now rests in how to convert a fore-and-aft trigger pull into a side-to-side sear pressure. The rear end of the sear engages with the bent as the bolt rides forward in its closing movement, causing the striker spring to be compressed; to release the striker the forward end of the sear has to be pressed inwards, rocking the rear end out of engagement with the bent. To achieve this change of direction of effort from trigger to sear, a bell crank is employed, hung on a cover plate which locks, dovetail-fashion, into the frame. The axis of this crank is parallel with the axis of the bore and the lower limb of the bell crank engages in a recess machined in the upper front of the trigger. Thus when the trigger is pulled and moves about its axis pin, the fore end moves down, taking the end of the crank with it. The crank pivots and the top end of the upper limb moves in and presses in the front end of the sear, causing it to rock and disengage the rear end from the striker bent. Elegant though it is, it has two major faults. First, the interacting surfaces and reversals of motion all contribute to an imprecise and 'creepy' trigger pull which is execrated by target shooters. Secondly, the fitting of the bell crank has to be precisely done for each pistol, for which reason the cover plate is inscribed with the pistol's serial number. Admittedly the design is of such precision that, in the majority of cases, cover plates and bell cranks can be changed from pistol to pistol and still function reasonably satisfactorily, but it is sometimes the case that a strange bell crank assembly will fail to operate at all. It is also worthy of note that attempts to 'improve' the trigger pull by bending or stoning the bell crank inevitably result in disaster.

The safety system used in the Parabellum is simplicity itself. When the safety catch is operated, it forces a flat steel plate out of a recess of the frame and covers the rear end of the sear, locking it firmly into engagement with the bent. Thus operation of the trigger will move the bell crank and press on the front end of the sear in the normal way, but, since the rear end is now firmly restrained, the rocking action cannot take place and the sear cannot disengage. Moreover, if the striker is forward and the safety catch applied, the toggle cannot be opened; this is due to the fact that as the toggle is opened so the striker is drawn back past the sear, forcing this outwards against a spring. Restraining the sear with the safety catch means that this action cannot take place.

The grip safety is in strange contrast to the rather elegant design of the rest of the weapon, being a simple piece of bent sheet metal protruding from the back of the butt in such a position that it must be depressed when the hand grips the butt for shooting. When not depressed, it is held by a spring in such a position that a hook-like projection at the top (concealed by the wooden grip) prevents movement of the sear.

The Parabellum's magazine is a single-column pattern carrying eight rounds and inserted in the butt, where it is held by a spring catch. On the right side is a slot in which rides a knurled button attached to the magazine platform. When loading this can be pulled down, either with the thumb or using the combination tool supplied with the weapon (and usually held in a pocket in the holster flap) to relieve spring pressure and facilitate the process. The bottom is formed by a wooden plug shaped to provide two finger grips to assist in withdrawal and which form a very ready identification of the magazine.

Extraction and ejection are performed by the extractor, a heavy spring-loaded arm lying in the upper surface of the bolt which is visibly raised when a round is chambered, and a light spring-steel ejector which is attached to the barrel extension's left side and brought into play by the retraction of the bolt. The extractor pulls the empty case from the chamber, and, as the bolt moves back, so it permits the ejector to move in and strike the case, knocking it out of

Parabellum 1900

Calibre	7.85mm Parabellum
Method of operation	Recoil, toggle lock, striker-fired, single-action
Safety devices	Manual safety catch on left rear of frame; grip safety
Magazine type	Single-column detachable box in butt
Position of catch	Left front edge of butt, behind trigger
Magazine capacity	8 rounds
Front sight	Fixed blade
Rear sight	Fixed V-notch
Overall length	9.31in (237mm)
Barrel length	4.72in (120mm)
Number of grooves	4
Direction of twist	Right-hand
Empty weight	31.4oz (890g)
Markings	'DWM' monogram on front toggle arm
Serial number	Full number on frame under barrel and on magazine; last two digits on practically every removable part

the feedway. As the bolt moves back to reload, so the ejector is pressed back into the barrel extension and the extractor is snapped over the rim of the next round as it chambers.

To strip the Parabellum is remarkably easy. After clearing the gun, removing the magazine and pressing the trigger, press the muzzle back against the pressure of the recoil spring for about 0.25in (6.5mm), either by using the hand or by pressing on some solid surface such as a table. At the front end of the frame, beneath the chamber, is a dismantling latch with a knurled head. Rotate this latch through 90°, swinging it down and forward until vertical. The cover plate and bell crank will now fall free and can be removed. The entire barrel, extension and toggle unit can be slid forward off the frame in one piece, the pendant hook beneath the rear toggle link disengaging itself from the recoil spring as it comes forward.

Once the barrel complex is removed, the axis pin of the rear toggle link is exposed; by pulling slightly upwards on the toggle to relieve pressure on the action, this pin can be pushed out to one side and the entire toggle unit and bolt can be slid from the arms of the extension. By using a small screwdriver, or the small end of the combination tool, the bayonet catch in the rear of the bolt can be depressed and given half a turn, releasing it and allowing the striker spring and striker to be removed. It is not advisable to attempt to dismantle the individual components of the bolt and toggle assembly. The grips can be removed from the butt by the removal of the two screws which retain them in place, whereupon the action of the safety catch and grip safety becomes apparent. The trigger can be lifted carefully from its pivot pin, taking care that the trigger return spring is not lost in the process.

Reassembly is the reverse of the above procedure. When the bolt is slid back into the barrel extension it is necessary to squeeze in the front end of the sear to allow the striker bent to pass and permit the toggle to lie flat so that the axis pin can be reinserted. When the barrel assembly is returned to the frame, it is advisable to hold the units upside down so that the recoil spring hook does not foul the frame. Once the barrel assembly is almost in place, bring everything the right way up and the hook will drop down and automatically engage with the stirrup at the top end of the recoil spring.

The foregoing description will have made it clear that the reliability and strength of Luger's system of operation are dependent upon the precise machining and accurate fitting of the various components of the toggle and bolt unit and the pins which link the various parts together. In addition to precision, the other requirement is first-class material and hardening. It is this demand which has made the Borchardt-Luger system one of the very few unpirated designs in the handgun world.

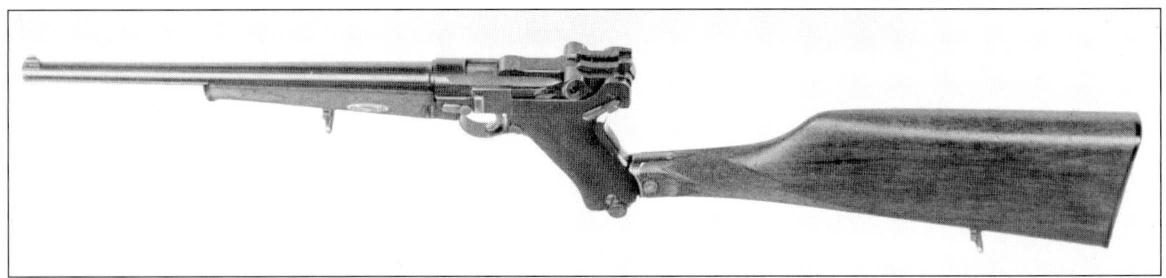

Above: The 1903 model carbine, complete with its butt.

Parabellum M02 and M03 (Carbine)

The 1900 model was followed by the 1902 model, which is almost identical except that the barrel is somewhat thicker. In 1903 came the first of the special Carbine models, virtually a longer-barrelled (11.81in/300mm) version of the Model 1900 with wooden fore end and a stock which attached to the butt. This stock is a properly shaped rifle-type stock, and not the more common holster stock device usually found with pistol adaptations. The recoil spring is somewhat heavier than in the short-barrel version and a special cartridge was provided which had a heavier granulation of the powder in order to achieve the desired ballistics in the longer barrel. A tangent ramp sight is fitted just ahead of the chamber. A small number of carbines are reputed to have been made for the then-experimental 9mm Parabellum cartridge, in support of which the entry in the DWM Cartridge Catalogue for 1904 is always quoted—'480D – 9mm Parabellum Carbine'. Unfortunately DWM were not averse to allotting numbers to cartridges which they might, one day, produce, and I suspect this to have been one of them. No ballistic details of the round are known and no specimen appears to exist—and neither does any specimen of the weapon. A prototype or two may have been made, but no more than that.

Parabellum M04

By 1904 Georg Luger was hard at work trying to sell his pistol to the German authorities and had met some sales resistance owing to the small 7.65mm bullet and the poor man-stopping capability of the round. In an attempt to overcome this, he, in consort with DWM ammunition experts, redesigned the cartridge, opening out the 7.65mm bottleneck to make a parallel-sided case and fitting a 9mm bullet into it—probably the most fortuitous piece of 'wild-catting' ever undertaken. Using the same truncated-cone type of bullet he had developed for the 7.65mm round, Luger now produced a service pistol to suit—the 1904 model, which was accepted by the German Navy. This again

Parabellum 1904 Naval

Calibre	9mm Parabellum
Safety devices	Manual safety on left rear of frame; grip safety until 1915
Magazine type	Single column detachable box in butt
Position of catch	Left front edge of butt, behind trigger
Magazine capacity	8 rounds
Front sight	Adjustable barleycorn
Rear sight	Two-position flip U-notch, for 100 and 200m
Overall length	10.50in (267mm)
Barrel length	5.90in (150mm)
Number of grooves	6
Direction of twist	Right-hand
Empty weight	35.6oz (1,010g)
Markings	'DWM' monogram on front toggle arm
Serial number	Full number on frame below barrel and on magazine; last two digits on most removable parts

was much the same as the 1900 model—except for the increase in calibre—but featured a 6in barrel and a two-range flip sight; it was also fitted to take a holster stock on a lug formed at the rear of the butt.

During 1904–05 Luger made some minor changes in design based on practical experience and the reports of owners over the previous four years, and changed the design into what was substantially the final form. The most important change was the adoption of a coiled spring for the recoil spring in place of the leaf spring used in the earlier designs. This was an easier manufacturing proposition, and was less difficult to fit to the pistol. A central link passed through the centre of the spring and acted as a

Below: Patent 13,147, 10 June 1904, Georg Luger. This covers the use of the extractor as a loaded-chamber indicator and is interesting because it shows three possible designs, one with a solid nose, one with a hook-like nose and one with an extended nose to provide extra leverage and a greater degree of rise. It is also of interest because it shows what appears to be a rifle design, rather than the Luger pistol on which it was to appear.

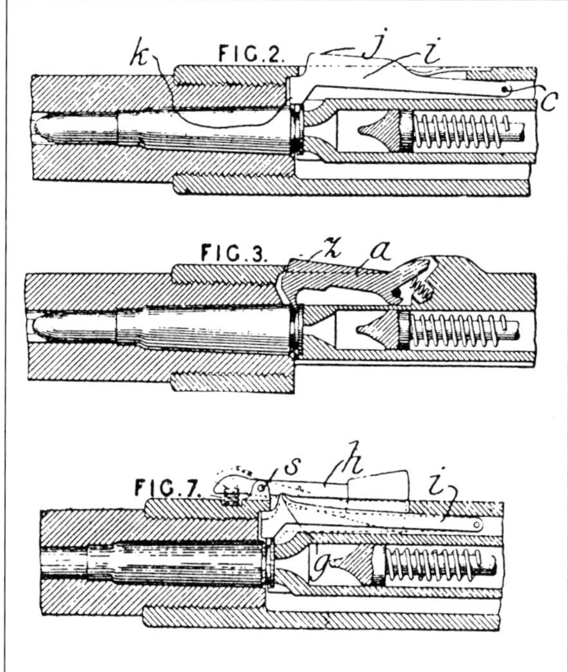

Above: The 1904 Marine Model.

connection to the hook on the rear toggle joint. The upper surface of the coil abutted against a shoulder in the butt frame and the action was such that recoil lifted the link, compressing the spring from the bottom. Another change was in the contour of the bolt: the early models all have a flat top, but the newer design exhibits a rounded top. Finally, the anti-bounce device was abandoned and the toggle can be broken by lifting instead of having to be drawn back first.

Parabellum M06

These changes were incorporated in the Model of 1906, which was a commercial design. It was produced in 7.65mm with a 4.75in (120mm) barrel or in 9mm with a 4in (102mm) barrel. No stock lug was fitted, but the grip safety was still in use. The safety catch was changed from the earlier design in that it now moved down to set 'safe', although its mechanical operation on the sear was exactly as before. Another addition in this model was a breech stop piece which, actuated by the magazine platform, holds the breech open after the last round in the magazine has been fired. A 1906 Naval model was also produced, in 9mm calibre with a stock lug and a two-range sight; what is sometimes called the Naval-Commercial Model, which was simply the Naval model but with civil proof marks, was also manufactured for commercial sale. The Naval models all had 6in (152mm) barrels and

Above: A typical issue Pistole '08.

Below: Left side of a Pistole '08.

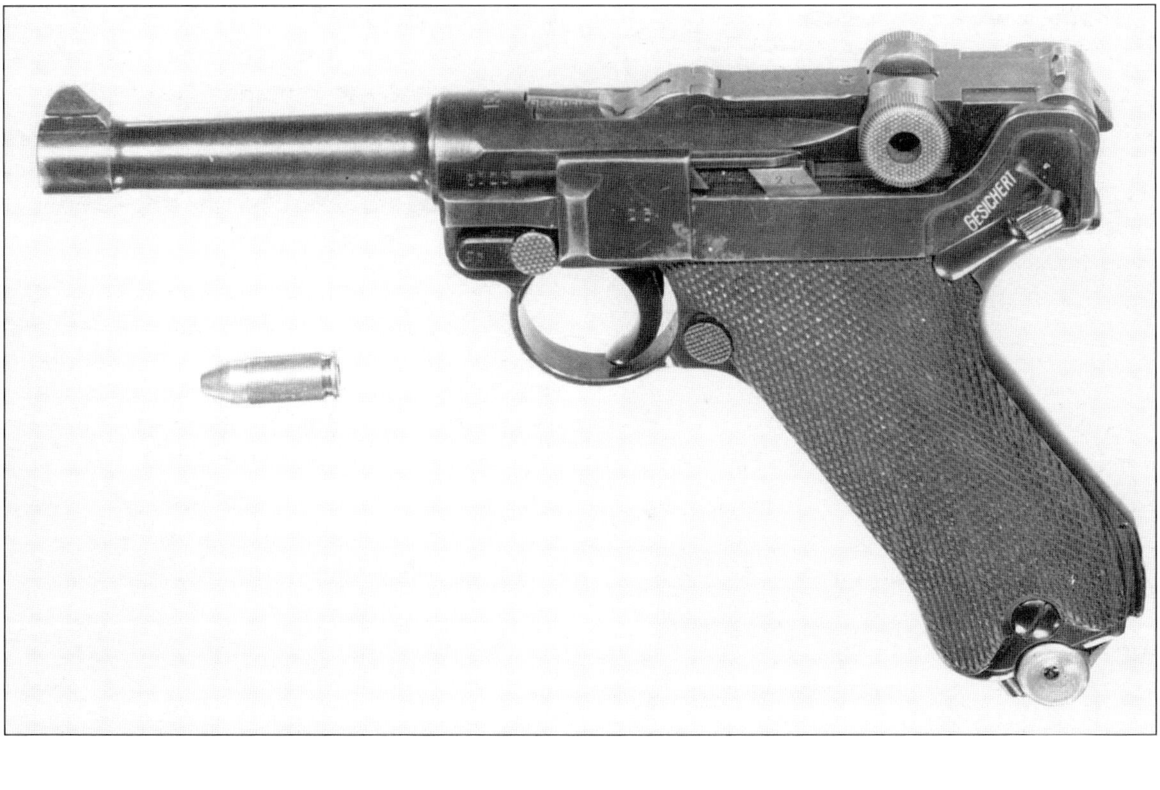

Parabellum Pistole '08

Maker	DWM, Erfurt
Calibre	9mm Parabellum
Method of operation	Recoil, toggle lock, striker-fired
Safety devices	Manual safety catch left rear of frame
Magazine type	Single-column detachable box in butt
Position of catch	Front left edge of butt, behind trigger
Magazine capacity	8 rounds
Front sight	Adjustable blade
Rear sight	Fixed V-notch
Overall length	8.75in (223mm)
Barrel length	4.00in (102mm)
Number of grooves	6
Direction of twist	Right-hand
Empty weight	30.0oz (850g)
Markings	See text
Serial number	Front of frame below barrel; magazine bottom; last two digits on most removable parts

the Naval-Commercial was available in 7.65mm or 9mm form.

In 1908 a commercial model with a 4in (9mm) barrel was produced. It was little different from the 1906 Model, but this was overshadowed by the official German Army adoption of the weapon in this year, which led to the nomenclature 'Pistole '08' in German service circles. This is the model most commonly met today, thousands and thousands having been produced for the German Army, a large proportion of which became souvenirs or 'war surplus' after both World Wars. There were three versions of the '08. First were those made by Deutsche Waffen- und Munitionsfabrik at Berlin. These have the year of manufacture engraved over the chamber, the DWM monogram on the toggle front link, no grip safety, a stock lug on the butt and a holding-open device, and the safety catch moves down to make safe. This is the most common model. The second version is the model built by the Königlich Gewehrfabrik (German Government Arsenal) at Erfurt. This has the year of manufacture over the chamber as on the DWM model, a crown and the word 'ERFURT' engraved on the toggle link, no grip safety, no holding-open device and no stock lug. So far as is known, no Erfurt manufacture took place after 1917, and models with dates later than 1915 are exceptionally rare. An even rarer variety is the Erfurt pattern—i. e. without hold-open or stock lug—but made by DWM and dated 1914. The third variant of the 1908 is the Bulgarian Model, which is virtually the DWM model described above but marked with the Bulgarian Royal Lion badge over the chamber and with the inscription 'Safe' under the safety catch and 'Loaded' on the side of the extractor in Cyrillic characters instead of the German words 'GESICHERT' and 'GELADEN' on the German models. This pistol was the official Bulgarian Army issue from 1910 to 1912 and, although precise figures are not available, it can be assumed that the total number made was no more than three or four thousand; in any event, it is a rare weapon today.

So far as the mechanism goes, the 1908 Model is identical with that of 1906 except for the reversed movement of the safety catch; it

Below: Phantom drawing of the internal arrangements of the Pistole '08.

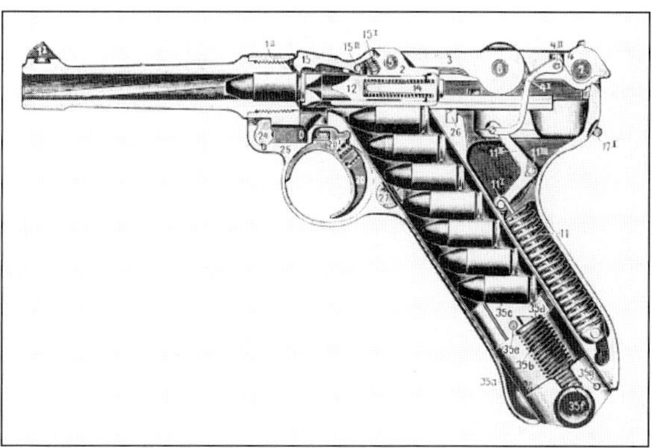

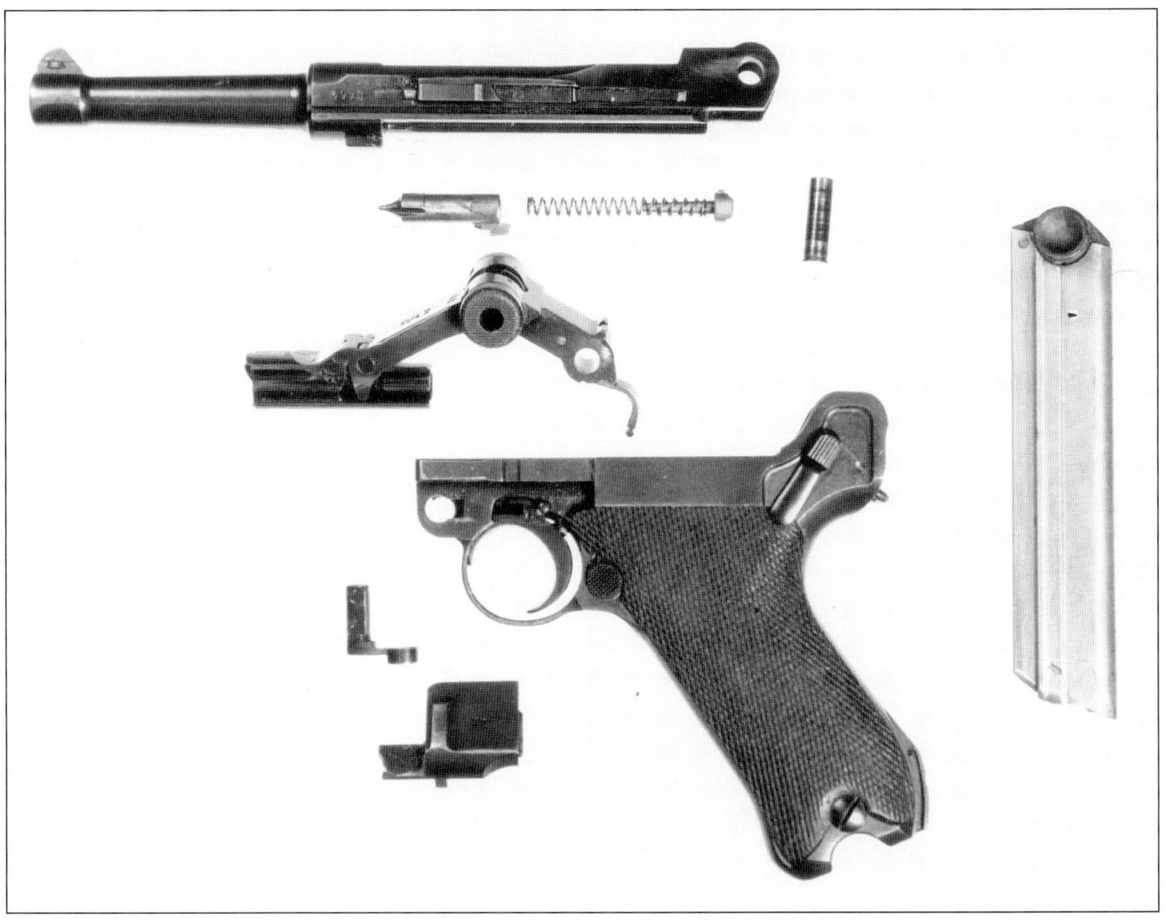

Above: A Pistole '08 field-stripped.

has the same coil-spring recoil spring and dispenses with the anti-bounce catch.

Parabellum M08 Naval

The year 1908 also saw the introduction of a Naval model, differing from the Army's '08 in having a longer barrel of 5.5in (140mm) instead of 4in (102mm). The chamber top is engraved with the Imperial Crown and 'M' for Marine and the 'DWM' monogram is on the toggle link. It has a grip safety and a hold-open device, the safety catch goes up for 'safe', and a two-range (100m and 200m) sight is fitted to the rear toggle link.

In 1914 the Naval model was slightly changed, now having the date above the chamber as the Army models, and the same year saw the modification of the '08 by slight changes in the sear contour.

The Long P '08

Also known as the Artillery Model, this weapon was, for many years, believed to date from 1916 or 1917, since the first specimens seen by Allied troops during the war came to light in September 1917. However, modern research has shown that it was, in fact, adopted in June 1913 and was in manufacture well before the war began.

The pistol is exactly as the '08 except that a 7.9in (200mm) barrel is fitted, together with a tangent back sight graduated up to 400m

Parabellum Lange Pistole '08

Maker	DWM, Erfurt
Calibre	9mm Parabellum
Method of operation	Recoil, toggle lock, striker-fired
Safety devices	Manual safety catch left rear of frame
Magazine type	Single-column detachable box in butt
Position of catch	Front left edge of butt, behind trigger
Magazine capacity	8 rounds
Front sight	Adjustable blade
Rear sight	Tangent V-notch, adjustable to 400m
Overall length	12.48in (317mm)
Barrel length	7.97in (200mm)
Number of grooves	6
Direction of twist	Right-hand
Empty weight	39.0oz (1,105g)
Markings	As for Pistole '08
Serial number	Front of frame below barrel; magazine bottom; last two digits on most removable parts

mounted on the barrel just ahead of the chamber. It was originally issued with the normal magazine, but in 1915 the DWM designers began working on helical-feed magazines for aerial weapons, and from this came the Trommelmagazin '08, popularly called the 'snail magazine'. For many years this was believed to have been based on patents taken out by Tatarek and von Benko in 1913, but more recent research had shown that the design owes more to wartime patents of Friedrich Blum. This magazine held 32 rounds in a spiral, ending in a straight section which fitted into the butt. A special loading tool was also provided. The magazine, together with the butt-stock holster, converted the pistol into something like a semi-automatic carbine, and these weapons were widely issued to NCOs of machine-gun units, artillery observers and shock troops prior to the advent of the Bergmann MP18, the first 'proper' submachine gun. The pistols were also used by the crews of motor torpedo-boats, who sometimes got close enough to their adversaries to exchange small-arms fire.

The 'snail magazine' was (and still is) difficult to load—impossible without the proper loading tool—and it was soon discovered that the conical bullet of the original pattern jammed very badly in it. At much the same time—late 1917—the German authorities began to have misgivings over the legality of the flat-tipped conical 9mm bullet *vis-à-vis* the Hague and St Petersburg Conventions. So, in order to solve both problems, the entire German production of 9mm Parabellum was changed over in 1918 to round-nosed bullets of the more conventional type, and, so far as military use went, the conical bullet died overnight.

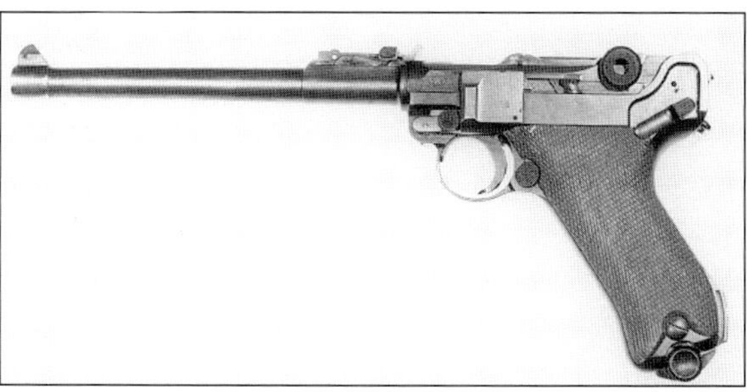

Left: The Long '08 or Artillery Model.

Post-World War I Developments

In 1920 DWM put together a large number of pistols based on the '08 model and made from the surplus or reconditioned components which they had on hand. In order to comply with the restrictions of the Versailles Treaty, the barrel blanks, although externally to the same dimensions as the 9mm '08, were rifled to 7.65mm calibre.

These models were distinguished by a poor quality of finish (compared with pre-war and later work), soft wooden grips and no date or other marks over the chamber, and the DWM marking may be absent from the toggle link. So far as is known, none was ever constructed using the Erfurt marked toggle link. In addition to the pistols a few 11.75in (300mm) barrel carbines were also constructed; these are readily distinguished from the earlier pattern by the fact that the toggle link on the post-war models has no anti-bounce provision.

The 1920s led to some quite remarkable offshoots of the Parabellum. First, in 1922 came a version which was virtually the '08, in both 9mm and 7.65mm calibre, made by Simson of Suhl. This was an export venture, under license from DWM, and these models are identified by the engraving 'SIMSON & CO SUHL' either on the chamber top or on the toggle front link. The finish is excellent, since these were all-new weapons, in contrast to the reconditioned pistols still being turned out by DWM at that time. Shortly after this DWM also turned over to the manufacture of new weapons for export and produced a bewildering variety: in calibres of 9mm or 7.65mm, they had barrels varying in length from 3.63in (92mm) to 16in (406mm), depending on the whim of the customer, and it was this weapon which led to the name Luger being applied to the gun.

From its inception the pistol had always been known in Europe as the Parabellum, a telegraphic code name devised by DWM; in German service circles it was either the Parabellum or, if specific identification was wanted, the '08 or the Long '08—terms which are still recognised in Germany today. It was also referred to as the Luger-Parabellum, probably to distinguish it from the Borchardt; British—and more particularly American—troops began to call it commonly the Luger. Large numbers of the 1923 model were imported into the United States by A. F. Stoeger & Co of New York and, in order to capitalise on the commonly known name among ex-soldiers in the US, they took the remarkable step of patenting the name 'Luger' for their own use in that country. They went further and had their imports engraved with the words 'LUGER A. F. STOEGER' on the right-hand side of the frame. Thus the name became legitimised in the English-speaking world, though it was still known as the Parabellum elsewhere. It was therefore possible for the Stoeger Arms Corporation, in the 1970s, to produce a .22 calibre Luger lookalike with an aluminium frame, fixed barrel and highly modified toggle mechanism and mark it 'LUGER' with perfect legality.

In 1924 two more odd variants appeared. The Swiss Government had always been a good customer for the Luger's pistol, arming both military and police with 7.65mm versions. Now they began manufacturing their own, with 4.75in (121mm) barrels, practically the same as their original 1906 models, and with the chamber engraved 'WAFFEN-FABRIK BERN'. At the same time the Dutch Government were in the market for a supply of 9mm Model 08 pistols, and these were supplied by the British company Vickers. These are an exact copy of the DWM '08 except for not being fitted with a stock lug and having the words 'VICKERS LTD' engraved on the toggle and Birmingham proof marks on the barrel. They are also marked with the Royal Dutch cypher, a script 'W', on the left side. There was no grip safety and the safety catch moved down to 'safe'. Six thousand of these pistols were supplied to the Dutch Government, most of them being sent to the Netherlands East Indies, and consequently this version is much more common in the Pacific area than it is in Europe. In fact the component parts for 6,000 pistols were made in the DWM factory; they were then shipped to Britain, where they were assembled at the Vickers factory in Crayford, Kent. They were then sent, minus their wooden grips, to the Netherlands early in 1922. Next they were sent to Fabrique National d'Armes de Guerre in Liège, Belgium, to be overhauled and adjusted, since, apparently, the Vickers workmanship had been poor, and when this had been done they went to Bavaria to have the wooden butt grips fitted before being finally issued to the Netherlands East Indies forces. All this, of course, was due to the provisions of the Versailles Treaty prohibiting the manufacture of 9mm pistols in Germany.

In 1934, when the rearmament of the German Army got under way, DWM were in no position to produce the volume required and Mauser were brought in to fill the demand. Eventually Mauser took over all the machinery and stock and became responsible for the entire production of P '08 pistols. Mauser were originally provided with jigs and drawings and were soon turning out both military and commercial models, the former in 9mm and the latter in both 9mm and 7.65mm calibres, the only difference between the two being that the military version bears the date of manufacture on the chamber top. All these models carry the Mauser badge on the toggle. At the same time another firm, Krieghoff of Suhl, also took up production on the same terms and produced similar models to Mauser, being differentiated from these by the engraving 'KRIEGHOFF SUHL' on the toggle, or 'HEINRICH KRIEGHOFF WAFFENFABRIK SUHL' on the chamber in the case of commercial models, while the military models have the date above the chamber and 'KRIEGHOFF SUHL' on the toggle. All 1934 models, irrespective of maker, have the inscription 'P '08' engraved on the left side of the barrel extension. A minor change in connection with the post-1934 production was the rationalisation of the magazine: the early design had the bottom of the magazine cut parallel with the axis of the gun and the wooden plug shaped to fit; post-1934 has the bottom of the metalwork cut at right angles to the front edge of the magazine and the bottom plug is slightly different in consequence. Additionally, bottom plugs of aluminium or other light alloy now made their appearance

It might be well, at this point, to clarify the matter of manufacturing by looking at the fundamental question: how many production lines existed? There were only ever three sets of production machine tools for the Parabellum pistol. These were, first, the original DWM production line set up in Berlin in 1900; secondly, the second production line set up in Erfurt in 1910–11; and thirdly, the production line established in Switzerland, at the Waffenfabrik Bern, in 1918. At the end of World War I the Erfurt arsenal was demilitarised and in 1922 the Parabellum machinery was moved to Simson & Co of Suhl in order that they could undertake the manufacture of 10,000 pistols for police and army use. The DWM line continued in use ostensibly to make pistols for commercial sale, but the company were also able to produce parts for assembly elsewhere, as the Vickers order and another for Finland proved. In 1930, in a rationalisation programme, this machinery was moved from Berlin to the Mauser factory at Oberndorf and DWM's involvement with the Parabellum pistol ceased. In 1935 the Simson company, being Jewish, was taken over by the State, and the Parabellum machinery ex-Erfurt was moved to the Heinrich Krieghoff company. Both the Mauser and Krieghoff lines were scrapped after World War II. The Swiss line remained in existence and was eventually sold to Mauser in 1967.

The Krieghoff variety was short-lived. Once the Wehrmacht had been stockpiled, production reverted entirely to Mauser. By 1938 security had raised its head and the engraving of the maker's name was forbidden; now a code was used to indicate the pistol's provenance. Thus 'byf' indicated Mauser manufacture, as did 'S', and the year of manufacture was no longer placed over the chamber. Instead, the practice arose of engraving the maker's code and the last two digits of the year of manufacture on the toggle front link. Mauser were still permitted to make and supply pistols to neutral countries up to 1943, and these weapons still bore the Mauser badge.

In 1938, after a search for a pistol which could be more easily mass-produced, the German army standardised on the Walther P-38 and, once production of this had built up, the Parabellum was phased out. Production of the two pistols ran side by side for a short time, but in mid-1942 the last Parabellum pistol was manufactured by Mauser and the long history of production came to an end. Even so, there was a sufficient stock of components to allow assembly of small orders from time to time until the war ended, and after the war, under French supervision, some 5,000 were assembled.

A word on serial numbers should be given. Some years ago in the United States, following a murder, the investigators of the crime advised foreign police forces, via Interpol, of sundry particulars of the wanted miscreant, and the serial number of the murder weapon—a Parabellum—was included. A conscientious British policeman, happening to check his firearms files, found that this number was registered to a local resident, who was most surprised to be visited by the posse and invited to explain. The fact of the matter is that dozens of Parabellum pistols will bear apparently identical serial numbers, particularly those of wartime manufacture. The number produced was so great that, had they been really serially numbered, the gun would probably have had to be redesigned in order to provide enough space for the astronomical figures involved. Consequently the standard practice was to start on the first of the month with '1' and work through, numbering serially, until the last day. Then the numbering started again at '1' on the first day of the next month. In order to distinguish months a script letter was also engraved below the barrel- 'a' for January, for example. In conjunction with the year date—openly engraved on military models, concealed and coded on civil models—and with the manufacturer's mark, this gave a distinct identity to each weapon but kept the numbers down to a reasonable size: I have never yet seen a serial number which reached five figures.

Another odd marking which sometimes raises questions is the small figure engraved under the barrel near the breech—'8,88' or '8,82' being examples before me. This is the actual, as opposed to the nominal, calibre in millimetres.

Parabellum Resurgum

In the 1960s it became apparent that there was a large body of gun collectors who were prepared to pay to obtain a brand-new, mint condition Parabellum pistol. Mauser saw an opportunity in this, and in 1967 acquired the Swiss arsenal machine tools which had been used for the manufacture of the Swiss service Parabellum pistols. These machines were overhauled and set up in the Mauser factory, and production of new Parabellum pistols began in November 1970. For further details, readers are referred to the Mauser entry.

PICKERT

Friedrich Pickert Waffenwerk, Zella Mehlis, Thuringia

The Pickert Waffenwerk was founded by a cousin of Carl Walther and produced a variety of revolvers in calibres ranging from 5.5mm to .38in, displaying innumerable variations on the same basic theme. They are often described as Arminius revolvers, since the head of this German hero was one of Pickert's trademarks, and the name beneath the engraved head is often the only identification on the weapon.

Essentially, the Pickert revolver is of the solid-frame non-ejecting pattern in which the cartridges are loaded into the cylinder through a gate on the right-hand side. A swinging ejector rod is fitted beneath the barrel, and this can be aligned with one chamber and pressed back to eject the empty case therein. The rod is then released and the chamber loaded. The cylinder is then revolved by hand to position the next chamber opposite the ejector and the cycle repeated.

The action may be of the usual hammer type, with double or single action, or it may be of the pseudo-hammerless class in which the hammer is concealed in the high-backed frame. This type operates double-action only, utilises a loose firing pin in the frame which is struck by the flat-faced hammer, and usually has a safety catch mounted on the left side of the frame. Another odd feature of most Pickert designs is the provision of a butt trap in which spare cartridges can be carried. In 0.32in (7.65mm) calibre, which is probably the most common, the trap is designed to accept a clip or charger which holds five—or six, depending on cylinder capacity—rounds of 7.65mm Auto ammunition. As this cartridge is semi-rimmed, it will fit into a clip and yet function in a revolver, though the weapons will handle most short .32in or .320in cartridges of the normal rimmed type.

The Pickert revolver cannot, by any stretch of the imagination, be classed as a target wea-

Below: A 6.35mm Pickert Model 3 revolver, typical of the hammerless pocket revolvers of the pre-1914 era.

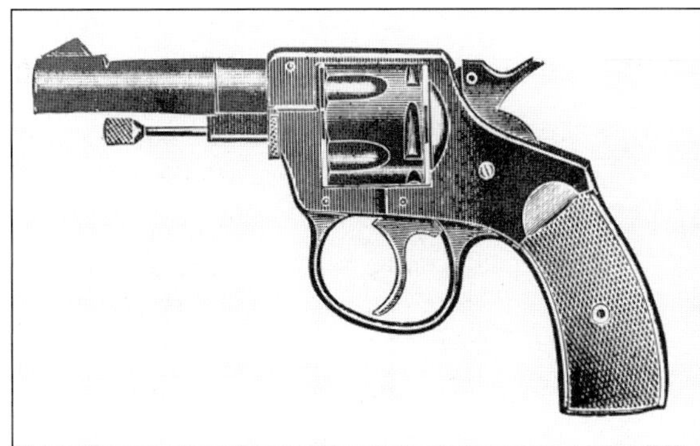

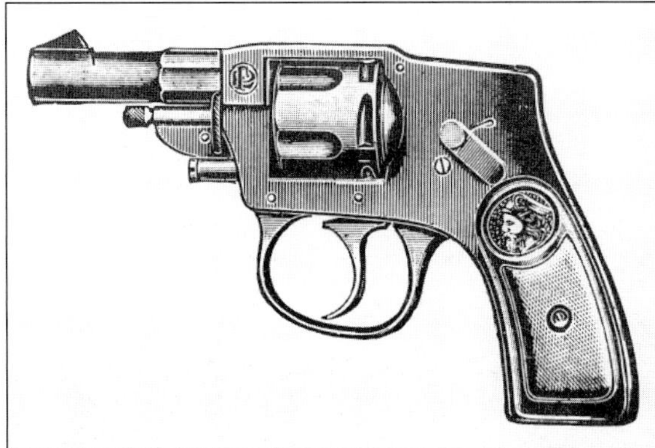

pon, nor is it sufficiently robust or rapid in use to be of much value as a police or military arm, but it found a ready sale in the early years of the century—until 1939, in fact—as a home and personal defence weapon. It was soundly enough made, of good materials, and retailed at a price below that of all but the very worst automatic pistols, and far below that of revolvers of the Smith & Wesson or Webley class.

Owing to the vast range of barrel lengths, weights, calibres, styles, number of chambers per cylinder, etc (all of which could be permuted and combined *ad infinitum*), a complete data table is impossible, but the accompanying short table gives the essential features of the basic Pickert models.

Left, upper: Pickert Arminius 7.65mm Model 9, gate-loaded with rod ejection.
Left, lower: Pickert Arminius 7.65mm Model 10—a slightly different hammerless design.
Below: One of the last Pickert products was this Model 13 in .38 calibre.

BASIC PICKERT MODELS

Model number	Type of action	Calibre and cartridge	Chambers	Barrel length (in/mm)	Weight (oz/kg)
1	Hammerless	0.22in Short and Long	7	1.97/50	7.8/0.22
3	Hammerless	0.25in/6.35mm	5	1.97/50	8.8/0.25
4	Hammerless	5.5mm Velo-Dog	5	1.97/50	10.6/0.30
5/1	Hammer	7.5mm Swiss Ordnance	5	2.56/65	13.6/0.38
5/2	Hammer	7.5mm Swiss Ordnance, 8mm French Ordnance (Lebel) or 7.5mm Nagant	5	3.15/80	17.6/0.50
7	Hammer	0.320in	5	2.36/60	11.7/0.33
8	Hammerless	0-320in	5	5.50/140	11.7/0.33
9	Hammer	0.32in/7.65mm Auto	5	2.36/60	11.4/0.32
9A	Hammer	0.32in/7.65mm Auto	5	2.36/60	12.3/0.35
10	Hammerless	0.32in/7.65mm Auto	5	2.36/60	12.8/0.36
13	Hammer	0.380in	5	2.56/65	16.5/0.46
13A	Hammer	0.22in Long	8	5.30/135	18.6/0.53
14	Hammerless	0-380in	5	2.56/65	16.5/0.46

RECK

Reck Sportwaffenfabrik Karl Arndt KG, Lauf a.d. Pegnitz

This company was set up in the early 1950s and rapidly became a major manufacturer of signal, blank and starting pistols, and in the late 1950s and 1960s Reck began manufacture of cartridge-firing weapons, including a Deringer-like .22 single-shot pistol and a solid-frame non-extracting 6-shot .22 revolver with a folding trigger called the 'Recky'.

Their principal model, however, was the P 8, a blowback automatic in 6.35mm calibre which was widely sold in the United States under such names as La Fury and Chicago Cub and in Europe as, among other names, the Gecado (q.v.). It was striker-fired weapon, made largely of alloy and available in a variety of finishes, and sold cheaply. Its final appearance seems to have been as the Rhöner Model SM 115 in 1987.

Above: The Reck P 8 6.35mm pistol appeared under innumerable names in both Europe and the United States in the 1960s.

As with many other cheap and small pistols, the US Gun Control Act of 1968 put an end to its importation into the United States, and the company turned to making a better grade of revolver for both export and home sales. The two principal models were the R 14, a Smith & Wesson style revolver available in .22, .32 or .38 calibres and with various barrel lengths; and the R 15, which was a Western-style single-action six-shot revolver based on the Colt M1873 and chambered for .22LR or .22 Mag-

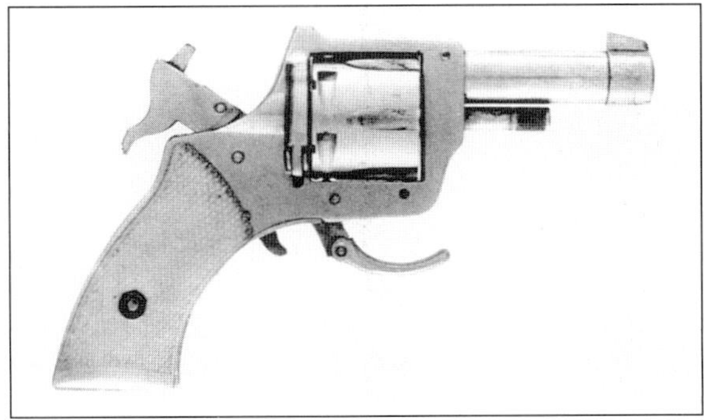

Reck P 8	
Calibre	6.35mm Browning
Method of operation	Blowback, striker-fired, single-action
Safety devices	Manual safety catch on left side of frame
Magazine type	Single-column detachable box in butt
Position of catch	At heel of butt
Magazine capacity	7 rounds
Front sight	Fixed blade
Rear sight	Fixed U-notch
Overall length	4.56in (116mm)
Barrel length	2.24in (57mm)
Number of grooves	6
Direction of twist	Right-hand
Empty weight	14.8oz (420g)
Markings	Left side of slide: 'RECK P 8 Kal. 6,35 mm Made in West - Germany [or with other names]'
Serial number	On right side of frame

Top: The Recky revolver, another of Reck's products sold under a wide variety of names in the United States but which fell foul of the 1968 Gun Control Act.
Above: One of Reck's more modern and higher-quality revolvers, the R 14 in .38 calibre is based upon the Smith & Wesson pattern.
Below: Reck's R 15 is a Western-style revolver in .22 calibre. Note that the characteristic muzzle reinforce seen on the 'Recky' is still apparent.

num rimfires. These were good-quality weapons, but increasing competition, together with growing restrictions on ownership of pistols, led the company to turn away from 'proper' firearms and concentrate more upon starting and alarm pistols. In the 1970s it was absorbed by a sporting-goods conglomerate and now operates as the Reck Division of Umarex-Sportwaffen of Arnsberg, making only starting and similar pistols.

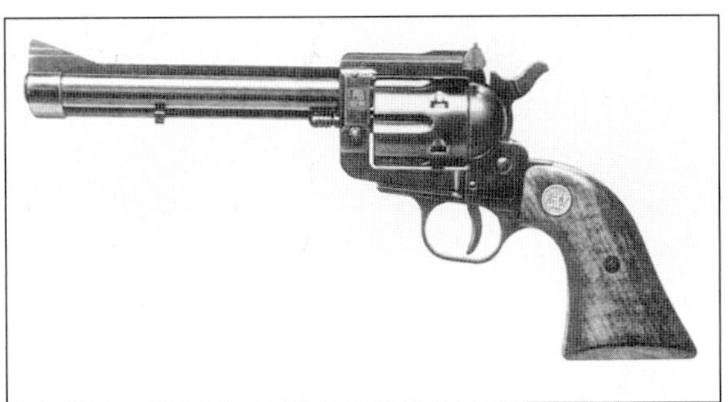

REFORM

August Schuler, Suhl

The Reform pistol is a repeating pistol of a type which was quite popular in the 1907–14 period, since it was light in weight, slim and easily pocketable, and very simple to use. This particular design has an unusual automatic ejecting feature not found on others of the class.

The weapon consists of a revolver-like butt and a box-like frame, with a self-cocking trigger and hammer mechanism. The frame is open at the front, and into it drops a block consisting of four superimposed barrels. To prepare the pistol for firing this block is removed, by lifting it from the frame, and the four chambers are loaded with 6.35mm Browning automatic pistol cartridges. The loaded block is then inserted into the frame, where it is held by a spring catch. To fire, the hammer is drawn back or the trigger pulled to cock the hammer and then release it. The cartridge in the topmost chamber is fired and the bullet departs through the top barrel. At the next cocking of the hammer a pawl lifts the block up so as to present the second barrel in front of the hammer. When this barrel is fired, some of the propelling gas escapes through a port leading up into the first barrel and blows the empty cartridge case out of the chamber—which must be rather disconcerting for the firer. The next cocking of the hammer lifts barrel number three into line, and firing that barrel causes the empty case to be blown out of number two. Finally barrel four is fired and ejects the case from barrel three. Now the block is lifted out of the frame and the spent case in chamber number four has to be manually ejected by either poking some instrument down the barrel or levering the case out with a penknife under its slight rim.

The design is the ultimate in simplicity and cheapness of manufacture, and slender and light enough to be carried in a pocket without much inconvenience. But one needs to be confident that one can stave off disaster with no more than four shots, for reloading looks like being a hazardous business if the enemy has not been subdued.

Dismantling the Reform is simply a matter of lifting out the barrel block and cleaning it; the only other useful step is to remove the grips, by removing the usual screws, to examine the lockwork, but repairing the lockwork would probably be a major task since the frame appears to be riveted together.

Reform	
Calibre	6.35mm Browning
Method of operation	Manual repeater, double-action
Safety devices	Manual safety catch on left side of frame
Magazine type	Barrel block
Magazine capacity	4 rounds
Front sight	Fixed blade
Rear sight	Fixed U-notch
Overall length	5.43in (138mm)
Barrel length	2.44in (62mm)
Number of grooves	4
Direction of twist	Right-hand
Empty weight	21.9oz (620g)
Markings	Left of barrel block: 'BREVETE D.R.P. 177025'
Serial number	None

Below: The Reform repeating pistol, a style very popular in the 1900s.

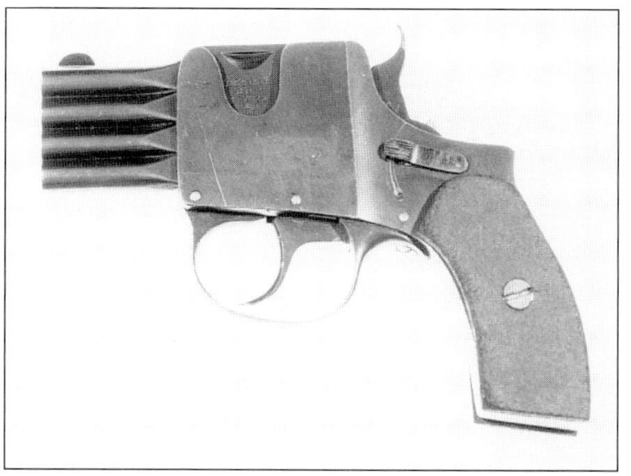

REGNUM

August Menz, Suhl

This is another four-barrelled mechanical repeating pistol of very similar appearance to the Reform described previously but considerably different in construction and operation. It bears no maker's marks and its attribution to Menz is based upon the fact that he owned the word 'Regnum' as one of his registered trademarks. It probably dates from the same 1907–14 period as the Reform pistol—a period which is determined by the fact that it fires the 6.35mm

Browning cartridge, which first appeared in 1906—and its production was abruptly ended by the outbreak of war in 1914.

The Regnum has the same sort of revolver butt and rectangular open frame as the Reform, but there is no visible hammer, the rear of the frame being carried up to enclose the firing mechanism. There is a block of four superimposed barrels, almost identical to the block used in the Reform, but in this case it is a fixture in the pistol, held there by a hinge screw at the lower front of the frame. By pressing a release catch on the left side of the frame, the block can be tipped forward, and the chambers are loaded with four 6.35mm cartridges and the weapon closed. There is a manual safety catch behind the barrel release catch which can be applied. To fire, the safety catch is released and the trigger pulled. A self-cocking mechanism drives a striker in the cap of the topmost cartridge and fires it. The next pull applies the firing pin to the second barrel, then the third and finally the bottom barrel. The release catch is pressed and the barrels tip forward; there is an automatic extractor system which eases the cartridges partially out of their chambers, very similar to a revolver, and a quick flip of the wrist will fling them clear of the gun to permit a reasonably quick reloading.

Regnum	
Calibre	6.35mm Browning
Method of operation	Manual repeater, self-cocking
Safety devices	Manual catch on left side of frame
Magazine type	Four-barrel block
Position of catch	Left side of frame
Front sight	Fixed blade
Rear sight	Groove in top of frame
Overall length	5.00in (127mm)
Barrel length	2.76in (70mm)
Number of grooves	4
Direction of twist	Right-hand
Empty weight	21.2oz (600g)
Markings	Left of frame: 'DRGM Auslands-PATENT' (although this marking is not always present)
Serial number	On side of trigger or right side of frame

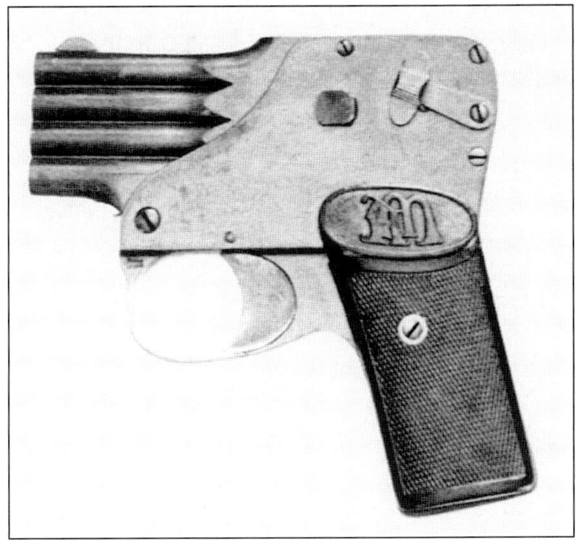

Above: The Regnum, another repeating pistol but one showing a slightly different method of approach to the problem.

Dismantling this pistol is not to be recommended. The essential dismantling of the barrel block for cleaning is simple enough, by removing the hinge screw in the frame, but the interior can only be gained by removing the grips and then by removing a number of screws, taking off the side plate. This reveals the self-cocking mechanism, which is best left alone.

REICHSREVOLVER

There is an old proverb to the effect that the camel wanted to be a horse but got designed by a committee: by and large, the implied moral of this holds good when contemplating committee-designed weapons. They generally manage to fall between two stools, being neither as up to date as the latest thinking in the

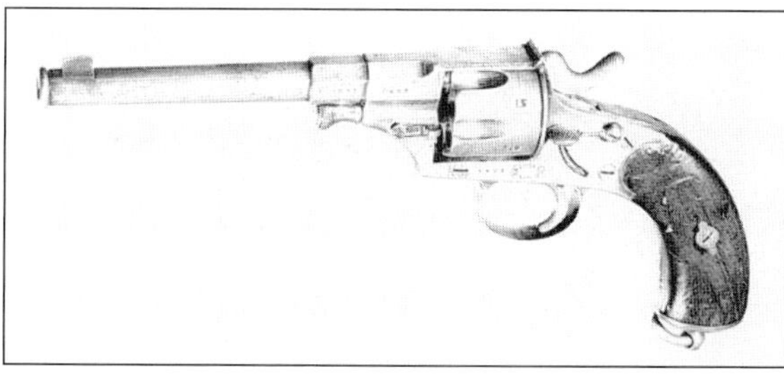

Above: The M1879 or Troopers' Model Reichsrevolver.

arms industry nor as combat-worthy as the users would like to see them. However, to its credit, the German Commissions of 1880 who were responsible for re-equipping the German Army when magazine weapons and metallic cartridges were making their appearance managed to produce quite creditable designs, and the two revolvers produced were sound and reliable handguns well up to the standard of their day.

There is a certain amount of confusion over the terminology applied to these two weapons, since they are variously called the M79, Cavalry or Troopers' Model in the case of the long-barrelled version and the M83, Infantry or Officers' Model in the case of the short-barrelled version.

The M83 shown here was manufactured at Suhl and bears the initials 'VCS CGH', indicating manufacture by a consortium which included V. C. Schilling and C. G. Haenel. It is a single-action, solid-frame revolver loading through an outward-hinging gate on the right side but, surprisingly, without means of cjccting the spent cases other than complete removal of the cylinder and punching out the cases one by one, using the cylinder axis pin. I say 'sur-

Below: The shorter M1883 or Officers' Model Reichsrevolver.

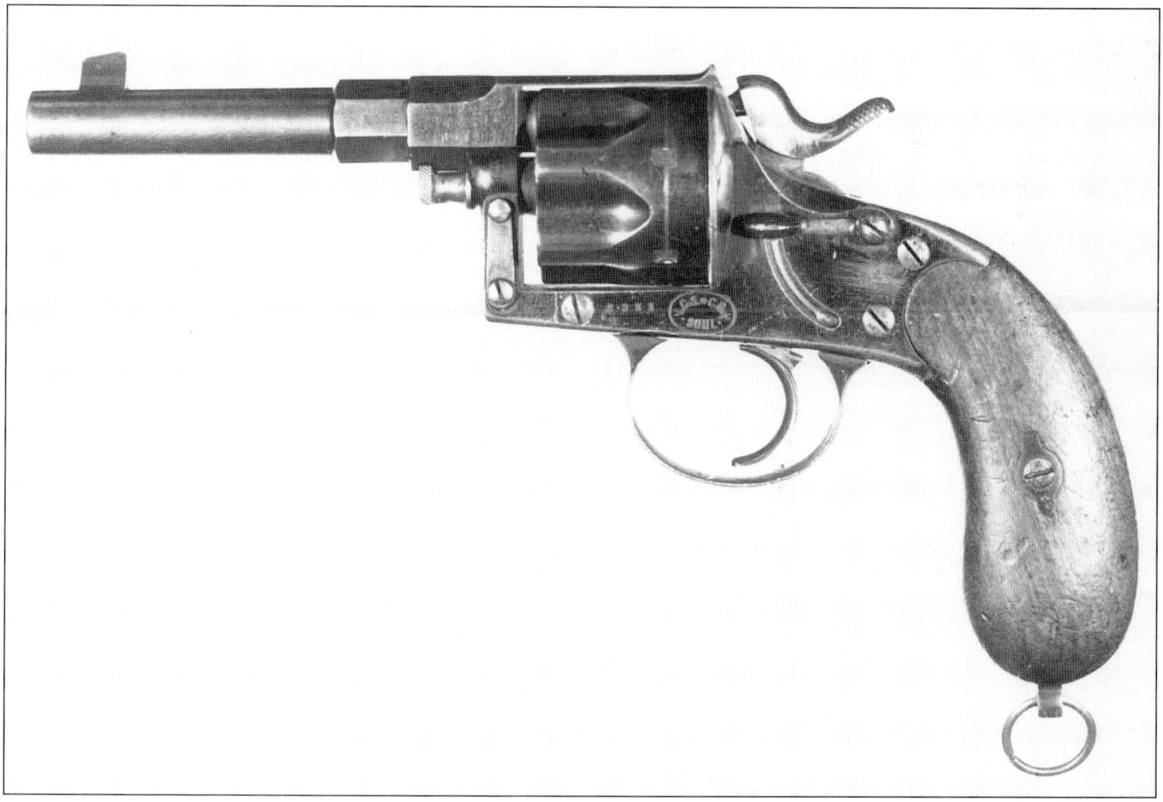

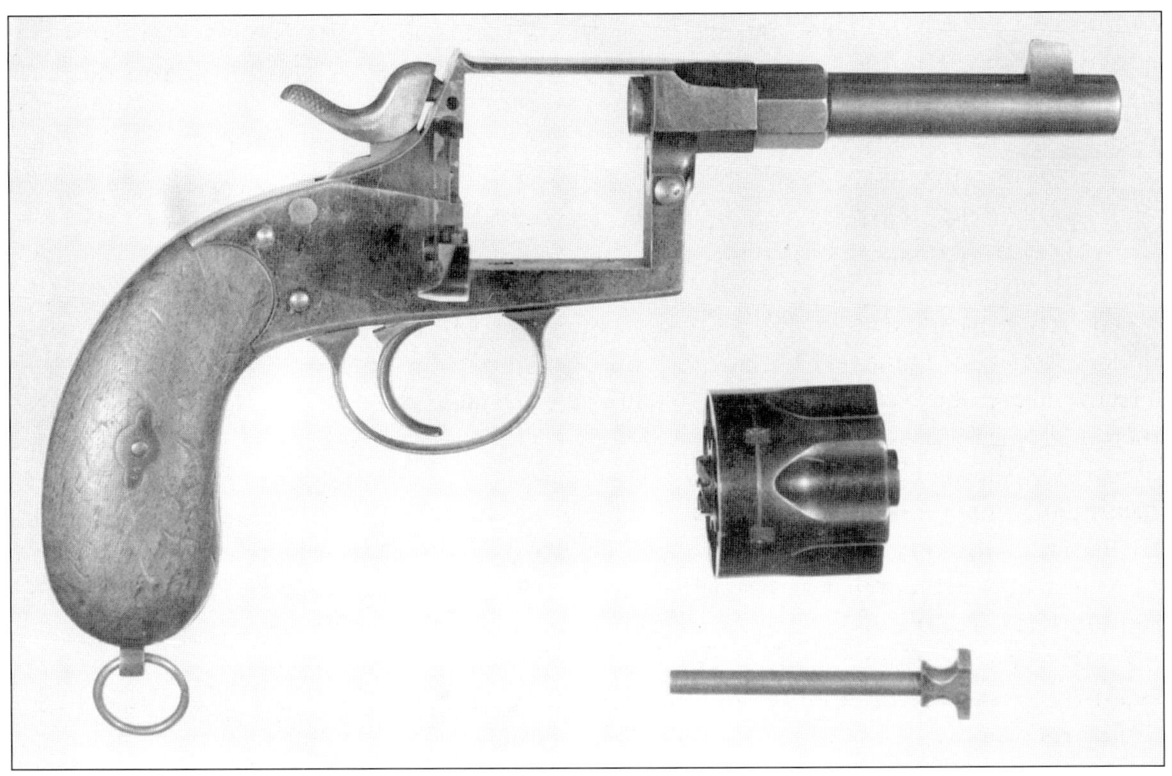

Above: Field-stripping a Reichsrevolver presents no great problems; it is also the quickest method of loading and unloading.

prisingly', since by 1880 there were a number of ejection systems available; it may well have been that the Commission subscribed to the contemporary theory that it was the duty of officers and NCOs to supervise the activity of the soldiers and not get themselves embroiled in personal combat. Therefore, since the revolver would only be used for one or two desperate shots when things got out of hand, rapid reloading was a luxury they could do without. Conversely, it may have been the case that all the practical ejection systems were well tied up with patents and the adoption of one might have cost money, although this point of view does not seem to have deterred the Commission when they were designing a rifle.

Another unusual feature of the revolver is the provision of a safety catch just below the hammer which is pressed down to make safe. This feature is rarely seen on military revolvers, but is more common on commercial designs. It always seems superfluous on a revolver and particularly so on a single-action type. A further safety feature is the provision of a half-cock notch on the hammer which is used to release the cylinder so that it revolves freely for loading through the gate.

The revolver is built up from a frame carrying the lock work and cylinder, with a short barrel stub into which the barrel is screwed and shrunk. The stub and rear section of the barrel are shaped into hexagonal form in order to facilitate assembly. The six-chambered cylinder is removed by pressing in the spring catch on the left front side of the frame ahead of the cylinder and pulling the cylinder axis pin forward. Opening the loading gate will allow the cylinder to drop out. It will be seen that the rear of each chamber is recessed in order completely to surround the head of the cartridge; this is a commendable safety measure in view of the state of the metallic cartridge in 1880 and was hailed as a great innovation when applied to .22in revolvers some forty years later. It will also be noted that each chamber is numbered on the outer surface of the cylinder—a feature of questionable utility.

The 10.6mm cartridges for this pistol appear under a variety of names—10.6mm, 10.8mm, 11mm and even 11.5mm being quoted here and there—but the figures '10,55' engraved on both the models shown here, together with similar measurements across the lands, appear to settle that question. The original ammunition is no longer obtainable, but it is possible to fire the Smith & Wesson .44in Russian cartridge from these pistols. Both are strong enough to stand up to the black-powder loading of this round, and the longer barrel of the M79 makes for accurate shooting. They should not, of course, be subjected to the force of a smokeless powder loading.

The makers' monogram will be found on the left side of the frame, above the trigger. The model shown here is marked with an oval containing the initials 'VCS CGH' and 'SUHL'. As for military markings, in many cases the life history of the pistol can be determined from those engraved on the back strap of the butt. This was the customary place for successive regiments to stamp their own identifying marks when the pistols formed part of their equipment. The model shown here is marked 'B.5.A.5.17', representing the 5th Bavarian Field Artillery Regiment, 5th Battery, weapon number 17. Serial numbers usually consist of two initial letters and a four-digit number and will be found on the barrel hexagon, the barrel stub hexagon, the frame side above the trigger guard, the loading gate front surface and the rear surface of the cylinder. In addition, the last two digits will be found on practically every removable part, for example the safety catch and all exposed screw-heads, and the number without initial letters will be found on the grip portion of the cylinder axis pin.

Reichsrevolver Model 1883

Calibre	10.6mm German Ordnance
Method of operation	Six-chambered, non-ejecting, single-action
Safety devices	Manual catch on left rear of frame
Magazine type	Six-chambered cylinder, right-hand gate loading
Position of catch	Axis pin removable
Front sight	Fixed blade
Rear sight	Fixed V-notch
Overall length	10.25in (260mm)
Barrel length	4.92in (125mm)
Number of grooves	6
Direction of twist	Right-hand
Empty weight	32.5oz (921g)
Markings	See text
Serial number	See text

M1879

This weapon differs from the M83 in dimensions. There is a slight difference in the cylinder pin retaining catch, this one having to be rotated downwards rather than pressed in to release the pin, and there is a prominent muzzle reinforce.

The regimental markings on this model are on the butt crown plate instead of the back strap, which is unusual. They consist of 'I.R.A.4.28' crossed through and 'I.M.27.40' (Infantry Munitions Column no 27, pistol no 40). The cypher of Wilhelm I, a crowned script 'W', also appears on the butt plate, and an inspection mark (a crown over a Gothic 'F') is stamped under the frame ahead of the trigger guard. The maker's mark on the frame is 'S & S VCS CGH SUHL', indicating the co-operative efforts of Spangenburg & Sauer, V. C. Schilling and C. G. Haenel.

Reichsrevolver M1879	
Calibre	10.6mm German Ordnance
Method of operation	Six-chambered, non-ejecting, single-action
Safety devices	Manual catch on left rear of frame
Magazine type	Six-chambered cylinder, right-hand gate loading
Position of catch	Centre axis pin
Front sight	Fixed blade
Rear sight	Fixed V-notch
Overall length	12.20in (310mm)
Barrel length	7.20in (183mm)
Number of grooves	6
Direction of twist	Right-hand
Empty weight	36.5oz (1,034g)
Markings	See text
Serial number	See text

The production history of these two revolvers is somewhat complex. The bulk of the initial production, from 1879 to about 1887, was by the commercial gunmakers Mauser of Oberndorf, Spangenburg & Sauer, Schilling and Haenel in Suhl and the Waffenfabrik von Dreyse in Sömmerda. This appears to have provided the Army with all the revolvers it needed and stocked the reserve arsenals as well. Thereafter production stopped for a few years, to recommence in about 1891 at the Königlich Gewehrfabrik Erfurt, where repair, refurbishment and the manufacture of occasional batches to keep the reserve up to strength continued until some time during World War I. The revolver production machinery was scrapped in 1919 when the arsenal was closed down by the Allied Disarmament Commission.

In addition to military production, several thousand revolvers were made for the civilian market by the Suhl factories after they had completed their military contracts. As a result of all this dispersed and prolonged activity, the actual number of Reichsrevolvers produced is not known with any degree of accuracy, but it was certainly not less than 100,000.

RHEINMETALL

The Rheinmetall pistol is the post-World War I offspring of the earlier Dreyse models, being made by the Rheinische Metallwaren- und Maschinenfabrik of Sömmerda, from the contraction of which title came 'Rheinmetall'. This company were later much more active in the manufacture of heavier military weapons, from machine guns up to the very heaviest artillery, and this pistol was probably their last excursion into the commercial market. Certainly, it was only made in very small numbers, and examples are particularly scarce today.

Although generally dismissed as simply another copy of the Browning 1910 design, with the return spring wrapped around the barrel and a more or less tubular front portion to the slide, the Rheinmetall conceals an unusual method of construction. The slide is actually in two parts, the rear section (with the finger grooving) being a separate component which carries

Rheinmetall 7.65mm	
Calibre	7.65mm Browning
Method of operation	Blowback, striker-fired
Safety devices	Manual catch at left rear of frame
Magazine type	Single-column detachable box in butt
Position of catch	Bottom rear of butt
Magazine capacity	8 rounds
Front sight	Fixed blade
Rear sight	Fixed U-notch
Overall length	6.50in (165mm)
Barrel length	3.65in (93mm)
Number of grooves	4
Direction of twist	Right-hand
Empty weight	23.5oz (666g)
Markings	Left of slide: 'RHEINMETALL ABT SOMMERDA' and the 'RM' trademark, a diamond within a circle
Serial number	See text

Above: The Rheinmetall pistol may look like the Browning 1910 but it is a good deal different inside.

the breech block and striker. The barrel is also a separate item, carried in a yoke in the frame.

All this becomes apparent when the pistol is dismantled. After removing the magazine and clearing the gun, pull back the slide until the safety catch can be turned up into the usual dismantling notch on the left side. With the slide locked back, it will now be possible to twist the rear section of the slide to loosen and remove it. Now grasp the rest of the slide and release the locking catch, allowing the slide to go forward until it can be slipped off the barrel and removed. The return spring and its collar now come off, leaving the barrel on the frame. Grasp the barrel and turn it through 90° so that the lip beneath the chamber mouth clears the restraining lug on the frame, and the barrel can then be removed to the rear.

Reassembly of the weapon is the reverse of stripping, assembling barrel and recoil spring into the frame first, placing the slide over the barrel and locking it in place, and then replacing the breech piece.

The full serial number is to be found underneath the muzzle end of the slide; the last four digits are inside the on the rear end of the frame and lower surface of the breech piece. An assembly number, bearing no relation to the register number, will be found on the underside of the breech piece and the underside of the rear end of the slide, where the breech piece fits, so that when assembled the two numbers are adjacent.

RÖHM

Röhm GmbH, Sontheim-an-der-Brenz

The Röhm company has produced a range of pistols under its own designations and then sold them under a dozen other names as well. All the following names refer to the same range of cheap revolvers, most of them being American sale names in the days before the 1968 Gun Control Act; the passage of that act, with its manifold restrictions on pistol dimensions, severely curtailed the import of Röhm pistols into the United States, and many of the sales names promptly ceased to exist.

Under the 'Röhm' heading we can consider the whole range of Röhm revolvers, identifiable by a round medallion in the grip carrying the letters 'RG' and sometimes the model number. Construction falls into three broad groups: the cheap, solid-frame models with gate-loading; the cheap, solid-frame models with swing-out cylinders; and the better-quality, solid-frame models with swing-out cylinders. It might be noted that Röhm also do a great deal of business in starting, gas and alarm pistols; these are numbered in the same way as bullet-firing weapons, and numbers missing from the following sequence may well be this class of weapon.

The first group—the cheap, solid-frame revolvers with gate-loading—were invariably in .22 rimfire calibre and were developed from the company's range of signal and blank cartridge starting pistols. They were of a somewhat angular appearance, with large and deeply serrated hammers and a prominent reinforce at the muzzle. These revolvers were primarily made for export, particularly to the United States, where they appeared under a variety of names—Burgo, EIG, Hy-Score, Thalco, Romo, Liberty, Vestpocket, Western Style, Zephyr and probably others not yet identified—for sale by various dealers. The 1968 US Gun Control Act put an end to their import into that country, which closed their major market, and their manufacture ceased shortly thereafter.

The models in this group were:

Model RG7 .22 Short, 1.25in barrel, solid-frame, gate-loaded, non-ejector.

Model RG10 By far the most common model, this was in .22 Short, a six-shot model with a 2.25in barrel. There were numerous minor variations in such details as finish, butt size, hammer spur and so forth, which do not appear to follow any recognisable system and were presumably added at the behest of various dealers to differentiate 'their' model from the others.

Model RG10s A variant with a trigger guard which is rounded, instead of the usual square shape, and with a much larger butt than normal.

Model RG11 .22LR, 3.625in barrel, solid-frame, non- ejector with finger grips formed into the front strap of the butt.

Model RG12 .22LR, 3.625in barrel, solid-frame, gate-loading, rod-ejection, with finger grip butt.

All these models can be identified by the medallion on the grip, which will either be

Below: The Rohm RG10 was another of the 1950s crop of cheap and cheerful .22 revolvers exported under a score of names.

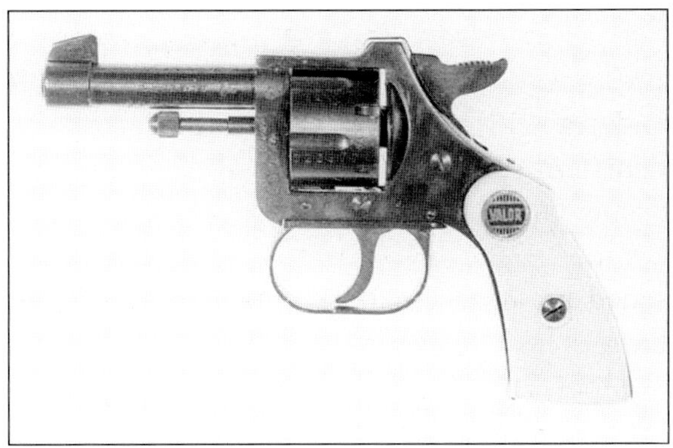

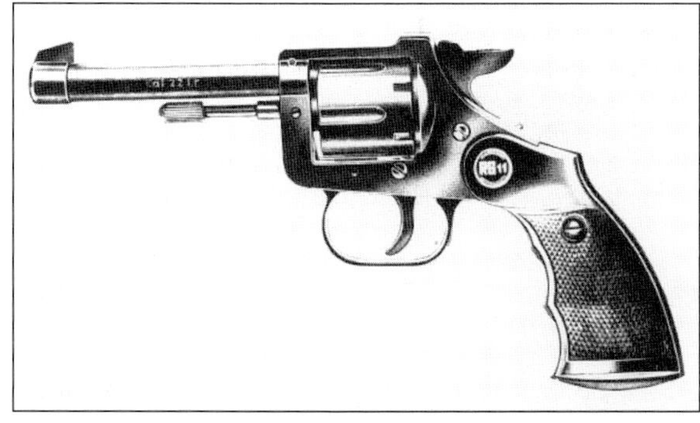

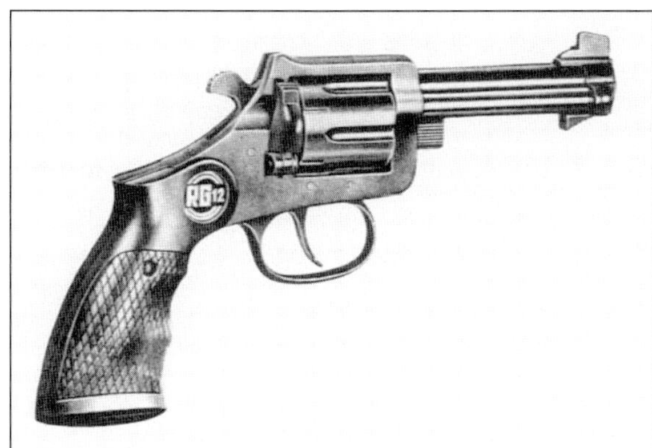

Top: The RG11 showed signs of improved design.
Above: The RG12 was a gate-loaded, rod-ejecting model.

marked with 'RG' and the model number or with the name adopted by the particular dealer. The barrel will usually be marked with the calibre and 'Made in Germany'.

The second group, which replaced the first group as the cheaper end of the Röhm range, use a simple swing-out cylinder mechanism which is locked in place by the ejector rod and released by pulling the rod forward. The general appearance of the weapons is more rounded and graceful, with ribbed barrels, less prominent hammers and oval or round trigger guards. Some still show the muzzle reinforce of the earlier models, but in general this has been superseded by a more robustly constructed ribbed barrel.

Models in this second range included the following:

Model RG14 .22LR, 1.75in barrel, six-shot, fixed sights.
Model RG20 .22 Short, 3in barrel, six-shot, fixed sights.
Model RG23 .22LR, 1.5in barrel, fixed sights.
Model RG24 As for RG23 but with 3.5in barrel.
Model RG31 .38 Special, 2in barrel, five-shot.

As a general rule this group carry the butt medallion with 'RG' and the model number and have 'Made in Germany' either on the barrel or on the right side of the frame and the cartridge on the left side of the barrel.

The third group are the best-quality group, based broadly on Smith & Wesson principles with a thumb-latch on the side of the frame, close to the hammer, to release the swing-out cylinder. Sights may be fixed or adjustable, ventilated ribs are common, anatomic grips appear on target models, and the company name appears on the left side of the barrel.

Model RG34 .22 Short. Best-quality solid-frame, with swing-out cylinder and ribbed barrel. The Model 34A has an adjustable rear sight and broadened hammer spur. The Model 34T has an adjustable rear sight, ramp front sight, heavy barrel, broad trigger and hammer spur and wooden anatomical grips.
Model RG35 As RG34 but in .22LR calibre.
Model RG36 As RG34 but in .32 S&W Long.
Model RG36T As for the RG34T but in .22 Winchester Magnum RF
Model RG38 As RG34 but in .38 Special. The Model 38S has adjustable rear sights and broad hammer spur; the Model 38T has ventilated rib and adjustable sights.
Model RG40 .38 Special, 2in barrel, six-shot.
Model RG57 A strengthened version of the RG34 available in .38 Special, .357 Magnum, .41 Magnum, .44 Special, .44 Magnum or .45

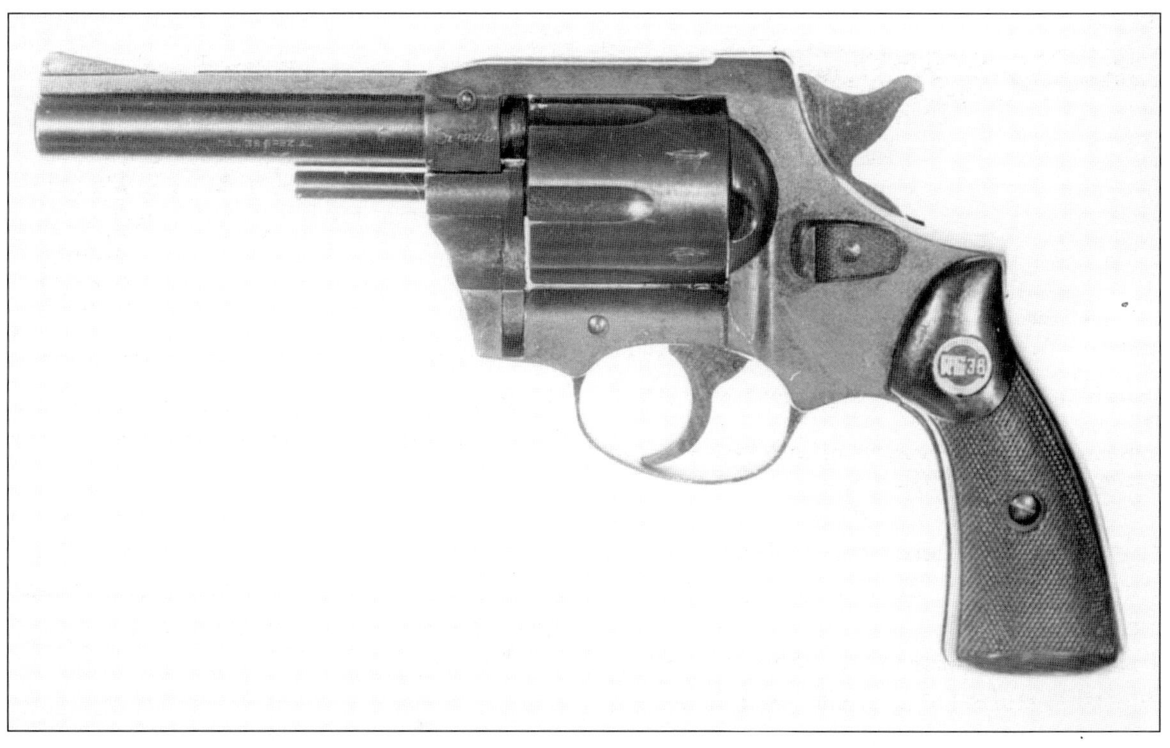

Above: With the RG38, Röhm entered the serious market with a side-opening .38 calibre revolver of good quality.
Below: The RG57 in .44 Magnum was Röhm's most powerful revolver.

Colt. Six-shot, with 4in or 6in barrel. The RG57T has adjustable sights.

Model RG88 A very high-quality .38/.357 Magnum six-shot revolver with ventilated rib and fixed sights. This model is distinguished by having the ejection rod concealed within a shroud, in Smith & Wesson fashion. The RG88T has adjustable sights. A 6in barrel is standard on both models, though shorter barrels are available to order. The Model 86T is the same pistol but with an adjustable rear sight.

There is also a fourth group which bears no similarity to the other three: this is the 'Western' style single-action group, all based broadly upon the familiar Colt Frontier model.

Röhm Model RG38

Calibre	.38 Special
Method of operation	Double-action revolver
Safety devices	None
Magazine type	Six-chambered cylinder
Position of catch	Left rear of frame
Front sight	Fixed blade
Rear sight	Fixed U-notch
Overall length	9.25in (235mm)
Barrel length	4.01in (102mm)
Number of grooves	6
Direction of twist	Right-hand
Empty weight	33.15oz (940g)
Markings	On left of barrel: 'RÖHM GMBH SONTHEIM/BRENZ MODEL 38 CAL. 38 SPECIAL'
Serial number	On right side of frame

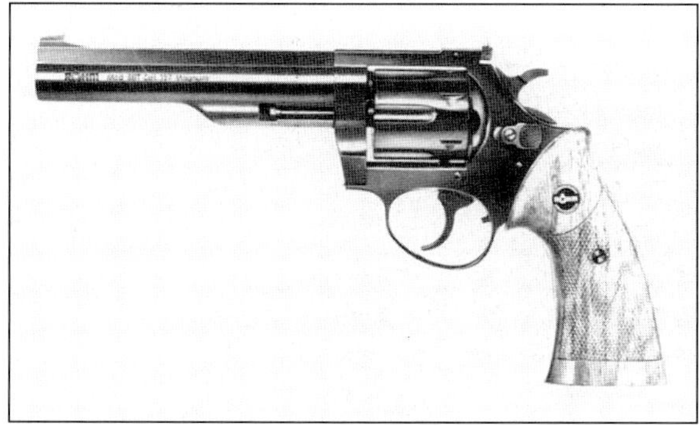

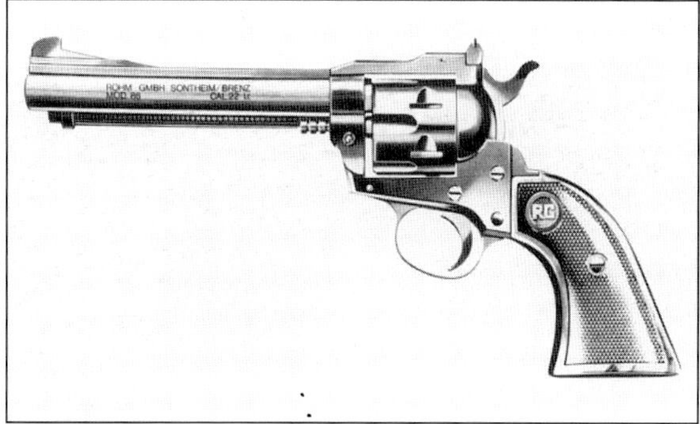

Above left: A popular choice for target shooting is the Röhm 88T . . .
Above right: . . . and, of course, the inevitable Western-style revolver, the Röhm 86T.

Model RG63 Western style single-action solid frame, available in .22, .32, .38, and .38 Special chambering.
Model RG66 Similar to the RG63 but with an adjustable rear sight and with interchangeable cylinders, offered in .22LR and .22WMRF combinations, with 4.75in or 6in barrel. The RG66T is a target version of this weapon, with adjustable sights and an adjustable trigger stop.

Röhm Model RG27

Calibre	6.35mm Browning
Method of operation	Blowback, hammer-fired, double-action
Safety devices	Manual safety catch on slide
Magazine type	Single-column detachable box in butt
Position of catch	Heel of butt
Magazine capacity	7 rounds
Front sight	Fixed blade
Rear sight	Fixed U-notch
Overall length	5.67in (140mm)
Barrel length	3.03in (77mm)
Number of grooves	6
Direction of twist	Right-hand
Empty weight	15.16oz (430g)
Markings	On left of slide: 'RÖHM GMBH SONTHEIM/BRENZ RG27 Kal. 6,35'
Serial number	On right side of frame

Model RG86 A strengthened version of the RG66 but with the same interchangeability of cylinders.

In the 1970s Röhm began producing blowback automatic pistols, the first of which was more or less based on their existing range of starting pistols.

Model RG26 This is a simple 6.35mm automatic, developed from an earlier starting pistol design, using an alloy frame and steel slide, and is striker-fired. It has a six-shot magazine.
Model RG27 This is a much more advanced design, with elements of the Walther TPH in it, having a double-action lock, an exposed hammer and a safety catch on the slide.

ROMER

Romerwerke GmbH, Suhl

This is a blowback pistol unusual in that it was normally supplied with two barrels, one for target shooting and one for self-defence, the target barrel being 6.5in long and the other 2.5in. The barrels can be interchanged rapidly without interfering with the rest of the weapon (and without even removing the magazine) by pressing the catch in the front end of the trigger guard; this withdraws a locking plate and allows the barrel to be slid forward out of the frame, and

Above: The Romer with its short barrel fitted.

the other barrel can then be slid back in. This interchangeability also facilitates cleaning.

The slide is also unusual in having a reduced-diameter forward section which is totally enclosed within the breech extension of the barrel when the weapon is loaded, thus completely concealing the cartridge case and insuring against accidents arising from burst rimfire cases. The magazine, in the butt, has its sides cut away and the platform fitted with grips so that it can be pulled down to make the insertion of rounds easier (which seems to be an unnecessary refinement on a pistol of this calibre).

Romer

Calibre	.22in Long Rifle rimfire
Method of operation	Blowback, striker-fired
Safety devices	Manual catch left rear of frame
Magazine type	Single-column detachable box in butt
Position of catch	Bottom rear of butt
Magazine capacity	7 rounds
Front sight	Blade; fixed on short barrel, adjustable on long barrel
Rear sight	Fixed U-notch
Overall length	9.50in (241mm) long-barrel model; 5.5in (140mm) short-barrel model
Barrel length	2.5 or 6.5in (63.5 or 165mm)
Number of grooves	6
Direction of twist	Right-hand
Empty weight	11.0oz (312g) short-barrel model
Markings	Left of barrel: 'KAL. .22 LONG RIFLE'; left of slide: 'ROMERWERKE SUHL'; grips: monogram of 'RWS' (see text)
Serial number	On left of slide, on left of frame, on bottom of barrels

Below: The Romer dismantled, showing how the barrel comes off and how the slide is shaped so as to enter the rear of the barrel block.

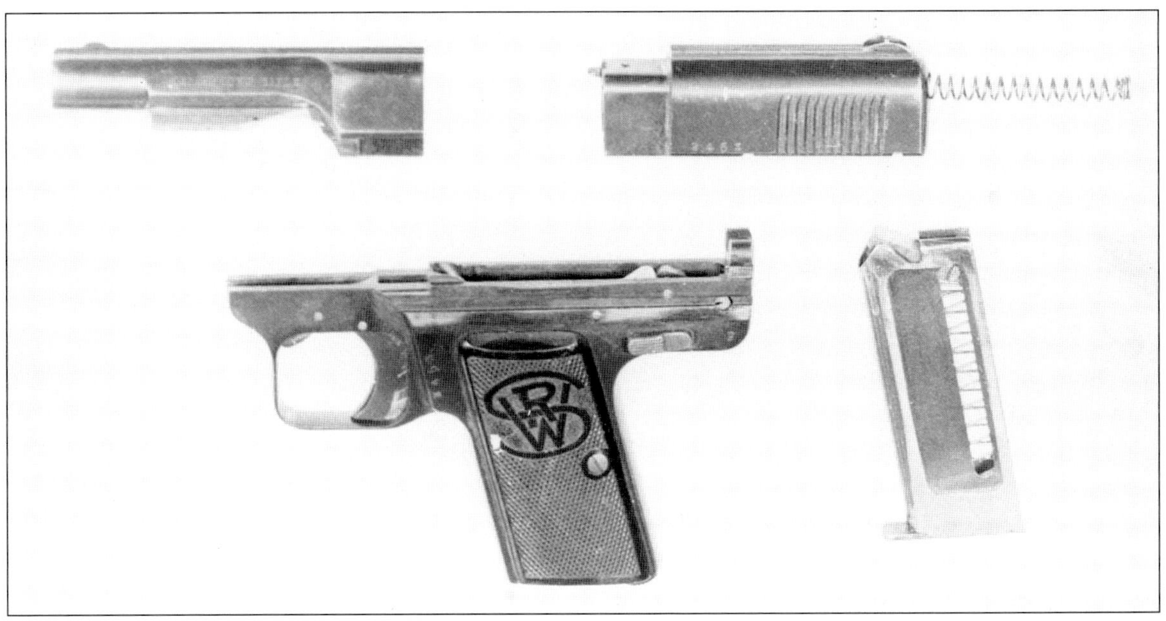

To strip the Romer, after clearing and removing the magazine, remove the barrel as explained above. The slide can then be removed by pulling back, lifting and easing it forwards.

Note that the monogram 'RWS' on the grip represents 'Romer Werke Suhl' and must not be confused with Rheinische Westfalische Sprengstoff, an ammunition and explosive manufacturer who used a similar monogram on their ammunition.

ROTH-SAUER

J. P. Sauer & Sohn, Suhl

George Roth, well-known as an Austrian ammunition manufacturer, was also a prolific designer both of complete weapons and of small details which could be incorporated into weapons. He was most active in consort with Frommer, (a Hungarian) and Krnka (a Bohemian), and the three of them seem to have been most intrigued with the 'long recoil' concept of operation. In this system the recoiling bolt takes the barrel with it for almost the full travel, certainly for a distance greater than the length of the cartridge. When this point is reached, the bolt is unlocked and held while the barrel is allowed to return to its forward position. Then the bolt is released and travels forward, chambering a round as it does so, until it meets the barrel and is locked once more. Very few pistols—or any other weapons for that matter—have been successfully designed around the long recoil principle. It is tolerable in a shoulder arm, but in anything other than a small and low-powered pistol the reciprocation of all that weight renders it a most uncomfortable performance for the firer. The all-time record in this respect was held by the British 'Mars' pistol, a long-recoil weapon of exceptionally powerful ballistics; when this was fired, the firer invariably finished with the pistol pointing straight up in the air, so violent was the transfer of weight above his hand.

Roth appears not to have been particularly interested in making the pistols which he designed, probably because an ammunition factory is not well adapted to mechanical engineering, and thus we find the Roth-Steyr, made in Austria to his design, the Frommer, made in Hungary, and the pistol considered here, the Roth-Sauer, made in Germany. This was manufactured by J. P. Sauer prior to World War I, and probably while they were perfecting their own designs of weapon. It is virtually a smaller 'pocket' edition of the much more powerful 8mm Roth-Steyr Austrian Service pistol which was adopted in 1907 and which had the distinction of being the first automatic pistol adopted by a major power for military use. It had several novel features which were reproduced in this Sauer version.

The cartridge used with this weapon was the 7.65mm Roth-Sauer, a special round developed for it by Roth. It is somewhat shorter than the normal 7.65mm auto round and rather less powerful. In spite of this, the pistol uses a locked-breech system. The breech bolt is locked

Below: The Roth-Sauer, a somewhat ornate design covering a somewhat complicated interior.

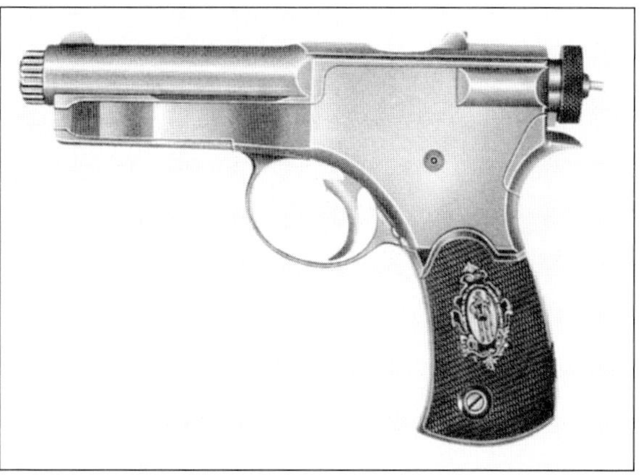

into the chamber recess by a single lug at the top of the bolt. Theoretically this is a bad thing, since it means that stresses and strains induced by firing are ill-balanced, but in a weapon such as this no harm is done. When the pistol is fired, the barrel and bolt recoil locked together. At the end of the recoil stroke the bolt is rotated by a cam through about 20° and held, permitting the barrel to run back under the force of the return spring. In doing so it pulls itself off the spent cartridge case, which of course is held by the extractor on the face of the bolt and then ejected. The barrel is held just before it reaches the firing position, and the bolt is, by the barrel's action, released to come forward under spring power. In coming forward it strips the next round from the magazine and loads it; the bolt lug enters its recess and the barrel and bolt move forward into the firing position, during which movement the bolt is rotated to lock.

The recoil action has also partially cocked the striker; completion of the cocking movement is done by the first action of the trigger. As the trigger is pulled through, the first portion of the movement causes the striker to be further cocked, placing more compression on the striker spring, until the sear is tripped and the striker released to hit the cartridge cap. However, contrary to common belief, this is not a double-action system: once the trigger has been pulled the action is uncocked and the trigger cannot be pulled again in the event of a misfire. The only way to re-cock is to operate the bolt manually. The object of this peculiar system is not an attempt at double-action, but a form of safety device. The Roth-Steyr, which is the father of this weapon, was a heavy cavalry pistol, and the Austro-Hungarian Army were afraid that a normal sear mechanism would lead to a trigger too sensitive for use by cavalry, since if the pistol were cocked, an inadvertent squeeze of the trigger (such as a trooper might make if his horse chose that moment to become skittish) would result in the pistol being fired—hence the design of this trigger and striker mechanism so that the cocking is not completed until the firer consciously and deliberately chooses to pull the trigger. It is for this reason, too, that no applied safety catch is found on these designs: with such a trigger they would be superfluous.

Roth-Sauer

Calibre	7.65 × 13mm Roth-Sauer
Method of operation	Long recoil, locked breech, rotating barrel, striker-fired
Safety devices	None
Magazine type	Integral in butt; charged loaded
Position of catch	Cartridge release catch on left side of frame
Magazine capacity	7 rounds
Front sight	Fixed blade
Rear sight	Fixed U-notch
Overall length	6.60in (168mm)
Barrel length	3.86in (98mm)
Number of grooves	6
Direction of twist	Right-hand
Empty weight	23.5oz (665g)
Markings	On top of frame: 'PATENT ROTH'; on grips: a medallion with the Sauer badge, a 'bearded savage hunter'
Serial number	On left side of barrel

As with many Frommer/Roth designs, the magazine lies in the pistol butt, but it is integral and not detachable. To load the pistol the bolt is drawn back as far as possible until the magazine platform rises and holds the action open. A charger of seven rounds is inserted into guides in the top frame, which blocks the movement of the bolt. This charger is fitted with a thumb piece to make loading easier. The rounds are swept out of the charger and into the butt magazine by pressure on this thumb piece and the empty charger is then removed, allowing the bolt to go forward and chamber the first round.

Should it be desired to empty the magazine without firing, one can either manipulate the bolt back and forth until the last round is ejected, or pull back and hold the bolt open and press in the stud on the left side of the frame. This pulls back the spring catch controlling feed from the magazine and permits the magazine spring to eject the entire contents of the magazine straight up and through the action—and usually into the nearest mud-puddle.

SAUER

J. P. Sauer und Sohn GmbH, Suhl (1733–1945)
J. P. Sauer & Sohn GmbH, Eckernförde (1946–)

This company were known and renowned for their high-class rifles and shotguns for many years before they entered into the pistol field. Their final pistol design prior to World War II was one of the most advanced weapons of its day and only the advent of war prevented it from becoming as famous as the Mauser or Walther. The first modern pistol to achieve commercial success was their 1914 model, generally known as the Old Model, and it formed the basic pattern for subsequent designs. But before that they had briefly flirted with an odd mechanical repeating pistol.

Bär Pistol

This repeating-pistol was the invention of Burkhard Behr, a Russian resident in Switzerland, who secured British Patent 11998 of 1898, together with patents in other countries, to cover the unusual features. The arrangements by which Sauer came to manufacture it are not known, but they placed it on the market in 1900, and it seems to have enjoyed a certain popularity for some years until the rise of the pocket automatic supplanted it as a personal defence pistol. The Bär was rather like a revolver in its layout, but the barrel unit was a flat, fluted block with two barrels, one above the other.

Sauer Bär Pistol

Calibre	7 × 15.5mm Bär or 6.35mm Browning
Method of operation	Manual repeater, self-cocking
Safety devices	None
Magazine type	4-chambered block
Position of catch	Top of frame
Magazine capacity	4 rounds
Front sight	Fixed blade
Rear sight	Fixed U-notch
Overall length	5.10in (155mm)
Barrel length	2.44in (62mm)
Number of grooves	4
Direction of twist	Right-hand
Empty weight	12.2oz (345g)
Markings	Top of barrel: 'BÄR PISTOLE'; left side of barrel; 'J. P. SAUER & SOHN SUHL'; side of chamber block: 'D.R.G.M. 104616 PATENT'
Serial number	On left side of frame in front of chamber block

Behind this, in the place where a revolver cylinder would go, was a flat block with four chambers arranged vertically, and with a longitudinal pivot passing through its centre, so that the two upper chambers were aligned with the two barrels. Behind the chambers lay a hammer, concealed in the rise of the frame above the butt, and this hammer carried a rotating firing-pin unit on its face. On pulling the folding trigger, the hammer was cocked and released, firing one of the upper chambers, the bullet passing through the corresponding barrel. Pulling the trigger again repeated the action, turning the firing pin unit during the cocking stroke, so that the pin descended on the unfired chamber and discharged the other bullet through its barrel. A catch on top of the frame was now pressed, and the chamber block rotated about its axis pin so that the two lower, loaded chambers were now aligned with the barrels and the two fired chambers were at the bottom, after which the two upper chambers could be fired in the same manner as before.

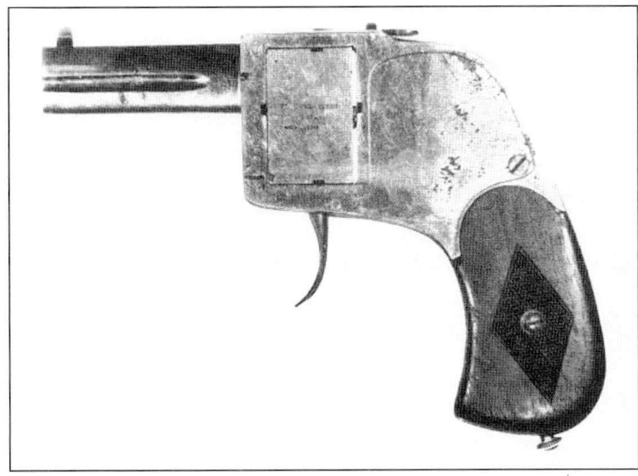

Above: Sauer's Bär pistol, an ingeniously simple design of four-shot repeater.

By giving only a half-turn to the chamber block, the chambers protruded at the sides to allow the empty cases to be punched out by using a pin carried in the butt, after which they could be re-loaded.

The Bär was originally produced chambered for a special 7mm rimmed cartridge, but after 1907 numbers were produced chambered for the 6.35mm Browning automatic pistol cartridge.

The only dismantling which can usefully be done is to remove the block axis pin and the chamber block. Withdrawing two screws will allow the grips to be removed, but that reveals nothing. A further three screws on the left side of the frame permit a cover plate to be removed, giving access to the lockwork.

Once the mechanical repeater began to lose its popularity, Sauer & Sohn set about developing their own design of automatic pistol, which appeared on the market late in 1913.

Below: The 7.65mm Sauer Model 1913 used a pressed slide with an inserted breech block.

Sauer M1914

Produced in both 6.35mm and 7.65mm calibres, both versions being alike except for dimensions, this is a simple blowback pistol but showing evidence of original thought in the design. Instead of the usual pattern of slide-cum-breech block, the Sauer model uses a separate block securely mounted in the slide; while the block itself is a complex piece of milling, it was probably an easier proposition from the production point of view than a combined unit.

To strip the Model 1914, after removing the magazine and clearing the gun, press down the spring-loaded back sight. This releases a catch engaged in the rim of the knurled cap at the rear of the slide. The cap can now be unscrewed, though while doing so the slide and frame should be securely gripped, as removal of the cap will release tension on the recoil spring. Take care also, with the final unscrewing, since

Sauer 6.35mm 1914	
Calibre	6.35mm Browning
Method of operation	Blowback, striker-fired
Safety devices	Manual catch at left rear of trigger guard
Magazine type	Single-column detachable box in butt
Position of catch	Bottom rear of butt
Magazine capacity	7 rounds
Front sight	Fixed blade
Rear sight	Fixed V-notch
Overall length	4.27in (108mm)
Barrel length	2.76in (70mm)
Number of grooves	6
Direction of twist	Right-hand
Empty weight	14.4oz (408g)
Markings	See 7.65mm M1914
Serial number	See text

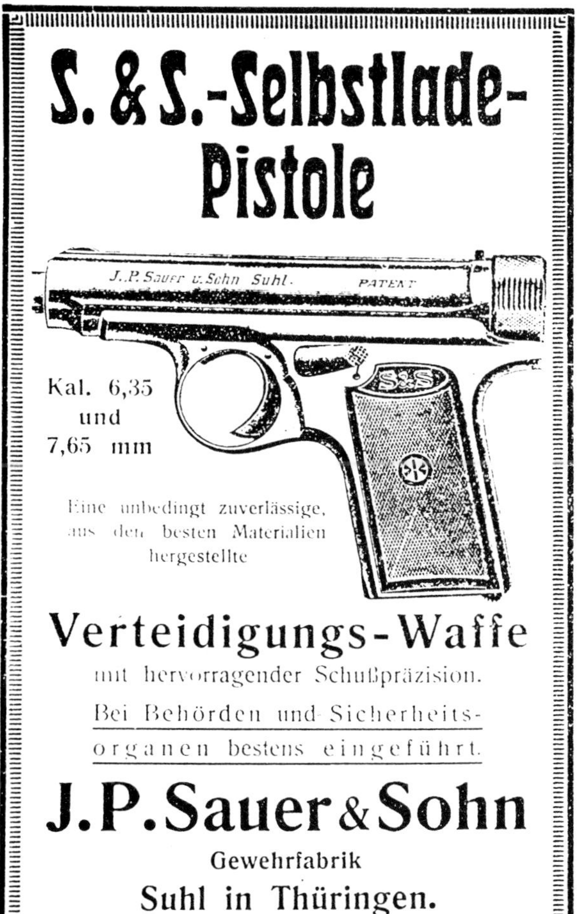

Left: A 1920s advertisement for the Sauer pistols.

Sauer 7.65mm 1914	
Calibre	7.65mm Browning
Method of operation	Blowback, striker-fired
Safety devices	Manual catch at left rear of trigger guard
Magazine type	Single-column detachable box in butt
Position of catch	Bottom rear of butt
Magazine capacity	7 rounds
Front sight	Fixed blade
Rear sight	Fixed V-notch
Overall length	5.67in (144mm)
Barrel length	2.95in (75mm)
Number of grooves	6
Direction of twist	Right-hand
Empty weight	20.3oz (575g)
Markings	Top of slide: 'J. P. SAUER & SOHN SUHL'; left of slide: 'PATENT'; right of slide: 'CAL. 7.65' or 'CAL. 6.35'; butt grips, left: 'SAUER, CAL. 7.65 [or CAL. 6.35]'; butt grips, right: 'S & S'
Serial number	See text

Left: The 7.65mm Behörden model of 1930 is similar to the 1913 model but has a few cosmetic changes.

the firing pin spring will push the cap off quite forcefully. Remove the cap, together with the firing pin spring, and allow the slide to move forward until it can be slipped completely off the frame. The breech block can now be slid backwards from the frame and the firing pin removed from it. The butt grips are secured, not by the usual screw into the frame, but by latches locking behind the frame and controlled by screws in the centre of each grip. Turning these through 90° until the screwdriver slot is parallel with the barrel will allow the plastic grips to be lifted off.

Reassembly is the reverse of the foregoing procedure. Care should be taken when screwing home the end cap to remember to depress the rear sight before the last few turns; care must also be taken to ensure that the sight catch is not released into the slotted portion of the cap but that the cap is turned on until the slotted section lies beneath the slide and out of sight.

The full serial number is found on the frame above the grip. However, when the weapon is dismantled, a completely different set of numbers will be found—a four-digit number at the back of the frame, with the last three digits repeated on the slide, on the breech block and inside the knurled cap. These numbers refer to the run of work in the factory, while the exterior number is the register or serial number of the weapon.

Sauer M1930

This is sometimes called the Behörden Modell or Authorities' Model, though I know of no official justification for this title other than the fact that, like many other pistols of this class, it was used by military and civil police units. In general appearance and construction it is practically the same as the 1914 Model, but the butt

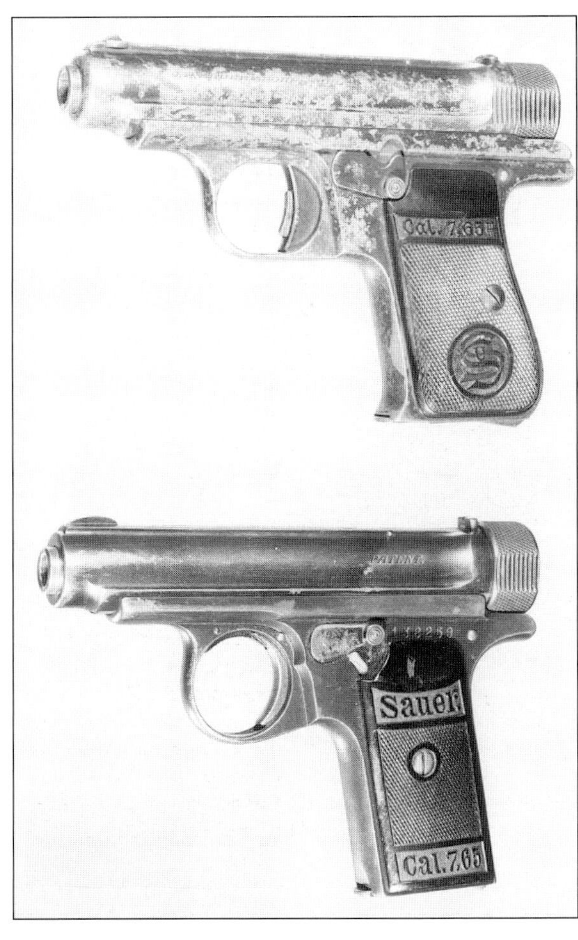

Right: The two Sauer 7.65mm pistols compared: the M1930 at the top, with the M1913 below.

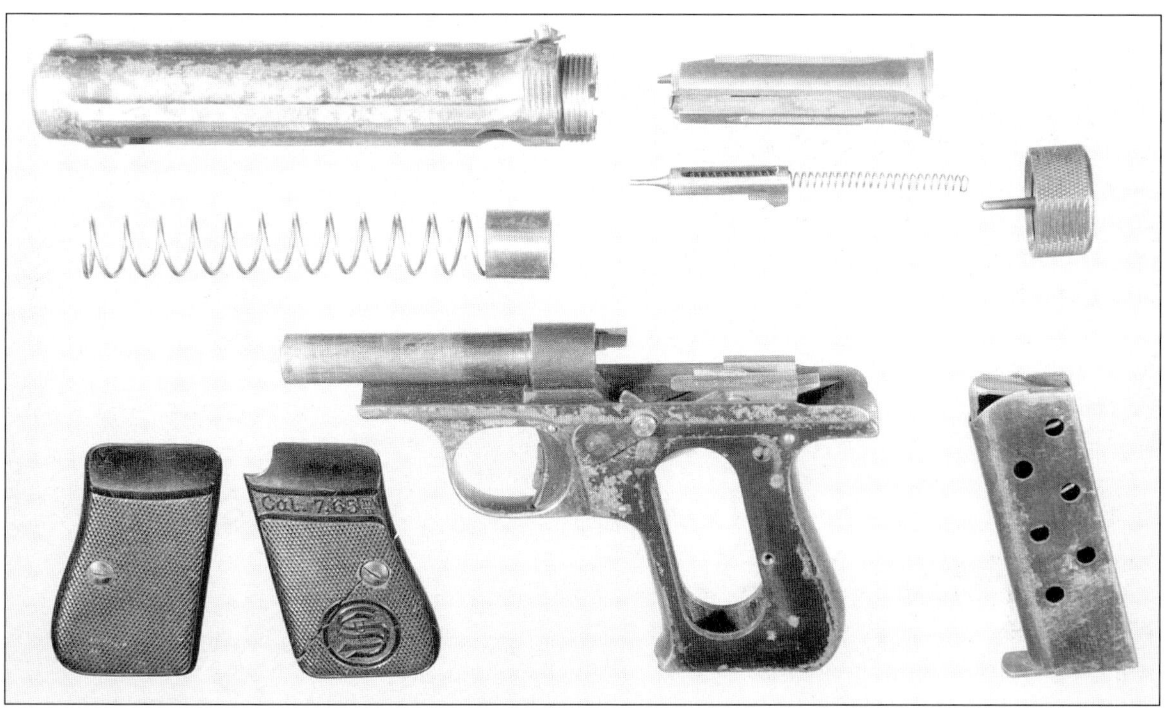

Above: A sadly corroded specimen of the Behörden model dismantled.

Sauer M1930

Calibre	7.65mm Browning
Method of operation	Blowback, striker-fired
Safety devices	Manual catch at left rear of trigger guard
Magazine type	Single-column detachable box in butt
Position of catch	Bottom rear of butt
Magazine capacity	7 rounds
Front sight	Fixed blade
Rear sight	Fixed V-notch
Overall length	5.75in (146mm)
Barrel length	3.03in (77mm)
Number of grooves	6
Direction of twist	Right-hand
Empty weight	22.0oz (630g)
Markings	As for 1914 Model with addition of 'S & S CAL. 7,65' on bottom plate of magazine; left grip has 'CAL. 7,65' and monogram of 'S u S'.
Serial number	Full number on right side of frame; last three digits on underside of slide (note that this model has the top of the slide knurled in order to provide a non-reflecting surface)

shows signs of having been designed with the intention of fitting the human hand rather better, there is a loose sleeve on the barrel to act as a bearing for the recoil spring, a signal pin is fitted to the bolt so as to protrude through the rear screwed cap when a round is chambered, and the trigger is much lighter in action due to the fitting of a sensitive catch plate. This last protrudes from the front edge of the trigger and unlocks on finger pressure to permit a very small amount of movement of the main trigger to fire the pistol. The 1914 Model had a long and creepy trigger pull; simply retaining the same mechanism and lightening the pull would have made it unsafe against a sudden jar or drop and was liable to lead to fully automatic functioning by the shock of the returning slide jarring off the trigger. The addition of the catch plate removes these dangers and ensures that only correct application of a finger can fire the pistol.

Stripping the 1930 Model is a similar procedure to that outlined above for the 1914 Model, with the addition that, when the bolt is removed, the signal link and pin can be slipped out against the pressure of the pin's spring; when doing this, place one finger over the top of the bolt and pin and then push back on the front end of the arrangement, allowing link and pin to pop up and be trapped by the finger—otherwise it tends to fly out for several feet and is small enough to be easily lost.

The Vest-Pocket Models

In 1923 there appeared the first of a series of *Westentaschenmodellen* or vest-pocket models, which bore no resemblance whatever to the 1914 pattern and might be said to be closer to the Walther Model 9 in both size and appearance. A small fixed-barrel blowback, the WTP was notable for the curious construction of the slide, with a large cutaway section in the middle which acted as the ejection port but exposed about half the length of the barrel. Another odd feature was the provision of finger grooves not only at the rear of the slide like virtually every other similar weapon but also at the front end of the slide like none other—although, of course, this may just have been a cosmetic feature.

Below: The Sauer WTP vest-pocket 6.35mm model.

Sauer WTM

Calibre	6.35mm Browning
Method of operation	Blowback, striker-fired
Safety devices	Manual safety catch on left grip
Magazine type	Single-column detachable box in butt
Position of catch	At heel of butt
Magazine capacity	6 rounds
Front sight	Fixed blade
Rear sight	Groove in slide top
Overall length	4.21in (107mm)
Barrel length	2.17in (55mm)
Number of grooves	6
Direction of twist	Right-hand
Empty weight	11.3oz (320g)
Markings	Left of slide: 'J. P. SAUER & SOHN SUHL PATENT'; right of slide: 'CAL. 6,35 PATENT'; bottom plate of magazine 'S & S CAL. 6,35 WTM'; grips, top: 'SAUER'; grips, bottom: 'CAL. 6,35'
Serial number	On right side of frame behind grip

The construction is also unique. The slide is actually open-topped for most of its length and carries a separate breech block which forms most of what appears to be the rear end of the slide. On the rear face of the slide there is a central signal pin (actually forming part of the firing pin assembly) which indicates that the pistol is cocked. Alongside it, to the right, is a small serrated catch which locks the breech block to the slide. By re-pressing this catch and drawing back the slide, the breech block will stay behind the chamber but the slide will move to the rear and expose the firing pin spring and signal pin. The slide can now be lifted at the rear and slipped forward over the barrel and removed. The breech block can now be simply lifted off the frame. The recoil spring can be taken from its guide rod beneath the barrel and the firing pin shaken out of the breech block, and the pistol is now stripped as far as is really necessary.

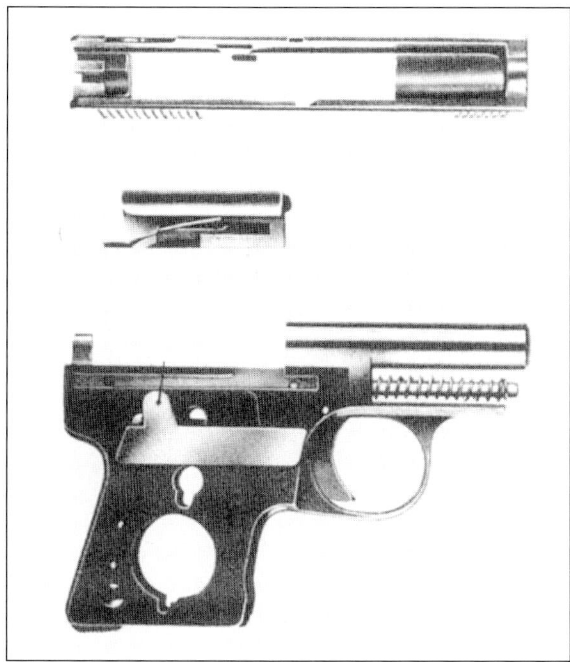

Above: The Sauer WTP stripped.

Reassembly is quite simple. Replace the return spring, insert the firing pin into the block, and replace the block in the frame, closing the chamber. Insert the firing pin spring and signal pin. Slip the slide over the barrel and spring, and lower the rear end and run it forward, allowing the signal pin to enter its hole and the breech block catch to engage.

Model WTM 28

In the early months of 1927 a new model was introduced, generally similar to the WTM but slightly smaller—the Model WTM 28. The most obvious external difference is that the serrations for the finger grips at the rear of the slide are now slightly oblique and more numerous, and those at the front of the slide have been removed. The inscription on the lower part of the grips now reads 'CAL. 6,35 28'. The construction differs considerably and is much simpler. The separate breech block has been discarded for the usual sort of block forming part of the slide, but the general appearance remains the same, with the large central cutaway portion acting as the ejection port. The signal pin is not longer present, and the firing pin is retained in the rear end of the slide by a bayonet catch cover.

Finally, in 1929 or 1930, the design was changed again. The slide now became the more conventional type which entirely covers the barrel and has an ejection port on the right-hand side. The return spring no longer has a guide rod and lies beneath the barrel, with an end cap which slips into a hole in the front of the slide. Dismantling is simply a matter of pulling the slide all the way back, lifting, and easing it forward over the barrel. The dimensions were changed slightly, the overall length now being 4.52in (115mm) and the barrel length 2.20in (56mm). The markings remained the same, and it appears that there was no change of designation. Production of the WTM continued until the latter 1930s, and serial numbers in the 250,000 range have been seen.

Sauer WTM 28	
Calibre	6.35mm Browning
Method of operation	Blowback, striker-fired
Safety devices	Manual safety on left grip
Magazine type	Single-column detachable box in butt
Position of catch	At heel of butt
Magazine capacity	6 rounds
Front sight	Fixed blade
Rear sight	Groove in slide top
Overall length	3.93in (100mm)
Barrel length	1.96in (50mm)
Number of grooves	6
Direction of twist	Right-hand
Empty weight	9.7oz (275g)
Markings	Left of slide: 'J. P. SAUER & SOHN SUHL'; right of slide: 'CAL. 6,35 D.R.P. 459854'; grips: top: 'SAUER'; grips, bottom: 'CAL. 6,35 28'
Serial number	On right side of slide behind grip

Sauer M38H

This was Sauer's last pre-war design, and I am of the opinion that, had the war not intervened, it might well have captured the world markets for pocket pistols, since it was outstandingly good. It was heavy enough to make a good shooting pistol in this calibre—most 7.65mm weapons err on the side of lightness, which does nothing for their accuracy—and it had many advanced features, some of which were not to be seen again until the 1980s.

It departs entirely from the tubular appearance of the previous models and reverts to the more usual practice of combining slide and breech block in one unit. A safety catch is fitted to the rear of the slide, convenient to the thumb for a right-handed firer, and a signal pin protrudes from the rear of the slide when a round is chambered. A magazine safety ensures that the weapon cannot be fired when the magazine is withdrawn. At the top of the left grip (just behind the trigger) is a thumb catch which at first sight appears to be a safety catch but is in fact Sauer's unique contribution to pistol design. This lever can be used to lower the cocked hammer on to a loaded chamber under control, or, if the hammer is already down, a sharp depression of the catch causes the hammer to be lifted and cocked. In addition, the lockwork is arranged for double-action firing, i.e. the slide can be pulled back to cock and load in the usual fashion, whereupon pressure on the trigger will release the hammer and fire the pistol; alternatively, after cocking, the thumb piece can be used to lower the hammer. Then, when needed, the first shot can be fired by a straight pull on the trigger—cocking and releasing the hammer

Below: The Sauer 38H of 1938, a double-action pistol with de-cocking lever.

Above: The Sauer 38H dismantled to show the location of the de-cocking lever.

Sauer Model 1938

Calibre	7.65mm Browning
Method of operation	Blowback, hammer-fired, double-action
Safety devices	Manual catch at left rear of slide; magazine safety
Magazine type	Single-column detachable box in butt
Position of catch	Top left butt grip
Magazine capacity	8 rounds
Front sight	Fixed blade
Rear sight	Adjustable U-notch
Overall length	6.75in (171 mm)
Barrel length	3.27in (83mm)
Number of grooves	4
Direction of twist	Right-hand
Empty weight	25.3oz (717g)
Markings	Left of slide: 'J. P. SAUER & SOHN SUHL CAL. 7,65'; right of slide: 'PATENT'; left butt grip: monogram 'S u S'; magazine bottom plate: monogram 'S u S' and 'CAL. 7,65'
Serial number	Full number on right rear of frame; last three digits on undersurface of slide

in one movement—or the thumb piece can be used once more to cock the hammer ready for a more deliberate release of the trigger. The double-action system is admirable for quick-draw combat use, but, if time is available for a more precise aim, then the second method can be used. Altogether, practically every eventuality seems to have been covered by this system.

To strip the 1938 Model, first remove the magazine by pressing the button just behind the trigger, clear the gun and lower the hammer using the thumb catch. Now pull down on the two milled wings protruding from the frame just ahead of the trigger and within the trigger guard. Pull back the slide to its fullest extent, lifting the rear end. This will bring the rear end clear of the frame and allow the slide to be eased forward and slipped off the barrel, leaving the recoil spring in place around the barrel. The grips can be removed by the usual type of screw to give access to the lockwork and thumb-piece. Close examination of the slide will reveal that, while for all practical purposes the breech block forms part of the slide, it is in fact a separate piece held into the slide by a transverse pin. Reassembly is simply the reverse of stripping.

Sauer Revolvers

After 1945, when Suhl vanished into the Soviet Zone of Occupation, J. P. Sauer & Sohn were broken up, and eventually re-formed in Echernförde/Holstein in the Federal Republic. There the company began the manufacture of a range of revolvers of high quality.

Revolver Model SR3

'SR' stands for Sport Revolver, and this was the basic Sauer pattern, based upon Smith & Wesson practice insofar as the ejector rod engaged with a lug beneath the barrel and the side-opening cylinder was released by pushing forward a catch on the left side of the frame, alongside the hammer. The barrel carried a ventilated rib, the sights were fully interchangeable and adjustable, and the grips were hand-filling chequered wood. The only major deviation from the Smith pattern was the use of a coil spring for the mainspring instead of the more usual leaf spring. The standard version was in .38 Special chambering, but a version in .22 LR rimfire was also available and differed only in being slightly heavier.

Revolver Model VR4

'VR' means Verteidigungs Revolver (defence revolver), and whilst the frame and cylinder are the same as those of the others in the series, the barrel is available in shorter lengths and the butt is of a smaller and more rounded pattern compatible with concealed carrying. Barrel lengths of 2, 3, 4 and 6in were produced, and the pistol was made in both .38 Special and .22LR chamberings.

Manufacture of these revolvers ceased in the late 1970s when the company's involvement with SIG and the manufacture of the SIG-Sauer pistols (described below) commenced. Subsequently the revolver designs were licensed to Sterling Armament of Great Britain, but in 1983, before they could get production properly established, this firm ran into financial prob-

Sauer Model SR3

Calibre	.38 Special or .22 Long Rifle rimfire
Method of operation	6-chambered, clockwise rotation, double-action
Safety devices	None
Magazine type	Rotating cylinder
Position of catch	Left side of frame
Magazine capacity	6 rounds
Front sight	Fixed replaceable blade
Rear sight	Adjustable V-notch
Overall length	10.50in (267mm)
Barrel length	5.00in (127mm)
Empty weight	37.3oz (1,057g)
Markings	Left side of barrel: 'J. P. SAUER & SOHN MADE IN WEST GERMANY'
Serial number	On bottom of grip frame

Sauer Model VR4

Calibre	.38 Special or .22 Long Rifle rimfire
Method of operation	6-chambered, clockwise rotation, double-action
Safety devices	None
Magazine type	Rotating cylinder
Position of catch	Left side of frame
Magazine capacity	6 rounds
Front sight	Fixed blade
Rear sight	Fixed V-notch
Overall length	10.60in (269mm)
Barrel length	5.40in (136mm)
Empty weight	26.5oz (750g)
Markings	Left side of barrel: 'J. P. SAUER & SOHN MADE IN WEST GERMANY'
Serial number	On bottom of grip frame

lems and was taken over, first by an Anglo-Canadian consortium and then by Royal Ordnance, and the entire revolver project was abandoned. The revolvers were then licensed to Armi San Paolo of Italy, who produced them for some years in the 1980s.

Western Six-Shooter

This Colt lookalike appeared in the 1950s when the 'fast-draw' craze was at its height and single-action revolvers of this type were being desperately sought by would-be gunslingers all over the world. This weapon, though, was of much better quality than most of the products which were hurriedly put on the market at this time. It generally resembles the Colt M1873 Frontier in appearance, with a shrouded hand ejector rod under the barrel, a loading gate on the right side and a prominent single-action hammer. The standard model had fixed sights and polished hardwood grips, while the 'target' version had an adjustable rear sight and walnut grips. Dimensions varied slightly according to calibre.

Sauer Western Six-Shooter

Calibre	.22 LR or .22 Magnum RF or .357 Magnum or .44 Magnum
Method of operation	6-chambered, clockwise rotation, single-action
Safety devices	None
Magazine type	Rotating cylinder
Position of catch	None
Magazine capacity	6 rounds
Front sight	Fixed blade
Rear sight	Fixed V-notch
Overall length	10.60in (269mm)
Barrel length	5.40in (136mm)
Empty weight	26.5oz (750g)
Markings	Left side of barrel: 'J. P. SAUER & SOHN'
Serial number	On right side of frame

The only dismantling which can be undertaken with this type of revolver is to withdraw the cylinder axis pin, by releasing a spring catch, so as to remove the cylinder. Access to the lockwork can be achieved by removing the screws and side plate but is not necessary for routine cleaning.

Below: A Sauer Western-style revolver of the 1970s.

SIG-Sauer Pistol P220

This was the first of a series of numbered pistols which were originally designed by Schweizerische Industriegesellschaft (SIG) of Neuhausen-am-Rheinfalls, Switzerland. These are, therefore, Swiss rather than German pistols; but such are the restrictions on the export of weapons from Switzerland that SIG set up a cooperative venture with Sauer for the pistols to be manufactured both in Switzerland and in Germany, and I have included this entry as representative of this collaboration. It will be seen that there are some distinctly Sauer features about these designs, even though SIG claim that they are entirely Swiss in origin. No doubt they are, but I feel that the SIG designers gave a nod towards the Sauer 38H at some stage of their work!

As might be expected of any product of either SIG or Sauer, the quality of the P220 (and the other members of the family) is superlative. Essentially, the weapon is based upon the Browning system of dropping the barrel out of engagement with the slide, using a shaped cam beneath the chamber riding across a fixed pin in the frame. However, instead of the usual two or three lugs on top of the barrel and mating grooves on the interior of the slide, the barrel, around the chamber, is formed into a rectangular block, and the ejection port on the slide is

Below: The SIG-Sauer P220, a combination of Swiss design and German manufacture. Does that de-cocking lever look familiar?

a rectangular hole in the slide top, into which this rectangular block fits. Slide and barrel are therefore held firmly together and recoil together until the cam, beneath the barrel, draws the rear end of the barrel down and thus withdraws the upper surface of the rectangular block from its place in the ejection port. The slide then continues to the rear, loading the recoil spring underneath the barrel and cocking the hammer. The return stroke loads a fresh round from the magazine and then the forward movement of the slide and barrel causes the rear end of the latter to ride up on its cam and bring the block back into engagement with the ejection port.

The trigger mechanism is essentially similar to that of the Sauer 38H in that it is double-action and there is a de-cocking lever in the left side grip. The pistol can be loaded and cocked by drawing back and releasing the slide in the usual manner. After that it can be fired by pulling the trigger, or, by using the de-cocking lever, the hammer can be lowered safely on to the loaded chamber. To fire, the trigger is pulled through for double-action operation; in this system the lever cannot be used to re-cock the hammer.

The hammer can be safely lowered since there is an automatic safety device incorporated in the firing pin housing. The firing pin is prevented from moving by a spring-loaded safety pin which presses down into a cutaway portion of the firing pin shank and prevents it from moving forward. The hammer can fall as much as it likes, but the pin will not move. When the trigger is pulled through, at the peak of the pull, fractionally before the hammer is released, an arm attached to the sear presses the safety pin upwards and thus frees the firing pin. It is held free as the hammer falls, and thus the firing pin strikes the cap and the pistol is fired. The movement of the slide on recoil disconnects the trigger mechanism, and the safety pin springs back, engaging with the cut-out as the firing pin is driven back into its housing by the firing pin spring.

Stripping the P220 is simple. After removing the magazine and operating the slide to ensure that no round is left in the chamber, pull back the slide to its stop and turn up the slide lock on the left side of the frame, behind the de-cocking lever. Now turn down the dismantling catch, on the left side immediately above the trigger, until it is vertical. Pull back the slide slightly so as to allow the slide catch to disengage, and then allow the slide to run forward off the frame. Invert the slide, remove the recoil spring and guide rod, then remove the barrel. No further dismantling is recommended. Reassembly is simply a reversal of the stripping procedure. Insert the barrel into the slide, followed by the recoil spring and guide rod. Fit

SIG-Sauer P220

Calibre	9mm Parabellum
Method of operation	Recoil, dropping barrel, double-action, hammer-fired
Safety devices	Manual de-cocking lever on left side of frame; automatic firing pin safety
Magazine type	Double-column detachable box in butt
Position of catch	Left side of butt, behind trigger
Magazine capacity	13 rounds
Front sight	Fixed blade
Rear sight	Fixed square notch
Overall length	7.09in (180mm)
Barrel length	3.86in (98mm)
Empty weight	30.0oz (850g)
Markings	Left side of slide: 'SIG-SAUER'; right side of slide: 'P220 MADE IN GERMANY [or W. GERMANY on earlier models]'; the calibre is marked on the side of the chamber, visible in the ejection port
Serial number	On right side of slide

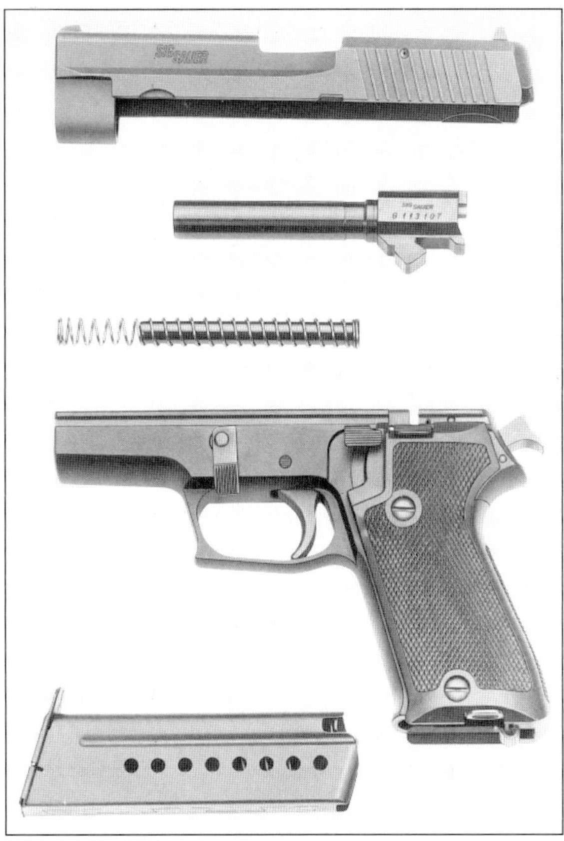

Above: The SIG-Sauer P220 dismantled, showing how the barrel is dropped by a shaped cam and how the chamber area is squared off to lock into the ejection port.

the slide into the frame and draw it fully back, turn up the slide catch and then turn up the dismantling catch. Draw back the slide to release the slide catch and allow it to go forward. Depress the de-cocking lever to release the hammer.

SCHLEGELMILCH

Königlich Gewehrfabrik, Spandau, Berlin

Louis Schlegelmilch was an employee of the Spandau Arsenal and is said to have been responsible for the design of the bolt for the Gewehr 88 service rifle; he later achieved the rank of Superintendent at the Arsenal. He spent some time in the 1880s working on a design of mechanical repeating pistol but abandoned it in favour of a self-loading design which he patented in 1894 (D.R.P.78,881). Very little is known about the design, and very few specimens exist, since it appears never to have got beyond a handful of prototypes. I have not been able to dismantle one, and therefore am guided only by the patent drawings and an external examination, but it appears to be a blowback weapon using a reciprocating bolt in the upper part of the receiver; this is blown back by the pressure of the cartridge explosion and, in running back, cocks the hammer. On the return stroke it collects a cartridge from the clip in the magazine ahead of the trigger, and the trigger can then be pressed to release the hammer to strike the firing in the bolt. A spring follower forces the cartridge up through the clip, and a lever on the left side forces the follower down to permit a fresh clip to be loaded. The cartridge is known to have been a rimmed, straight-sided case, but no specimen is believed to exist and no dimensions are available.

Schlegelmilch	
Calibre	8mm Schlegelmilch (or Spandau)
Method of operation	Blowback, single-action, hammer-fired
Safety devices	Manual catch on right side of frame
Magazine type	Clip-loaded box magazine
Position of catch	None; integral with frame
Magazine capacity	5 rounds
Front sight	Fixed blade
Rear sight	Fixed U-notch
Overall length	10.82in (275mm)
Barrel length	4.68in (119mm)
Number of grooves	4
Direction of twist	Right-hand
Empty weight	30.0oz (850g)
Markings	None on specimen seen
Serial number	On left side of frame

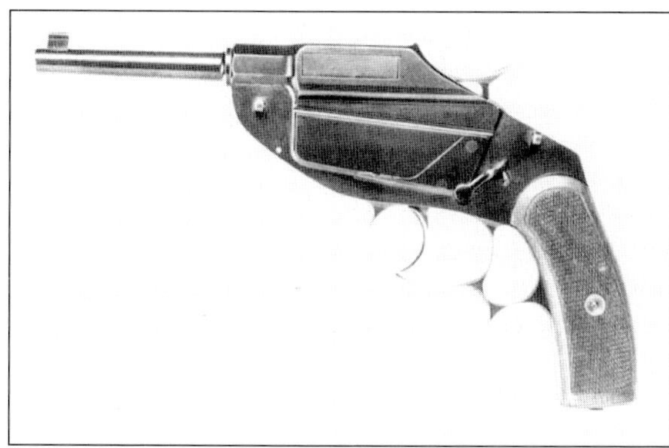

Above: A rare specimen of the Schlegelmilch.

SCHMIDT

Herbert Shmidt, Ostheim-a-d-Rhon

Herbert Schmidt has produced revolvers under a bewildering variety of names—Amco, Bison, Buffalo Scout, Cheyenne Scout, Deputy Adjuster, Deputy Magnum, Deputy Marshal, EIG, Eusta, Geroco, Indian Scout, LA's Deputy, Liberty Scout, Madison, NATO, Omega, Spesco, Texas Scout, Valor, Vol, Western and probably a few more I have not yet caught up with.

When the weapons are examined more closely, however, it can be seen that these are all variations on the same handful of designs, the different names being applied to guns destined for particuar markets. Spesco, for example, applies only to guns markted by the Speco Corporation of Atlanta, Georgia.

The Model 11 is a simple six-shot, double-action, solid-frame .22 revolver with swing-out cylinder and 2.5in barrel, sold in the United States as the Liberty Model 11 and the EIG E8. There was also a version of this with a 5.5in barrel and adjustable rear sights, sold as a target revolver.

Perhaps the most widely distributed of Schmidt's revolvers was the Western model, which appeared in the late 1950s in order to meet the demand for single-action Colt Frontier lookalikes created by the 'quick-draw' craze which swept the United States. This was the usual style of Frontier gun in .22 Long Rifle calibre and with a 6in barrel and appeared in two versions. The cheaper model had solid recoil shields and was loaded and unloaded by removing the cylinder arbor pin so as to release the cylinder; the more expensive version had a loading gate on the right side and a spring-loaded rod ejector mounted Colt-style under the barrel. The more obvious Western titles (Marshal, Deputy and so forth) in the above list attached to these two pistols.

Finally—and perhaps a more serious weapon than the .22 offerings—came the HS38, a Smith

Below: The Herbert Schmidt Model 11 revolver—a solid-frame .22 weapon sold under various names in the United States during the 1960s.
Bottom: The Schmidt Western, another popular export model which had a variety of suitable names.

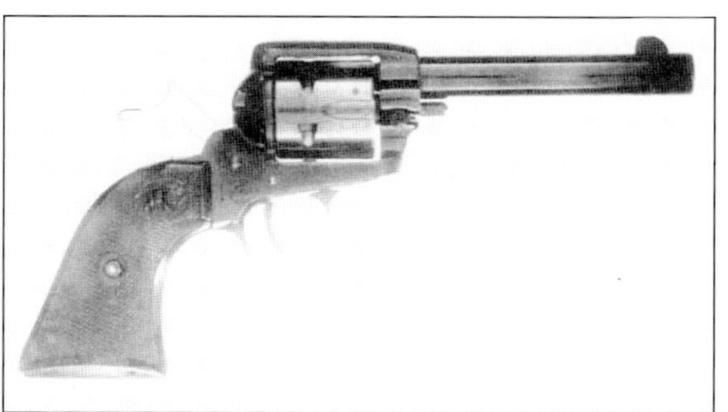

Left: The Schmidt HS38 was a better-quality home defence revolver firing the .38 Special cartridge.

Schmidt HS38

Calibre	.38 Special
Method of operation	Double-action revolver
Safety devices	None
Magazine type	6-shot cylinder
Position of catch	Left side of frame
Front sight	Fixed blade
Rear sight	Fixed U-notch
Overall length	8.00in (203mm)
Barrel length	4.00in (102mm)
Number of grooves	6
Direction of twist	Right-hand
Empty weight	31.2oz (885g)
Markings	Vary according to what dealer's name was being used, but all Schmidt revolvers have 'H. SCHMIDT' stamped into the grip frame, visible when the grips are removed
Serial number	On left side of frame, below cylinder

& Wesson style revolver in .38 Special chambering. This was of distinctly better quality than the earlier weapons, but it is not believed to have had much sales success. Specimens are not as common as those of the other two models.

SCHWARZLOSE

Andreas W. Schwarzlose GmbH (1893–1919)

Andreas Schwarzlose served as an armourer in the Austro-Hungarian Army, then went to Suhl for some practical gunmaking experience. In the early 1890s he began designing automatic pistols, and he later developed a blowback machine gun which was adopted by the Austro-Hungarian Army and remained in use until 1945. He opened a factory in Berlin to make the machine gun and various pistols, but this was closed down by the Disarmament Commission in 1919. He then went to work as a consultant for other firearms firms, and he died in 1936. For all that, he deserves to be remembered more for his pistol designs, for each of them was a testimony to his originality of thought and thorough grasp of engineering principles. His first design, patented in 1892, used a recoiling barrel together with a degree of delayed blowback functioning owing to the breech block, which pivoted to the rear and down, acting as a rudimentary form of lock. An example of this pistol was reputed to be in a Belgian Museum before the war, but few were made and it was never offered commercially.

In 1895 he patented a long-recoil weapon, i.e. one in which the barrel and breech block recoil together for the whole length of the cartridge, after which the breech is unlocked and held while the barrel returns to its original position; the breech block is then released to go forward and chamber the next round. Few successful long-recoil pistols have ever been marketed, the best-known and most common example being the Hungarian Frommer. Schwarzlose's design certainly never reached the public.

Abandoning this system, he then produced his Military Model 1896, but he managed to market it just as the Mauser and then the Mannlicher were being offered. Since these designs appeared superior to the Schwarzlose, few of

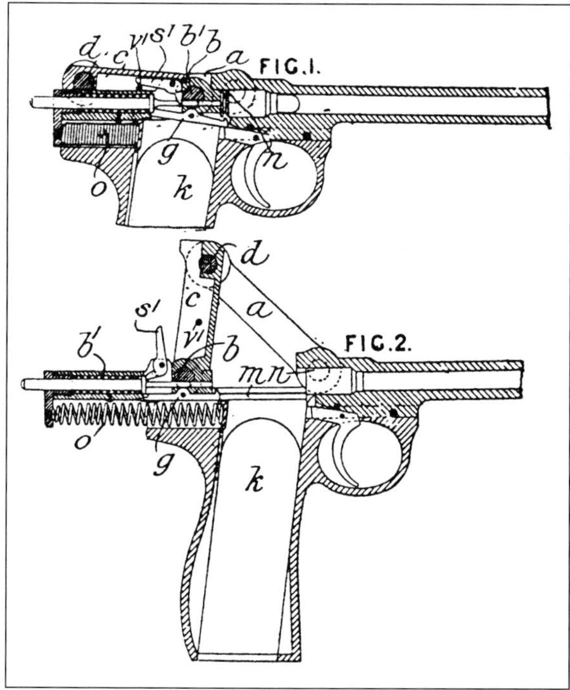

Left: Patent 6,056, 31 March 1900, Andreas W. Schwarzlose. This design never saw production, but it is an interesting variation on the toggle-lock method of breech closure. The toggle is actually folded up (Fig. 1) when the breech is closed, with the arms lying side by side. It then unfolds (Fig. 2) as the breech block is driven backwards; the effort required to unfold the toggle is considerable at the start of the opening movement but gets easier as it goes further, so that there is a progressive form of delayed blowback in operation.

the latter were sold. An interesting story is told to the effect that when the Russian revolutionaries of 1905 were seeking a supply of automatic pistols they chanced on a Berlin salesman who had a large stock of Schwarzlose pistols on his hands. Offered, no doubt, at clearance prices, they were duly purchased and shipped to Russia. A few reached the revolutionaries, but the greater part of the shipment was seized by the authorities. Faced with this windfall they issued them to various units of the Imperial and Frontier Police and the Schwarzlose consequently became more common in Russia than anywhere else—which accounts for its scarcity in the West.

Schwarzlose Military M96

This is a locked-breech pistol, as might be expected with such a powerful cartridge as the 7.63mm Mauser; breech and barrel recoil, locked together, for about 0.75in (19mm), while the bolt is rotated through 45° by a cam track in the frame. Once the bolt is unlocked it continues to the rear, compressing its return spring, while the barrel moves forwards for about 0.2in (6mm), where it is held by a catch. The recoil spring now returns the bolt, chambering the next round from the butt-mounted magazine as it does so, and the bolt locks back into the breech aperture by the same cam action. As the bolt locks, so the barrel catch is released, and the barrel and breech go forward into battery locked securely together.

There are innumerable points of interest on this pistol, all evidence of the designer's ingenuity and of his love of making one device serve more than one purpose. Thus the striker and bolt return springs are combined in one unit, and the striker and extractor ride forward together when the trigger is pressed so that the extractor snaps into place on the rim of the cartridge at much the same time as the striker hits the cap—a system which makes it difficult to extract a round without firing it. The ejector is

Below: The 7.65mm Schwarzlose model of 1896—an elegant weapon which deserved better success.

Schwarzlose Model 1896

Calibre	7.63mm Mauser
Method of operation	Recoil, locked breech, rotary bolt locking; striker-fired
Safety devices	Manual catch left side of frame
Magazine type	Single-column detachable box in butt
Position of catch	Bottom rear of butt
Magazine capacity	7 rounds
Front sight	Fixed blade
Rear sight	Adjustable U-notch
Overall length	10.75in (273mm)
Barrel length	6.43in (163mm)
Number of grooves	4
Direction of twist	Right-hand
Empty weight	33.0oz (936g)
Markings	'A.W.S.' on left side of barrel
Serial number	On left side of frame, ahead of trigger

a positive operator, rather than a passive one as in most pistols, being pivoted below the bolt and being driven up by the recoiling bolt so as to knock the empty case forcibly upward from the gun. A hold-open device is fitted, but not a completely automatic one: the magazine holds the bolt open after the last round in the magazine has been fired, but withdrawing the magazine allows the bolt to close. However, a slide or bolt stop lever is fitted on the left side of the frame, and if this is pushed up before the magazine is withdrawn then the bolt remains open. On inserting a fresh magazine nothing happens until this bolt stop lever is pushed down, when the bolt closes and chambers the first round. The other lever on the frame—the forward lever of the two visible—is a combination device, being both the action lock pin and the safety catch.

Had Schwarzlose been able to get this pistol on the market some four or five years earlier, there is every chance that it might now be as well-known and common as the Mauser, for doubtless some of the minor shortcomings—such as the two-stage holding open catch—would have been redesigned in the light of user experience. As it was, the demand was so slight that he appears not to have pursued the matter and proceeded to develop fresh ideas instead, with the result that the Model 1896 is now a most desirable collector's piece.

The next pistol design of Schwarzlose was a modified toggle-lock project, in which the toggle was folded up when the breech was closed but unfolded during recoil almost like a reversal of Luger's action and bearing a similarity to the Maxim machine gun lock. Although the subject of patents, it seems never to have been manufactured, and the next production pistol was the Model 1908.

Schwarzlose M08

This, again, is a completely different design from anything Schwarzlose had done before, and also completely different from anything which anybody else was doing at that time. Instead of the well-known blowback action, Schwarzlose elected to use a 'blow-forward' system, in which the breech is solid with the frame and the explosion of the cartridge causes the barrel to slide forward on the frame, pulling itself clear of the fired cartridge case against

Below: Patent 18,188, 12 August 1907, Andreas W. Schwarzlose. The basic features of the Schwarzlose blow-forward pistol of 1908 are covered in this patent. Later applications expanded on it, with details of safety devices, stripping methods and so forth, but this covers the fundamental operating principle.

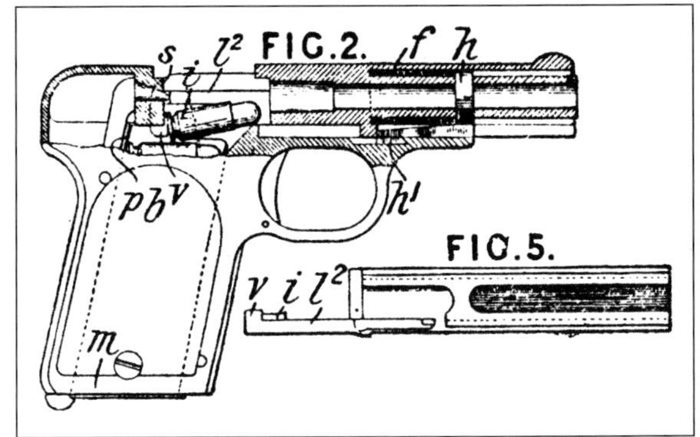

the pressure of a heavy return spring. In addition, the barrel itself is longer than usual and relatively heavy, all adding to the inertia to be overcome in the opening action. A mechanical ejector, similar in concept to that on the Model 1896, flings the empty case clear, and the return spring then runs the barrel back to the breech, picking up the bullet of the next round and gathering it into the chamber en route. At the same time the returning barrel cocks the hammer by means of a mechanical linkage.

Beneath the trigger, in the front edge of the butt, is a grip safety with a heavy spring controlling it. This must be firmly grasped in order to allow the trigger to be released, but it can be locked into the 'fire' position by a press-button catch in much the same way as on the later

Schwarzlose Model 1908

Calibre	7.65mm Browning
Method of operation	Blow-forward, hammer-fired
Safety devices	Grip safety front edge of butt, spring retention to 'fire'
Magazine type	Single-column detachable box in butt
Position of catch	Bottom rear of butt
Magazine capacity	7 rounds
Front sight	Fixed blade
Rear sight	Fixed U-notch
Overall length	5.50in (140mm)
Barrel length	4.13in (105mm)
Number of grooves	4
Direction of twist	Right-hand
Empty weight	18.5oz (525g)
Markings	Right rear of frame: 'SCHWARZLOSE' over engraving of machine gun; or 'A. W. Schwarzlose GmbH Berlin' in flowing script on left side of slide; see text
Serial number	On right of frame

Below: One of the most eccentric designs ever to prosper: the Schwarzlose 'blow-forward' pistol of 1908.

Ortgies design. Loading the pistol feels awkward at first, owing to the requirement to push the barrel forward and release it rather than the accustomed opposite action. In spite of the odd concept, it fires well, with a relatively gentle recoil, and is quite accurate—due, no doubt, to the extra barrel length.

Owing to the simplicity of this design, stripping is particularly easy. After removing the magazine and clearing the gun, take a fine screwdriver, drift or even paper clip and pass it through the hole in the return spring guide rod which protrudes below the muzzle. This rod is attached to a block at its far end which bears against a stop face just under the breech. The return spring is coiled round the rod so that, as the barrel goes forward, the stop face pushes against the block and forces the guide rod forward, compressing the spring. In the bottom surface of the frame, under the return spring, is a machined step. Pulling the recoil rod out and up, then releasing it gently, will allow the block to anchor itself against this step and below the level of the barrel stop face. The barrel unit can now be slid from the front of the frame. If desired, the recoil spring rod can be unhooked from its step and allowed to move back in the frame until it can be removed. No further work is needed, since the gun is now, for all practical purposes, stripped. Reassembly is simply a matter of reversing the process.

It is reported that these pistols have been seen with no Schwarzlose identification, with gunsmith's or retailer' name engraved.

SIMPLEX

Th. Bergmann/V. C. Schilling, Suhl

This pistol was patented by Bergmann in 1901 (British Patent 23808); although resembling the large military Bergmann-Bayard in general out-

Below: The Bergmann parentage of the Simplex is fairly obvious, the weapon resembling a junior Bergmann-Bayard.

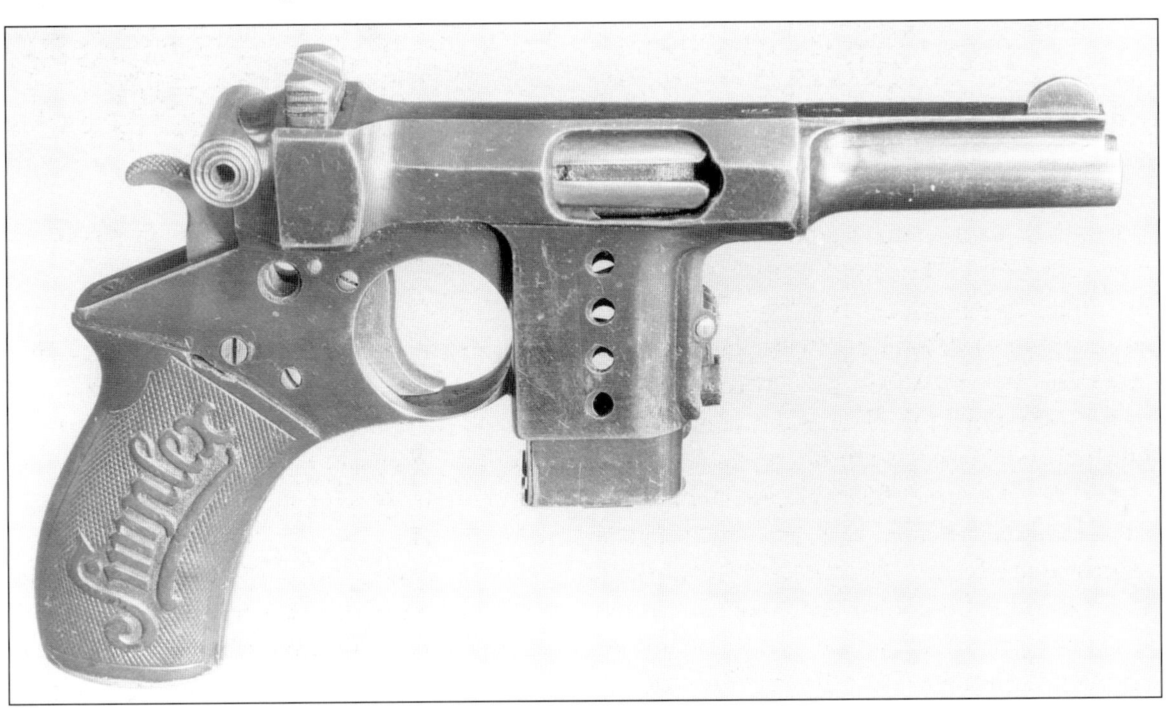

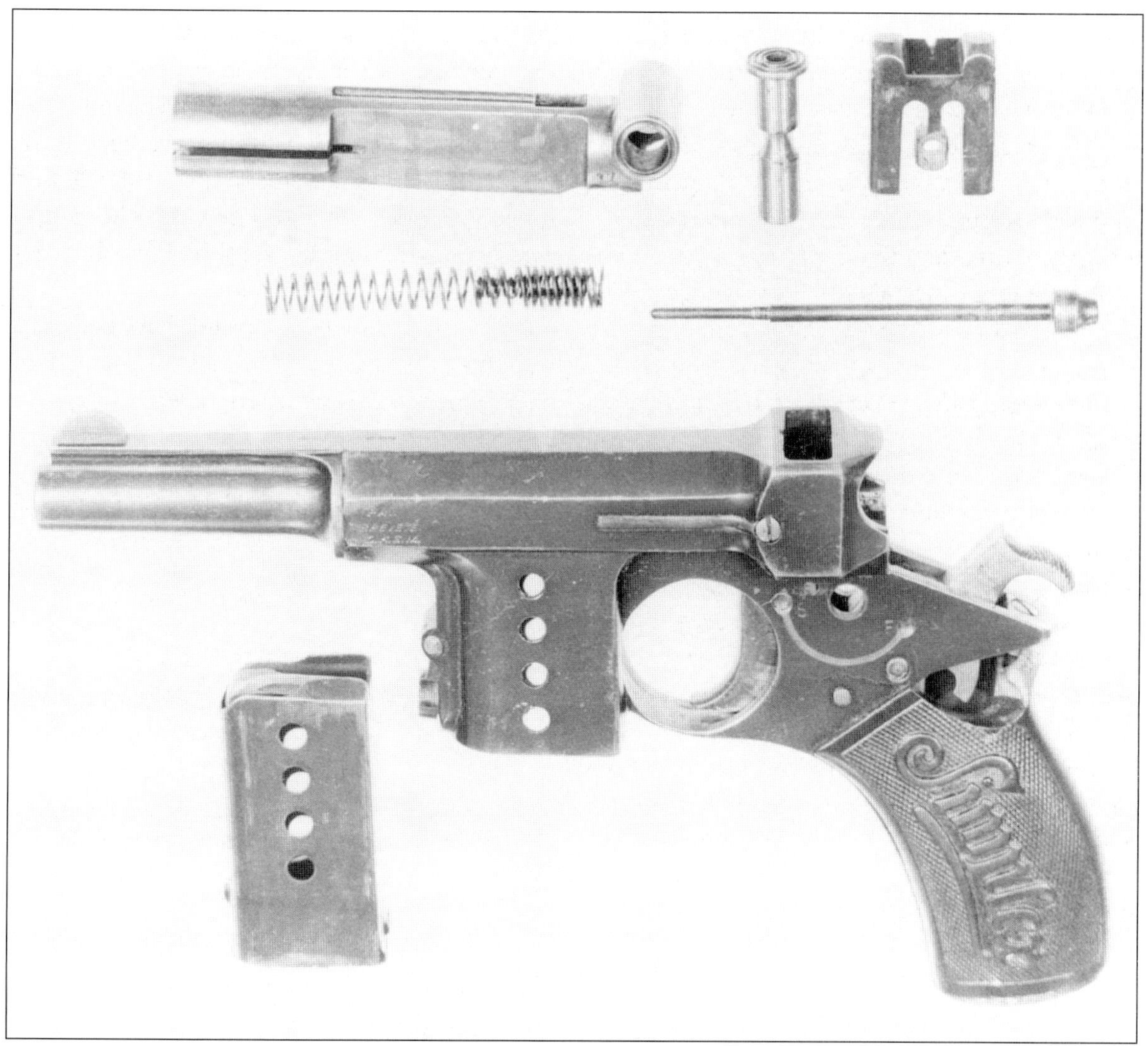

Above: The Simplex stripped. The safety catch was missing from this specimen.

line, it is in fact a much simpler and cheaper blowback pistol. About 3,000 pistols were made by V. C. Schilling of Suhl, Bergmann's subcontractor, in 1902–03, and they were marketed in Britain by the Wilkinson Sword Company from 1904 onwards. The 8mm calibre is an unusual one, for which ammunition is no longer obtainable. A review of this weapon in the magazine *Arms and Explosives* for April 1904 said: 'It stands apart from other pistols owing to the extraordinary simplicity of its parts . . . The simplicity of its mechanism will go far to recommend it in the eyes of the man who likes to be able to take a pistol to pieces without indulging in the mysteries of a Chinese puzzle.' In view of the complexity of the general run of automatic pistols existing at that date, this was fair enough comment, but later developments showed that it could be improved upon.

The operation of the Simplex is much the same as that of the earlier Bergmann pistols, having a bolt reciprocating in the frame together with a magazine mounted ahead of the trigger,

Simplex	
Calibre	8mm Simplex
Method of operation	Blowback, hammer-fired
Safety devices	Manual catch at left rear of frame
Magazine type	Double-column detachable box in front of trigger
Position of catch	Front of trigger guard
Magazine capacity	6 or 8 rounds
Front sight	Fixed blade
Rear sight	Fixed V-notch
Overall length	8.00in (203mm)
Barrel length	2.75in (70mm)
Number of grooves	6
Direction of twist	Right-hand
Empty weight	21.0oz (595g)
Markings	Left of breech: 'PAT. BREVETE D.R.G.M.'; moulded into grips: 'SIMPLEX'
Serial number	Under trigger guard and on bottom of butt frame

though this magazine is a removable box and much more efficient than the original clip-loaded Bergmann pattern.

To strip the weapon, after removing the magazine clear the gun and, with the hammer cocked, push in the rear end of the firing pin and slide the cross-bolt out to the right. Remove the firing pin and its spring; originally these springs were flat riband-section coils, though later replacements are usually ordinary wire. Now lift out the rear sight from its slot in the frame; this releases the bolt, which can now be pulled out to the rear. No further stripping is necessary, and reassembly is simply a reversal of the foregoing procedure.

SIMSON

Waffenfabrik Simson & Co, Suhl (ca 1880–1934)

Simson Models 1922 and 1927

At the beginning of the 1920s the German Army and police began to feel the need for re-

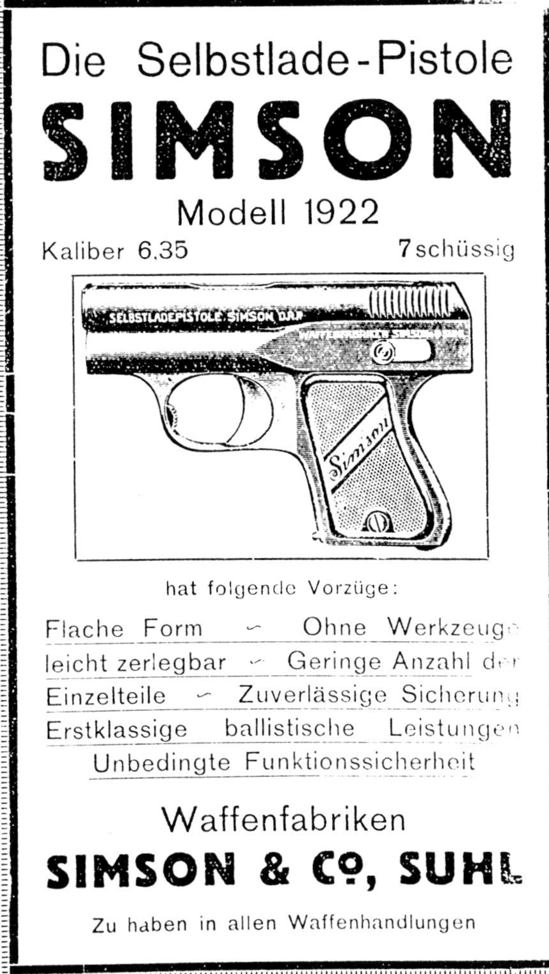

Above: A 1923 advertisement for the Simson Model 1922. Notice the different contours of the frame in this model compared to the later weapons.

placement or repaired pistols. As things stood, the Allied Disarmament Commission had forbidden the manufacture of 9mm military pistols; but, faced with this request—which, given the state of civil disturbance at the time, appeared to be a quite reasonable one—they were adamant that the major military gunmakers should not be given the chance to regain their former monopolistic position. They therefore arranged for the Parabellum machinery from Erfurt Arsenal to be sent to a small firm in Suhl

Above: The Simson Model 1927 pistol had a number of interesting features: note the stripping catch in the forward edge of the trigger guard.

called Simson, who had hitherto manufactured sporting rifles and shotguns. The firm were now awarded a contract to supply the German services with Parabellum pistols, and most of the contract involved refurbishing wartime weapons; more were assembled from wartime parts stocks, and a small number were actually made in the Simson plant. The pistols can be recognised by the Simson mark of an 'S' in three triangles or by 'Simson & Co Suhl' on the toggle.

This contract must have aroused Simson's interest in pistol manufacture, for they produced a 6.35mm blowback of their own design in 1922, and in 1927 a modified version appeared. Both pistols were of good quality, but in 1934 the company (which had Jewish ownership) was sequestered by the State and became part of the Gustloff Werke. The Parabellum machinery was removed and sent to Krieghoff and the production of the Simson pistol ceased. The company name was revived after 1945 as part of the East German nationalised gunmaking industry, and the firm now makes shotguns.

Although both models are simple enough blowback 6.35mm weapons, they are exceptionally well made and display features of construction which show that the designer was no mere copyist. The principal difference between the 1922 and 1927 models is the exterior shape, the only other change being in the design of certain of the lockwork components, and a description of the 1927 will suffice to cover both weapons.

The 1927 is distinguished from the 1922 by being flat-sided throughout its length, whereas the slide of the 1922 swelled into a rounded section from the trigger guard to the muzzle.

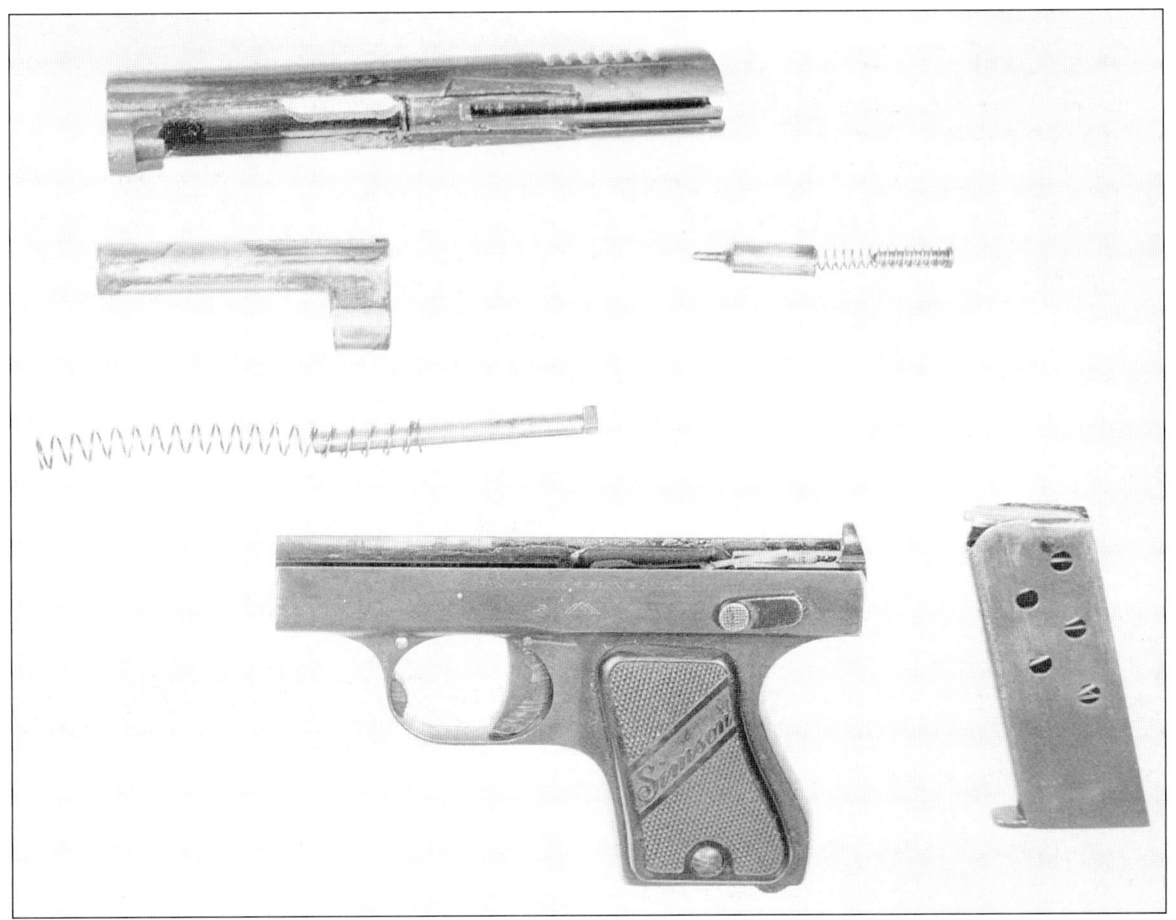

Above: The Simson 1927 dismantled.

The grip is well shaped and the pistol feels much more comfortable than does the usual run of pocket pistols.

To dismantle, clear the gun and press the trigger. Hold the pistol in the right hand with the right thumb pressing on the rear of the slide and with the left thumb press forward the catch in the front edge of the trigger guard. The pressure of the right thumb will push the slide forward once the catch is released, and it can then be removed from the front—one of the easiest and quickest methods of stripping ever designed. The slide, it will now be seen, is unusual in being almost circular in section; the striker and spring can be removed from the rear, and the recoil spring guide rod can be pushed out of engagement and pulled through the barrel lug to the rear. With the rod removed the spring can be twisted and lifted from engagement with the barrel lug at the rear and the slide at the front, and the rear end of the barrel can be lifted to allow the barrel to be pulled clear of the slide. The lockwork can be completely removed by pushing the safety catch through the frame from right to left until it is held by a spring plunger just short of complete exit from the frame. The stirrup can be lifted from the magazine well and the sear support block can be lifted from the frame, taking care not to lose the small spring which pressed the sear upwards. Now it can be seen that the lock of the Simson is of the ultimate simplicity: movement of the trigger

Simson Model 1927	
Calibre	6.35mm Browning
Method of operation	Blowback, striker-fired
Safety devices	Manual catch at left rear of frame
Magazine type	Single-column detachable box in butt
Position of catch	Bottom rear of butt
Magazine capacity	6 rounds
Front sight	Fixed blade
Rear sight	Fixed V-notch
Overall length	4.50in (114mm)
Barrel length	2.20in (56mm)
Number of grooves	6
Direction of twist	Right-hand
Empty weight	13.0oz (368g)
Markings	See text
Serial number	Full number on frame, at front edge of butt.; last four digits on right of slide and on barrel lug

pushes up the front end of the stirrup, levering on the support block, and the rear end moves down to free the striker. When the slide recoils, the notched cut-outs in its lower edge engage with the upstanding ears of the stirrup and push it backward into the magazine well, disengaging the front end from the trigger. As the slide returns, the small spring at the rear of the sear serves two purposes, first to return the stirrup to engagement with the trigger ready for the next shot and secondly to push the sear up to hold the striker bent and cock the striker. The safety catch shank is cut away on one side so that rotation into the 'safe' position securely locks the sear into engagement with the striker.

The magazine is straightforward sheet metal, but with perforations to allow the contents to be checked and counted—a procedure common enough in large-calibre pistols but not all that common in the small-calibre weapons where even the cost of drilling a few holes in the magazine would make the accountants wince.

Reassembly is simply the reverse of stripping; there are no hidden snags. Markings comprise, on the left of the frame, 'WAFFENFABRIK SIMSON & CO. SUHL' and a monogram consisting of the letter 'S' inside three overlapping triangles (the specimen under review also has what appears to be a Belgian lion engraved at the extreme rear of the frame, but this is more probably a retailer's mark). On the right of the slide is 'SELBSTLADEPISTOLE SIMSON D.R.P.'; on top of barrel, visible through ejection port, is 'CAL. 6,35'; and moulded into the butt grips on each side is the word 'Simson'.

All in all, the Simson is one of the better pistols of its type, and one which is quite safe to use today, and it can only be regretted that Simson & Co were never able to go further in the pistol field.

STERN

Albin Wahl, Zella Mehlis

As well as producing pistols under his own name (see the entry for Wahl), Albin Wahl also made this 6.35mm pocket pistol, a completely different weapon from his 7.65mm model and equally

Below: A 6.35mm Stern pistol, now rarely encountered.

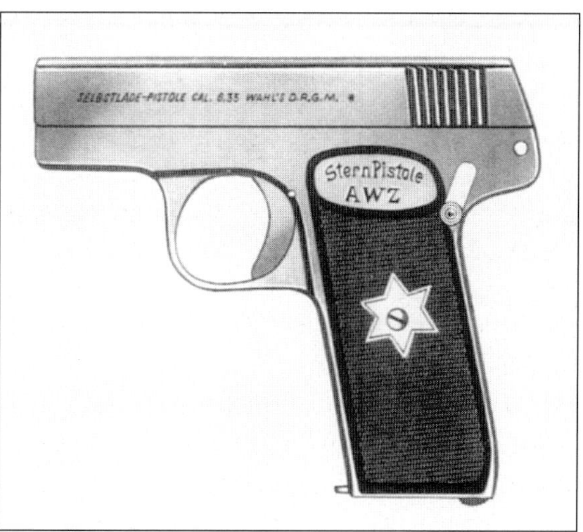

uncommon. The Stern Pistole is a conventional blowback pocket automatic, distinguished by the long butt, allowing a much greater magazine capacity than is usual in this class, and by the very slab-sided appearance of the slide and frame, with none of the usual taper or relief towards the muzzle end. Two versions of this pistol are known to exist: one has an oval cross-pin passing through the slide just above the front edge of the grips, while the other has a similar pin inserted from the right side but not showing on the left side. Since I have been unable to find a specimen, the significance of this difference and the purpose of this cross-pin are not known. It is possible that the slide contains a separate breech block and that this pin retains it in place, but this is pure supposition. Dating this pistol (and the Wahl) is difficult, but the six-pointed star on the butt suggests that it would not have been much in evidence after 1934, and a period around 1928–33 seems most probable.

Stern Pistole	
Calibre	6.35mm Browning
Method of operation	Blowback, single-action, striker-fired
Safety devices	Manual safety catch on left side of frame
Magazine type	Single-column detachable box in butt
Position of catch	Heel of butt
Magazine capacity	10
Front sight	Fixed blade
Rear sight	Fixed U-notch
Overall length	4.906in (125mm)
Barrel length	2.42in (61.5mm)
Number of grooves	6
Direction of twist	Right-hand
Empty weight	15.5oz (440g)
Markings	On left of slide: 'SELBSTLADE-PISTOLE CAL. 6,35 WAHL'S D.R.G.M.'; butt grips: oval at top with 'SternPistole AWZ'; six-pointed star central, surrounding the fixing screws
Serial number	On right side of frame

STOCK

Franz Stock Maschinen- und Werkbaufabrik, Berlin (1915–1938)

This is a well-made and reliable pistol of conventional blowback type. It was made in two calibres, 6.35mm and 7.65mm, and except for the dimensions the two weapons were the same. It was marketed just after World War I but fell from sight in the 1930s and was never revived or redesigned. The design was patented by Walter Decker and licensed to Stock.

Stripping the Stock can be quite a puzzle, although a clue is afforded by the usual German feature of a stripping notch in the lower

Right, upper: The 7.65mm Stock, a well-built pistol with some unusual design features.
Right, lower: Starting to dismantle the Stock, showing the extent of the slide, which incorporates a barrel jacket, and how to remove the breech block.

Stock 6.35mm	
Calibre	6.35mm Browning
Method of operation	Blowback, striker-fired
Safety devices	Manual catch on left rear of frame
Magazine type	Single-column detachable box in butt
Position of catch	Bottom rear of butt
Magazine capacity	7 rounds
Front sight	Fixed blade
Rear sight	Fixed V-notch
Overall length	4.75in (121mm)
Barrel length	2.48in (63mm)
Number of grooves	4
Direction of twist	Right-hand
Empty weight	12.5oz (355g)
Markings	Left side of slide: 'FRANZ STOCK - BERLIN'; moulded into grips: 'STOCK'
Serial number	On left of receiver above grip; last three digits in front of slide, beneath barrel shroud; last two digits on breech block

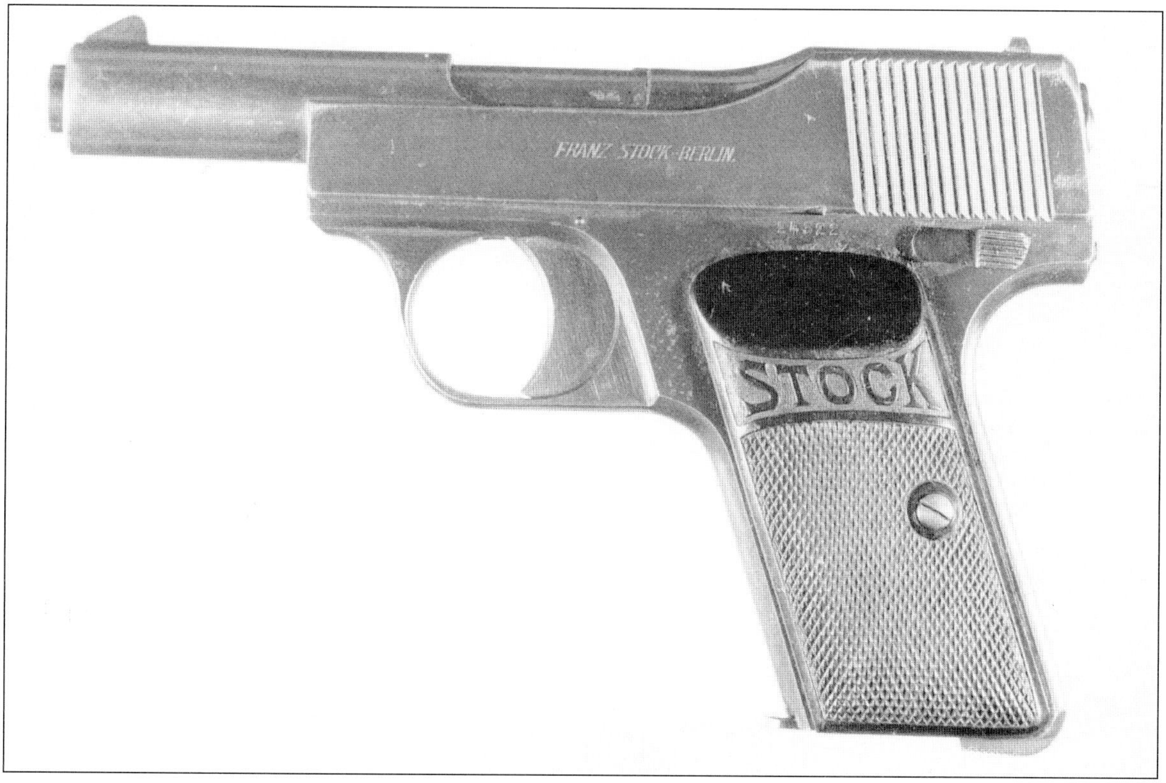
FRANZ STOCK-BERLIN.
STOCK

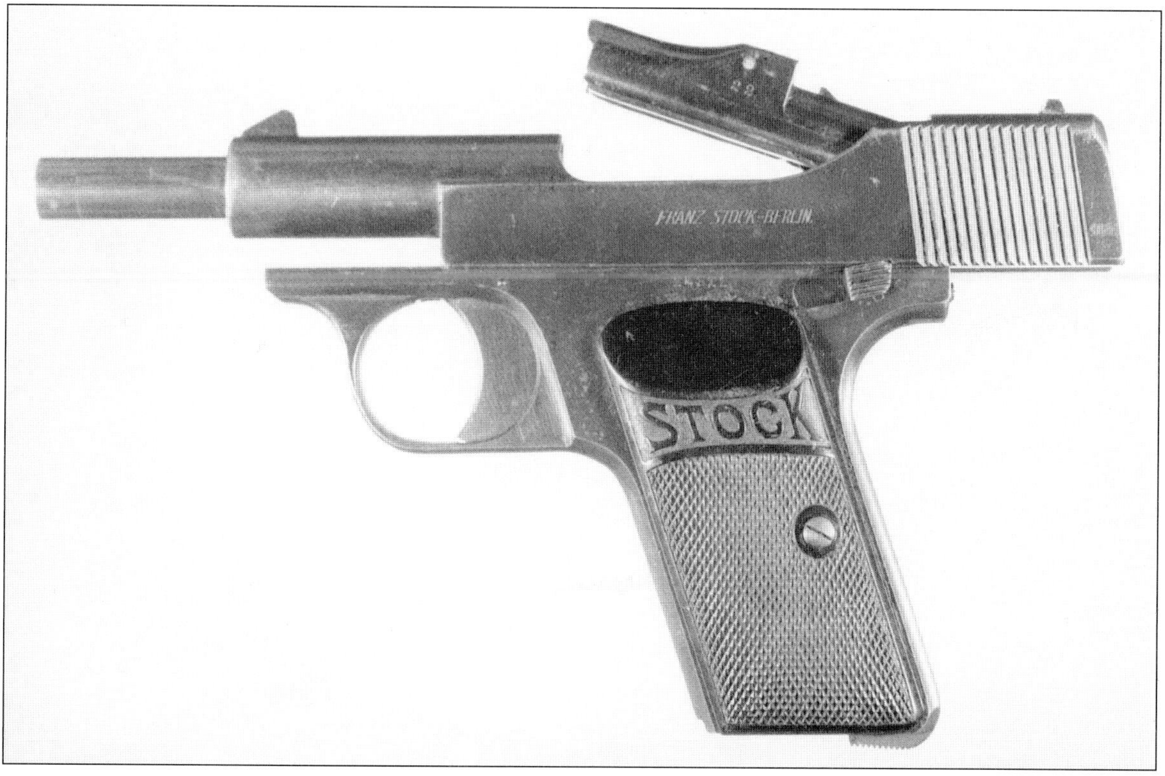
FRANZ STOCK-BERLIN.
STOCK

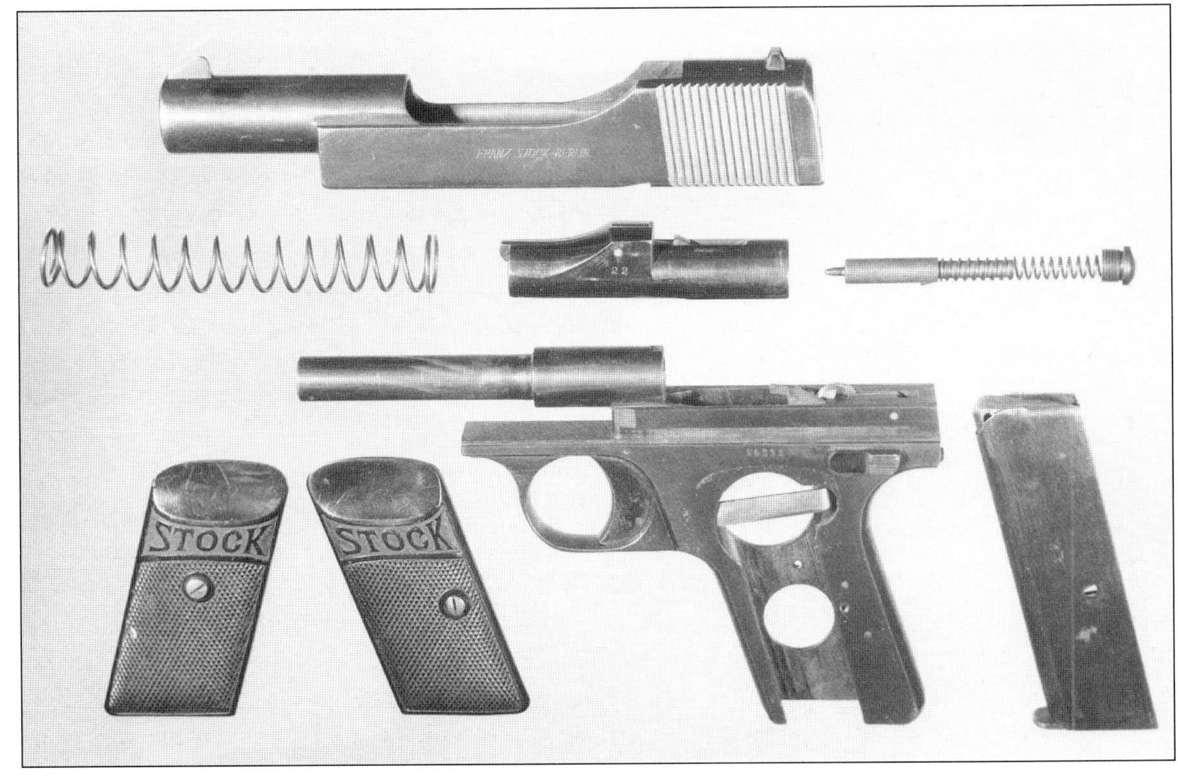

Above: The Stock pistol completely dismantled.

edge of the slide. Pulling the slide back against the recoil spring allows the safety catch to be turned up into this notch to hold the slide in place. Gripping the pistol in the normal way, place a thumb against the large screwhead in the rear of the slide. With a finger of the same hand, pull up on the tip of the extractor and push with the thumb. The entire breech block, with the firing pin, spring and extractor, will now come free and can be 'wangled' out of the open top of the slide. Now grip the slide, depress the safety catch and allow the slide to slip off the front of the frame. Withdrawing the grip screws allows the grips to be removed and the lockwork oiled, but dismantling the lock demands driving out pins and is not to be recommended. Removal of the screw in the rear of the breech block allows the firing pin and spring to be removed; the extractor is pinned in place. Reassembly is simply the reverse of the foregoing procedure.

Stock 7.65mm

Calibre	7.65mm Browning
Method of operation	Blowback, striker-fired
Safety devices	Manual catch at left rear of frame
Magazine type	Single-column detachable box in butt
Position of catch	Bottom rear of butt
Magazine capacity	8 rounds
Front sight	Fixed blade
Rear sight	Fixed U-notch
Overall length	6.81in (173mm)
Barrel length	3.62in (92mm)
Number of grooves	4
Direction of twist	Right-hand
Empty weight	23.5oz (666g)
Markings	Left side of slide: 'FRANZ STOCK - BERLIN'; moulded into grips: 'STOCK'
Serial number	On left of receiver above grip; last three digits in front of slide, beneath barrel shroud; last two digits on breech block

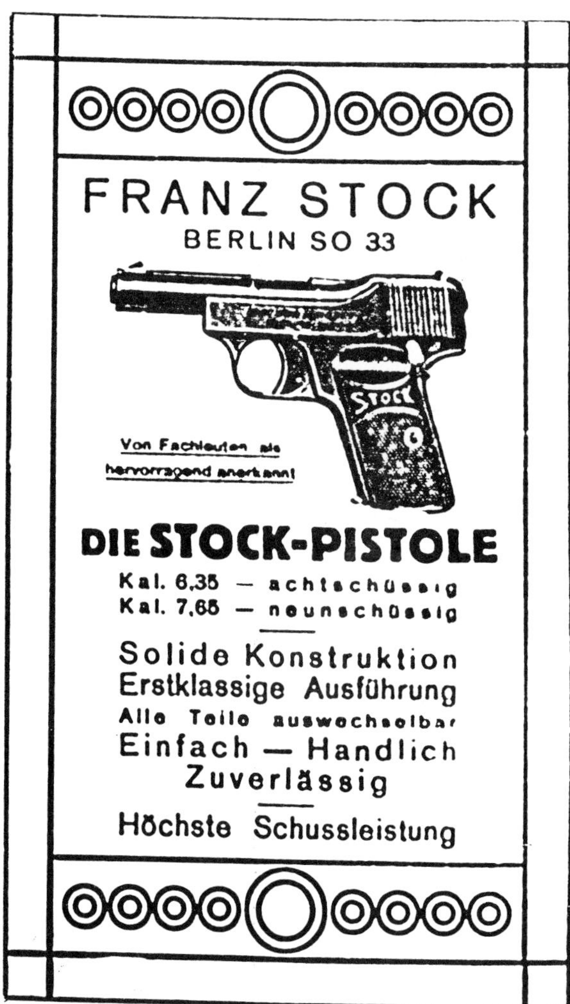

Above: A 1920s advertisement for Franz Stock.

VOLKSPISTOLE

Gustloffwerke, Suhl
Mauserwerke, Oberndorf-am-Neckar
Carl Walther, Zella Mehlis

This title covers a number of designs which were under development in 1945 in response to a demand for cheap and quickly produced weapons with which to arm guerrillas, 'Werewolves', stay-behind parties and other figments of the imagination of the Nazi hierarchy; the German citizens had more sense, and these last-ditch organisations never materialised. Nor, for that matter, did their armaments, the Volkspistole and its putative partner the Volksgewehr.

The full story of the Volkspistole development is unlikely ever to be known, since the chaotic state of affairs in Germany in the closing months of the war meant that accurate records were either destroyed or not kept in the first place; little information was discovered during the interrogation of ordnance engineers and manufacturers, simply because they had little information themselves. The entire Volkswaffen project was meant to be secret, and the German habit of concealing development projects not only from Germany's enemies but even from other branches of the German war effort ensured that very few people ever knew much more than their own small part of the programme. Little has ever been published about it, and, strangely, no manufacturer has ever come forward and explained his part in the business.

However, across the years items of information have appeared, often within the context of something entirely different, and it has become possible to piece together the skeleton and even put flesh on some of the limbs. Without en-

Below: A prototype Walther design, largely of pressed steel construction, which is generally held to be the company's proposal for the Volkspistole programme.

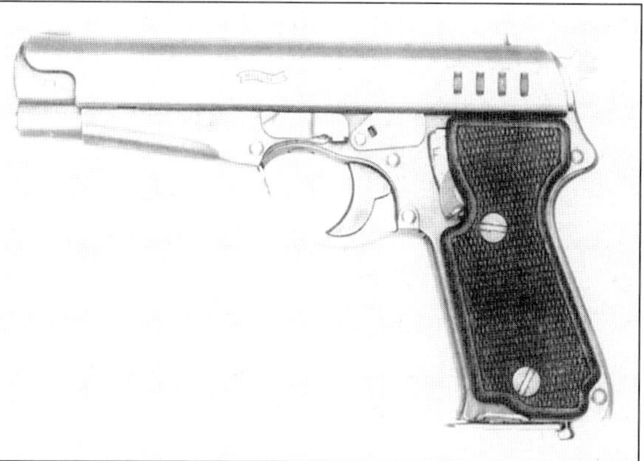

quiring into the origins of the Volkssturm movement, let us just say that the pistol programme began with a request to manufacturers for a cheap and quickly made pistol capable of firing the standard 9mm Parabellum cartridge with sufficient accuracy to hit a 20cm square target at a range of 15m. Beyond demanding that it be safe to handle, use the readily available P38 pistol magazine and not demand high-quality steel or expensive machining processes, there were no other restrictions or demands placed on the makers. Mauser, Walther and the Gustloffwerke in Suhl (formerly the Simson factory) all accepted the challenge.

During the war almost all German military arms makers had experimented to some degree with metal pressings and stampings, welding, brazing and other time-saving techniques. Some of these techniques had appeared in production weapons, such as the MG42 and the Sturmgewehr 44, but not in pistols This is quite remarkable, bearing in mind the Jäger pistol (q.v.), which had appeared before 1914 and was entirely of stamped metal, but it may simply be a recognition of the fact that a soldier will (reluctantly) accept a sheet-metal and wire spring wonder in an assault rifle or submachine gun but will balk at having a pistol with all the hallmarks of 'cheap and nasty'. Whatever the reason may have been, the stamped pistol had not appeared in German military circles by late 1944.

The Volkspistole programme, though, practically demanded stamped metal manufacture, and the various manufacturers all followed this route. Walther produced a quite handsome pistol of conventional appearance, utilising recoil operation with the breech locked by the familiar Colt/Browning cam-controlled dropping barrel. The slide was of sheet metal, pressed into shape, with a machined breech block pinned inside it. The Walther P38 double-action firing mechanism was incorporated, but with a butt-mounted safety/de-cocking lever similar to that of the Sauer 38H.

Dismantling follows the same line as the Browning High-Power or any other of the dropping-barrel breed, the principal change being that the slide stop lever is, like almost every other part except the barrel and breech block, a stamped and not a machined component. Serial numbers suggest that perhaps as many as 40 of these pistols may have been manufactured, but only a handful are known to have survived and all are in private collections. I have been unable to examine one or obtain dimensions.

Mauser planned a blowback pistol vaguely resembling the P38. It was to be entirely of stamped metal except for a cold-forged barrel and, presumably, a machined breech block. Beyond the fact that it had a self-cocking, striker-fired action, we know very little of this weapon. The only known drawing comes from a post-war interrogation report and it is not believed that a complete pistol was ever made before the war ended. Certainly no example is known to have survived.

The last specimen is subject to some debate. On the evidence of various design features, it is

Below: A drawing, from an interrogation report, of the proposed Mauser Volkspistole design.

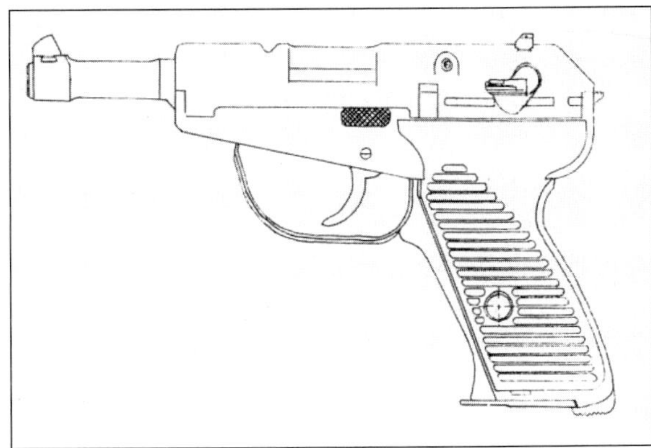

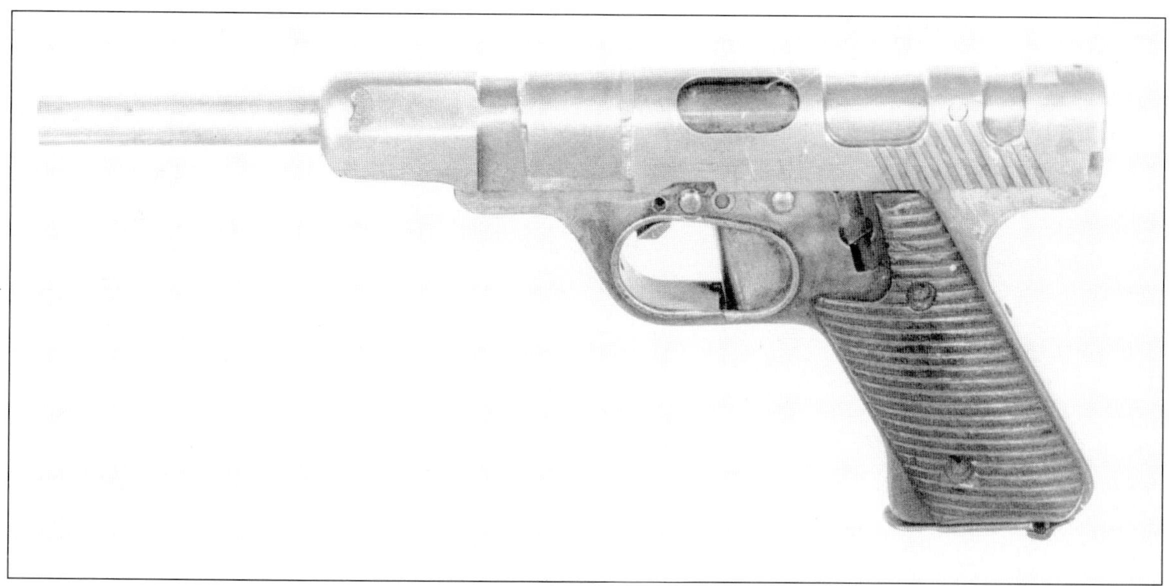

Above: The delayed blowback pistol which appears to be the Gustloffwerke entry into the Volkspistole contest.

generally understood to have come from the Gustloffwerke, but there is a body of opinion which avers that it was a Mauser design, basing this view on the fact that it resembles the Mauser drawing. One might also aver that the Ford Granada is a Rolls-Royce design because it has a wheel at each corner.

Although there is no manufacturer's mark to indicate what the parentage is, an examination of it enables some reasonable conclusions to be drawn. So far as is known, only three specimens exist: the one dealt with here is in the Pattern Room of the Royal Small Arms Factory, while two others are reputed to be in the collection of the Aberdeen Proving Ground in the United States. The Enfield version appears to be unique, differing from the two held in Aberdeen. The general outline is reminiscent of some of the earlier Walther weapons, and although at first appearance it seems to be a commonplace blowback weapon, closer examination shows that it is in fact a delayed blowback type; the delay is achieved by tapping off gas from the chamber and directing it forward in two fine jets to impinge on surfaces in the underside of the slide. The pressure thus generated causes the slide to delay opening until the bullet has moved well up the bore and the chamber pressure has dropped to a safe level. This system of delayed blowback action is the same as that developed by Barnetzke of Gustloffwerke for the Volkssturm-Gewehr semi-automatic rifle, developed as part of the same programme, and is obviously a very strong argument for believing that the pistol came from the same factory.

The slide is a combination of metal pressings brazed together to provide the requisite strength and carries a machined breech block pinned in place. The frame is also a combination of pressings, and the various levers and parts of the firing mechanism are all stamped parts.

An unusual feature is the provision of a smooth-bore extension to the barrel, screwed to the muzzle, almost doubling the effective barrel length. This could be an economy measure, in that only half as much rifled barrel would have to be made per weapon; it might have been added in order to try and improve the accuracy in the hands of untrained firers; or it may even have been merely a flash hider/slide bearing. Another possible reason for the feature is to extend the pressure-time curve and so ensure that the delayed blowback system delays a sufficient length of time by keeping the pressure built up for a longer time than would have been possible with the shorter rifled barrel. This model is 'in the white'—exactly as finished in the toolroom with no form of blueing or other protective finish, with rough welds apparent and without a mark of any kind upon it—no marker's name, no monogram, no serial number or proof marks and no inspector's stamps. So there is nothing to confirm or deny the foregoing conjectures. To sum up, it appears to be an emergency weapon, based on Barnetzke's breech design, probably put together by the Gustloffwerke.

Volkspistole

Calibre	9mm Parabellum
Method of operation	Delayed blowback by gas pressure, striker-fired
Safety devices	None
Magazine type	Single-column detachable box in butt—ex P38 Walther
Position of catch	Bottom rear of butt
Magazine capacity	8 rounds
Front sight	None
Rear sight	None (though provision had been made on the specimen examined)
Overall length	11.25in (286mm)
Barrel length	5.13in (130mm) without extension sleeve (which adds 3.00in, 76mm, to these figures)
Number of grooves	6
Direction of twist	Right-hand
Empty weight	34.0oz (963g)
Markings	None
Serial number	None

Below: The Gustloff Volkspistole dismantled.

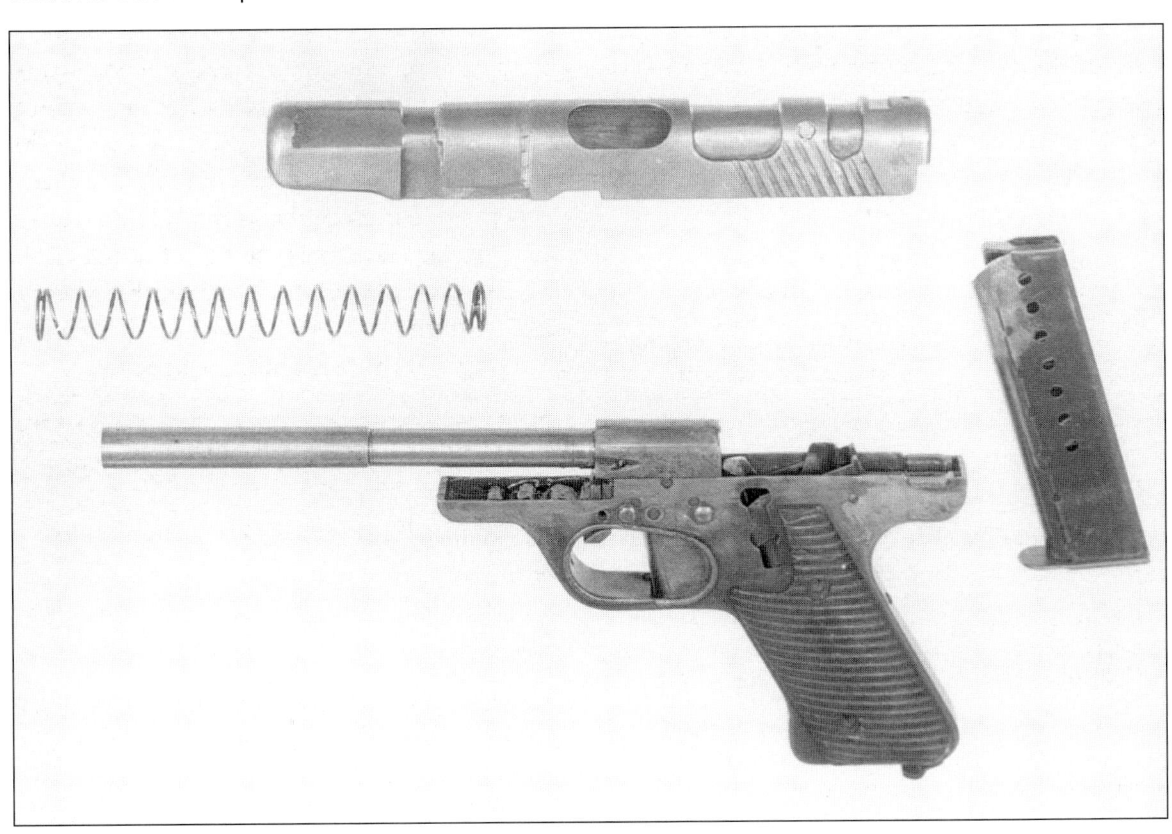

WAHL

Albin Wahl GmbH, Zella Mehlis

This 7.65mm automatic pistol is an extremely rare weapon; it was made in small numbers in the early 1930s but failed to achieve any great success, even though it was well made and finished and exhibited some interesting features.

The Wahl is a fixed-barrel blowback pistol with the return spring wrapped around the barrel and with the front end of the slide tapered up rather like the Browning 1910 model. The butt is unusually deep, giving a larger than normal magazine capacity, and there is a prominent grip safety behind the butt.

Dismantling is fairly straightforward: the whole weapon is virtually held together by one nut, the hexagonal nut which surrounds the muzzle. After removing the magazine and clearing the gun, grip the slide and frame firmly and unscrew the nut; it may need the application of a wrench if the gun has been undisturbed for years. Note that behind the nut is the return spring under compression, so be prepared for the nut to come loose rather violently. Release the spring pressure as you remove the nut, and then withdraw the spring. Now pull back the slide to its maximum travel, lift the rear end, and slide it forward to remove it from around the barrel. The usual sort of screws hold the grips in place, and with these removed the working of the grip safety in preventing movement of the sear can be seen. The lockwork and grip safety levers can be removed, but this is not recommended. Reassembly is simply a matter of replacing the slide over the barrel, lowering it into engagement with the frame, pushing it forward, inserting the return spring and screwing the hexagonal nut back into the slide.

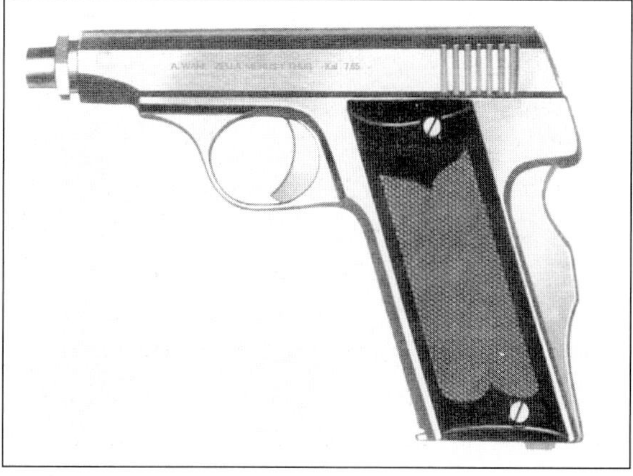

Above: The safety of the Wahl pistol relies entirely upon its oversized grip safety.

Wahl	
Calibre	7.65mm Browning
Method of operation	Blowback, striker-fired
Safety devices	Grip safety; there is no manual safety catch
Magazine type	Single-column detachable box in butt
Position of catch	At heel of butt
Magazine capacity	9 rounds
Front sight	Fixed blade
Rear sight	Fixed V-notch
Overall length	6.10in (155mm)
Barrel length	3.124in (80mm)
Number of grooves	6
Direction of twist	Right-hand
Empty weight	21.4oz (607g)
Markings	Left of slide: 'A. WAHL ZELLA MEHLIS i THUR Kal. 7,65'; right side of frame: 'WAHL D.R.G.M. & AUST. PAT.'
Serial number	On right side of frame

WALTHER

Carl Walther Waffenfabrik, Zella Mehlis (1888–1945)

Carl Walther Waffenfabrik, Ulm-an-der-Donau (1950–)

Carl Walther and his son Fritz designed the first Walther pistol and placed it on the market in 1906 as the Model 1. This method of titling was carried on until the Model 9 and was then

Above: The first Walther, the Model 1, carries its barrel in a carefully concealed jacket.

dropped in favour of more descriptive initial letters, such as the PP, PPK, MP, HP and so forth. After 1945 the Soviet occupation of Zella Mehlis put an end to the firm's long connection with the town, the factory and its machinery being dismantled and taken to Russia as the spoils of war, while, regrettably, most of the unique Walther collection of firearms was looted and dispersed all over the world.

The company was re-formed in Ulm in the early 1950s. As it still owned the relevant patents it was able to license manufacture of the PP and PPK pistols to Manurhin of France, which allowed Walther to go back into business making calculating machines. With the relaxation of post-war restrictions the company were able to return to firearms manufacture in the late 1950s, and received something of a boost when the newly formed Bundeswehr demanded that the P38 pistol be put back into production as their standard sidearm.

Walther Model 1

Walther's first pistol was a simple blowback which showed a good deal of originality; the design is akin to the early Mannlicher in that the breech block is formed with arms reaching alongside the barrel and joined underneath to contain the recoil spring. Close examination of the muzzle and top surface of the barrel will show that the barrel proper is surrounded by the three-quarter length jacket carrying the front sight and prevented from rotating by a key engaging in the slide. Until this feature is seen and understood, dismantling is impossible. There

Above: The Walther Model 1 dismantled.

appear to have been two models of the Model 1 without any distinguishing mark other than the addition of a dismantling button on the frame of the later version. The specimen shown here, serial number 30790, is of the second type, while one with number 11251 is of the first pattern. An unusual feature is the cross-bolt type of safety catch running through the frame; to set for firing it is pushed across from left to right.

To strip the model shown here, first remove the magazine and clear the gun, then set the safety catch to 'safe' and pull back the slide. At the same time press in the serrated catch in the front of the trigger guard; this causes a catch to rise in the frame and hold the slide back. Now grasp the muzzle and unscrew the barrel jacket; the locating key will be seen to move away from its alignment with the slide slot. Once the jacket is removed, pull and release the slide, allowing it to return to the closed position. Now press in the stripping button located on the right rear of the frame, behind the safety catch, and pull the slide back about 0.5in (12mm), pulling upwards at the same time. As the slide comes back, so it will come free from the frame and can be eased forward, taking the recoil spring and its guide rod with it. The striker and striker spring will fall out of their hole in the slide. With the slide off, the important parts of the lockwork are exposed and there is no need to remove the butt grips. Reassembling the weapon is the reverse of stripping.

Walther Model 2

The Model 1 was commercially successful, but Walther felt that it was capable of improvement

Walther Model 1

Calibre	6.35mm Browning
Method of operation	Blowback, striker-fired
Safety devices	Cross bolt manual safety at rear of slide
Magazine type	Single-column detachable box in butt
Position of catch	Bottom rear of butt
Magazine capacity	6 rounds
Front sight	Fixed blade
Rear sight	Groove in slide top
Overall length	4.50in (114mm)
Barrel length	2.05in (52mm)
Number of grooves	4
Direction of twist	Right-hand
Empty weight	13.0oz (366g)
Markings	Left of slide: 'SELBSTLADE-PISTOLE CAL. 6,35. WALTHER'S PATENT.' (later models also have the Walther badge beneath); on each butt grip, moulded in, a monogram of 'CW'
Serial number	Full number on left rear of frame; last two digits on barrel jacket and undersurface of breech block section of slide

Above: The Walther Model 2 simplified and improved upon the Model 1.

Walther Model 3

Introduced in 1910, this is little more than a Model 2 in 7.65mm calibre. A peculiar feature of the model (which was repeated on the later Model 4) is the placing of the ejection opening in the slide on the left-hand side, so that the empties are thrown across the firer's front—a

and followed it very rapidly with the Model 2 of 1909. Here we see the introduction of a feature which has been common to most Walthers ever since—the use of the barrel as a guide for the recoil spring. Another interesting feature is the use of the rear sight as an indicator as to whether the gun is loaded or not; with a round in the chamber the sight is up and can be used, but with the chamber empty the sight drops into a recess in the slide and cannot be sighted over. The more usual type of safety catch replaces the cross-bolt and the peculiar method of stripping is abandoned.

To dismantle the Model 2, after the usual safety checks grasp the knurled collar around the muzzle and, with due care for the compressed recoil spring, unscrew and remove it. Slip the recoil spring out, then draw back the slide, lift, and slip it forward from the frame over the top of the barrel.

Walther Model 2

Calibre	6.35mm Browning
Method of operation	Blowback, hammer-fired
Safety devices	Manual catch left rear of frame
Magazine type	Single-column detachable box in butt
Position of catch	Bottom rear of butt
Magazine capacity	6 rounds
Front sight	Grooved slide
Rear sight	Grooved slide
Overall length	4.30in (109mm)
Barrel length	2.12in (54mm)
Number of grooves	6
Direction of twist	Right-hand
Empty weight	9.75oz (280g)
Markings	Left of slide: 'SELBSTLADE-PISTOLE CAL. 6,35. WALTHER'S PATENT.'; right of slide: 'CARL WALTHER WAFFENFABRIK ZELLA ST BLASII'; grips: 'CW' monogram
Serial number	On right side of trigger guard

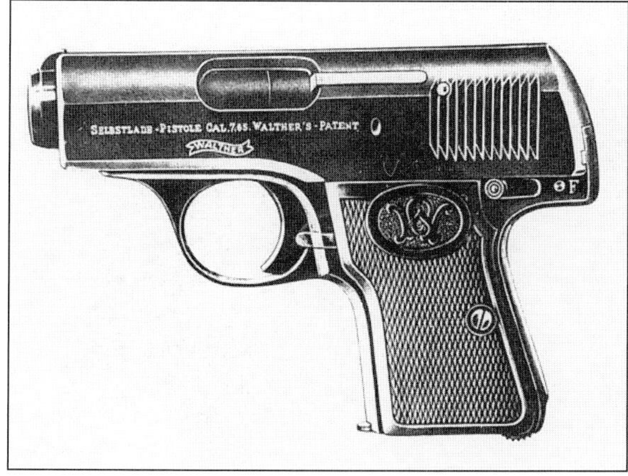

Above: For reasons which no doubt seemed good at the time, the 7.65mm Walther Model 3 had its ejection port on the left side of the slide.

disconcerting performance. Stripping is exactly as for the Model 2.

Walther Model 4

This model shows Walther's first move towards a heavier weapon suited to military or police use, and many were so employed. It was particularly popular as a pocket weapon for staff officers of the German Army in World War I. It is really a logical enlargement of the Model 3 with the barrel extended to give better accuracy and the butt extended to give a better grip and greater magazine capacity. In order to simplify manufacture, the same slide as the Model 3 was used, but lengthened by a light metal shroud to cover the longer barrel.

To dismantle the weapon, clear the gun, remove the magazine and then press in the metal slide extension or muzzle shroud, unlocking it by a quarter-turn. The recoil spring will then push it out, and the spring, shroud and spring bushing can all be removed. Now pull back the slide—lifting as it reaches the end of its travel—and remove it from the frame. This is all the stripping normally necessary; the essential fea-

Walther Model 3

Calibre	7.65mm Browning
Method of operation	Blowback, hammer-fired
Safety devices	Manual catch at left rear of frame
Magazine type	Single-column detachable box in butt
Position of catch	Bottom rear of butt
Magazine capacity	6 rounds
Front sight	Fixed blade
Rear sight	Fixed U-notch
Overall length	5.00in (127mm)
Barrel length	2.62in (67mm)
Number of grooves	6
Direction of twist	Right-hand
Empty weight	16.5oz (467g)
Markings	As Model 1, except for change in calibre designation, though late models may have the address 'ZELLA MEHLIS'
Serial number	As for Model 2

Walther Model 4

Calibre	7.65mm Browning
Method of operation	Blowback, hammer-fired
Safety devices	Manual catch at left rear of frame
Magazine type	Single-column detachable box in butt
Position of catch	Bottom rear of butt
Magazine capacity	8 rounds
Front sight	Fixed blade
Rear sight	Adjustable V-notch
Overall length	6.00in (152mm)
Barrel length	3.35in (85mm)
Number of grooves	4
Direction of twist	Right-hand
Empty weight	19.5oz (553g)
Markings	Left side of slide: 'SELBSTLADE-PISTOLE CAL. 7,65. WALTHER'S PATENT.', with the Walther badge beneath; right side of slide: 'CARL WALTHER WAFFENFABRIK/ZELLA ST. BLASII'; moulded into both grips: monogram of 'CW'
Serial number	Full number on right of frame; last three digits beneath slide

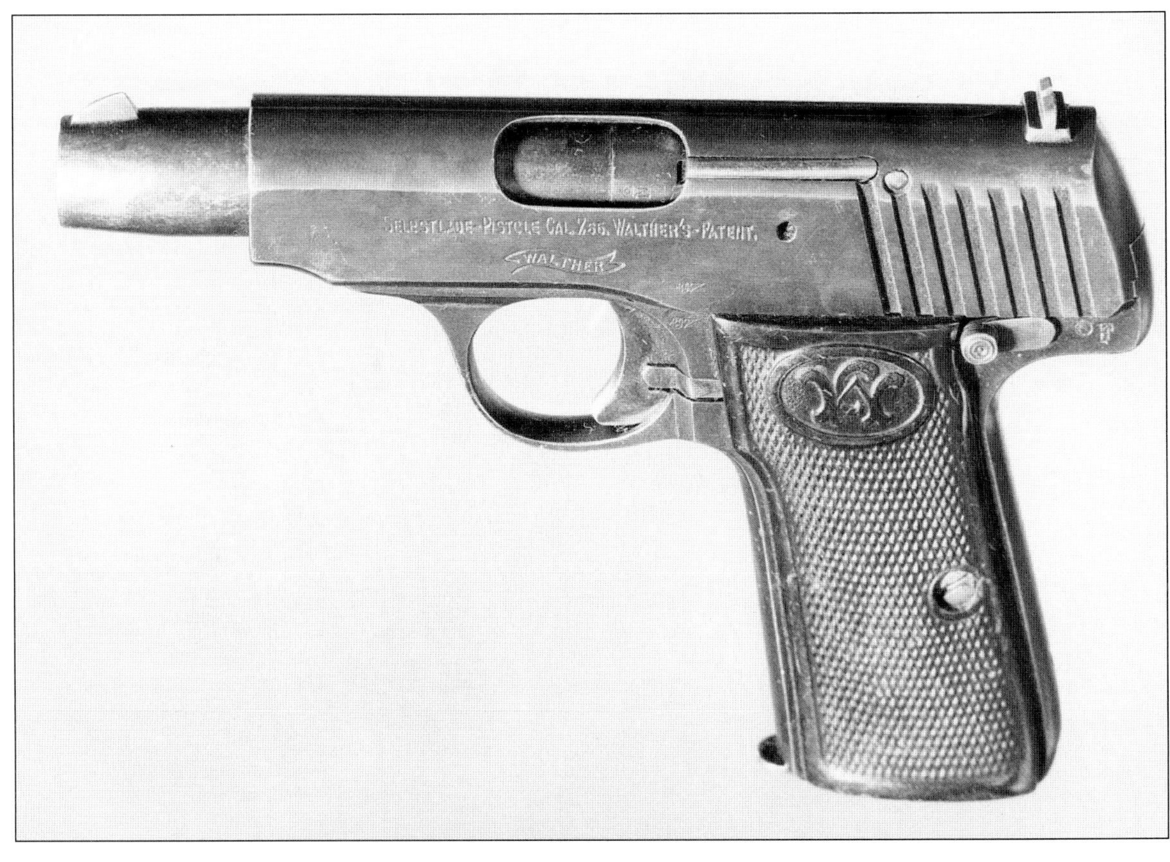

Above: Walther's Model 4 was a 3 with a longer barrel and an extended slide.
Right, upper: The Walther 5 was simply the Model 2 built to a higher standard and given fore and rear sights instead of just a groove in the slide.
Right, lower: The Model 5 dismantled.

Walther Model 5

Calibre	6.35mm Browning
Method of operation	Blowback, striker-fired
Safety devices	Manual catch at left rear of frame
Magazine type	Single-column detachable box in butt
Position of catch	Bottom rear of butt
Magazine capacity	6 rounds
Front sight	Fixed blade
Rear sight	Fixed U-notch
Overall length	4.25in (108mm)
Barrel length	2.12in (54mm)
Number of grooves	4
Direction of twist	Right-hand
Empty weight	9.75oz (276g)
Markings	Left of slide: 'WALTHER'S-PATENT CAL. 6,35' and Walther banner; right of slide: 'WAFFENFABRIK WALTHER ZELLA MEHLIS'
Serial number	On right side of frame

tures of the lockwork can be seen after removal of the slide, and the firing pin can be removed by driving out the cross-pin which locks it in place and which is visible just behind the extractor spring.

Walther Model 5

This model, introduced in 1913, is nothing more than the Model 2 built to a slightly higher standard of workmanship. It can be distinguished from the Model 2 only by having fore and rear sights and a change of inscription on the slide to 'WALTHER'S-PATENT 6,35' and the

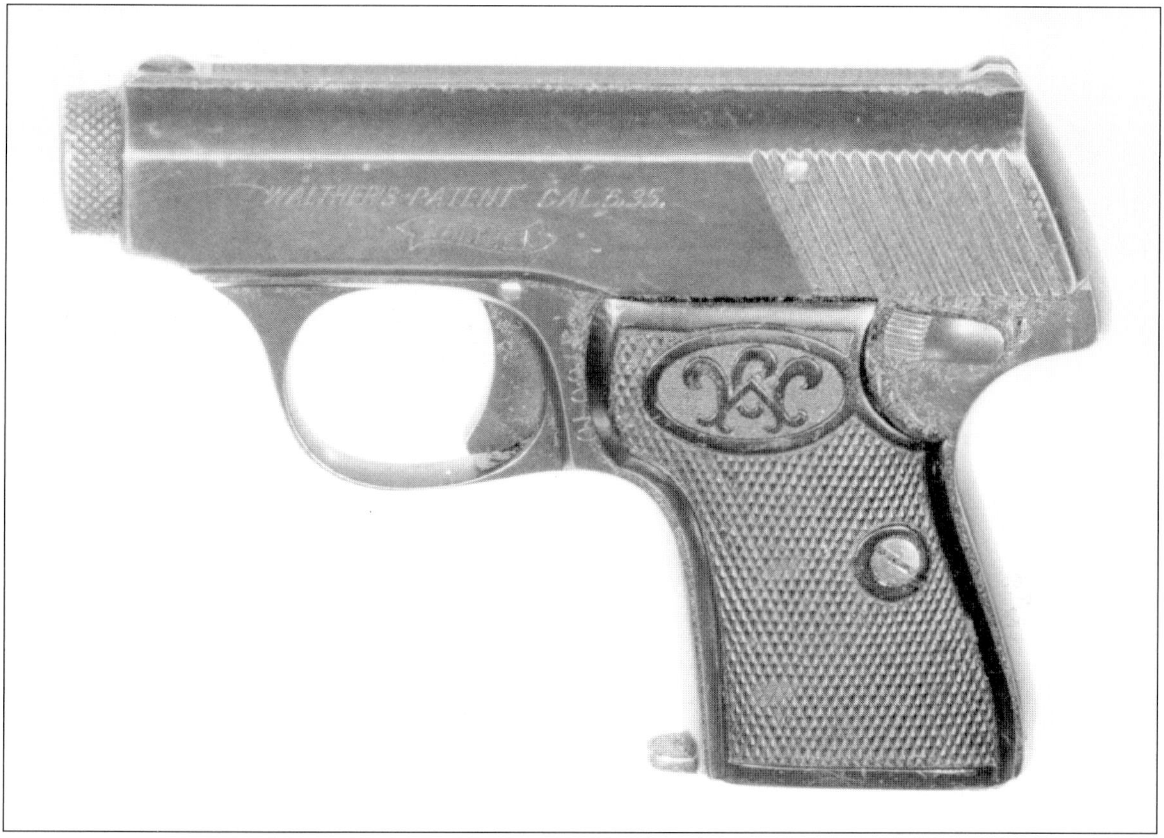

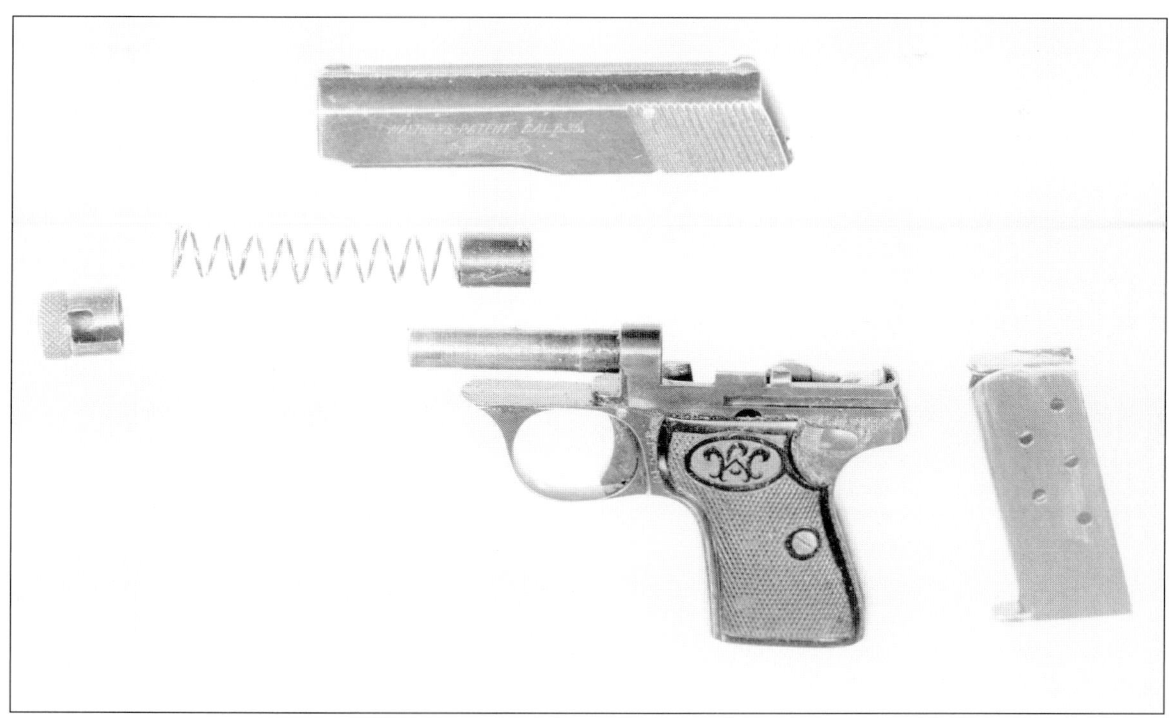

Walther badge. The barrel is rifled with only four grooves instead of the six of the Model 2, but in all other respects the characteristics are the same.

Walther Model 6

This was a wartime expedient, produced in an endeavour to provide a substitute standard pistol for the German Army. In 1915 the standard Army issue weapon was the P '08, chambered for 9mm Parabellum; since these were difficult to mass-produce, Walther simply enlarged his Model 4 to accept the more powerful and larger 9mm cartridge. It was a straight blowback design, and this meant using a heavy slide and very strong spring to withstand the heavier recoil, and the Model 6 is one of the few pure blowback pistols in this calibre. Construction, assembly and stripping are exactly the same as for the Model 4. Relatively few of these weapons were made, and manufacture was discontinued in 1917. The only change from the Model 4 is that the ejection is now to the right.

Walther Model 6	
Calibre	9mm Parabellum
Method of operation	Blowback, hammer-fired
Safety devices	Manual catch at left rear of frame
Magazine type	Single-column detachable box in butt
Position of catch	Bottom rear of butt
Magazine capacity	8 rounds
Front sight	Fixed blade
Rear sight	Adjustable U-notch
Overall length	8.25in (209mm)
Barrel length	4.75in (121mm)
Number of grooves	4
Direction of twist	Right-hand
Empty weight	34.0oz (963g)
Markings	Left side of slide: 'Selbstlade-Pistole Cal. 9m/m. Walther's-Patent' with the Walther banner
Serial number	On right side of frame

Above: The Model 6 was an attempt to fire 9mm Parabellum out of a blowback pistol. It worked, but customers were not enthusiastic.

Walther Model 7

Provided in 1917 as a staff officers' pocket pistol, this is simply a smaller copy of the Model

Walther Model 7	
Calibre	6.35mm Browning
Method of operation	Blowback, hammer-fired
Safety devices	Manual catch left rear of frame
Magazine type	Single-column detachable box in butt
Position of catch	Bottom rear of butt
Magazine capacity	8 rounds
Front sight	Fixed blade
Rear sight	Adjustable V-notch
Overall length	5.25in (133mm)
Barrel length	3.03in (77mm)
Number of grooves	4
Direction of twist	Right-hand
Empty weight	12.0oz (340g)
Markings	Left side of slide: 'Selbstlade Pistole Cal. 6,35 Walther's Patent' and banner; right of slide: 'Carl Walther Waffenfabrik Zella St. Blasii'; moulded into both grips: 'CW' monogram
Serial number	Full number on right side of frame and front of trigger guard; last three digits beneath slide at muzzle end

Right: The Walther Model 7, showing how the slide extension fits in place.
Below: The Model 7 dismantled.

6, with the same right-side ejection and with the lockwork on the right side of the frame. Stripping and handling are exactly the same as for the Model 4.

Walther Model 8

Developed in 1920, the Model 8 shows several advances on previous designs and also foreshadows later designs in its generally streamlined appearance. The overall concept is still that of a simple blowback with the recoil spring concentric with the barrel, but it introduces the Walther system of a trigger-guard lock for stripping, has the safety catch mounted in a much more convenient position in the front edge of the butt grip, and can be found in a nickelled or blued finish.

To strip this model, after the usual safety precautions have been taken press down the small serrated spring catch on the right front of the trigger guard and pull the entire guard down away from the slide. It will come completely free from the slide and frame, and can be re-

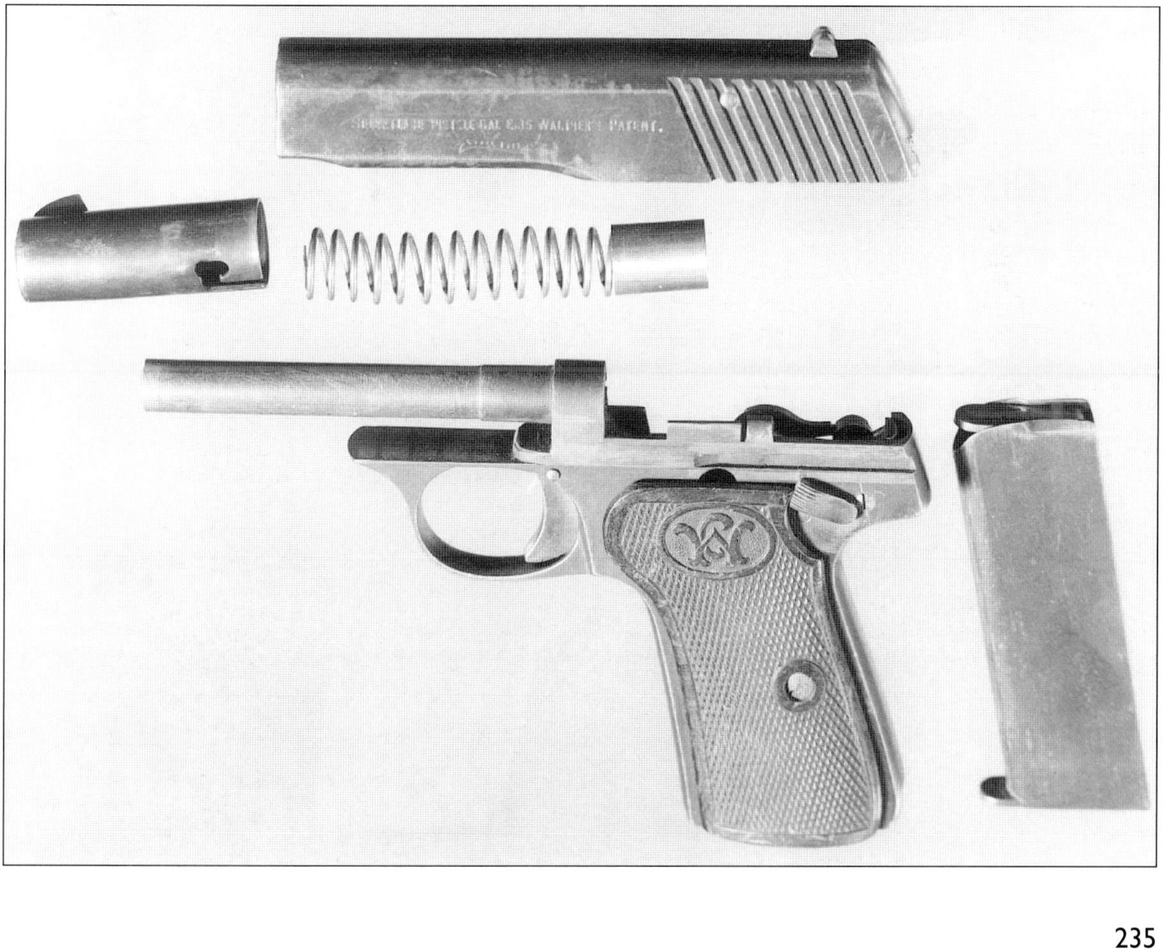

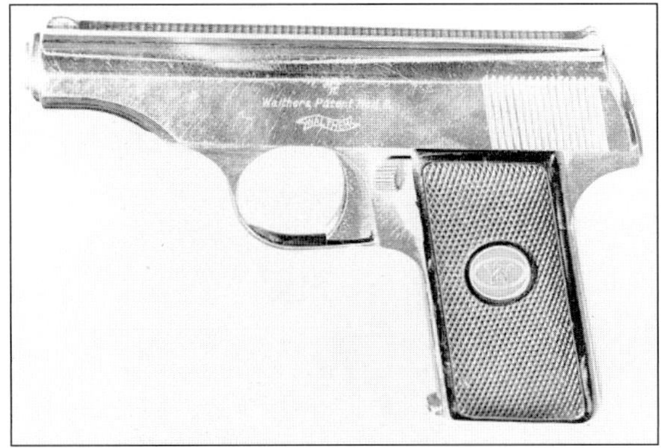

Left: The Walther Model 8 in a highly polished nickel finish. Below: The Model 8 dismantled, showing the first application of the trigger guard as the stripping catch.

moved. Now pull back the slide and lift it free, then allow it to pass forward over the barrel and remove it. To remove the grips a special tool is needed, though a small pair of circlip pliers will serve if used carefully. The monogram on the right-hand grip will be seen to have two small holes in its perimeter. Place the pins of the tool, or the circlip pliers, into these holes and unscrew the monogram plate, which will release both grips. The breech block is a separate unit within the slide and can be removed by releasing the extractor from its locking groove. How this is done depends on the age of the pistol: early versions require a thin blade to be forced between the extractor and the slide side wall, but later models need a fine drift to be pressed against the retaining pin through a hole in the slide wall, while the extractor is hooked out by some suitable implement. The firing pins also vary: in early models they are retained by the extractor, and, once the breech block is freed, the extractor will slip out without further ef-

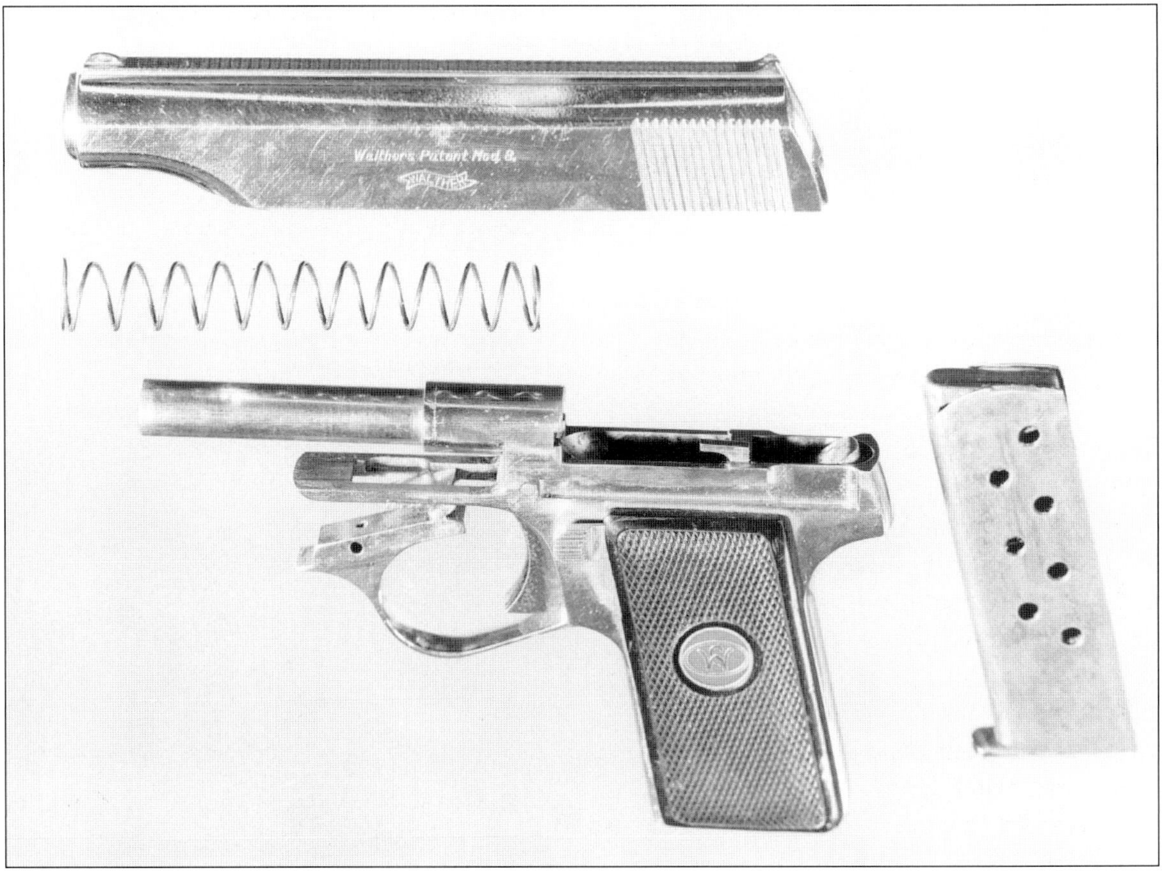

Walther Model 8

Calibre	6.35mm Browning
Method of operation	Blowback, hammer-fired
Safety devices	Manual catch in front edge of left butt grip
Magazine type	Single-column detachable box in butt
Position of catch	Bottom rear of butt
Magazine capacity	8 rounds
Front sight	Fixed blade
Rear sight	Fixed U-notch, with sight base knurled to reduce reflection
Overall length	5.13in (130mm)
Barrel length	2.83in (72mm)
Number of grooves	6
Direction of twist	Right-hand
Empty weight	13.0oz (368g)
Markings	Left side of slide: 'Walther's Patent Mod. 8' and badge; right side of slide: 'Waffenfabrik Walther Zella-Mehlis (Thür.)'; blue and silver medallions in centre of butt grips; in left side a 'CW' monogram in an oval, on right side '6,35' in an oval; bottom of magazine: Walther badge
Serial number	Full number on right rear of frame

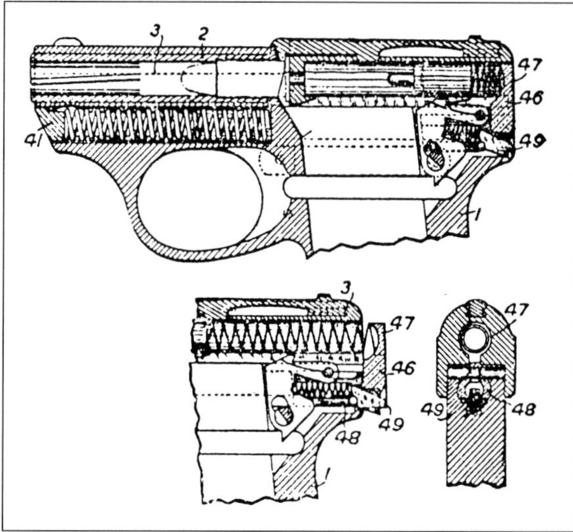

Above: Patent 182,410, 21 April 1921, Fritz Walther. A pistol patent from Walther first appeared in July 1920 and was something of a rag-bag of ideas, most of which were never seen again because the application was cancelled before the final specification was due to be filed. He came up with this one in 1921, covering the method of assembly of the Model 9 pistol.

fort. In the later models they are retained by a keeper plate and screw which can be removed without disturbing the extractor or breech block.

Walther Model 9

This vest-pocket pistol was Walther's 1921 version of the original Model 1. It shows a reversion to the Model 1 outline and general appearance, but the method of stripping is unusual and the workmanship is generally better than that exhibited in the Model 1. It is a simple blowback in 6.35mm calibre, with the safety catch in the front edge of the butt—a feature inaugurated on the Model 8.

To strip, after the usual safety checks, use the lip on the bottom plate of the magazine to

Walther Model 9

Calibre	6.35mm Browning
Method of operation	Blowback, striker-fired
Safety devices	Manual catch in front edge of butt grip
Magazine type	Single-column detachable box in butt
Position of catch	Bottom rear of butt
Magazine capacity	6 rounds
Front sight	Fixed blade
Rear sight	Groove on slide top
Overall length	4.02in (102mm)
Barrel length	2.01in (51mm)
Number of grooves	6
Direction of twist	Right-hand
Empty weight	9.25oz (262g)
Markings	Left side of slide: 'Walther's Patent Mod. 9.' and banner; right side of slide: 'Waffenfabrik Walther Zella-Mehlis (Thür.)'; on lower edge of each grip and on bottom plate of magazine: Walther banner
Serial number	Full number on right side of frame

WALTHER

Left, upper: The Model 9, Walther's candidate for the vest-pocket market.
Left, lower: The Model 9 dismantled.

push up the tiny spring catch protruding from the rear end of the frame below the slide. This releases the dumb-bell shaped striker anchorage and allows it to come out about 0.33in (8mm) and release the slide. The slide can be lifted straight up and slipped forward from the barrel; it will be seen that the barrel proper is a thin insert in a barrel housing which is an integral part of the frame and not, as on every other Walther design, a separate component pinned to the frame.

Reassembly is the opposite of stripping. When the slide has been replaced, the striker anchorage can be pressed back into engagement with the frame and everything is locked together once more. When the weapon is cocked the rear end of the firing pin protrudes through a hole in the striker anchorage as a signal.

The Model 9, the last of the numbered Walther pistols, remained in production until 1945.

Walther Model PP (Polizei Pistole)

The introduction of this model in 1929 rendered every other self-loading pistol obsolete overnight, so advanced was its design. For the first time a popular self-loader was produced by a major manufacturer with a workable and reliable double-action mechanism—a device which had tempted designers and eluded inventors since the beginning of the century. Several other minor innovations were married together in this pistol, which will be examined during the section on stripping.

Originally produced as a police pistol (and hence the initials) for uniformed officers—i.e. for carrying in a holster—this handgun was later adopted by the German services in large numbers, and manufacture continued throughout the war. It has since been manufactured under licence in France and Turkey and copied without licence in several other countries, and it is still being manufactured today. In addition to the standard versions, special models were turned out in which the slide was of light alloy, and numerous examples of plating and ornamental engraving exist.

In addition to the standard 7.65mm calibre, models were also made in 0.22in Long Rifle, in 6.35mm calibre and in 9mm Short/0.380in Auto calibre. Except for the calibre of the barrel, the dimensions and external appearance of these variants are almost identical.

Another new feature on the Model PP is the provision of a signal pin which floats in the slide and is pressed back by the rim of the chambered round so that its end protrudes through the slide just above the hammer, where it can

Walther Model PP .22in

Calibre	.22in Long Rifle (rimfire)
Method of operation	Blowback, hammer-fired
Safety devices	Manual catch on left rear of slide
Magazine type	Single-column detachable box in butt
Position of catch	Left butt, to rear of trigger
Magazine capacity	10 rounds
Front sight	Fixed blade
Rear sight	Fixed U-notch
Overall length	6.38in (162mm)
Barrel length	3.82in (97mm)
Number of grooves	6
Direction of twist	Right-hand
Empty weight	22.5oz (637g)
Markings	Left side of slide: 'Waffenfabrik Walther Zella-Mehlis (Thür.) Walther's Patent Cal. 6.35m/m Mod. PP [or as appropriate]' and Walther banner; top of grips and bottom plate of magazine: Walther banner
Serial number	On right side of frame behind trigger guard

WALTHER
Waffenfabrik Walther, Zella-Mehlis (Thür)
Walther's Patent Cal. 7,65 %
Mod. PP
WALTHER

Left, upper: Walther's 1929 surprise: the double-action Model PP.
Left, lower: The dismantled Model PP, showing the double-action mechanism.

be both seen and felt. This feature is not used on the 0.22in model, since, of course, the 0.22in cartridge is a rimfire; moreover, it is not always present on the other models. In some cases it was omitted during the stress of wartime manufacture as being an unnecessary luxury but it is absent from pre-war commercial models also, though the rules governing its presence or absence have not been determined.

The double-action feature means that pulling the trigger first causes the hammer to rise and then fall to strike the firing pin. In the normal action it is necessary to pull back the slide to cock the weapon initially and load the chamber. Once this is done, the user has two alternatives should he not wish to fire the pistol at once: he can either put the safety catch on and carry the pistol with the hammer cocked, or he can carefully lower the hammer and carry the pistol like that, having to thumb the hammer back before firing. With the Walther design, initial loading and cocking is the same, but, after that, application of the safety catch causes the hammer to drop—quite safely, since the first movement of the safety catch interposes a steel guard which takes the hammer blow and prevents the firing pin from being struck—and then locks the striker. To fire, all that needs be done is to move the safety catch forward and then pull the trigger through to cock and fire in one action.

Stripping the PP is quite simple. After the usual safety checks, pull down on the front of

Walther Model PP 7.65mm

Calibre	7.65mm Browning
Method of operation	Blowback, hammer-fired
Safety devices	Manual catch on left rear of slide
Magazine type	Single-column detachable box in butt
Position of catch	Left butt, to rear of trigger
Magazine capacity	8 rounds
Front sight	Fixed blade
Rear sight	Fixed U-notch
Overall length	6.38in (162mm)
Barrel length	3.35in (85mm)
Number of grooves	6
Direction of twist	Right-hand
Empty weight	25.0oz (708g)
Markings	As PP .22in
Serial number	As PP .22in

Walther Model PP 6.35mm

Calibre	6.35mm Browning
Method of operation	Blowback, hammer-fired
Safety devices	Manual catch on left rear of slide
Magazine type	Single-column detachable box in butt
Position of catch	Left butt, to rear of trigger
Magazine capacity	8 rounds
Front sight	Fixed blade
Rear sight	Fixed U-notch
Overall length	6.38in (162mm)
Barrel length	3.35in (85mm)
Number of grooves	6
Direction of twist	Right-hand
Empty weight	25.5oz (722g)
Markings	As PP .22in
Serial number	As PP .22in

Walther Model PP 9mm

Calibre	9mm Short/.380in Auto Pistol
Method of operation	Blowback, hammer-fired
Safety devices	Manual catch on left rear of slide
Magazine type	Single-column detachable box in butt
Position of catch	Left butt, to rear of trigger
Magazine capacity	7 rounds
Front sight	Fixed blade
Rear sight	Fixed U-notch
Overall length	6.38in (162mm)
Barrel length	3.35in (85mm)
Number of grooves	6
Direction of twist	Right-hand
Empty weight	25.5oz (722g)
Markings	As PP .22in
Serial number	As PP .22in

the trigger guard and swing it sideways a fraction of an inch so that it lodges on the bottom of the frame and is prevented from returning to its slot. Then pull back to withdraw the slide from the frame by lifting and easing it forward over the barrel. Removal of the grips enables the lockwork to be cleaned.

Walther Model PPK

This is a smaller edition of the PP, intended for use by plain-clothes police instead of a holster gun—hence PPK, for 'Polizei Pistole Kriminal' (although there seems an equally good case to be made out for calling it 'Polizei Pistole Kurz', i.e. 'short'). In mechanism, construction and

Walther Model PPK .22in

Calibre	.22in Long Rifle (rimfire)
Method of operation	Blowback, hammer-fired
Safety devices	Manual catch on left rear of slide
Magazine type	Single-column detachable box in butt
Position of catch	Left butt, to rear of trigger
Magazine capacity	9 rounds
Front sight	Fixed blade
Rear sight	Fixed U-notch
Overall length	5.85in (148mm)
Barrel length	3.15in (80mm)
Number of grooves	6
Direction of twist	Right-hand
Empty weight	17.5oz (496g)
Markings	As for Model PP except that slide inscription reads 'Mod. PPK'
Serial number	As PP .22in

Walther Model PPK 6.35mm

Calibre	6.35mm Browning
Method of operation	Blowback, hammer-fired
Safety devices	Manual catch on left rear of slide
Magazine type	Single-column detachable box in butt
Position of catch	Left butt, to rear of trigger
Magazine capacity	7 rounds
Front sight	Fixed blade
Rear sight	Fixed U-notch
Overall length	5.83in (146mm)
Barrel length	3.15in (80mm)
Number of grooves	6
Direction of twist	Right-hand
Empty weight	19.0oz (538g)
Markings	As for Model PP except that slide inscription reads 'Mod. PPK'
Serial number	As PP .22in

Walther Model PPK 7.65mm

Calibre	7.65mm Browning
Method of operation	Blowback, hammer-fired
Safety devices	Manual catch on left rear of slide
Magazine type	Single-column detachable box in butt
Position of catch	Left butt, to rear of trigger
Magazine capacity	7 rounds
Front sight	Fixed blade
Rear sight	Fixed U-notch
Overall length	5.83in (148mm)
Barrel length	3.15in (80mm)
Number of grooves	6
Direction of twist	Right-hand
Empty weight	20.5oz (587g)
Markings	As for Model PP except that slide inscription reads 'Mod. PPK'
Serial number	As PP .22in

Walther Model PPK 9mm

Calibre	9mm Short/.380in Auto Pistol
Method of operation	Blowback, hammer-fired
Safety devices	Manual catch on left rear of slide
Magazine type	Single-column detachable box in butt
Position of catch	Left butt, to rear of trigger
Magazine capacity	6 rounds
Front sight	Fixed blade
Rear sight	Fixed U-notch
Overall length	5.83in (148mm)
Barrel length	3.15in (80mm)
Number of grooves	6
Direction of twist	Right hand
Empty weight	21.0oz (595g)
Markings	As for Model PP except that slide inscription reads 'Mod. PPK'
Serial number	As PP .22in

disassembly detail it is almost exactly the same as the Model PP, the major difference being in the dimensions. There is also a minor difference in the construction of the grip. In the PP the outline of the butt is a forged part of the frame; in the PPK, except for a very few early models, the frame forging for the butt is rectangular and the necessary shaping for the hand is done by the one-piece plastic grip.

Above: The Model PPK with magazine extension to give the little finger something to lean on.

Walther Model MP

In the same way as the Model Four was 'up-calibred' to the Model 6 for service use, so the Model PP was increased in size and chambered for the 9mm Parabellum round as the Model MP (Militärische Pistole). Few were made and fewer still exist today, since the gun was never accepted as a service weapon. Being a simple blowback design, it was viewed with some mistrust by the military authorities responsible for the selection of service weapons, and it was turned down in favour of the later HP and P38 designs.

The general construction is the same as that of the Model PP, and the markings—except for

Below: Comparison between the PP (top) and PPK frame shapes.

Walther Model MP

Calibre	9mm Parabellum
Method of operation	Blowback, striker-fired
Safety devices	Manual catch on left rear of slide
Magazine type	Single-column detachable box in butt
Position of catch	Left butt grip, behind trigger
Magazine capacity	8 rounds
Front sight	Fixed blade
Rear sight	Adjustable U-notch
Overall length	8.07in (205mm)
Barrel length	5.00in (127mm)
Number of grooves	6
Direction of twist	Right-hand
Empty weight	39.0oz (1,110g)
Markings	Left side of slide; 'Waffenfabrik Walther Zella-Mehlis (Thür.) Walther's Patent Cal. 9m/m Mod. MP' and Walther banner
Serial number	On right side of frame behind trigger

Walther Model AP

Calibre	9mm Parabellum
Method of operation	Recoil, locked breech, hammer-fired
Safety devices	Manual catch left rear of slide
Magazine type	Single-column detachable box in butt
Position of catch	Bottom rear of butt
Magazine capacity	8 rounds
Front sight	Fixed blade
Rear sight	Adjustable V-notch
Overall length	8.50in (215.9mm)
Barrel length	4.75in (120.7mm)
Number of grooves	6
Direction of twist	Right-hand
Empty weight	27.8oz (790g)
Markings	Left side of slide: 'Waffenfabrik Walther Zella-Mehlis (Thür.) Armee-Pistole Cal. 9m/m' and Walther banner; at top of grips and bottom of magazine plate: Walther banner
Serial number	On front edge of barrel lug; on left side of frame and slide

the alteration of the slide inscription to read 'Cal. 9mm' and 'Mod. MP'—are the same.

Walther Model AP

This was developed in the early 1930s as a military pistol and represents a complete change of Walther design. For the first time, the firm produced a pistol with a locked breech capable of firing 9mm Parabellum and similar powerful rounds. The barrel was no longer pinned to the frame but was free to recoil, locked to the slide, for a short distance until breech pressure dropped. Then the barrel stopped and was unlocked from the slide, and the slide continued to recoil, cocking the hammer and being returned by two recoil springs. The double-action feature of the PP and PPK was also used, suitably strengthened, but the hammer in this

Below: The Armee Pistole with shoulder stock.

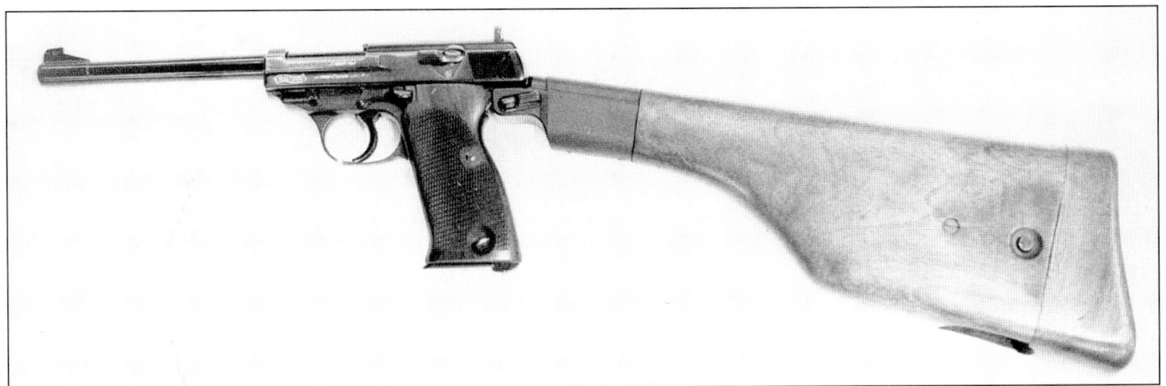

model was completely enclosed within the slide and frame.

Only a small number—probably not more than two hundred—of the Model AP (Armee Pistole) were made, and it was then dropped in favour of the Model HP, which is virtually the same weapon but with an external hammer. Since construction and assembly are practically the same as for the P38, these topics are not covered separately here.

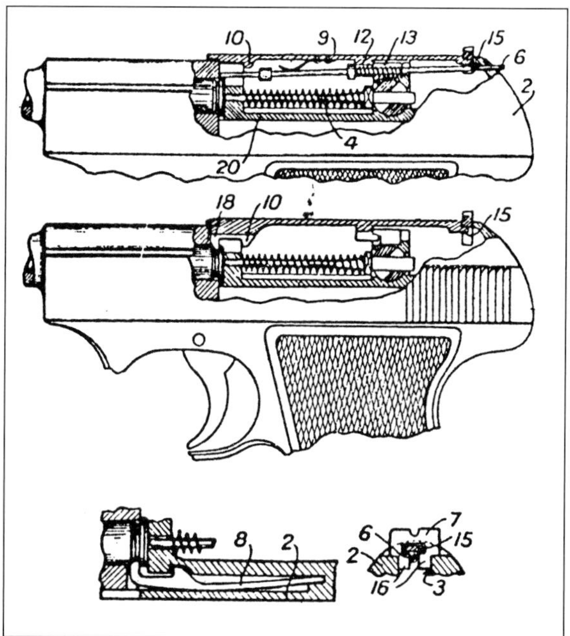

Above: Patent 485,514, 18 April 1937, E. and G. Walther. This patent illustrated the construction of the breech block, cover and signal pin used on the HP and P38 Walther pistols.

Walther Model HP

Model HP (for 'Heeres Pistole') was the successor to the Model AP and was the same pistol except for the change in mechanism to use an external hammer. It is double action and has the usual Walther signal pin in the slide to indicate when the chamber is loaded. Except for minor dimensional changes in the lockwork to facilitate mass-production, the Model HP is identical with the Model P38; indeed, the P38 was, for a very short period, sold on the commercial market as the Model HP.

Walther Model P38

After being offered the AP, the military authorities expressed a preference for a visible hammer and it was redesigned as the HP, and this model was accepted as the standard pistol of the German Army from 1938 onwards. Upon this official acceptance its title became P38, only the early models—a few of which were released to the commercial market—bearing the name HP. The Walther was chosen to supplement and later replace the P '08 as the standard military sidearm, since it promised to be a pistol more amenable to mass production, less liable to derangement in the strain of battle and less critical of the ammunition supplied to it. Since the war, the weapon has been revived as the official pistol for the Bundeswehr under the nomenclature of P1.

In addition to its adoption by the German Army, the P38 was also adopted in 1939 by the Swedish Army as their P39, but the outbreak of war brought supplies to a stop after about 2,000 pistols had been delivered. Immediately after the war ended the Mauser factory, which had been making P38 pistols, was taken under French control and began making P38s for the French Army. About 37,000 were produced, and were marked with the normal wartime German markings though were identified as French by means of a five-pointed star stamped into the right side of the slide. Production continued until May 1946, after which the factory was dismantled.

The P38 consists essentially of three component groups, the barrel, the slide and the frame. The underside of the barrel is formed so as to carry a separate locking block and a buffer. The slide is formed into the usual breech block section at the rear, carrying firing pin, safety catch and extractor, but has the front third cut away at the top. When the gun is assembled the barrel fits into this cutaway section so that the breech abuts against the breech block. The barrel unit moves in specially prepared grooves in the slide, while the slide moves in grooves on the frame. The frame carries the magazine, hammer, trigger and lockwork, together with two recoil springs which fit in grooves on the top of the frame on each side of the magazine recess.

The locking block beneath the barrel is pivoted at its front end; its sides are shaped to form a continuation of the barrel unit bearing surfaces which ride in the slide, and the rear end engages in a buffer pin. The cutaway section of the slide has two rectangular slots, one on each side, and these slots match the upward-facing lugs on the locking block. The bottom of the locking block is shaped into a cam which is controlled by bearing surfaces in the forward section of the frame.

Below: Patent 490,091, 22 May 1937, F.Walther and F. Barthelmes. This completed the patent protection for the HP and P38 pistol designs and details the barrel/slide assembly and the breech locking system. It will have been noted that Walther patented very little of his early design work: he appears to have been unworried by potential piracy, relying upon superior workmanship to keep him ahead of the competition.

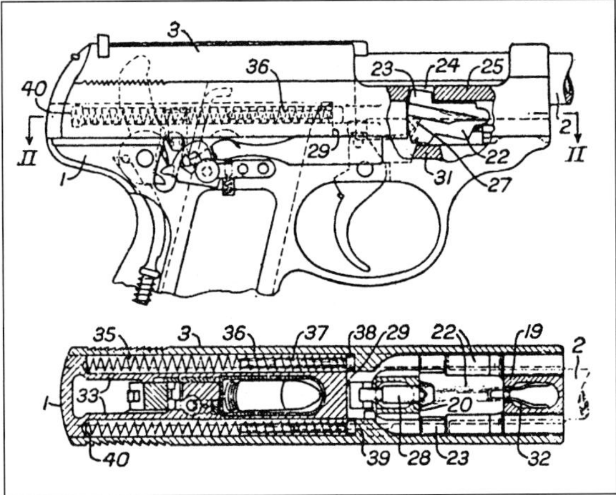

With the pistol ready to fire, the frame bearing surfaces push up the locking block so that the lugs enter the recesses in the slide and firmly lock barrel and slide together. When the cartridge is fired, the recoil drives the unit back along the frame until the buffer pin on the barrel assembly strikes a transom on the frame, immediately ahead of the magazine recess. Pressure on this buffer pin forces the locking cam downwards and releases the lugs from the slide. Owing to the locating spring of the locking block acting as a shock absorber, the barrel is brought to rest comparatively softly, but the slide is now free to continue backwards, compressing the recoil springs and cocking the hammer. On the return stroke of the slide, as soon as the breech block loads the fresh cartridge and exerts pressure on the barrel unit, the two move forward. Owing to the cam in the frame, the locking block is now forced back up to return the lugs to the recesses and securely lock barrel and breech together once more.

The double-action mechanism is virtually the same as that used in the PP and PPK, suitably strengthened and enlarged, as befits a combat weapon. The slide contains a signal pin to indicate when the chamber is loaded and the safety catch and its associate devices are also in the slide. The catch physically locks the firing pin when applied and also, by pressure on a decocking lever, releases the hammer and permits it to fall on the locked pin. In addition, there is an automatic safety feature in that a small lever connected to the hammer presses against a spring-loaded plunger running vertically alongside the firing pin. When the hammer is in any other position than fully cocked, this plunger is allowed to drop under spring pressure and locks the firing pin against forward movement. When the hammer is cocked, and only then, the plunger is pressed up and the firing pin is free to move; during the fall of the hammer this

Above: The Walther P38—the pistol that brought double-action into the large-calibre league.

safety plunger is kept out of action by the controlling lever being held up by a connection to the sear. So long as the trigger is pressed, and the sear moved to the firing position, the auto-safety plunger will be held up out of engagement with the firing pin.

To strip the P38 proceed as follows. After clearing the gun and removing the magazine, pull the slide back and lock it by pushing up the slide lock latch on the left of the frame, just above the trigger. Now rotate the locking pin on the left front of the frame down and forwards. Press down the slide latch while gripping the slide, and allow the slide to move forward until it is in the normal firing position. Then press the trigger and allow the hammer to fall—unless this is done, the automatic safety plunger control lever will be raised into its recess in the slide and will not allow the slide to be removed. Now ease the slide and the barrel off the frame.

Owing to the cam action of the locking block, the two will be securely locked together when removed. Turn the unit upside down and press in the end of the buffer pin; this will release the lock and force the barrel out of the slide. The recoil springs in the frame should not be disturbed: unnecessary removal leads to kinked springs and eventual breakage. The grips are secured by a single screw passing in from the left-hand side, and, with these removed, the action of the lockwork and the automatic safety plate can be seen. The firing pin, safety plunger, safety catch and indicator pin are all contained in the slide and can be examined and replaced by placing the tip of a screwdriver under the overhanging lip of the spring steel plate which forms the top of the slide and springing it forwards and upwards. This releases the rear sight

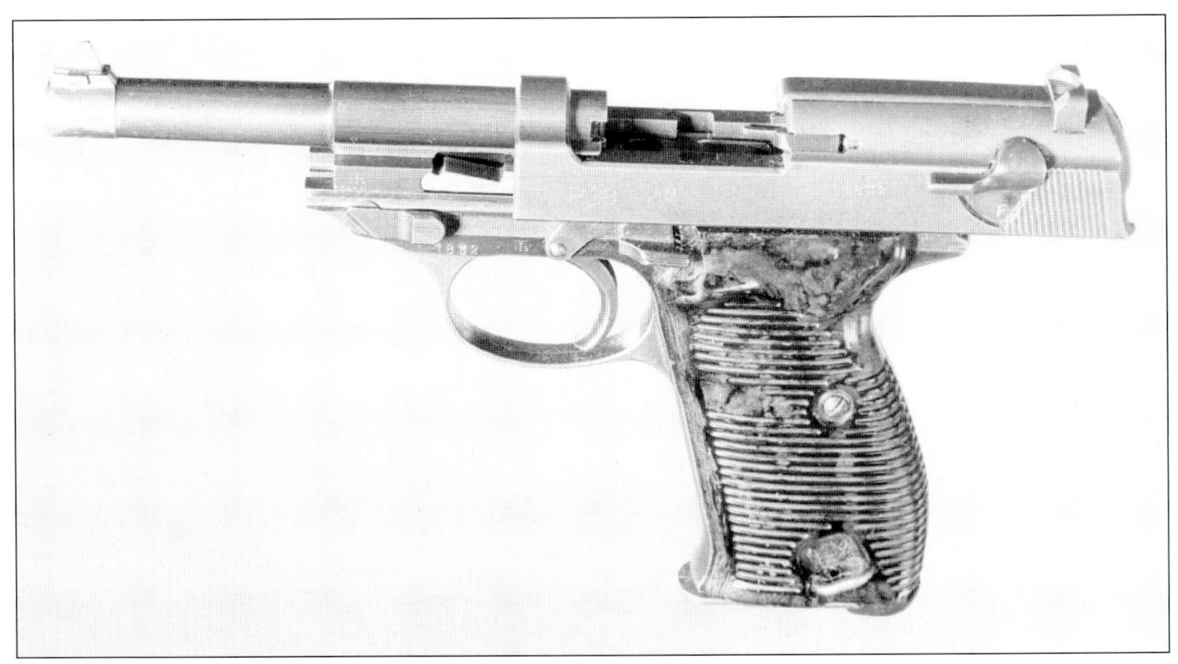

Left, upper: The P38 with its slide locked back to show the breech locking wedge under the barrel.
Left, lower: The P38 dismantled into its basic units.

block, which can be lifted out: beneath this block are the automatic safety plunger with its small spring and, on the other side of the firing pin, the firing pin locating stop. The indicator pin rides across the whole assembly. Removal of these various components is fairly obvious once they are exposed.

When reassembling the P38 there are one or two points to be watched. First, it is possible—though scarcely probable—to reassemble it with the locking block missing: the gun fits together reasonably well, but is thus converted into a form of delayed-action blowback pistol which, with a 9mm Parabellum cartridge, is dangerous. The recoil springs were not designed for this type of functioning. However, when so assembled, the barrel rattles about and emits alarming clanking noises when the slide is pulled back, so that there is little likelihood of the condition escaping the notice of anyone used to firearms. Secondly, examination of the frame when stripped will show that, if it is inverted, three metal plates—the automatic safety, the safety trip lever and the ejector—will protrude past the surface of the frame. These must all be below the surface of the frame before attempting to reassemble, otherwise they will jam the slide and, if one persists in trying to force the slide on, will be bent or broken. Thirdly, owing to the action of the automatic safety, the hammer must be in the fired position.

Having got these three points clear, reassembly is virtually the reverse of disassembly. If the spring plate on top of the slide has been removed, it should be replaced as follows. Press the back sight block down into its bed and drop the spring plate into the recess in the slide, making sure that the rear end is engaged in the groove in the rear sight block. Place the slide on a firm surface and press down hard on the plate about one inch (25mm) in front of the rear sight and then, keeping up this pressure, press the plate backwards towards the rear sight. It will then snap into position, locking both itself and the rear sight. Take up the barrel unit and press in the buffer to bring the locking lugs into line with the bearing surfaces milled in the side of the barrel body. Slide the barrel unit into the front end of the slide—inspection will show that there is only one way in which it will fit. Once the two are together and the barrel fully occupying the cutaway part of the slide, push up on the bottom cam surface of the locking block, thus locking barrel and slide together. Now, making sure that the three plates mentioned above are depressed into the frame and the hammer is in the fired position, slip the slide/barrel assembly on to the frame. If it sticks half way, the cause is invariably the locking block, which will have dropped from the locked position: press it back with the thumb as the barrel

Walther Models HP and P38

Calibre	9mm Parabellum (a few were made in 7.65mm Browning)
Method of operation	Recoil, locked breech, double-action, hammer-fired
Safety devices	Manual catch left rear of slide
Magazine type	Single-column detachable box in butt
Position of catch	Bottom rear of butt
Magazine capacity	8 rounds
Front sight	Adjustable blade
Rear sight	Fixed U-notch
Overall length	8.38in (213mm)
Barrel length	5.00in (127mm)
Number of grooves	6
Direction of twist	Right-hand
Empty weight	29.5oz (840g)
Markings	See text
Serial number	Full serial number on front edge of barrel block, left side of slide and left side of frame; may have suffix letter to show month of manufacture

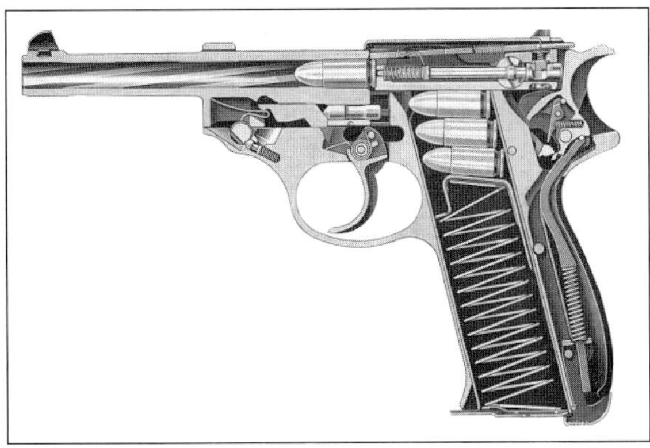

Above: A sectioned drawing of the P38 mechanism.

is eased on to the frame. Having got the complete assembly on, pull the slide all the way back, cocking the hammer, and lock it there with the slide lock latch, rotate the locking pin back and up and depress the slide lock latch, allowing the slide to run forward, and the gun is ready for use.

The markings on the left side of the slide vary according to the date of manufacture, whether the weapon was for military use or commercial sale, and whether it was made by Walther or a wartime contractor.

The first production models for the Army carried the Walther badge, together with the inscription 'P38' and a serial number beginning with '0'. When manufacturers' code numbers were allotted, to counter economic intelligence being garnered by the Allies, Walther were given the code '480', and a small number of weapons made during the last months of 1939 may be found with '480 P38' on the slide. In 1940 the '480' was dropped and the letter group 'ac' was allotted to Walther. Additionally, the last two digits of the year of manufacture were stamped below this letter group. Another change was the addition of a suffix letter to the serial number in order to keep the numbers within bounds. The system was the same as that described for the Parabellum, in which each month had an identifying letter. Early in 1941 the Mauser company began production of P38 pistols, and their products are identified by the letters 'byf' or 'svw'. Later, production was also organised in the factories of Spreewerke GmbH at Berlin-Spandau and Kratzau, Bohemia, and these pistols are identified by the letter groups 'cyq' and 'nho' respectively. Towards the end of the war, production was dispersed to several small factories, though not many were able to do much beyond getting organised before the war ended. Other letter codes which may be found on late-model P38 pistols, their magazines and their component parts can be identified from the details given in Appendix III.

Finally, a word about variations on the P38. From time to time these weapons are reported: some in 7.65mm; a single-action-only version; models with special wood butt grips; models with peculiar sighting arrangements; the list never seems to end. None of these was ever a production model and they are probably some of the flotsam from the looting of Zella Mehlis coming to the surface after sixty years of submergence.

Walther Olympia-Pistole

In 1932 Walther designed a .22in automatic pistol for use in the Olympic Games; the weapon was of basic Walther blowback design, mechanically similar to the Model 9, but of a suitable size to give a reasonable grip for target shooting, and with a barrel 9in (229mm) long. It was later made available for commercial sale in a number of shorter barrel lengths, the 5in (127mm) probably being the most common.

It is dismantled by depressing the catch in the front edge of the trigger guard, pulling the slide back and up and then slipping it forward over the barrel in the usual Walther way. Precise data are not tabulated since the model came in numerous variations to cater for the target

Above: The Walther Olympia-Pistole in .22 calibre.

shooter's whims, but the basic Olympia Modell had an overall length of 12.95in (330mm) and weighed 35oz (1kg) empty.

For the next Games in 1936 an improved weapon was produced and called the 'Olympia-Pistole'. Mechanical arrangements were much the same as those of the previous model, but this weapon uses a hammer instead of a striker, since hammer mechanisms can be engineered to give better trigger pulls than can striker types and this is certainly borne out when comparing the two types. The wooden grip of the Olympia fills the hand well, and is extended downwards for balance and sureness of grip, the magazine having a wooden block attached to its bottom plate to match.

The Olympia is stripped on the same system as the PP and PPK models, by pulling down the front end of the trigger guard to unlock the slide, which can then be pulled to the rear and up to free it from the frame. The recoil spring will be seen to be a very small diameter coil, anchored snugly in the frame, very much like one of the recoil springs of the later P38 model. It is neither necessary nor desirable to disturb it.

The standard model shown here has an overall length of 7.88in (200mm), weighs 27oz

Below: The Olympia-Pistole dismantled, showing the location of the recoil spring inside the frame.

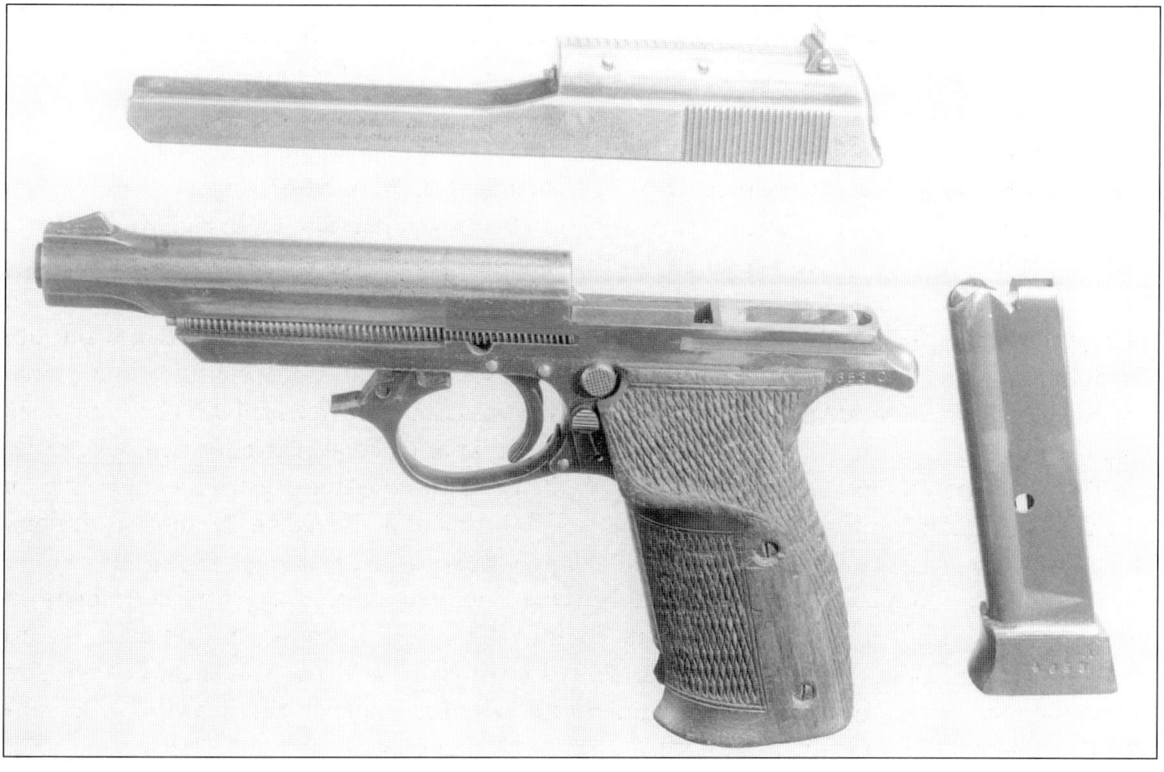

Walther Olympia-Pistole

Calibre	0.22in Long Rifle (rimfire)
Method of operation	Blowback, hammer-fired
Safety devices	Manual catch on front edge of left butt grip
Magazine type	Single-column detachable box in butt
Position of catch	Left side of butt, behind trigger
Magazine capacity	10 rounds
Front sight	Adjustable blade
Rear sight	Adjustable U-notch
Overall length	7.83in (200mm)
Barrel length	4.75in (120mm)
Number of grooves	6
Direction of twist	Right-hand
Empty weight	27.0oz (766g)
Markings	Walther banner; 'Waffenfabrik Walther Zella-Mehlis (Thür.) Walther's Patent Olympia-Pistole'
Serial number	On right side of frame

(766g) and has a 4.75in (120mm) long barrel rifled with six grooves on a right-hand twist. Magazine capacity is ten rounds of .22in Long Rifle. Numerous variations were made, again to suit the desires of marksmen, and models with barrels up to 7.5in (190mm), with or without adjustable or fixed balance weights hung beneath the barrel, with variations in sights and with more or less fancy grips can be met. They are all the same weapon under the skin, except that a few were made, or subsequently modified, to chamber the .22in Short cartridge.

CARL WALTHER OF ULM

In 1945 Zella Mehlis vanished into the Soviet Zone of Occupation and the Walther factory was thoroughly looted and then gutted of its machinery. In the late 1940s the company reformed as Carl Walther in Ulm-an-der-Donau, and began manufacturing calculating machines once more. It was also the owner of a number of patents and was able to licence manufacture of the PP and PPK pistols to the French company Manurhin (Manufacture de Machines du Haut-Rhin, Mulhouse). Whilst identical in construction to the pre-1945 articles, these can be distinguished by the slide inscription, which reads: 'MANUFACTURE DE MACHINES DU HAUT-RHIN – MANURHIN – LIC. EXCL. WALTHER Mod PP [or PPK] Cal. 7.675m/m [or other] MADE IN FRANCE'. The grips have the Manurhin name at the top and 'LIC. WALTHER PP [or PPK]' at the bottom. Both standard models as described above, and long-barrelled 'Sport Models' with adjustable sights, were made until 1964, when manufacture returned to the Walther factory in Ulm. It is understood that some numbers of pistols were actually made by Manurhin but marked in the Walther manner for sale by Walther until their production line was up and running.

Pistole P1

What propelled Walther back into the firearms business was the establishment of the Bundeswehr, the Federal German Army, in 1954. Originally outfitted with American arms, the new force immediately set about organising German weapons, and for their service pistol they specified a return to the P38. Walther therefore set about re-tooling and the new pistol was introduced as the P1. Due to the fresh tooling, there were some very slight differences in dimensions and finish, and the new design uses an alloy frame, but for all practical purposes the new P1 and the old P38 are twins.

Pistol P38

Once the P1 was in production, Walther, very astutely, realised that there was a wide market for the wartime pistol and placed the design on the commercial market as the P38. For reasons

Walther Pistole I	
Calibre	9mm Parabellum
Method of operation	Recoil, wedge-locked breech, double-action, hammer-fired
Safety devices	Manual catch left rear of slide
Magazine type	Single-column detachable box in butt
Position of catch	Bottom rear of butt
Magazine capacity	8 rounds
Front sight	Adjustable blade
Rear sight	Fixed U-notch
Overall length	8.58in (218mm)
Barrel length	4.88in (124mm)
Number of grooves	6
Direction of twist	Right-hand
Empty weight	27.2oz (772g)
Markings	'Carl Walther Waffenfabrik Ulm/Donau' with Walther banner and 'P1 KAL. 9m/m' below, on left side of slide
Serial number	On left side of slide ahead of trigger

Walther Model P38	
Calibre	.22LR, 7.65mmP or 9mmP
Method of operation	Blowback .22LR; recoil 7.65mm, 9mm
Safety devices	Safety/de-cocking lever at rear of slide
Magazine type	Single-column detachable box in butt
Position of catch	Bottom rear of butt
Magazine capacity	8 rounds
Front sight	Fixed blade
Rear sight	Fixed square notch
Overall length	8.50in (216mm)
Barrel length	5.07in (129mm) .22LR; 4.92in (125mm) 7.65mm, 9mm
Number of grooves	6
Direction of twist	Right-hand
Empty weight	28.2oz (800g)
Markings	Left side of slide: Walther banner, 'Carl Walther Waffenfabrik Ulm/Do. P38 Kal. XXX'
Serial number	On left side of frame above trigger

which are not entirely clear, there are some very slight dimensional differences between the military P1 and the commercial P38, but apart from that they are virtually one and the same weapon: everything works the same way, everything looks the same, and they come to pieces in the same manner.

However, one major difference is that the commercial P38 was available in .22 Long Rifle or 7.65mm Parabellum chambering as well as the standard 9mm Parabellum. The 7.65mm is the same as the 9mm model, but the .22 version is, of course, purely a blowback design and has no locking wedge or signal pin to indicate a loaded chamber. Remarkably, the dimensions for all three are almost identical.

Left: The post-1945 P38 was better finished and had a different set of markings, but was mechanically the same as the pre-1945 model.

Pistol P1A1

The P1A1 was announced in 1989 and was an improved model of the P5 (see below) and thus a cousin of the P38. The principal change was the adoption of a cross-bolt safety catch in the slide instead of the familiar safety and de-cocking lever. This operated directly upon the firing pin: when the bolt was pushed to the left, the firing pin was positively locked and also pushed down so that it was aligned with a cut-out portion on the face of the hammer. Thus, if the hammer fell, the firing pin would not be touched and, in any case, was positively locked

Above: The P1A1 was intended to replace the P38, but circumstances change ...

against movement. Pushing the cross-bolt to the right would unlock the firing pin and permit it to rise so that it was aligned with the solid part of the hammer face. There was a de-cocking lever on the left side of the butt which could be used to drop the hammer safely on to a loaded chamber.

Walther P1A1

Calibre	9mm Parabellum
Method of operation	Recoil, locked breech, double-action, hammer-fired
Safety devices	Cross-bolt in rear part of slide; de-cocking lever on left grip
Magazine type	Single-column detachable box in butt
Position of catch	Bottom rear of butt
Magazine capacity	8 rounds
Front sight	Adjustable blade
Rear sight	Fixed U-notch
Overall length	7.05in (179mm)
Barrel length	3.54in (90mm)
Number of grooves	6
Direction of twist	Right-hand
Empty weight	28.5oz (808g)
Markings	Left side of slide: Walther banner, 'P1A1 Kal. 9m/m'
Serial number	Full number on left side of both slide and frame

The P1A1 was intended as a possible replacement for the P1 in the German Army, but its arrival coincided with the restoration of Germany's eastern provinces, which absorbed much of the funding earmarked for the Bundeswehr. The idea was dropped and the design was not put into production.

Pistol P4

The P4 appeared in the late 1970s and was essentially a P38 with a shorter barrel and with an entirely new semi-automatic safety system. The slide carried the same safety lever as the P38/P1 models but when applied it moved the firing pin out of line with the hammer, locked it, and then allowed the hammer to fall safely. When the catch was released, it sprang back to the upper position. When ready to fire, the trigger was pulled and this raised the hammer and also released the firing pin from its locked position in such a way that it would be struck by the falling hammer. The significant difference be-

Walther P4

Calibre	9mm Parabellum
Method of operation	Recoil, locked breech, double-action, hammer-fired
Safety devices	Safety and de-cocking lever on left rear of slide
Magazine type	Single-column detachable box in butt
Position of catch	Bottom rear of butt
Magazine capacity	8 rounds
Front sight	Fixed blade
Rear sight	Adjustable square notch
Overall length	7.87in (200mm)
Barrel length	4.33in (110mm)
Number of grooves	6
Direction of twist	Right-hand
Empty weight	29.1oz (825g)
Markings	Left side of slide: Walther banner, 'Carl Walther Waffenfabrik Ulm/Do. P4 Kal 9m/m'
Serial number	On left side of frame above trigger

Above: The P4 is really a P-38 with an alloy frame, a shorter barrel and a new set of safety devices.

tween this and the system used later in the P5 is that the firing pin stays in the aligned position until the safety is re-applied; in the P5 it springs back into the 'safe' position after each shot and must be released by the trigger action again for the next shot. Apart from this and an alloy frame, the construction, operation and stripping is the same as that for the P38 pistol.

Walther Model P38K

Calibre	9mm Parabellum.
Method of operation	Recoil, locked breech, double-action, hammer-fired
Safety devices	De-cocking lever on left rear of slide
Magazine type	Single-column detachable box in butt
Position of catch	Bottom rear of butt
Magazine capacity	8 rounds
Front sight	Fixed blade
Rear sight	Adjustable square notch
Overall length	6.30in (160mm)
Barrel length	2.75in (70mm)
Number of grooves	6
Direction of twist	Right-hand
Empty weight	27.9oz (790g)
Markings	Left side of slide: Walther banner, 'Carl Walther Waffenfabrik Ulm/Do. P38K Kal. 9m/m'
Serial number	On left side of frame above trigger

Pistole P38K

This was produced at the same time as the P4 and was an even shorter form, with the barrel ending just in front of the slide and with the front sight blade mounted on the slide. The semi-automatic firing pin safety system of the P4 was incorporated, and the frame was of light alloy.

Pistole P5

In spite of the numbering, this appeared after the P1 and before the P1A1 and is essentially a shortened and modernised form of the P38/P1 design intended for police and security forces, by whom it has been widely adopted.

The basic mechanical features are the same as those of the P38, using a wedge beneath a moving barrel to lock the breech, but the slide is all-enveloping and the barrel is shorter. An automatic firing pin safety system has been incorporated, in which the pin is not free to move nor is it aligned with the hammer, except when the trigger is being correctly pulled.

The de-cocking lever has been removed from the slide and placed on the left grip and now functions only as a hammer release; it no longer

Below: The P38K is simply a P4 made even shorter—the barrel so short that the fore sight had to go on the slide.

has any safety feature and, of course, no influence on the firing pin. After loading the pistol, the slide is pulled back and released to put a round into the chamber; the de-cocking lever is then pressed down and released. This allows the hammer to drop and strike the slide, a recessed portion in the face of the hammer enclosing, but not touching, the end of the firing pin. The pistol may now be carried in perfect safety; when required, all that is needed is to pull the trigger, which will raise the hammer, unlock and align the firing pin and then release the hammer to fire the round in the chamber. Thereafter the hammer will remain at full cock after each shot, but the firing pin automatically returns to the 'safe' position until the trigger is again pressed to release the cocked hammer.

Dismantling the P5 is similar to dismantling the P38. After removing the magazine and clearing the gun, press the muzzle against some soft but resistant surface until it reaches its recoil stop. Then turn up the dismantling catch on the left front of the frame and release the pressure so as to permit the barrel and slide to come off the frame forwards. The barrel can be removed from the slide by pressing forward the locking pin against the wedge. No further dismantling should be attempted, and reassembly is simply a reversal of the procedure.

Walther Model P5

Calibre	9mm Parabellum
Method of operation	Recoil, locked breech, double-action, hammer-fired
Safety devices	Cross-bolt in rear part of slide; de-cocking lever on left grip
Magazine type	Single-column detachable box in butt
Position of catch	Left front of butt behind trigger
Magazine capacity	8 rounds
Front sight	Fixed blade
Rear sight	Adjustable square notch
Overall length	7.05in (179mm)
Barrel length	3.54in (90mm)
Number of grooves	6
Direction of twist	Right-hand
Empty weight	28.5oz (808g)
Markings	Left side of slide: Walther banner, 'P5 Carl Walther Waffenfabrik Ulm/Do.'
Serial number	On left side of frame above trigger

Pistol P5 Compact

As the name suggests, this is simply a shorter and lighter version of the P5, making it more convenient for concealed carrying. The pistol has an alloy frame and wooden grips, and the

Below left: The P5 is more or less the P4 mechanism clad in a new outer skin, giving it a more modern appearance. Below right: The P5 Compact is just that—a P5 with a shorter barrel.

Walther Model P5 Compact

Calibre	9mm Parabellum
Method of operation	Recoil, locked breech, double-action, hammer-fired
Safety devices	Cross-bolt in rear part of slide; de-cocking lever on left grip
Magazine type	Single-column detachable box in butt
Position of catch	Left front edge of butt behind trigger
Magazine capacity	8 rounds
Front sight	Fixed blade
Rear sight	Adjustable square notch
Overall length	6.61in (168mm)
Barrel length	3.11in (79mm)
Number of grooves	6
Direction of twist	Right-hand
Empty weight	27.5oz (780g)
Markings	Left side of slide: Walther banner, 'P5 COMPACT Carl Walther Waffenfabrik Ulm/ Do.'
Serial number	On left side of frame above trigger

hammer is rounded so as not to catch in clothing. The operation, safety devices and dismantling procedure are all exactly the same as for the P5.

Pistol P88

In 1988 Walther surprised everybody by abandoning their wedge lock which had served them for fifty years and producing this design, which uses the Browning dropping barrel method of locking the breech. The shape, also, reverts to the general 'Browning' type, though the butt and grips show a distinct Walther family resemblance. The breech locking is in the modern idiom, pioneered by SIG of Switzerland, in which the chamber area of the barrel is formed into a rectangular block which, when it rises in the frame, locks into a large rectangular ejection opening in the slide that completely spans the top and extends slightly down each side. This produces a very solid lock and is a good deal easier to manufacture than the internal slide ribs and grooves of the original Browning design.

The mechanism is that of the P5, with automatic firing pin safety and a de-cocking lever, but in this case the de-cocking lever is 'ambidextrous' and appears on both sides of the frame, as does the magazine release, so that the gun can be used with either hand with equal facility.

Dismantling is, again, very much in the usual Browning style. After removing the magazine and clearing the gun, press the muzzle against some soft but solid surface until the barrel and slide have moved back to their stop. Turn down the slide stop pin on the left side of the frame and withdraw it to the left. Now ease up on the pressure and the slide, barrel and return spring will slip off the front of the frame. Invert the unit and remove the barrel, spring and guide rod. Reassembly is simply a reversal of the stripping process.

Walther Model P88

Calibre	9mm Parabellum.
Method of operation	Recoil, locked breech, double-action, hammer-fired
Safety devices	De-cocking lever both sides of butt
Magazine type	Double-column detachable box in butt
Position of catch	Front edge of butt, both sides
Magazine capacity	15 rounds
Front sight	Fixed blade
Rear sight	Adjustable square notch
Overall length	7.36in (187mm)
Barrel length	4.01in (102mm)
Number of grooves	6
Direction of twist	Right-hand
Empty weight	31.7oz (900g)
Markings	Left side of slide: Walther banner, 'P88 Made in Germany'; right side of barrel, visible through ejection port: Walther banner, '9 × 19m/m'
Serial number	On left side of frame above trigger

Left: The P88 caused a minor sensation when it appeared, since it was the first Walther to adopt the Browning system of breech locking. This is the Compact version.

Pistole P88 Compact

This appeared in 1992 and completely replaced the P88 described above. It is generally to the same design, but smaller and lighter, and with a change in the safety devices. Instead of having the de-cocking lever on the frame, it has been moved up to the 'traditional' Walther position on the rear of the slide, and is duplicated, appearing on both sides. The position formerly occupied by the de-cocking lever now has a slide release lever which allows the slide to go forward after loading a fresh magazine.

Operation and dismantling are the same as for the original P88.

The P88 Compact is also available chambered for the 9 × 21mm IMI cartridge; the dimensions are the same except that the magazine will hold only fourteen rounds.

Walther Model P88 Compact	
Calibre	9mm Parabellum
Method of operation	Recoil, locked breech, double-action, hammer-fired
Safety devices	De-cocking lever both sides of slide
Magazine type	Double-column detachable box in butt
Position of catch	Front edge of butt, both sides, behind trigger
Magazine capacity	16 rounds
Front sight	Fixed blade
Rear sight	Adjustable square notch
Overall length	7.12in (181mm)
Barrel length	3.82in (97mm)
Number of grooves	6
Direction of twist	Right-hand
Empty weight	29.0oz (822g)
Markings	Walther banner, 'P88 COMPACT Made in Germany'
Serial number	On left side of frame above trigger

Pistole P88 Competition

This is based upon the P88 Compact but with the mechanism considerably modified. It is now a single-action hammer, and thus the de-cocking function is no longer present and the safety catch on the slide is purely a safety de-

Walther Model P88 Competition	
Calibre	9mm Parabellum.
Method of operation	Recoil, locked breech, single-action, hammer-fired
Safety devices	Manual safety catch at rear of slide
Magazine type	Double-column detachable box in butt
Position of catch	Front left edge of butt, behind trigger
Magazine capacity	14 rounds
Front sight	Fixed blade
Rear sight	Adjustable square notch
Overall length	8.30in (211mm) with long barrel
Barrel length	3.93in (100mm) or 4.92in (125mm)
Number of grooves	6
Direction of twist	Right-hand
Empty weight	28.2oz (800g) with long barrel
Markings	Left side of slide: Walther banner, 'P88 COMPETITION'; right side of slide: 'Made in Germany'
Serial number	On left side of frame above trigger

Above left: The Competition P88 pistol has competition sights and trigger.
Above right: The PP-Super is an enlarged Model PP, designed to fire the 9 × 18 Police cartridge and incorporating the new safety systems introduced in the P5.

vice, locking the hammer and firing mechanism when applied. It is available with two lengths of barrel, the longer protruding from the slide.

Pistol PP-Super

As might be imagined by the title, this is a PP pistol but it incorporates the improved safety system of the P5 and is chambered only for the 9 × 18mm Police cartridge. It can be readily distinguished from the original PP by the squared-off trigger guard, for the currently fashionable two-handed grip. Operation, except for the modified de-cocking switch, and stripping are exactly the same as for the original PP model.

Walther Model PP-Super

Calibre	9 × 18mm Police
Method of operation	Blowback, double-action, hammer-fired
Safety devices	Automatic firing pin safety, de-cocking lever on left grip
Magazine type	Single-column detachable box in butt
Position of catch	Front left edge of butt, behind trigger
Magazine capacity	7 rounds
Front sight	Fixed blade
Rear sight	Fixed square notch
Overall length	6.92in (176mm)
Barrel length	3.23in (82mm)
Number of grooves	6
Direction of twist	Right-hand
Empty weight	27.5oz (780g)
Markings	Left side of slide: Walther banner, 'Carl Walther Waffenfabrik Ulm/Do. PP-SUPER Kal. 9m/m'
Serial number	On left side of frame above trigger

Model PPK/S

This was a rather odd weapon which came into being as a method of circumventing one of the more ridiculous provisions of the US Gun Control Act of 1968, which used the height of the weapon as one of the criteria for admission to the United States, the minimum depth being 4in. The PP, a very popular weapon with off-duty police officers in the US, was, under this regulation, prohibited, since it measured 3.9in from the bottom of the magazine to the top of the slide. Walther therefore manufactured this hybrid, which is, according to how you look at it, either a PP with a shorter slide and barrel or a PPK with a deeper butt frame. It was, in fact, the frame of the PP carrying the slide and barrel of the PPK. This increased the depth of the butt to 4.1in, honour was satisfied and the gun

Above: The PPK/S is a special weapon designed to bring the PPK within the permitted area of the American 1968 Gun Control Act.

was granted entry to the United States. Production began in late 1969. It is currently manufactured in 9mm Short/.380 Auto calibre and marketed in the US only.

Model SC

This was the Model PP in .22LR and with a 150mm or 210mm barrel, a ten-shot magazine and target grips, an adjustable rear sight and an extended hammer spur. The object was to produce a target pistol of adequate quality but stopping short of the refinements demanded by ISU and Olympic-class shooters. A variant model in .22 Short was produced by Manurhin at about the same time. It does not appear to have been marketed for very long—from 1956 to 1963.

Model TP

'TP' stands for Taschenpistole—Pocket Pistol—and this was a post-war revival of the 6.35mm Model 9 but with a more modern shape and one which gave the pistol a distinct family likeness to the PP and PPK. The grip was better shaped and raked back , and the slide and barrel were shaped generally to resemble the PPK. The safety catch was most unusual, a manual catch mounted on the left side of the slide but close to the front edge of the breech block—a convenient place for the thumb to reach but a most unusual position for a safety catch.

Introduced in 1963, the weapon was withdrawn after only about 15,000 had been sold

Below: The Sport-PP was an interesting target pistol developed by Manurhin during their license period in the 1950s.

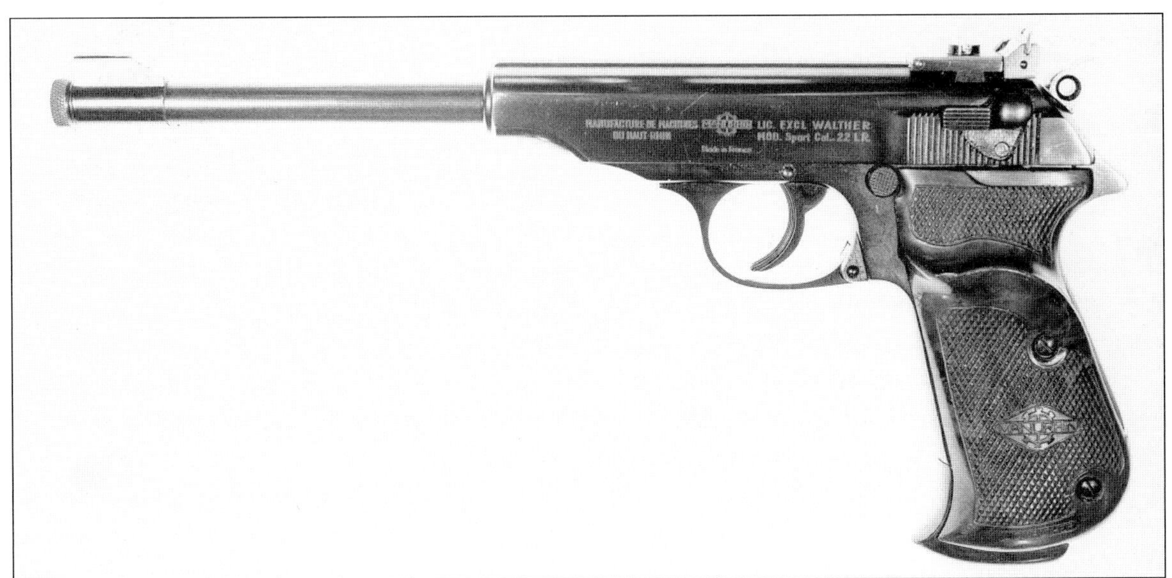

Walther Model TP

Calibre	6.35mm Browning
Method of operation	Blowback, single-action, concealed hammer-fired
Safety devices	Manual safety catch left side of slide
Magazine type	Single-column detachable box in butt
Position of catch	At heel of butt
Magazine capacity	6 rounds
Front sight	Fixed blade
Rear sight	Groove in slide top
Overall length	5.25in (133mm)
Barrel length	2.56in (65mm)
Number of grooves	6
Direction of twist	Right-hand
Empty weight	11.0oz (310g)
Markings	Left side of slide: Walther banner, 'TP Cal. 6.35 Ulm/Do'; right side of slide: 'Made in West Germany'; on grips: Walther banner at the bottom; a stylised globe with the Walther banner across it central on both sides
Serial number	On right side of frame

Walther Model TPH

Calibre	.22 Long Rifle or 6.35mm Browning
Method of operation	Blowback, double-action, hammer-fired
Safety devices	Safety catch and de-cocking lever left rear of slide
Magazine type	Single-column detachable box in butt
Position of catch	Left front edge of butt, behind trigger
Magazine capacity	6 rounds
Front sight	Fixed blade
Rear sight	Fixed square notch
Overall length	5.31in (135mm)
Barrel length	2.79in (71mm)
Number of grooves	6
Direction of twist	Right-hand
Empty weight	11.46oz (325g)
Markings	Left side of slide: Walther banner, 'Carl Walther Waffenfabrik Ulm/Do. Cal. .22 LR [Cal. 6.35m/m]'; right side of slide: 'Made in Germany'
Serial number	On left side of frame above trigger

since it failed to meet the dimensional requirements of the US Gun Control Act of 1968, thus closing its principal market. The pistol is dismantled in exactly the same way as the Model 9.

Model TPH

'TPH' means Taschenpistole mit Hahn—Pocket Pistol with Hammer—and the weapon is really a diminutive version of the PP and PPK design and which replaced the TP model. It was introduced in 1968 and has continued in production ever since. Like its larger cousins, it is a double-action pistol, with a safety and de-cocking lever on the left rear of the slide. This, applied when the hammer is cocked, will make the firing pin safe and interpose a solid block between it and the falling hammer. When required, the safety is pushed up to the 'fire' position and the trigger pulled to raise and release the hammer.

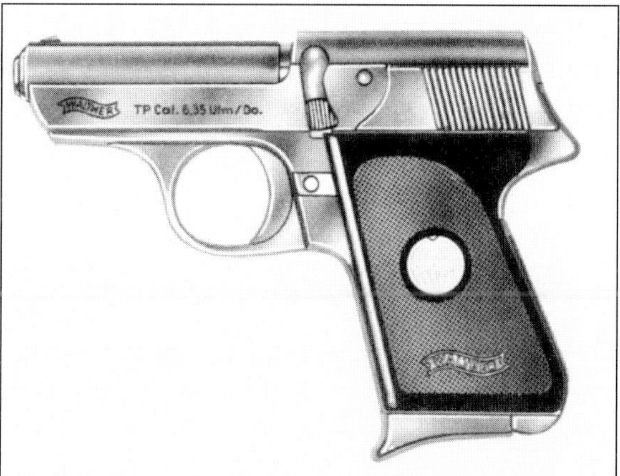

Above: The Taschenpistole is the modern equivalent of the pre-1945 Model 9.

Dismantling the Model TPH follows exactly the same procedure as for the PP: remove the magazine, clear the gun, spring down the trigger guard and then pull back and lift off the slide.

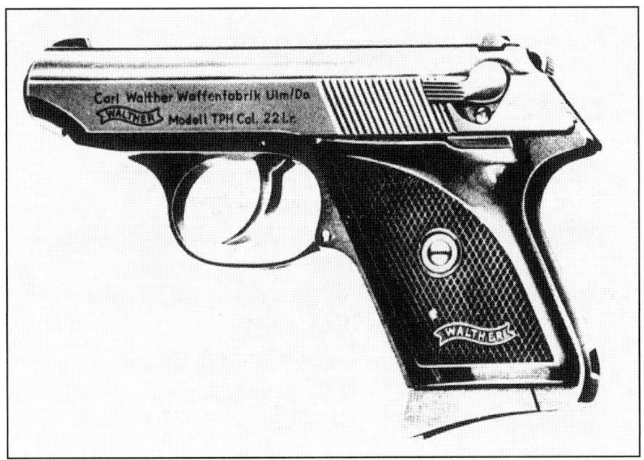

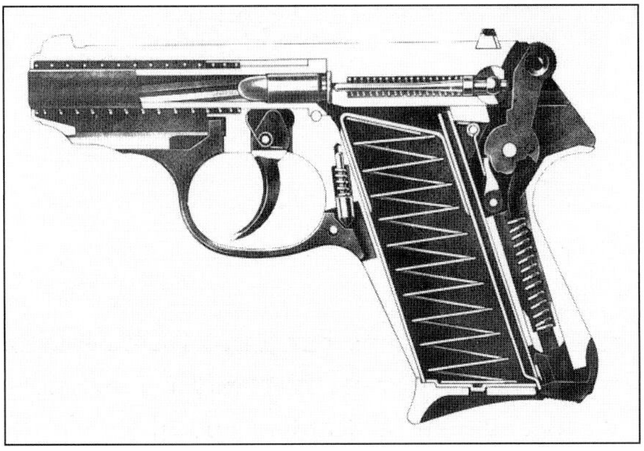

Left, upper: The TPH is the TP but with a double-action hammer mechanism—in effect a shrunken PPK.
Left, lower: Inside the Model TPH.

Owing to the import restrictions of the US Gun Control Act, manufacture of the TPH in the United States under licence commenced in 1989. The gun was manufactured by the Ranger Manufacturing Co of Gadsden, Alabama, and marketed by Interarms of Alexandria, Virginia. The pistol is identical to the German-made version but is marked on the right side of the slide 'MADE IN USA INTERARMS ALEXANDRIA VIRGINIA'.

Model GSP

The Model GSP—Gebrauchs und Sport Pistole (Utility and Sport Pistol)—is primarily a purpose-built competition pistol. Introduced in 1967, it has proved popular and highly effective in winning prizes. The gun is a slab-sided blowback pistol with its magazine ahead of the trigger—which, uniquely, pivots at the bottom—and is available firing either the .22 Long Rifle or the .32 Smith & Wesson Long cartridge, the latter with wadcutter bullets. The mechanism uses a bolt moving inside the receiver. A range of accessories, such as balance weights, sights, dry-firing trigger units and adjustable trigger units, is available and a dedicated enthusiast could virtually build up his pistol to his own personal desires whilst staying within the bounds of competition regulations.

Dismantling the GSP is not difficult, but neither is the process readily evident. Remove the magazine and pull back the bolt to eject any round in the chamber. Uncock the pistol by pulling back the bolt and then letting it forward under control while pulling the trigger. Push in the locking spring below the slide locking lever (on the left side of the frame, in front of the magazine) and rotate the lever upwards and

Walther Model GSP

Calibre	.22 LR; .32 S&W Long
Method of operation	Blowback, hammer-fired
Safety devices	None
Magazine type	Single-column detachable box
Position of catch	Bottom rear of magazine
Magazine capacity	5 rounds
Front sight	Fixed blade
Rear sight	Micro-adjustable square notch
Overall length	11.50in (292mm)
Barrel length	4.21in (107mm)
Number of grooves	6
Direction of twist	Right-hand
Empty weight	41.6oz (1,180g) .22; 45.1oz (1,290g) .32
Markings	Left side of receiver: Walther banner, 'GSP .32 Su.W long Wadcutter [or GSP Cal .22 LR] Carl Walther Waffenfabrik Ulm/Do.'
Serial number	On right side of frame

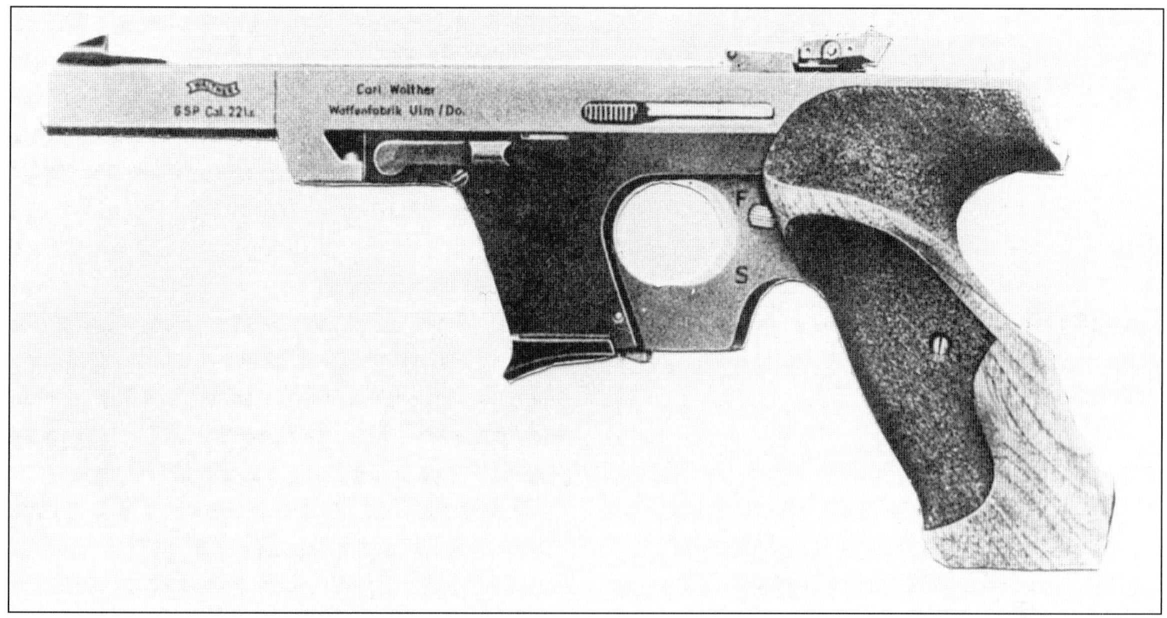

Above: The Model GSP-22 target pistol.

forwards to its stop. Now push the barrel and receiver forward for a short distance and lift it from the frame. *Do not* invert the barrel receiver unit: turn it on its side and loosen the barrel locking screw, using the Allen key supplied with the pistol, until the cocking piece lock pin can be seen through the hole in the base of the receiver. Now, using a drift or fine screwdriver, push in the spring-loaded pin and at the same time push on one side of the cocking piece so as to force it from the receiver; or, on the .22 version, pull out the cocking knob. Swing the hinged ejector open, and then continue loosening the barrel locking screw until the barrel can be removed. With the barrel out, the breech bolt can be removed from the receiver. Now locate the locking pin on the left side of the frame, between the magazine and the trigger. Using a screwdriver, rotate this through 180°, then grip the hammer and lift the entire trigger unit out of the frame.

Below: The Model GSP-32 fires the .32 S&W cartridge.

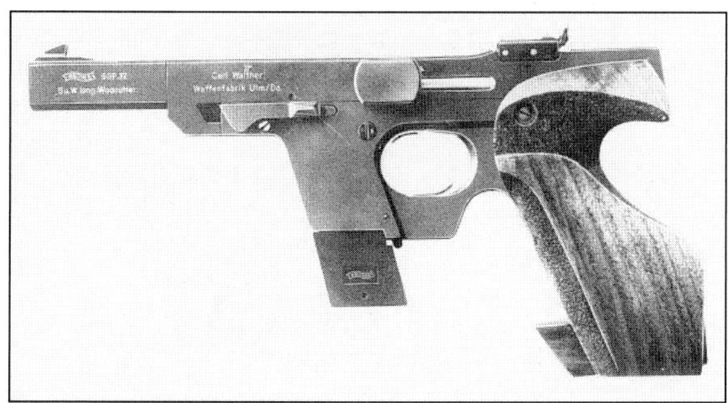

To reassemble the weapon the procedure is reversed. Re-insert the breech block into the receiver. Insert the barrel and manipulate the barrel holding screw to hold the barrel until the cocking piece can be inserted. Tighten the barrel locking screw and turn back the ejector. Lower the trigger unit into the frame and rotate the locking pin until the mark faces forward. Lower the receiver on to the frame, about 8mm forward of the normal rest position, then push backwards and rotate the slide locking lever fully back.

Model OSP

'OSP' stands for Olympic Sport Pistol, and this is exactly the same pistol as the GSP described

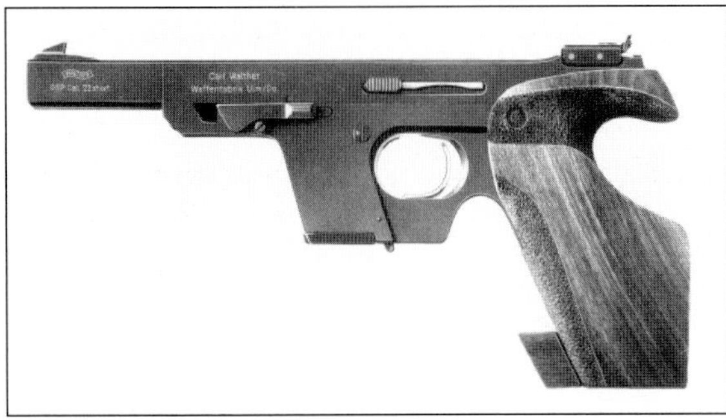

Above: The OSP is built to fire the .22 Short cartridge for international shooting contests.

above except that it is chambered for the .22 Short cartridge so as to meet the requirements for Olympic competitions. Construction, operation and dismantling are all exactly the same. The dimensions differ only in the length of barrel, 108mm instead of 107mm, and weight, 39.5oz (1,120g). The markings are similar except that the calibre notation reads 'OSP Cal .22 Short'.

Model FP

Entirely different from the rest of the company's products, the FP is a Free Pistol, a single-shot weapon using a Martini-type dropping block operated by a lever on the right side of the frame. The firing circuit is electronic: a solenoid firing pin is actuated by a trigger switch and a 9-volt battery. Opening the breech breaks the firing circuit; closing the breech restores the circuit and charges a capacitor which provides the power for the solenoid. This also operates a 'ready' light, which illuminates when the pistol is ready to fire.

The Ultra Pistols

In the 1930s Walther began questioning the utility of the existing standard pocket pistol calibres—6.35mm, 7.65mm and 9mm Short—and, in conjunction with the Gustav Genschow Patronenfabrik of Durlach, began development of three new cartridges known as the Ultra series. These were in 6.45mm, 8mm and 9mm calibre and were designed to extract the maximum performance without demanding a locked breech. Special models of the PP and PPK pistols were chambered to suit, and the designs were finalised in 1938. The military authorities, however, were reluctant to change to a range of new calibres, and the international situation at the time was such that commercial exploitation appeared to hold little promise. The project was shelved, and the war effectively killed it.

Below: The little-known Walther FP Free Pistol for competition work.

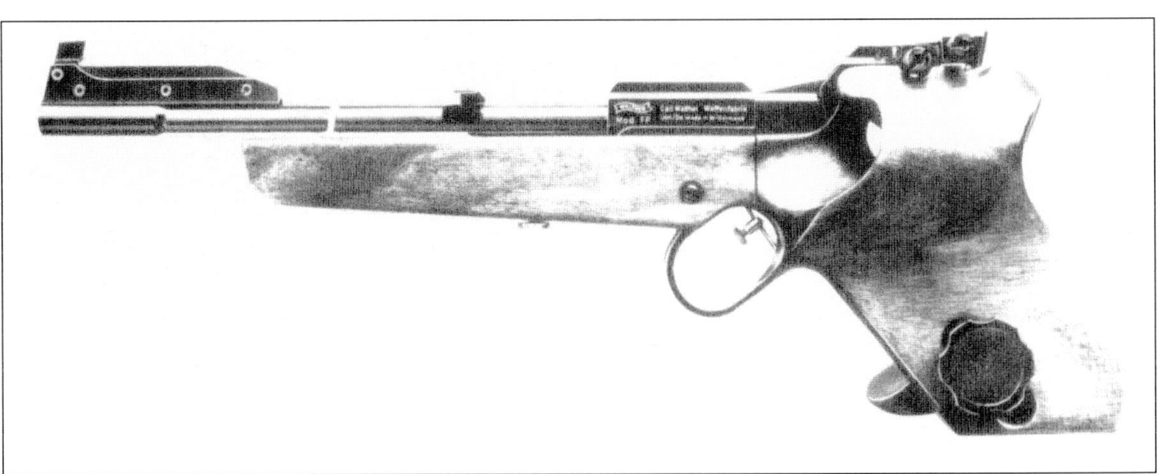

It is said that batches of 20,000 rounds in each calibre were made, most of which were used up in testing. The special pistols were likewise tested virtually to destruction. The remaining pistols were probably dispersed in 1945, and at least one, in 9mm Ultra, is in an American collection. The ammunition is similarly scarce.

The project was not entirely forgotten, however, and it is generally accepted that the 9 × 18mm Makarov and 9 × 18mm Police cartridges which appeared in the late 1970s were both inspired by knowledge of the Ultra programme.

WEIRAUCH

Herman Weirauch Waffenfabrik, Mellrichstadt, Germany

Weirauch was originally located in Zella Mehlis as a maker of bicycles and sporting guns but fled to the West when Thuringia came under Soviet control after 1945. He produced air rifles and sporting guns and then began to manufacture a range of revolvers using Pickert's old tradename of Arminius; however, the circumstances by which he acquired rights to this name are unknown.

The Weirach Arminius weapons are very different from those of Pickert, being side-opening hand ejector models based more or less on the lines of Smith & Wesson or Colt designs, and are substantial pistols of good quality. All models carry the Arminius trademark on the frame, a bearded head with winged helmet—a stylised version of the Pickert trademark used before 1939. The model number is engraved on the cylinder crane and the calibre and cartridge on the barrel; 'Made in Germany' usually appears on the frame.

Below: The Weirauch Arminius HW3 revolver.

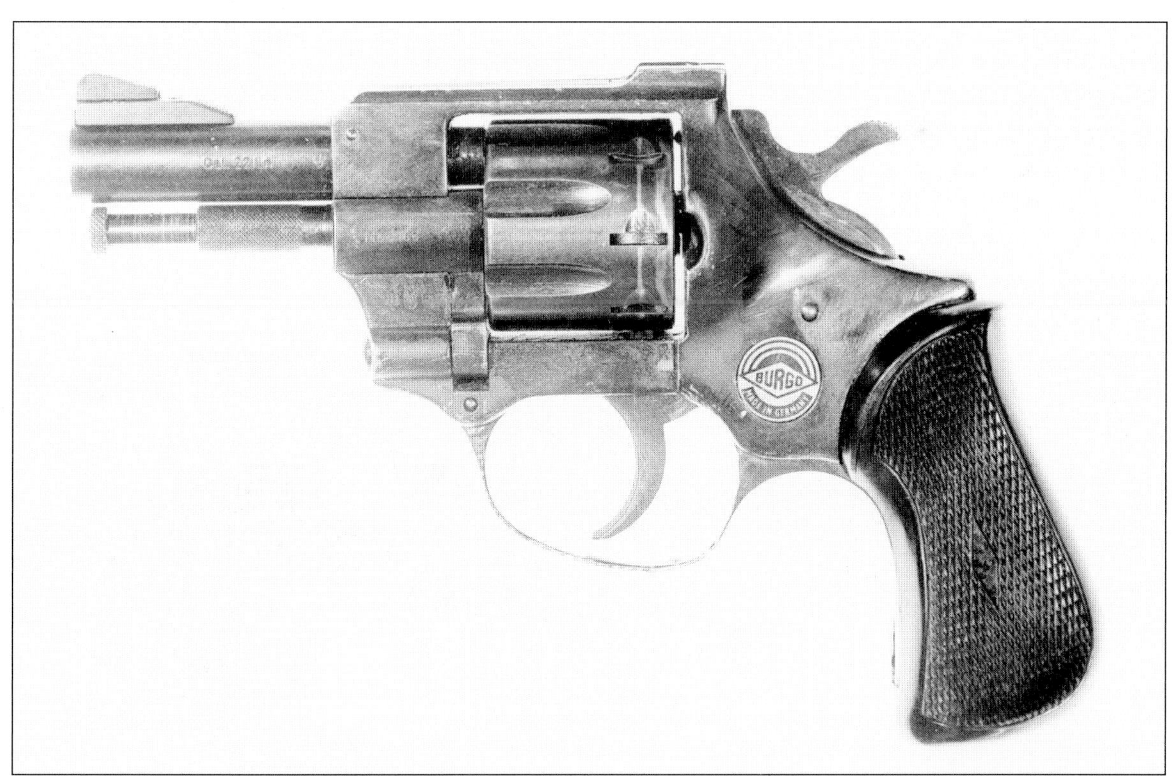

Weirauch Model HW3	
Calibre	.32 S&W Long
Method of operation	7-shot double-action revolver
Safety devices	None
Magazine type	7-chambered cylinder
Position of catch	Left side of frame
Front sight	Fixed blade
Rear sight	Fixed U-notch
Overall length	6.92in (176mm)
Barrel length	2.75in (70mm)
Number of grooves	6
Direction of twist	Right-hand
Empty weight	24.4oz (693g)
Markings	On left of barrel: '.32 S&W'; on left side crane arm: 'HW3'; on left of frame above butt: Arminius badge in circle
Serial number	On bottom of butt frame

Model HW3

This is a short-barrel model with rounded butt. It is normally found in .22LR calibre, although some early models could also be had in .32 S&W Long. In .22 the cylinder holds eight rounds, in .32 seven. It was also sold in Europe under the name Gecado and in the United States as the Dickson Bulldog in the 1960s.

Weirauch Model HW7	
Calibre	.22 Long Rifle RF
Method of operation	Double-action solid-frame revolver
Safety devices	None
Magazine type	6-chambered cylinder
Position of catch	Left side of frame
Front sight	Fixed blade
Rear sight	Adjustable U-notch
Overall length	10.43in (265mm)
Barrel length	5.91in (150mm)
Number of grooves	6
Direction of twist	Right-hand
Empty weight	36.7oz (1,040g)
Markings	Left side of barrel: 'CAL. .22 LR'; left side of frame: 'ARMINIUS HW9' and Arminius badge
Serial number	On bottom of grip frame

Weirauch Model HW7	
Calibre	.22 Long Rifle RF
Method of operation	Double-action solid-frame revolver
Safety devices	None
Magazine type	7-chambered cylinder
Position of catch	Left side of frame
Front sight	Fixed blade
Rear sight	Fixed U-notch
Overall length	10.43in (265mm)
Barrel length	5.91in (150mm)
Number of grooves	6
Direction of twist	Right-hand
Empty weight	31.9oz (905g)
Markings	Left side of barrel: 'CAL. .22 LR'; left side of frame: 'ARMINIUS HW7' and Arminius badge
Serial number	On bottom of grip frame

Model HW4

Another .22 pistol, available with a 2.5in, 4in or 6in barrel and blue or chromed finish and a square or flared butt or with anatomical target grips.

Model HW5

Using interchangeable cylinders, this can fire either .22LR or .22WMRF. It is generally similar to the HW3 but with a 4in barrel and a larger grip. A .32 S&W Long version was sold in the United States as the Omega in the 1960s.

Model HW7

This has a 6in barrel and ventilated rib and is generally an enlarged HW5 with the same calibre options.

Model HW9

This is a .22LR revolver intended for competitive use; it has a ventilated rib, target sights, an adjustable trigger with shoe and thumb-rest grips. The standard model has an alloy frame; the HW9ST variant has a steel frame.

Right: The Weirauch HW38 is very much a police and law enforcement weapon.

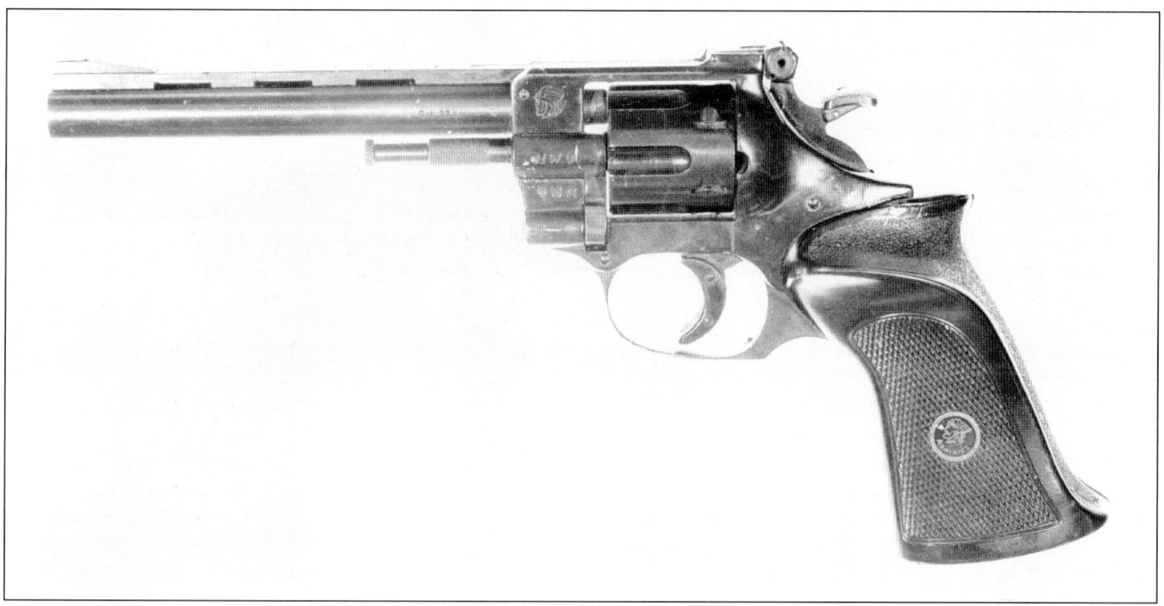

Above: The Weirauch HW9 revolver, with micro-adjustable sights and a ribbed barrel

Model HW38

As the name suggests, this is a .38 calibre revolver produced in three different barrel lengths, all with ventilated ribs.

Model HW68

A lightweight version of the HW4 with a 2.5in barrel and an alloy frame with a black anodised finish. It has interchangeable cylinders and can fire the .22LR or .22WMRF cartridges.

Model HW357

Much the same as the HW38 but chambered for the .357 Magnum cartridge. It is mainly a personal defence weapon, with fixed sights, but is available with target sights for competition work.

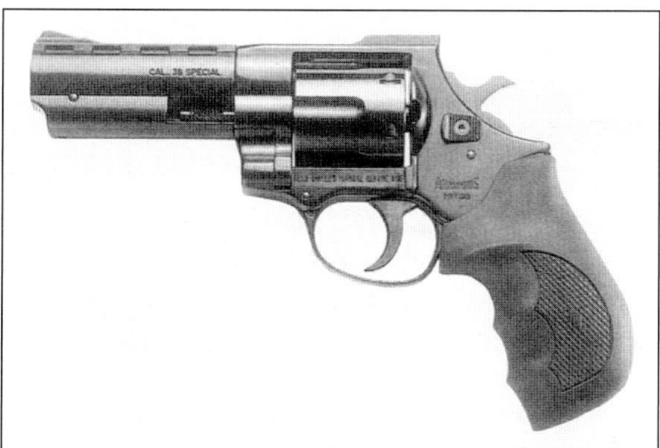

Western Six-Shooter

Not to be confused with the Sauer product of the same name, this is a similar Colt near-copy

Weirauch Model HW38

Calibre	.38 Special
Method of operation	Double-action solid-frame revolver
Safety devices	None
Magazine type	6-chambered cylinder
Position of catch	Left side of frame
Front sight	Fixed blade
Rear sight	Fixed U-notch
Overall length	8.86in (225mm)
Barrel length	4.00in (102mm)
Number of grooves	6
Direction of twist	Right-hand
Empty weight	30.8oz (875g)
Markings	Left side of barrel: 'CAL. 38 SPL'; left side of frame: 'ARMINIUS HW38' and Arminius badge
Serial number	On bottom of grip frame

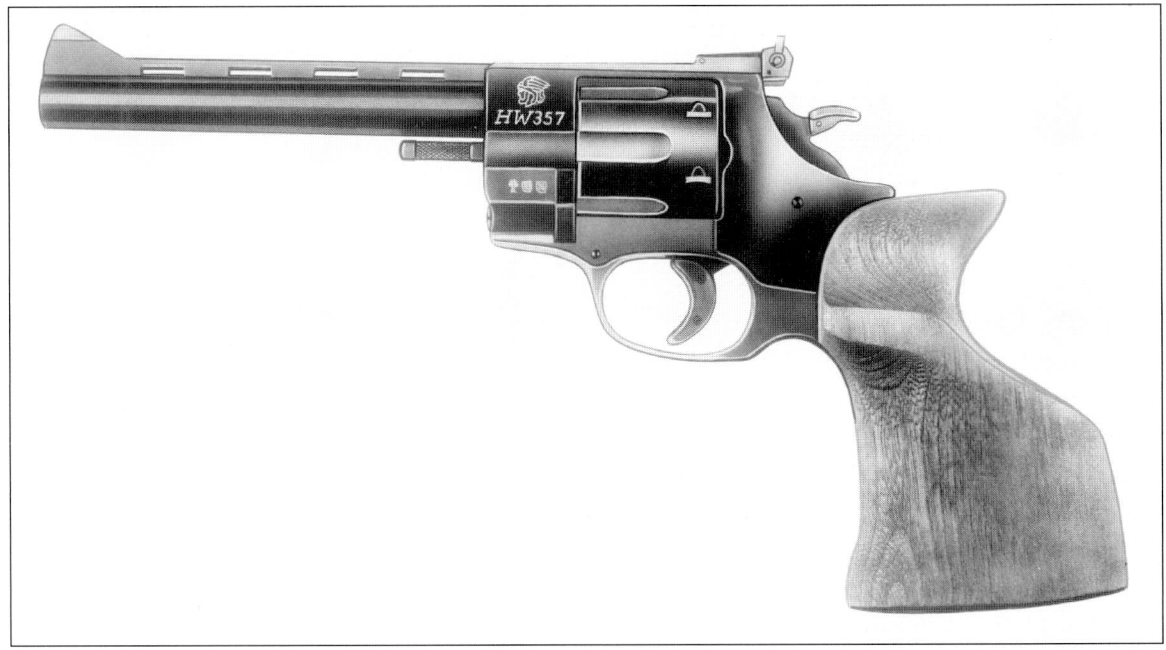

Above: The HW357 fires the .357 Magnum cartridge but is nevertheless a competition pistol with target sights and an anatomical grip.

based upon the M1873 Single-Action Army model. Produced in .357 Magnum, .44 Magnum and .45 Long Colt chambering, these differ from the Colt original by having a transfer bar hammer system with a floating firing pin in the standing breech, principally in order to comply with the US Gun Control Act of 1968. The Target Six-Shooter is a variant model with adjustable rear sight.

Below: The Weirauch Target Six-Shooter, a single-action model loosely based on the Colt 1873 Frontier but with adjustable sights.

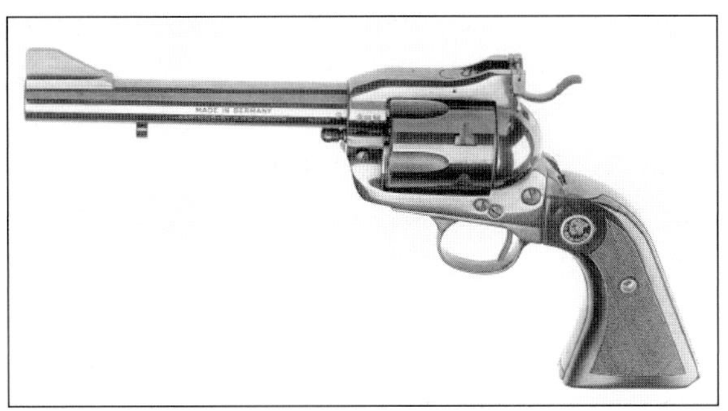

WERDER

Königlich Bayrische Gewehrfabrik, Amberg, Bavaria

This design was the invention of Johann Werder and the mechanism appeared first on an infantry rifle; it was then adopted for a carbine and for this pistol, which was generally issued to cavalry troopers and later appears to have spread to other parts of the Bavarian Army.

The weapons were all known under the popular title of Bavarian Lightning pistol or rifle, due to the speed of operation of the breech. The method of breech closure was, in fact, the well known Peabody system of a hinged block which lowered its front edge to expose the chamber, a system perhaps better known today under the name of Martini, who made some significant improvements in later years. The Peabody system relied upon a lever beneath the rifle butt being forced down so as to operate the breech. This was all very well for hunters and target shooters, and it would have been all very well for soldiers too some fifty years before, but by the middle 1860s the idea of lying down to shoot, so presenting the enemy with a more difficult target, was beginning to take root in European armies, and the Peabody rifle was awkward to operate when lying on the ground owing to the clearance demanded by the lever.

Werder took the same breech block but gave it a thumb-actuated operating lever which stood up alongside the breech and by some clever arrangement of leverage allowed the soldier to open the breech by a simple movement of the hand rather than a long downward sweep of a lever. With a little training the soldier could flick open the breech, reload, flick the breech closed and fire far faster than with any other contemporary single-shot weapon.

Werder pistols are not common today, and the ammunition is, of course, long obsolete. The pistols are notable for their plain appearance at a time when ornate decoration was the norm. Their immediate recognition feature is the twin 'triggers' in the trigger guard and the single upstanding lever in a housing to the right side of the action body. The barrel is ribbed, and the butt grips are of plain wood. To operate the pistol the front trigger is pushed forward; this removes a prop from beneath the breech block, allowing it to fall open, and also brings an extractor into play to eject the spent case from the chamber. As the block opens, so the thumb lever moves forward. After a fresh cartridge has been loaded, pulling back on the thumb lever closes the block and restores the prop beneath it and also cocks the firing pin inside the block. The rear trigger then releases the firing pin when pulled.

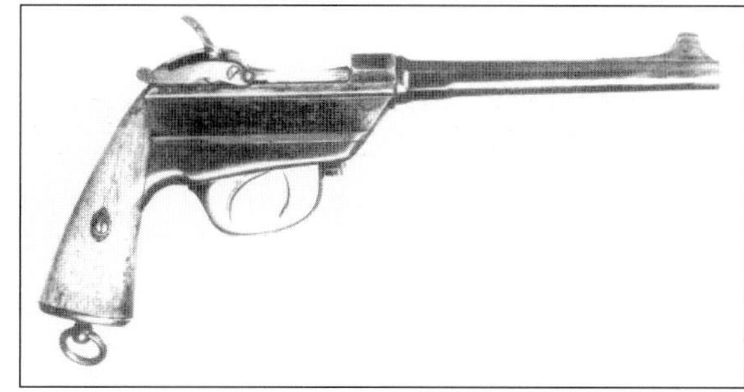

Above: The Werder Bavarian Lightning pistol, showing the front trigger which unlocks the breech and the thumb lever which is ready to be pulled back to close it and cock the action.

Werder Pistol

Calibre	11 × 35R Werder pistol
Method of operation	Manual, dropping block, single-shot
Safety devices	Manual lever on right side of action body
Front sight	Fixed blade
Rear sight	Fixed U-notch
Overall length	14.84in (377mm)
Barrel length	8.86in (225mm)
Number of grooves	4
Direction of twist	Right-hand
Empty weight	58.0oz (1,645g)
Markings	None
Serial number	On left side of action body and barrel

ZEHNA

Emil Zehner Waffenfabrik, Suhl

This is a small 6.35mm pocket pistol of the usual blowback type made between 1921 and 1926. It has one or two minor features of interest in its construction, and is robustly made of good materials. It is noteworthy that early models (up to serial number 5000 or thereabouts) were of relatively poor finish and were marked differently from the later production models, which were of much better quality and carried the maker's name. Total production is thought to have been in the region of 20,000 pistols.

The interesting features become apparent during dismantling. After clearing the gun and pressing the trigger, turn the safety catch to the

Above: The Zehna, a neat and robust 6.35mm pocket pistol.

rear and pull the slide back until the upturned safety catch engages in a small notch on the lower edge of the slide. Now grasp the flat plate beneath the muzzle with the fingernails and pull it outwards (against the pressure of the recoil spring) for about half an inch (12mm). It will be seen that there is a locating pin on this plate which engages with a hole drilled in the barrel forging just below the muzzle. When the plate has been withdrawn sufficiently to clear this pin from its hole, it can be rotated through 90° and released, so that the locating pin now abuts on the front of the frame with the plate held away from it. This action has pulled the recoil spring guide rod—which is attached to the plate—out of engagement with a lug on the barrel forging beneath the breech, and the barrel can now be lifted clear of the pistol. This method of barrel attachment has some points of similarity to the Mauser system.

Below: Dismantling the Zehna, showing the method of barrel removal.

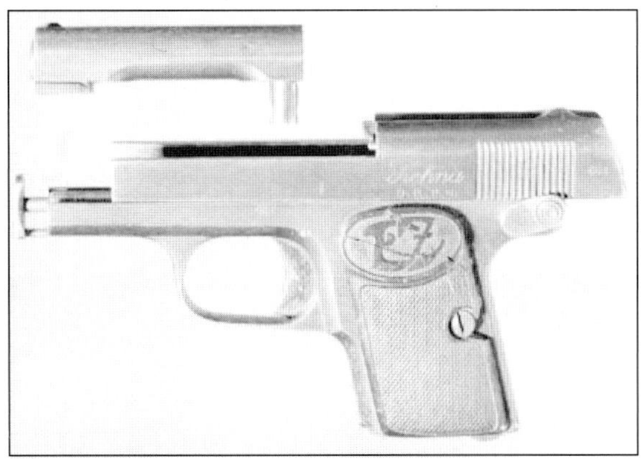

With the barrel clear, take up the spring pressure on the slide and release the safety catch; the slide will go forward and can be removed from the frame. The striker and spring can be slipped from their recess in the slide, and the recoil spring and rod can, if desired, be worked

Zehna	
Calibre	6.35mm Browning
Method of operation	Blowback, striker-fired
Safety devices	Manual safety catch on left rear of frame
Magazine type	Single-column detachable box in butt
Position of catch	At heel of butt
Magazine capacity	6 rounds
Front sight	Fixed blade
Rear sight	Fixed V-notch
Overall length	4.72in (120mm)
Barrel length	2.40in (61mm)
Number of grooves	4
Direction of twist	Right-hand
Empty weight	13.0oz (368g)
Markings	Left side of slide: (early models) 'Zehna D.R.Pa.', (later models) 'Zehna Cal. 6,35 D.R.Pa. E. Zehner Suhl Made in Germany'; top of butt grips: monogram of 'EZ'
Serial number	On right side of frame above trigger; last three digits on underside of slide and underside of barrel near muzzle

free of the slotted lump in which they fit, although there is no real need for their removal. Removing the usual screws allows the grips to be taken off; the lockwork (what there is of it) is carried in a separate component which forms the rear edge of the butt grip, and can be removed by driving out, firstly, a small pin at the bottom rear corner of the butt frame and, secondly, the safety catch. With these two removed, the unit can be driven out of the gun frame in a downward direction. Except for the repair of broken parts—which should be unlikely—there is no real need to perform this last part of the stripping; one factor weighing against it is that owing to the age of these pistols they usually have the butt corner somewhat battered, and removal of the pin can be a difficult task.

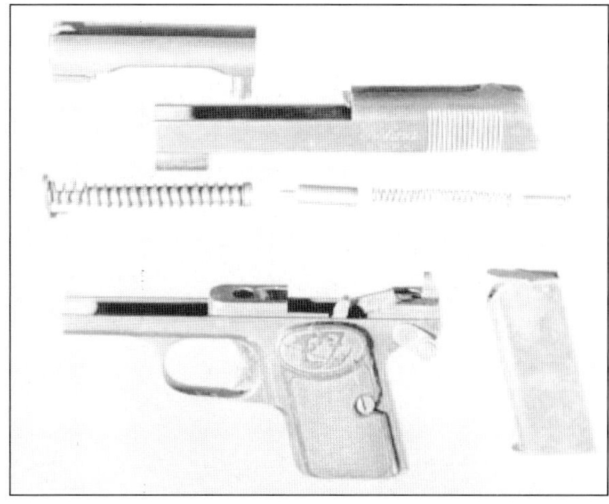

Above: The Zehna dismantled.

Reassembly of the pistol is the opposite of dismantling. If the lock carrier has been removed, tapered drifts will be needed to line up the holes for the safety catch and locating pin.

APPENDICES

APPENDIX I: TABLE OF DIMENSIONS (in alphabetical order and metric units)

Name	Calibre (mm)	Type	Length (overall) (mm)	Length (barrel) (mm)	Weight (empty) (g)	Rounds	Muzzle velocity (m/sec)
Adler	7.25	Auto	102	85	685	8	245
Anschutz	5.6	Target	492	254	2,504	5	740
Bär	7.0	Rep	155	62	345	4	225
Beholla	7.65	Auto	140	73	637	7	300
Bergmann No 2	5.0	Auto	280	135	1,030	5	180
Bergmann No 3	6.5	Auto	265	112	830	5	215
Bergmann No. 5	7.8	Auto	270	100	1,155	5	381
Berg-Bayard	9.0	Auto	250	102	1,015	6	395
Berg Erben 2	6.35	Auto	124	66	410	7	230
Borchardt	7.65	Auto	279	165	1,160	8	370
Continental (1)	6.35	Auto	121	53	400	7	230
Continental (2)	7.65	Auto	167	100	570	8	300
Dreyse 1907	6.35	Auto	114	52	400	6	230
Dreyse 1907	7.65	Auto	160	93	710	7	300
Dreyse	9.0	Auto	206	126	1,050	8	345
DWM	7.65	Auto	152	88	570	7	300
Em-Ge 220KS	.22LR	Rev	170	63	450	6	265
Em-Ge 300	.32	Rev	270	150	970	6	235
Erma Old	.22LR	Target	230	110	992	10	265
Erma New	.22LR	Target	390	300	1,100	10	265
Erma EP22	.22LR	Auto	183	83	1,010	8	250
Erma KGP-68A	7.65	Auto	187	88	640	6	300
Erma KGP-69	.22LR	Auto	196	199	840	8	250
Erma EP457	7.65	Auto	160	82	620	8	300
Erma EP5522	.22LR	Auto	138	73	410	7	250
Erma EP-25	6.35	Auto	135	70	570	7	230
Erma EP-65A	.22LR	Target	254	152	1,163	8	250
Erma ER440	.38S	Rev	150	76	620	5	235
Gecado	7.65	Auto	132	65	587	7	300
Gecado 11	6.35	Auto	116	57	425	6	230

Gustloff	7.65	Auto	168	95	768	8	300
Haenel 1	6.35	Auto	120	63	383	6	230
Haenel 2	6.35	Auto	100	52	335	6	230
H&K HK4	7.65	Auto	157	85	520	9	300
H&K P9S	9.0	Auto	192	102	875	9	350
H&K VP70	9.0	Auto	205	116	820	18	360
H&K P7M8	9.0	Auto	171	105	855	8	350
H&K P7M13	9.0	Auto	169	105	975	13	350
H&K P7K3	7.65	Auto	160	97	760	8	300
H&K P7M10	.40	Auto	175	105	850	10	285
H&K P7PT8	9.0	Auto	170	105	790	8	400
H&K P11-ZUB	7.62	Rep	200	?	1,200	5	n/a
H&K USP	9.0	Auto	194	108	770	15	350
H&K Mk 23	.45	Auto	245	149	120	12	270
Heim	6.35	Auto	108	55	310	6	230
Helfricht 3	6.35	Auto	120	51	323	6	230
Helfricht 4	6.35	Auto	109	46	340	6	230
Heym Detective	.22LR	Rev	200	51	690	6	260
Jäger	7.65	Auto	155	79	646	7	300
Kesslet	7.65	Auto	164	95	646	7	300
Kommer 2	6.35	Auto	108	51	368	7	300
Kommer 4	7.65	Auto	140	76	565	7	300
Korriphila TY70	6.35	Auto	117	55	348	6	230
Korriphila HSP	9.0	Auto	183	102	990	9	350
Korth Sport	.357	Rev	283	150	1,160	6	435
Korth Combat	.357	Rev	210	76	950	6	435
Korth	9.0	Auto	231	127	1,240	10	350
Langenhan 2	6.35	Auto	145	80	502	7	230
Langenhan 3	6.35	Auto	121	58	468	5	230
Langenhan Army	7.65	Auto	168	105	666	8	300
Lignose 2	6.35	Auto	114	53	405	6	230
Lignose 2A	6.35	Auto	121	55	385	6	230
Lignose 4	7.65	Auto	126	60	535	8	300
Lignose 5	9.0	Auto	126	60	535	7	285
Mann WTP	6.35	Auto	105	42	255	5	230
Mann TM	7.65	Auto	121	60	354	5	300
Mauser M1878	9.0	Rev	269	136	750	6	240
Mauser 1896	7.63	Auto	295	140	1,120	10	442
Mauser M1916	9.0	Auto	296	140	1,120	10	365
Mauser Bolo	7.63	Auto	251	99	1,045	10	420
Mauser 1930	7.53	Auto	286	130	1,150	10	442
Mauser 711	7.63	Auto	286	133	1,206	10/20	442
Mauser Nickl	9.0	Auto	152	91	700	8	285
Mauser 1910	6.35	Auto	116	80	425	9	230
Mauser 1914	7.65	Auto	152	87	595	8	300
Mauser 1934	7.65	Auto	152	87	595	8	300

Mauser WTP1	6.35	Auto	114	60	326	6	230
Mauser WTP2	6.35	Auto	102	55	298	6	230
Mauser HSc	7.65	Auto	192	86	595	8	300
Mauser HSP	9.0	Auto	165	85	750	8	360
Mauser 80SA	9.0	Auto	203	118	900	14	350
Mauser 90DA	9.0	Auto	203	118	1,000	14	350
Mauser 90DAC	9.0	Auto	188	105	950	13	340
Mauser Trident	.38	Rev	175	64	660	6	320
Mauser 29/70	9.0	Auto	215	100	907	8	345
Mayer Mod 22	.22	Rev	195	76	585	6	265
Menta	6.35	Auto	118	63	384	6	230
Menta	7.65	Auto	140	73	637	7	300
Menz VP	6.35	Auto	118	60	425	6	230
Menz Liliput	6.35	Auto	102	51	284	6	230
Menz Mod 2	7.65	Auto	130	68	435	6	300
Menz P&B 3	7.65	Auto	157	89	700	8	300
Menz P&B Spl	7.65	Auto	158	85	745	8	300
Nordheim	7.65	Auto	156	92	595	7	300
Ortgies	6.35	Auto	133	69	396	7	230
Ortgies	7.65	Auto	165	87	638	8	300
Ortgies	9.0	Auto	165	87	595	7	285
Parabellum 00	7.65	Auto	237	120	890	8	335
Parabellum 04	9.0	Auto	267	150	1,010	8	345
Parabellum 08	9.0	Auto	223	102	850	8	345
Parabellum L'08	9.0	Auto	317	200	1,105	8	380
Pickert 1	.22	Rev	135	50	220	7	250
Pickert 2	.22	Rev	210	150	245	7	250
Pickert 3	6.35	Rev	135	50	250	5	210
Pickert 4	5.5	Rev	130	50	300	5	180
Pickert 5/1	7.5	Rev	170	65	380	5	200
Pickert 5/2	7.5	Rev	170	60	400	5	200
Pickert 7	.32	Rev	148	65	400	5	155
Pickert 8	.32	Rev	135	64	400	5	155
Pickert 9	7.65	Rev	168	60	320	5	280
Pickert 9A	7.65	Rev	155	60	350	5	280
Pickert 10	7.65	Rev	145	60	360	5	280
Pickert 13	.380	Rev	155	65	460	5	220
Pickert 13A	.22	Rev	200	135	550	8	275
Pickert 14	.380	Rev	160	65	460	5	220
P. Mod 12(ö)	9.0	Auto	216	128	992	8	345
P. Mod 27(t)	7.65	Auto	165	97	710	8	300
P. Mod 35(p)	9.0	Auto	211	115	1,050	8	345
P. Mod 37(ü)	7.65	Auto	182	110	765	7	300
P. Mod 39(t)	9.0	Auto	206	118	935	8	290
P. Mod 615(r)	7.62	Auto	196	116	850	8	420
P. Mod 640(b)	9.0	Auto	196	112	965	13	345

P. Mod 641(b)	9.0	Auto	178	114	708	9	285
Reck P-8	6.35	Auto	116	57	420	7	230
Reform	6.35	Rep	138	62	620	4	230
Regnum	6.35	Rep	127	70	600	4	230
Reichsrev. M79	10.6	Rev	310	183	1,034	6	235
Reichsrev. M83	10.6	Rev	260	125	921	6	225
Rheinmetall	7.65	Auto	165	93	666	8	300
Röhm RG38	.38	Rev	235	102	940	6	320
Röhm RG27	6.35	Auto	140	77	430	7	230
Romer	.22	Auto	140	64	312	7	250
Roth-Sauer	7.65	A|uto	168	98	665	7	300
Sauer 1914	6.36	Auto	108	70	408	7	230
Sauer 1014	7.65	Auto	144	75	575	7	300
Sauer 1930	7.65	Auto	146	77	630	7	300
Sauer WTM	6.35	Auto	107	55	320	6	230
Sauer WTM28	6.35	Auto	100	50	275	6	230
Sauer 38H	7.65	Auto	171	83	717	8	300
Sauer SR3	.38	Rev	267	127	1,057	6	320
Sauer VR4	.38	Rev	269	136	750	6	320
Sauer Western	.357	Rev	269	136	750	6	430
SIG-Sauer P220	9.0	Auto	180	96	850	13	360
Schlegelmilch	8.0	Rep	275	119	850	5	n/a
Schmidt HS38	.38	Rev	203	102	885	6	310
Schwarzlose 96	7.65	Auto	273	163	936	7	440
Schwarzlose 08	7.65	Auto	140	105	525	7	300
Simplex	8.0	Auto	203	70	595	6	259
Simson 22	6.35	Auto	114	56	368	6	230
Stern	6.35	Auto	125	61	440	10	230
Stock	6.35	Auto	121	63	355	7	230
Stock	7.65	Auto	173	92	666	8	300
Volkspistole	9.0	Auto	266	130	963	8	n/a
Wahl	7.65	Auto	155	80	607	9	300
Walther 1	6.35	Auto	114	52	366	6	230
Walther 2	6.35	Auto	109	54	280	6	230
Walther 3	7.65	Auto	127	67	427	6	300
Walther 4	7.65	Auto	152	85	553	8	300
Walther 5	6.35	Auto	108	54	276	6	230
Walther 6	9.0	Auto	209	121	963	8	345
Walther 7	6.35	Auto	133	77	340	8	230
Walther 8	6.35	Auto	130	72	368	8	230
Walther 9	6.35	Auto	102	51	262	6	230
Walther PP	7.65	Auto	162	85	708	8	300
Walther PPK	7.65	Auto	148	80	587	7	300
Walther MP	9.0	Auto	205	127	1,110	8	350
Walther AP	9.0	Auto	215	120	790	8	350
Walther P38	9.0	Auto	213	127	840	8	350

Walther Olympia	.22	Target	200	120	766	10	265
Walther P1	9.0	Auto	218	124	772	8	360
Walther P38	7.65	Auto	215	125	800	8	300
Walther P38K	9.0	Auto	160	70	790	7	340
Walther P1A1	9.0	Auto	179	90	808	8	36-
Walther P4	9.0	Auto	200	110	825	8	365
Walther P5	9.0	Auto	179	90	808	8	360
Walther P5 Com	9.0	Auto	168	79	780	8	350
Walther P88	9.0	Auto	197	102	900	15	360
Walther P88 Com	9.0	Auto	181	97	822	16	355
Walther P88 Cp	9.0	Target	211	125	800	14	365
Walther PP Sup	9.0	Auto	176	82	780	7	350
Walther TP	6.35	Auto	133	65	319	6	230
Walther TPH	6.35	Auto	135	71	325	6	230
Walther GSP	.32	Target	292	107	1,290	5	235
Walther OSP	.22	Target	292	108	1,120	5	265
Weirauch HW3	.32	Rev	176	70	693	7	230
Weirauch HW7	.22	Rev	265	150	905	7	260
Weirauch HW38	.38	Rev	225	102	875	6	320
Werder	11	SS	377	225	1,645	1	220
Zehna	6.35	Auto	120	61	368	6	230

APPENDIX II: TABLE OF DIMENSIONS
(in ascending order of calibre and weight)

Name	Calibre (mm)	Type	Length (overall) (mm)	Length (barrel) (mm)	Weight (empty) (g)	Rounds	Muzzle velocity (m/sec)
Bergmann No 2	5.0	Auto	280	135	1,030	5	180
Pickert 4	5.5	Rev	130	50	300	5	180
Pickert 1	.22	Rev	135	50	220	7	250
Pickert 2	.22	Rev	210	150	245	7	250
Romer	.22	Auto	140	64	312	7	250
Erma EP5522	.22	Auto	138	73	410	7	250
Em-Ge 220KS	.22	Rev	170	63	450	6	265
Pickert 13A	.22	Rev	200	135	550	8	275
Mayer Mod 22	.22	Rev	195	76	585	6	265
Heym Detective	.22	Rev	200	51	690	6	260
Walther Olumpia	.22	Target	200	120	766	10	265
Erma KGP-69	.22	Auto	196	199	840	8	250
Weirauch HW7	.22	Rev	265	150	905	7	260
Erma Old	.22	Target	230	110	992	10	265

Erma EP22	.22	Auto	183	83	1,010	8	250
Erma New	.22	Tarfet	390	300	1,100	10	265
Walther OSP	.22	Target	292	108	1,120	5	265
Erma EP-65A	.22	Target	254	152	1,163	8	250
Anschutz	5.6	Target	492	254	2,504	5	740
Pickert 3	6.35	Rev	135	50	250	5	210
Mann WTP	6.35	Auto	105	42	255	5	230
Walther 9	6.35	Auto	102	51	262	6	230
Sauer WTM28	6.35	Auto	100	50	275	6	230
Walther 5	6.35	Auto	108	54	276	6	230
Walther 2	6.35	Auto	109	54	280	6	230
Liliput	6.35	Auto	102	51	284	6	230
Mauser WTP2	6.35	Auto	102	55	298	6	230
Heim	6.35	Auto	108	55	310	6	230
Walther TP	6.35	Auto	133	65	319	6	230
Sauer WTM	6.35	Auto	107	55	320	6	230
Helfricht 3	6.35	Auto	120	51	323	6	230
Walther TPH	6.35	Auto	135	71	325	6	230
Mauser WTP1	6.35	Auto	114	60	326	6	230
Haenel 2	6.35	Auto	100	52	335	6	230
Helfricht 4	6.35	Auto	109	46	340	6	230
Korriphila TY70	6.35	Auto	117	55	348	6	230
Walther 7	6.35	Auto	133	77	340	8	230
Stock	6.35	Auto	121	63	355	7	230
Walther 1	6.35	Auto	114	52	366	6	230
Kommer 2	6.35	Auto	108	51	368	7	300
Walther 8	6.35	Auto	130	72	368	8	230
Simson 22	6.35	Auto	114	56	368	6	230
Zehna	6.35	Auto	120	61	368	6	230
Haenel 1	6.35	Auto	120	63	383	6	230
Menta	6.35	Auto	118	63	384	6	230
Lignose 2A	6.35	Auto	121	55	385	6	230
Ortgies	6.35	Auto	133	69	396	7	230
Continental (1)	6.35	Auto	121	53	400	7	230
Dreyse 1907	6.35	Auto	114	52	400	6	230
Lignose 2	6.35	Auto	114	53	405	6	230
Sauer 1914	6.36	Auto	108	70	408	7	230
Berg Erben 2	6.35	Auto	124	66	410	7	230
Reck P-8	6.35	Auto	116	57	420	7	230
Gecado 11	6.35	Auto	116	57	425	6	230
Mauser 1910	6.35	Auto	116	80	425	9	230
Menz VP	6.35	Auto	118	60	425	6	230
Röhm RG27	6.35	Auto	140	77	430	7	230
Stern	6.35	Auto	125	61	440	10	230

Langenhan 3	6.35	Auto	121	58	468	5	230
Langenhan 2	6.35	Auto	145	80	502	7	230
Erma Ep-25	6.35	Auto	135	70	570	7	230
Regnum	6.35	Rep	127	70	600	4	230
Reform	6.35	Rep	138	62	620	4	230
Bergmann No 3	6.5	Auto	265	112	830	5	215
Bär	7.0	Rep	155	62	345	4	225
Adler	7.25	Auto	102	85	685	8	245
Pickert 5/1	7.5	Rev	170	65	380	5	200
Pickert 5.2	7.5	Rev	170	60	400	5	200
P. Mod 615(r)	7.62	Auto	196	116	850	8	420
H&K P11-ZUB	7.62	Rep	200	?	1,200	5	n/a
Schwarzlose 96	7.65	Auto	273	163	936	7	440
Mauser Bolo	7.63	Auto	251	99	1,045	10	420
Mauser 1896	7.63	Auto	295	140	1,120	10	442
Mauser 1930	7.63	Auto	286	130	1,150	10	442
Mauser 711	7.63	Auto	286	133	1,206	10/20	442
Pickert 9	7.65	Rev	168	60	320	5	280
Pickert 9A	7.65	Rev	155	60	350	5	280
Mann TM	7.65	Auto	121	60	354	5	300
Pickert 10	7.65	Rev	145	60	360	5	280
Walther 3	7.65	Auto	127	67	427	6	300
Menz Mod 2	7.65	Auto	130	68	435	6	300
H&K HK4	7.65	Auto	157	85	520	9	300
Schwarzlose 08	7.65	Auto	140	105	525	7	300
Lignose 4	7.65	Auto	126	60	535	8	300
Walther 4	7.65	Auto	152	85	553	8	300
Kommer 4	7.65	Auto	140	76	565	7	300
Continental (2)	7.65	Auto	167	100	570	8	300
DWM	7.65	Auto	152	88	570	7	300
Sauer 1014	7.65	Auto	144	75	575	7	300
Gecado	7.65	Auto	132	65	587	7	300
Walther PPK	7.65	Auto	148	80	587	7	300
Mauser 1914	7.65	Auto	152	87	595	8	300
Mauser 1934	7.65	Auto	152	87	595	8	300
Mauser HSc	7.65	Auto	192	86	595	8	300
Nordheim	7.65	Auto	156	92	595	7	300
Wahl	7.65	Auto	155	80	607	9	300
Erma EP457	7.65	Auto	160	82	620	8	300

Sauer 1930	7.65	Auto	146	77	630	7	300
Beholla	7.65	Auto	140	73	637	7	300
Menta	7.65	Auto	140	73	637	7	300
Ortgies	7.65	Auto	165	87	638	8	300
Erma KGP-68A	7.65	Auto	187	88	640	6	300
Jäger	7.65	Auto	155	79	646	7	300
Kesslet	7.65	Auto	164	95	646	7	300
Roth-Sauer	7.65	Auto	168	98	665	7	300
Langenhan Army	7.65	Auto	168	105	666	8	300
Rheinmetall	7.65	Auto	165	93	666	8	300
Stock	7.65	Auto	173	92	666	8	300
Menz P&B 3	7.65	Auto	157	89	700	8	300
Walther PP	7.65	Auto	162	85	708	8	300
Dreyse 1907	7.65	Auto	160	93	710	7	300
P. Mod 27(t)	7.65	Auto	165	97	710	8	300
Sauer 38H	7.65	Auto	171	83	717	8	300
Menz P&B Spl	7,65	Auto	158	85	745	8	300
H&K P7K3	7.65	Auto	160	97	760	8	300
P.Mod 37(ü)	7.65	Auto	182	110	765	7	300
Gustloff	7.65	Auto	168	95	768	8	300
Walther P38	7.65	Auto	215	125	800	8	300
Parabellum 00	7.65	Auto	237	120	890	8	335
Borchardt	7.65	Auto	279	165	1,160	8	370
Pickert 7	.32	Rev	148	65	400	5	155
Pickert 8	.32	Rev	135	64	400	5	155
Weirauch HW3	.32	Rev	176	70	693	7	230
Em-Ge 300	.32	Rev	270	150	970	6	235
Walther GSP	.32	Target	292	107	1,290	5	235
Bergmann No 5	7.8	Auto	270	100	1,155	5	381
Simplex	8.0	Auto	203	70	595	6	259
Schlegelmilch	8.0	Rep	275	119	850	5	n/a
Lignose 5	9.0	Auto	126	60	535	7	285
Ortgies	9.0	Auto	165	87	595	7	285
Mauser Nickl	9.0	Auto	152	91	700	8	285
P. Mod 641(b)	9.0	Auto	178	114	708	9	285
Mauser HSP	9.0	Auto	165	85	750	8	360
Mauser M1878	9.0	Rev	269	136	750	6	240
H&K USP	9.0	Auto	194	108	770	15	350
Walther P1	9.0	Auto	218	124	772	8	360
Walther P5 Com	9.0	Auto	168	79	780	8	350
Walther P5 Com	9.0	Auto	168	79	780	8	350

Walther PP Sup	9.0	Auto	176	82	780	7	350
H&K P7PT8	9.0	Auto	170	105	790	8	400
Walther AP	9.0	Auto	215	120	790	8	350
Walther P38K	9.0	Auto	160	70	790	7	340
Walther P38K	9.0	Auto	160	70	790	7	340
Walther P88 Cp	9.0	Target	211	125	800	14	365
Walther P1A1	9.0	Auto	179	90	808	8	360
Walther P5	9.0	Auto	179	90	808	8	360
Walther P1A1	9.0	Auto	179	90	808	8	360
Walther P5	9.0	Auto	179	90	808	8	360
H&K VP70	9.0	Auto	205	116	820	18	360
Walther P88 Com	9.0	Auto	181	97	822	16	355
Walther P4	9.0	Auto	200	110	825	8	365
Walther P4	9.0	Auto	200	110	825	8	365
Walther P38	9.0	Auto	213	127	840	8	350
Parabellum 08	9.0	Auto	223	102	850	8	345
SIG-Sauer P220	9.0	Auto	180	96	850	13	360
H&K P7M8	9.0	Auto	171	105	855	8	350
H&K P9S	9.0	Auto	192	102	875	9	350
Mauser 80SA	9.0	Auto	203	118	900	14	350
Walther P88	9.0	Auto	197	102	900	15	360
Mauser 29/70	9.0	Auto	215	100	907	8	345
P. Mod 39(t)	9.0	Auto	206	118	935	8	290
Mauser 90DAC	9.0	Auto	188	105	950	13	340
Volkspistole (1)	9.0	Auto	266	130	963	8	n/a
Walther 6	9.0	Auto	209	121	963	8	345
P. Mod 640(b)	9.0	Auto	196	112	965	13	345
H&K P7M13	9.0	Auto	169	105	975	13	350
Korriphila HSP	9.0	Auto	183	102	990	9	350
P. Mod 12(ö)	9.0	Auto	216	128	992	8	345
Mauser 90DA	9.0	Auto	203	118	1,000	14	350
Parabellum 04	9.0	Auto	267	150	1,010	8	345
Berg-Bayard	9.0	Auto	250	102	1,015	6	395
Dreyse	9.0	Auto	206	126	1,050	8	345
P. Mod 35(p)	9.0	Auto	211	115	1,050	8	345
Parabellum L'08	9.0	Auto	317	200	1,105	8	380
Walther MP	9.0	Auto	205	127	1,110	8	350
Mauser M1916	9.0	Auto	296	140	1,120	10	365
Korth	9.0	Auto	231	127	1,240	10	350
Sauer Western	.357	Rev	269	136	750	6	430
Korth Combat	.357	Rev	210	76	950	6	435
Korth Sport	.357	Rev	283	150	1,160	6	435
Pickert 13	.380	Rev	155	65	460	5	220
Pickert 14	.380	Rev	160	65	460	5	220

Erma ER440	.38	Rev	150	76	620	5	235
Mauser Trident	.38	Rev	175	64	660	6	320
Sauer VR4	.38	Rev	269	136	750	6	320
Schmidt HS38	.38	Rev	203	102	885	6	310
Weirauch HW38	.38	Rev	225	102	875	6	320
Röhm RG38	.38	Rev	235	102	940	6	320
Sauer SR3	.38	Rev	267	127	1,057	6	320
H&K P7M10	.40	Auto	175	105	850	10	285
Reichsrev. M83	10.6	Rev	260	125	921	6	225
Reichsrev. M79	10.6	Rev	310	183	1,034	6	235
Werder	11	SS	377	225	1,645	1	220
H&K Mk23	.45	Auto	245	149	120	12	270

APPENDIX III: MANUFACTURERS AND THEIR WARTIME CODES

The following list details theWorld War II code markings used by the principal manufacturers of small arms and major contractors for small-arms components; small firms making minor components have not been identified. It also includes the code markings adopted by foreign factories impressed into German service

aak	Waffenwerk Brünn AG, Prague, Czechoslovakia
abc	Deutsche Metallwerk, Neustadt-an-der Weinstrasse
ac	Carl Walther GmbH, Zelia-Mehlis
aek	F. Dusek Waffenerzeugung, Opocno bei Nachod, Czechoslovakia
afo	MIAG: Mühlembau und Industrie AG, Frankfurt-am-Main
ah	Carl Merta, Stetten bei Hechingen
ajf	Junker und Ruh AG, Karlsruhe-im-Baden
akj	Vorwerk & Co, Wuppertal/Barmen
amn	Mauser-Werke AG, Werk Neuweid, Neuweid
amo	Mauser-Werke AG, Werk Waldeck, Waldeck, Bezirk Kassel
aop	Maschinenfabrik Germania, Chemnitz
ar	Mauser-Werke AG, Berlin-Borsigwalde
asb	Deutsche Waffen- und Munitionsfabrik, Berlin-Borsigwalde
auc	Mauser-Werke AG, Köln-Ehrenfeld
auf	Metall-, Güss- und Presswerk H. Diehl, Nuremberg
avy	Oskar Schleicher Maschinenfabrik und Eisengiesserei, Greiz
awt	Württembergische Metallwarenfabrik AG, Geislingen-Steige
ax	Feinmechanische Werke GmbH, Erfurt
ayf	B. Geipel, GmbH, Waffenfabrik 'Erma', Erfurt

aym	Carl Hoffman Maschinenfabrik, Aue/Sachsen
baa	Keller & Knappisch GmbH, Augsburg
baz	Netersener Maschinenfabrik M. Hatrase, Netersen
bcd	Gustloffwerk, Weimar
bej	Maschinenfabrik Buckau, R. Wolff AG, Magdeburg
bga	Präzisionswerke Brüninghaus & Co, Bielefeld
bh	Brünner Waffenwerke AG, Brünn (Brno), Czechoslovakia
bky	Böhmische Waffenfabrik AG, Ukershy Brod, Czechoslovakia
bmv	Rheinmetall-Borsig AG, Sömmerda
bnz	Steyr-Daimler-Puch AG, Steyr
bpr	Grossfuss Metall- und Lackierwarenfabrik, Döbeln
bvl	Th. Bergmann Automaten und Metallwarenfabrik, Hamburg-Altona
byf	Mauser-Werke, Oberndorf-am-Neckar
bym	Genossenschafts Maschinenhaus der Büchsenmacher, Ferlach
bzt	Fritz Wolf Gewehrfabrik, Zella Mehlis
ce	J. P. Sauer & Sohn Gewehrfabrik, Suhl
ch	Fabrique National d'Armes de Guerre, Herstal, Belgium
chd	Deutsche Industriewerk AG, Berlin-Spandau
cnd	National Krupp Registierkassen GmbH, Berlin
con	Franz Stock Maschinen- und Werkzeugfabrik, Berlin-Neuköln
cos	Merz Brothers, Frankfurt-am-Main
cpj	Havelwerk GmbH, Brandenburg/Havel
cpo	Rheinmetall-Borsig, Berlin-Marienfelde
cpp	Rheinmetall-Borsig, Breslau
cpq	Rheinmetall-Borsig, Guben, Poland
csm	Knorr-Bremse AG, Berlin-Lichtenberg
cxq	Liegnitzer Eisengiesserei und Maschinenfabrik Teichert & Sohn, Liegnitz
cyq	Spreewerk GmbH Metallwarenfabrik, Berlin-Spandau
dfb	Gustloff-Werk, Waffenwerke Suhl
dot	Waffenwerk Brünn AG, Brno, Czechoslovakia
dou	Waffenwerk Brünn AG, Bystrica, Czechoslovakia
dov	Waffenwerk Brünn AG, Vsetin, Czechoslovakia
dow	Waffenwerk Brünn, Prerau, Czechoslovakia
dox	Waffenfabrik Brünn AG, Podbrezova, Czechoslovakia
dsh	Waffenfabrik Ing. Janacek, Prague, Czechoslovakia
duv	Berliner-Lübecker Maschinenfabrik, Lübeck
edt	Metallwarenfabrik vormals H. Wissner, Zella Mehlis
eea	Hermann Weirauch Gewehr- und Fahrradteilfabrik, Zella Mehlis
eeo	Deutsche Waffen- und Munitionsfabrik, Poznan, Poland
fa	Mansfeld AG, Hettstedt
fnh	Böhmische Waffenfabrik AG, Strakonitz

fwh	Norddeutsche Maschinenfabrik GmbH, Berlin
fxo	C. G. Haenel Waffen- und Fahrradfabrik, Suhl
fzs	Heinrich Krieghoff Waffenfabrik, Suhl
ghf	Fritz Kiess & Co GmbH Waffenfabrik, Suhl
gsb	Rheinmetall-Borsig AG, Louvain, Belgium
hee	Ilaria-Werke GmbH, Velten/Mark
hew	Waffenfabrik Ing. F. Janacek Werk, Prague-Nusle
hhg	Rheinmetall-Borsig AG, Berlin-Tegel
jhv	Metallwaren-, Waffen- und Maschinenfabrik AG, Budapest
jkg	Königlich Üngarnische Staatlische Eisen-, Stahl- und Maschinenfabrik, Budapest
jua	Danuvia Waffen- und Muntionsfabrik AG, Budapest
jwh	Manufacture Nationale d'Armes Chatellerault, Chatellerault, France
kfk	Dansk Industrie Syndikat (Dansk Rekylriffel Syndikat), Copenhagen
kls	Steyr-Daimler-Puch AG, Warsaw, Poland
ksb	Manufacture Nationale d'Armes de Lavallois, Paris
kur	Steyr-Daimler-Puch AG, Graz, Austria
kyo	Interprinderile Metalurgie, Brasov, Romania (Romanian national arsenal under German control)
lza	Mauserwerke, Karlruhe
moc	Johann Springer Erben Gewehrfabrik, Vienna
mrb	Aktiengesellschaft (formerly Skoda) Prague, Czechoslovakia
myx	Rheinmetall-Borsig, Sömmerda
nea	Walther Steiner Eisenkonstructionen, Suhl
nec	Waffenfabrik Brünn AG, Gurein, Czechoslovakia
nhr	Rheinmetall-Borsig AG, Sömmerda
nyw	Gustloff-Werke AG, Meiningen
orp	Königliche Ungarnische Staatliche Eisen-, Stahl- und Maschinenfabrik, Diosgyor, Hungary (Hungarian state arsenal under German control)
pcd	Theodor Bergmann AG, Bernauwerk, Berlin
qve	Carl Walther GmbH, Zella Mehlis
svw	Mauser-Werke, Oberndorf-am-Neckar
swp	Waffenwerk Brünn unknown factory
ta	Dürner Metallwerk GmbH, Berlin

xa	Busch-Jäger-Lüdenscheider Metallwerke AG, Lüdenscheid/Westfalia
ya	Sachsiche Metallwarenfabrik August Wellner und Sohn, Aue/Sachsen
27	B. Geipel, GmbH, Waffenfabrik 'Erma', Erfurt (superseded by 'ayf' above)
42	Mauser-Werke, Oberndorf-am-Neckar (superseded by 'byf' above)
122	C. G. Haenel Waffen- und Fahrradfabrik, Suhl (superseded by 'fxo' above)
147	J. P. Sauer & Sohn, Suhl. (superseded by 'ce' above)
237	Berlin-Lübecker Maschinenfabrik, Lübeck (superseded by 'duv' above)
243	Mauser-Werke AG, Berlin-Borsigwalde (superseded by 'ar' above)
480	Carl Walther GmbH, Zella Mehlis (superseded by 'ac' above)
660	Steyr-Daimler-Puch AG, Steyr (superseded by 'bnz' above)

APPENDIX IV: GERMAN SMALL-ARMS AMMUNITION HEADSTAMPS

COMMERCIAL

H. BARELLA	J. H. Barella. Gunsmith, Berlin; cases made by DWM.
BB	Braun & Bloem, Düsseldorf.
B&B	Braun & Bloem, Düsseldorf.
B&BD	Braun & Bloem, Düsseldorf.
BRENNEKE	Wilhelm Brenneke, Leipzig (pre-1939) or Berlin (post-1945).
B & S	Basse & Selve, Hamburg-Altona.
C. STUSCHE	Carl Stusche, Niesse, Silesia. Gunmaker; cases made by DWM.
D	Gustav Genschow, Durlach.
DM, DMK	Deutsche Metallpatronenfabrik, Karlsruhe. The firm became part of DWM in 1896 but continued to use these marks for several years.
DWA	Deutsche Werke AG, Berlin (1920s).
DWM	Deutsche Waffen- und Munitionsfabrik, Karlsruhe.
DWM-B or -BB	DWM Berlin-Borsigwalde.
DWM-K or -KT	DWM Karlsruhe.
DWM-L	DWM Lübeck.
EGESTORFF	George Egestorff, Linden-bei-Hannover.
F	Frister & Rossman, Berlin (1888–93).
⋆G⋆	Gustav Genschow, Durlach.
GE	George Egestorff, Linden-bei-Hannover.
GE&Co	George Egestorff, Linden-bei-Hannover.
GECADO	G. C. Dornheim, Suhl.
GECO	Gustav Genschow, Durlach.
Ge D	Gustav Genschow, Durlach.
GEL	George Egestorff, Linden-bei-Hannover.
GELbH	George Egestorff, Linden-bei-Hannover.
GGC	Gustav Genschow, Durlach.
GGCC	Gustav Genschow, Durlach.

GG&Co	Gustav Genschow, Durlach.
HE&C	Henri Ehrmann & Co, Karlsruhe.
HOFFMAN	Hoffman, Waffen und Munitions, Berlin. Gunmaker; cartridges made to his order by DWM.
HU	H. Utendorffer Patronenfabrik, Nuremberg. Company was absorbed by RWS in 1888 but the headstamp continued in use for many years afterwards, to differentiate the products of the Nuremberg factory.
J. PETER	Johann Peter, Stuttgart. Gunmaker; cartridges probably made by DWM.
KARLSRUHE	Lorenz Patronenfabrik, Karlsruhe (1878–89).
KRLSR	DWM, Karlsruhe.
L	Lignose Pulverfabrik AG, Berlin. Usually found with the calibre marking, which distinguishes it from the military 'L' which is generally found with a batch number and year date.
LORENZ	Deutsche Metallpatronenfabrik Lorenz, Karlsruhe.
MWS	Munitionswerke Schönebeck, Schönebeck-an-der-Elbe. The Sellier & Bellot factory, returned to private ownership after 1918 subsequent to its use for military production.
NAGEL & MENZ	Nagel & Menz. Gunmakers, Baden.
NICORRO	DWM, Karlsruhe. Trademark denoting the use of a non-corrosive primer in the cartridge.
NIMROD	Nimrod Gewehrfabrik GmbH, Suhl. Cases actually made by RWS.
P	Polte, Magdeburg
PATR FABR	Lorenz Deutsche Patronenfabrik, Karlsruhe. Used in the period 1880–90.
PM	Polte, Magdeburg. Uused 1900–10.
P&S	Potz und Sand, Mannheim.
R	RWS Nuremberg. Letter in a shield or circle on rimfire cartridges.
RM	Rheinisch Metallwaren und Maschinenfabrik, Sömmerda.
RMS	Rheinisch Metallwaren und Maschinenfabrik, Sömmerda.
RWS	Rheinisch-Westfalische Sprengstoff AG, Nuremberg.
RWS-N	Rheinisch-Westfalische Sprengstoff AG, Nuremberg.
RWS-T	Rheinisch-Westfalische Sprengstoff AG, Troisdorf.
SB	Made in the East German state factory at Schönebeck-an-der-Elbe 1950–90. This was originally a Sellier & Bellot factory, and the headstamp resembles the pre-1936 S&B headstamp except that it uses rosettes instead of stars.
SB PRUSSIA	Mark used on rimfire cartridge made in the Sellier & Bellot factory at Magdeburg prior to 1914.
SBR	Sellier & Bellot factory, Riga, pre-1914.
SBS	Sellier & Bellot factory, Schönebeck-an-der-Elbe, pre-1914.
SCH	August Schuler, Suhl. Gunmaker; cartridges made byRWS.
SCHURK	Adolf Schurk, Munich. Gunmaker; cartridges made by ?
SKD	Selve-Kronbiegel Dornheim AG Munitionsfabrik, Sömmerda.
ST	B. Stahul Metallhulsenfabrik, Suhl.
SU	G. C. Dornheim, Suhl.
TB	Th. Bergmann & Co GmbH, Berlin. Cases made by DWM.
U..U	H. Utendorffer, Nuremberg. Early mark, ca 1880.

Vom Hofe	E. A. Vom Hofe, Berlin. Gunmaker; cases made by DWM and others.
VZ	Vereinigte Zünder und Kabellwerke AG, Meissen-an-der-Elbe. On rimfires.
VZK	Vereinigte Zünder und Kabellwerke AG, Meissen-an-der-Elbe. On centrefires.
W GEHMANN	Walter Gehmann, Stuttgart. Gunmaker; Cases made by IWK. Post-1950.
WM	In a shield, backed by crossed arrows: Walbinger, Mauschel & Co, Bischweiler. Pre-1914.

MILITARY, pre-1918

BMF	Berndorffer Metallwarenfabrik, Berndorf, Austria. In monogram form.
C	Patronenfabrik Cleebronn, Heidelberg.
D	Königlich Munitionfabrik, Danzig. Or Dresden; there is no easy way of telling the two apart, though it seems probable that if the primer is stabbed in three places, the cartridge came from Dresden. It can also stand for Gustav Genschow's factory at Durlach, which supplied 7.92mm and 9mm ammunition to the Army on contract during World War I.
DW	Deutsche Werke AG, Berlin.
E	In script form. Erfurter Patronenfabrik, Erfurt.
E	Preceding the factory identifier or the year mark, indicates a case made of steel. Example: EG, where G is the factory identifier.
ez	In cursive script; believed to be 'Erfurt Zeugamt' but unconfirmed.
G	Waffen- und Munitionsfabrik Gieslingen.
GD	Gustav Genschow, Durlach.
Ge	Gustav Genschow, Durlach.
GM	Grünberger Metallgesellschaft, Grünberg.
H	H. Huck Metallwarenfabrik, Nuremberg.
J	Bayrische Hauptlaboratorium, Ingoldstadt. 1911–18.
K67	Marking used to indicate an armour-piercing bullet round (K for 'kern') using a case made of 67% copper and 33% zinc. 1916–18.
L	Lindener Zündhütchen und Thorwarenfabrik, Linden-bei-Hannover. The company was taken over by Dynamit Nobel in 1927, and it seems probable that it was originally the Military Ammunition Department of the George Egestorff factory. Usually found with a batch number and the last two digits of the year.
LDP	Lorenz Deutsche Patronenfabrik, Karlsruhe. Often with two stars.
MW	Munitonswerke, Schönebeck-an-der-Elbe. Formerly the Sellier & Bellot commercial ammunition factory taken over by the German government for military production during World War I.
N	Rheinisch-Westfalisch Sprengstoff AG, Nuremberg. On World War I 7.92mm Mauser ammunition. This mark was used to differentiate military from commercial production.
N&S	Niebecker & Schumacher, Iserlohn.
P	Polte, Magdeburg.
PE	Polte, Magdeburg; the 'E' indicates the experimental use of steel cartridge cases in the period 1900–05.
PMF	Pulver und Munitionsfabrik, Dachau.

S	Königlich Munitionsfabrik, Berlin-Spandau.
S67	Marking used to indicate pointed bullet ('S' for Spitzer) in a cartridge case containing 67% copper and 33% zinc. 1916–18.
SC, SD, SE, SH, SS	All found on 7.92mm Mauser cartridges with 1914–18 dates; believed to be Berlin-Spandau but not confirmed.
SE	When accompanied by a maker's mark, on 1916–18 ammunition, indicates a steel cartridge case.
SO	Superimposed as a monogram: Sprengstoffwerke Oberschlesiem, Ober-Lazisk, Silesia.
T	Dynamit AG, Troisdorf. Ca 1890–1900.
U	In Gothic form: H. Utendorffer, Nuremberg.
UN	H. Utendorffer, Nuremberg.

MILITARY, 1918–45

abc	Deutsche Metallwerk, Neustadt/Weinstrasse.
acb	Rheinische-Wesfalische Kunststoffwerke GmbH, Kettwing, Mulheim.
acc	Sprengstoffwerke Oberschliesen GmbH, Ober-Lazisk, Silesia. Used this mark 1940–41, then changed to 'ola'.
acd	Hümmel & Sohn, Bingen-bei-Laufenberg, Bavaria.
ad	Patronen-, Zundhutchen und Metallwarenfabrik GmbH, Schönebeck-an-der-Elbe. Originally a factory of Sellier & Bellot, the Czech commercial firm; became independent as the Munitionswerke Schönebeck and was then taken over by the German state in the late 1930s and given this title.
adc	Wilhelm Pryn, Stollberg/Rhein.
ade	Schmidt und Lautenbach Metallwarenfabrik, Oberstein.
aeu	Prozsnitzr Maschinenfabrik Wichtel & Kovarics, Prozsnitz, Poland.
afp	Maschinenfabrik Wilhelm Korders HG, Lette-bei-Oelde, Minden.
agl	Stahlwerk Braunschweig, Starachowitz, Poland.
agw	Berg- und Huttenwerke Karwin-Trzynietz AG, Trzynietz, Poland.
ah	Carl Merz Maschinenfabrik, Stetten-bei-Hechingen.
ahg	Stahlgiesserei Wozniak, Sosnowitz, Poland. Used 'jwc' until late 1943.
aj	Sorensen & Koster, Aluminium und Metallwerke, Neumuster-i-Holstein.
ajn	Union Sprengstoff und Zundmittelwerke, Alt Berum, Upper Silesia.
ak	Munitionsfabrik Vlasim, Vlasim, Czechoslovakia. Originally the principal factory of Sellier & Bellot, Czech commercial ammunition manufacturers, it was newly built in 1937 and taken over by the German authorities upon the occupation of Bohemia in 1939 and used solely for military production. Used 'P90D' until mid-1940.
aks	Schneider & Korb Metallwarenfabrik, Bernsbach.
al	Deutsche Leucht und Signalmittelwerk Dr Feistel KG, Werk Schonhage, Berlin-Charlottenberg.
am	Otto Eberhardt Patronenfabrik, Hirtenberg, Austria. Actually the Hirtenberg Patronenfabrik GmbH factory but taken over in 1939 and absorbed into the Gustloffwerke organisation.
amh	Bullmanwerke Hans Bullman, Gablonz, Sudetenland.

an	C. Beutenmuller & Co GmbH Metallwarenfabrik, Bretten/Baden.
any	Gebrüder Unger Maschinenfabrik AG, Chemnitz.
aon	Detona GmbH, Bohuslavice, Czechoslovakia. Early mark; changed to 'boh' in late 1940.
ap	Deutsche Leucht und Signalmittelwerk Dr Feistel KG, Werk Ronsdorf, Wuppertal.
asb	Deutsche Waffen- und Munitionsfabrik, Berlin-Borsigwalde.
asc	Druckma Schnellpressenfabrik GmbH, Leipzig.
asf	Erich und Greitz AG Metallwarenfabrik, Berlin.
aso	Fichtel & Sachs, Schweinfurt.
asr	Hanseatische Kettenwerke GmbH, Hamburg.
ast	Johann Hoff Maschinenfabrik, Berlin-Lichterfeld.
aue	Metall und Eisen GmbH, Nuremberg.
auj	Monheimer Ketten und Metallwarenindustrie Pötz & Sand, Monheim-Düsseldorf.
auu	Patronenhülsen und Metallwarenfabrik, Rokycany bei Pilsen, Czechoslovakia.
auv	Julius Pintsch K-G, Werk Fürstenwalde/Spree.
aux	Poltewerke, Magdeburg. One of the largest German cartridge companies. Originally used 'ava'; adopted 'aux' in late 1940.
auy	Poltewerke, Werk Grünberg.
auz	Poltewerke, Werk Arnstadt.
av	VDN-Halbzeugwerke GmbH, Werdol.
ava	Poltewerke, Magdeburg. Early mark; used 'aux' after late 1940.
ave	Preuss und Heinrich Blechwarenfabrik, Döbeln.
avt	Silva Metallwerk GmbH, Werk Magdeburg.
avu	Silva Metallwerk GmbH, Werk Genthin.
awt	Württembergischer Metallwarenfabrik AG, Gieslingen-Steige.
axq	Erfurter Ladenindustrie, Erfurt.
axs	Berndorffer Metallwarenfabrik AG, Amstetten.
az	VDM-Halbzeurwerke GmbH, Altena.
azy	Maschinenfabrik Sangerhausen AG, Sangerhausen.
ba	Sundwiger Messingwerk, Sundwig, Iserlohn.
bb	A. Laue, Werk Reinickendorf, Berlin.
bc	Kupfer & Messingwerke K-G, Becker & Co, Langemberg.
bcn	Kordt & Rosch Press-, Stanz- und Hammerwerke, Wipperfürth, Ruhr.
bd	F. A. Lange Metallwerke AG, Bodenbach/Sudetenland.
be	Berndorffer Metallwarenfabrik, Berndorf, Austria. Austrian company taken over and operated by A. Krupp on German contracts.
bh	Waffenwerk Brünn, Brno, Czechslovakia.
bk	Metall-, Walz- und Platierwarenfabrik Hindrichs-Aufferman AG, Wuppertal.
bkt	Kabel- und Metallwerk Neumayer AG, Nuremberg. Early mark; changed to 'va' in late 1940.
blu	Sprengstoffwerke Blumau AG, Blumau bei Felixdorf, Austria.

bmb	Metallwarenfabrik Reichertshofen Carl Binder, Reichertshofen.
bne	Metallwerk Odertal GmbH, Odertal, Austria.
bnf	Metallwerk Wolfenbüttel GmbH, Wolfenbüttel.
boh	Detona GmbH, Bohuslavice, Czechoslovakia.. Mark changed from 'aom' in late 1940.
bpo	Johann Jackl & Co Metallwarenfabrik GmbH, Schwenningen-an-der-Nahe.
brb	Richard Rinker GmbH, Menden, Iselohn.
bsy	Hugo Schneider AG (HASAG), Leipzig. Changed to 'wa' in late 1940.
btn	Ernst Gosser, Metallwaren und Kunstharzpresswerk, Iserlohn.
btr	Metall und Presswerke Gablonz, Gablonz, Czechoslovakia.
bts	Matthias Ochsler & Sohn GmbH, Metallwarenfabrik, Riegersdorf, Sudeten.
bxm	Vereinigte Zünder und Kabellwerke AG, Meissen-an-der-Elbe.
bye	Hannover Maschinenbau AG (HANOMAG), Hannover-Linden. The old George Egestorff cartridge factory taken over and being run by Hanomag.
bzb	Wilhelm Schüren KG, Press-, Stanz- und Ziehwerk, Gevelsberg.
cao	Broteroder Metallwarenfabrik Weustenfeld & Co, Broterode.
cf	Westfalische Anhaltische Sprengstoff AG (WASAG), Oranienburg.
cg	Finower Industriewerk GmbH, Finow.
ck	Metallwerk Neumeyer München GmbH, Munich.
cmf	Fertigungsgemeinschaft Strager & Co, Maschinienfabrik Pini & Kai, Vienna.
cop	Carl Urban Stanzwerk und Metallwarenfabrik, Velbert.
cvg	VDM-Halbzeurwerke GmbH, Heddenheim, Frankfurt-am-Main.
cwg	Westfalische Anhaltische Sprengstoff AG (WASAG), Coswig.
cxm	Gustav Genschow AG, Berlin.
cxw	Ludwig Braun Metallwarenfabrik, Schmalkalden.
czo	Heeres Zeugamt Geschosswerkstatt (Army Board of Ordnance Ammunition Workshop), Königsberg, East Prussia.
dc	Uta-Werkstatten Uta & Co, Auerbacj.
de	Munitionswerke Schönbecke, Schönebecke-an-der-Elbe.
dma	Geeres Munitionanstalt Geschosswerkstatt (Army Munitions Establishment Ammunition Workshop), Zeithain.
dnf	Westfalische Anhaltische Sprengstoff AG (WASAG), Stadeln, Nuremberg.
dng	Dynamit-AG, Werk Empelde, Hanover. Mark replaced by 'emp' in late 1940.
dnh	Rheinische Westfälische Srengstoffwerke AG, Durlach.
dom	Westfalische Metallindustrie AG, Lippstadt.
dou	Waffenwerk Brünn AG, Povaska Bystrica, Czechslovakia.
drv	Hugo Schneider AG (HASAG), Tschenstochau (Czestochowa), Poland.
dxs	August Thyssen-Hütte AG, Duisburg-Hamborn.
ea	Trierer Walzwerke AG, Trier.
eba	Metallwerke Schafenburg & Teubert GmbH, Breitungen/Werra.
edq	DWN, Lübeck-Schlutup. Changed to 'tko' in late 1944.
edt	Metallwarenfabrik vormals H. Wisser AG, Zella Mehlis.

eej	Märkisches Walzwerk GmbH, Strausberg/Potsdam.
eel	Metallwarenfabrik vormals H. Wisser AG, Broterode.
eem	Selve-Kronbiegel Dornheim AG Munitionsfabrik, Sömmerda.
eeo	DWM, Poznan, Poland.
eex	Teuto Metallwerke GmvH, Osnabrück. Changed to 'oxo' late 1940.
eey	Metallwarenfabrik Treuenbreitzen GmbH, Röderhof.
efg	Heinrich Huhn Stanz-, Press- und Ziehwerk, Hützemert/Westfalia.
eh	Trierer Walzwerke AG, Burg bez Magdeburg.
ehe	H. Rommler Presstoffwerk AG, Spremberg.
ek	C. Beutenmüller & Co, GmbH Metallwarenfabrik, Breiten, Baden.
elg	Westfalische Anhaltische Sprengstoff AG (WASAG), Elsnig.
emh	George Allgaier Stanz- und Presswerke, Uhingen.
emp	Dynamit-AG, Werk Empelde, Hannover. Formerly 'dng'.
eom	H. Huck Metallwarenfabrik, Nuremberg.
erm	W. G. Dinkelmeyer Metallwarenfabrik, Kötzting. Early mark; changed to 'ern' to avoid confuision with 'Erma'.
eva	Press-, Stanz- und Ziehwerke Rudolf Chillingworth AG, Nuremberg.
faa	DWM, Karlsruhe. Abandoned; replace by 'suk' in late 1944.
fb	Mansfeld Metallwarenfabrik AG, Rothenburg.
fd	Stollberger Metallwerke AG, Von Asten, Lyman & Schleicher, Stollberg/Rhld.
fde	Dynamit AG, Werk Förde.
fer	Metallwerke Wandhofen GmbH, Schwerte.
foc	Bebrit-Presstoffwerk, Bebra.
foz	Hansa-Metallwerk AG, Möhringen, Stuttgart.
fva	Draht- und Metallwarenfabrik GmbH, Salzwedel.
ga	Hirsch Kupfer- und Messingwerke AG, Finow.
gew	August Berghaus Press- und Stanzwerke, Oberbrügge.
gtb	J. E. Eisfeld Pulver- und Pyrotechnischefabrik GmbH, Güntersberge.
gyu	Michera AG, Stara-Tura, Czechoslovakia.
gyw	Tausz Armaturen und Metallwarenfabrik, Myjava, Czechoslovakia.
gyx	Elektro-Mechanik GmbH, Reichenberg, Sudetenland.
ham	Dynamit-AG, Werke Hamm.
has	Pulverfabrik Hasloch, Hasloch-am-Main.
HASAG	Framed in a diamond: Hugo Schneider AG, Leipzig, Werk Skatzysko-Kamienna, Poland. Former Polish military ammunition plant operated under German occupation by the HASAG company.
hhu	Metallwarenfabrik H. A. Erbe AG, Schmalkalden.
hhw	Metallwerke Silberhütte GmbH, St Andreasberg.
hla	Metallwarenfabrik Treuenbrietzen GmbH, Sebaldushof.
hlb	Metallwarenfabrik Treuenbrietzen GmbH, Selterhof.
hlc	Zieh und Stanzwerk GmbH, Schleusingen.
hou	Press-, Stanz- und Ziehwerke GmbH, Velbert.

hrg	Gustav Genschow, Durlach. This code was reallocated to an engine manufacturer in late 1944 and may never have been used on ammunition.
hrn	Presswerke GmbH, Metgethen, East Prussia.
htg	Poltewerk, Duderstadt.
jjp	VDM-Halbzeurwerke Gmbh, Hildesheim.
jjw	Wirrth & Schirp Presswerk, Rodt-Müllenbach.
jlj	Heeres Zeugamt, Ingoldstadt.
jne	Presswerk Mollberg & Co, Hofgeismar, Kassel.
jvh	Presswerk Westfälen Friedrich Hefendehl, Hierspe-Bahnhof/West.
kam	Hugo Schneider AG (HASAG), Leipzig, operating the Polish Army factory at Skarzysko Kamienna, Poland, under German occupation.
kea	Karl Wüst Press- und Stanzwerk, Felbach, Stuttgart.
krd	Sprengstoffwerke Oberschliesen GmbH, formerly Lignose AG, Kriewald.
krl	Dynamit AG, Krummel.
kru	Lignose Sprengstoffwerke, Kruppamuhle.
ktr	Vereinigte Deutsche Metallwerke AG, Gross-Auhem.
kwd	Jagdpatronen, Zundhutchen und Metallwarenfabrik AG, Budapest. The small-arms ammunition section of the Hungarian national arsenal which produced German service ammunition under German supervision.
kyn	'Astra' Fabrica Romana de Vagoane, Motorane, Armament si Munitiuni, Brasov, Romania. Romanian arsenal producing German service ammunition under German supervision.
laz	F. A. Lange Metallwerke AG, Obernhaus-Grünthal.
ldb	Deutsche Pyrotechnische Fabriken GmbH, Berlin-Malchow. Formerly Lechfeld & Depyfag AG.
ldc	Deutsche Pyrotechnische Fabriken GmbH, Cleebron. Formerly Lechfeld & Depyfag AG.
ldn	Deutsche Pyrotechnische Fabriken GmbH, Neumarkt-i-d-Oberpfalz. Formerly Lechfeld & Depyfag AG.
lge	Kugelfabrik Schulte & Co, Tente.
lkb	Staats Rustungwerke, Warsaw. Polish arsenal under German occupation.
lkm	Munitionsfabrik Prague-Veltsberg, Czechoslovakia. Sellier & Bellot commercial ammunition factory taken over for German military production.
mhr	Vereinigte Oberschliessische Hüttenwerke, Werk Hermanshütte, Laband, Silesia.
mkf	Trierer Walzwerke AG, Wuppertal-Langerfeld.
mkv	Kupfer und Messingwerke Moosach GmbH, Munich.
mog	Deutsche Sprengchemie, Moschwig.
mpl	Östpreussische Blechdosenfabrik F. C. R. Unger & Sohn, Braunsberg, East Prussia.

na	Westfalische Kupfer- und Messingwerke AG, formerly Casper Noell, Lüdenscheid.
nbe	Hugo Schneider AG (HASAG) Eiden und Metallwerke GmbH, Tschenstochau (Czestochowa), Poland.
nbp	Maschinenfabrik Lindenhof, Meissner & Co, Bunzlau (now Bloselawiec, Poland).
nfx	Rheinisch-Westfalische Sprengstoff GmbH, Munitionsfabrik Warsaw-Praga, Poland.
nkq	Wilhelm Tausch Stanz- und Ziehwerke, Oederan.
nqb	Zieh- und Presswerke Carl Froh, Hachen.
ntn	Fema Metallwarenfabrik AG, Bromberg (now Bydgoszcz, Poland).
nua	Press- und Stanzwerke GmbH, Reichenbach-Vilshofen.
nwo	Hans Bullman Werke, Tannwald bei Gablonz (now Jablonec, Czech Republic).
nwp	Hans Bullman Werke, Proschwitz.
oa	Huck Metallwarenfabrik, Lüdenscheid.
ogt	Usine Manufacture Generale de Munitions, Valence, France. On German contract ammunition 1940–44.
ola	Sprengstoff Oberschliesen GmbH, Ober Lazisk, Silesia (now Laziska Gorne, Poland). Late mark; previously used 'acc'.
oxo	Teuto Metallwerke GmbH, Osnabrück. Late mark; previously used 'eex'.
P14	Waffenwerke Brünn, Povaska Bystrica, Czechoslovakia. Later used 'dou'.
P25	Metallwarenfabrik Treuenbreitzen GmbH, Sebaldushof. Later used 'hla'.
P28	DWM, Karlsruhe. Later used 'faa'.
P67	RWS, Nuremberg. Later used 'dnf'.
P69	Patronen, Zundhütchen und Metallwarenfabrik GmbH, Schonebeck-an-der-Elbe. Later used 'ad'.
P90D	Munitionsfabrik Vlasim, Vlasim, Czechoslovakia. Later used 'ak'.
P94	Kabel- und Metallwerke Neumeyer AG, Nuremberg. Later used 'bkt', then 'va'.
P120	Dynamit AG, Empelde. Later adopted 'dng' then, 'emp'.
P131	DWM Berlin-Borsigwalde. Later adopted 'asb'.
P132	Metallwerke Wandhofen, Schwerte. Also used 'P491' and later adopted 'fer'.
P151	RWS, Stadlen, Nuremberg. Later adopted 'dnf'.
P154	Poltewerke, Grünberg (now Zielona Gora, Poland). Later used 'auy'.
P162	Presswerke GmbH, Metgethen, East Prussia. Later used 'hrn'.
P165	Metallwarenfabrik Treuenbrietzen GmbH, Selterhof. Later used 'hlb'.
P181	Hugo Schneider AG (HASAG), Altenburg. Later used 'wg'.
P186	Metallwerke Wolfenbüttel GmbH, Wolfenbüttel. Later used 'bnf'.
P198	Metallwarenfabrik Treuenbrietzen GmbH, Belsig.
P207	Metallwerke Odertal GmbH, Odertal. Later used 'bne'.
P249	Finower Industrie GmbH, Finow/Mark. Later used 'cg'.
P315	Märkisch Walzwerke GmbH, Strausburg/Potsdam. Later used 'eej'.

P316	Westfalische Metallindustrie GmbH, Lippstadt. Later used 'don'.
P334	Mansfeld Metallwarenfabrik AG, Rothenburg. Later used 'fb'.
P340	Metallwerke Silberhütte GmbH, St Andreasburg. Later used 'hhw'.
P346	H. Huck Metallwarenfabrik, Nuremberg. Later used 'eom'.
P369	Teuto Metallwerke GmbH, Osnabrück. Later used 'eex', then 'oxo'.
P370	Poltewerke, Magdeburg. Later used 'aux'.
P379	Metallwarenfabrik Scharfenburg & Teubert, Breitungen. Later used 'eba'.
P405	Dynamit AG, Durlach. Later used 'dnh'.
P412	DWM, Lübeck-Schlutup. Later used 'edq', then 'tko'.
P442	Zieh- und Stanzwerke Gmbh, Schleusingen. Later used 'hlc'.
P490	Poltewerke, Magdeburg. Later used 'aux'.
P491	Metallwerke Wandhofen, Schwerte. Also used 'P132', then adopted 'fer'.
P635	Munitionsfabrik Wollerdorf, Vienna, Austria.
pa	Stollberg Metallwerke KG, Von Asten, Lyman & Schleicher, Stollberg.
Pak	Munitionsfabrik Vlasim, Vlasim, Czechoslovakia. An intermediate mark used briefly between 'P90D and 'ak'.
pcd	Th. Bergmann & Co KG, Waffen- und Munitionsfabrik, Bernau, Berlin.
Pcdp	Th. Bergmann & Co, KG, Bernau. Intermediate mark used between the 'P' system and the three-letter system, probably because of a misunderstanding of how the new system was to be worked. Seen on 7.92mm ammunition dated 1940.
pjj	Copenhagen Arsenal, Denmark. On 9mm Paraberllum ammunition made under German occupation 1940–45.
qa	Wilhelm Pryn Metallhalbfabrikat, Stollberg.
ra	Deutsche Messingwerke Carl Eveking AG, Berlin-Niederschönweide.
S*	Mark used to indicate a cartridge case made of 72 % copper and 18% zinc.
she	Unknown; found on 9mm Parabellum with 1944 dates.
skd	Selve-Kronbiegel Dornheim AG Munitionsfabrik, Sömmerda.
SS-TV	'Schutz Staffel-Technische Verwaltung'. Found on ammunition supplied to SS training establishments 1935–45. Manufactured by DWM. The letters 'SS' are in Nordic rune form.
St	Indicates the use of steel case metal. 'St+' indicates reinforced case design; 'St–' indicates a single flash hole.
suk	DWM, Karlsruhe. Adopted late 1944 in place of 'faa'.
tko	DWM, Lübeck-Schlutup. Adopted late 1944 in place of 'edq'.
ua	Osnabrücker Kupfer- und Drahtwerke AG, Osnabrück.
va	Kabell- und Metallwerk Neumeyer AG, Nuremberg.
vzg	Vereinigte Zünder und Kabellwerke AG, Meissen-a-d-Elbe.
wa	Hugo Schneider AG (HASAG), Leipzig.

wb	Hugo Schneider AG (HASAG), Köpenick, Berlin.
wc	Hugo Schneider AG (HASAG), Meuselwitz.
wd	Hugo Schneider AG (HASAG), Taucha.
we	Hugo Schneider AG (HASAG), Langewiesen.
wf	Hugo Schneider AG (HASAG), Kielce, Poland.
wg	Hugo Schneider AG (HASAG), Altenburg.
wh	Hugo Schneider AG (HASAG), Eisenach.
wj	Hugo Schneider AG (HASAG), Oberweissbach.
wk	Hugo Schneider AG (HASAG), Schlieben.
wm	Hugo Schneider AG (HASAG), Dermbach.
X	In addition to the standard four-item marking on 9mm Parabellum, indicates subsonic cartridge for silenced weapons.
xa	Busch-Jäger Lüdenscheider Metallwerke, Lüdenscheid.
y	Jagdpatronen-, Zundhutchen- und Metallwarenfabrik AG, Werk Nagyteny, Budapest. Hungarian arsenal under German supervision 1942–45.
ya	Sächsische Metallwarenfabrik August Wellner Söhne AG, Aue.
zb	Kupferwerke Ilsenburg AG, Ilsenburg.

MILITARY, post-1945

DAG	Dynamit-AG, Empelde, Hannover.
DNG	Dynamit-Nobel-Genschow AG, Durlach.
EN	Maschinenfabrik Elisenhütte, Nassau.
GCO	Gustav Genschow, Cologne; on US contract ammunition.
IWK	Industriewerk Karlsruhe.
ME	Maschinenfabrik Elisenhütte, Nassau.
MEN	Maschinenfabrik Elisenhütte, Nassau.
MN	Maschinenfabrik Elisenhütte, Nassau.
MS	Manusaal-Diehl, Bubingen.

APPENDIX V: AMMUNITION

The following notes give details of the ammunition used in the various pistols discussed in the body of this book. The dimensions given are the mean of a number of rounds measured. No charge weight is given since smokeless powder is of varying quality and efficiency from batch to batch, as well as from maker to maker, and pistol ammunition is generally loaded to give a specified chamber pressure and velocity in a test barrel. The muzzle velocity and energy will vary depending upon the nature and weight of the propellant, the length of the barrel used, the ambient temperature and pressure and the method used in measuring. Thus the figures quoted here are nominal values, but they are based upon actual measurements wherever possible and are those values to be expected from standard ammunition fired in a pistol with the normal length of barrel. Under 'synonyms', the initials 'DWM' indicate the index number in the Deutsche Waffen und Munitionsfabrik catalogues before 1939 and the letters 'GR' the index number in the catalogues of George Roth of Vienna prior to 1929 when that company was bought out by Ceskoslovensaka Zbrojovka and the numbering system ceased. Both companies included these numbers in the cartridge case headstamp.

4.25mm Liliput

Synonyms: 4.25mm Erika

Case type	Rimless, straight
Round length	0.600in (15.25mm)
Case length	0.411in (10.44mm)
Rim diameter	0.198in (5.03mm)
Bullet type	Jacketed roundnose
Bullet diameter	0.68in (4.5mm)
Bullet weight	12gr (0.77g)
Charge type	Mixed black and smokeless
Muzzle velocity	750ft/sec (228m/sec)
Muzzle energy	14.7ft-lb (20J)

Originally produced for an Austrian pistol, the Erika, in about 1910. In 1920 the cartridge was adopted by August Menz of Suhl for his 'Liliput' automatic pistol, which continued in production until about 1928. By then Menz had realised that the peculiar cartridge was doing nothing to help sales, and he modified his pistol to accept the more common 6.35mm ACP cartridge. Presumably manufacture of the 4.25mm cartridge came to an end in the early 1930s.

The bullet was jacketed and averaged about 0.8g in weight. It might possibly be lethal at very close range, but at ten feet it will only just penetrate a half-inch wooden plank. The propelling charge was a curious mixture of smokeless and black powder which produced a very loud report and a large cloud of smoke on discharge, probably for psychological effect. The muzzle velocity is that claimed by the makers of the pistol: the bullet is so small that it fails to register on a conventional sky-screen chronograph.

5mm Bergmann No 2, M1894

Synonyms: DWM 416

Case type	Rimless, grooveless, sharply tapered
Round length	0.856in (21.75mm)
Case length	0.596in (15.14mm)
Rim diameter	0.274in (6.95mm)
Bullet type	Roundnose lead or jacketed or softnose
Bullet diameter	0.203in (5.15mm)
Bullet weight	35gr (2.25g)
Charge type	Smokeless
Muzzle velocity	590ft/sec (180m/sec)
Muzzle energy	29ft-lb (36J)

This round was developed by Theodor Bergmann for his early self-loading pistol in 1894 and was without an extraction rim of any kind. These early model pistols relied on residual pressure to blow the case out of the chamber when the breech opened, this action being aided by the sharp taper of the case. Attractive as the idea seemed, it was not entirely practical: extraction was usually satisfactory, but ejection from the pistol was spasmodic and the empty case often remained in the feedway and jammed the bolt. The bullet is unusual in being much longer in relation to its calibre than is the commonly accepted ratio and, as a result, its flight is usually unstable, the bullet tending to turn end-over-end. The ammunition is no longer manufactured.

5mm Bergmann No 2, M1896

Synonyms: DWM 416A

Case type	Rimless, straight taper
Round length	0.856in (21.75mm)
Case length	0.590in (15mm)
Rim diameter	0.270in (6.85mm)
Bullet type	Roundnose lead or jacketed or softnose
Bullet diameter	0.205in (5.21mm)
Bullet weight	35gr (2.25g)
Charge type	Smokeless

Muzzle velocity	590ft/sec (180m/sec)
Muzzle energy	29ft-lb (36J)

The extraction-ejection system on the M1894 Bergmann pistol proved unreliable, and in 1896 the pistol was redesigned to incorporate a positive extraction system; to suit this, the cartridge was similarly changed, giving the case an extracting groove. Bullet weight and ballistic performance remained the same. These later cases could be used in either type of pistol, since the blow-out extraction on the earlier models would still function. The 5mm Bergmann was a moderately popular target pistol, and the ammunition was manufactured, principally by Deutsche Metallpatronenfabrik and their successors, DWM, until the early 1930s.

5mm Pickert Revolver

Synonyms: DWM 416B; 5.2 × 16.5R

Case type	Rimmed, straight taper
Round length	0.868in (22.55mm)
Case length	0.642in (16.30mm)
Rim diameter	0.333in (8.45mm)
Bullet type	Roundnose lead or jacketed or softnose
Bullet diameter	0.205in (5.20mm)
Bullet weight	34gr (2.20g)
Charge type	Smokeless
Muzzle velocity	492ft/sec (150m/sec)
Muzzle energy:	18ft-lb (25 J)

Friedrich Pickert of Zella Mehlis was a prolific producer of cheap revolvers under the trade-name 'Arminius', and this cartridge was developed about the turn of the century to suit one of them. This was, it would seem, designed to compete with Bergmann's 5mm automatic pistols, and this cartridge is little more than the Bergmann 5mm No 2 of 1894 with an upstanding conventional rim added. It failed to attract much attention and did not survive World War I.

Bullets were either fully or partially jacketed and around 34gr (2.2g) in weight, though a plain lead bullet is sometimes encountered.

5.5mm Velo-Dog

Synonyms: 6mm Velo-Dog; DWM 382; GR 646

Case type	Rimmed, straight, brass
Round length	1.385in (35.20mm)
Case length	1.157in (29.40mm)
Rim diameter	0.300in (7.62mm)
Bullet type	Jacketed roundnose or soft-point
Bullet diameter	0.226in (5.74mm)
Bullet weight	43gr (2.75g)
Charge type	Smokeless
Muzzle velocity	672ft/sec (205m/sec)
Muzzle energy	43ft-lb (57J)

'Velo' means velocipede, or bicycle; 'Dog' means one of those great slavering things with fangs which lurk in French farmyards and which delighted in chasing cyclists in the 1890s. So for protection against dogs the 'Velo-Dog' revolver appeared, and this cartridge was developed for it.

It was an elegant little round, astonishingly long for its calibre, but made that way so as to obtain a slender cylinder for the revolver, allowing it to be easily carried in the pocket. As a result, many pocket revolvers were chambered for it, and it is still popular in the more remote areas of Spain and Portugal—though not necessarily for protecting cyclists any more. It was invariably found with a jacketed roundnose bullet, though soft-points were also popular and there was also a bird-shot charge, presumably for smaller and less evil-minded dogs.

.22 Long Rimfire

Synonyms: none

Case type	Rimmed, copper, rimfire-primed
Round length	0.880in (22.35mm)
Case length	0.595in (15.11mm)
Rim diameter	0.275in (6.98mm)
Bullet type	Lead, roundnose or hollow-point

Bullet diameter	0.223in (5.66mm)
Bullet weight	20gr (1.29g)
Charge type	Black or smokeless
Muzzle velocity	870ft/sec (265m/sec)
Muzzle energy	33ft-lb (42J)

This originally appeared in 1871 as a black-powder loading to improve upon the current .22 Short, using the same bullet. Some years later is was overtaken by the .22 Long Rifle round, since when the .22 Long has been something of a misfit. However, it appears here because of its use in some of the early Pickert revolvers, and the figures quoted above are taken from documents of the period and reflect the performance to be expected at that time in a small revolver. Modern high-velocity loadings give far better performance, but the fact remains that the .22 Long Rifle can outperform it and is more accurate into the bargain.

.22 Long Rifle Rimfire

Synonyms: none

Case type	Rimmed, copper or steel, rimfire-primed
Round length	0.975in (24.76mm)
Case length	0.595in (15.11mm)
Rim diameter	0.275in (6.98mm)
Bullet type	Lead, ogival or hollow-point
Bullet diameter	0.223in (5.66mm)
Bullet weight	40gr (2.60g)
Charge type	Smokeless
Muzzle velocity	722ft/sec (220m/sec)
Muzzle energy	46ft-lb (63J)

In contrast to the previous entry, the figures above are based upon current production standard velocity rounds as used in target shooting, since this cartridge is internationally recognised for competition purposes. It dates from 1887 and in its original form was simply the existing .22 Long carrying a 40-grain bullet instead of the then-normal 20-grain. In black powder days is was outperformed by the .22 Long so far as hitting power went, but it outperformed practically everything else when it came to accuracy, and once smokeless powder gave it superior velocity it rapidly became the commonest .22 sporting cartridge. There are innumerable brands and varieties. The high-velocity rifle rounds can deliver more power than shown above, which is based upon pistol performance with current German ammunition.

.22 Hornet

Synonyms: 5.6 × 35R Hornet; DWM 578: GR808

Case type	Rimmed, bottlenecked, brass
Round length	1.720in (43.70mm)
Case length	1.396in (35.45mm)
Rim diameter	0.344in (8.75mm)
Bullet type	Ogival, jacketed, soft- or hollow-point
Bullet diameter	0.218in (5.55mm)
Bullet weight	46gr (3.00g)
Charge type	Smokeless
Muzzle velocity	2,428ft/sec (740m/sec)
Muzzle energy	606ft-lb (820J)

As might be surmised from the velocity figure, this is actually a high-velocity rifle cartridge, and it finds its place here due to its adoption in a long-range target pistol made by Anschutz and based upon the bolt action of one of their rifles. Even though the pistol is heavy and the bullet light, it must be something of a handful to fire. It was designed principally as a small game cartridge, and the most common bullets are therefore the soft- and hollow-point varieties, but the target shooter has generally adopted the well-streamlined full-jacketed variety.

6.35mm Browning

Synonyms: .25 ACP; .25 Colt; 6.35 × 16; DWM 508A; GR 757

Case type	Semi-rimmed, straight
Round length	0.910in (23.11mm)
Case length	0.612in (15.55mm)
Rim diameter	0.301in (7.65mm)
Bullet type	Roundnose jacketed or soft-point
Bullet diameter	0.251 (6.37mm)
Bullet weight	50gr (3.24g)
Charge type	Smokeless powder
Muzzle velocity	755ft/sec (230m/sec)
Muzzle energy	63ft-lb (85.5J)

This round was developed by Fabrique National of Liège, Belgium, for the first 'Baby Browning' pistol in 1906 and has since become widely adopted throughout the world, being also well-known under the designation '.25 Auto'. It is of that peculiar class known as semi-rimmed, in which, although there is a pronounced extractor groove, careful examination will show that the cartridge rim is of greater diameter than the rest of the case.

It is an attempt to have the best of both worlds: a rimmed case is positioned in the chamber by its rim, which makes the gun designer's task easy; a rimless round must be positioned by the front edge of the case or by the bottleneck if one is present, which makes design rather more critical. On the other hand, a rimmed round is difficult to feed through an automatic mechanism, particularly in small pistol calibres, while a rimless round is, of course, less of a problem. But rimless designs in small calibres mean small extractor grooves and the possibility of faulty extraction, and so an enlargement of the cartridge base to the semi-rimmed form gives the extractor a larger bearing surface without bringing the rim out to the point where it begins to cause trouble in the feeding mechanism.

The 6.35mm round has been made by just about every manufacturer in the world and, as a result, has had just about every possible type of bullet and powder tried in it. The most usual patterns encountered are the normal jacketed or soft-point types of bullet, and in spite of their sophisticated appearance they are, in fact, rather less deadly than the common .22 Long Rifle rimfire cartridge.

6.35mm Pickert Revolver

Synonyms; 6.35mm Revolver; .25 Revolver CF

Case type	Rimmed, straight, brass
Round length	0.893in (22.70mm)
Case length	0.608in (15.45mm)
Rim diameter	0.309in (7.85mm)
Bullet type	Roundnose, jacketed
Bullet diameter	0.25in (6.35mm)
Bullet weight	49gr (3.20g)
Charge type	Smokeless
Muzzle velocity	755ft/sec (230m/sec)
Muzzle energy	62ft-lb (84J)

Pickert was just one of many European manufacturers who produced 6.35mm revolvers chambered so as to accept the standard 6.35mm Browning auto pistol cartridge. Fiocchi of Italy considered that this was a lucrative market for a cheaper alternative and manufactured these cartridges, which were to the same dimensions and with the same performance as the 6.35mm Browning but were inside primed and conventionally rimmed, making them somewhat cheaper. Manufacture appears to have been confined to the 1920s and early 1930s.

6.5mm Bergmann No 3 M1894

Synonyms: DWM 413

Case type	Rimless, grooveless, bottle-necked
Round length	1.215in (30.85mm)
Case length	0.858in (21.79mm)
Rim diameter	0.370in (9.39mm)
Bullet type	Roundnose, jacketed or lead
Bullet diameter	0.265in (6.73mm)
Bullet weight	65gr (4.20g)
Charge type	Smokeless
Muzzle velocity	705ft/sec (215m/sec)
Muzzle energy	75.7ft-lb (102 J)

Like the 5mm Bergmann No 2, this was produced for one of the early Bergmann automatic pistols which relied on breech gas pressure to eject the case from the chamber, and consequently no extraction rim or groove was provided. The usual bullet was a jacketed roundnose type of about 65gr (4.2g) weight, but plain lead and flatnosed soft-point have also been recorded. Moreover, like the 5mm No 2, the lack of an extraction rim proved to be a liability (how do you unload an unfired round?), and two years later the design was abandoned in favour of a more conventional type of rimless case.

6.5mm Bergmann No 3 M1896

Synonyms: DWM 413A; GR 658

Case type	Rimless, bottlenecked
Round length	1.198in (30.45mm)
Case length	0.858in (21.80mm)
Rim diameter	0.372in (9.45mm)
Bullet type	Jacketed roundnose or flat nose or lead heeled
Bullet diameter	0.288 (6.80mm)
Bullet weight	65gr (4.20g)
Charge type	Smokeless
Muzzle velocity	705ft/sec (215m/sec)
Muzzle energy	72ft-lb (97J)

This replaced the M1894 (above) and differs in having an extraction rim. It was to remain in manufacture until the early 1930s, being produced by most European ammunition firms with a variety of bullets, lead and jacketed, flat- and roundnosed. The standard loading was the same as that for the M1894 pattern.

6.5mm Parabellum

Synonyms: 6.5 × 21.6; DWM 550

Case type	Rimless, bottlenecked, brass
Round length	1.167in (29.65mm)
Case length	0.848in (21.50mm)
Rim diameter	0.394in (10mm)
Bullet type	Jacketed roundnose
Bullet diameter	0.263in (6.70mm)
Bullet weight	113gr (4.50g)
Charge type	Smokeless

This cartridge appeared in the 1904 DWM catalogue as being for an experimental Parabellum pistol. It is, in fact, a 7.65mm Parabellum case necked down to take a 6.5mm Bergmann bullet, and the object in view was presumably to step up the velocity and reduce the size of the pistol. In order to equal the energy of the 7.65mm Parabellum, this round would have had to exceed 425m/sec, which would probably have been feasible but at the expense of considerable muzzle blast. In any event, nothing more was heard of the project. The cartridge was apparently loaded with a jacketed bullet weighing 113gr (4.5g), but no performance figures can even be estimated.

7mm Bär

Synonyms: none

Case type	Rimmed, straight
Round length	0.905in (23.00mm)
Case length	0.610in (15.5mm)
Rim diameter	0.303in (7.70mm)
Bullet type	Roundnose lead
Bullet diameter	0.266in (6.75mm)
Bullet weight	55gr (3.50g)
Charge type	Smokeless
Muzzle velocity	738ft/sec (225m/sec)
Muzzle energy	65ft-lb (88J)

The Bär pistol was patented in 1898 by a Russian, Burkhardt Behr, resident in Switzerland, and was manufactured by J. P. Sauer & Sohn of Suhl from 1900 onward. The pistol was a mechanical repeater of great simplicity; it enjoyed a certain amount of popularity as a home and personal defence weapon and was manufactured until

1914, though after 1907 it was chambered for the 6.35mm ACP cartridge. This 7mm rimmed round was in production during the years 1900 to 1907.

7.25mm Adler

Synonyms: 7.25 × 17.5

Case type	Rimless, bottlenecked, brass
Round length	0.964in (24.50mm)
Case length	0.696in (17.70mm)
Rim diameter	0.338 (8.60mm)
Bullet type	Roundnose, brass-jacketed
Bullet diameter	0.280in (7.10mm)
Bullet weight	62gr (4.02g)
Charge type	Smokeless
Muzzle velocity	804ft/sec (245m/sec)
Muzzle energy	89ft-lb (120J)

The Adler automatic pistol appeared in 1905, the subject of patents by Haussler and Hermsdorff. It was not a particularly good design and survived for less than two years, as a result of which the ammunition is extremely scarce. The bottlenecked cartridge can be mistaken for the 7mm Charola, equally scarce, the principal difference being in the position of the case shoulder. The bullet is unusual, being jacketed in brass instead of the usual copper or nickel-plated steel of the period. The only specimens seen carried the RM headstamp of the Rheinische Metallwaren und Maschinenfabrik of Sömmerda.

7.5mm Bergmann No 4A

Synonyms: 7.5 × 22; DWM 451A

Case type	Rimless, straight taper
Round length	1.198in (30.45mm)
Case length	0.866in (22.00mm)
Rim diameter	0.372in (9.45mm)
Bullet type	Roundnose lead or semi-jacketed flatnose
Bullet diameter	0.307in (7.80mm)
Bullet weight	90gr (5.80g)
Charge type	Smokeless

This cartridge was developed for a 7.5mm Bergmann pistol in about 1896 but neither pistol nor cartridge were ever commercially marketed. The cartridge seems to have survived in the DWM catalogues until 1904 or later, but too much should not be read into that. The cartridge is characteristically Bergmann, with its sharp taper, and lead or softnosed semi-jacketed bullets of 83gr (5.4g) to 91gr (5.9g) weight have been reported. All recorded specimens have been of DWM manufacture and have the case number 451A included in the headstamp. No performance figures have been traced for this round.

7.5mm Bergmann No 7A

Synonyms: 7.5 × 20; DWM 460A

Case type	Rimless, straight taper
Round length	1.12in (28.50mm)
Case length	0.787in (20.00mm)
Rim diameter	0.372in (9.45mm)
Bullet type	Lead, roundnose, heeled
Bullet diameter	0.307in (7.80mm)
Bullet weight	90gr (5.83g)
Charge type	Smokeless

Another experimental Bergmann cartridge from 1896, like the 4A this lingered in catalogues for a further decade even though it was never commercially produced in any quantity. No performance figures are available, but it is reasonable to suppose that they were well below those of the 7.63mm Mauser and that the cartridge suffered thereby.

7.5mm Swiss Ordnance

Synonyms: 7.5mm Schmidt; 7.5mm Swiss Nagant; DWM421

Case type	Rimmed, straight, brass
Round length	1.352in ((34.35mm)
Case length	0.857in (21.76mm)
Rim diameter	0.409in (10.38mm)
Bullet type	Roundnose, lead or jacketed
Bullet diameter	0.315in (8.00mm)
Bullet weight	105gr (6.80g)

Charge type	Smokeless
Muzzle velocity	722ft/sec (220m/sec)
Muzzle energy	121ft-lb (164J)

Although this originated as the official Swiss Army revolver cartridge in 1882, it soon came to be adopted by commercial gunmakers as a convenient and reasonably powerful round for pocket revolvers. It was replaced in Swiss service when they adopted the Luger pistol in 1901, but it has remained in use there as a target cartridge and is still made, from time to time, by the Swiss Government cartridge factory. For those shooters outside Switzerland, Fiocchi of Italy also turn some out at intervals. The round is normally found with a lead roundnose bullet, although jacketed and soft-point types are also met and very early Swiss production examples had a paper patch or sleeve around the bullet.

7.5mm Nagant

Synonyms: 7.5 Norwegian Nagant; 7.5 Swedish Nagant; DWM 482; GR 609

Case type	Rimmed, straight, brass
Round length	1.215in (30.85mm)
Case length	0.883in (22.43mm)
Rim diameter	0.405in (10.28mm)
Bullet type	Roundnose, lead or jacketed
Bullet diameter	0.324in (8.23mm)
Bullet weight	103gr (5.58g)
Charge type	Smokeless
Muzzle velocity	738ft/sec (225m/sec)
Muzzle energy	104ft-lb (141J)

Another of the European military cartridges adopted for commercial use by various gunmakers, notably Pickert, this round is interchangeable with the 7.5mm Swiss Ordnance round, revolvers chambered for either one being capable of firing the other, and one wonders why Pickert even bothered to specify which one to use with his Arminius No 5 revolvers. This cartridge was introduced in the middle 1880s by the Belgian maker Nagant, and was widely adopted as a military round in Scandinavia and also in Luxembourg. The usual bullet was the standard sort of roundnosed lead military type, but jacketed and patched bullets can also be found.

7.6mm Mauser Revolver

Synonyms: 7.6 × 20R; DWM 5; GR 620

Case type	Rimmed, straight
Round length	1.212in (30.80mm)
Case length	0.798in (20.27mm)
Rim diameter	0.378in (9.60mm)
Bullet type	Roundnose, lead or jacketed
Bullet diameter	0.313in (7.95mm)
Bullet weight	98gr (6.35g)
Charge type	Black powder
Muzzle velocity	722ft/sec (220m/sec)
Muzzle energy	113ft-lb (153J)

This is the smallest of a series of three cartridges (7.6, 9 and 10.6mm) for the Mauser 'Zig-Zag' revolver of 1878. The 7.6mm was offered as a commercial venture; the two larger pistols were aimed at the military market. They failed in this latter attempt and all three sizes were offered commercially; all were eventually superseded by the Mauser automatic pistol. The 7.6mm version seems to have been the least popular of the three and thus the cartridges are less common today. They will usually be found with DWM, Roth or Keller headstamps. The usual loading is a lead bullet of about 98gr (6.35g) weight, though jacketed bullets have occasionally been seen.

A long-case version of this cartridge (7.6 × 25R) was also developed, listed by DWM under the reference number 5A, but no corresponding revolver was made for sale and it can be assumed that this was a development model which never passed the prototype stage.

7.63mm Mauser Pistol

Synonyms: 7.63 × 25mm; DWM403; GR 829; .30 Mauser

Case type	Rimless, bottlenecked
Round length	1.350in (34.29mm)
Case length	0.990in (25.14mm)
Rim diameter	0.393in (9.98mm)
Bullet type	Various, but usually roundnose full-jacketed
Bullet diameter	0.309in (7.85mm)
Bullet weight	85gr (5.50g)
Charge type	Smokeless
Muzzle velocity	1,450ft/sec (442m/sec)
Muzzle energy	396ft-lb (536J)

The oldest automatic pistol cartridge still in regular service, this was for many years also the most powerful one. It began life as a design attributed to Borchardt—although it appears that Georg Luger might have had a lot to do with it—and was produced for the original Borchardt pistol in 1893. Mauser then took it as the round for his military model pistol introduced in 1896; it has to be admitted that, given the cartridge, the development of the pistol was much easier.

While credit accrues to Borchardt and Luger for their pistol designs, much more honour is due to them for the perfection of various designs of pistol cartridge, without which the development of automatic pistols would have been a much longer and more tedious process. They led; others followed. However, Mauser did not accept the Borchardt round as it stood. He made some very slight dimensional changes (no doubt for his own good reasons—probably to facilitate mass production) and also altered the bullet seating. These changes are so small that the difference between a Mauser and a Borchardt cartridge can disappear inside the manufacturer's tolerances. The principal difference is that the Mauser round is loaded to work at a higher pressure than the Borchardt. Since Borchardt cartridges are now in the category of collectors' pieces, the differences are not vital for the shooting man.

Bullets of every conceivable type have been loaded into Mauser rounds, from flat-nosed soft-point, through fully jacketed, to a peculiar Westley-Richards design in which the soft-point opened out in front of the half-jacket and gave the appearance of a reversed cone stuck into the nose of the bullet. This, while giving fatal results on game, refused to function in the automatic feed cycle and had to be individually loaded for every shot; it was therefore replaced by another pattern in which a hollow ogival cap covered the exposed nose.

The Mauser pistol is notoriously hard on its ammunition, tending to hammer the bullets back into their cartridge cases while the rounds are in the pistol's magazine. This is due to the small clearance between the front wall of the magazine and the bullet nose, allied to the violent recoil of the pistol on firing. Pistols using detachable magazines—in which the separate unit acts as a sort of shock absorber—have less trouble with this defect. The Mauser's faults are well recognised by ammunition manufacturers, who invariably go to great lengths to anchor the bullet positively in the cartridge case by stabbing case metal into the bullet or canneluring the case to form a bullet seating stop—or even combining both methods.

Although actually 7.65mm calibre, this round is known throughout the world as 7.63mm Mauser. This differential was deliberate Mauser policy in order to avoid confusion between his round and the rounds for 7.65mm Borchardt, Mannlicher, Browning and other pistols, all of which had the same calibre designation but were of different chamber shapes, dimensions and ballistic properties.

7.65mm Bergmann No 8

Synonyms: 7.65 × 21; DWM 475;

Case type	Rimless, bottlenecked
Round length	1.159in (29.45mm)
Case length	0.827in (21.0mm)
Rim diameter	0.346in (8.80mm)
Bullet type	Jacketed roundnose
Bullet diameter	0.307in (7.80mm)
Bullet weight	85gr (5.50g)
Charge type	Smokeless
Muzzle velocity	1,210ft/sec (368m/sec)

Muzzle energy	279ft-lb (372J)

This was another of Bergmann's less successful cartridges; it was developed in 1899 for a No 8 version of the pistol which had originally appeared as the 8mm No 6. It was a reversion to an earlier design, and for this reason it failed to compete with better pistols which were, by then, available. It therefore faded from production quite quickly and only a handful of pistols were ever made in this chambering.

The standard bullet was a jacketed roundnose type weighing 85gr (5.5g); softnose and hollowpoint bullets are understood to have been catalogued, but none has ever been encountered. The cartridge was made only by DWM, the identifying number being 475; it is easily confused with the Austrian 7.65mm Mannlicher, a far more common round.

7.65mm Borchardt

Synonyms: none

Case type	Rimless, bottlenecked, brass
Round length	1.342in (34.10mm)
Case length	0.990in (25.14mm)
Rim diameter	0.392in (9.95mm)
Bullet type	Jacketed or soft-point, round- or flatnose
Bullet diameter	0.306in (7.77mm)
Bullet weight	86gr (5.55g)
Charge type	Smokeless
Muzzle velocity	1,214ft/sec (370m/sec)
Muzzle energy	280ft-lb (379J)

This was the cartridge developed by Borchardt and the Deutsche Metallpatronenfabrik Karlsruhe to work with Borchardt's automatic pistol of 1893. In fact, in the eyes of more than one observer, the cartridge was a more significant development than the pistol, since it was the first 'modern' cartridge to be developed specifically to suit an automatic pistol, and it formed the foundation upon which other experimenters were able to build. As a result, there is a more than coincidental similarity between this cartridge and the 7.63mm Mauser, 7.65mm Mannlicher, 7.62mm Tokarev and 7.8mm Bergmann.

The bullet generally used was an 86gr (5.55g) jacketed roundnose type, though soft-point bullets of 82gr (5.3g) to 87gr (5.64g) can be encountered. It was loaded to a lesser velocity than the later Mauser cartridge, and although 7.65mm Borchardt and 7.63mm Mauser cartridges are interchangeable, the use of either in the other pistol is not recommended. (This is perhaps an academic point, since nobody in his right mind would fire a Borchardt pistol or its ammunition today.)

Initial manufacture of Borchardt ammunition was by the Deutsche Metallpatronenfabrik Karlsruhe; this became DWM in 1897, and subsequent manufacture bore the appropriate marking, but no identifying number has ever been traced. It has been alleged that Borchardt ammunition was made by other German firms and also in the United States, but no specimens have ever been encountered.

7.65mm Browning

Synonyms: 7.65 × 17SR; 7.65mm ACP; .32 ACP; .32 Browning; DWM 479; GR 619

Case type	Semi-rimmed, straight
Round length	0.975in (24.76mm)
Case length	0.680in (17.27mm)
Rim diameter	0.352in (8.94mm)
Bullet type	Jacketed, soft-point or solid lead
Bullet diameter	0.309in (7.85mm)
Bullet weight	73gr (4.73g)
Charge type	Smokeless
Muzzle velocity	984ft/sec (300m/sec)
Muzzle energy	157ft-lb (212J)

This is another cartridge which has been made in every country and by every manufacturer. It dates from 1900 and, like the 6.35mm Browning round, was a development of Fabrique Nationale of Belgium for their Browning-designed automatic pistol. Like the 6.35mm, it is a semi-rimmed design, and due to the slight rim it can also be used in some .32in revolvers. Also like the 6.35mm, it is somewhat inefficient as far as stopping power goes. Its principal virtue lies in this very lack of power, since for many years it was the highest-powered round which could safely be used in blowback pistols, so much so that it has been estimated that fully 80 per cent of the automatic pistols in the world have been chambered for it and that, more than any other factor, it was responsible for the wide distribution of cheap pocket automatics in the 1920s and 1930s.

The usual loading is a jacketed roundnose bullet weighing about 73gr (4.73g), but soft-point and solid lead bullets are also common. Cases are of brass or steel, and in recent years plastic rounds have been developed for indoor target practice.

7.65mm Parabellum

Synonyms: 7.65 × 21.5mm; DWM 471; GR 924; .30 Luger

Case type	Rimless, bottlenecked
Round length	1.145in (29.08mm)
Case length	0.850in (21.50mm)
Rim diameter	0.393in (9.98mm)
Bullet type	Jacketed; flat-, round- or conical nose
Bullet diameter	0.309in (7.84mm)
Bullet weight	93gr (6.03g)
Charge type	Smokeless
Muzzle velocity	1,100ft/sec (335m/sec)
Muzzle energy	250ft-lb (338J)

When Georg Luger redesigned the Borchardt pistol and turned it into the less cumbersome Parabellum, he chambered it for the same 7.63mm Borchardt cartridge. When tested by the Swiss Army, with a view to adoption as their service pistol, they opined that the action was a little too violent and the consistency poor, and that these defects might well vanish if a slightly less powerful cartridge were adopted. Luger therefore shortened the Borchardt case and produced the 7.65mm Parabellum; as the Swiss had foretold, this improved the pistol's behaviour and in 1901 they formally adopted both pistol and cartridge. Following upon this, the pistol was placed on commercial sale and then became the service sidearm of several other countries, as a result of which the ammunition has been produced by most of the major ammunition companies at one time or another. It is still made by, among others, Winchester-Olin, Sako, Norma, Lapua, Dynamit Nobel and Fiocchi.

The original military loading was a 93gr (6.025g) steel-jacketed cylindro-conoidal bullet with a flat nose, the latter feature being intended to improve the stopping power. This developed a 1,158ft/sec (353m/sec) muzzle velocity, but it was superseded during World War I by a roundnose bullet of about 92gr (5.96g) weight. This change followed the similar change in shape of the 9mm Parabellum (q.v.) and was probably due to misgivings about the legality of a flatnose bullet *vis-à-vis* the Hague Convention. For commercial sale the usual variety of soft-point, hollow-point, cylindro-conoidal lead and jacketed ogival flatnose bullets have been produced.

In addition to the Parabellum pistol, it has been used in one or two submachine guns and offered as an optional chambering with some SIG and Beretta pistols, but it has never reached any great degree of popularity, probably owing to the fact that it is powerful enough to demand a fully locked breech; in this calibre a simpler solution is to use the normal 7.65mm Auto Pistol round and a simple blowback design, while if a locked breech is acceptable one might as well go up and use a more lethal calibre.

7.65mm Parabellum Carbine

Synonyms: DWM 471A

As was fashionable in pre-1914 days, a long-barrelled and stocked version of the Parabellum pistol was produced as the Model 1903 carbine. Since the Parabellum's toggle action is exceptionally sensitive to changes in breech pressure, this version failed to work reliably with the standard pistol cartridge and therefore a more powerful loading was developed for the carbine. This had a 15 per cent increase in charge and developed a velocity of 1,510ft/sec (460m/sec) in the 11.81in (300mm) carbine barrel. In order to distinguish this extra-power cartridge, the brass case was chemically blackened by immersion in silver nitrate; it is also recognisable by the DWM case number 471A in the headstamp, since so far as can be ascertained only DWM made these carbine cartridges.

Dimensions and details are similar to those of the 7.65mm Parabellum cartridge, but the charge weight is slightly heavier and the granulation of the powder different in order to give the desired ballistic performance in the long barrel. It is worth noting that silver nitrate treatment has a long-term effect which weakens the case metal; it is not advisable to fire this ammunition, nor is it safe to reload cases marked with silver nitrate.

7.65mm Pickert Revolver

Synonyms: 7.65 × 17R; .32 Revolver CF

Case type	Rimmed, straight
Round length	0.975in (24.76mm)
Case length	0.680in (17.27mm)
Rim diameter	0.352in (8.94mm)
Bullet type	Jacketed, soft-point or solid lead
Bullet diameter	0.309in (7.85mm)
Bullet weight	74gr (4.80g)
Charge type	Smokeless
Muzzle velocity	984ft/sec (300m/sec)
Muzzle energy	160ft-lb (215J)

As is the 6.35mm Pickert (q.v.), this is a rimmed equivalent of the 7.65mm Browning automatic pistol cartridge, and it was produced by Fiocchi of Italy to suit the numerous cheap European revolvers chambered for the Browning cartridge. The brass cases are inside-primed and carry a 74gr (4.8g) jacketed bullet, giving slightly different performance. Like the smaller round, production appears to have been confined to the period 1920–35.

7.65mm Roth-Sauer

Synonyms: 7.65 × 13nn; GR703

Case type	Rimless, straight taper
Round length	0.837in (21.25mm)
Case length	0.508in (12.90mm)
Rim diameter	0.333in (8.45mm)
Bullet type	Roundnose, jacketed
Bullet diameter	0.308in (7.82mm)
Bullet weight	72gr (4.65g)
Charge type	Smokeless powder
Muzzle velocity	1,070ft/sec (326m/sec)
Muzzle energy	182ft-lb (246J)

This was developed from the Hungarian 7.65mm Frommer cartridge, designed for the Roth-Frommer long-recoil pistol which demanded a fairly powerful charge to guarantee correct functioning, but the Roth-Sauer used a rotating-barrel locking system for which the Frommer loading was too powerful. The charge was therefore reduced to suit the mechanism of the Roth-Sauer pistol, and this weaker cartridge became known by the same name. The only reliable way to distinguish between the two is by the headstamp: rounds with Fegyvergyar of Budapest markings (FGY:BP) are Frommer; those with any other markings—notably Roth, Keller, RWS or American—are Roth-Sauer. (Numbers of Roth-Sauer pistols were exported to the United States prior to 1914 and ammunition was made there for a few years.) Production of the Roth-Sauer cartridge in Europe appears to have ended in 1939. The bullet was a jacketed roundnose type of 72gr (4.65g) weight.

.32 Smith & Wesson Long

Synonyms: GR 931

Case type	Rimmed, straight, brass

Round length	1.265in (32.15mm)
Case length	0.915in (23.25mm)
Rim diameter	0.375in (9.55mm)
Bullet type	Lead wadcutter, or roundnose, lead or jacketed
Bullet diameter	0.311in (7.90mm)
Bullet weight	98gr (6.35g)
Charge type	Smokeless
Muzzle velocity	686ft/sec (210m/sec)
Muzzle energy	103ft-lb (149J)

Smith & Wesson developed this cartridge in 1896 for their Hand Ejector revolver and it became quite popular, particularly as a police cartridge in the early part of the twentieth century. It then fell from favour, but it was rediscovered because with a wadcutter bullet it proved to be an extremely accurate and consistent round, which then became an international competition standard. Sporting ammunition can be found with the usual variety of lead or jacketed roundnose bullets in the 85–100-grain area, but the competition round is that quoted above, a 98gr wadcutter moving at 210m/sec.

.320 Short C.F.

Synonyms: .320 Revolver; .320 Bulldog; DWM 194; GR 97

Case type	Rimmed, straight, brass, centrefire
Round length	0.982in (24.95mm)
Case length	0.650in (16.50mm)
Rim diameter	0.359 (9.12mm)
Bullet type	Lead, roundnose
Bullet diameter	.303in (7.70mm)
Bullet weight	85gr (5.51g)
Charge type	Black or smokeless
Muzzle velocity	550ft/sec (168m/sec)
Muzzle energy	57ft-lb (78J)

This was developed in England in about 1870 and first used in early Webley revolvers, but it soon spread to the rest of Europe and became extremely popular for use in pocket revolvers in the latter part of the nineteenth century. It has long been superseded by more modern .32 cartridges, but it is still made in small batches for use by revolver enthusiasts. The usual loading is a roundnose lead bullet of anything between 65 and 90gr (4.2–5.8g), though jacketed bullets are occasionally seen and there was also a shot loading—quite a common loading for revolvers in the 1880–1910 period.

7.8mm Bergmann No 5

7.8 × 25; DWM 461

Case type	Rimless, bottlenecked
Round length	1.338in (34.00mm)
Case length	0.980in (24.90mm)
Rim diameter	0.392in (9.95mm)
Bullet type	Jacketed roundnose and others
Bullet diameter	0.308in (7.82mm)
Bullet weight	85gr (5.50g)
Charge type	Smokeless
Muzzle velocity	1,250ft/sec (381m/sec)
Muzzle energy	295ft-lb (398J)

This is another cartridge which owed much to the 7.65mm Borchardt for its inspiration. The dimensions are almost identical, except that the shoulders on the Bergmann round are about 2mm further back than on the Borchardt. It was developed for Bergmann's 1897 Military pistol, his first locked-breech model and his first to use a detachable box magazine in front of the trigger. The pistol was, in fact, of 7.65mm calibre, but it was called '7.8mm' after the bullet diameter and in order to distinguish it from the many other 7.63mm and 7.65mm cartridges which were clamouring for attention in the late 1890s. However, it failed to generate any military enthusiasm, and after being sold in small numbers for a few years the pistol was dropped from production. At the same time a few long-barrelled 'carbine' pistols had been made, but these were equally unsuccessful. The cartridge was produced by DWM until 1914.

The usual loading was an 85gr (5.5g) jacketed roundnose bullet, but a wide variety of sporting bullets have been recorded, from simple soft-point to semi-jacketed flatnose with slit jackets, ogival soft-point, hollow-point, and even the Westley-Richards 'All-Range' bullet. Considering the few pistols and fewer carbines made, this diversity is quite remarkable.

8mm Bergmann No I

Synonym: 8mm Bergmann-Schmeisser

Case type	Rimless, grooveless, tapered, brass
Round length	1.329in (33.75mm)
Case length	0.905in (23.00mm)
Base diameter	0.419in (10.50mm)
Bullet type	Jacketed, roundnose
Bullet diameter	0.200in (8.10mm)
Bullet weight	88gr (5.75g)
Charge type	Smokeless

Little is known about this cartridge since very few were made. It was the largest of three (5mm, 6.5mm and 8mm) rimless and grooveless rounds produced for the original Bergmann pistols introduced in 1894. The two smaller calibres attained some popularity, but the 8mm did not, and in consequence specimens of either pistol or ammunition are exceedingly rare. It was replaced in 1896 by the 8mm No 4 (below).

8mm Bergmann No 4

Synonyms: 8 × 22mm; DWM 451

Case type	Rimless, straight, brass
Round length	1.198in (30.45mm)
Case length	0.866in (22.00mm)
Rim diameter	0.372in (9.45mm)
Bullet type	Roundnose, lead, jacketed or softnose
Bullet diameter:	0.315in (8.00mm)
Bullet weight	88gr (5.75g)
Charge type	Smokeless

This is the rim-and-groove version of the 8mm No 1, using an almost straight-sided case, which was developed for the 1896 model of the Bergmann No 4 pistol. This, like the 5mm and 6.5mm 1896 pistols, employed positive extraction. The standard bullet was an 88gr (5.75g) jacketed ogival type, though soft-point and pure lead roundnose bullets have also been recorded. Even this improvement failed to generate much interest in the 8mm calibre, and the ammunition was off the market before 1914.

8mm Bergmann No 7

Synonyms: 8 × 20mm; DWM 460

Case type	Rimless, straight, brass
Round length	1.120in (28.45mm)
Case length	0.707in (20.00mm)
Rim diameter	0.372in (9.45mm)
Bullet type	Roundnose, jacketed, lead or softnose
Bullet diameter	0.315in (8.00mm)
Bullet weight	88gr (5.75g)
Charge type	Smokeless

In spite of (or perhaps because of) the relative lack of success of the 8mm No 4 pistol, Bergmann returned to this calibre in 1899 with his No 7 pistol. This was a hybrid design, using the locked breech of the 7.8mm No 5 but reverting to the side-opening, clip-loaded magazine of the Nos 1 to 4 pistols. The cartridge was a shortened version of the No 4, using the same 88gr (5.75g) jacketed bullet as standard, and with similar soft-point and solid lead alternatives. But this pistol turned out to be even less of a success than his earlier one, since it was of poor design and was universally rejected.

8mm Bergmann Simplex

Synonyms: 8 × 18mm; 8mm Simplex; DWM 488

Case type	Rimless, straight taper
Round length	1.014in (25.75mm)
Case length	0.711in (18.06mm)
Rim diameter	0.356in (9.04mm)
Bullet type	Roundnose, full jacketed or soft-point
Bullet diameter	0.316in (8.02mm)
Bullet weight	72gr (4.6gm)
Charge type	Smokeless
Muzzle velocity	800ft/sec (259m/sec)
Muzzle energy	114ft-lb (154J)

The origins of this cartridge are shrouded in mystery. Various writers have asserted that it was 'designed for the Bergmann pistol of 1895'. The only drawback to this statement appears to be that Bergmann did not produce any design of pistol in 1895 and at that time was still turning out pistols for his original grooveless, rimless, sharply tapered cartridges. What we might call 'conventional' cartridges did not appear in the Bergmann repertoire until 1897.

The next common observation is that it was 'adapted to the Simplex pistol in 1897', but since we know that Bergmann did not take out the patents covering the Simplex until 1901, it seems safe to say the Simplex pistol did not see the light of day until 1900 at the very earliest and more probably 1902. R. K. Wilson (*Textbook of Automatic Pistols, 1943)* suggests 1896 for its origin, but then goes on to suggest that it was the basis of the 7.65mm Browning cartridge—an idea that might well have caused John M. Browning to suck his teeth had he ever seen it.

I am inclined to think that there has been some confusion between this and the 8mm Bergmann No 7 cartridge, which, as noted above, had a brief span of life in the 1890s. I think it was abandoned but then redesigned in a shorter and less powerful form, to suit the Simplex pistol, and that the Simplex cartridge therefore dates from about 1900. The cartridge seems to have been made by the Cartoucherie Belge in the first instance but was then taken up by DWM, who continued to produce it until the early 1930s. It does bear some resemblance to the 7.65mm Browning but I do not think that too much significance should be placed on that.

8mm Ultra

Synonyms: 8 × 21

Case type	Rimless, straight, brass
Round length	1.102in (28.00mm)
Case length	0.821in (20.85mm)
Rim diameter	0.360in (9.15mm)
Bullet type	Jacketed, flatnose
Bullet diameter	0.315in (8.00mm)
Bullet weight	88gr (5.75g)
Charge type	Smokeless
Muzzle velocity	1,050ft/sec (320m/sec)
Muzzle energy	217ft-lb (294J)

In the mid-1930s the Gustav Genschow company of Durlach, in collaboration with Walther Waffenfabrik, began top develop of a range of pistol cartridges intended to replace the existing 6.35mm, 7.65mm and 9mm Short Browning rounds with rounds more powerful but still suited to use in blowback pistols. A range of Walther PP pistols was modified to fire these cartridges, but before the idea could be perfected the war intervened and the project was abandoned. The 8mm Ultra, intended to replace the 7.65mm Browning, used a jacketed flatnose bullet, no doubt to improve the stopping ability, and gave a 28 per cent increase in muzzle energy.

9mm Bergmann No 6

Synonyms: 9 × 23mm; 9mm Mars No 6; DWM456

Case type	Rimless, straight, brass
Round length	1.377in (35.00mm)
Case length	0.905in (23.00mm)
Rim diameter	0.393in 10.00mm)
Bullet type	Jacketed roundnose
Bullet diameter	0.358in (9.10mm)
Bullet weight	135gr (8.80g)

Charge type	Smokeless
Muzzle velocity	1,115ft/sec (340m/sec)
Muzzle energy	376ft-lb (508J)

Yet another of the numbered series of Bergmann designs, the No 6 was produced in 1901 to go with an improved No 5 pattern pistol with locked breech. It was submitted to various armies for trial and was also sold commercially as the Bergmann 'Mars' . With this model Bergmann finally achieved his aim of military recognition when the Spanish Army decided to adopt the pistol. However, in Bergmann's hour of triumph, the sub-contractor who was to make the pistols sold out to a competitor of Bergmann, the new owner cancelled the contract and Bergmann was obliged to sell his rights in the pistol to a Belgian firm, Pieper of Liège, who produced it as the Bergmann-Bayard Model 1906 for the Spanish. In the process they made slight manufacturing changes to both pistol and cartridge.

The Bergmann No 6 cartridge, which used a 136gr (8.8g) jacketed roundnose bullet, went out of production within a very few years of its inception and specimens are uncommon. It can be distinguished from the Bergmann-Bayard cartridge by having the bullet set less deeply into the case, giving it an abnormally long appearance.

9mm Bergmann-Bayard

Synonyms: 9 × 23mm; 9mm Largo; DWM 456B, 456C; 9mm Danish pistol

Case type	Rimless, straight, brass
Round length	1.319in (33.50mm)
Case length	0.910in (23.10mm)
Rim diameter	0.388in (9.85mm)
Bullet type	Roundnose, jacketed or soft-point
Bullet diameter	0.355in (9.01mm)
Bullet weight	127gr (8.23g)
Charge type	Smokeless
Muzzle velocity	1,300ft/sec (395m/sec)
Muzzle energy	474ft-lb (640J)

This was the Bergmann 9mm No 6 cartridge after being modified by Pieper of Belgium. He wisely seated the bullet rather more deeply into the case, which not only made it more resistant to life's little misfortunes but also improved the charge/space ratio and thus the combustion characteristics to give the pistol a somewhat better ballistic performance. The reduction in length was small—1 to 1.5mm, depending upon the type of bullet—but it was sufficient to create a new cartridge, which became the Bergmann-Bayard. The pistol did not survive much after 1920 in the Spanish Army, but the cartridge, which they called the 9mm Largo, remained their service round until the 1970s. The Bergmann-Bayard pistol did better under Danish ownership, being retained by them until the 1950s, but when they abandoned it the manufacture of the cartridge ceased outside Spain and is now confined to Italy, where the public-spirited Fiocchi company produce batches from time to time.

The standard commercial bullet is a 135gr (8.8g) jacketed roundnose type; the standard Spanish military round used a 130gr (8.42g) jacketed ogival bullet loaded to give 1,148ft/sec (350m/sec) in the service Astra 400 pistol. Hollow-point and softnose bullets were also available commercially, but these have not been made since 1939. The cartridge can be found with Spanish, Danish, German or Belgian headstamps. It is similar in appearance and dimensions to the 9mm Steyr round, but distinguishable because the Steyr bullet is more pointed and was invariably made with a plain steel jacket.

9mm Short

Synonyms: 9 × 17SR; 9mm Browning Short; .380 Auto; DWM 540; GR 929

Case type	Rimless, straight taper
Round length	0.980in (24.90mm)
Case length	0.675in (17.15mm)
Rim diameter	0.374in (9.50mm)
Bullet type	Jacketed or soft-point, roundnose

Bullet diameter	0.356in (9.04mm)
Bullet weight	94gr (6.10g)
Charge type	Smokeless powder
Muzzle velocity	935ft/sec (285m/sec)
Muzzle energy	183ft-lb (247J)

This round is also known as the .380in Auto Pistol in the United States and Britain, as the 9mm Corto in Italy, as the 9mm Kurz in Germany and by a variety of other names elsewhere. In Europe it was originally called the 9mm Browning Short, to distinguish it from the 9mm Browning Long, and was first produced in the United States (as the 0.380in Auto) for the Colt Company's 1908 pistol. So far as can be ascertained it was introduced into Europe by Fabrique Nationale in about 1910. It represents about the largest practicable calibre for an unlocked blowback pistol, though locked-breech examples can be found, and it has been accepted as a military service cartridge by many countries. Theoretically it is a low-powered round, but in practice it has sufficient performance to make it effective, and it is a better pocket pistol cartridge than the more common 7.65mm Browning round since it has better impact characteristics owing to its greater cross-section.

Loads vary considerably and depend upon the whims of the various makers. A series of tests carried out with a variety of makes displayed velocities ranging from 845ft/sec (259m/sec) to 985ft/sec (300m/sec); the values quoted above represent mean figures based upon the standard 94gr (6.10g) bullet. Bullet types run from full-jacketed roundnose or ogival, through various semi-jacketed and soft-points, hollow-points and flat-tips, to plain lead roundnose, though a three-quarters jacketed soft-point or a jacketed roundnose seem to be the most common.

9mm Mauser Export

Synonyms: 9 × 25mm; DWM 487;

Case type	Rimless, straight, brass
Round length	1.378in (35.00mm)
Case length	0.981in (24.91mm)
Rim diameter	0.391in (9.93mm)
Bullet type	Ogival, jacketed or soft-point
Bullet diameter	0.355in (9.01mm)
Bullet weight	127gr (8.23g)
Charge type	Smokeless
Muzzle velocity	1,362ft/sec (415m/sec)
Muzzle energy	523ft-lb (707J)

This enlarged version of the 7.63mm Mauser cartridge was developed for the 1912 Export Model pistol. For a number of years it was virtually unobtainable, manufacture for Mauser by DWM having stopped in 1914, but in the early 1930s its size and power were rediscovered and some submachine guns were designed around it, leading to a resumption of manufacture on a large scale from 1936 until 1945. The case is of the same length as the 7.63mm cartridge, but straight instead of bottlenecked and thus carrying a powerful charge. It has never been used in any other pistol, and the only other weapons chambered for it are Swiss and Hungarian submachine guns.

As can be seen from the figures above, this is a very potent cartridge and I find it surprising, in view of the modern enthusiasm for 'magnum' rounds, that it has not been revived. The normal bullet was a full-jacketed ogival type weighing 127gr (8.23g), though soft-point types have been recorded. When used in submachine guns it showed a muzzle velocity of about 1,493ft/sec (455m/sec).

9mm Mauser Revolver

Synonyms: 9 × 25R; DWM 6;

Case type	Rimmed, straight
Round length	1.398in (35.52mm)
Case length	0.970in (24.63mm)
Rim diameter	0.455in (11.55mm)
Bullet type	Jacketed or solid lead, roundnose
Bullet diameter	0.370in (9.39mm)
Bullet weight	162gr (10.50g)

Charge type	Black powder
Muzzle velocity	787ft/sec (240m/s)
Muzzle energy	223ft-lb (302J)

The 'middle man' in the Mauser 1878 revolver series, this is of conventional pattern and was most usually seen with a solid lead bullet, though jacketed types are known. It never achieved military adoption but was perhaps the most popular of the Mauser revolver cartridges. Manufacture of these rounds ceased between 1900 and 1910.

9mm Parabellum

Synonyms: 9 × 19mm; 9mm Luger; DWM 480; GR 927

Case type	Rimless, straight, brass or steel
Round length	1.149in (29.16mm)
Case length	0.747in (18.97mm)
Rim diameter	0.391in (9.93mm)
Bullet type	Truncated cone, jacketed, ogival jacketed or soft-point
Bullet diameter	0.354in (8.93mm)
Bullet weight	124gr (8.0g)
Charge type	Smokeless
Muzzle velocity	1,132ft/sec (345m/sec)
Muzzle energy	352ft-lb (475J)

This cartridge, which is probably the most widely distributed pistol and submachine gun round in the world today, was originally produced by DWM for the 9mm Parabellum pistol and is sometimes called the 9mm Luger round, particularly in the United States. Its development was largely due to the fact that the German Army was reluctant to accept the 7.65mm bullet as a combat load, since it appeared to be insufficiently powerful as a man- stopper. Georg Luger simply expanded the mouth of the 7.65mm case and DWM produced a suitable bullet; in this way they avoided a major redesign of the pistol, since the rim and case dimensions remained the same and only the barrel of the pistol needed to be changed. The magazine and bolt would function equally well with either round.

The original German bullet was of a truncated cone shape, probably copied directly from Luger's 7.65mm bullet and intended to obtain the best anti-personnel effect. A great deal of ammunition made in other countries, notably the United States and Switzerland, retained this contour, but the German Army changed to the more usual ogival-nose pattern in 1917. In that year the long-barrelled Parabellum with the 'snail' magazine was introduced, and the flat-point bullet was found to work badly through this magazine, giving frequent jams and malfunctions. At more or less the same time there were misgivings about the legality of the flat-tipped bullet *vis-à-vis* the Hague and St Petersburg Conventions, and in order to avoid any accusations of using prohibited bullets the German Army decided to change to the ogival bullet. Since that time all German production, both military and civil, has been of the round-nose pattern, and today it is fairly safe to say that the roundnose has completely displaced the earlier pattern of bullet.

In addition to these two standard bullets, others have been produced at various times. Georg Luger himself patented a double- bulletted round as early as 1906 and a small number of these were produced, the theory being that if you missed with the first bullet, the second might well save the day. Another unusual variation was a streamlined (or boat-tailed) bullet produced by DWM in 1913 for use in the Mauser 1912/14 Military blowback pistol. During World War II the German Army produced semi-armour-piercing bullets for use against light armoured vehicles, and also a substitute (*ersatz*) ball bullet made from compressed, sintered iron as an economy measure. These can be distinguished from the general run of gilding-metal-jacket ball bullets, since the semi-AP type are coated in a shiny black varnish while the sintered iron bullets are a dull grey.

World War II also saw the manufacture of this round in vast numbers in many countries which had hitherto never manufactured it in bulk or for military use, and thus there are hundreds of different 9mm Parabellum rounds available today. By and large they are all of reasonable quality and safety, but there are a few jokers in the pack which can lead the unwary into trouble. Two dangerous cartridges which frequently turn up in souvenir packages are the German proof charges, using high-pressure loadings which were for testing weapons under suitable precautions. These can be identified by the word 'BESCHUSS' included in the head- stamp, or by virtue of the base of the case being enamelled bright green. On the other hand, a round with the case completely painted green, base and sides, indicates a reduced charge loading for use in silenced submachine guns.

To make life even more complicated, there are one or two rounds which have the appearance of standard Parabellum but which were designed for different weapons and thus have peculiar ballistics of their own. One of the most common is the Italian round for the 9mm Glisenti pistol. This has identical dimensions to the Parabellum round and the same truncated-cone bullet, but the powder charge is considerably less since the design of the Glisenti was not suited to ammunition of the Parabellum's power. Any truncated-cone cartridge bearing Italian headstamps can be taken as being a 9mm Glisenti.

A variation frequently quoted is the round for the 9mm Parabellum pistol-carbine. As in the case of the 7.65mm carbine round, these are said to be loaded to a greater power and identified by the blackened case with the headstamp 'DWM 480D'. Unfortunately, there is no evidence that these were ever manufactured, their existence being based solely upon their appearance in the August 1904 edition of the DWM catalogue. Since there does not appear ever to have been a 9mm Parabellum pistol-carbine, it follows that the existence of ammunition for such a weapon is unlikely and that DWM merely catalogued it in anticipation of a development which never took place.

It should be noted that the performance figures quoted above are based upon the 1914 Pistole Patrone '08, all measurements being taken from several specimens and averaged. They do not correspond with data for the current NATO standard 9mm round.

9mm Police

Synonyms: 9 × 18mm; 9mm Ultra

Case type	Rimless, straight, brass or steel
Round length	0.990in (25.14mm)
Case length	0.709in (18.00mm)
Rim diameter	0.374in (9.50mm)
Bullet type	Jacketed ogival
Bullet diameter	0.355in (9.01mm)
Bullet weight	94gr (6.09g)
Charge type	Smokeless
Muzzle velocity	1,082ft/sec (330m/sec)
Muzzle energy	244ft-lb (331J)

This cartridge was developed in Germany in the early 1970s in order to improve on the 9mm Short without going so far as to demand a locked-breech pistol. Although it is nominally the same size as the Soviet 9 × 18mm Makarov, the two cartridges differ in essential dimensions and are not interchangeable.

It will be readily appreciated that the object of this and the pre-war 'Ultra' range of cartridges was the same, and the Genschow company took the comparison a stage further by calling their production 'Geco 9mm Ultra' and so marking it in the headstamp. The Hirtenberg company, however, marked theirs '9mm Police', and that is the title which stuck, Genschow later abandoning their name.

An indication of the small, but vital, advances in powder technology and ammunition design which took place in the twentieth century become apparent when one compares the dimensions and performance of this cartridge with the pre-war 9mm Ultra described below: the 9mm Police shows an increase in power of 11 per cent over the 9mm Ultra (designed in 1936) and of 48 per cent over the 9mm Short (designed in 1908).

Type: 9mm Geco Ultra

Synonyms: none

Case type	Rimless, straight, brass
Round length	1.024in (26.00mm)
Case length	0.728in (18.50mm)
Rim diameter	0.374in (9.50mm)
Bullet type	Jacketed, ogival, flatnose
Bullet diameter	0.354in (9.00mm)
Bullet weight	108gr (7.00g)
Charge type	Smokeless
Muzzle velocity	951ft/sec (290m/sec)
Muzzle energy	217ft-lb (294J)

This was another of the experimental cartridges developed by Gustav Genschow in co-operation with Walther in 1938–39. This one was intended to be superior to the 9mm Short and was tested by the German Army. The test reports were unfavourable—which is scarcely surprising when one realises that the muzzle energy was the same as that of the smaller 8mm Ultra round—and, since the war had by that time claimed the undivided attention of the German ammunition-makers, the project was dropped. Specially chambered models of standard Walther pistols were manufactured to suit these rounds, but to the best of my knowledge any of these weapons which exist today are tucked away in private collections and the ammunition is extremely rare.

.380 Short Revolver

Synonyms: .380 Short, Long Case; .380 English; DWM 193; GR 100

Case type	Rimmed, straight, brass or lacquered steel
Round length	1.018in (25.85mm)
Case length	0.707in (17.95mm)
Rim diameter	0.427in (10.84mm)
Bullet type	Roundnose, lead
Bullet diameter	0.360in (9.14mm)
Bullet weight	124gr (8.03g)
Charge type	Smokeless
Muzzle velocity	623ft/sec (190m/sec)
Muzzle energy	107ft-lb (144J)

Developed in England in about 1870, this cartridge soon spread across Europe and was widely manufactured for pocket revolvers. It has been entirely superseded by more modern .38 loadings, but small quantities of .380 Short are still produced from time to time by ammunition firms specialising in the collector and enthusiast market. It is normally found with a plain lead roundnose bullet of various weights, but there was also a cylindrical, flat-headed 'manstopper' bullet, as well as a number of bird shot loadings.

10mm Bergmann

Synonyms: 10 × 21mm; DWM 478

Case type	Rimless, straight, brass
Round length	1.220in (31.70mm)
Case length	0.827in (21.00mm)
Rim diameter	0.439in (11.00mm)
Bullet type	Ogival, hollow-based
Bullet diameter	0.394in (10.00mm)
Bullet weight	105gr (6.80g)
Charge type	Smokeless
Muzzle velocity	870ft/sec (265m/sec)
Muzzle energy	176ft-lb (238J)

This cartridge, which has been the source of much confusion in the past, was developed by DWM for a special version of the Bergmann No 6 automatic pistol which was submitted for British Army testing in 1902. The British Small Arms Committee always stood out for a cartridge of at least 12.96mm calibre firing a 200gr (12.96gm) bullet, but designers were slow in working up to this and persisted in submitting cartridges which did not meet the specification in the hope of producing sufficient performance to persuade the Committee to relent. Bergmann took a leaf out of Schouboe's book here and submitted a 10mm bullet which was internally hollowed out until it was little more than a thin jacket lined with lead. This gave good velocity, since it weighed only

6.87gm, but the bullet failed to expand on impact and the Committee threw it out.

Much of the confusion over this cartridge has arisen from a remark by Wilson in his *Textbook of Automatic Pistols*, in which he quoted two bullets, one the light and hollow type and one the conventional type of 9.65g. But careful study of the actual report of the Small Arms Committee shows that only the light bullet was ever submitted for trial in 1902, the heavy bullet not being seen until 1903, when it was submitted for trial as the 11mm Bergmann. The cases of these two rounds are very close in dimensions, and I am quite convinced that Wilson, in this instance, was the unfortunate victim of honest error.

.40 Smith & Wesson

Synonyms: none

Case type	Rimless, straight, brass
Round length	1.130in (28.70mm)
Case length	0.850in (21.60mm)
Rim diameter	0.424in (10.76mm)
Bullet type	Ogival, jacketed, soft-point or hollow-point
Bullet diameter	0.398in (10.11mm)
Bullet weight	178gr (11.53g)
Charge type	Smokeless
Muzzle velocity	968ft/sec (295m/sec)
Muzzle energy	370ft-lb (500J)

After Bergmann gave up trying to sell the idea of a 10mm round in the 1900s, there was an abortive attempt by the BSA Company in 1920, after which nothing was heard of the calibre until the late 1970s. By the middle 1980s it had gained momentum, but the dimensions of the 10mm Auto cartridge made conversion of a 9mm pistol design into 10mm an expensive process. Smith & Wesson developed this round to provide the 10mm shooter with a cartridge delivering reasonable power but in a size that allowed makers of 9mm automatic pistols to convert them with minimal alteration. It has since gained in stature and is now widely used in pistols and submachine guns. It earns its place here on the strength of various SIG-Sauer and Heckler & Koch pistols which can be optionally chambered for this round. There are currently about 60 versions of this cartridge, with the usual variety of jacketed, soft-point or hollow-point bullets.

10.6mm Ordnance Revolver

Synonyms: DWM 200

Case type	Rimmed, straight taper
Round length	1.434in (36.42mm)
Case length	0.970in (24.64mm)
Rim diameter	0.510in/12.95mm
Bullet type	Roundnose, solid lead
Bullet diameter	0.433in (11.00mm)
Bullet weight	262gr (16.97g)
Charge type	Black or smokeless powders
Muzzle velocity	672ft/sec (205m/sec) black; 750ft/sec (229m/sec) smokeless
Muzzle energy	263ft-lb (356J) black; 329ft-lb (444J) smokeless

This cartridge is of conventional pattern, but for some reason or other seems to be the source of much confusion, various authorities quoting the calibre as anything from 10.5 through 10.6, 10.8, 10.85 and 11.0 to 11.5mm. Since, as mentioned in the section on the revolver, the barrels are engraved '10,55', I have taken 10.6 as the correct nomenclature for my purpose here.

The cartridge was introduced in 1879 when the Reichsrevolver was developed, and it remained in service throughout the life of the weapon. After World War I manufacture virtually ceased, but so many of the guns remained in use in private hands that one enterprising company found it worthwhile to restart production using a reduced charge of smokeless powder and a modern non-corrosive primer, this production continuing until 1939. The issue cartridge was loaded with a 17g lead roundnose bullet, but various other weights of bullet were loaded commercially.

10.6mm Mauser revolver

Synonyms: 10.6 × 25R; DWM 7; GR 352

Case type	Rimmed, straight
Round length	1.457in (37.00mm)
Case length	0.980in (24.90mm)
Rim diameter	0.512in (13.00mm)
Bullet type	Roundnose, jacketed or lead
Bullet diameter	0.433in (11.00mm)
Bullet weight	256gr (16.60g)
Charge type	Black powder
Muzzle velocity	705ft/sec (215m/sec)
Muzzle enenegy	283ft-lb (372J)

This closely resembles the 10.6mm German Ordnance cartridge and was designed for the largest Mauser 'Zig-Zag' revolver in the hope of obtaining military acceptance. Instead, the Reichsrevolver was accepted, and so relatively few 10.6mm Mauser revolvers were made. The cartridge uses a similar bullet to the Reichsrevolver cartridge's; positive identification is best carried out by the DWM number 7 in the headstamp, whereas Reichsrevolver cartridges carry the number 200.

11mm Bergmann

Synonyms:11 × 23mm; DWM 490

Case type	Rimless, straight, brass
Round length	1.309in (33.25mm)
Case length	0.895in (22.75mm)
Rim diameter	0.472in (12.00mm)
Bullet type	Jacketed, ogival, flat tip
Bullet diameter	0.440in (11.20mm)
Bullet weight	148gr (9.59g)
Charge type	Smokeless

When discussing the 10mm Bergmann I commented upon Wilson's error in attributing to it a 148gr (9.59g) bullet. This 11mm cartridge is the cause of the confusion. It closely resembles the 10mm round, but uses a more conventional form of jacketed bullet. It was submitted to the Small Arms Committee by the British agents for Bergmann in January 1903; they suggested that the SAC might test it to prove that it worked satisfactorily, after which the agents would be happy to instruct Bergmann to develop a fresh cartridge with a 12.96g bullet (the SAC's 200gr standard), though, in fact, they knew that Bergmann would much prefer to develop an 11.2g (175gr) bullet.

However, by this time the SAC were tired of people submitting ammunition not in accordance with their 11.40mm/200gr condition and they flatly refused to countenance testing the Bergmann in any form. That appears to have been the end of that. Bergmann took his pistol back and went on to develop a cartridge with an 11.2g bullet, and it seems that this combination is the only one ever encountered by collectors. Furthermore, since the British refused to test the 9.59g cartridge, we have no idea what the performance was.

11mm Werder

Synonyms: 11.5 × 35R; DWM 9; GR 45

Case type	Rimmed, brass, bottlenecked
Round length	1.962in (49.85mm)
Case length	1.305in (35.20mm)
Rim diameter	0.590in (15.20mm)
Bullet type	Lead, roundnose
Bullet diameter	0.457in (11.60mm)
Bullet weight	336gr (21.75g)
Charge type	Black powder
Muzzle velocity	720ft/sec (220m/sec)
Muzzle energy	389ft-lb (525J)

Three Werder weapons were produced in 1869, the rifle, the carbine and the pistol, and they each fired a separate cartridge, the pistol round being the smallest of the three and also the only bottlenecked round. It is frequently called the 'pistol and carbine' cartridge, but this seems to be a misnomer based upon the fact that it also became a popular commercial cartridge for use with target rifles; it might have been possible to fire it from the Werder carbine but it would not have been advisable, nor would it have produced much in the way of accuracy.

This cartridge appeared in 1869, early days for a centrefire cartridge, and the state-manufactured cartridges used the 'folded head' form of construction with a Berdan primer based on Berdan's American Patent 53338 of 1866. In later years, when both the pistol and a similar carbine passed into the civil market and commercial manufacture of ammunition began, Mauser- and conventional flat-based cases were used. The standard bullet was of a roundnose lead pattern, with lubricating groove, weighing about 340gr (22.0g). Commercial production came to an end in about 1910, but military production appears to have lasted longer, since numbers of the pistols were still in the hands of troops at the outbreak of war in 1914.

APPENDIX VI: PARABELLUM PISTOLS
Variations Recognised by Collectors

Model date	Type	Calibre (mm)	Barrel length (mm)	Other details
1900	Commercial	7.65	120	Grip safety.
1900	Swiss Military	7.65	120	Grip safety, Swiss Cross on chamber.
1900	American Commercial	7.65	120	Grip safety, American Eagle on chamber.
1903	Commercial	7.65	101	Grip safety. May have American Eagle. This model has a much thicker barrel than the 1900 models.
1903	Carbine	7 -65	300	Wooden fore-end; recoiling barrel; grip safety; sighted to 800m.
1904	Naval	9	152	Two-range sight; extractor marked 'GELADEN: GESICHERT' under safety catch; stock lug; grip safety.
1905	Bulgarian Army	7.65	129	Bulgar lion over chamber.

All the foregoing models are the original pattern with anti-bounce lock, flat-topped bolt, and leaf-type recoil spring.

Model date	Type	Calibre (mm)	Barrel length (mm)	Other details
1906	US Army Trial	0.45in	127	Reputedly only one exists today.
1 906	Commercial	7.65	120	Grip safety; no stock lug.
1906	Commercial	9	101	Grip safety.
1906	Naval	9	152	No grip safety, stock lug; two-range sight.
1906	Naval-Commercial	7.65	152	As above, with civil proof marks.
1906	Naval-Commercial	9	152	As above.

The foregoing models have the safety catch moving upwards to 'safe'. Subsequent models have it moving down to 'safe'.

Model date	Type	Calibre (mm)	Barrel length (mm)	Other details
1907	Bulgarian Army	7.65	120	Extractor and safety both marked in Cyrillic characters.

1908	Commercial	9	101	
1908	Military Model '08	9	101	May be DWM or ERFURT: may have hold-open, may not have stock lug.
1906	Swiss Military	7.65	120	Grip safety; Swiss Cross over chamber.
1906	Swiss Police	7.65	120	Swiss cross on a shield over chamber.
1907	Swiss Commercial	7.65	120	Extractor marked 'GELADEN'.
1907	US Commercial	7.65	120	Extractor = 'LOADED'; safety = 'SAFE'.
1907	US Commercial	9	100	Extractor = 'LOADED'; safety = 'SAFE'.
1908	Naval	9	152	As Naval '06 but with grip safety.
1908	Russian Commercial	9	100	Extractor and saety marked in Cyrillic.
1909	Portuguese Army	7.65	120	Extractor marked 'CARREGA'.
1909	Portuguese National Guard	7.65	120	Extractor = 'CARREGADAL'; safety = 'SEGURANÇA'.
1910	Bulgarian Army	9	100	Bulgarian lion over chamber.
1910	Portuguese Navy	9	100	Extractor marked 'CARREGADA'.
1911	Bolivian Army	9	100	Eaxtractor marked 'CARGADO'.
1911	Brazilian Army	7.65	120	Extractor marked 'CARREGADA'.
1911	Dutch East Indies Army	9	100	Extractor = 'GELADEN'; safety = 'RUST'.
1914	Naval	9	152	As Naval '08 but chamber is dated.
1914	Military	9	101	Dated; DWM or ERFURT; modified sear contour.
1914	Long '08 Military	9	203	Dated; DWM; tangent backsight.
1920	Commercial	9	100	DWM or ERFURT; no date; civil proof.
1920	Commercial	7.65	152	Ex-military weapons, re-worked.
1920	Carbine	7.65	300	Ex-factory spare stocks. Very few made.
1922	Commercial	7.65	98	DWM
1922	Commercial	9	98	DWM
1925	Commercial	9	101	'SIMSON & CO SUHL'.
1925	Commercial	7.65	101	'SIMSON & CO SUHL'.
1923	Finland – Army	7.65	100	Extractor/safety unmarked.
1923	Finland – Prison Service	7.65	100	Extractor/safety unmarked.
1924	Dutch Army	9	100	Marked 'VICKERS LTD' on toggle.
1928	Swiss Model 06/24	7.65	120	Marked 'WAFFENFABRIK BERN'. Grip safety.
1927	Dutch Navy	9	100	BKIW. Safety = 'RUST'; extractor = 'GELADEN'.
1929	Swiss Model 06/29	7.65	120	Small Swiss cross on toggle. Grip safety.
1930	Dutch Navy	9	100	Mauser. 'RUST'/'GELADEN'.
1934	Commercial	7.65	10	Mauser badge on toggle.
1934	Mauser Military '08	9	101	Dated, Mauser badge.
1934	Mauser Commercial	9	101	Undated, Mauser badge; civil proofs.
1934	Krieghoff Military '08	9	101	Dated; 'KRIEGHOFF SUHL' marking.
1935	German Luftwaffe	9	101	Krieghoff; as P '08.
1936	Commercial	9	100	Krieghoff.
1936	Persian Army	9	100	Mauser; Arabic markings.
1936	Turkish Army	9	100	Mauser.

1937	Siamese Police	9	100	Mauser.
1937	Siamese Police	9	200	Mauser.
1937	Dutch Navy	9	100	Mauser 'RUST'/'GELADEN'.
1940	Swiss 06/29 Commercial	7.65	120	'WAFFENFABRIK BERN' and Swiss cross.
1934	German Army P '08	9	100	The model manufactured in 1934 remained in production until 1943, but later models were marked with code groups.
1943	Portuguese Army	9	100	Mauser; German markings.
1970	Mauser 29/70	Both	100	Based on Swiss 06/29; Swiss butt.
1973	Mauser 06/73	Both	100	Based on Swiss 06/29 but with German butt.

Note that the various 'commemorative' models made by Mauser in the 1970s have not been listed. These were simply replicas of the Swiss, German, Russian and Bulgarian models with the appropriate badges and markings.